BTEC
Level 3

edexcel
advancing learning, changing lives

BUSINESS LEVEL 3

Book 1

BTEC National

John Bevan | Helen Coupland-Smith
Rob Dransfield | John Goymer | Catherine Richards

Published by Pearson Education Limited, a company incorporated in England and Wales, having its registered office at Edinburgh Gate, Harlow, Essex, CM20 2JE. Registered company number: 872828

www.pearsonschoolsandfecolleges.co.uk

Edexcel is a registered trademark of Edexcel Limited.

Text © John Bevan, Helen Coupland-Smith, Rob Dransfield, John Goymer, Catherine Richards 2010

First published 2010

17 16 15 14

11 10 9 8

British Library Cataloguing in Publication Data

A catalogue record for this book is available from the British Library.

ISBN 978 1846906 34 3

Edited by Juliet Mozley
Designed by Wooden Ark
Typeset by Phoenix Photosetting, Chatham, Kent
Original illustrations © Pearson Education Limited 2010
Illustrated by KJA-artists.com
Cover design by Visual Philosophy, created by eMC Design
Picture research by Ginny Stroud-Lewis
Copyright requests by Hardwick Studios
Cover images Front: **Image Source Ltd**; Back: **Pearson Education Ltd:** Gareth Boden cr,
Shutterstock: Dean Mitchell tl, Keith Gentry tr
Printed in Slovakia by Neografia

Websites

The websites used in this book were correct and up to date at the time of publication. It is essential for tutors to preview each website before using it in class so as to ensure that the URL is still accurate, relevant and appropriate. We suggest that tutors bookmark useful websites and consider enabling learners to access them through the school/college intranet.

Disclaimer

This material has been published on behalf of Edexcel and offers high-quality support for the delivery of Edexcel qualifications.

This does not mean that the material is essential to achieve any Edexcel qualification, nor does it mean that it is the only suitable material available to support any Edexcel qualification. Edexcel material will not be used verbatim in setting any Edexcel examination or assessment. Any resource lists produced by Edexcel shall include this and other appropriate resources.

Copies of official specifications for all Edexcel qualifications may be found on the Edexcel website: www.edexcel.com

Contents

About the authors v

About your **BTEC Level 3 National Business** vi

Unit	Credit value	Title	Author	Page
1	10	The business environment	Rob Dransfield	1
2	10	Business resources	Catherine Richards	47
3	10	Introduction to marketing	John Bevan	83
4	10	Business communication	John Bevan	123
5	10	Business accounting	Helen Coupland-Smith	163
9	10	Creative product promotion	John Bevan	197
10	10	Market research in business	Rob Dransfield	235
12	10	Internet marketing in business	John Goymer	279
13	10	Recruitment and selection in business	Catherine Richards	319
19	10	Developing teams in business	Rob Dransfield	355
33	10	The impact of communications technology on business	John Goymer	395
34	10	Website design strategy	John Goymer	439

Glossary 477

Bibliography 482

Index 488

Also available

There are many different optional units in your BTEC Level 3 National Business qualification, which you may use to form specialist pathways or to build a broader programme of learning. This student book covers enough units for the Edexcel BTEC Level 3 National Diploma in Business, but if you want a bigger choice of optional units or if you are completing the Edexcel BTEC Level 3 National Diploma in Business, you may be interested in Student Book 2.

Written in the same accessible style with the same useful features to support you through your learning and assessment, *BTEC Level 3 National Student Book 2* (ISBN: 978 1846906 35 0) covers the following units:

Unit	Credit value	Title
16	10	Human resource management in business
18	10	Managing a business event
21	10	Aspects of contract and business law
27	10	Understanding health and safety in the business workplace
29	10	Understanding retailing
36	10	Starting a small business
37	10	Understanding business ethics
38	10	Business and the economic environment

BTEC Level 3 National Business Student Book 2, ISBN: 978 1846906 35 0

Available direct from www.pearsonfe.co.uk/btec2010 and can be ordered from all good bookshops.

About the authors

John Bevan, Helen Coupland-Smith, Rob Dransfield, John Goymer and Catherine Richards have all brought a wealth of experience to their writing. The author team combines verifying, specification writing, pedagogical excellence and best-selling authors to bring you a range of engaging and motivating BTEC resources for the 2010 specifications.

Credits

The publishers would like to thank the following for their kind permission to reproduce their photographs:

(Key: b-bottom; c-centre; l-left; r-right; t-top)

Alamy Images: Adrian Sherratt page 252; Alex Segre page 1; Alistair Heap page 171; Alistair Laming page 18; Asia Images Group Pte Ltd pages 395, 418; Buzz Pictures page 185; BWAC Images page 151; Colin Palmer Photography page 444; David Willis page 341; Errol Rait page 59; Hugh Threlfall page 105; Image page 361; ImageState page 333; Jack Sullivan pages 88, 247; John Rensten page 73; Johner Images page 468; Keith Morris page 168tl; Peter Titmuss page 182; RazorPix page 206; Richard Levine page 197; SS Studios page 89; Vstock page 83; Woodystock pages 51, 347; **Blackberry:** page 402; **Corbis:** Holger Scheibe page 345; Radius Images page 168bl; REUTERS / Danny Moloshok (UNITED STATES ENTERTAINMENT) page 376bc; Rune Hellestad page 30; Smart Creatives page 319; **Getty Images:** AFP page 463, Alex Wong page 376tl, Bloomberg 7; George Rose page 200; Image Bank page 126; Matthew Peters / Manchester United via Getty Images page 203; Photographer's Choice pages 47, 65, Yoshikazu Tsuno / AFP page 227; **H.J. Heinz Company Limited:** page 95; **iStockphoto:** Vikram Raghuvanshi page 49; **Kobal Collection Ltd:** Film page 4 / Celador Films / Pathe International page 39; **Masterfile UK Ltd:** Michael Goldman page 163; **Pearson Education Ltd:** Clark Wiseman; Studio 8 page 237; David Sanderson page 55, Gareth Boden pages 3, 85, 165, 232, 281, 441; Jules Selmes pages 174, 321, 357; **Rex Features:** Copetti / Photofab 376tr, 389, ITV 221, Masatoshi Okauchi 119; Nicholas Bailey 136; Nick Rogers page 376bl; Sipa Press page 376tc, 376br; **Science Photo Library Ltd:** Michael Donne page 262; **Shutterstock:** Andre Blais page 199; Apollofoto page 125; ardni page 4; Castka page 255; Dean Mitchell page 331; Denis and Yulia Pogostins pages 279, 428; Evok20 page 265; Gluestock page 288; Gualtiero Boffi pages 101, IKO 123, 158; Keith Gentry pages 235, 287; Kharidehal Abhirama Ashwin page 397; London Eye page 326; Maksim Toome page 128; Monkey Business Images page 297; Pable Eder page 213; Petros Tsonis page 117; Ricardo A Alves page 170; Roman Sigaev page 439; Ronen page 103; Stephen Orsillo page 312; Vladimir Wrangel page 355.

Cover images: *Front:* **Image Source Ltd**; *Back:* **Pearson Education Ltd:** Gareth Boden cr, **Shutterstock:** Dean Mitchell tl, Keith Gentry tr

The authors and publishers would also like to thank the following individuals and organisations for their approval and permission to reproduce material:

www.poundland.co.uk page 8; Oxfam International, www.innocentdrinks.co.uk page 18; Audit Commission page 23; www.purbeckicecream.co.uk page 62; www.securedbydesign.com page 67; Natural Sleep Innovations Limited page 69; Mid and West Wales Fire Service page 88; Tesco Stores Limited pages 91, 207, 303; www.skoda-auto.com page 128; Microsoft page 135; American Marketing Association page 202; Mail on Sunday page 239; Motor Cycle Industry Association page 265; © 2010 Amazon.com Inc. and its affiliates. All rights reserved. pages 244, 291, 424; www.internetworldstats.com pages 315, 316, 407; The Nielsen Company page 306; www.clickz.com pages 288, 289, 292, 402, 406, 410, 411, 415; www.dell.com page 292; www.telegraph.co.uk page 439; Dave Chaffey/www.marketing-insights.co.uk page 311; Card Corporation page 302; BT Business Club page 306; Sylvia Carr/Wolters Kluwer page 314; Ibstock Brick Ltd page 295; www.fightback.com page 296; www.egg.com page 301; www.4retail.com pages 301, 444; Hey Banner Banner Web & Print Advertising Design page 308; B&Q plc page 455; Southampton City Council page 350; Office of Harriet Harman QC MP page 390; www.saveanddrive.co.uk page 425; Andrew Woolley, Woolley & Co solicitors (www.family-lawfirm.co.uk) page 437; © RS Components Ltd Courtesy of RS Components Ltd page 404; Next page 404; © The Co-operative Bank p.l.c. page 405; Digg page 411; Campsite Directory page 415; Go-Ahead Group plc page 445; South Tyneside Council page 446; Crown Copyright click-use licence number C2008002221 page 447; Copyright Guardian News and Media Ltd 2007, www.greenphase.co.uk page 448; www.othermedia.com page 460; Bells Fish and Chips, www.grsites.com page 462.

Every effort has been made to trace the copyright holders and we apologise in advance for any unintentional omissions. We would be pleased to insert the appropriate acknowledgement in any subsequent edition of this publication.

About your BTEC Level 3 National Business

BTEC Level 3 National Business is one of the few qualifications that will help you succeed in your future career no matter what you go on to do. The principles of business that you will learn here underpin every organisation – from presenting positive marketing messages and developing effective interpersonal skills to operating within a legal framework and accurate accounting.

Your BTEC Level 3 National in Business is a **vocational** or **work-related** qualification. This doesn't mean that it will give you all the skills you need to do a job, but it does mean that you'll have the opportunity to gain specific knowledge, understanding and skills that are relevant to your chosen subject or area of work.

What will you be doing?

The qualification is structured into **mandatory units** (M) (ones that you must do) and your choice of **optional units** (O). How many units you do and which ones you cover depend on the type of qualification you are working towards.

- BTEC Level 3 National Certificate in Business: two mandatory units and one optional unit to provide a total of 30 credits

- BTEC Level 3 National Subsidiary Diploma in Business: four mandatory units and two optional units to provide a total of 60 credits

- BTEC Level 3 National Diploma: four mandatory units and eight optional units to provide a total of 120 credits

- BTEC Level 3 National Extended Diploma: four mandatory units and 14 optional units to provide a total of 180 credits

The table below shows how the units covered by the books in this series cover the different types of BTEC qualifications.

Unit number	Credit value	Unit name	Cert.	Sub Dip.	Dip.	Ext. Dip.
1	10	The business environment	M	M	M	M
2	10	Business resources	M	M	M	M
3	10	Introduction to marketing	O	M	M	M
4	10	Business communication	O	M	M	M
5	10	Business accounting		O	O	O
9	10	Creative product promotion		O	O	O
10	10	Market research in business		O	O	O
12	10	Internet marketing in business		O	O	O
13	10	Recruitment and selection in business		O	O	O
16	10	Human resource management in business		O	O	O
18	10	Managing a business event		O	O	O
19	10	Developing teams in business		O	O	O
21	10	Aspects of contract and business law		O	O	O
27	10	Understanding health and safety in the business workplace		O	O	O
29	10	Understanding retailing		O	O	O
33	10	The impact of communications technology on business		O	O	O
34	10	Website design strategy		O	O	O
36	10	Starting a small business		O	O	O
37	10	Understanding business ethics		O	O	O
38	10	Business and the economic environment		O	O	O

Units in green are covered in this book. Units in yellow are covered in *BTEC Level 3 National Business Student Book 2* (ISBN: 978 1846906 35 0)

How to use this book

This book is designed to help you through your BTEC Level 3 National Business course. It contains many features that will help you develop and apply your skills and knowledge in work-related situations and assist you in getting the most from your course.

Introduction •———————

These introductions give you a snapshot of what to expect from each unit – and what you should be aiming for by the time you finish it!

Assessment and grading •——————— criteria

This table explains what you must do to achieve each of the assessment criteria for each of the mandatory and optional units. For each assessment criterion, shown by the grade buttons **P1**, **M1**, **D1**, etc., there is an assessment activity.

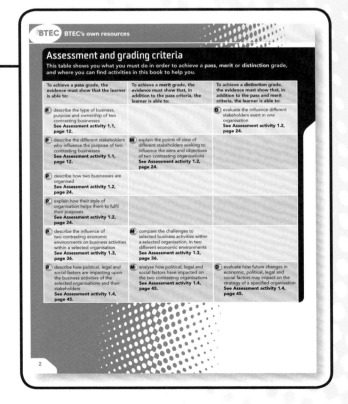

Assessment

Your tutor will set **assignments** throughout your course for you to complete. These may take a variety of forms including business reports, presentations and case studies. The important thing is that you evidence your skills and knowledge to date.

Learner experience

Stuck for ideas? Daunted by your first assignment? These learners have all been through it before…

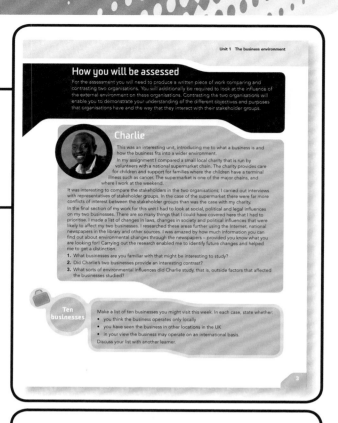

Activities

There are different types of activities for you to do:
Assessment activities are suggestions for tasks that you might do as part of your assignment and will help you develop your knowledge, skills and understanding.
Grading tips clearly explain what you need to do in order to achieve a pass, merit or distinction grade.

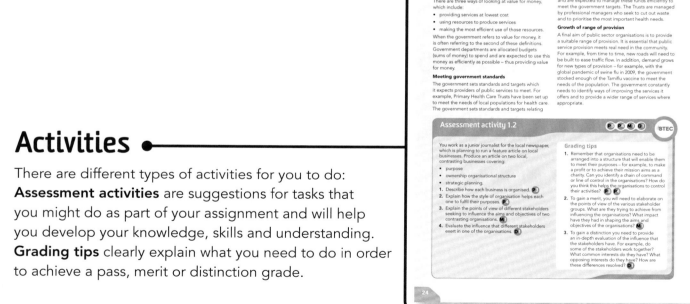

There are also suggestions for activities that will give you a broader grasp of the business world, stretch your understanding and develop your skills.

Personal, learning and thinking skills •

Throughout your BTEC Level 3 National Business course there are lots of opportunities to develop your personal, learning and thinking skills. These will help you work in a team, manage yourself effectively and develop your all-important interpersonal skills. Look out for these as you progress.

PLTS

Working with other learners, carrying out the research and making the presentation will require careful planning of teamwork tasks.

Functional skills •

It's important that you have good English, maths and ICT skills – they're vital in the modern business world and are skills that employers value highly. Use these to help develop and stretch your skills; it might just give you the edge in a job interview!

Functional skills

ICT: this activity will allow you to demonstrate your search skills.

Key terms •

Technical words and phrases are easy to spot. The terms and definitions are also in the glossary at the back of the book.

Key term

Privatised – when the ownership of a business has been transferred from the government to private owners

WorkSpace •

WorkSpace provides snapshots of real-world business issues and shows you how the knowledge and skills you are developing through your course can be applied in your future career.

WorkSpace — Mission statements of well-known organisations

Most organisations, including your places of study, work and leisure, have a mission statement, which is a statement setting out the purpose of the organisation. This is so that all members of the organisation can pull in the same direction. Here are the mission statements of two well-known British businesses.

1. *'Oxfam International is an international group of independent non-governmental organisations dedicated to fighting poverty and related injustice around the world.'* Oxfam International is a confederation of 14 organisations working together in over 100 countries to find lasting solutions to poverty and injustice.
Note that the emphasis is on fighting poverty and injustice rather than any mention of profits. It is an international organisation.

2. *'innocent: The Earth's favourite little food company. A company that makes delicious, healthy, natural, ethical food universally available for all.'*
Note the emphasis that the company seeks to provide healthy and good products which are available across the globe. Note also the emphasis on not behaving like a giant company.

Different types of organisations will emphasise different points in their mission statements. For example, a fashionable hairstyling company would emphasise being at the leading edge of fashion and hair dressing. Other organisations will emphasise aspects such as quality (for example a precision engineering firm), value for money (a supermarket) or customer/client focus (a health centre or medical practice). The mission will also emphasise whether the organisation sees itself as a local, national or international business. The mission should be easy to understand and should be shared with employees and other stakeholders in the business.
Both the Oxfam and innocent mission statements provide a clear purpose for the organisation and its members to work towards.

Think about it!

1. Why do organisations need to have a mission statement?
2. What do the mission statements above tell us about the differences between these organisations?
3. Which of the mission statements do you think is most likely to give a sense of purpose to stakeholders? Justify your answer.
4. Find out whether an organisation that you work for or are a member of has a mission statement. Are people who work for the organisation familiar with the mission, and if so, how does this affect their actions? Interview two or three people at different levels within the organisation to find this out.

Just checking •────────────────────

When you see this sort of activity, take stock! These quick activities and questions are there to check your knowledge. You can use them to see how much progress you've made and to identify any areas where you need to refresh your knowledge.

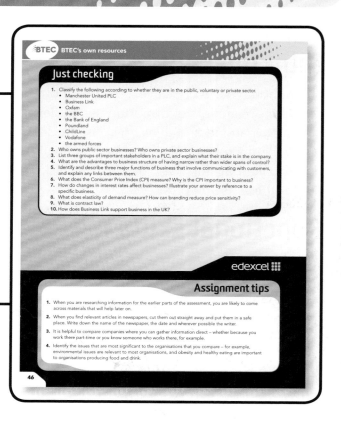

Edexcel's assignment tips •──────

At the end of each unit, you'll find hints and tips to help you get the best mark you can, such as the best websites to go to, checklists to help you remember processes and useful reminders to avoid common mistakes. You might want to read this information before starting your assignment.

Don't miss out on these resources to help you!

Have you read your **BTEC Level 3 National Study Skills Guide**? It's full of advice on study skills, putting your assignments together and making the most of being a BTEC Business student.

Ask your tutor about extra materials to help you through your course. You'll find interesting videos, activities, presentations and information about the world of business.

Your book is just part of the exciting resources from Edexcel to help you succeed in your BTEC course.

Visit:
* www.edexcel.com/btec or
* www.pearsonfe.co.uk/btec2010

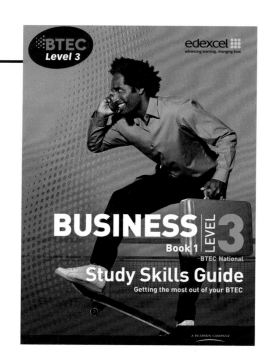

1 The business environment

You will be familiar with many of your local businesses, such as the local corner shop, as well as national businesses, such as Poundland and Wilkinsons. You will have some knowledge of international businesses, such as Costa Coffee and Virgin, which operate in many countries across the world, whether as a customer or perhaps as an employee. This unit provides a background picture of these organisations and will help you understand what their owners, managers and stakeholders are trying to achieve. The unit also shows you how these organisations are structured and how plans are made to guide business activity.

You will examine how businesses are affected by outside change. We have recently experienced a global recession that affected all businesses. Most people across the world felt that their jobs were less secure. However, there are other factors that businesses need to be aware of. These include changes in laws, and changes in society such as population structures and the way in which consumers spend their money. You will investigate this changing business environment.

Learning outcomes

After completing this unit, you should:

1. know the range of different businesses and their ownership
2. understand how businesses are organised to achieve their purposes
3. know the impact of the economic environment on businesses
4. know how political, legal and social factors impact on business.

Assessment and grading criteria

This table shows you what you must do in order to achieve a **pass**, **merit** or **distinction** grade, and where you can find activities in this book to help you.

To achieve a **pass** grade, the evidence must show that the learner is able to:	To achieve a **merit** grade, the evidence must show that, in addition to the pass criteria, the learner is able to:	To achieve a **distinction** grade, the evidence must show that, in addition to the pass and merit criteria, the learner is able to:
P1 describe the type of business, purpose and ownership of two contrasting businesses **See Assessment activity 1.1, page 12.**		**D1** evaluate the influence different stakeholders exert in one organisation **See Assessment activity 1.2, page 24.**
P2 describe the different stakeholders who influence the purpose of two contrasting businesses **See Assessment activity 1.1, page 12.**	**M1** explain the points of view of different stakeholders seeking to influence the aims and objectives of two contrasting organisations **See Assessment activity 1.2, page 24.**	
P3 describe how two businesses are organised **See Assessment activity 1.2, page 24.**		
P4 explain how their style of organisation helps them to fulfil their purposes **See Assessment activity 1.2, page 24.**		
P5 describe the influence of two contrasting economic environments on business activities within a selected organisation **See Assessment activity 1.3, page 36.**	**M2** compare the challenges to selected business activities within a selected organisation, in two different economic environments **See Assessment activity 1.3, page 36.**	
P6 describe how political, legal and social factors are impacting upon the business activities of the selected organisations and their stakeholders **See Assessment activity 1.4, page 45.**	**M3** analyse how political, legal and social factors have impacted on the two contrasting organisations **See Assessment activity 1.4, page 45.**	**D2** evaluate how future changes in economic, political, legal and social factors may impact on the strategy of a specified organisation **See Assessment activity 1.4, page 45.**

How you will be assessed

For the assessment you will need to produce a written piece of work comparing and contrasting two organisations. You will additionally be required to look at the influence of the external environment on these organisations. Contrasting the two organisations will enable you to demonstrate your understanding of the different objectives and purposes that organisations have and the way that they interact with their stakeholder groups.

Charlie

This was an interesting unit, introducing me to what a business is and how the business fits into a wider environment.

In my assignment I compared a small local charity that is run by volunteers with a national supermarket chain. The charity provides care for children and support for families where the children have a terminal illness such as cancer. The supermarket is one of the major chains, and where I work at the weekend.

It was interesting to compare the stakeholders in the two organisations; I carried out interviews with representatives of stakeholder groups. In the case of the supermarket there were far more conflicts of interest between the stakeholder groups than was the case with my charity.

In the final section of my work for this unit I had to look at social, political and legal influences on my two businesses. There are so many things that I could have covered here that I had to prioritise. I made a list of changes in laws, changes in society and political influences that were likely to affect my two businesses. I researched these areas further using the Internet, national newspapers in the library and other sources. I was amazed by how much information you can find out about environmental changes through the newspapers – provided you know what you are looking for! Carrying out the research enabled me to identify future changes and helped me to get a distinction.

1. What businesses are you familiar with that might be interesting to study?
2. Did Charlie's two businesses provide an interesting contrast?
3. What sorts of environmental influences did Charlie study, that is, outside factors that affected the businesses studied?

Ten businesses

Make a list of ten businesses you might visit this week. In each case, state whether:

- you think the business operates only locally
- you have seen the business in other locations in the UK
- in your view the business may operate on an international basis.

Discuss your list with another learner.

1. Know the range of different businesses and their ownership

1.1 Range of different businesses

There are many different types of business that you come across as a customer or employee or that you hear about in news stories. It is helpful to develop a picture of the **range of businesses**.

> ### Key term
>
> **Range of businesses** – the variety of different types of business. Three useful ways of classifying business are: according to where they operate; what the businesses are trying to achieve; and the sector of business activity they are involved in

Local, national, international and global businesses

A new business that sets up in your town is a local business. However, one day it may set up outlets in other parts of Britain so that it becomes a national business. Soon after, it might start to sell its products overseas – becoming an international business. Finally, it may produce goods and develop selling outlets across the globe – by which time it will be a global business. Toni & Guy is an example of a business that has expanded very quickly.

Marks & Spencer and the Body Shop are good examples of British organisations that started off as small local businesses. Both then went on to become national, international and global businesses. However, both have also faced difficulties – particularly in developing an international presence. In 2006 the Body Shop was taken over by a larger global business, the cosmetics giant L'Oréal.

Public and private businesses

Public sector businesses are those that have been set up or taken over by the government. Private businesses are owned by private citizens. In many countries, the majority of businesses are owned by private individuals. Public sector businesses are less likely to take risks, because they operate for the benefit of the wider public rather than just to make a profit. Large private sector businesses, like the mobile phone company Vodafone, are owned by shareholders. Anyone can buy shares in Vodafone.

Case study: Hair Fashion

The Hair Fashion chain was originally a simple local family business. Now it has almost 500 salons spread across the globe, many of which are on a franchise basis. In addition to this, the chain sells a range of hair care and styling products worth hundreds of millions of pounds each year. The latest part of the strategy has been the setting up of a website to market these products.

The business started with the father, Luigi, who emigrated from Italy to England in the 1960s. He taught his two sons the hairdressing trade. They set up their own salon in London, and created the world's best-known brand in hairdressing. The daughter, Maria, set up a Hair Fashion salon in the United States in the 1990s. The chain is now owned by the brothers and their sister.

1. At what point did Hair Fashion become an international business?
2. What benefits do you think that businesses

like Hair Fashion gain from becoming national rather than local businesses?

3. What difficulties might arise from becoming an international business?
4. How might the website help the business to succeed globally?

Many people believe that businesses are run better when they are privately owned. Private owners risk their own money, so are determined for their business to succeed. However, they may take too many risks or be too greedy, as with the financial crisis in 2008–09 when many banks got into difficulty because they had lent too much in order to try to make higher profits.

In the UK there are very few public businesses left. Most businesses have been **privatised**.

Key term

Privatised – when the ownership of a business has been transferred from the government to private owners

Examples of public sector businesses include:

- Her Majesty's Customs and Revenue – the UK's tax-collecting body.
- National Archives – the body responsible for looking after government records and records from the courts of law.

Examples of private businesses include Virgin, Innocent, Tesco and lastminute.com.

In some countries, the public sector continues to play a major part in the economy. For example, the biggest employer in India is Indian Railways, and millions of people work for the government in departments such as the Public Works Department (PWD), maintaining roads, looking after government buildings and doing other important work.

Activity: Football teams

What do you think would be the advantages and disadvantages of top football teams, such as Arsenal men's or women's football teams, being owned by the government rather than by private shareholders? Discuss this with another learner.

Not-for-profit/voluntary businessess

Not all businesses are set up to make a profit. Many organisations are set up for quite different purposes. For example, the international charity Médecins sans Frontières provides doctors and nurses across the globe to areas where there are wars, famines and other situations in which people are suffering. The organisation runs on business lines (for example, seeking to use the money it receives in donations as efficiently as possible) and has many paid workers, but it does not seek to make a profit, just to cover the cost of running.

A voluntary organisation is also a not-for-profit organisation. It is set up, organised, staffed and run by people who are working purely on a voluntary basis, usually for a good cause. Examples of voluntary organisations are the Women's Royal Voluntary Service (WRVS) and Voluntary Service Overseas (VSO).

Case study: Voluntary Service Overseas

Voluntary Service Overseas (VSO) is an example of a not-for-profit global organisation. It is UK-based and seeks to match volunteers with projects in areas of the world that need help. For example, a volunteer might teach English to children in an African country, or teach them how to use computers. Many volunteers are young people, but volunteers include older people with specialist skills who can make a real difference to the lives of people in need.

1. Why do you think that voluntary organisations work on a not-for-profit basis?
2. To what extent would you say that it is important for voluntary organisations to be businesslike?
3. What sorts of people are most likely to work for voluntary organisations and why?
4. Visit the VSO website at www.vso.org.uk and set out four examples of ways in which VSO can be said to operate in a businesslike way.

Did you know?

To become a charity in the UK, an organisation has to meet tight requirements set out by law. It must register with the Charity Commission and present a set of accounts each year. Charities have to be set up for a specific purpose, such as to provide educational benefits or humanitarian aid.

Primary, secondary and tertiary sectors

Most of you will have tasted fresh orange juice drinks which appear as branded drinks under names such as Tropicana or innocent. The production of fresh orange drinks in plastic bottles and cartons provides a good example of the three sectors of business activity.

The **primary sector** stage is concerned with extracting the primary products of nature. Oranges are grown on trees by orange farmers. Oranges typically grow in a Mediterranean-type climate in countries like Spain, Morocco or Israel. When the oranges are ripe they are transported to market.

The second stage of producing a fresh orange drink is to remove the skin and pips, and to squeeze the oranges. Bottling, packing and labelling the finished fresh orange drinks is part of this process in the **secondary sector**.

Bringing the finished product to your local supermarket involves the **tertiary sector**. Tertiary activities involve providing services – both to businesses and to consumers. Examples of services involved in providing fresh orange drinks include:

- transporting the oranges and the finished drinks
- selling the fresh orange juice in a shop or supermarket
- advertising the fresh orange juice
- providing insurance services to the transport, **manufacturing** and **retailing** companies.

Activity: Classification

Classify the following lists into primary, secondary and tertiary sector businesses:

- a mining company
- a newspaper
- an advertising agency
- a newspaper delivery business
- a canning factory
- a forestry business
- an oyster-gathering business
- a furniture manufacturer
- a building company
- a second-hand furniture shop.

Key terms

Primary sector – extracting raw products from nature

Secondary sector – transforming those raw products into finished or part-finished goods

Tertiary sector – providing services to individuals and businesses

Manufacturing – making things (in the secondary sector)

Retailing – selling things in small quantities (shops in the tertiary sector)

1.2 Business purposes
Supply of products or services

Business activity typically involves one person or organisation providing a product or service that they supply to someone else. Usually this involves payment. Think of the things that you might have needed or wanted this week. Business activity helps you to meet these requirements and various businesses have been set up to do this, as Table 1.1 shows.

Table 1.1: Examples of products or services supplied.

Product or service	Want or need that it satisfies	Business
Internet music download	For entertainment	Online music store
Sandwich	Because you were hungry	Bakery or supermarket
Tooth filling	Because a filling had come out and was causing pain	Dentist
Haircut	Because you wanted to look more attractive	Hair salon

The growth of expensive hair salons in Britain provide a good illustration of the way in which private businesses have responded to the increased demand for such services from customers. People in Britain spend more money on their hair than anywhere else in Europe, and many are prepared to pay £100 or more to have their hair cut in an expensive salon. Another type of business that has responded to growing customer demand is coffee shop chains like Costa Coffee and Starbucks.

Costa Coffee is a business that has expanded nationally and internationally in response to growing customer demand.

A physical product is an item that you can touch and see, like a loaf of bread or a jar of coffee. A service is something that provides satisfaction to the buyer because it is helpful to them, but does not consist of a physical item. Good examples of services are insurance and banking.

A visit to a coffee shop will provide you with both a physical product and a service. The physical product is the cake that you eat or the coffee that you drink, and the service includes being waited on and having your drink poured for you.

Profit and not-for-profit organisations

Many businesses are set up to make a profit. To make a profit, a business needs to make sure that the money it receives from sales activities more than cover all of its **running costs**. The business needs to provide goods that customers are willing to buy at prices that are higher than the costs of supplying those goods. Everywhere you look, you will find businesses seeking to make profits, ranging from huge international oil companies like British Petroleum (BP) to big supermarkets like Tesco. While BP has generated record profits for a UK-based business in recent years, its profits fluctuate considerably. While Tesco is responsible for £1 in every £7 of retail sales in the UK, it only makes seven pence profit for every pound's worth of goods that it sells. Even these giant businesses suffer in periods of recession such as the downturn in business activity in 2008–09.

Key term

Running costs – day-to-day costs incurred in operating a firm or facility

Case study: Poundland

Poundland is a good example of a profit organisation that boomed during the recession in 2009 – reporting a doubling of its profits to £400 million. Poundland, based in the West Midlands was established in April 1990, opening its first store in Burton-on-Trent by two businessmen, Steve Smith and Dave Dodd. The company was taken over by a company (Advent International) that bought up the shares in Poundland.

Since then Poundland has grown from strength to strength and is now Europe's biggest single price discount retailer with 254 stores nationwide, which includes eight stores in Northern Ireland.

Poundland is an irresistible shopping experience where shoppers are guaranteed to find quality brands and something new each time they visit. Customers are spread across all age groups, but recently it has seen an increase in professional and managerial classes to 22 per cent.

The secret of Poundland's success is the quality of the products it offers, as well as the £1 price point. Poundland offers 3000 everyday product lines across 16 categories, including food and drink, health and beauty, household, baby, pets, party and DIY. It also offers 1,000 top brands, including Cadbury, Pampers, Colgate, Walkers and Kodak.

Poundland is able to buy in bulk from suppliers because it has over 2.5 million customers every day and has excellent relationships with its supplier base. Stock falls into three main categories: main lines bought direct from manufacturers, seasonal ranges and clearance stock. 65 per cent of Poundland's products are bought from British suppliers.

1. Why do you think that 2.5 million customers shop at Poundland every day?

2. How is Poundland able to make a profit despite selling items at only £1 each?

3. Is Poundland a local, national, international or global business? Justify your choice.

4. To what extent would the recession of 2008–09 have affected Poundland's profits?

PLTS

This case study encourages you to reflect on what you have learned so far about private sector businesses. Think about how you introduce concepts like demand, profit, risk and size of business into your answers.

To show how a business makes a profit, we can take the example of a bookshop selling a dictionary for £20. It may have paid the book supplier only £12 for the dictionary. However, the difference between the £20 selling price and the £12 buying price is not profit. The bookshop also has to deduct from the money that it receives part of the cost of running the shop (electricity, rates, and so on) and the wages of staff. These costs need to be spread across all of the books that the bookshop sells. If the bookshop has worked out that these costs come to £6 for each book sold, then the profit from the dictionary will only be £2.

Businesses do not always seek to sell their products for a profit. Sometimes they do so 'at cost'. Supplying at cost occurs when the money received from selling a product is equal to the cost of supplying that product and may be done for a variety of reasons. For example,

the England Netball Association may offer schools low-cost seats at an England netball fixture to increase interest in the sport.

Another good example of a not-for-profit organisation is Oxfam. Oxfam raises money for famine relief. However, it is not just a charity, it is also a highly professional organisation. Oxfam shops sell second-hand items on high streets and other retail locations. As a charity, Oxfam receives an 80 per cent business rates reduction. This makes it very competitive and because of the high quality of its service and its low cost of operation, it has

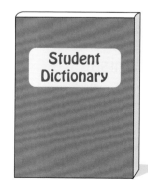

Price:	£ 20.00
Cost of buying from bookseller:	£ 12.00
Contribution to cost of running the shop:	£ 6.00
Profit:	£ 2.00

Fig. 1.1: How a business makes a profit.

recently driven a number of independent second-hand book sellers out of business.

1.3 Ownership

Public, private and voluntary sectors

In the public sector, businesses are owned by the government or by agencies appointed by the government to provide a service. In the private sector, businesses are owned by individuals. An individual owner is typically a single owner or a group of partners, or the owners will be shareholders. In the voluntary sector, organisations typically have groups of trustees responsible for overseeing the work of the organisation.

Table 1.2: Owners and objectives of businesses.

Sector	Owners	Objectives
Private	Owned by individuals or shareholders	Profit is often the major driving force
Public	Owned by government	Has wider objectives than profit – often has wider social service aims
Voluntary	Supervised by trustees	Usually set up to provide a service to the wider community

Types of ownership

Owners are the people to whom a business belongs. For example, Fred's corner store may be owned by Fred on his own – he is a sole trader. In contrast, the solicitors Makepeace, Patel and Amin would be a partnership.

Sole trader and partnership businesses are not only owned by the owners, they are also controlled by them. Control refers to decision making. Fred makes his own decisions about what he sells, whom he employs and when he opens and shuts his shop.

In companies, however, there is a distinction between the ownership and the control of the business. Companies are owned by shareholders but it is often directors or managers who make decisions and hence control the business.

Shareholders are people who put capital (money) into a business. They receive a reward for the risk they take

in the form of a return called a dividend, which is paid out from company profits.

Sole traders

A sole trader business is owned and controlled by one person. It is the most common type of business and is found in a wide range of activities (for example, window cleaning, plumbing, electrical work). No complicated work is required to set up a sole trader business. Decisions can be made quickly and close contact can be kept with customers and employees, and all profits go to the sole trader.

But there are disadvantages. As a sole trader you have to make all the decisions yourself, and you may have to work long hours. (Then what happens if you are ill or want a holiday?) Another disadvantage is that you do not have the legal protection of limited liability. This means that should the business run up debts, these become the responsibility of the business owner and may be unlimited. The sole trader typically provides much of their own finance, although they may also borrow from a bank or friends. As a sole trader you need to be a jack-of-all-trades, to cover all aspects of the business.

Partnerships

A partnership is usually formed by signing a Deed of Partnership (which sets out how profits will be shared and the different responsibilities and payments to partners) with the paperwork being supervised by a solicitor. Partnerships are typically found in professional work, for example, a medical or dental practice, or a group of accountants or solicitors. People in business partnerships can share knowledge, skills and workload, and it may be easier to raise the capital needed. When one of the partners is ill or goes on holiday, the business can cope.

The main disadvantages of partnerships are that:

- people can fall out ('she doesn't work as hard as me!')
- ordinary partnerships do not have limited liability
- partnerships can rarely borrow or raise large amounts of capital
- business decisions may be more difficult (and slower) to make because of the need to consult all the partners
- there may be disagreements about how things should be done
- profits have to be shared.

A 'limited liability partnership' was created in Britain in 2003. This exists in businesses like accounting and the law, where there are hundreds of partners. This is to protect individual partners, should another partner's actions cause the partnership trouble.

Public and private limited companies

A limited company has to be registered before it can start to operate. The owners of the limited company are its shareholders. They elect directors to represent their interests. A managing director is the senior director on the Board. The Board consists of executive directors who make the major policy decisions about the business, and some non-executive directors. These provide specialist advice and offer links with other businesses.

Shareholders put funds into a limited company by buying shares. They are able to have a say about the way the limited company is run when they attend an Annual General Meeting (AGM) each year. At this AGM, highlights of the Annual Report will be presented to shareholders as well as the annual accounts. At this meeting the shareholders are able to question company policy, vote out the directors and take actions such as refusing to approve pay rises to directors.

There are two main types of limited company.

- **Private limited companies** tend to be smaller than public ones (below) and are often family businesses. There must be at least two shareholders but there is no maximum number. Shares in private limited companies cannot be traded on the stock exchange, and often shares can only be bought with the permission of the Board of Directors. Private limited companies may find it possible to raise more cash (by selling shares) than unlimited-liability businesses. The shareholders can also have the protection of limited liability.

- **Public limited companies** have their shares bought and sold on the stock exchange. The main advantage of these are that large amounts of capital can be raised very quickly. One disadvantage is that control of a business can be lost by the original shareholders if large quantities of shares are purchased as part of a 'takeover bid'. It is also costly to have shares quoted on the stock exchange.

Government departments and agencies

A government department like the Department for Customs and Revenue operates on behalf of the government and is staffed by civil servants, known in this department as customs and revenue officers. Their job is to collect income tax and other taxes on behalf of the government, to collect repayments on student loans and to make payments known as tax credits. Rather than seeking to make a profit, they will want to collect taxes efficiently and make sure that taxpayers get a fair deal.

Government agencies are more independent than government departments. The government sets these up to take responsibility for a particular activity. For example, the Child Protection Agency is a government-funded body responsible for looking after the rights of children. Although it is funded by government and accountable to government, it has considerable freedom to manage its own affairs. These bodies are set up with tight guidelines, but in the interest of fairness they need to be seen to operate in an independent way.

Did you know?

Local councils are responsible for supervising and, in a small number of cases, owning local services. What is your local council? In their specific area, the local authority will give contracts to private companies to run certain services such as refuse collection or street lighting. It is the job of the council to oversee the efficient running of these services. Local councils also own and supervise the collection of rents and repairs to social housing.

Worker co-operatives

A worker co-operative is a body that is owned by the people who work for it. A worker co-operative has limited liability. To become a member of a worker co-operative, an employee would have to buy a share in the organisation. Each member has one vote in making decisions. This is democratic and prevents one individual or a few individuals gaining control. Members receive a share of the profits of the business in the form of a dividend. When they leave the co-operative, they can take their funds back. The basic principle behind a worker co-operative is that those who do the work should get the rewards. They tend to be small-scale, local enterprises.

Charitable trusts

A charity is an organisation that is set up to raise funds and support other people or a good cause. The business objective of charities is to create a surplus to use for helping others. A surplus occurs when the revenue (money coming into the charity) is greater than the costs of running the charity.

The management of charity work is overseen by a group of trustees, who are volunteers with reputations as responsible citizens. Many will have a range of experience in both charity and business activities. Charities have to register as such and must produce annual accounts that are available to be viewed.

Charities employ paid managers and workers (unlike voluntary organisations, which rely on the goodwill of their staff).

1.4 Key stakeholders

In 1988 the giant Swiss global company Nestlé took over the UK company Rowntree Macintosh. Rowntree's of York was famous for producing confectionery such as Smarties, Quality Street and a range of other leading brands. In September 2006 Nestlé announced that it would be losing almost 650 jobs at its York plant and that a number of brands would be cut back. Smarties would now be made in Hamburg.

Which individuals and groups do you think were affected by this decision – for better or worse?

People who have an interest in the decisions that businesses make are called stakeholders. Most decisions affect a number of stakeholders. Fig. 1.2 below shows a number of stakeholders in Nestlé's decision to pull out of York.

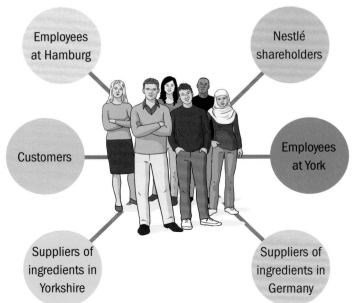

Fig. 1.2: How would Nestlé's decision have affected stakeholders?

You can see from the Smarties example that stakeholders' interests are intertwined. Sometimes a decision is good for a range of stakeholders. Sometimes a decision is good for some stakeholders and bad for others.

The key stakeholders in a business include the following.

1. **Customers** – They want a company to produce high-quality, value-for-money products. Customers often identify with the brands they buy. They like to see improvements that give them better value for money.

2. **Employees** – Their stake is that the company provides them with a livelihood. They seek security of employment, promotion opportunities and good rates of reward. They may also want to work for a company that they are proud of.

3. **Suppliers** – They want steady orders and prompt payment. They also want to feel valued by the company that they supply.

4. **Owners** – This may be a sole trader or a partnership. In a company it would be the shareholders. Owners are often thought to be the most important stakeholders because they might have put a good part of their life into setting up a business. They see themselves as being the principal risk takers. Owners like to see their share of profit increasing, and the value of their business rising.

5. **Trade unions** – These represent the interests of groups of employees. They seek to secure higher wages and better working conditions for their members.

6. **Employer associations** – These are the employer's equivalent of the trade unions. There are employer associations representing the interests of employers in specific industries.

7. **Local and national communities** – The actions of business can have a dramatic effect on communities. For example, the oil giant Shell has built vast pipelines in Nigeria, which run through the lands of various tribal people. The pipelines can be very dangerous and cause local pollution. Community leaders therefore represent important interest groups.

8. **Governments** – These want business to be successful, to create jobs and to pay taxes. They want to see prosperous businesses that take a full responsibility in looking after the welfare of society.

Influence of stakeholders on organisations

A business needs to take account of the interests of all of its stakeholder groupings. These interests are all linked together. For example, if Richard Branson decides to run his Virgin trains using greener fuels, this means that the cost of journeys on Virgin trains increases.

This may be seen as a bad thing because:

- customers may have to pay higher fares
- shareholders may get lower profits
- Virgin buys from new suppliers rather than the old ones

- some jobs may be at risk
- the government may lose taxes.

However, it may be seen as a good thing because:

- it is better for the environment
- more people may want to travel by train because it is greener
- employees feel better about working for a greener transport company
- the company may increase sales and make more profits.

Activity: Researching local businesses

You should base the following task on research carried out in your local town supported by knowledge that learners in your group acquire from work experience and part-time jobs.

Make a study of a sole trader, partnership, private limited company and public limited company.

1. Who own``s these businesses?
2. How much capital does each have? (If you cannot find out the exact sum, give a

breakdown of the main forms of capital it relies on, for example, x per cent owner's capital, y per cent borrowings.)

3. What are the advantages and disadvantages of this organisational form for this particular business organisation?

As a group, you could present the work as a newspaper feature using a desktop publishing package.

Assessment activity 1.1

 BTEC

Carry out an investigation into two contrasting types of business organisation from different sectors (you could choose one in the private sector and one in the public sector or voluntary sector). You should consider stakeholder influence in the two organisations, and your report should focus on:

- business activity, for example, local, national, global
- business sector
- business purpose
- ownership of the business
- key stakeholders of the business.

1. Describe the type of business, purpose and ownership of two contrasting organisations. **P1**
2. Describe the different stakeholders who influence the purpose of these contrasting organisations. **P2**

Grading tips

1. An Internet search using the name of the business/organisation will be a good starting point. You should send off for a company report for any private sector company –

addresses will be supplied on the company website. You should also study recent news reports to get the latest changes in the activities of these organisations. Make sure you describe the activities of the two organisations. You should not spend too much time on the history, but it may be helpful to give a brief introduction showing how and why the business was set up, and how it has changed to become what it is today. **P1**

2. Reading company reports about your chosen organisations and other literature they produce will give you a good idea of who the main stakeholders are in these organisations. Look through the report to identify specific mentions of stakeholder groups and ways that the organisation is seeking to engage with these groups, for example, through meetings and other communications. What sorts of relationships is the company seeking to build with different groups? You may feel that some groups get more attention than others. Why do you think this happens? **P2**

2. Understand how businesses are organised to achieve their purposes

2.1 Organisational structures

Organisations like Oxfam, innocent and Poundland need to be organised into a structure that will enable them to meet their purposes – to provide famine relief, to create excellent smoothies or to provide bargains for shoppers. For example, Oxfam will have a section concerned with media and public relations, another with managing its shops and others concerned with organising famine relief in various parts of the world.

Purpose

An organisation's structure should be designed to:

- divide up the work to be done
- establish lines of **control** and communication.

For example, innocent is organised into teams that:

- procure supplies of fresh fruit for producing the smoothies
- deal directly with retailers to organise supplies to shops, cafés and restaurants
- recruit new people to work for innocent and look after their training and development at work
- find out about customer preferences and manage promotion and advertising.

Dividing up the work in this way means that people are clear about who does what in the organisation and that all of the tasks required are performed.

Organisational structure is also important in controlling organisational activities, to avoid conflict and individuals making decisions that contradict others. Organisational structure therefore creates patterns through which decisions and activities can be controlled. This often involves some form of chain of command, or **line of control**. Individuals lower down the organisation will often have to report to a senior before taking action or making particular decisions.

Key terms

Control – the process of making sure that things are done in expected ways

Line of control – where individuals are responsible to a line manager or supervisor. The senior colleague will be responsible for making more important decisions

Organisational structures also set out important aspects of how communication will take place. Lines of communication refer to who will talk to whom in an organisation. Some decisions and plans will need to be made through a team communicating with each other. In other situations, communication may be top down – that is, a senior tells a junior what needs to be done.

Types of organisation structure

There are a number of ways of structuring organisations, which include:

- **function:** this is a discrete part of an organisation designed to meet a specific purpose such as production, marketing or accounts
- **geographical area:** for example, North West, Wales, Midlands, London
- **product groups:** for example, a confectionery and sweets manufacturer may have separate divisions for chewing gum, chocolate and sweets or ice cream
- **type of customer:** for example, many banks have sections that deal directly with individual customers and those that deal entirely with business customers.

Activity: Organisational structure

Carry out an Internet search for a well-known organisation, for example, World Vision, Oxfam, Boots, M&S or Shell, and see if you can identify the organisation structure. You may want to print off a copy of their organisation chart so as to be able to discuss this structure with others.

Typically at the top of the home page you will find a box that you can click on which has a heading such as 'About Us' or 'Organisational Structure'.

Functional skills

ICT: this activity will allow you to demonstrate your search skills.

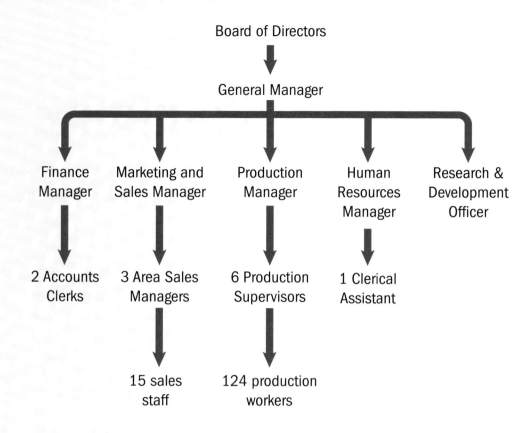

Fig. 1.3: Organisational chart for a manufacturing company.

Organisational charts

An organisational chart shows the main parts of the organisation, and the relationship between the various parts.

For example, Fig. 1.3 shows the structure of a manufacturing company making office furniture. Note that important parts of the structure are the production department and the sales department selling direct to other businesses.

When you look at an organisational chart, it should give you a clear picture of what the relevant sections of the organisation are and who reports to whom.

Line management refers to a person who is directly responsible for somebody else. For example, the production manager reports to the general manager. The production supervisors report to the production manager. The production supervisors supervise the work of the production workers.

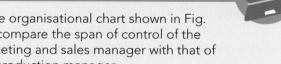

Activity: Span of control

In the organisational chart shown in Fig. 1.3, compare the span of control of the marketing and sales manager with that of the production manager.

1. Why do you think that their spans of control are different?

2. Which individuals within the organisation have the greatest span of control?

3. Why do you think this is?

Span of control

The span of control is the number of people that individuals are responsible for in an organisation. The wider the span of control, the greater the number of people for whom the individual is responsible. A manager who tries to supervise too many people may be so overworked that their staff in turn are unable to perform their duties effectively. On the other hand, if a manager has too few people to supervise, their time may be wasted – for example, in explaining things to a single individual.

2.2 Functional areas

The functional areas are the specialist areas of activity within an organisation. These include:

- finance
- marketing
- production
- customer service
- sales
- human resources.

Finance

Finance department functions include:

- keeping records of financial activity, for example, sales made by the business
- providing managers with information that they can use in decision making, for example, the cost of creating products.

The chief accountant supervises the work of the accounts department. The managers of an organisation need to be constantly aware of the financial state of the business and the likely financial impact of decisions that they make.

Accounts can be subdivided into two sections.

- Financial accounting is responsible for keeping records of financial events as they occur – for example, the sale of a car in a salesroom. This section will also produce the annual accounts and keep VAT records.
- Management accounting is responsible for supplying information that helps managers make decisions. This includes working out production costs. Management accountants also set out budgets.

Marketing

The marketing function is responsible for identifying, anticipating and satisfying customer requirements.

Marketing involves carrying out market research to find out which types of customer make up a particular market, what they want, where they want it, how they

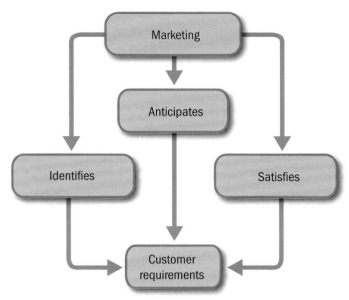

Fig. 1.4: The role of marketing.

like it and at what price. Marketing works closely with production. This is so that the wishes of customers can be linked to new product development.

Marketers will have an important say in deciding:

- the **products** that the company produces
- the **prices** charged
- the **promotions** designed to encourage customers
- the **place** where goods are sold.

These are called the four Ps of marketing.

Production

Production organises who makes the goods and how and when they are made.

The production manager of a company is responsible for making sure raw materials are processed into finished goods well. They must make sure work is carried out to an appropriate standard, and must supervise work activity.

Production managers will decide how goods will be produced – that is, the methods of production. They will also be responsible for working out who does what and when. This involves creating schedules for when employees will carry out particular tasks. The production manager will typically have production supervisors working under them.

Customer service

Customer service is concerned with looking after customers at all stages of their relationship with a company (see Table 1.3).

Table 1.3: Stages of customers' relationship with a company.

Stage	Details
Prior to making purchase	Providing customers with details about offers, and making sure they are given personal attention
During purchase	Making sure that customers are listened to and valued
Post-purchase	Attending to customer complaints, providing after-sales service such as servicing of goods, spare parts or information about new products

When you visit your local supermarket, the first area that you will find when you enter the store is usually the customer service department. Customer service also carries out frequent survey work to find out how customers rate the service they have received.

Many large organisations have customer service call centres dedicated to dealing with customer service issues. The centre is overseen by a manager, and typically call centre employees will work in teams.

Sales

This function is responsible for getting customers to buy what the company produces. It liaises closely with the marketing department. While the role of marketing is to find out what customers want and then to provide the right mix of price, product, promotion and place, the role of sales is to get customers to buy what the business produces.

The main responsibility of the sales department is to create orders for goods and services. Some organisations employ a large force on a regional basis, for example, businesses selling photocopiers

or cars. Other organisations depend on advertising to stimulate sales and only employ a small sales team. The sales team will try to identify 'prospects' – potential customers – and then follow this up to try to close the sale.

Human resources

Human resource managers are responsible for all aspects of people management in an organisation. The type of work covered in the human resource function might include a:

- policy-making role – creating major policies about people in the organisation, for example, a policy about retirement
- welfare role – concerned with looking after people and their needs
- supportive role – helping other functional managers to develop their work, such as helping them in the processes involved in recruiting new employees
- bargaining and negotiating role – acting as an intermediary between different groups, for example, trade unions and managers
- administrative role – paying wages and supervising health and safety requirements
- educational and development role – helping to train and develop employees.

Activity: Organisational functions

Identify the various functions of a local organisation.

1. How many people are involved in each of these functional areas?
2. Which of these functions does the organisation believe are the most important, and why?

Did you know?

One criticism made of some organisations is that they 'work in silos'. A silo is a tall container. If you imagine an organisation made up of a lot of silos, then you would see a situation in which there would be poor communication between departments. In modern business practice, it is important to break down these silos so that the various parts of the organisation work together.

Human Resources Management

Fig. 1.5: Human resources covers many aspects of people management.

Fig. 1.6: Why is communication poor in organisations where staff work in 'silos'?

2.3 Strategic planning

The aims of organisations depend on the type of business they are. For example, the aims of a charity organisation will be quite different from those of a for-profit global business.

A business needs to have a clear sense of direction, which must be clearly communicated to all stakeholders. This is the aim of the business which can then be broken down into smaller aims, and objectives.

Strategic planning is of central importance in giving direction to organisations.

A strategic plan is drawn up for a relatively long period of time, typically by senior managers. The plan will cover a five-year period or longer.

The plan needs to be shaped by the mission and values of the organisation.

Key term

Strategic planning – planning for the whole organisation, setting out its aims and the major resources that will be used to achieve these

Mission and values

Most organisations today set out two statements that guide their actions. These are:

- a **mission statement** setting out the purpose of the organisation, usually in one or a small number of sentences. It needs to be clear to communicate the key purpose of the organisation to all stakeholders

- a **values statement** setting out the core values of the organisation and what it believes in. These values should shape all of the relationships between members of the organisation and other stakeholders.

WorkSpace Mission statements of well-known organisations

Most organisations, including your places of study, work and leisure, have a mission statement, which is a statement setting out the purpose of the organisation. This is so that all members of the organisation can pull in the same direction. Here are the mission statements of two well-known British businesses.

1. 'Oxfam International is an international group of independent non-governmental organisations dedicated to fighting poverty and related injustice around the world.'
Oxfam International is a confederation of 14 organisations working together in over 100 countries to find lasting solutions to poverty and injustice. Note that the emphasis is on fighting poverty and injustice rather than any mention of profits. It is an international organisation.

2. 'innocent: The Earth's favourite little food company. A company that makes delicious, healthy, natural, ethical food universally available for all.'

Note the emphasis that the company seeks to provide healthy and good products which are available across the globe. Note also the emphasis on not behaving like a giant company.

Different types of organisations will emphasise different points in their mission statements. For example, a fashionable hairstyling company would emphasise being at the leading edge of fashion and hair dressing. Other organisations will emphasise aspects such as quality (for example a precision engineering firm), value for money (a supermarket) or customer/client focus (a health centre or medical practice). The mission will also emphasise whether the organisation sees itself as a local, national or international business. The mission should be easy to understand and should be shared with employees and other stakeholders in the business.

Both the Oxfam and innocent mission statements provide a clear purpose for the organisation and its members to work towards.

Think about it!

1. Why do organisations need to have a mission statement?
2. What do the mission statements above tell us about the differences between these organisations?
3. Which of the mission statements do you think is most likely to give a sense of purpose to stakeholders? Justify your answer.
4. Find out whether an organisation that you work for or are a member of has a mission statement. Are people who work for the organisation familiar with the mission, and if so, how does this affect their actions? Interview two or three people at different levels within the organisation to find this out.

Activity: Values

Does your college or school have a set of values? As a stakeholder, do you think that the values are appropriate and that members of the organisation live the values?

Development of strategic aims and objectives

While the mission of an organisation sets out its purpose and the values that it stands for, its aims set out in broad terms what the organisation seeks to achieve through its strategic plan. The aims of an organisation are closely tied to the mission, and give a general sense of direction for planning.

The aims of the organisation can then be broken down into more specific objectives. The objectives are goals that the organisation seeks to achieve during the period of the strategic plan.

For example, the aim of Ryanair is to be Europe's number one low-cost airline.

Ryanair's objectives include:

- to undercut the fares of rivals
- to take over similar airlines
- to increase sales and destinations flown to each year.

Did you know?

Sometimes an organisation has to revise its objectives in the light of what is happening in the economy. For example, for 2009 and 2010, Ryanair cut a number of its routes because of the decrease in numbers of passengers travelling by air due to the economic downturn.

Cascading of objectives

The objectives that are set for the organisation as a whole **cascade** down into objectives set for the various components of the organisation as follows.

Key term

Cascade – to pass information on to a succession of others

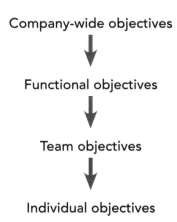

Company-wide objectives

↓

Functional objectives

↓

Team objectives

↓

Individual objectives

Fig. 1.7: Cascading of objectives.

For example, a department store sets itself the objective to increase sales by ten per cent. Then this becomes an objective for each of the departments, for example, the Sportswear Department. Teams within this department are given the objective of increasing sales by ten per cent and each individual member of the sales team is given this target of a ten per cent increase. If the objectives are carefully cascaded down, even a junior salesperson should have the target communicated to them by their team leader. The salesperson's performance in meeting this target can be reviewed at a monthly, quarterly or annual review meeting.

The strategic planning process

The strategic planning process of an organisation is the process through which major plans are created. Strategic plans involve major decision makers and major resources in the organisation. Strategic managers meet together to identify broad aims and more specific objectives to work towards. Then they create the major plans that will help the organisation to meet objectives. Performance measures are established early on to measure the success of the plan.

Use of SMART objectives

In business a good set of objectives should be SMART. This acronym stands for:

- Specific
- Measurable
- Achievable
- Realistic
- Time related.

19

Case study: SMART objectives

Sales of goods by an organisation, which is one of the top three supermarket chains, have been increasing by at least five per cent a year for the last ten years. It therefore set itself the objectives in its strategic plan for 2010–15:

- to retain its position in the top three
- to increase annual sales by five per cent a year between 2010 and 2015.

The first objective is clearly SMART. It is specific – to retain its position. It is measurable (staying within the top three) and achievable, as it is already there. It appears to be realistic and it relates to the time period 2010–15.

1. Why is it important to write SMART objectives?
2. Think about the objective to increase annual sales by five per cent a year. Do you think that it is a SMART objective? Discuss this with another learner.
3. What other SMART objectives might it be suitable for a large supermarket chain to have?
4. Why do you think that competing organisations might be interested to find out these objectives?

2.4 Influencing factors

Three main factors influence the strategic plan:

- stakeholders
- business environment
- business type and who owns it.

Stakeholders

Different organisations have different groups of stakeholders. The influence of these stakeholders varies with the type of organisation.

For example, important stakeholders in Oxfam include:

- donors providing funds for Oxfam, who donate because they believe that it will make a difference in fighting poverty
- volunteers working for Oxfam, who give up their time because they believe in social justice
- people living in poverty, who appreciate the difference that Oxfam is making to their lives.

Important stakeholders in innocent include:

- customers, who want the option of buying ethical, natural food and drink
- employees, who have chosen to work for an organisation that cares about environmental and health issues
- supermarket chains, which are keen to partner with popular brands.

When you examine these stakeholder groupings and what they expect from these organisations, it is clear that they have a lot of influence on the strategic plans of the organisation – its mission, values and objectives.

Activity: Objectives and values

Examine the objectives and values of a specific organisation. Identify the key stakeholders in the organisation.

How are the stakeholders likely to have influenced the objectives and values of that organisation?

Business environment

What is happening outside a business will affect its strategic plan – this is the **business environment**. Businesses need to keep in touch continually with external changes because they can have a dramatic impact. For example, in recent years, car manufacturers have had to change car designs because of legislation affecting how cars are fuelled, as well as a growing consumer preference for cars that are more energy efficient. The objectives of some major car manufacturers such as Toyota and Honda have moved towards focusing on becoming world leaders in environmentally efficient cars.

Another major impact that the business environment has on strategic planning is whether the economy

Key term

Business environment – all of the outside influences on a business. These include government actions, actions by competitors and changes in the law

is booming or in recession. When an economy is booming with consumers spending more money, businesses have expansion strategies, whereas in a recession they may cut back their labour force and range of products.

Business type and ownership

Another major influence of business strategy is the owner and the nature of the business. The owners of for-profit businesses will want to see a good return on the money they have invested in their business. In contrast, those who set up and work for not-for-profit organisations are simply concerned with making sure that their organisation runs well and meets a range of different objectives – for example, providing education, fighting homelessness and poverty, and helping children in need. Where a private business is a sole trader, partnership or family company, the original owners will have considerable influence in shaping the strategic plan. In a public company the plan is more likely to be shaped by directors.

2.5 Different aims

You have seen that aims are an important part of strategic planning in business. We will now look at how aims vary between private and public sector organisations.

Private sector aims

The expectations of shareholders and other owners have a major influence on the aims of private sector businesses.

This section outlines four major strategies of private sector organisations:

- break-even
- survival
- profit maximisation
- growth.

Break-even

Breaking even is essential for business survival in the short term.

We can look at break-even by examining a fictional business, Café Smoothie. This business sells luxury smoothies, which cost £2 each to produce. The costs that arise directly from producing each luxury smoothie

include raw materials – the plastic bottle and label, and the fruit mix. The smoothies are sold for £3 each. On the face of it, it seems that the business is making a profit of £1 on each smoothie sold.

However, we have only accounted for **variable costs** so far – how much it costs directly to produce each smoothie. We have not included the **fixed costs**, which are the costs of running the business – regardless of how many smoothies are sold.

These fixed costs include the rent on the premises on which the smoothies are made, local business taxes, fuel bills, insurance and wages. In this example, these fixed costs add up to exactly £20,000 per year. The business has to sell enough smoothies to cover these fixed costs too, or it will make a loss.

As we saw above, every smoothie sold brings in (or makes a **contribution** of) £1 towards covering the fixed costs. The business therefore has to sell 20,000 smoothies per year to cover all of its fixed costs: £3 (selling price) minus £2 (production costs) equals £1 (contribution) (£20,000 divided by £1 = 20,000 smoothies).

Key terms

Variable costs – costs that vary with the level of output or sales

Fixed costs – the costs of running a business, such as rent and wages

Contribution – how much money each unit of an item sold brings in towards paying off the fixed costs of a business (revenue, or income, minus variable cost)

If the business is open for 50 weeks in the year (being closed for two weeks' holiday) this means that 400 smoothies will need to be sold on average each week (20,000 divided by 50 weeks) for Café Smoothie to be safe.

Break-even analysis can be converted into the following formula.

$$\text{break-even sales} = \frac{\text{fixed cost}}{\text{contribution}}$$

In this case:

$$\text{break-even} = \frac{£20,000}{(£3 \text{ (selling price)} - £2 \text{ (production costs)} = £1 \text{ (contribution)})}$$

$$= 20,000 \text{ smoothies}$$

Survival

Walk down any high street and you will find a selection of businesses that have been there a long time – they have survived. Some of the survivors, like M&S or WH Smith, may have seen better days. Up until the 1990s M&S went from strength to strength and represented the very best of British quality. However, by the 1990s many other new stores were springing up and there was a rapid change in consumers' tastes and a desire to become more fashionable. M&S was left behind and its profits started to suffer. In recent years it has completely revamped many of its stores and employed top designers to make its clothing desirable (for example, the Per Una range has been particularly successful). For example, it has:

- changed its name to M&S because very few people use the term Marks & Spencer
- created new attractive store layouts
- carried out some successful advertising using top models like Twiggy and Elizabeth Jagger.

Profit maximisation

Many people believe that the main objective of businesses is to maximise their profits. Although businesses probably seek to achieve high profits in the longer term, they may have different short-term objectives. For example, in order to gain market

leadership, a business may have to invest heavily in the short period so that short-term profits fall. By sacrificing short-term profit maximising, a business can secure long-term profit growth.

When calculating profits, it is helpful to look at the profit figure when all costs have been taken away from the value of sales made by a business. This is shown by the following formula.

sales revenue – costs of running the business = profit

Growth

Businesses can grow in a number of ways, such as by:

- growing existing sales, which can take sales away from rivals and reduce your costs of producing each unit – for example, Amazon.co.uk has increasingly taken a larger share of the books, music and film markets
- growing into new markets, by producing and selling a wider variety of goods – for example, in recent years, Poundland stores have been selling 10,000 new goods per year

Functional skills

Mathematics: Carrying out the calculations involved with the table in the case study will help you to develop your ability to interpret real business figures.

Case study: Profits at Sainsbury

J Sainsbury PLC is one of the UK's major supermarket chains and has been very successful in recent years. The following figures show how Sainsbury has been increasing its profits over the last five years.

It shows:

- the amount of profit made before tax
- how that profit has been increasing as a percentage figure from year to year

- the amount of profit that Sainsbury makes for every £1 of goods that it sells.

1. What has been happening to Sainsbury's profits over the five years shown?
2. To what extent are these results encouraging?
3. Do any of the figures suggest that the growth in profits is slowing? Explain your answer.
4. What explanation could you provide for the change in profits between 2008 and 2009?

Table 1.4: Sainsbury's profits for the years 2005–09.

Year	2009	2008	2007	2006	2005
Profit before tax	543	488	380	267	238
Increase on previous year %	11.3%	28.4%	42.3%	12.2%	Not available
Profit for each £1 of sales made	3.26p	3.00p	2.54p	2.24p	Not available

- increasing the number of retail outlets or production facilities – for example, in 2009, Poundland set out plans to increase the number of its outlets from 220 to 250, including the purchase of a number of prime Woolworth's sites (taking over another business is a quick way to grow)
- increasing the number of employees and other resources used – for example, after opening new stores, Poundland will need to recruit new employees
- expanding into overseas markets – for example, Tesco has such an extensive hold of the UK market that in 2008–09 it launched new fresh&easy outlets in the United States, Thailand and elsewhere, providing locally sourced fresh food in small neighbourhood stores.

Growth can be carried out:

- internally by using profits to expand the business within
- externally by joining together with other businesses either through mutual agreement (a merger) or by takeover (buying up at least 51 per cent of the shares of the other business).

Public sector aims

Organisations in the public sector have broader aims than just focusing on profitability. A key reason for this is that important stakeholder groupings include national and local government and everyone that makes up society including taxpayers.

Service provision

The public sector typically has more of an emphasis on **public service**.

A national example of a public sector business is the BBC. The BBC charges an annual licence fee to watch TV programmes. Its purpose is not to make a profit, but to broadcast a wide range of information and entertainment.

All sorts of people provide services on behalf of the government. Tax officials check tax returns, midwives deliver babies, teachers educate you and so on. Another example of a public sector business is the National Health Service. Central government funds this organisation to enable it to provide services. There are many other local services, such as those provided by local council officers who organise national and local elections and who make sure that services provided to your house by private contractors such as bin collection are carried out efficiently.

Cost limitation

Government is responsible for about half of all spending in Britain. Government revenue (income) is largely raised through taxation although some also comes from borrowing. Government therefore has a responsibility to taxpayers (an important stakeholder in government) to use money carefully. This also means government needs to be accountable for its spending. Regular checks identify ways to reduce unnecessary costs. The Audit Commission works on behalf of the government to identify these ways.

Case study: The Audit Commission

An audit is a formal examination of a set of accounts to see that they are true and fair; it identifies areas of concerns and reports issues, which results in greater efficiency and higher levels of service. The Audit Commission is an independent public body that seeks to make sure that public money in areas such as housing, health, and the fire and rescue services is used properly. Although the body is independent, it is sponsored by Communities and Local Government, a government department. The Commission also checks for fraud where requested, using a system of cross-referencing called the National Fraud Initiative.

1. Why is it important to have service level agreements – an agreement between a funder and a public service provider that the provider will meet the set standards?

2. How does it help those providing services to have service level agreements?

3. How does it help customers when there are service level agreements?

4. What is the role of the Audit Commission in making sure that the public gets the service it deserves? How could this role be enhanced?

Key term

Public service – emphasis on providing high-quality service to the public rather than focusing on narrow self-interest

Value for money

In recent years the government has stressed the importance of 'value for money' from public services. There are three ways of looking at value for money, which include:

- providing services at lowest cost
- using resources to produce services
- making the most efficient use of those resources.

When the government refers to value for money, it is often referring to the second of these definitions. Government departments are allocated budgets (sums of money) to spend and are expected to use this money as efficiently as possible – thus providing value for money.

Meeting government standards

The government sets standards and targets which it expects providers of public services to meet. For example, Primary Health Care Trusts have been set up to meet the needs of local populations for health care. The government sets standards and targets relating to how quickly patients should be treated and other factors that can be measured, such as hospital waiting lists. The Trusts receive funds from the government and are expected to manage these funds efficiently to meet the government targets. The Trusts are managed by professional managers who seek to cut out waste and to prioritise the most important health needs.

Growth of range of provision

A final aim of public sector organisations is to provide a suitable range of provision. It is essential that public service provision meets real need in the community. For example, from time to time, new roads will need to be built to ease traffic flow. In addition, demand grows for new types of provision – for example, with the global pandemic of swine flu in 2009, the government stocked enough of the Tamiflu vaccine to meet the needs of the population. The government constantly needs to identify ways of improving the services it offers and to provide a wider range of services where appropriate.

Assessment activity 1.2

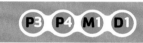

You work as a junior journalist for the local newspaper, which is planning to run a feature article on local businesses. Produce an article on two local, contrasting businesses covering:

- purpose
- ownership organisational structure
- strategic planning.

1. Describe how each business is organised. **P3**
2. Explain how the style of organisation helps each one to fulfil their purposes. **P4**
3. Explain the points of view of different stakeholders seeking to influence the aims and objectives of two contrasting organisations. **M1**
4. Evaluate the influence that different stakeholders exert in one of the organisations. **D1**

Grading tips

1. Remember that organisations need to be arranged into a structure that will enable them to meet their purposes – for example, to make a profit or to achieve their mission aims as a charity. Can you identify a chain of command or line of control in the organisations? How do you think this helps the organisations to control their activities? **P3 P4**

2. To gain a merit, you will need to elaborate on the points of view of the various stakeholder groups. What are they trying to achieve from influencing the organisations? What impact have they had in shaping the aims and objectives of the organisations? **M1**

3. To gain a distinction you need to provide an in-depth evaluation of the influence that the stakeholders have. For example, do some of the stakeholders work together? What common interests do they have? What opposing interests do they have? How are these differences resolved? **D1**

3. Know the impact of the economic environment on businesses

The business environment consists of a range of major influences that are outside a business. These include political, social and legal changes that affect business. However, most business people will tell you that it is changes in economic factors that they fear most because they can have such a dramatic effect, as witnessed by the global economic crisis of 2008–09.

Activity: Economic factors

1. Interview one local business person to find out what economic factors have the most impact on their business. Then reflect on ways in which these economic factors are likely to affect other businesses that you are familiar with.

2. Use the example of the business that you are familiar with to draw out relationships between changes in the economy and businesses more widely. Think of examples of other businesses and how they are likely to be affected by some of the influences mentioned by your business person.

3.1 Economic environment

The economy is made up of millions of individual decision makers who buy and sell goods, borrow and lend money, and raise taxes and change interest rates. From the business point of view, the most important of these decision makers are:

- **consumers**
- **suppliers.**

I buy goods and usually look for value for money.

I supply goods to other businesses and to customers.

fresh supplies

Case study: What happened in the global economic crisis?

In 2007, Jim Smith's business, Premier Autosupplies, had made record profits of £5 million. Jim was confident that this success story would continue. However, in America a large number of householders were falling behind in their mortgage repayments and were having their houses repossessed. Soon these stories become more and more regular, and by 2008 some of the US banks that had lent large sums of money for mortgages and other loans were finding that the money was not being repaid – these are called bad debts. This soon impacted on some large UK banks like the Bank of Scotland; HBOS, its holding company, had invested heavily in the United States and it became apparent the value of these investments were falling rapidly. These banks were in trouble and were running short of the cash that they need to run their businesses. All of the UK banks were therefore cutting back on their lending. With less lending, consumers across the UK had

less money to spend (for example, because they were able to borrow less on their credit cards) and were reducing their purchases of items like motor cars.

This affected Jim as:

- his bank was now reducing his credit card and overdraft limits
- his creditors were asking for quicker settlement of debts
- his order books were reduced from record levels to nearly zero.

1. What other businesses might have suffered in the same way as Jim's in 2008–09?

2. Who was responsible for Jim's difficulties?

3. Is there anything that Jim and business people like him could have done to prevent these difficulties from arising?

- **Bankers and other lenders**

I lend money to businesses and to households.

- **The government**

I set taxes and also decide how much money different parts of government should be spending.

Chancellor of the Exchequer

- **The Monetary Policy Committee**

We decide on the levels of interest rates in the country.

Monetary Policy Committee

Although the economy is made up of millions of separate decision makers, there are clear patterns to the types of decisions they make. For example, at times of consumer confidence, most consumers will raise their levels of spending and businesses will increase their supply of goods.

Importance of stability

Business people like stable economic conditions. Stability exists when business people can make forecasts for the short and medium term about likely demand for their products in the near future. Stability involves being able to make deals secure in the knowledge that people you supply to on credit will pay you back at the price agreed. When you borrow money, you expect the repayments to be for the agreed amounts.

Did you know?

In the African country of Zimbabwe, the economy is highly unstable. Prices rise on a daily basis, and there are long queues for petrol and sometimes food. Money has become virtually worthless as it loses value so quickly. In this environment, many businesses are reluctant to invest for the future.

Impact of changes in the economic environment

The case study of Jim Smith on the previous page illustrates some of the effects on business resulting from changes in the wider economic environment.

Growth

The opposite of a recession is a period of **economic growth**. Growth occurs when more goods are being produced and consumed, and incomes are rising.

Economic growth is associated with a ripple effect (see Fig. 1.8). Because people have more money to spend, they will buy more goods. Producers will make more goods. They will hire more labour and invest in new machinery and equipment. This leads to increases in demand for firms producing machinery and equipment, so they take on more labour.

Key term

Economic growth – a period of month-by-month increase in goods produced and consumed in an economy, coupled with rises in average incomes

Recession

Recession occurs when people involved in business become more cautious and:

* customers cut back on spending, and start to save more
* manufacturers and sellers cut back on their orders, produce fewer goods and start to cut back costs in general, including by laying off workers.

Key term

Recession – when for two quarters (a quarter is three months) in a row, the value of all the goods sold in the economy falls

Fig. 1.8: How could the changes affecting Jim in the case study on page 25 be seen as part of a ripple effect?

A ripple effect

The onset of a recession has a ripple effect, which is shown in Fig. 1.8.

The years 2008 and 2009 saw one of the biggest recessions in the UK in recent history. Industries that were hit particularly badly were building and construction and banking, as well as high street retailing. Full-time jobs for school leavers became harder to find and in August 2009 there were so many students seeking places at university that there was a shortage of university places.

Levels of inflation

Inflation occurs when there is a general rise in the price of goods in the whole economy. Not every price will be rising but average prices will. In the UK, average prices are measured by the government using a measure known as the Consumer Price Index (CPI).

Inflation damages business because it creates uncertainty. A rise in the rate of inflation might reflect a rise in the costs they have to pay: employees will want more wages, costs of materials may go up and the cost of fuel and energy may also rise. Rising costs eat into profit. Businesses then have a choice:

* keep prices constant and see profits fall
* raise prices and perhaps lose out to competitors.

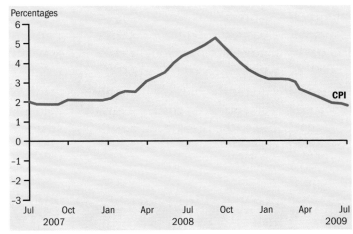

Fig. 1.9: CPI inflation.

Activity: Office for National Statistics

Carry out a search on the Internet for:

* the UK Consumer Price Index (CPI)
* UK consumer spending.

Both of these searches should take you to the Office for National Statistics website. There you will be able to see what the current rate of inflation is in the UK and the current state of consumer spending. Compare these figures with previous months to find out whether they are rising or falling, and the likely impact on UK business.

Key term

Inflation – the general increase in prices in an economy

Availability and cost of credit

The cost of credit (borrowing money) is the rate of interest. It is expressed as a percentage (%). For example, if a business borrows £1,000 for a year at a five per cent interest rate, it would expect to pay back £1,050, as £50 is five per cent of £1,000.

When interest rates rise, this will harm business profits (because it is an additional cost). If a business is already operating close to the break-even point, this additional cost can be crucial.

Case study: The credit crunch

In 2008 the newspapers created a new term: 'the credit crunch'. Banks and other lenders started calling in their loans to businesses and households so that they could meet their own debts.

This hit business hard because a lot of business activity is based on credit. Businesses need to borrow to:

• set up a new enterprise

• invest in new machinery, equipment and research

• pay for wages and supplies.

Without credit, business activity quickly grinds down. Businesses require credit and they need to be able to borrow cheaply.

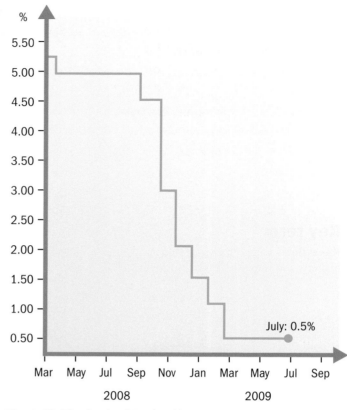

Fig. 1.10: The Bank of England base rate (interest rate) (source: Bank of England).

facing businesses and was trying to make it easier for businesses to get credit on favourable terms.

In Fig. 1.10, you can see that in 2009, the MPC had recommended a very low interest rate, 0.5 per cent, by the summer of 2009.

Interest rates are determined by an independent body called the Monetary Policy Committee (MPC). This is made up of men and women with a good understanding of the economy. It votes to determine the Bank of England interest rate each month. This is determined by majority decision. During the recession, the interest rate was very low. This was because the MPC understood the difficult situation

Labour

For most businesses, the wage bill makes up about 70 per cent of all costs. Businesses need to employ labour with the skills required for the job at an affordable wage rate. In a period of growth, it is more difficult to recruit enough labour with the right type of skills. For the first six or seven years of the new millennium, the British economy was growing steadily. A number of labour market shortages occurred and wages were rising. Fortunately, Britain was able to recruit additional labour from all over the world to fill the gaps.

In a period of recession, it becomes much easier for employers to obtain labour with the required skills.

Changes in government policy

The government has a major responsibility for managing the economy of a country. Good management should ensure that:

• there is stability and growth

• inflation is low

• there is available credit and low interest rates

• businesses have access to suitable supplies of labour.

The main tools that the government uses to manage the economy are taxation and spending.

We have already seen how the interest rate affects business. Through **monetary policy** the government can also change the quantity of money available. For example, in 2009 the Bank of England (working for the government) increased the amount of money in Britain. This was referred to as **quantitative easing**. The government provided more money to the banks to encourage them to lend to businesses.

Fiscal policy involves the government altering its taxes and spending in light of what is happening in the economy. For example, in a recession the government can reduce business taxes and other taxes to make it easier for businesses to make a profit or reduce business losses. It can give businesses more time to pay their tax bills. The government can also spend more in a time of recession. In 2009 this spending involved pumping a lot of government money into banks to encourage them to keep lending.

The government also influences business through the laws that it passes. In particular we have seen a range of new government laws restricting business creation of waste and pollution. We will look in greater detail at government and the law on page 37.

3.2 Demand

The term 'demand' is used to describe the quantity of a good or service that consumers will buy at a particular price. Consumers will buy more of the same product when it is cheaper than when it is more expensive.

This relationship between demand and price can be illustrated in a demand curve. A leisure club has carried out market research and found out that for a membership subscription of £20 per month, 1,000 people will want to join. At £10 a month the figure would be 2,000 and for £30 a month it would only attract 500 members.

There are a number of factors influencing demand, including:

• affordability

• competition and availability of substitutes

• level of income

• needs and aspirations of consumers.

Affordability

At lower prices goods are more affordable. As customers we are aware of what we can afford to buy.

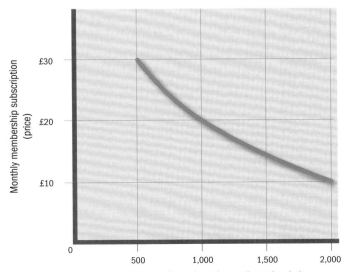

Fig. 1.11: Demand for membership at a leisure centre at different prices.

Key terms

Labour market – this consists of employers requiring (demand) employees and people seeking work (supply)

Monetary policy – policies related to money available in the economy. The government can change the quantity of available money or the cost of borrowing money (interest rate) as a result of advice from the Monetary Policy Committee

Quantitative easing – increasing the quantity of money in the economy

Fiscal policy – policies involving changes in government spending and government taxation

We demand those products that we can afford but not those that are too expensive. For example, as the price of leisure centre membership falls, it becomes affordable to more and more people. Businesses need to find out about levels of demand for their products at different prices. By making products affordable for the target audience, businesses are best placed to make sales.

Competition and availability of substitutes

Sellers of goods compete for our purchases. For example, there are many different competing firms providing chocolate bars. This affects the demand for a particular type of chocolate bar. Potential buyers will compare its price with those of alternatives. When there is a lot of choice, demand for individual products will be lower unless they really stand out. Products that compete with each other are called substitutes. In the mobile phone market there is a wide variety of substitutes.

Activity: Substitutes

Can you identify products where there are lots of substitutes and ones where there are few or no substitutes? How do businesses compete with each other to win demand in markets where there are lots of competitors?

Level of Gross Domestic Product

A person's income is a major determinant of demand. The higher a person's income, the more they are likely to spend on consumer goods (just think of celebrities and how much they spend on clothes and cars).

The same principle applies to levels of income in a country. The total amount of all incomes is called the Gross Domestic Product (GDP) or national income (Gross Domestic Income). Countries with a higher GDP will spend more than those where GDP is lower. The countries with the highest GDP are the United States and China, followed by Japan and India. Demand in these economies is huge. As GDP rises in these economies, so too does expenditure.

Needs and aspirations of consumers

Consumers buy some goods because they need them. We all need to eat, drink and have somewhere to live.

We all need some level of education and a minimum standard of health care. However, on top of this there is a demand for many aspirational goods. People may aspire to have a better car than their neighbours, dress and have their hair styled like celebrities, and go on holiday to exotic destinations.

Aspirational demand is based on consumers' aspirations to achieve success through copying the purchases of celebrities like Cheryl Cole.

Did you know?

One of Britain's most successful clothing websites is ASOS. ASOS originally stood for As Seen On Screen. Many of the clothes sold through the site were modelled on those worn by celebrities and pandered to the British public's fascination with and attempt to look like celebrities.

3.3 Supply

The 'supply' of a product is the quantity that a supplier is willing to provide at different prices. Typically suppliers will supply more at higher than at lower prices.

For example, a charter airline might run six planes a day between Stansted and Paris when business passengers are prepared to pay £200 each for the return journey. However, if business passengers are willing to pay £300 each, then the airline might buy more planes and run nine planes a day. At £400 each, they might run twelve planes. Supply can be illustrated on a supply curve as Fig. 1.12 shows. Note how it rises upwards from the bottom left corner to the top right corner of the illustration.

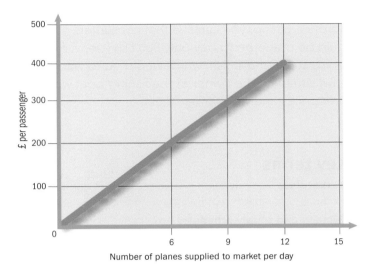

Fig. 1.12: Supply curve.

When demand for a product increases, then businesses will usually try to supply more. The ease with which they can increase supply depends on:

- availability of raw materials and labour
- logistics
- ability to produce profitably
- competition for raw materials
- government support.

Availability of raw materials and labour

When raw materials and labour are freely available then it is quite easy to increase supply. For example, after a recession there will be lots of builders looking for work and it should be easy to buy bricks, cement and other building equipment. Supply therefore could increase quite quickly. However, when extra raw materials and labour are scarce, during a boom period in building then it may be quite difficult to increase supply.

Logistics

The ability of a business to get goods to customers depends on the quality of its supply chain. The supply chain consists of the various stages of moving raw materials to where they will be made into goods, then on to storage and finally distribution to the end customer. **Logistics** is concerned with organising this

supply chain. Today this is usually managed using computer databases and electronic systems.

Ability to produce profitably

Businesses supply in response to demand when they can make a profit from doing so. Consumers often consume large quantities of goods when they are free, for example, downloading pirated music from the Internet. However, once they have to start paying for the music, they are far more cautious in making purchases. Businesses will only supply if demand is at high enough prices for a profit to be made.

Competition for raw materials

Businesses and countries compete with each other for supplies of raw materials. This affects prices at which these materials can be obtained. From a business point of view, the aim is to secure steady supplies at as low a cost as possible. A feature of the first decade of the 21st century is that there is increased competition in global markets for raw materials. The Chinese and Indian economies have been growing at a very fast rate. These economies have over a billion consumers. Huge construction and development projects in these countries have required vast quantities of oil, gas, metals, cement, plastics and a range of other raw materials. These requirements have pushed up the global prices of these and other items (including food).

Government support

Many products and industries receive government **subsidies**. A good example of this is farming in the European Union where farmers receive subsidies for the growing of certain agricultural products and the purchase of farm machinery. The greater the level of subsidy, the more of these products will be supplied. A subsidy has the same effect as lowering the cost of production.

Key terms

Logistics – processes involved in moving and supplying goods to where they are required. Logistics involves organising transport and storage of goods

Subsidies – money provided by government to provide additional finance for a business to support selected activities

3.4 Changes in supply and demand

In the **marketplace**, the forces of demand and supply will interact to create a market price. Table 1.5 shows a fictional daily **demand and supply schedule** for fish in a small fishing village.

Table 1.5: Demand and supply for fish in a small fishing village.

Price of fish (pence)	Quantity demanded	Quantity supplied
35	800	350
40	700	400
45	600	450
50	500	500
55	400	550
60	300	600

When the price of fish is high, the owner of the only fishing boat will spend more time fishing than when prices are low. Conversely, consumers will want to purchase more fish at low than at high prices.

The data can then be plotted on a graph, as Fig. 1.13 shows.

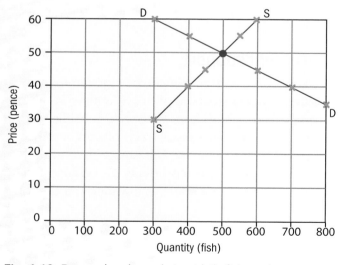

Fig. 1.13: Demand and supply in a daily fish market.

In this graph, there is only one price at which the wishes of consumers and suppliers coincides: 50p. At this price the quantity that will be bought and sold is 500.

We can see that the market provides a mechanism for automatically bringing the decisions of consumers and producers into line, even though the two groups have different motives.

We can see how the process of forming an **equilibrium** price comes about by considering a disequilibrium situation.

At a price of 60p, you can see that consumers of fish would be prepared to buy only 300 fish – leaving a surplus stock of 300 fish, which would go to waste. In this situation, the owner of the fishing boat would lower prices and work fewer hours.

Key terms

Marketplace – any situation in which customers demanding products interact with suppliers supplying products

Demand and supply schedules – tables showing quantities that will be supplied and demanded at different prices

Equilibrium – position at which demand equals supply, so that producers and consumers are happy; disequilibrium is the opposite

Activity: Disequilibrium

Explain in your own words why a price of 40p for fish would be a disequilibrium position, and what is likely to happen in this situation.

Changes in supply and demand curves

Demand

Supply and demand curves change position regularly. For example, the demand curve for a product shifts to the right when more of the good is demanded at a given price. For example, demand for *Hello!* magazine might increase when:

- it becomes 'the one to read' – because it is seen as being very fashionable to do so
- consumers' incomes rise so that they have more money to spend on magazines.

In these situations, demand for *Hello!* would shift to the right as illustrated on the next page in Fig. 1.14.

Supply

The supply curve can also shift to the right (increased supply at each price) and to the left (decreased supply at each price).

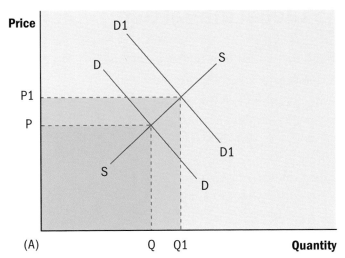

Fig. 1.14: A shift to the right in demand.

Factors leading to increases in supply include:

- for agricultural crops – good weather leading to better harvests, higher milk yields and so on
- for most goods – improvements in technology. For example, using computers to design and make products leads to much lower levels of waste material, with a tremendous impact on supply.

Fig. 1.15 illustrates the shift in supply. You can see that when a supply curve shifts to the right, this leads to a lowering in price.

Elasticity of demand

Elasticity of demand is a measure of how much the quantity demanded of a product responds to a change in price.

If quantity demanded is very responsive to price changes, then a small change in price will lead to a relatively large change in quantity demanded. In this case we would say that demand is elastic. For example, if the price of a standard washing powder rose by two or three pence, then customers could easily switch to cheaper substitutes such as other standard washing powder.

Where quantity demanded is relatively unresponsive to price change, demand is inelastic. An example of this is Lemsip (lemon-flavoured paracetamol) for colds and sore throats. Even though the price is relatively high, people are prepared to buy Lemsip because when they are feeling unwell, they feel confident that they will get value for money from this palatable way of taking paracetamol.

Elasticity of demand can be shown by the following formula.

$$\text{elasticity of demand} = \frac{\text{\% change in quantity demanded}}{\text{\% change in price}}$$

Elastic demand is represented by figures which are higher than 1. In other words, when the price changes by a given percentage, the percentage change in quantity demanded will be greater.

Inelastic demand is represented by figures of less than 1 – that is, the percentage change in quantity demanded is less than the percentage change in price.

Price sensitivity

Price elasticity tells a business person how sensitive demand is to changes in price. Pricing is one of

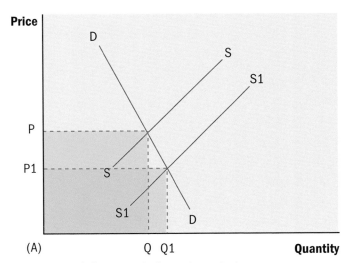

Fig. 1.15: A shift in supply (lowering price).

the most important decisions a business makes. Overcharge or undercharge, and you will lose valuable revenue.

Some goods have more sensitive prices than others. These include goods that:

- have lots of substitutes (competing products)
- are regarded to be optional extras or luxuries rather than necessities
- have been around a long time and are being replaced by more up-to-date products.

Activity: Elasticity of demand

1. Can you identify items which if their prices rose a little you would have:
   - an elastic demand for them
   - an inelastic demand for the product?
2. Which of the goods listed below are likely to have the most elastic demand resulting from a rise in price? Explain your answers.
   - The iPhone
   - Swan Vestas matches
   - The *Daily Mail* newspaper
   - A container of Saxo table salt
   - A packet of cereal.

Influence of branding on price sensitivity

One of the main purposes of branding products is to create a relatively inelastic demand for the product. The more consumers consider the brand to have unique qualities, the less sensitive demand will be to price changes. Coca-Cola has successfully used brand imaging for many years to create inelastic demand. As a result, Coca-Cola still sells at premium prices. Aspects that make the brand special include:

- the unique Coca-Cola lettering on packaging
- the distinct shape of bottles and cans
- the secret formula of the drink
- the billions of pounds that have been spent on advertising and promoting the brand.

3.5 Global interaction

Globalisation involves the creation of global markets, global businesses and global products.

Key aspects of globalisation include:

- the creation of global brands – people round the world instantly recognise global brands like Sony Playstation, the Apple iPhone and Cadbury's Dairy Milk
- the creation of global products and global advertising – for example, global advertising for Coca-Cola or the Volkswagen Beetle
- instant global communications through the Internet; airlines move passengers rapidly round the globe and the speed of bulk shipping transport has rapidly increased
- huge economies like China and India now being part of the global market – the fact that these huge economies are able to produce large quantities of products at very low costs makes life difficult for British-based competitors producing similar lines.

Levels and types of interdependence

Interdependence takes place at a number of levels as Fig. 1.17 illustrates.

Interdependence takes place at a:

- **local level:** an organisation like Tesco gets many of its supplies of fresh vegetables from local growers, and recruits staff for supermarkets locally
- **national level:** much of Tesco's supplies of meat and fish will be provided by suppliers within Britain
- **international level:** increasingly supplies come from all over the world – Tesco accesses supplies of oranges, grapefruit, bananas and kiwi fruit from a range of countries including Spain, Israel, Egypt, New Zealand and the West Indies.

Supply chains

Large businesses today rely on global **supply chains**. For example, much of the chocolate we consume is processed from cocoa beans from West Africa. The

Key terms

Interdependence – the linking together and mutual dependence of parts of a system on each other

Supply chains – made up of a series of links starting with raw materials, and converting them into finished products

Magnum ice cream   is produced by global company Unilever   and is manufactured and sold across the globe.

Fig. 1.16: An example of globalisation.

cocoa is grown on small farms in countries like Ghana and the Ivory Coast, then sold to a processor in these countries who processes the cocoa beans before selling them on to the chocolate manufacturers like Cadbury's and Nestlé. The cocoa powder is then mixed with milk and sugar in factories in the UK and elsewhere to produce the chocolate products that we are familiar with.

Ownership of businesses

A multinational company owns at least 50 per cent of the shares in at least one overseas business. The overseas business that is part owned or fully owned is then called a subsidiary. The Japanese car manufacturers Honda, Toyota and Nissan have large manufacturing units in the UK. Tesco has set up a chain of supermarkets in the United States, Thailand and elsewhere.

Creating a foreign subsidiary can take place through:

- 'greenfield investment' of setting up a new plant – for example, when Toyota set up its car factory near Derby
- acquisition of an existing firm.

Another popular form of ownership for multinationals is the creation of a joint venture. This is when companies based in two countries will create and share ownership of a new company. Many European companies entering the Chinese and Indian markets have created joint ventures. This is because the local partner will have a good knowledge of the local market as well as being able to make contacts with government and other key stakeholders.

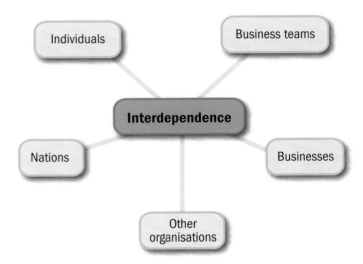

Fig. 1.17: Levels of interdependence.

Movement of capital and business operations

Businesses need **capital** to build factories and retail units, and to invest in research and new technology. In today's world, capital flows freely between countries. International investors are on the lookout for good investments in business.

Key term

Capital – funds that are invested in business

The term Foreign Direct Investment (FDI) refers to an investment in a foreign company where the investor holds at least ten per cent of the shares in a company with the purpose of securing a lasting interest in that company. A good example of FDI is where rich foreign investors have bought most of the shares in the main Premier League football clubs in the UK.

One of the problems of multinational enterprise is that the companies do not have a particular loyalty to specific countries. They are more concerned with producing close to their markets at locations where costs are lowest. For example, British companies like BT have moved their call centres to India and elsewhere, where labour costs are lower.

Reducing ability of government to regulate global business

From a government point of view, a major advantage of having foreign multinationals operating in their country is that they bring jobs and investment, and pay business taxes. The disadvantage is that foreign companies are more difficult to regulate. These wealthy companies can switch production very quickly to new locations because modern factories can be built and set up within months. Governments try to keep on the right side of management of multinationals, sometimes at the expense of other stakeholders in these businesses.

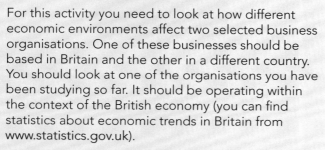

Assessment activity 1.3   P5 M2 BTEC

For this activity you need to look at how different economic environments affect two selected business organisations. One of these businesses should be based in Britain and the other in a different country. You should look at one of the organisations you have been studying so far. It should be operating within the context of the British economy (you can find statistics about economic trends in Britain from www.statistics.gov.uk).

The second organisation should be operating in a different country. You can research it by examining its annual report, which you should be able to obtain online. You can then look at statistics for inflation, employment and GDP for the organisation's country by using the latest statistics produced by the national statistical office in that country.

The types of issues you should be looking at include:

* the economic environment facing the business (for example, recession, rising demand and so on)
* levels of inflation
* government policy in relation to business
* changes in GDP and in demand in economies studied
* changes in conditions of supply.

You should also examine issues involving global interdependence that affect the business, including the supply chain and ownership of the business, as well as how it acquires capital for its activities.

1. Describe the influence of two contrasting economic environments on business activities within a selected organisation. **P5**

2. Compare the challenges to selected business activities within a selected organisation in two different economic environments. **M2**

Grading tips

1. Use newspapers, and data from the Internet setting out economic data. Every day newspapers and the BBC produce economic updates on what is happening to consumer spending, GDP, inflation rates, interest rates and so on. You should study reports in newspapers like the *Guardian* and the *Independent* to identify current economic trends. To find an up-to-date graph illustrating such data you can access Google Images, and search for the data you require, for example: 'UK Consumer Price Index March 2010'. **P5**

2. You will need to analyse the data that you gather for P5. You will soon get a picture of whether national demand and GDP are rising or falling, whether changes in interest rates favour business or not, and so on. You then need to make sense of this data to identify the key challenges to your two businesses. **M2**

4. Know how political, legal and social factors impact on business

Business people need to know about changes that are taking place as a result of:

- political decisions made by government
- changes in the law
- changes that take place in society over time.

4.1 Political factors

Politicians make important decisions. At national level the UK is governed by the political party that secures the most Members of Parliament in a general election. The ruling party is led by the Prime Minister who appoints the Cabinet of senior Ministers in charge of key areas of government – for example, education, health, industry and so on.

At international level, Britain is a member of the European Union. This body makes political decisions that increasingly affect what can be done within member states.

At local level, councils are the elected representatives of their populations and make decisions about local issues on their behalf.

Political decisions involve making choices that affect large numbers of people and businesses. The choices made by politicians, for example, in creating new laws, will tend to favour some groups at the expense of others. Sometimes these decisions favour business, for example, in the granting of a subsidy or an exemption from paying taxes (not having to pay them). At other times political decisions restrain business, for example, when business taxes are raised or businesses are stopped from carrying out given activities.

Political stability

Periods of political stability favour business. A political party is usually elected (at national level) to office for up to five years. Once elected, it will seek to put its manifesto (plans) into action. Plans are made public. This helps business planning. Businesses are able to use the government manifesto to identify likely changes and how these will affect them. It provides business with a degree of certainty for the next few years. For example, in recent years the Labour government has been raising environmental taxes, particularly on larger vehicles. As a result, businesses

in the car industry know that it is sensible to plan to produce a higher number of smaller fuel-efficient cars and energy-efficient vehicles such as electric cars and **hybrid vehicles**.

> ### Key term
> **Hybrid vehicles** – cars that run on a combination of petrol and alternative fuels such as battery-powered electricity; they can switch between the two

Government support for different types of organisation

Government supports different types of business in different ways.

For the private sector, the government tries to create an environment in which businesses can compete with each other on level terms regardless of size. Where firms appear to be too large or powerful, the Competition Commission or Restrictive Practices Court will investigate and take action through the courts against businesses if they are found to be abusing their position. In addition, government provides various incentives such as grants to start up a new enterprise.

In the voluntary sector, government support involves various cash grants such as those provided by the National Lottery Commission for activities that benefit the wider community, and tax relief on premises owned by these organisations. Charity organisations receive similar support.

In the public sector, the government covers the losses made by government-owned organisations. Government effectively subsidises a number of non-profit-making activities such as maintaining roads or ferry services to remote communities, and funds welfare, education and health services.

Taxation

Taxes are levied by national government (for example, income taxes) and local government (for example, business rates).

Taxation helps government to raise revenue and also enables it to discourage various activities and to encourage others (through lower rates of tax and subsidies).

Examples of these include high taxes on:

- cigarettes to discourage smoking
- high fuel consumption cars to discourage pollution.

The main types of tax that affect business are shown in Table 1.6.

Businesses see taxes as a cost that eats into profit. Business people are thus very interested in what government is going to do to tax rates. These are sometimes changed, particularly in the Annual Budget in March – when the government announces its tax plans for the year. For a small business, paying tax is a particular burden because there are a lot of forms and paperwork that need to be filled in. A large business will have its own accounts department, but this is an unaffordable luxury for most small businesses.

Direct support

Government provides direct support to specific types of businesses and for specific business activities in the forms of grants and loans.

A grant is a sum of money that the government gives to a business that is not repaid. The government gives the grant because the business activity supports government policy. For example, sometimes the government gives grants to employers to take on and train young and previously unemployed workers. A government may give a grant to a farmer to purchase up-to-date farming machinery.

The government also gives loans to businesses for specific purposes. Government loans are at a much lower rate of interest than those of other sources such as banks.

The government subsidises certain activities to encourage them.

Did you know?

In Britain, the film industry is subsidised by the government. British film companies with budgets of up to £20 million for a film are entitled to a subsidy of £4 million a film. The British film industry is regarded as very important and the government wants to give priority to it.

Table 1.6: Taxes that affect business.

Corporation tax	Income tax	National Insurance	VAT (value-added tax)	Customs duty
A tax on company profits	A tax on the incomes of the self-employed and other income earners	A compulsory deduction to pay for pensions, sickness and unemployment benefits	A tax on the value added to products by businesses	A tax on imports and exports of goods and services

Case study: Business taxes

Charneeta Kaur runs a small printing business in the Midlands. The business provides printing services to local companies, for example, leaflets and brochures, as well as printing a newspaper targeted at the Sikh community in Britain. The business only started up last year. As it was a start-up business, Charneeta was able to gain a rate reduction of 50 per cent for the first two years of running the business from the local council.

In the latest budget, the Chancellor of the Exchequer announced that the profit level at which small businesses would have to start to pay tax would be raised by £5,000. However, at the same time it was announced that VAT would now be charged on certain printed items that previously

had been exempt. Charneeta's business previously delivered newspapers to newsagents using a large van, but she has now decided to economise by purchasing a hybrid car.

1. Identify four different types of tax that affected Charneeta's business.

2. Explain how recent changes in two of these taxes would have benefited her printing business.

3. Explain how recent changes in another of the taxes mentioned might have had a negative impact on the business.

4. What other business taxes might have affected Charneeta's business and how?

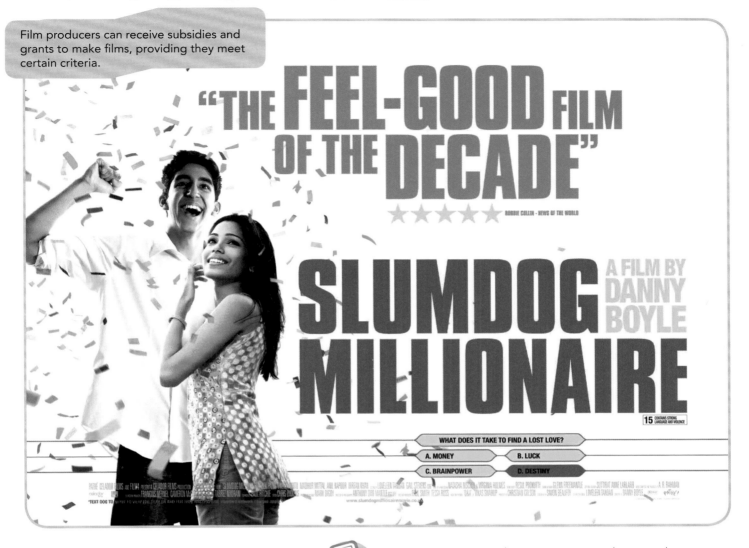

Film producers can receive subsidies and grants to make films, providing they meet certain criteria.

Did you know?

In 2009 the government created a car scrappage scheme in the UK to create demand in the car industry during the recession. Anyone trading in a second-hand car that was over ten years old was entitled to a £2,000 reduction in the price of a new car. The government paid £1,000 and the car dealer £1,000. This was effectively a government grant to car buyers.

Providing infrastructure

The government provides the central **infrastructure** of the economy. It builds and maintains motorways and other major transport links. Local government is responsible for local roads. The government also owns and maintains the railway lines and railway stations.

Until the 1980s it also owned the telecommunications system, but this has been privatised. However, the government provides support to make sure that these facilities are provided for all. For example, the government's policy of 'Broadband Britain' is designed to support private providers like BT in making broadband Internet links available to all. The government has paid for Internet facilities to be installed in libraries and other public locations to make the Internet accessible to households that cannot afford the Internet at home. A number of local government authorities in Britain have made their cities 'wireless zones'. Within these cities, which include Edinburgh and Bristol, anyone can access the Internet wirelessly.

Key term

Infrastructure – the skeleton of the economic system which supports the rest of the economy. It includes communication links such as transport networks, and Internet and telephone systems

Enhancing the skills of the population

Education and training help to increase the skills of the working population and those preparing for the world of work. The government creates the educational framework, including the types of qualification on offer, such as Apprenticeships or NVQs.

At the same time, the government provides a range of training courses that are available through various industry training schemes, for example, the construction industry, motor vehicle manufacture and so on.

The government carries out research into labour market trends to identify which industries are likely to grow in the future, so that they can target education and training to meet the changing needs of the economy.

Organisations to support businesses

The government runs a variety of organisations designed to support business. Perhaps the best example of an organisation that helps business is the government's Business Link, which is a very useful resource for you during your BTEC award. You can access Business Link at www.businesslink.gov.uk, and find a range of services offered, and a link to grants and loans provided by the government for businesses. It is a service providing business people with a wealth of information about business; for example, how to set up, how to choose a business name, how to carry out marketing, how to create a business plan, how to apply for government loans, how to fill in tax returns and so on. The government runs Business Link offices from all of the regions of the UK. It is a free service designed to help business become more efficient and provides a source of support for every business in the UK.

Membership of international trading communities

Another important political factor affecting business is in creating international links, particularly in relation to trading. The UK is an important member of the European Union. Britain imports and exports more within the European Union than with all of the other countries in the world added together. European Union countries like France, Italy, the Netherlands and Germany are advanced industrial economies which buy the complex modern goods and services that we produce in this country.

Britain therefore benefits substantially from being a member of this trading group. Within the European Union, there is free movement of:

- goods
- capital (money)
- labour.

British business benefits from being able to trade goods with minimal paperwork. Britain also benefits from the free flow of skilled and unskilled workers coming to Britain to seek jobs.

In 2010 there are 27 members of the EU. The most recent countries to join included Poland, Hungary and the Czech Republic.

4.2 Legal factors

Businesses must operate within the framework of the law. Failure to do so can lead to fines and even imprisonment of directors. Businesses therefore give high priority to making sure they comply with the law. There are thousands of separate pieces of legislation (laws) that affect business. Here we just focus on three important areas (shown in Table 1.7).

Table 1.7: Laws affecting business.

Type of law	Governs
Company	how businesses are set up and run
Contract	the contracts that businesses make with employees, consumers, suppliers and so on
Competition	how businesses deal with employees, consumers, suppliers and so on, and how businesses are allowed to compete with each other

Providing a framework for business (company law)

There are rules about who can set up a business, the steps and paperwork involved in setting up, and the reports a business makes, including how it presents its accounts. Much of this is covered by company law. The most important piece of legislation is the Company Act, covering a range of important matters.

For example, on page 9 we mentioned limited liability. This is legal protection that limits how much a shareholder in a company can lose, should the company become bankrupt. Similarly there are laws about 'business names' – for example, you cannot use a name already used by an existing business. Law sets out the steps required to register a private or public company, and how the company should report to its shareholders.

Businesses are required to keep certain 'books' including a register of shareholders and directors. Shareholders are entitled by law to sell their shares to others, receive notice of company meetings and receive a copy of the company annual report.

A company's annual accounts need to be approved by the Board of Directors and signed on behalf of the board by a director. The accounts should then be delivered to the Registrar of Companies.

Did you know?

Company law sets out what businesses can call themselves. Companies are not allowed to use names which make it appear that they are associated with government. They cannot use a name already registered by another company, or too similar to another company – for example, 'The Body Shops' or 'Virgins Records'. Offensive names are illegal.

Protecting consumers and employees (contract law)

Businesses form **contracts** with many different individuals, groups and bodies outside the business.

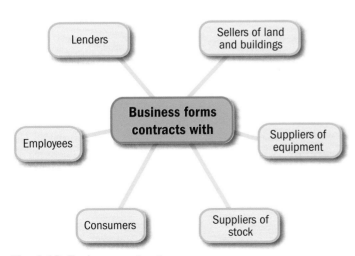

Fig. 1.18: Business contracts.

Contract law can be illustrated by examining two of the main types of contract affecting business – contracts with consumers, and contracts with employees.

Consumer protection

The most frequent contract that a business makes is for the sale of goods. This is covered by the Sale of Goods Act, which says that goods must be:

- 'of satisfactory quality', which means free from significant faults except defaults which are brought to your attention by the seller (for instance, if goods are declared to be 'shop soiled')
- 'fit for purpose', including any particular purpose mentioned by you to the seller. For example, if you ask for a jumper that is machine washable, you should not be sold one that has to be hand-washed
- 'as described' on the package or sales literature, or verbally by the seller. If you are told that a shirt is 100 per cent silk, then it should not turn out to be a mix of silk and something else.

The law also protects consumers when buying a service, for example, from a dry cleaner, travel agent, hairdresser or personal trainer. You are entitled to certain standards. A service should be carried out:

- with reasonable care and skills – for example, you would not expect a hairstylist to colour your hair pink when you ask for it to be dyed green
- within a reasonable time – if you have your car repaired you would not expect the repair to drag on for months
- at a reasonable charge, if no price has been fixed in advance.

The second major contract that businesses make with customers is for selling goods on credit. The Consumer Credit Act covers 'credit agreements made between an individual ("the debtor") and any other person ("the creditor") by which the creditor provides the debtor with credit'.

Key term

Contracts – legally binding agreements between two or more parties, who promise to give and receive something from each other

Types of credit include:

- **bank loan**
- **overdraft**
- credit cards
- store cards.

The Consumer Credit Act sets out that those giving credit must be licensed, and that advertisements and offers of credit must set out the true cost to the borrower. The business giving credit must give information about the:

- total charge for credit, for example, £1,000 over two years.
- Annual Percentage Rate (APR), for example, 20 per cent APR
- price at which goods could be bought for cash.

Other consumer protection laws which affect business activity include:

- the Trades Description Act
- the Weights and Measures Act
- the General Product Safety Regulations.

Did you know?

You can find out more about consumer legislation by visiting www.consumerdirect.gov.uk

Employment law

Employees are also protected at work and employers need to update themselves continually on changes in legislation relating to employees.

A key component of employment protection is in the creation of a contract of employment.

A contract of employment should include details such as:

- names of employer and employee
- job title and/or job description
- date employment started, the place of work and the address of the employer
- amount of pay and how it will be paid
- hours of work
- holiday pay entitlement
- notice period required.

The contract is a binding agreement.

Employment legislation consists of UK and EU **regulations** and **directives** that concern employees and employers.

The EU has put into force a number of employment directives, including:

- the Working Time Directive, which sets out that there should be: a minimum rest period of 11 consecutive hours in every 24-hour period; a rest break if the working day is longer than six hours; a minimum rest period of one day in every seven; a minimum of four weeks' paid annual leave
- Minimum Wage Regulations, which set out that employees should be entitled to a minimum hourly rate of pay. In the UK, the rate is monitored by an independent body called the Low Pay Commission
- the Equal Treatment Directive, which sets out that there should be no discrimination on grounds of sex, nor by reference to marital or family status, in access to employment, training, working conditions, promotion or dismissal
- the Equal Pay Directive, which states that all discrimination on the grounds of sex in respect to pay should be removed
- the EU Employment Directive, which requires member states to implement laws prohibiting discrimination on grounds of sexual orientation and religious discrimination and now age discrimination
- the EU Race Directive, which is concerned with principles of equal treatment of people, irrespective of their racial or ethnic background.

Key terms

Bank loan – a sum of money borrowed by an individual or organisation for a period of time, and then paid back at so much a month which includes repayment of the sum borrowed plus interest

Overdraft – when more money is taken out of a bank account than is in it, making the account overdrawn

Regulations – laws that are directly binding on member states created at European Union level

Directives – these bind member states to objectives to be achieved within a certain time limit. However, it is left to national authorities to decide how to implement them. Directives have to be implemented through national law

Ensuring fair and honest trading (competition law)

There are also laws governing how businesses can compete with each other – for example:

- laws against restrictive business practices to reduce competition – for example, two or more sellers agreeing to set prices

- monopoly and merger legislation to stop businesses from dominating a particular market. For example, the big four supermarket chains account for three-quarters of all food sales in the UK and have been regularly investigated by the government's Competition Commission, which so far has ruled that the supermarkets do actually compete quite vigorously with each other

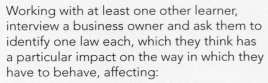

Activity: Contract and competition law

Working with at least one other learner, interview a business owner and ask them to identify one law each, which they think has a particular impact on the way in which they have to behave, affecting:

- their relationship with consumers
- their relationship with employees
- the way they much compete with rivals.

Produce your findings in the form of a poster and present it to your class. In each instance, carry out some further research to find out the precise details of the laws that your business owner mentions.

PLTS

Working with other learners, carrying out the research and making the presentation will require careful planning of teamwork tasks.

Functional skills

English: Preparing your poster and presentation requires the structuring of ideas into a clear and focused presentation, which involves careful consideration of communicating to a target audience.

- laws against Resale Price Maintenance, stopping a manufacturer from controlling the price at which a retailer can sell their goods.

4.3 Social factors

Over time many changes take place in society which are relevant for business organisations, such as in:

- demographic (population) issues
- changes in structure
- household and families
- education
- attitudes to work
- religions
- attitudes to male and female roles
- ethics.

Demographic (population) issues

When the population of a country is growing, there is an increase in:

- demand for goods and services
- the numbers of people making themselves available for work.

The first decade of the 21st century has seen an increase in the UK population at a faster rate than in previous decades. Part of this has been as a result of the boom in the economy which has encouraged the government to make immigration of labour to the UK relatively easier. Large numbers of workers from the new EU states like Poland have settled in Britain to work. Many of these workers are relatively highly skilled. In addition, young people and learners from overseas have provided a ready pool of labour for important UK industries such as catering and hotel work.

Changes in structure

The number of older people in Britain is increasing fast. Statisticians predict that during the next century there will be a substantial increase in those living to be over 100. According to recent estimates, the number of people over 60 could rise by 40 per cent in the next 30 years. In 1995 there were less than nine million people over 65 – by 2030 there may be about 13 million.

People tend to work and save when they are young, and live off the proceeds when they retire. As the population ages, we may see more people spending the proceeds of their previous earnings. They are also likely to have different spending patterns to the young. For example, there may be greater demand for stair lifts, anti-ageing creams, botox injections and world cruises. New businesses will spring up to cater for the needs of the elderly and e-commerce will be a particularly useful vehicle for selling directly into the homes of people in this group. There will be a profound impact for the pharmaceutical and health industries, which will need to expand to meet the needs of the ageing population.

Household and families

Another aspect of the UK's changing population has been the rise in single-person households. The average age of marriage is increasing and many people now live alone. Many single people are high-income earners with high disposable incomes.

Education

The level of education of the workforce is important. Many modern jobs require good educational qualifications. In nearly all industries, employees are expected to have good information technology, mathematics, and English skills. They may be required to work with databases, analyse sets of figures and make presentations. Vocational qualifications like a BTEC award in business are seen by employers to be particularly good preparation for supervisory and management posts at work.

The current Labour government has set a target for 50 per cent of the population to attend university and gain a university-level award.

Business in general is keen to support these initiatives and play an active part in helping to design new qualifications. Business people can suggest the types of skills that they are looking for in preparing learners to fit into the world of work today and in the future. For example, Apprenticeship awards involve learners working with an employer and a local educational institution to develop the knowledge and skills required to make a better contribution at work.

Attitudes to work

Attitudes to work influence the important relationship between a business and its employees. In recent years,

Britain has developed a 'long hours culture' compared with some other European countries such as France and Italy. However, hours worked in Britain are lower than in many South East Asian countries.

Table 1.8: Hours worked by employees in 2008 (per week).

Country	Hours worked
South Korea	45
Hong Kong	42
UK	38
France	35

Other aspects include the care with which employees do their work, their attitude to customers and their relationship with the employer.

Religions

Some countries are made up of people belonging largely to the same or similar religious groups. Others, like Britain, consist of many different religious groups. Each religious group has its own beliefs and values. These beliefs and values affect the types of goods that customers purchase and use, and behaviours in the workplace. For example, the Muslim religion requires believers to fast during daylight hours at a certain time of the year and to pray at given hours of the day. It is essential that employers are familiar with these religious requirements so that they can make appropriate allowances. They need to apply similar sensitivities to products and materials that people of different religions may touch and handle, and days of the week on which they can work. For example, some Christians will not work on Sundays.

Attitudes to male and female roles

Male and female roles in society have been shifting over the last fifty years. This is witnessed by the facts that today 50 per cent of the working population is female and that over half of new entrants to careers in medicine, the law and some other professions are females. The only level where substantial change has yet to occur is at director level within British businesses, where the majority of directors tend to be older males.

Changing gender roles have also had an impact on consumption patterns. For example, the rapid rise in the 'ready meals' market is partly a response to families where both parents work and there are growing numbers of 'cash rich, time poor' individuals. Increasingly, people are also putting off having a family, creating new markets for a range of consumer goods and services such as fitness clubs and gyms and a range of entertainment equipment.

Ethics

Business ethics are the values and principles held by those that run businesses. Ethics help to shape the actions of a business and the decisions it makes. Ethical principles should go beyond legal requirements.

Key ethical issues include:

- fair trade – offering fair prices to suppliers, often in poorer countries. For example, do the prices they get for their products enable them to send their children to school, and to feed and clothe them?

- environment – using resources well and minimising waste. There is strong pressure on businesses to reduce their **carbon footprint**

- not misleading customers or cheating them in any way

- providing customers with what is good and useful to them, rather than what is harmful.

The term corporate social responsibility (CSR) describes a thoughtful approach by business to the society in which it operates. Modern businesses develop policies and carry out actions that are responsible. For example, the CSR policy of Manchester United includes:

- working with other institutions to ensure that there is no room for racism in football

- working with local communities to provide education and training facilities using the Old Trafford Football ground training rooms

- working with local schools to develop football training

- cleaning up around the football ground immediately after home matches are completed

- making sure that away supporters are stewarded to and from games.

Key term

Carbon footprint – this measures the impact of an activity on the environment by doing things like burning fossil fuels to heat factory buildings. A carbon footprint is measured in tonnes or kilograms of carbon dioxide equivalent

Assessment activity 1.4

For the assignment, you have been examining two contrasting business organisations. The final part of the assessment asks you to examine how your chosen organisations are affected by changes in their political, legal and social environments.

1. Describe how political, legal and social factors are impacting upon the business activities of selected organisations and their stakeholders. **P6**

2. Analyse how political, legal and social factors have impacted on two contrasting organisations. **M3**

3. Evaluate how future changes in economic, political, legal and social factors may impact on the strategy of a specified organisation. **D2**

Grading tips

1. You only need to examine the main political, legal and social factors that affect your business. It is helpful to use the three headings but remember that there will be a certain amount of overlap between the three areas.

To achieve a pass you simply need to describe some of the important changes that are taking place using appropriate facts and figures. **P6**

2. You need to analyse the changes. For example, which of the factors are most significant and what sort of impact are they having on the business? What sorts of changes in business planning have resulted from these external changes? How is the business coping with these changes? **M3**

3. You have already looked at how changes are currently affecting your business. But what about the future? What are likely to be the new challenges facing the business? Can you find predictions and forecasts about likely changes in the economy, possible implications of a change in government policy, new laws that are likely to come in and changes that are taking place in society and are likely to continue in the future? **D2**

Just checking

1. Classify the following according to whether they are in the public, voluntary or private sector.
   - Manchester United PLC
   - Business Link
   - Oxfam
   - the BBC
   - the Bank of England
   - Poundland
   - ChildLine
   - Vodafone
   - the armed forces
2. Who owns public sector businesses? Who owns private sector businesses?
3. List three groups of important stakeholders in a PLC, and explain what their stake is in the company.
4. What are the advantages to business structure of having narrow rather than wider spans of control?
5. Identify and describe three major functions of business that involve communicating with customers, and explain any links between them.
6. What does the Consumer Price Index (CPI) measure? Why is the CPI important to business?
7. How do changes in interest rates affect businesses? Illustrate your answer by reference to a specific business.
8. What does elasticity of demand measure? How can branding reduce price sensitivity?
9. What is contract law?
10. How does Business Link support business in the UK?

edexcel

Assignment tips

1. When you are researching information for the earlier parts of the assessment, you are likely to come across materials that will help later on.

2. When you find relevant articles in newspapers, cut them out straight away and put them in a safe place. Write down the name of the newspaper, the date and wherever possible the writer.

3. It is helpful to compare companies where you can gather information direct – whether because you work there part-time or you know someone who works there, for example.

4. Identify the issues that are most significant to the organisations that you compare – for example, environmental issues are relevant to most organisations, and obesity and healthy eating are important to organisations producing food and drink.

2 Business resources

You may have noticed – through work experience or a part-time job – the different types of resources that businesses use to perform effectively. These resources come from four different areas: human, physical, technological and financial. Human resources are anything that relates to people in the business – for example, staff and managers. Physical resources are those that are physically used by the business – for example, land, raw materials, buildings or equipment. Technological resources are those that make use of technology – for example, computers, software or systems. Financial resources are any aspects of the business relating to money, such as money owed to or by the business.

It is essential for any business to control, manage and make the best use of these resources in order to achieve the best possible results. This unit will help you to investigate these resources by looking at how they are managed, what they are used for, how they can be sourced and finally the way in which data can be used to see if they are being used to their full potential.

The unit starts by investigating human resources and the way that people are recruited and allocated to different departments and teams. It then goes on to consider the use of technology within the workplace and its many issues and benefits, including legal requirements to protect business ideas. Finance represents a huge area of resource management, and you will learn how financial statements and budgeting are used. You will also find out how to take those financial statements and view trends or changes by applying accounting ratios to compare the performance of a business with others in its market.

Learning outcomes

After completing this unit, you should:

1. know how human resources are managed
2. know the purpose of managing physical and technological resources
3. know how to access sources of finance
4. be able to interpret financial statements.

Assessment and grading criteria

This table shows you what you must do in order to achieve a **pass**, **merit** or **distinction** grade, and where you can find activities in this book to help you.

To achieve a **pass** grade, the evidence must show that the learner is able to:	To achieve a **merit** grade, the evidence must show that, in addition to the pass criteria, the learner is able to:	To achieve a **distinction** grade, the evidence must show that, in addition to the pass and merit criteria, the learner is able to:
P1 describe the recruitment documentation used in a selected organisation **See Assessment activity 2.1, page 64.**	**M1** explain how the management of human, physical and technological resources can improve the performance of a selected organisation **See Assessment activity 2.2, page 69.**	**D1** evaluate how managing resources and controlling budget costs can improve the performance of a business **See Assessment activity 2.4, page 81.**
P2 describe the main employability, personal and communication skills required when applying for a specific job role **See Assessment activity 2.1, page 64.**	**M2** assess the importance of employability and personal skills in the recruitment and retention of staff in a selected organisation **See Assessment activity 2.1, page 64.**	
P3 describe the main physical and technological resources required in the operation of a selected organisation **See Assessment activity 2.2, page 69.**		
P4 describe sources of internal and external finance for a selected business **See Assessment activity 2.3, page 71.**		
P5 interpret the contents of a trading and profit and loss account and balance sheet for a selected company **See Assessment activity 2.4, page 81.**	**M3** interpret the contents of a trading and profit and loss account and balance sheet for a selected company explaining how accounting ratios can be used to monitor the financial performance of the organisation **See Assessment activity 2.4, page 81.**	**D2** evaluate the adequacy of accounting ratios as a means of monitoring the state of the business in a selected organisation, using examples **See Assessment activity 2.4, page 81.**
P6 illustrate the use of budgets as a means of exercising financial control of a selected company **See Assessment activity 2.4, page 81.**	**M4** analyse the reasons why costs need to be controlled to budget **See Assessment activity 2.4, page 81.**	**D3** evaluate the problems they have identified from unmonitored costs and budgets **See Assessment activity 2.4, page 81.**
P7 illustrate the financial state of a given business **See Assessment activity 2.4, page 81.**		

How you will be assessed

To achieve Unit 2, you will investigate businesses that operate in your local area and nationally, and find out how changes in the business environment can affect them. Your assessment could include both practical and written tasks as well as presentations. The assessment activities in this book will help you prepare for this.

Rajinder

My parents have always wanted me to run my own business, so knowing about the resources in a business is really important to me.

Knowing a bit more about how to manage people has been really useful – it has made me think about how I should treat my staff when I start my own business. I now know that giving incentives to my employees might be a useful way to motivate them. I really enjoyed the physical and financial resource aspects of this unit, and in particular the interpretation of the profit and loss and balance sheet. Maths wasn't my strength in school, but I think the business context has helped – I'm doing the sums for a reason.

My recommendation to anyone studying this unit is not to be put off by the figures. Approach them carefully and really apply them in the business situation. Understanding the accounting side of things also means that when people are talking about liquidity and cash flow on business programmes or on the news, I understand what they are talking about and take an interest. I'm now working towards an accounting qualification.

The most important resource

Some people think that the most important resource in any organisation is the human resource. In two groups, have a whole-class discussion about this statement, with one half of the class supporting this view and the other opposing the view. Which is the strongest argument?

1. Know how human resources are managed

Human resources are managed in two main ways. First, it is important for organisations to recruit the right people, monitor them and then decide how they can best be used. Then resources have to be provided for these employees in order to maintain an effective business operation.

1.1 Human resources

Employees are a business's human resource and need careful management. Unlike financial or physical resources, human resources need to be dealt with sensitively. If a machine is no longer useful, it could be thrown away or replaced. People cannot be treated in the same way because they are protected by **legislation**, so it is important to recruit, employ and treat them appropriately. More information on human resources can be found in Unit 13 Recruitment and selection in business (page 319).

Staffing to meet changing business demands

Suitably qualified staff may be recruited or they may be trained within the organisation when they first join in order to have the right level of skills. The level and type of staffing also needs to change to keep up with the changing demands of the business, and this is likely to affect the number of employees needed and the skills that they need to have.

Many businesses keep a Human Resource Information System (HRIS) that stores computerised records of the training and experience that employees have. This helps the business to plan to expand or reduce (contract) the number of employees that they need.

It can also help the business plan for the future – this is known as **succession planning**. A junior employee may receive management training to prepare them to take over the running of a team or department. Businesses that plan well are less likely to have problems when

Key terms

Legislation – UK and EU laws

Succession planning – when employees are recruited and developed to fill each key role within the company

Activity: Self-service scanning

In 2009, Tesco reported 25 per cent of all shopping at its stores was done through self-scanning.

At Asda, 3.6 million customers used the self-checkout systems per week, which is an increase of 60 per cent from 2007.

1. What impact is self-scanning likely to have on the human resources required at Tesco and Asda?

2. What are the advantages of this change in customer behaviour?

3. What are the disadvantages?

4. How should these businesses plan for the future?

5. Carry out research into other businesses that have included more self-service online or offline – for example, Ryanair – and consider the impact on these businesses.

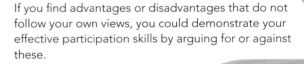

PLTS

If you find advantages or disadvantages that do not follow your own views, you could demonstrate your effective participation skills by arguing for or against these.

their needs change. You will study technological change in more detail later in this unit. Many businesses are changing the way that they trade and are making greater use of online methods of handling customers. This means that employees need training to be able to carry out different tasks.

Co-ordination of team resources to meet targets

As well as making sure that individual employees are managed within the organisation, it is essential that resources are used effectively within teams to meet the targets that the company sets.

The resources might be skills within the team, experience or even financial resources that will help the team to achieve what it needs to. Some organisations may appoint team leaders to help managers to look after team members on a day-to-day basis, so that the manager can just oversee the whole process.

Co-ordination of team resources may also involve deciding which members of the team can use training resources to improve the performance of the team and how this training can then be shared. As long as the team is working together in a co-ordinated way, then it should meet targets.

Monitoring of team performance

Co-ordinating a team is likely to mean that a company knows what employees should be doing to work towards their targets; but it is also essential to monitor the team's performance to make sure that they are actually making progress. One way to measure performance is for the business to monitor how closely the team has met targets. This might involve measuring sales figures, seeing how much the team has spent (under or over budget) or considering the number of customer complaints during a time period.

Regular team meetings can give an indication of how the team members are feeling about their targets and if all is going well. Individual and team appraisals may be carried out to see what can be done to improve the way the team works together and sharing ideas can give the team themselves the opportunity to suggest how things can be improved.

Managing team working means monitoring a set of individuals rather than one person. It needs to be done carefully to make sure that all the team are performing equally and that no one is being lazy or working too hard. Sometimes managers give their employees incentives, such as a bonus or prize for achieving good results in a team. This helps to reward hard-working teams. The same is true of teams performing badly: managers would need to follow the disciplinary procedures to deal with a team that gets poor results or may even have to break up the team altogether.

Why is it important to monitor not just individual performance but also team performance?

Liaison with other departments

Large organisations may have hundreds of different teams working across the organisation. Unless each is able to work with other teams and departments and co-ordinate as a whole organisation, there will be conflict or unsatisfactory performance. Departments may be responsible for different functions within the business, such as finance, marketing or human resources, and each will need to work with the others to ensure the smooth running of the business.

One way to make sure that employees work together effectively with other departments is to have cross-functional teams. This means that members who are working at the same level in the organisation are taken from each department so that they can work together to understand what each part of the business does. These teams do not have to meet physically – sometimes organisations choose to use virtual cross-functional teams where employees meet over the Internet, using technology such as web conferencing. This type of team structure is already being used by a number of different large organisations including BA and IBM.

Establishment of professional culture

Professional culture means the way that employees behave in the organisation, including the level of formality that is used between employees. You will already have noticed differences in formality at social events you have been to, such as weddings or parties, or the different way that teachers speak to you if you have moved from school to college. The language and the way you address people changes depending on where you are; the same is true of business.

Some businesses are very formal and managers will refer to each other using their title, such as Mr, Mrs or Dr. Other organisations will only use first names. Professional culture may also relate to the unwritten expectations that an employer might have of its employees, such as whether or not people are expected to stay late in the office on a Friday or whether they can go home early.

The same differences also occur within organisations when comparing work and personal lives. Some organisations make sure that people's home lives and work lives are completely separate. This may include only having social activities for staff members and not their families, or discouraging relationships between employees. Other organisations may allow activities or relationships to be brought into the organisation. An example of this is pub management, where job vacancies are often advertised as for 'couples' rather than single people.

Different formalities and work/personal life activities are just part of managing human resources in the workplace. The whole process is complex and it can be hard for management to be objective (that is, acting without letting their personal feelings and opinions affect situations).

As well as taking into account personal relationships at work, it is also necessary to make it clear to employees whether or not they are allowed to work outside the organisation in a second job or do another job in the evening. Taking on a second job is known as 'moonlighting'. Some employers are happy to allow their staff to take on another job in a non-related capacity – for example, an office administrator working in a bar. Other employers may choose to ban such practices by writing express terms in their contract that require employees to ask permission before taking a second job. This helps to protect an employer from employees taking business from them in the evening or not being able to cope with their usual working hours due to tiredness.

Providing appropriate incentives

To manage human resources effectively, managers may decide to use **incentives** to encourage employees to work harder or to produce work of a higher quality.

At school or college you may have noticed your tutors using incentives, such as allowing you to finish the lesson five minutes early if you have worked particularly hard, or giving prizes at the end of the year. Employers are the same; they need to think of different ways to encourage their employees to work harder (see Table 2.1).

It is most important that the incentives offered by an organisation are appropriate for the employees involved, because if employees are not convinced that the incentives are worth working for, they will

Key term

Incentives – additional rewards or payments that employers give to employees as a reward for working even harder or better

Table 2.1: Main ways of rewarding employees.

Performance-related pay	This is when an employee receives extra money for working harder, either as a one-off payment, such as a bonus, or an increase in their salary.
Share schemes	These are when employees are offered shares in the company either freely or at a reduced rate, depending on company performance and how long they have worked there.
Desirable treats	Some organisations choose not to use pay as an incentive for employees but use treats to encourage staff to work harder. These treats might be anything from a voucher for a weekend in a health spa to giving employees microwaves or televisions. The treats may be awarded after appraisals or given on a points system so that employees can keep earning points to work towards the treat of their choice.
Working hours or home–work balance	Employees with families or other outside commitments may prefer to have time off in lieu rather than extra money or treats. Some organisations offer time off for good performance. This may mean being able to leave early on certain days or take extra holidays.
Social events	Providing an office party or a trip to a sports game can also be an incentive for employees. As they can be used with whole departments of employees, these events can increase morale in the workplace, which leads to even more work being completed.
Useful benefits	These include other products that employees might find useful but are not considered treats. These might be free pension funds, insurance payments, discounts at retailers, free gym membership or free parking. All of these benefits can save the employee money.

not work harder to get them. To help make sure this does not happen, employers can provide a package of different incentives that employees can choose from; that way employees can decide what they want to work towards. Employers must also be careful, when offering any incentives, to find out whether or not employees will need to pay tax on these benefits to the Inland Revenue.

Encouraging creativity and initiative

Businesses that are able to change quickly and adapt to customer needs are more likely to be successful. This is now even more important because the Internet allows businesses to compete all over the world. Two ways for businesses to become more adaptable include:

- being more creative
- showing initiative.

This means that organisations allow their employees to develop new ideas and solutions so that they can get better and better.

It is sometimes more difficult to develop new ideas quickly in larger organisations, because so many people are involved in the decision making. Some business people believe that smaller businesses find it easier to adapt and that in future there will be more businesses, but they will be smaller. Sometimes businesses start out small and become much larger by being creative and using initiative. Yahoo! is one well-known example.

Outsourcing versus in-house decisions

Organisations can either make use of their own services (in-house) or the services of external agencies doing work for them (outsourcing). You will need to be aware of the differences between these options and the issues and benefits associated with each.

It may be more expensive to employ people within an organisation to undertake project work or provide maintenance than to ask another company to do this work. This is because the business will need to recruit these people, employ them on a contract, pay them for a given time, and provide them with benefits and office space or equipment. Outsourcing pushes all those issues across to the outsourcing company in exchange for a fee. Another reason that companies may outsource is if their employees in-house do not have the expertise and it would cost a lot of money to train or employ someone. Using another company to do this work means the organisation can use workers as and when they are needed, rather than employing people permanently.

Outsourcing can be used in many different ways to manage human resources for everything from recruiting employees in the first place to bringing cleaners in to keep the workplace clean and tidy.

Outsourcing has many advantages (for example, it may offer cost and/or time savings, frees up in-house resources, allows access to wider knowledge and skills) and disadvantages (for example, quality risks, lack of company knowledge, may risk security of company information) compared to having the work done in-house, so it is important to consider the reasons why outsourcing might be used and the length of the project involved. If this method is used carefully, it can be an effective way of working for a business, but it could result in higher costs for the business than if the work had been done in-house.

1.2 Maintenance of operation

Maintaining business operations is critical for any organisation. Unless the business can carry out its day-to-day activities efficiently, it will lose customers or clients.

Adequate resources to meet tasks

Resources need to be available for employees and there must be sufficient employees using those resources to provide good service.

Staffing

If there are not enough staff working, tasks cannot be done. For example, a restaurant without a chef, waiting staff or kitchen assistants cannot operate effectively and may end up with complaints from customers. Therefore all businesses need to manage their human resources carefully. They need to make sure that:

- there are enough staff
- they have adequate skills to carry out their jobs
- they are working to the best of their ability.

It is a careful balancing act to ensure that there are enough employees. Too many staff will cost a business a lot of money and potentially damage profits, while too few staff could lower quality, damaging the reputation of a business and so also damage profits. Staffing may need to change according to the seasons, so there may need to be a mixture of permanent and temporary staff to meet different levels of demand over the year. Holiday company Pontin's employs 300 permanent staff and then takes on temporary staff to

fill another 1,600 roles during the spring and summer months. The company encourages temporary staff to keep returning by offering good training and other incentives. This helps to avoid some of the costs of recruiting new staff each year.

In other organisations, such as the NHS, there is clear guidance for minimum staff levels based on ratios. There may, for example, need to be one nurse for five patients on one ward or one nurse per patient on another. Getting the right number of staff for each ward is essential for the effective operation of that hospital.

The skills of staff employed are also critical. There is no point having staff available if they are not qualified to do the jobs that need to be carried out. There may also be a problem due to skills shortages in different sectors, which can prevent work from being carried out.

You have already learned that it is important to have the right number of properly trained staff. Employees also need the resources to do their jobs in order to allow the business to operate effectively. You will learn more about the physical, technological and financial resources that are needed later on in this unit. However, initially it is important to consider four resources that are needed by workers for the business to operate successfully:

- equipment
- working capital
- facilities
- administration.

Equipment

This is important in order for employees to be able to carry out their daily duties. Equipment might take the form of machinery, or **consumables** that are part of their everyday work, or could simply be the uniform that they need to wear.

For some jobs, equipment is required by law. Employees working in the print room of an organisation might need to wear ear defenders

Key term

Consumables – goods that customers have to buy regularly because they wear out or are used up, for example, food and clothing

to protect their hearing under the Health and Safety at Work Act 1974. Those working in a factory may need to wear eye shields to protect themselves while they are working. A lack of equipment could mean employees are unable to do their jobs effectively, but also that the organisation is breaking the law, because they have a duty of care to their employees. Therefore some equipment must be provided free of charge if needed.

Working capital

This is a form of resource – the day-to-day money needed to pay the bills for the business to remain trading. Working capital is the current assets of the business minus its current liabilities (the debts that must be paid in the short term). It is important to estimate how much working capital is needed by the business in order to make sure it can continue trading.

Working capital needs careful management within a business – too much working capital will mean that the business has lots of cash available that is not being best used. This is an interest cost to the business as this money could have gained interest from alternative investments. On the other hand, not enough working capital in the business means that a business will not be able to pay its bills and may become insolvent.

Factors that influence how much working capital a business has include:

- the level of sales – high sales mean that money needs to be available to buy more supplies or stock
- trade credit – the time offered by suppliers to pay for purchases – for example, one month or two months – and whether that payback is with or without interest
- payment time – how long it takes to get payment from customers
- the level of inflation in the economy – if levels are high, then working capital needs to be higher to allow for price and wage increases.

Ensuring the business has enough working capital is essential as this is needed to pay staff and keep the business running.

Facilities

Facilities are essential for the operation of any business. They can be anything from the provision of buildings and equipment to services that are offered for staff to support them at work or places for customers to access. Like equipment, some facilities are required to be offered by law for staff. For example, employers must provide:

- toilet and washing facilities
- access to drinking water
- a rest area or room for breaks
- facilities for preparing or obtaining a hot drink.

Can you think of equipment required by law for specific jobs?

You will learn more about facilities within this unit when you consider physical resources on page 64.

Administration

An organisation needs administration to make sure that everything runs smoothly. Through administration, resources are controlled and managed by the use of systems or processes that help to keep everyone organised. Administration covers a number of different areas, as Fig. 2.1 shows. It is important for the smooth running of the business that administration is carried out effectively. Large organisations may have specific departments that work on part of the administration process, whereas in smaller organisations one individual might have responsibility for a number of different aspects.

Monitoring

Monitoring takes place in two main ways within a business. This is through **formal monitoring** and **informal monitoring**.

Key terms

Formal monitoring – when managers are officially checking, watching or recording the employee in some way

Informal monitoring – when managers are making more subtle judgements about how an employee is fitting in or if they have a problem

Some organisations have very strict monitoring policies so that employees are monitored at all times throughout their working day – for example, in customer service/call centres where employees are constantly dealing with customer enquiries. Supervisors in this case often listen in to calls to monitor customer service or record calls to check at a later date. Managers will often monitor emails sent or have CCTV showing employees at the workplace. Employers have to make employees aware that monitoring is taking place.

Formal monitoring may also be necessary in order to comply with the law; for example, the Data Protection Act 1998 requires employers to ensure that personal information is protected and is only accessed if necessary. Some employers also carry out drug and health tests as part of monitoring in the workplace; for example, hospitals may test their medical workers for diseases like tuberculosis so they do not pass them on to patients, or organisations that require employees to use machinery may test for drugs.

Staff may also be monitored to see how often they are absent (for example, through sickness), how often they are late, how much work they produce during a day or how often those in particular roles leave and need to be replaced.

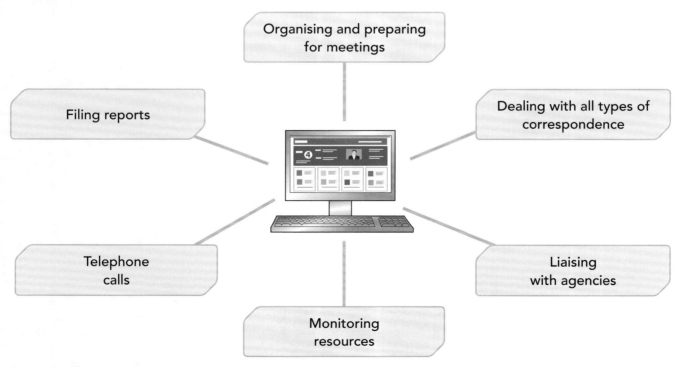

Fig. 2.1: Different aspects of administration.

This is a much less scientific approach to monitoring and needs extra care and attention in order that the manager does not intrude too much on an employee's privacy. All monitoring may feel uncomfortable for an employee (you will know yourself how it feels to be monitored by invigilators in examinations), so it is important that employees feel happy with it and know why it is happening. Informal monitoring may be used for managers to assist their employees in ways to improve or at review times during the year.

It is essential that monitoring is very carefully carried out, whether formal or informal. This is because by being intrusive, an employer may breach the Human Rights Act 2000. Changes in technology have made monitoring seem much more menacing in some organisations, where all email exchanges and Internet access are logged, but it is important for managers to make sure that employees understand when and why they are being monitored.

Troubleshooting and problem solving

Troubleshooting and problem solving are important but vary widely from one organisation to another. Something that is a problem for one manager may not be for another. The extent to which troubleshooting and problem-solving skills are needed will depend on the size of the organisation and the skills and competence of the managers involved. Managers may:

- look for problems
- solve problems as they happen.

Looking for problems is a proactive approach. It means the organisation is constantly looking for ways to improve its business and by solving smaller issues, hopes to avoid big problems altogether. This is known as continuous improvement. These processes require everyone in the organisation to seek to make improvements in some small way so that the quality of the product or service is continually improved. The extent to which this can happen effectively will depend on the culture and resources within the organisation.

The method of solving problems as they arise, in order of how urgent they are, may also be used by some organisations. For example, a restaurant manager may have a number of problems to deal with, but the issue of someone ringing in that they are unwell and cannot work would be dealt with before a problem with the food order for next week, as it is more important. If a manager has too many problems in one go, and keeps having to deal with one after another, it is known as 'firefighting', as it is like trying to put out a fire where new flames appear as quickly as the ones you have just put out. Working in an environment where firefighting is a common management technique for problem solving can be very stressful and tiring.

1.3 Human resources
Recruitment and retention

The first area of human resources (HR) that is essential to the business is **recruitment** and **retention** of people with the right skills to do their jobs. Finding suitable staff to work within the organisation is critical, as without the right people it is unlikely that good business decisions will be made. There are many different ways that businesses can attract staff. Traditional methods to make people aware of job vacancies now have to compete with Internet-based methods of recruitment. Table 2.2 shows different types of traditional and online methods of recruitment that organisations can use to find the best staff to work for them.

Key terms

Recruitment – taking on employees

Retention – keeping employees at the workplace for as long as possible, to benefit from their experience

Table 2.2: Different types of traditional and online methods of recruitment.

Traditional methods	Internet-based methods
Newspaper advertisement	Online application form
Paper-based curriculum vitae (CV)	Online curriculum vitae
Letter	Email
Word of mouth	Web advertisement
Paper-based application form	Web page with curriculum vitae details
Careers fair	Web page with job board
Poster	Web page pop-up

Recruitment online is much faster than traditional methods and has a number of benefits over using paper. It is possible to monitor how many people have gone on to a website to look at a job. The business can see how many of those people then go on to apply for the job, so they know whether or not this method of recruitment is the best way for them to encourage people to work for them. By using online application forms, data supplied by applicants can be put straight into computer software.

Retaining staff is also extremely important. When a business has spent a lot of time and effort recruiting staff, they need to make sure that the employees are going to stay with the organisation and work to the best of their ability. If an employee joins a business, but decides to leave soon after, the business will have to pay recruitment costs again and give training to another member of staff. This can cost a lot of money, so the business will want to avoid this. It can also leave other workers in the business feeling fed up and unhappy if they have to do extra work until a new employee is appointed.

Businesses can use measurements to work out how long staff are staying with them and work out targets to maintain or improve the trend. The key measurement that they can use is known as staff turnover. This is where the number of staff leaving during a year is worked out as a percentage of all the staff employed in that year.

$$\frac{\text{Number of staff leaving in a year}}{\text{Average number of staff employed in that year}} \times 100$$

This helps the business to see how many staff are leaving, if there is a potential problem with their human resources and what could be done about it if so.

Functional skills

ICT: Remember to evaluate information for its fitness for purpose (how relevant it is) when using ICT to search for information.

Activity: Creative Solutions Ltd

Creative Solutions Ltd is a small IT specialist organisation considering online recruitment.

1. Using research from the web (a useful website list is provided below) and classroom-based resources, produce a poster in pairs showing the advantages or disadvantages of using online recruitment.

   - www.oneclickhr.com
   - www.reed.co.uk
   - www.onrec.com

2. Discuss your results with other members of your class.

3. Produce a written report giving a judgement about the importance of choosing the right method of recruitment for a business like Creative Solutions Ltd, to help it manage its resources.

In August 2009, Asda announced that it had reduced its staff turnover rate to less than 20 per cent per year. This is approximately 10 per cent lower than the average turnover for other industries such as hotel and leisure, and production. The company suggested that it had made these reductions through a number of different methods including the share scheme that it offers to employees. Asda also announced other key retention information about their staff including that:

- there had been a 10 per cent increase in the number of colleagues with at least five years' service since August 2008
- more than 67,000 colleagues had now worked at Asda for at least five years
- 23 shop floor colleagues were being promoted to management roles every month
- the longest-serving colleague, Paul Higgins, working at the Blackpool store, had 43 years of service under his belt
- there were a further 2,433 colleagues who also had completed 25 or more years of service.

Find out more about Asda by accessing their website, then answer the following questions.

Think about it!

1. Which factors did Asda suggest were affecting the average staff turnover?
2. What are the advantages of having an increasing number of colleagues with at least five years' service? Are there any possible disadvantages?
3. What effect was the 23 shop floor colleagues being promoted every month likely to have had on Asda?
4. Make a judgement about the retention tactics that Asda are using for employees to stay with the company compared with those of other organisations in the retail sector.

Suitably skilled staff

Having suitably skilled staff is not just about recruiting new people. It is also about making sure that staff already working for the organisation are being trained and updated. It is important that they are developing new skills to cope with changes in their jobs or the way that the work is completed. Without suitably skilled staff, a business cannot operate and will need to get additional help, or it will lose money if it cannot carry out its day-to-day business.

There are three main elements to making sure a business has suitably skilled staff:

- attracting the right staff
- training staff while in work
- educating people in the first place to leave full-time education with the right level of skills.

All three elements must be put into place to ensure that businesses are able to make use of suitably skilled staff.

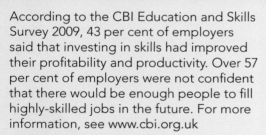

Activity: CBI Education and Skills Survey 2009

According to the CBI Education and Skills Survey 2009, 43 per cent of employers said that investing in skills had improved their profitability and productivity. Over 57 per cent of employers were not confident that there would be enough people to fill highly-skilled jobs in the future. For more information, see www.cbi.org.uk

In small groups, discuss these views.

1. Do you agree or disagree with them?
2. What are the advantages of having a highly skilled workforce?
3. Which other factors need to be taken into account when training employees for the future?

Contracts of employment and job descriptions

An employee should have been given a **job description** as part of the recruitment process. This is the final stage for the employer and employee to check that they are happy with all aspects of the job. Once this is agreed, the new employee is asked to sign

a contract which is the legal agreement made between the employer and employee. All of the essential elements of the job are made clear – for example, salary or working hours.

The main rights and duties of both employers and employees will be specified in the terms of the contract of employment. The contract of employment exists to protect both the employer and the employee so that they both know what is expected of them. The Employment Rights Act 1996 states that all employees should receive a written contract of employment within eight weeks of the start of their employment. The contract itself will contain important terms. These terms can be either express terms or implied terms.

Express terms are the main part of the individual contract and will have been discussed at an interview and confirmed in writing. They will include pay, hours and holidays.

The implied terms are provisions that are not included as written terms, as they are understood to be included automatically. These will include terms such as the right to equal pay and the right not to suffer discrimination. Some terms may be included in a contract through custom or tradition – for example, the business might close every Wednesday afternoon but will be open every Saturday morning, and those times form part of your contract of employment.

There is more information about job descriptions and contracts of employment in Unit 13 Recruitment and selection in business (page 334).

1.4 Employability skills

Each job requires the person doing it to possess a range of specialist skills. However, there are also skills that are useful to a wide variety of careers and are therefore transferable between jobs. These are known as employability skills and they are essential for employees to be able to work effectively in a modern workplace. Each of these areas is important, and they include:

- suitable qualifications
- experience in a similar role

Key term

Job description – a list of working conditions that come with a job – for example, pay, hours or duties

- knowledge of products and services
- experience of specific industry
- effectiveness in meeting personal and team targets
- ability to observe and raise professional standards.

Suitable qualifications

Different jobs require different types of qualifications. Some employers will be happy to take on applicants with GCSE qualifications, while others may require more specific skills, such as NVQ qualifications. For professional careers such as accountancy, marketing and human resources, employers will often look for candidates with problem-solving and critical skills, meaning they will often need candidates with at least A levels or a BTEC National.

To be useful to an employer, it is important that you have the correct level of qualifications and in the right subjects. Completing a BTEC National in Business is a good start towards a wide range of professional jobs and a rewarding career.

Did you know?

According to the CIPD Annual Recruitment, Retention and Turnover Survey 2009, the most common reason for people not being able to recruit staff was a lack of specialist skills (73 per cent). The next most common reason was lack of experience (39 per cent). You can find out more from www.cipd.co.uk

Experience in a similar role

Experience in a similar role can make the difference when an employer is choosing a new employee. If you can show that you have done similar work before, for another company, it should indicate that you can do it again for the new organisation. When applying for a job, you should think carefully about any previous experience that might show how you already have some of the skills required to be successful in the new role. If you have already worked in that industry, you need to make this very clear in your letter of application or CV, as the prospective employer is likely to value such experience.

Knowledge of products and services

Product and service knowledge is vital, especially if you intend to work in a customer service role. You will improve your chances of obtaining a job if you can demonstrate knowledge of the products or services that the business delivers.

Experience of specific industry

If you have worked in an industry before, you should make this very clear to a prospective employer when applying for a job. Experience of a particular industrial sector is highly valued by employers, as employees can bring with them hints, tips and information that can be used in the new business. Sometimes changing employer in the same industry may mean that your new employer is able to find out more about their competitors by employing you.

Effectiveness in meeting personal and team targets

Meeting targets is vital for business success. Individual employees must be able to meet targets too. If you can demonstrate that you can meet targets and deadlines, this is likely to make you stand out at interview.

If you have worked to targets in previous jobs with targets that were either your own or given as part of a team, an employer will find you even more employable. Some team targets are easier to meet than others. The ease of meeting them often depends on the structure of the organisation and how well employees get on with each other.

Ability to observe and raise professional standards

An employee who is able to work consistently to the standards required by the organisation will be valued by the employer. One who seeks to improve standards by suggesting and implementing better ways of doing the job is even more useful. Employers will want to employ people with high professional standards. Standards are often drawn up by organisations that represent different professions and members need to agree to follow those standards when they are working.

1.5 Personal skills

Certain skills will be beneficial regardless of the job or career that you pursue. These transferable personal skills make a candidate attractive to a new employer.

Patient and hard-working

Patience is required in many jobs, especially if you are dealing with members of the public. Employees

Case study: Purbeck Ice Cream

Purbeck Ice Cream is an award-winning producer of different ice creams ranging from more traditional flavours like vanilla bean to more outlandish flavours such as cracked black pepper, chilli or liquorice.

Peter and Hazel Hartle, who own the company, suggest that one of the reasons it is so successful is because of their team-working ethos. Although the business is quite small, with less than 15 employees, by encouraging employees to work more closely together and through careful monitoring the team has become stronger as individuals have developed themselves and taken on new skills to improve the team as a whole.

The team still needs to be co-ordinated into relevant areas to ensure that progress is being made to the right level in every part of the business such as production, marketing and administration. It is also essential, however, to ensure that everyone is involved in making plans for the future. Working in this way has certainly helped Purbeck Ice Cream move from a small enterprise to one that now supplies supermarket chains all over Dorset. It even distributes its award-winning products to wine bars and top hotels in London.

1. How has team working helped Purbeck Ice Cream to be a success?

2. What might the disadvantages of close team working be to a small organisation like Purbeck Ice Cream?

3. Discuss the view that team working and the monitoring of team performance is less important in a smaller organisation than a larger one.

For more information on Purbeck Ice Cream, see www.purbeckicecream.co.uk

---

who can remain patient in very difficult situations and get the job done are highly valued by employers. Being patient with people is not always easy, and it is undoubtedly easier with some people than with others. Patience is an important skill for a business person. Rushed decisions are rarely the best ones; it is usually much better to consider options and potential consequences before making decisions.

Someone who gets lots of work done is also valued, whereas employees who spend too much time talking, answering their mobile phones or surfing the Internet during working hours will not make a good impression. It can be very difficult to avoid distractions at work, but it is important that any employee, including you, is able to avoid them and do the job that they have been employed to do. This may also mean staying late sometimes if it is necessary to ensure that a job is completed on time.

Team worker

Another personal skill that is very important is to work as part of a team. You have already learned about team working on page 50 of this unit and Unit 19 Developing teams in business (page 355) also gives you more information about how to work effectively as part of a team.

Interpersonal skills

Interpersonal skills enable us to get on with other people, promote positive relationships in the workplace and so enable the job to be done better or more efficiently. Some people are naturally good at getting on with others and encouraging colleagues, but it is possible to learn good interpersonal skills. If you think your skills might be lacking in this area, it would be worth working on them – such abilities will make you more employable and will also enable you to do a better job at work.

Some interpersonal skills are very simple: such as smiling. A cheerful smile can break down barriers and encourage someone to listen and talk to you, so remembering to smile is a good start to improving your interpersonal skills.

Co-operation

Line managers expect employees to co-operate with their ideas and wishes. As an employee, you should

Key term

Interpersonal skills – skills that enable us to get on with other people and promote positive relationships in the workplace

Case study: Chartered Institute of Marketing (CIM)

In line with CIM's Professional Marketing Standards, CIM members must adhere to a strict code of professional practice.

This code requires each individual to:

- demonstrate integrity, bringing credit to the profession of marketing
- be fair and equitable towards other marketing professionals
- be honest in dealing with customers, clients, employers and employees
- avoid the dissemination of false or misleading information
- demonstrate current knowledge of the latest developments and show competence in their application
- avoid conflicts of interest and commitment to maintaining impartiality
- treat sensitive information in complete confidence

- negotiate business in a professional and ethical manner
- demonstrate knowledge and observation of the requirements of other codes of practice
- demonstrate due diligence in using third party endorsement, which must have prior approval
- comply with the governing laws of the relevant country concerned.

1. Discuss the CIM code of professional practice by considering the advantages of having such a code and any possible disadvantages. For more information about the code, go to www.cim.co.uk

2. Look up another code of professional practice and compare it to this one. What do you notice about the two? Which elements are the same and which are different?

---

work co-operatively with other colleagues wherever possible. This also means that if you are asked to do something at work, you get on with doing it in a positive and constructive way rather than moaning about it to other people.

Negotiation

Another useful skill for an employee is the ability to negotiate effectively. Negotiating involves discussing a topic in order to produce some agreement or common ground. At the start of negotiations, the parties involved usually have quite different opinions on what should happen. The art of negotiation is in finding common ground that both parties can agree upon – making it a 'win-win' situation. Negotiation is the process of seeking agreement and can therefore be useful for resolving conflicts between members of staff, agreeing personal or departmental targets, agreeing budget allocations and during interviews, especially for new staff members. Negotiating can also be personally useful for achieving pay rises or better working conditions.

Conflict can be very destructive in a work environment, so taking steps to avoid it (or positively to resolve conflict) is a useful skill. You can do this by being respectful to others, respecting differences in other people, thinking carefully before you speak (so many

conflicts have been caused by ill-advised, hasty and confrontational comments), being patient and empathising with others.

Negotiation is also really important when agreeing targets for an individual or a team of people. This is because sometimes targets may be set very high and therefore need to be further developed between the line manager and employee. Other times they may be too low and need to be worked up.

When agreeing budgets, the level of negotiation will depend on the type of budgeting being used. For example, if zero budgeting is being used, a budget holder will need to negotiate with their line manager the amount of money that they are likely to request or bid for. With an allocated budget they are given a budget, but may still need to negotiate to try to get more money if they think the budget is too small.

Interviewing skills

Interviewing skills can be useful in a number of contexts. Being able to interview customers or clients effectively to encourage sales or improve customer relationships will be useful to many organisations. In addition, it will be an asset to identify the best candidates effectively when interviewing potential new employees or to deal with appraisal situations for current members of staff.

Activity: Interviewing

In pairs, think of an interview situation that you have been in. The situation may have been in the workplace, in school or college, or in another context.

1. What type of questions did you have to answer?
2. How complicated was the interview?
3. How long did it last?

4. Which skills did you require?
5. Which skills did your interviewer need in order to interview you?

When you have worked through these questions, write up a poster or information sheet about interviewing skills. Include some advice for interviewers and interviewees in the interview situation.

PLTS

To really stretch your reflective skills, try to be as honest as you can about what you found difficult and what you think you can improve.

Assessment activity 2.1

For the first part of the assessed work for this unit, you must demonstrate that you have gained understanding of the way human resources are managed in a specific organisation. Before you start the tasks, think carefully about the organisation that you would like to study and for which you will complete assessed work.

1. Describe the recruitment documentation used in a selected organisation. **P1**
2. Describe the main employability, personal and communication skills required when applying for a specific job role. **P2**

3. Assess the importance of employability, and personal skills in the recruitment and retention of staff in a selected organisation. **M2**

Grading tips

1. When you describe, remember to include all the relevant information that relates to the documentation and skills. **P1** **P2**
2. When assessing, you will need to think about how the skills are important but also when they might be less important in the business context that you are studying. **M2**

2. Know the purpose of managing physical and technological resources

Both physical and technological resources need to be managed carefully in an organisation. Physical resources include the building, maintenance and security of the premises. Technological resources include the physical equipment and designs and drawings.

2.1 Physical resources

These are the resources that the business needs to maintain in order to carry out its activities. They include things like the buildings, facilities, **plant** and machinery. Management of physical resources involves planning maintenance and refurbishment, and includes

organising insurance and security to keep those resources safe.

Buildings and facilities

Any business will need to have premises from where it can operate. This may range from a person's home, when the business first starts operating, to tower block offices all over the world. Buildings play an important role in the image of a business and can make potential customers want to work with the business even more. The building that is used by Lloyds is so famous that it has become a tourist attraction to many visitors from London. Many financial institutions still have their head offices in central London near the Stock Exchange so that they can still maintain links with clients' suppliers in person as well as online.

When customers enter the building, facilities need to be arranged for them, such as meeting rooms or front desks. Banks, for example, often have desks or rooms where clients can talk to an advisor about financial products, such as loans or mortgages, as well as a screened area from which money is given out or paid in.

For some businesses, the attractiveness of the building is not as important as the inside because customers are never expected to see what goes on there. For example, Amazon.co.uk (www.amazon.co.uk) and Ocado, Waitrose's home shopping service (www.ocado.com), run massive warehouses with high levels of automation (use of automatic equipment). The public do not go there so the buildings are designed to be as efficient as possible and do not necessarily look attractive. Other businesses may use the building and facilities to market the type of services or products that they are offering. Ikea in Croydon, for example, painted the chimneys of the former Croydon Power Station in the company colours in 2003. These blue and yellow chimneys can be seen for miles around and remind people that the store is there, while still keeping something of the history of the building.

The location of buildings is important when a business considers its distribution network. If a business locates to a place that is as accessible to as many customers as possible, its profits can increase. This might be

What role does the Lloyds building play in the image of the company?

achieved, for example, by businesses that trade throughout Europe locating in countries in central Europe, from where they can easily distribute to more countries.

Materials and waste

The materials that are needed by a business will very much depend on the type of operation it is running and the people working there. A car-making factory will need access to steel, paint, plastics and so on to make cars. An office will have to provide computers, pens, paper and telephones for their employees to use. Some businesses will use materials that are renewable or recyclable, such as paper, while others use non-renewable materials such as oil. All businesses need to be careful about how much they use and try to avoid wasting materials so as to keep their costs low and help the environment. Some companies have made excellent use of initiatives to reduce the amount of materials they use and so save money. For example, the Oxford Group (www.oxfordgroup.co.uk) saved £40,000 a year by reducing the amount of paper used.

The waste that a business produces has to be taken away by another agency such as the council or a private company. It makes good business sense to reduce the amount of waste as this cuts waste disposal costs, which should help lead to higher profits for the business. The government sees waste reduction as important for the environment and has funded the Envirowise campaign, giving tips on ways to do this.

Plant and machinery

Like materials and buildings, each business has specific requirements for the type of plant and machinery that it might need. A business may spend thousands of pounds on its factory and machinery by buying everything that is needed. For other businesses, it may be easier and more cost effective to lease what is needed.

Equipment including IT

Equipment is essential for a business to operate smoothly. For example, your tutor may be unable to work effectively without a board marker or access to the register to check who is present. Equipment is critical for profit and not-for-profit organisations alike. In some types of organisations, lack of equipment means that a job or service cannot be carried out. A hospital without bed trolleys or wheelchairs is unable to move patients. A catering business without access to mixers and ovens is unable to produce food. Many organisations include information technology (IT) within their list of essential equipment, as both hardware (physical computer components) and software (computer programs) are becoming essential pieces of kit.

Some traditional businesses have also taken to using IT to help support and enhance their methods of working. Cows in the UK and Australia are, in some cases, doing self-milking, and researchers at the University of Nottingham are investigating the benefits of using more technology on farms. This means cows choose when to be milked and robots conduct the process. This may seem like a crazy idea but it has been found to lead to happier cows and an increase in the amount of milk that they produce.

Activity: Reducing waste

Using the Envirowise website www.envirowise.gov.uk to help you, produce an information pack on ways that a business of your choice could reduce the amount of materials they need and waste they produce. You should include:

- ten tips for waste reduction for that business
- issues that the business may face when trying to reduce waste
- a judgement about the impact on the business of not reducing waste in the future.

Activity: Comparing plant and machinery use

Produce a table to compare three different organisations near you. Include a column for each of these headings:

- name of business
- type of business
- location of buildings
- plant and machinery used
- costs of buildings and plant/machinery (low or high).

What do you notice about the different requirements for the buildings and plant of each business?

Planned maintenance and refurbishment

All buildings, plant and machinery require regular maintenance and updating. Even factories that work using flow production (where a product moves through successive processes in a single direction) 24 hours a day have to allow time to check that machines are working properly and make minor adjustments to them if necessary. If this maintenance does not take place, machines may break down, stopping production and leading to a loss of profits. Building maintenance, such as regular cleaning and painting, is also needed to keep buildings in good order, clean and safe.

A good working environment is likely to make staff happier, work harder and stay with the company longer. **Refurbishment** can help the environment if the new resources are eco-friendly or energy saving, such as installing solar panels, and this can give a good image for the company as well as saving energy and therefore reducing costs.

Key term

Refurbishment – when a business gives a new look to its offices or stores. It can help keep staff and customers happy

Emergency provision

The Health and Safety at Work Act 1974 requires organisations to draw up policies and provisions for what should happen in the event of an emergency within a building. This means that evacuation training must be given to employees and clear instructions provided about what to do in the event of a fire or other incident within the building. The organisation must also provide other equipment within the building, including fire alarms to detect fire, fire escapes for use in high buildings and fire extinguishers.

Regular audits of health and safety provision must take place so that any new equipment can be provided. It is not just the employer's responsibility to ensure that the building is safe; employees must also inform their employer about any hazards that exist so that they can be dealt with. Employers also have a duty of care towards any customers or visitors who come into the workplace, so emergency provision is a high priority for any organisation.

Insurance

All buildings owned or leased by businesses must have insurance. If the business owns the building, it will arrange this cover itself, but if the building is leased, it is often arranged with the landlord. A fee is paid each month and then protection is given to the business in the event that something happens to or within the building such as:

- a flood, fire, earthquake or storm that damages the building and stock
- damage to any equipment
- theft from the building
- vandalism
- leaking pipes
- collision by vehicles.

The type of insurance coverage and the amount of money paid will depend on the policy that the business takes out. The business is also required to have some other types of insurance.

Employers' liability insurance is compulsory by law. It provides insurance in case employers have to pay any employee or their family as a result of accidental death, bodily injury or disease as a result of an individual's employment.

Public liability insurance must be paid by employers to cover any payments to the public for injuries suffered or property damaged as a result of the business.

There are also other types of insurance that businesses can take out, including product liability insurance, professional indemnity insurance and so on. Choosing the right policy for the organisation can be complicated and specialist advice may be required.

Security

The building must be made secure and looked after, even when employees have gone home. Some businesses employ full-time security staff to do this and they patrol the building, sometimes using dogs to help them. Other organisations use security cameras and alarms, which are linked to police stations. There are now many schemes for businesses including Beating Business Crime (in Warwickshire, for example) and the national Business Watch, working with the police. These organisations give help and advice on how to keep buildings and stock secure, such as installing safe letter boxes, fitting appropriate doors and only holding a limited amount of cash or stock within the building.

2.2 Technological resources

Technological resources are more than just equipment. Computer hardware, such as a modem or router and monitor, is a physical resource and is treated as such. Technological resources in this instance are things like

Case study: Secured by Design

Secured by Design (www.securedbydesign.com) is a police-owned initiative that aims to reduce crime by changing the design of many building projects (ranging from commercial properties, hospitals, schools to new homes and play areas).

Their network of police officers (which are called Crime Prevention Design Advisors) gives free advice to businesses and organisations on how to secure a property, how to design new buildings in a way that makes it harder for criminals to break in and even how to use cameras in order to monitor people who are visiting the premises.

One of the ways that organisations can increase their security with relatively low expense is to grow 'defensive planting' around the outside of their buildings. This means planting very thorny plants such as hawthorn or berberis that will scratch criminals as they try to enter or leave the premises.

In pairs or small groups, think of any business premises that are near you that have very thorny plants outside of them.

1. What do you think the advantages of using defensive planting might be?
2. Are there any disadvantages?

software, music or text. These resources are owned, like physical resources, and have to be managed in the same way. Technological resources can be considered in four main areas:

- intellectual property
- accumulated experience and skills
- software licences
- protection via patents and copyright.

Intellectual property

Intellectual property rights allow people to own ideas and have rights concerning what happens to these ideas, including how often they are used, what they are associated with and if they have permission to be copied. There are considered to be five different types of intellectual property (see Table 2.3).

All of these different types of communication are covered within copyright and patenting law, and have to be protected like any other copyrighted material.

Accumulated experience and skills

Accumulated experience means experience gained over a number of years when a person has come across lots of different issues to do with the job. If the business can keep people in their jobs, the level of experience in the business can grow. Experienced employees are more likely to be able to do a good job in an organisation and should be managed carefully. Sometimes this might mean paying people more or giving them special conditions.

It is important to build up a person's skills but organisations have to be careful not to create a situation where, for example, only one person can operate a piece of machinery or fix a software program. If that person then leaves the organisation, it is difficult to maintain that resource and the business may not function effectively. Organisations have to make sure that there is backup available for specialist employees dealing with such resources and that they **cascade** training. This means that others receive training on how to look after that resource.

Key term

Cascade – to pass information on to a succession of others

Table 2.3: The five different types of intellectual property.

Designs	Covers the features or decoration of products such as colours, lines, materials, shape or texture
Drawings	Covers the drawings of a product, including the drawing of a patent
Text	Covers the actual style and content of text that is used, including data written on websites
Music	Covers the use of music for public or private performances and its copying
Video	Covers the use of video clips within websites or whole films, and the protection against copying or performances in public places

Software licences

Many businesses invest a lot of money in software and its day-to-day use. Sometimes bespoke (made to order or for a specific purpose) software will be designed for a business or they will use someone else's software and pay a licence fee to use it. For example, if a computer you use when completing your BTEC National course has Word or Excel on it, these items of software are licensed to Microsoft, so money has to be paid to Microsoft to use that software. Licences may allow the software to be installed on one computer, a limited number of computers or even a whole site so that everyone can use the software. The licence may also allow employees to have the software installed on laptops or at home. Universities often have multiple user licences so that tutors and learners can gain access to cheaper licences for educational purposes.

If businesses do not buy a licence or are 'under-licensed' (meaning that they run software on more computers than they have a licence for), they are breaking the law. Sometimes businesses may find themselves in the opposite position, where they are over-licensing. This may be because a number of different departments have bought software individually. By applying for a whole site licence, the business may be able to save money. Businesses should therefore carry out a software audit where each computer is checked for software and a central database kept by the IT department.

Protection via patents and copyright

It can be difficult and costly for businesses to protect technological resources. Legislation can help to protect these resources, but it is sometimes difficult to prove if someone has taken your idea and used it. Patents and copyright are two areas of intellectual property law.

A patent gives an inventor the legal rights to stop someone else copying or using part of their invention without their permission. This helps to ensure that

Did you know?

According to the Alliance Against Intellectual Property Theft (www.allianceagainstiptheft.co.uk), the Rogers Review suggests that £1.3 billion of intellectual property crime took place in 2006 and £900 million of that money went directly to organised criminals.

new ideas can be given time to be developed and manufactured once the idea has been registered with the UK Intellectual Property Office (www.ipo.gov.uk).

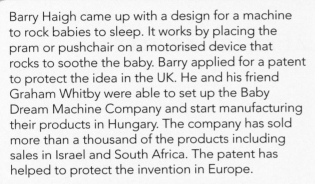

Case study: The Baby Dream Machine and Hushbye Baby Rocker

Barry Haigh came up with a design for a machine to rock babies to sleep. It works by placing the pram or pushchair on a motorised device that rocks to soothe the baby. Barry applied for a patent to protect the idea in the UK. He and his friend Graham Whitby were able to set up the Baby Dream Machine Company and start manufacturing their products in Hungary. The company has sold more than a thousand of the products including sales in Israel and South Africa. The patent has helped to protect the invention in Europe.

Meanwhile, in Australia, Newton McMahon was designing an automatic baby rocker that works with prams, pushchairs or even cots. His device also includes a micro-motion device that checks whether or not the baby is breathing and alerts the carer if they are not. This product, called the Hushbye Baby Rocker, is similar to the Baby Dream Machine.

Sometimes within patenting law it is difficult to prove whether or not something is similar to another product. A patent taken out in the UK will also only provide protection within the UK unless the inventor has taken out an International Patent protecting it throughout the world. Patents are not free in the UK; the first stages of applying for a patent costs at least £200 and the licence needs to be reviewed every year. It usually takes between two and three years to grant a patent and so the invention is also not protected during this time.

1. **What is meant by a patent and what is its purpose?**
2. **What are the limitations of a patent?**
3. **To what extent has online shopping and the use of international purchasing habits by UK citizens limited the effectiveness of UK patenting law?**

Assessment activity 2.2

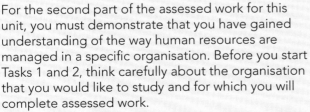

For the second part of the assessed work for this unit, you must demonstrate that you have gained understanding of the way human resources are managed in a specific organisation. Before you start Tasks 1 and 2, think carefully about the organisation that you would like to study and for which you will complete assessed work.

1. Describe the main physical and technological resources required in the operation of a selected organisation. **P3**
2. Explain how the management of human, physical and technological resources can improve the performance of a selected organisation. **M1**

Grading tips

1. You must make sure that you include a range of resources that cover both topic areas to achieve a pass. **P3**
2. For merit work, you need to show understanding, so remember to include clear explanation in your own words of how the management clearly improves the performance. **M1**

3. Know how to access sources of finance

There are two main ways that businesses can access financial resources:

- from within the business (internal source)
- from outside the business (external source).

3.1 Internal sources

Internal sources of finance can be from the business owner's savings or from profits.

Owner's savings

The owner of a business often has to use their own personal savings to start the business, particularly if they are a new sole trader (a person who owns and runs their business). This is because banks may not be willing to take a risk and invest in them. Savings are a good source of finance for a business, as interest does not need to be paid to someone else while the money is being used, and the business remains totally in the control of the owner.

Capital from profits

Once a business is operating it may be able to invest the money that it makes as profits back in the business. This means that even greater profits may be made in the future. The amount of profit to invest back in the business – or in new businesses – will depend on how much profit the owner(s) want to keep for themselves against how much they want the business to expand. For some businesses it is not possible to use capital from profits – for example, if they are a charity or not-for-profit organisation.

3.2 External sources

There are a number of different external sources that can be used to fund a business. Table 2.4 outlines some of these.

Table 2.4: Some external sources to fund a business.

Source	Details
Banks	Banks are able to offer loans, business accounts, commercial mortgages and overdraft facilities based on the business plan. Interest is payable based on the predicted risk. Some security will need to be provided, for example, assets such as a house.
Building societies	Building societies are also able to offer loans, business accounts, commercial mortgages and overdraft facilities based on the business plan. Interest is payable based on the risk of the venture. As with banks, some security will need to be provided, such as assets.
Hire purchase	Hire purchase means that resources can be used by the business while they are being paid for to a finance company. Until the last payment is made on the agreement, the goods are not owned by the business, and if payments are not made the finance company can take them back.
Leasing	Leasing means that a business can make use of resources and pay to use them every month. The business does not own the goods at the end of the lease. Leasing is often used by companies for vehicles.
Venture capitalists	These are people who invest in new and up-and-coming risky ventures, usually in return for a share of the ownership.
Factoring	Debt factoring means that the business sells its debts to another company and receives some of the money immediately. The debt factoring company collects the debts and takes a percentage cut for this service.

continued

Table 2.4: Some external sources to fund a business – *continued.*

Source	Details
Share issues	Issuing shares is a good way for many companies to raise finance. Small businesses will issue shares when they move from being a sole trader/partnership to become limited (ltd). The shares are not offered publicly but business contacts, friends or family can buy them. Limited companies are then able to sell shares on the stock exchange if they become public limited companies (PLC). This is known as floating on the stock exchange. Sometimes large PLCs will have a new share issue as well when they want to invest in a large project and these are also floated on the stock exchange.
Friends or family	Money from friends and family may either be invested in the business in exchange for ltd shares or paid back as a loan – often at a lower rate than would be payable to a bank or other lender.
Government grants and Prince's Trust loans and grants	These are available from the EU, national government and local government. A grant is money given to an entrepreneur that does not have to be paid back and the amount of that money will depend on where it is coming from (for more information, see www.businesslink.gov.uk). Businesses run by people between the age of 18 and 30 can apply for low-interest loans from the Prince's Trust (www.princes-trust.org.uk).

Activity: Dina's Silk Flowers

Dina de Santos is thinking of setting up her own silk flower-making business. She needs more information about where to access funds to help her get her business off the ground.

Produce an information pack for her describing where she can obtain different sources of finance.

Assessment activity 2.3   P4   BTEC

For the third part of the assessed work for this unit, you must demonstrate that you have gained understanding of the way human resources are managed in a specific organisation. Before you start the task, think carefully about the organisation that you would like to study and for which you will complete assessed work.

Describe sources of internal and external finance for a selected business. **P4**

Grading tip

Make sure that you really describe each source of finance – a simple description will not be enough. You must describe the sources in the context of the business you have chosen. **P4**

4. Be able to interpret financial statements

As part of your understanding of resources, you will need to be able to use financial statements and work out how a business is managing financial resources in three main ways:

- costs and budgets
- financial statements
- basic ratios.

4.1 Costs and budgets

The management of costs is a very important aspect of managing financial resources. If costs are not managed effectively, this can lead to profits being damaged and the business being potentially unable to pay its expenses. Keeping within a budget, increasing income in order to cope with change, making sure that working capital is available and making sure that money set aside for emergencies is all part of the balancing exercise.

Costs managed to budget

There are two main costs that need to be managed to budget: fixed costs and variable costs.

Fixed costs are costs that do not change, regardless of the number of goods that are sold or services that are offered. These costs include rent, insurance and salaries. Whether the business makes 100 or 10,000 products, these costs must be paid.

Variable costs are costs that change according to output. These costs change directly according to how many products are made; for example, a business

producing footballs will have varying requirements for amounts of leather, rubber, thread and valves, depending on how many footballs it makes.

Budgeting is a difficult process because it seeks to give a guide to how much the business thinks it will spend in a given area in the future. Some businesses will choose to use zero budgeting. This is when departments are given no budget, but have to ask their managers for money based on what they believe they will need for that year.

Allocated budgeting is the opposite; this is when money is allocated for a budget and divided according to how many departments and people are working there. The budget is usually set at the start of the financial year and the business must ensure each month that it is sticking to its predictions. If sales are higher than budgeted, this is likely to be positive for the business, but if costs are higher this could lead to lower profits or even problems with paying the business's expenses.

Measuring the difference between what is budgeted and the actual costs or sales revenue that has been received is known as variance analysis. If the result is better than expected – for example, sales revenues are higher or costs are lower – this variance is known as favourable (F). If sales are lower or costs are higher than expected, this variance is known as adverse (A). Monitoring the variances is really important as if the business notices them early enough, it can make changes to get back on track.

Activity: Smell the Dough

Smell the Dough is a small business producing dough that has a variety of different flavours from smoked cheese to lemonade. The dough is sold in hand-painted pots. The business is run from a unit rented on an industrial estate. Each pot is hand painted by local people in their spare time. They are paid £2 per pot. The pots are ordered at a minimum level and the levels depend on the sales already made that month.

Electricity and gas is paid monthly. Smell the Dough has a website that advertises their products and a web master is paid monthly to maintain it and process the orders. The dough ingredients are

bought in bulk and are stored until they are ready to be used and filled into the completed pots. Orders are received by email and by phone.

1. Write a list of the fixed costs that Smell the Dough must pay.
2. Write a list of the variable costs that Smell the Dough must pay.
3. Can you think of any additional costs they may incur that are not included above?
4. 'It is essential to keep variable costs as low as possible in order to increase profits.' Discuss this view.

Case study: Hair for Wear Ltd

Hair for Wear Ltd is a company specialising in making hair extensions, which are delivered to hairdressing salons. Below is the budget for November, December and January.

Table 2.5: Budget for Hair for Wear Ltd.

Cost	Nov £	Dec £	Jan £
Materials	300	300	200
Petrol	200	200	200
Wages	800	800	800
Advertising	200	200	200
Insurance	300	300	300
Factory rental	400	400	400
Bank loan payment	350	350	350
Van payment	250	250	250
Total	**2,800**	**2,800**	**2,700**

The actual costs for November, December and January are given as follows.

- Materials were £200, £300 and £250.
- Petrol costs were £100, £150 and £100.
- Wages were as expected.
- Advertising cost £250 every month.
- Insurance was more expensive than predicted, at £400 per month.

Variance analysis is useful for any business.

- The factory rental was reduced by 50 per cent for January only.
- The bank loan payment was £375 every month.
- The van repayment was £230 per month.

1. Calculate the variances against the actual costs using the information given.
2. What recommendations would you make to Hair for Wear Ltd based on the variance analysis that you have just conducted?
3. Discuss the usefulness of variance analysis to a company like Hair for Wear Ltd.

Break-even

Businesses can use the calculations that they make of fixed costs, variable costs and sales to work out the point at which their costs equal their sales. This point is known as break-even and shows how many products they need to produce and sell, or services they need to offer, to get to the point where they are neither making a profit or a loss.

The break-even point (BEP) can be worked out as follows:

$$BEP = \frac{\text{fixed costs}}{\text{unit contribution}}$$

The unit contribution is the selling price minus the variable cost per unit.

Calculating break-even allows a business to work out how many products they need to sell before they can actually start to make a profit.

The margin of safety (MOS) can also be calculated to allow the business to work out the amount of units by which sales can fall before the business starts to make a loss. This is calculated with the following formula.

MOS = actual sales in units − BEP in units

A break-even chart enables a business to identify the:

- BEP in sales units and sales revenue
- MOS
- amount of profit or loss made at different levels of sales
- effect of changes in fixed costs, variable costs and selling prices.

The chart displays the revenue and costs at future levels of output. It enables the user to identify the break-even point.

Using a break-even chart, it is also possible to work out the contribution that a product or service makes to fixed costs. This is worked out in the following way.

unit contribution = selling price – variable cost

This is useful as it allows individual products or services to be viewed in terms of how much they contribute towards overall overhead costs or if they actually have a negative contribution and might be losing the business money.

Profit can also be worked out by multiplying the margin of safety by unit contribution. This is useful when comparing different products or services within the business.

There are some benefits and limitations of break-even that you should be aware of, as Table 2.6 shows.

Table 2.6: Benefits and limitations of break-even.

Benefits	Limitations
It can provide very quick results for display either by hand or on a computer.	It can oversimplify the situation in terms of pricing as often businesses will offer different prices to different customers, for example, discounts or trade prices.
It can be used to help investors decide whether or not to invest in a small business.	It is only useful for a short amount of time as both costs and prices may change rapidly.
It allows small businesses to forecast what might happen to their business if sales go down or costs go up.	It is only as useful as the data that is put into it in terms of future costs and sales.
It is easy to apply with a minimum amount of training.	It does not take into account economies of scale, where the cost per unit starts to reduce at higher levels of product output.
	It may be difficult to use if the business sells a range of different products that cover the fixed costs in differing amounts.
	It needs to be supported with relevant market research and economic predictions in order to be useful.

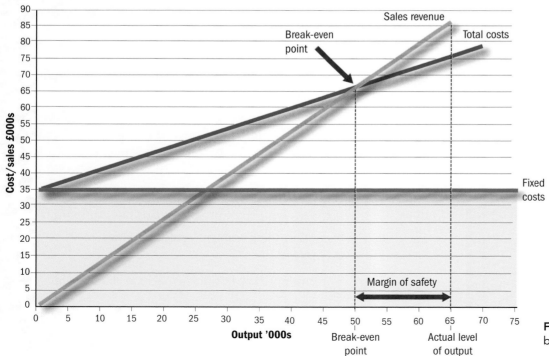

Fig. 2.2: An example of a break-even chart.

Activity: Deluxe Car Wash Services

Produce a break-even chart and check your workings using the break-even formula for the following car wash business.

- Car wash price = £12.50 per car
- Overhead costs = £175 per week
- Labour costs per wash = £4.50 per car
- Materials and water cost = £1.00 per car

1. Make sure you label your graph in full and include the break-even formula to show you are right.

2. Deluxe Car Wash Services averaged 30 cars per week during July – work out the margin of safety.

3. How much profit would Deluxe Car Wash Services make if they did 20 car washes during one week, and what recommendations would you make to them about this?

Once the business has worked out its break-even point, it knows the levels which it must reach or keep to in order to become profitable.

Bidding to increase future resources

Sometimes businesses realise that they do not have enough money available in their budgets to expand or buy new equipment, for example. Therefore they may choose to bid for additional funding through a capital grant or ask others to invest in the business. This type of budget funding is particularly important for organisations that work within the public sector, as they are often funded on a short-term basis and a certain amount is put in to pay for resources – for example, wages for employees.

A business may also choose to increase future resources by asking others to invest in the business. This means that the business owner(s) gets the use of the money invested and in return offers a percentage stake in the business. A private limited or public limited company may choose to do this by offering shares.

Other businesses may not have investment from large organisations or may not want another big company to be involved. They need to raise money in other ways, so may choose to go to their bank for a loan or may try to raise finance by getting a grant. National or local

government agencies can give businesses grants for many different reasons, including:

- where the business is located
- how big the business is
- if the business is in an industry that has problems.

The most common organisations to receive grants currently are those in farming, manufacturing or tourism.

Activity: The Prince's Trust

Some organisations like the Prince's Trust (www.princes-trust.org.uk) give out grants to young people to help them set up in business.

1. Using websites like the Prince's Trust, research three different types of grant that are available to people starting up in business.

2. Compare the different types of grants by considering their advantages and disadvantages.

3. Give a judgement about the effectiveness of grants compared to loans for a new small business.

Appropriate liquidity/working capital

Working capital is the day-to-day money needed to pay the bills so the business can continue to trade. It is the difference between the current assets (cash plus debtors due to settle their accounts plus stock) that the business has and its current liabilities (the debts that must be paid in the short term). Table 2.7 shows the example of Bob's Construction Ltd.

Table 2.7: Figures for Bob's Construction Ltd.

	Current assets £	Current liabilities £
Cash	4,000	
Debtors (people that owe money)	500	
Stock	100	
Creditors (people whom money is owed to)		1,600
Bank loan		2,000
Total	4,600	3,600

The working capital figure for Bob's business would be £4,600 – £3,600 = £1,000.

Working capital is extremely important to businesses because it puts them into a position where they can pay their bills. Large businesses may make things more difficult for smaller businesses by negotiating long payment periods. For example, if a small business is offering a window cleaning service to a large company, that company may negotiate payment after 14 days, which means that costs will be incurred at least two weeks before payment is received.

It is quite common for debtors to fail to settle invoices within the time negotiated, so there needs to be extremely careful cash flow management. The higher the level of **liquidity**, the easier it is for the business to access extra funds and so be able to pay off any debts that it has.

Activity: Pet supplies

Brains Pet Food Ltd		Kipper Fish Snax Ltd	
Bank	£200	Bank	£500
Creditors	£400	Creditors	£200
Loan from bank	£2,000	Loan from bank	£750
Debtors	£750	Debtors	£300
Stock	£600	Stock	£1,000
Cash	£300	Cash	£250

1. Calculate the working capital figure for each business.
2. Explain what the working capital figure shows for each business.
3. What recommendations would you make for each business?

Appropriate reserves to address emergencies/crises

Businesses, like the rest of us, have to keep some money back at the end of every month as reserves, in case an emergency should happen. This ensures that if they do have problems, such as an unexpected expense, or there is a downturn in their market due to world events or a natural disaster, they have enough funds to continue in business.

Some analysts recommend that reserves should be maintained that will allow the business to continue for at least three months in the event of an emergency. It is also important for businesses to have some reserves in the early stages of their budget planning, as it may be difficult to make accurate budget predictions and costs, and income calculations may need to be adjusted. An emergency budget will keep extra funds to allow for additional expenses.

4.2 Financial statements

Financial statements allow businesses to measure their financial resources. Public limited companies (PLCs) must publish their accounts so that investors can see how well they are doing and judge whether or not to buy their shares on the stock exchange. The two main types of financial statement you need to learn about are the profit and loss account and the balance sheet.

Profit and loss

The profit and loss account is a useful tool as it shows how much has been made at the end of a financial year. It can therefore help a bank or other lender to decide whether or not it is worth the risk to invest in a business. For smaller businesses, such as private limited companies (ltd) and sole traders, it is useful to be able to see how much profit has been made at the end of the year. Often businesses will use projected profit and loss accounts to help them to plan their finances. This can help with budget setting.

Fig. 2.3 shows a very simplified version of a service-based profit and loss account. This business is a consultancy offering business services. You can see how sales are shown and then expenses deducted, giving the net profit left over.

Fig. 2.4 on page 78 shows a profit and loss account for Khalida's Fashions Ltd; this also shows stock and gives a **gross profit** figure. Gross profit is when the cost of the sales has been taken away from the sales total. Expenses are then deducted to give the

Key terms

Liquidity – measure of a firm's ability to meet short-term cash payments

Gross profit – sales revenue minus cost of goods sold (the cost of the actual materials used to produce the quantity of goods sold)

Case study: Speed Ferries

Speed Ferries was introduced in May 2004 as a new concept in low-cost ferry services. In 2005, it won the 'Best European Crossing Operator' Award at the Telegraph Travel Awards. A press release in 2006 announced its services were up to 50 per cent cheaper than those of other operators, and that it had captured 12 per cent of the market.

In November 2008, administrators were appointed as the company was having cash flow difficulties. An extract from the Administrator's Statement of Proposals that was published in January 2009 reads:

'From 2004, the Company has incurred after tax losses in each year, with the most significant loss being £3.4m for the nine months to September 2008. The company suffered accumulated trading losses of c.£15m from inception to July 2008. Recent financial performance suffered due to an increase in the cost of fuel (£2.8m spend for the 12 months to December 2007 compared to £3.7m spend for the nine month period to September 2008) and a decline in revenue over the nine-month period to September 2008 (£10.3m compared to original forecast of £14.6m).

'In October 2008 the Company then experienced cash flow difficulties, as it was unable to hedge against fuel prices during a period of unprecedented price volatility

and was not in a position to pass on these costs to customers. Lower than forecast ticket and retail sales also impacted on the business. While previous losses had been funded by shareholders, these shareholders subsequently declined to provide further support to the Company. Management then sought new equity investment in the business and entered discussions with c.20 potential investors. Management formally instructed BDO Corporate Finance to assist them in their equity fund-raising initiatives. During these discussions the Company received a legal summons from the Port of Boulogne [PoB] for payment of unpaid harbour fees of c.£1.3m on 20 October 2008. The SpeedOne was subsequently arrested by PoB on 6 November 2008. As a result of the above, and the inability of the Company to trade while the ship remained arrested, A. Swarbrick and T. Burton of Ernst & Young LLP were appointed as Joint Administrators of the Companies on 12 November 2008 by the Company's directors.'

1. Using this information and www.speedferries.com, consider the issues that a business starting up with high fixed costs and investment needed may have regarding their cash flow, working capital and liquidity position.

Key term

Net profit – gross profit minus other expenses – for example, rent and advertising

net profit figure. You will learn more about using gross and net profit calculations to check the financial health of a business in this unit on page 79.

Shannon Coleman Business Services

Profit and loss account for the year ended April 2010

	£	£
Sales		19,500
Less expenses:		
Overheads	10,660	
Labour	7,020	17,680
Net profit before tax		1,820

Fig. 2.3: Profit and loss account for the year ended April.

Profit and loss accounts produced by large public limited companies can be extremely complicated and make use of many different accounting principles. You will learn more about financial information in Unit 5 Business accounting, but it is worth remembering that a profit and loss account shows the business and people that are interested in it, and how much profit the business is able to generate. The higher the profitability of a business, the better the performance that business has had. Tesco PLC in 2005 announced annual profits of more than £2 billion. This shows how effectively it had performed in that year to be able to make such large profits.

Balance sheet

The balance sheet is important because it gives a snapshot showing:

* assets (things a business owns)
* liabilities (debts a business owes)
* equity (the amount invested in the business).

Khalida's Fashions Ltd

Profit and loss account for the year ended April 2010
£

Sales		150,000
Less cost of sales		
Opening stock	5,000	
Purchases	51,000	
Less closing stock	6,000	50,000
Gross profit		**100,000**
Less expenses		
Rent and business rates	15,600	
Advertising	2,000	
Wages and salaries	28,000	
Administration	1,000	
Insurance	2,000	
Interest on loans	2,100	
Telephone	600	
Accountancy fees	900	
Legal fees	1,000	
Bank charges	400	
Depreciation	500	
Repairs and maintenance	300	
Heat and light	600	
Miscellaneous	300	
		55,300
Net profit before tax		**44,700**

Fig. 2.4: Profit and loss account for Khalida's Fashions Ltd.

Fixed assets are assets that are owned and expected to be retained for one year or more – for example, land, buildings, vehicles or equipment. Current assets are those that can be converted into cash more easily and are only retained for a short time.

Producing a balance sheet is important as it shows how the business is financed, whether through the investor's own money or through loans from other people, known as creditors. Because the balance sheet shows the assets of the business, it also gives the investor a snapshot of how much the business is actually worth. The balance sheet shown in Fig. 2.5 is a simplified version for a limited company. A balance sheet must balance! Here this is shown with the figure £93,000.

Public limited companies must publish balance sheets, and by looking at the data contained within them it is possible to value a business and estimate the net worth of a company. All sorts of other organisations use balance sheets as well, including the Inland Revenue, potential shareholders and companies taking over other organisations.

4.3 Basic ratios

One of the ways a business can measure how it is doing is through ratio analysis. Ratios can help the business to see how it is doing now and how it compares to last year or the year before and against other competitors. For these ratios to be useful, they should be compared over time to see if there are any trends and also compared between businesses within the same industry (competitors).

Solvency

Businesses can use ratios to work out their **solvency** by using the current ratio and acid test ratio (see page 79). These ratios allow businesses and potential investors to see how well they are able to meet their liabilities.

$$\text{current ratio} = \frac{\text{current assets}}{\text{current liabilities}}$$

This ratio (shown as x:1) shows how many assets a business has compared to liabilities – in other words,

Key term

Solvency – when a business is able to pay its expenses as it has money available within the business

Better Books Ltd

Start-Up balance sheet
£

Fixed assets		
Shop premises		75,000
Fixtures and fittings		5,000
		80,000
Current assets		
Stock	15,000	
Bank	3,000	
Cash	2,000	
	20,000	
Less current liabilities		
Creditors	7,000	7,000
Working capital		13,000
Total assets less current liabilities		**93,000**
Financed by		
Long-term liabilities		
Bank loan	10,000	
Mortgage	60,000	70,000
Capital and reserves		
Capital		23,000
Capital employed		93,000

Fig. 2.5: Start-up balance sheet.

how easily it would be able to pay its creditors. If the figure is just over 1, then the organisation may be in a difficult position for payment, as its current assets would be virtually equal to its liabilities. It is considered good practice to have a figure between 1.5 and 2, so that the business can be sure it can pay its liabilities easily. A figure higher than 2 would not be good as the money should be placed elsewhere to improve the business.

$$\text{acid test ratio} = \frac{\text{current assets} - \text{stock}}{\text{current liabilities}}$$

The acid test ratio shows the assets compared to liabilities, like the current ratio, but by taking out the stock figure from the current assets, it shows how well a business can meet its liabilities without having to sell stock. Again, the figure should be higher than 1 but not higher than 2.

Profitability

Ratios can also show how profitable a business really is – either as a snapshot or over time. There are three ways of working out how profitable a business really is:

- gross profit percentage
- net profit percentage
- return on capital employed (ROCE).

Gross profit percentage

This calculation shows gross profit as a percentage of the turnover (sales and any other income that a business gets). For example, if the gross profit is £1,000

and the turnover of the business is £2,000 the gross profit percentage would be as follows.

$$\frac{£1,000}{£2,000} \times 100 = 50\%$$

Gross profit percentage is also sometimes called gross profit margin. The calculation shows how well the business is managing its purchases of stock. A high gross profit percentage shows the business is doing well, as it is controlling the cost of its purchases.

Net profit percentage

This calculation takes the idea of profitability one stage further by actually considering the profit as a percentage of turnover after all the other expenses have been taken out. It is worked out as follows.

$$\frac{\text{net profit}}{\text{turnover}} \times 100 = \text{net profit percentage}$$

This shows the profit that the business has made before tax has been taken off. This calculation shows how well the business manages its other expenses, especially when it is compared to the gross profit percentage. If a business has a high gross profit percentage but a low net profit percentage, its operating costs (day-to-day running costs such as wages, rent and insurance) are too high, as they are taking out too much profit from the business. Sometimes it is possible to have a business where the gross profit percentage is good but the net profit percentage might be extremely low or even show a

Case study: Sweet ratios

Compare the following two businesses using both the current ratio and the acid test ratio. Both businesses are in the confectionery industry and the figures are taken from their annual accounts as at the end of April 2009.

Delicious Delights Ltd		Scrumptious Toffees Ltd	
Bank	£200	Bank	£500
Creditors	£400	Creditors	£200
Loan from bank	£2,000	Loan from bank	£750
Debtors	£750	Debtors	£300
Stock	£600	Stock	£1,000
Cash	£300	Cash	£250

1. Work out for each business which are the current assets and current liabilities.

2. Calculate the current ratio and acid test ratio for each business.

3. How do the ratios compare? What difference does stock make to their ability to pay their liabilities?

4. Make recommendations to each business about what they could do to improve their position in the future.

Table 2.8: The two calculations for stock turnover.

Stock turnover shown in number of times	Stock turnover shown in days
$\dfrac{\text{cost of sales}}{\text{average stock}} = \text{stock turnover (number of times)}$	$\dfrac{\text{average stock}}{\text{cost of sales}} \times 365 = \text{stock turnover (days)}$

loss. This would mean that the business would need to take action to reduce operating costs.

Return on capital employed (ROCE)

This is the final calculation that a business might use to judge profitability. It is worked out by considering the net profit as a percentage of the capital employed by that business. The reason this ratio is useful is because it shows the amount of money an investor is receiving back on their capital as a percentage. This means they can compare the percentage received against what they would have received if they had put the money into the bank.

$$\frac{\text{net profit before interest and tax}}{\text{capital employed (including shareholder funds)}} \times 100 = \text{ROCE (\%)}$$

If the interest rate at the bank is higher than that shown in the ROCE, it would make more sense for the investors to put their money there.

Determining performance

The final set of ratios that a business might want to use are those that determine performance. These show the stock turnover, **debtors'** collection period and asset turnover.

There are two main ways to work out the stock turnover ratio and they show how quickly the business has sold its stock. This is a useful way of measuring efficiency, as the faster the stock is turned over, the more likely the business is to be efficient. This is also extremely important if the goods being sold are perishable (for example, food).

The calculation for stock turnover can be shown either as a percentage or in days. Both show how quickly that stock is turned around and therefore how effective the stock control system is.

The debtors' collection period looks at the link between the number of debtors and how long on

Key terms

Debtors – customers who have purchased goods or services on credit, meaning they are in debt to the business as they owe it money

Average stock – the opening stock plus the closing stock, divided by two

Case study: Car businesses

The following three businesses all sell accessories and parts for cars. Kar Partz is run online and Dean's Motors and Jumpin' Jax are both run from the high street. The only variable costs that all three shops have are for the car parts themselves (stock).

	Kar Partz £	Dean's Motors £	Jumpin' Jax £
Fixed costs (operating costs)	500	600	800
Variable costs (stock)	300	400	600
Revenue (sales)	900	1,200	1,000

1. Which one has the best gross profit percentage?

2. Which one has the best net profit percentage?

3. Which business do you think is performing the best? Give reasons for your justification.

4. 'Gross profit is less important than net profit.' Give a judgement about this view, using real examples of companies you have studied to illustrate your thinking.

average it takes the business to collect its debts. The fewer the number of days means the business has better credit control, because it collects what is owed more quickly. If information about credit sales is not available, the calculation can still be worked out by using the total sales figure. The debtors' collection period can be shown in the following formula.

$$\frac{\text{debtors}}{\text{credit sales}} \times 365 = \frac{\text{total number of days it}}{\text{takes debtors to pay}}$$

The final ratio that can help to work out the performance of a business is asset turnover. This ratio looks at the sales as a percentage of the total assets that a business owns.

$$\frac{\text{sales}}{\text{total assets}} = \text{asset turnover}$$

By dividing the sales by the total assets, the business is able to work out how many pounds it earns for every pound invested in total assets. The following example demonstrates this.

$$\frac{30,000}{10,000} = \text{asset turnover}$$

This means for every £1 of assets, the business was able to generate £3 of sales.

The asset turnover ratio can also be broken down further as follows.

The fixed asset turnover ratio can show how much money has been invested in land and buildings. If the business is investing a lot in recent months, this is likely to be lower. Current assets such as stock, debtors or cash can be used within the current asset turnover calculation to see how many pounds of sales are generated per pound of current assets.

Asset-based ratio analysis can be very useful to businesses looking at trends in their performance to see how well they are making use of their assets. It is also important to consider the industry that the business is working in, to be able to tell how well they are doing. Some industries require a lot of investment in assets – for example, an engineering works or manufacturing plant. For others the investment might be relatively low – for example, an online business operating from home. It is important to make comparisons about asset turnover with relevant competitors and look at trends to see how well the business is doing.

Assessment activity 2.4   P5 P6 P7 M3 M4 D1 D2 D3   BTEC

For the last part of the assessed work for this unit, you must demonstrate that you have gained understanding of the way human resources are managed in a specific organisation. Before you start the tasks, think carefully about the organisation that you would like to study and for which you will complete assessed work.

1. Interpret the contents of a trading and profit and loss account and balance sheet for a selected company. **P5**

2. Interpret the contents of a trading and profit and loss account and balance sheet for a selected company, explaining how accounting ratios can be used to monitor the financial performance of the organisation. **M3**

3. Evaluate the adequacy of accounting ratios as a means of monitoring the state of the business in a selected organisation, using examples. **D2**

4. Illustrate the use of budgets as a means of exercising financial control of a selected company. **P6**

5. Analyse the reasons why costs need to be controlled to budget. **M4**

6. Evaluate the problems you have identified from unmonitored costs and budgets. **D3**

7. Illustrate the financial state of a given business. **P7**

8. Evaluate how managing resources and controlling budget costs can improve the performance of a business. **D1**

Grading tips

1. Make sure you build your answers up so that you can include descriptions to cover the pass elements of each criterion before you enhance your work to move towards merit and distinction. **P5 P6 P7**

2. For merit and distinction work, you should include the set of accounts that you have used for your interpretation as appendices at the end of your work. **M3 M4 D1 D2 D3**

Just checking

1. Name two different types of document that are used for recruitment.
2. Why are communication skills important at work?
3. Name three different ways that a business can offer incentives to employees.
4. Which personal skills are important at work?
5. What is the difference between planned maintenance and refurbishment?
6. Why is it important for an organisation to have public liability insurance?
7. To what extent can intellectual property be protected in the workplace?
8. How is break-even used to monitor and manage costs in an organisation?
9. What are meant by reserves?
10. Why is liquidity very important?
11. What is the different between the profit and loss account and the balance sheet of an organisation?
12. Name two ratios that can be applied to profitability, and explain the difference between the two.
13. What does ROCE stand for, and when is used?

Assignment tips

1. Make sure you include the paperwork that you have researched in your work in your appendices and reference information, using a bibliography.

2. It is useful to look at all the physical and technological resources that are around you at school or college. These may give you ideas for that part of your assessed work.

3. When you are working at distinction level you will see that the word 'evaluate' is used a lot. This means make a judgement, so you will need to ensure that you complete your pass and merit work thoroughly first so that you have enough evidence, including references, to make an appropriate judgement.

3 Introduction to marketing

The world is changing at an accelerating pace. As marketing is largely about identifying and meeting human and social needs, it plays a key role in any organisation's ability to survive and grow. Marketing is equally important to the non-commercial, public and voluntary sectors as it is to profit-making businesses.

The customer is the most important person to any business and this unit will introduce you to the various ways in which a business is able to analyse its customers and make important strategic decisions to ensure its survival and growth. Marketers are constantly faced with questions such as how to identify the correct group of customers to target, how to make a product or service different to customers, what price to charge, how to compete against similar products or services and how to build stronger brands. All these issues are examined in the unit.

You will explore how different types of organisations use marketing principles to meet the needs of their customers and achieve the organisation's objectives. You will study the laws which constrain the activities of marketers and protect consumers, as well as the voluntary codes that affect marketers.

Marketing involves making informed decisions, which requires information. Market research finds out answers to questions about whether or not there is a market for a product or service, which could be about price, quality, quantity and so on. This valuable information leads on to marketing planning. An effective marketing plan can help to identify sources of competitive advantage, gain commitment to a strategy, get resources needed to invest in and build the business, inform stakeholders, set objectives and strategies, and measure performance.

You will explore the segmentation and targeting of groups of customers, which are key marketing techniques. This includes the different bases for segmentation of both consumer and business markets. To effectively meet the needs and aspirations of a targeted group of customers, a marketing mix needs to be developed and the unit will show you how to do this for a new product or service.

Learning outcomes

After completing this unit, you should:

1. know the role of marketing in organisations
2. be able to use marketing research and marketing planning
3. understand how and why customer groups are targeted
4. be able to develop a coherent marketing mix.

Assessment and grading criteria

This table shows you what you must do in order to achieve a **pass**, **merit** or **distinction** grade, and where you can find activities in this book to help you.

To achieve a **pass** grade, the evidence must show that the learner is able to:	To achieve a **merit** grade, the evidence must show that, in addition to the pass criteria, the learner is able to:	To achieve a **distinction** grade, the evidence must show that, in addition to the pass and merit criteria, the learner is able to:
P1 describe how marketing techniques are used to market products in two organisations **See Assessment activity 3.1, page 96.**	**M1** compare marketing techniques used in marketing products in two organisations **See Assessment activity 3.1, page 96.**	**D1** evaluate the effectiveness of the use of techniques used in marketing products in one organisation **See Assessment activity 3.1, page 96.**
P2 describe the limitations and constraints of marketing **See Assessment activity 3.1, page 96.**		
P3 describe how a selected organisation uses marketing research to contribute to the development of its marketing plans **See Assessment activity 3.2, page 106.**	**M2** explain the limitations of marketing research used to contribute to the development of a selected organisation's marketing plans **See Assessment activity 3.2, page 106.**	**D2** make justified recommendations for improving the validity of the marketing research used to contribute to the development of a selected organisation's marketing plans **See Assessment activity 3.2, page 106.**
P4 use marketing research for marketing planning **See Assessment activity 3.2, page 106.**		
P5 explain how and why groups of customers are targeted for selected products **See Assessment activity 3.3, page 111.**		
P6 develop a coherent marketing mix for a new product or service **See Assessment activity 3.4, page 121.**	**M3** develop a coherent marketing mix that is targeted at a defined group of potential customers **See Assessment activity 3.4, page 121.**	

How you will be assessed

This unit will be assessed by an internal assignment that will be designed and marked by the staff at your centre. It may be subject to sampling by your centre's External Verifier as part of Edexcel's ongoing quality assurance procedures. The assignment is designed to allow you to show your understanding of the unit outcomes. These relate to what you should be able to do after completing this unit.

Your assessment could be in the form of presentations, case studies, practical tasks and written assignments.

Dafina

This unit helped me to understand that marketing is not just about selling products. It reaches every part of the business in order to understand what the customer actually wants and then to answer that need.

I enjoyed looking at different parts of the marketing mix and trying to think of products and how the mix of product, price, promotion and place combine to make the product successful.

There were lots of practical tasks and activities for this unit – the bit I enjoyed most was seeing how research assists the process of producing a marketing plan. I liked participating in different activities that helped me understand how the different parts of marketing all fit together. We looked at how leading businesses go about the business of marketing and it was fascinating to see how professional these organisations are at answering the needs of customers.

1. What areas of this unit might you find challenging?
2. Which section of the unit are you most looking forward to?
3. What preparation can you do in readiness for the unit assessment(s)?

Why do we buy certain products?

We all have our own priorities when buying. While some of us may be most concerned with having the latest branded clothes to impress people and to fit in, others are more concerned with buying things which simply serve a purpose. Try to think of the reasons why you were enticed into buying a product recently.

1. Why did not you buy a similar product made by another company?
2. Is the product advertised on television?
3. Do your friends and family also buy that product?

Discuss your answers in small groups and compare your answers.

1.   Know the role of marketing in organisations

1.1 What is the role of marketing?

Overall concept

The philosophy behind the marketing efforts of most modern businesses is that the company should identify the needs of their customers and produce products and services to satisfy those needs. This way, the customer is at the centre of the business and the decision-making process. A business following this philosophy is marketing-orientated.

However, there are alternative orientations for businesses, which you may come across in the course of your studies or in your future career. These include:

- **the production concept** – this is where a business focuses on creating economies of scale in production and distribution of a product or service. This assumes that customers will purchase lower-priced items, so demand is driven by availability. Examples of this practice can be found in construction suppliers, where construction firms will purchase cheaper building materials to increase their profit margins

- **the sales concept** – this is commonly known as 'the hard sell', where a product or service is produced and personal selling and other high-pressure selling techniques are used to convince customers to part with their money. You might see examples of this in a company specialising in double-glazing.

The **marketing concept**, unlike the alternatives above, puts the customer at the centre of all decisions before the product or service is developed. This can make a business more efficient, by focusing investment on products that customers will need and use rather than investing in products that customers may not buy.

Marketing definitions

Marketing plays an important part in ensuring the products that customers want are readily available.

Key term

Marketing concept – philosophy practised by producers of goods and services that focus on satisfying the needs of consumers

---

Did you know?

In the Middle Ages, many people could not read. In order to promote their goods, shopkeepers began using signs with simple images to advertise their businesses. A cobbler would have a sign illustrating a boot and the milliner would have a picture of a hat. Town criers were employed for the purpose of vocal advertising in the open-air markets, informing the consumer where to go and find certain products.

Activity: Concepts

Below are descriptions of three business activities. What concept best describes each activity?

1. A business produces a low-priced, low-quality corkscrew which people will buy based purely on price and need.

2. A firm that manufactures replacement windows send its sales force out to cold-call and sell the product to residential households.

3. A firm undertakes extensive market research to see how it can improve its product, which is an electric can opener.

PLTS

Through this activity you will investigate the marketing of business organisations through appropriate planning in order to carry out effective research into the marketing of organisations.

There are many definitions of marketing. The better definitions are focused upon customer orientation and satisfaction of customer needs.

- Marketing is the social process by which individuals and groups obtain what they need and want through creating and exchanging products and value with others (Kotler).

- Marketing is the management process that identifies, anticipates and satisfies customer requirements profitably (the Chartered Institute of Marketing, CIM).

- The right product, in the right place, at the right time, at the right price (Adcock).

From these definitions, marketing is about meeting the needs and wants of customers. It is a business-wide function – it is not something that operates alone from other business activities. It is about understanding customers and finding ways to provide products or services which customers demand.

1.2 Objectives
Private sector aims and objectives

The broad **business objectives** of an organisation in the private sector will be survival or growth.

When a business is first started, the objective is usually survival. A lot of investment is needed to launch a company, and it may take the business a significant amount of time to recoup the money. However, some companies find themselves forced to set survival objectives if there is a recession or problems with their industry. For example, in 2009 many well-established car manufacturers set themselves the objective of survival as the global economy was in recession and demand for cars had shrunk.

Key term

Business objectives – the goals a business sets to increase productivity and sales

Once a business is confident in its survival, it will often set a growth objective. Private sector companies are set up to make a profit, and growth means that they can maximise their profits by reinvesting in the business. Growth can mean expanding the business (for example, a cleaning company might take on more staff), duplicating the business (opening another shop so it becomes a chain, or expanding a chain) or increasing supply and distribution (producing more of a product and/or selling to different markets).

When businesses set objectives, they need to make sure these are SMART, which stands for:

- **S**pecific – the objective must be clearly stated and focused
- **M**easurable – in order for the business to see how it is performing against its objectives, it needs to be able to quantify its performance
- **A**chievable – for an objective to be useful, it needs to be something that the business is in a position to achieve
- **R**ealistic – it is no good for a business to set itself unrealistic goals because it will inevitably fail; this is bad for morale, and worse for share prices
- **T**ime-related – the objectives must be related to a timescale, otherwise there will be no real impetus behind the objective and measurements of the performance will be unreliable.

So, a SMART objective for a retailer might be 'to sell 20 per cent more confectionery each week in six months' time'.

Fig. 3.1: Key elements of marketing.

Activity: SMART objectives

With a partner, turn these aims into SMART objectives.

1. We want to increase sales next year.
2. The company wants to produce a new product.
3. We need a bigger sales force.
4. We need to make people more aware of our product.

Public and voluntary sector aims and objectives

Organisations in the public and voluntary sector are not run for profit. They therefore have a different range of objectives, based on efficiency, quality and philosophical targets.

Public sector organisations are owned by local or national government and are funded by the taxpayer. It would be inappropriate and unpopular for these organisations to aim to make a profit, so they often set objectives based on:

- providing a service or range of services in the first instance, with some expanding the range of services they offer (for example, a local council may consider expanding the range of waste they recycle)

- limiting costs and improving efficiency of service – it is important for public sector organisations to represent good value for money

- meeting quality standards to demonstrate the quality of the service provided – this also relates to the need to represent good value for money.

Aims of the Mid and West Wales Fire Service

1. To save lives and protect communities.
2. To be trusted and respected by our communities.
3. To be seen as more than an emergency service.
4. To manage within budget.
5. To make efficiencies year on year.
6. To match our resources to priorities.
7. To seek out and utilise alternative resources.
8. To manage our people effectively.
9. To fully develop risk reduction planning.
10. To develop effective partnership working.
11. To develop our workforce into effective and empowered people.

How do the aims of the Mid and West Wales Fire Service translate into SMART objectives?

These aims are then translated into specific SMART objectives.

The voluntary sector consists of charities, which may represent local, national or international causes. Ultimately, a charity may set itself a range of objectives, such as to:

- raise money to purchase equipment or services for a given cause (for example, providing protection against malaria in Africa or carers for disabled people in the local community)

- raise awareness of a given cause, which may in turn result in more money raised to support the cause

- create a surplus – for example, to generate more money than it takes to operate its fund-raising activities, which can be spent on the supported cause.

Marketing objectives

Marketing objectives are different from a business's objectives. While both will be SMART, marketing objectives may be based on factors other than survival and growth. However, as we will see, they should support the business's overall objectives – indeed, it may be necessary to achieve a marketing objective in order to achieve the business's overall objective of growth.

Market leadership

Market leadership is the position of a business with the largest market share in a given market for goods and services. Market share may be measured by either the volume of goods sold or the value of those goods. For example, Tesco is the market leader in the UK supermarket marketplace. It is the largest in terms of value of goods sold. Similarly, Pedigree Petfoods is the market leader in the pet food market, with successful brands such as Whiskas cat food.

Being a market leader can be a significant advantage for a business – suppliers will want to stock your product and it is likely that your customers will think about your products first. For example, if you wanted to buy a can of baked beans, there is a good chance you would look for Heinz, although you could buy Branston, or a supermarket's own brand.

What does 'market leadership' mean?

Key terms

Market leadership – position of a company with the largest market share or highest profitability margin in a given market for goods and services

Brand awareness – extent to which a brand is recognised by potential customers, and is correctly associated with a particular product

Brand awareness

A common marketing objective is to raise customers' **brand awareness**. This might relate to a business's overall brand (for example, BMW) or to a product brand within the company (for example, Mini).

Successful raising of brand awareness can raise sales because customers will subconsciously or consciously seek out a brand when purchasing an item or service. A high level of brand awareness exists where consumers start to use the brand name in place of the product type. For example, if you were to talk about domestic appliances, would you say 'vacuum cleaner' or 'Hoover'?

Perceptions of customers or users

A customer's perception of a business or brand often affects their purchasing decisions. For example, your business may have very high brand awareness, but if your customers perceive your business as offering low-quality products, they may decide to purchase a competitor's product.

If a company develops a bad name, it can take a lot of time, effort and money to change customers' perceptions. For example, Škoda had a reputation for producing cheap but unreliable vehicles before it was bought by Volkswagen in 1991. Since then, it has benefited from Volkswagen's reputation for reliable vehicles, combined with low prices. More recently, fast-food chains such as McDonald's and KFC have tried to emphasise healthier or fresher aspects of their menus to appeal to changing consumer tastes.

> **Did you know?**
>
> The symbol of Mercedes-Benz is a three-pointed star in a ring, which originally symbolised earth, sea and sky, the ambition of the car-maker for universal motorisation.

Link between organisational objectives and marketing objectives

Marketing objectives should not contradict a business's broader objectives, but should contribute to achieving those objectives. A business is unlikely to succeed if it is pulling in two directions. It is helpful to think of the business's objectives as a road map – this is the direction in which the organisation intends to go – and the marketing objectives as a vehicle – they are the means of getting to the destination.

For example, a business may have a corporate objective of increasing sales by ten per cent by the end of the current year. The marketing department will the set their own objectives to try to achieve this corporate objective. This may include increasing the sales force, increasing the advertising spends or introducing a new product. The cascading of the corporate objectives down to functional levels, which in turn create their own objectives to ensure the corporate objectives are met, is known as a hierarchy of objectives.

1.3 Marketing techniques available

Growth strategies

Igor Ansoff developed one of the best-known descriptions of the strategies available for growing a business in 1957. He identified four categories for growth.

- **Market penetration:** A market is a group of customers who may purchase a product, so if you were producing a video game for the Wii to be sold in the UK, your market would consist of people in the UK who owned Wii consoles. You could grow your business by increasing the number of people in the market who bought your product.

- **Market development:** This is when a company markets an existing product to a new market. So, in the example of the Wii game, you might sell your product in America. Nothing about the product has changed; it is just being sold to a different market.

- **Product development:** This is where a business develops a new product to sell to existing customers. So, once customers have bought your Wii game, you might sell them an expansion pack that offers more content, for example.

- **Diversification:** This is where a business markets new products to new customers. This can work in two ways – the business may produce a new product in an area that it understands (to continue the example, a new Wii game unrelated to the previous one), or it may enter a completely new, unrelated area.

Ansoff used these four categories in a matrix to show how the opportunities differ in terms of new and existing products and markets, as Table 3.1 shows.

Table 3.1: Ansoff's product/market matrix.

Product / Market	Present	New
Present	Market penetration	Product development
New	Market development	Diversification

Survival strategies

Many businesses are often faced with having to develop strategies just to survive. This could include downsizing the business to reduce costs. It could mean coming out of less profitable markets, discontinuing less profitable lines and making some employees redundant in order to balance the books.

Branding

Branding often consists of a brand name (such as Nike), a logo (the Nike 'swoosh'), a slogan ('Just do it')

> **Key term**
>
> **Branding** – entire process involved in creating a unique name and image for a product in the consumers' minds, through advertising campaigns with a consistent theme

Case study: Tesco PLC

Tesco PLC is one of the UK's most successful businesses. Over the last 20 years it has consistently increased its market share of the UK grocery market at the expense of its main competitors – Asda and Sainsbury's. It has over the last few years moved into the expanding convenience store market with its Tesco Express format and developed its stores overseas, in particular the Far East. It has also made inroads into the financial services marketplace, offering loans, credit cards and insurance. In addition, it is increasing the number of petrol stations at its stores. Recently, Tesco has been considering getting involved in education in some shape or form.

From the information given, answer the following questions.

1. What strategy can be described as market penetration?

2. What strategy can be described as diversification?

3. What type of strategy is the decision by Tesco PLC to:

   a) move into the convenience store market and to expand overseas

   b) develop financial services and expand petrol sales?

and guidelines for how the branding can be used. Some or all of these elements may be trademarked to prevent competitors from using similar branding. In some instances, the branding will dictate colours and shapes that should be used; in other instances, the brand can be used more flexibly.

A brand can be a powerful selling tool and can help achieve marketing objectives such as gaining market leadership and raising customer awareness.

Of course, a strong brand can be a commodity in itself. Dolce & Gabbana, Calvin Klein and Christian Dior are well-known designer brands that are able to charge a premium for their products because their brands are so desirable.

Once a brand builds strength, it can help a business either enter new markets or sell into existing markets with less risk of failure. If a customer has a good experience of a specific brand, they are likely to purchase something else from the same brand.

Activity: Brand images

Below are three well-known brands. Discuss in groups what images are conjured up in your mind when you think of these brands.

1. Marks & Spencer's (more commonly known as M&S these days)

2. Matalan

3. Benetton

The importance of branding in influencing buyer behaviour

Branding can exert a considerable influence over **buyer behaviour**. A strong brand can stick in a customer's mind and help to link products with a particular supplier or manufacturer. For example, Morris Drake's 1967 slogan 'beanz meanz Heinz' is credited as being one of the most successful advertising campaigns ever.

How does a strong brand benefit businesses?

Key term

Buyer behaviour – how people behave in certain ways before and when making a purchase

Brand building and positioning

It takes time, effort and investment for **brand building** and maintenance. A business must first identify its brand values – the central messages that it wants its customers to implicitly understand when they think of the brand. For example, Mercedes-Benz stands for high performance, safety and prestige.

The business then considers how to convey this message to their customers. This can be through methods such as:

- adopting a specific and consistent style in their promotional material
- using specific fonts, wording or images and layout in their emails
- training staff to present a specific image to the customer.

Ultimately, consistency is key to building and maintaining a brand. However, the business also needs to make sure it is delivering the promises of its brand. If it develops and implements a brand based on quality, but the products it is marketing under the brand are sub-standard, the brand may be seriously damaged.

In building and developing the brand, the business will consider how this is positioned within the market. This is most common in a competitive market where the competitor brands are well known, and can help differentiate the businesses for the customer.

Did you know?

In 2007 Apple produced a series of adverts featuring comedians David Mitchell ('I'm a PC') and Robert Webb ('I'm a Mac') to position Apple as a cooler personal computer than a PC, and less prone to viruses. However, in 2008, Microsoft took the 'I'm a PC' line from the Apple advert to demonstrate that their products were powerful and easy to use. Compare the adverts on YouTube to see how brands can be positioned against each other.

Brand extension

Once a brand is established, a business might reduce the risk associated with developing a new product by **brand extension**. For example, Richard Branson's Virgin group started as a record label and has expanded to include aeroplanes, trains and mobile

Key terms

Brand building – enhancing a brand's equity directly through advertising campaigns and indirectly through promotions such as supporting causes or event sponsorship

Brand extension – a marketing strategy in which a firm marketing a product with a well-developed image uses the same brand name in a different product category

phones. Similarly, Nike has extended its brand from sports clothes and shoes to include electronics with the Nike+ product range.

Extending a brand is more cost effective than developing a new brand for a new product range, and also reduces some of the risk of failure. If a business is looking at diversification as a growth strategy for producing a new product for a market that they do not currently operate in, there is a high chance of failure. However, if the business is able to launch the new product in the new market using an existing brand, customer awareness will grow much more quickly. This strategy does not guarantee success, though – despite being launched under a well-known brand in the 1990s, Virgin Cola has achieved very low market penetration in a competitive market.

Relationship marketing

Relationship marketing is where a business focuses on the long-term value of a customer. This basically means identifying valuable customers (or segments of a market), initiating relationships, maintaining, enhancing and (if necessary) terminating them to generate a sustainable profit.

Banks often use relationship marketing to attract lifetime or long-term customers. For example, a bank will advertise a current account, which will attract customers but will earn the bank relatively little. However, once a customer relationship has been established, the bank will use customer service (free financial advice, for example), promotions (exclusive rates on loans and mortgages) and quality service (online banking and so on) to maintain the relationship and attract the customer to more profitable products (for example, insurance or credit cards).

Transactional marketing is the alternative to relationship marketing. This is where the marketing effort is focused on the sale of an item or service, with little expectation of a relationship developing with the customer. An example of this might be when you buy a DVD from a high-street store; their marketing will have attracted you to the point of sale, but there is little expectation that you will have any other contact with the business unless you are expected to make another purchase.

A business that focuses on transactional marketing will expect to make a certain amount of profit from each sale, but will need to make a sustained effort to attract customers, although it makes little difference whether they are new customers or returning customers. A business that uses relationship marketing relies on the lifetime value of a customer. In the example above, the money spent on marketing a current account may not bring in big profits immediately, but over the course of the relationship, a good customer can be worth a lot.

Did you know?

Research has shown that it costs five times more to acquire new customers than to satisfy and keep current customers.

1.4 Limitations and constraints on marketing activities

Consumer law

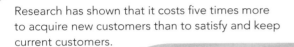

Businesses need to make sure that their marketing activities are within the constraints of the law. The European Union has strengthened consumer protection law in recent years, and businesses must keep up to date with changes in the law and landmark (significant) rulings that might make their activities illegal.

Sale of Goods Act 1979

This Act requires traders to sell goods that are as they are described and of satisfactory quality. This directly affects marketing activity because it means that any marketing should describe the product accurately and be able to substantiate any claims.

For example, a business that produces a 'lighter option' cereal could not claim that consuming their product will make you lose weight – it might help, but it will not guarantee you will.

Consumer Protection from Unfair Trading Regulations 2008

This Act entitles all customers to fair treatment and honesty from businesses they deal with. This relatively

Activity: Jack's car

A local garage sold a car to Jack. The car was advertised as 'in immaculate condition' and showed just 15,000 miles on the clock. In fact, the car had done over 100,000 miles and there were several faults, so that Jack had to spend £500 making it roadworthy.

Does Jack have a claim against the local garage? Explain your answer.

recent piece of legislation should not have affected most businesses, but was targeted at businesses that do not always treat their customers well.

Under this Act, businesses cannot use aggressive sales tactics, or put on dishonest promotions (such as closing-down sales when the business is not actually closing down).

Consumer Credit Acts 1974 and 2006

These Acts apply to businesses offering goods or services on credit, or companies that lend money to consumers. Businesses in these categories need to be licensed by the Office of Fair Trading (OFT) and any complaints between the business and a customer are settled by the Financial Ombudsman Service (FOS).

The Act requires businesses that provide credit or loans to give their customers regular updates on their account (for example, an annual statement). If a customer falls into arrears (falls behind on repayments), the FOS may extend the period of time for the customer to repay the debt. This helps to prevent predatory lending, where a business quickly resorts to bailiffs or threatening tactics when a customer struggles with repayments.

Did you know?

One of the earliest advertising success stories was that of Pears Soap. The famous soap company realised that they needed to be more aggressive about pushing their products if they were going to compete with their rivals. They launched a series of advertisements featuring cherubic children, which firmly established the brand. They used images considered 'fine art' to represent the brand's quality, purity and simplicity. They are often referred to as the founders of modern advertising.

Consumer Protection (Distance Selling) Regulations 2000

Distance selling is any form of selling where there is no face-to-face contact between the customer and the business, for example, an e-commerce website or a mail-order catalogue. The Regulations require the business to provide clear information so customers can make informed decisions about their purchases.

The business must give the consumer information about the:

- business
- goods or services they are selling
- payment arrangements
- delivery arrangements
- consumers' right to cancel their orders where appropriate.

Data Protection Act 1998

The Data Protection Act 1998 is designed to protect customers from unfair use of their personal information. This Act impacts on any business that keeps a database of customer information, so is very important for any marketing department that sends out direct mail. The information in the databases must be:

- obtained fairly and lawfully
- used only for the purposes stated during collection
- adequate, relevant and not excessive in relation to the intended use.
- accurate and where necessary kept up to date
- not kept for longer than necessary
- processed in line with your rights
- subject to procedures to prevent unlawful processing, accidental loss, destruction and damage to personal data
- protected from transfer to an area outside the European Economic Area (EEA) unless adequate protection exists for that data in the area.

When you register your details with a business (for example, when purchasing an item online), you will usually be given the option to 'opt in' and receive information about future offers. This is a legal requirement, as it would be illegal for the business to send you information you have not requested.

Voluntary codes of advertising practice

In addition to the legislation affecting what a business can and cannot say about its products and services, marketing activities are policed by the independent Advertising Standards Authority (ASA).

The ASA is an industry body, rather than a part of the legal framework, and it promotes and maintains the British Code of Advertising, Sales Promotion and Direct Marketing (CAP). This is a set of rules and standards that businesses follow when marketing to:

- keep within the legal framework
- protect customers from misleading claims
- create an even footing for advertisers.

The principles of the code are that advertising should be legal, decent, honest and truthful, and that businesses preparing advertising should do so with a sense of responsibility to both the consumer and society. So, businesses should not produce advertisements that mislead or offend customers.

If an advertiser breaches the code of practice, the ASA can:

- insist that it approves any advertising before it is published or broadcast
- refer the advertiser to the Office of Fair Trading
- ask TV stations, radio stations and publishers to withdraw the advertising from their broadcasts and publications.

Pressure groups

A pressure group is an organised group working to influence the behaviours and beliefs of government and/or business. There are thousands of pressure groups, of varying sizes, operating in the UK for thousands of different causes.

They will typically try to raise the profile of their cause in the media and to raise public awareness in order to exert pressure on government or business to change. This can result in negative publicity for the business involved, which can be damaging for both the business's reputation and its sales.

Did you know?

TV chef Hugh Fearnley-Whittingstall tried to pressure big supermarkets like Tesco into stocking only free-range chickens and eggs by raising awareness of battery farming. However, he was not entirely successful because of the high price of free-range poultry products.

Some examples of the many British pressure groups are:

- British Union for the Abolition of Vivisection – campaigning to halt the breeding and use of animals in experiments
- British Roads Federation – aiming to focus attention for a higher standard of service from the UK road network

- Earth First – campaigning against the destruction of the environment
- Liberty – campaigning to defend and extend human rights and civil liberties.

Consumerism

Consumerism is a social movement that is giving consumers some powers over businesses. It identifies the rights for consumers to:

- be safe
- choose
- be informed
- be heard.

TV programmes such as *Watchdog* and consumer-rights organisations such as Which? all help consumerism by forcing businesses to be accountable for their practices and products. The Office of Fair Trading also plays a role in consumerism by enforcing consumer legislation and taking action against unfair traders.

Acceptable language

Advertising, as we have seen, needs to avoid offending consumers. However, acceptable language can be subjective, and reactions to the same text may vary depending on the images that accompany it and the context in which it is used.

The Advertising Standards Authority (ASA) has identified the key areas where some people find the use of language unacceptable, which are when they:

- refer to sex
- use strong language or swear words
- mock religion or people's beliefs
- show people in a demeaning way and offend on the grounds of gender, race, religion, sexuality, age or disability.

The language chosen for advertising also needs to be accessible to your audience. If you are delivering a message as a text to a mobile phone, the chances are that the recipient will understand 'txt spk'. However, if you were advertising something on a billboard that had nothing to do with mobile phones, text language might be inappropriate for your audience. It all depends on your message and your audience.

Assessment activity 3.1

You work for a professional organisation for marketers. One of the activities that the organisation undertakes is to evaluate the marketing activities of different companies and produce a list of 'A'-classed marketers. You are asked to carry out research into two possible contenders for inclusion on the list. You need to complete the following tasks as part of your research project.

1. Describe how marketing techniques such as branding and relationship marketing are used to market products in two organisations. You need to choose one product or service from each organisation to undertake this task. **P1**

2. Compare, discussing the similarities and differences, the marketing techniques described in Task 1 used for the product or service chosen in each organisation. **M1**

3. Evaluate the effectiveness of the use of techniques in marketing products or services in one of your selected organisations. You need to judge the effectiveness by weighing up the pros and cons of the techniques used. **D1**

4. Describe the constraints and limitations under which marketers operate, making use of examples to explain your points. **P2**

Grading tips

1. Make sure that you understand the various techniques that are listed in the content section of the specification. Try to find out if the companies you choose use any of these techniques. **P1**

2. For this task, you need to find out the similarities and differences that exist between these techniques and discuss these in relation to the two products. Try to stay focused on answering the question and do not end up writing all you know about the techniques. **M1**

3. Evaluation is about considering in detail the advantages and disadvantages of something, and coming to conclusions as a result of this analysis. All the techniques can be criticised concerning their usefulness. Find out what these are and then make judgements about the effectiveness of the techniques used. **D1**

4. Try to find examples of where these laws have been contravened (broken to any degree). Useful websites are those belonging to Trading Standards and the Advertising Standards Authority. **P2**

2.   Be able to use marketing research and marketing planning

2.1 Marketing research

Marketing research informs a business's decisions by helping it to understand the changing dynamics of its market. This involves finding out more about customers, competitors and the overall marketing environment.

Key term

Marketing research – systematic gathering, recording and analysis of data about issues relating to marketing products and services

For example, a business promoting a consumer dining magazine would need to know about its audience's interests – it would need to know the kind of dining experiences its customers are used to (Pizza Hut or Heston Blumenthal's Fat Duck?). The magazine would also need to understand its competitors – if there was a similar magazine catering for the kind of consumer who goes to the Fat Duck, how could the business differentiate its product? Finally, the overall environment would allow the business to test the size of the market – whether the product would be better as an online subscription site, for example – and whether anything beyond the control of the business might affect the business plan.

Primary and secondary research

There are two types of research: primary and secondary. The difference between them relates to whether the research is original to the organisation conducting the research (they gathered the data) or whether it came from another source (the data had already been gathered). Within these categories, information can either be internal – from inside the organisation – or external – from another organisation or source outside of the organisation.

Primary research is data and information that the business has gathered first-hand and has not been gathered before. Internal primary research data sources include:

- sales figures for the business's own products
- customer data held on a central database.

External primary research methods include:

- questionnaires and surveys
- interviews and focus groups
- mystery shoppers, and other observation techniques.

Secondary research uses data and information that has been collected before, either from within the organisation (internal) or by another organisation (external). Secondary research is sometimes referred to as 'desk research' and sources include:

- reports from sales and regional representatives (internal)
- previous marketing research (internal)
- trade journals and websites (external)
- books and newspapers (external)
- industry reports from industry associations and government departments (external)
- census data and public records (external).

Activity: Research methods

1. Which of the following research methods are suitable for attaining primary data?
    - library
    - questionnaires
    - websites
    - customer interviews
    - newspapers.
2. Using the Internet, search for information regarding the different careers associated with market research. Create a short report stating the different types of jobs available in this sector and the key job specifications required.

Functional skills

ICT: If you use ICT to present your findings, you may have interacted independently using ICT for a complex task. You may also have entered, developed and formatted information independently to suit its meaning and purpose using text and tables, images, numbers and records.

It is more cost-effective for a business to conduct secondary research before it starts conducting primary research. This allows it to build an understanding of the market and identify any major barriers before committing to expensive research. It also allows the business to develop some assumptions (for example, people interested in video games are also likely to be interested in MP3 players and other consumer electronics), which means the business can use the primary research to test its assumptions. This helps to restrict the scope of the primary research, which can be expensive and is rarely able to answer all questions about a particular market.

However, the business needs to be aware of the limitations of secondary research. For example:

- the information may be old
- the information may be biased to promote a particular cause
- the collection methods may have been unreliable.

Qualitative and quantitative research

Research methods can be qualitative, quantitative or include elements of both (see Table 3.2). Well-planned marketing research often involves a combination as they can reveal different things about the same market.

Qualitative research is subjective and often open-ended. It often involves interviews with customers or focus groups and generally results in a wide range of answers based on personal experience and feelings. A qualitative question might ask you why you bought a specific product and allow you to provide an open answer.

Table 3.2: The differences between quantitative and qualitative research.

Quantitative	Qualitative
Objective	Subjective
Research questions: How many? What percentage?	Research questions: What? Why?
Tests theory	Develops theory
Focus is concise and narrow	Focus is complex and broad
Measurable	Interpretive
Basic element of analysis is numbers	Basic element of analysis is words/ideas
Reasoning is logical and deductive (concluding)	Reasoning is dialectic (for example, involving opinions) and inductive (leading)
Establishes relationships, causation	Describes meaning, discovery
Highly controlled setting: experimental setting (outcome oriented)	Flexible approach: natural setting (process oriented)

This kind of research can be used to:

- find out how customers perceive an organisation or brand
- understand how changes in price, or other variables, might affect consumer spending decisions
- investigate customer preferences, interests, aspirations and other variables.

Quantitative research, on the other hand, relates to numbers and figures that can be analysed mathematically and/or presented graphically. This can includes sales figures, market values and so on,

Case study: Feelbetter Ltd

Feelbetter Ltd manufactures and markets toiletry products for men, which are largely aimed at the 35+ age group. The organisation feels that that they need to develop and market new deodorants targeted at the 18 to 30 age group. They are going to survey 5,000 men in this age group to find out about possible fragrances, price points and names of product. They have also purchased from a market research agency a detailed new report on future trends in the deodorant market. They plan to run a number of focus groups around the country to find out this age group's views on deodorant products. A focus group is where six

to ten members of the target group are invited to attend a meeting, which a member of the research team will chair, and the group are asked what improved product characteristics they would like to see in a new deodorant.

1. Which parts of this case study are referring to primary research?

2. Which parts are referring to secondary research?

3. What other forms of secondary research could Feelbetter Ltd use in their market research?

Activity: Quantitative or qualitative?

1. Are the following statements quantitative, qualitative or a mix of the two? Tick the appropriate columns.

	Quantitative	Qualitative	Both
Ninety-five per cent of teenagers use the Internet.			
The older generation worry about their retirement, as they perceive a lower income will have a detrimental effect on their lifestyle.			
Research shows that the police believe CCTV is an excellent deterrent against street crime because they find that it discourages potential criminals. Eighty-five per cent do believe it is a useful tool when used responsibly.			
One in three people in the UK own a pet.			

2. Using either a business of your choice or a college/school as an example, find out from the workforce/colleagues what their perceptions are of the food on offer in the cafeteria. Work in groups and try to gain as much qualitative information as possible. Write a short report from conclusions from the research.

Functional skills

English: This activity allows you to read about business information, using it to gather information, ideas, arguments and opinions.

PLTS

Through this activity you will investigate the marketing of business organisations through appropriate planning in order to carry out effective research into the marketing of organisations.

You should attempt to generate original and creative ideas about marketing in business organisations in order to determine how organisations market their products and services.

Express carefully considered thoughts regarding the impact of marketing in business. Set your own goals when undertaking research and invite feedback on your work, considering it objectively and evaluating any outcomes to enhance your current and future learning experience.

but can also include responses from customers. For example, in a questionnaire, a question that gives you a series of answers to choose from can be used to produce quantitative data (for example, 75 per cent of customers indicating they liked the colour green).

Uses of marketing research

The information gathered for **market research** reduces the chances of the business making the wrong decision. If a product designer develops a new product without conducting research, then the business is just relying on guesswork as to whether customers will want and need the product. Effective market research therefore improves the chances of success and reduces risk.

A business can also effectively measure progress over time. For example, a business could carry out market

Key term

Market research – systematic, objective collection and analysis of data about a particular target market, competition and/or environment

Activity: Questionnaire techniques

1. What are the advantages and disadvantages to each of the following questionnaire techniques?

Technique	Advantages	Disadvantages
Interviewing a small group		
Conducting an interview over the telephone		
Email questionnaire		
Postal questionnaire		

2. Write a short report stating the preferred technique(s) for gaining information for a survey targeting teenagers. Remember, your time is limited and your costs have to remain low.

Functional skills

English: This activity allows you to read about business information, using it to gather information, ideas, arguments and opinions.

research to measure the awareness of a product before conducting a national advertising campaign. After the campaign, research can be conducted to see if awareness of the product has increased. Market research can be effective in measuring progress and the effects of marketing activities.

Limitations of market research – costs, effectiveness, and validity of data collected

No matter how small or large a market research project may be, any type of research performed poorly will not give relevant results. In fact, all research, no matter how well controlled, carries the potential to be wrong. There are many reasons why research may not give good results but a common problem is deciding whether the research is really measuring what it claims to be measuring.

Marketers must decide how reliable is the information obtained. Would similar results be obtained if another group containing different respondents or a different

set of data points were used? For example, if 50 customers participate in a research study focusing on customer service, is the information obtained from these 50 customers sufficient to conclude how all customers feel about the company's level of customer service? What if the same study was done again with 50 different customers – would the responses be similar? Reliability is chiefly concerned with making sure the method of data gathering leads to consistent results.

Validity asks whether the research measured what it intended to. Validity implies reliability: a valid measure must be reliable. But reliability does not necessarily imply validity: a reliable measure need not be valid.

- Reliability estimates the degree to which an instrument measures the same way each time it is used in under the same conditions with the same subjects.

- Validity involves the degree of accuracy of your measurement.

Validity is usually considered more important than reliability, because if an instrument does not accurately measure what it is supposed to, there is no reason to use it even if it measures reliably.

For example, imagine you have a piece of string that is three metres long. You measure it once with a tape measure – you get a measurement of three metres. Measure it repeatedly and you consistently get the same measurement. The tape measure offers reliable results.

A tape measure that has been created with accurate spacing for millimetres, centimetres and so on should offer valid results as well. Measuring this piece of string with a 'good' tape measure should produce a correct measurement of the string's length.

In research, we want to use measurement tools that are both reliable and valid. We want questions that offer consistent responses when asked multiple times – this is reliability. Similarly, we want questions that get accurate responses from respondents – this is validity.

Costs are also an important consideration in market research, as one has to weigh up the cost of undertaking the research against the potential benefits that may result. You could spend a lot of time and effort in trying to solve a problem through market research, only to find that the solution may not be worth implementing.

PLTS

In this case study you will investigate the marketing of business organisations through appropriate planning in order to carry out effective research into the marketing of organisations.

You should attempt to generate original and creative ideas about marketing in business organisations in order to determine how organisations market their products and services.

Functional skills

English: This case study allows you to read about business information, using it to gather information, ideas, arguments and opinions.

Case study: T&B Bedrooms

When T&B Bedrooms first started their furniture business, customers were very few and far between. It was a new company in the market, and it took a while for customers to discover their excellent products and service. Business was so slow that the owners decided to sit down and discuss how to resolve the situation. After thinking about their customers' buying habits and their competitors' businesses, they decided that they needed to extend their business services to include a design and installation service.

This would involve extra finances for employment of skilled personnel, resources and further promotion of the business. T&B Bedrooms realised that if this new venture failed, the extra money may have been better spent on their core business. Therefore, before spending any further money, they decided to carry out some research to establish whether the new idea was feasible.

Working in groups, discuss how you think the owners of T&B Bedrooms should go about their research. Make a short report describing how you would undertake this project, taking account of the following.

1. What type of customers should they be looking for?
2. Where should they look for this type of customer?
3. What should they know about their competitors?
4. What type of research should they use?
5. How will they use the results?

Design five questions suitable for use in their questionnaire.

2.2 Marketing planning

Marketing planning is concerned with establishing objectives and goals, allocating resources to meet these and setting out a clear plan of action. It also involves setting out ways of evaluating performance against marketing targets.

Typically, the marketing planning process involves:

- a PESTLE audit
- a SWOT analysis
- setting SMART objectives
- determining strategy and tactics
- implementing strategy and tactics
- evaluating effectiveness of marketing activity.

We will explore these different stages in more detail below.

Did you know?

In 4000 BC, in South America, South Africa and Asia, wall paintings were used to promote the politicians and commerce of the day.

Marketing planning process model – PESTLE and SWOT

As part of the marketing planning process, a business has to analyse its external environment. One useful way of analysing the external environment is by grouping external forces into six areas using a PESTLE analysis. PESTLE stands for political, economic, social, technological, legal and environmental influences.

Fig. 3.2: The external business environment.

Key term

Marketing planning – developing marketing strategies that will help a business attain its overall objectives

Political factors that affect a business are usually beyond the control of the organisation. However, the business needs to anticipate changes and identify the action it needs to take to either make the most of an opportunity or mitigate a threat. For example, during a recession, any banks or financial services providers would have to consider the likely government scrutiny of their business decisions.

Economic factors can affect the performance of a business. These relate to the national – or international – economy, which goes through periods of prosperity (when high employment and income drives demand), recession (when demand falls, leading to lower income and employment) and recovery (when demand, income and employment gradually rise).

Social factors relate to the values and beliefs of society. This includes the population's demographics (for example, size, gender, ethnicity, income, education, occupation). This provides useful information for businesses targeting their services at broad segments of the population, such as newspapers and magazines.

Technological developments can affect businesses in a range of ways. For example, the development of e-commerce benefited Amazon.co.uk, but eventually took business away from traditional bookshops that developed e-commerce websites later.

Legal developments, as we have seen (page 93), affect businesses in a range of ways. For example, any changes to the Data Protection Act would affect any business that holds customer data. Similarly, pubs and restaurants were affected by the introduction of the smoking law, which has led to many building shelters outside their premises to try to keep smokers' custom.

Environmental factors can relate to the social, political and legal aspects affecting a business. For example, a business may decide to package their food products in recyclable packaging. This may prove to be popular with consumers if there is a growing level of concern over waste. Similarly, the government may put pressure on businesses to increase the amount of recycling.

David
Market Research Analyst

During his BTEC Diploma in Business, David found the unit on marketing involved aspects of market research which caught his imagination, such as how and why brands engage people, and the investigative side of processing, analysing and presenting information in both statistical and report form.

After leaving college, David secured a position as an assistant in the market research department of a large supermarket chain. Day-to-day tasks were more administrative than research, but David learned a lot about the way the company used the information gained through customer surveys, interviews and questionnaires. After a year, David's supervisor, knowing his great interest in the field, showed him how they analysed and presented the information into a usable form. David realised he needed to further his education to advance in this field and subsequently decided to go to university and do a marketing degree.

He found his current role at Fanshaw Consultancy via a university careers service. He was particularly attracted to agency life as it would involve being engaged in a range of projects for a variety of clients. Originally the position was that of a trainee, but David found his previous experience and qualifications as well as his logical, methodical and problem-solving approach to work ensured his rapid promotion after just 12 months to Market Research Analyst.

Fanshaw Consultancy is a small agency and David can find himself liaising with market research interviewers and data input staff as well as doing his specific job of analysing, interpreting and presenting the data so that it can be readily understood by the client. David has to establish reasons for the final recommendations and conclusions, which may be used to help make decisions on issues like product design and advertising policy.

His company is now funding his part-time postgraduate degree in social research methods. David is ambitious and aspires to become a research executive in the next few years. He believes this passion for market research was fuelled by his time on the BTEC Diploma in Business.

Think about it!

1. What experience would you recommend other aspiring market researchers attain to enhance their qualifications?

2. What particular personal skills are essential for a market research analyst?

3. There are several methods used by market research interviewers in obtaining information from customers. Can you list the different methods used?

4. Working in groups, discuss the different areas within the business sector where market research is important. Each group should present their findings in a five-minute PowerPoint presentation to the class.

SWOT analysis

A useful approach to examining the relationship between a business and its marketing environment is by conducting a SWOT analysis. SWOT stands for:

- **S**trengths
- **W**eaknesses
- **O**pportunities
- **T**hreats.

Strengths and weaknesses are internal to the business and can include issues such as the buildings, quality of the staff, IT systems and so on. The external element looks at the opportunities and threats present in the environment in which the organisation operates.

Carrying out a SWOT analysis requires research into an organisation's current and future position. The idea is to match an organisation's strengths and weaknesses with the external forces (opportunities and threats).

SWOT analysis draws together all the evidence from the various analytical techniques used. It is a way of producing a summary, which then provides the basis for developing marketing objectives or aims and ultimately strategies or plans.

- **Strengths** refer to the internal features of an organisation, which provide a competitive advantage. An example could be a highly efficient IT system.
- **Weaknesses** are internal aspects of the organisation, which may not stand comparison with competition or are not performing effectively. An example might be not having staff effectively trained on systems and procedures.
- **Opportunities** focus on events and developments external to an organisation. This might include new territories for a product or service, or a new segment of a market.
- **Threats** are developments external to the organisations, which could damage overall performance. These threats can originate from governmental policy, such as an increase in corporation tax or new laws.

Once key issues have been identified with your SWOT analysis, they feed into marketing objectives.

SMART objectives

All businesses set objectives. These can be at a variety of levels, from a whole-company objective (for example, grow revenue by 20 per cent), to a small-scale objective that will be achieved through a promotional campaign (for example, raise awareness of the product by 15 per cent in the target market).

To be effective and measurable, objectives should follow the SMART principles (see page 87).

Activity: SMART or not?

Remind yourself of the principles of SMART objectives (page 87) and decide whether the objectives in the list below are SMART or not.

1. To sell more tins of cat food by February.
2. To answer all customer service phone calls within three rings within six months.
3. To increase profit margins by 30 per cent.
4. To raise awareness of Nokia products in the 24–35 age group by 15 per cent within the next 12 months.
5. To become market leader.

Case study: NIKE, Inc.

NIKE, Inc., named after the Greek goddess of victory, is a major USA sportswear and equipment supplier. The publicly traded company is the world's leading supplier of athletic shoes and clothing, as well as a major manufacturer of sports equipment. With revenue of nearly 19 million, it employs more than 30,000 people worldwide. The company was founded in 1964 by a University of Oregon track coach, Bill Bowerman, and a middle distance runner, Phil Knight. The original company was called Blue Ribbon Sports and Bowerman and Knight began importing the Japanese brand 'Onitsuka Tiger' running shoes (known today as ASICs). In 1978 the company was renamed Nike, Inc. and now markets its products under their own brand name as well as others such as Nike Pro, Nike +, Nike Golf, Air Jordan and Nike Skateboarding. They also market products under subsidiaries including Hurley International LLC, Converse Inc., Cole Haan and NIKE Bauer Hockey Corp. (between 1995 and 2008).

The company not only manufactures sportswear and equipment; it has retail outlets marketed under the Niketown brand name. Using highly recognised trademarks such as the swoosh logo and 'Just do it', the company sponsors well-known sports teams and individual athletes worldwide. Over the years, Nike has become a global brand and has subsequently developed into the number one sports brand in the world. The swoosh logo is recognised all over the world, but it is not without its competitors. Reebok and Adidas are global brands with their familiar logos.

The company itself is lean with a strategy of operating on a relatively low-cost basis. It manages this by not operating from expensive business premises and does not employ any manufacturing personnel. Instead, NIKE, Inc. subcontracts the manufacturing process to other companies that produce their high-quality products for a competitively low price. As a company, NIKE, Inc. is continuously carrying out extensive research and development, ensuring innovative new products are constantly being developed. Nike is known for having a diverse product range, but the majority of its income is derived from the footwear market and selling to retailers.

Working in groups, answer the following questions.

1. Identify NIKE, Inc.'s strengths and weaknesses.
2. Identify its threats and opportunities.
3. What can it do to turn its weaknesses into strengths and its threats into opportunities?

PLTS

In this case study you will investigate the marketing of business organisations through appropriate planning in order to carry out effective research into the marketing of organisations.

You should attempt to generate original and creative ideas about marketing in business organisations in order to determine how organisations market their products and services.

Remember to contribute to group or teamwork by applying a proactive approach to planning and carrying out research into the marketing of organisations.

Determination of strategy and tactics – implement changes and evaluation

Marketing **strategy** encompasses selecting and analysing the target market(s) and creating and maintaining an appropriate marketing mix (the four Ps or the seven Ps – see page 112) that satisfies the target market and the business. A marketing strategy articulates a plan for the best use of the organisation's resources and **tactics** to meet its objectives. A marketing plan will include:

- executive summary
- situation analysis – SWOT
- company resources
- marketing objectives

Key terms

Strategy – a long-term plan for success

Tactics – the plans and methods used to achieve a particular short-term aim

- marketing strategies which will include:
  - identification of the target market
  - development of a marketing mix to reach the target market
  - making financial projections, in terms of what returns will be expected from the plan and the costs involved in administering the plan
  - putting in place control systems and evaluation criteria – marketing control processes consist of establishing performance standards, evaluating the actual performance against what was planned and reducing the difference.

The rolling out of the marketing plan may involve the implementation of changes which could affect any of the marketing mix elements. These have to be carefully planned and executed. It is also essential that all activity is measured and evaluated, and corrective courses of action are put in place if anything deviates from what was planned.

Assessment activity 3.2

This assignment builds upon your work for the previous assignment. You need to choose one of your selected organisations and investigate its use of market research. You need to complete the following tasks as part of the continuation of your research project.

1. Describe how your selected organisation or any other organisation uses market research to contribute to its development plans. **P3**
2. Explain the limitations of the market research used to contribute to the development of your selected organisation's marketing plans. **M2**
3. Make three justified recommendations for improving the validity of the marketing research used to contribute to the development of your selected organisation's marketing plans. **D2**
4. The results of a questionnaire given to 200 customers of a local fresh sandwich bar to find out about the current range of sandwiches on offer and the standard of service included findings that:
   - 75 per cent want more children's sandwiches
   - 82 per cent want the shop to be open longer
   - 65 per cent said that the staff were unfriendly
   - 50 per cent said that the contents of the sandwiches should be fresher
   - 80 per cent said they would prefer more wraps.

Use the results of this market research to produce part of the marketing plan in terms of objectives to be set. **P4**

Grading tips

1. Remember that market research covers a wide area and you can include everything the business does to collect information about its marketplace. **P3**
2. Think about the reliability of the research methods used – could they be easily affected by strong personalities, closed questions, incentives, etc.? **M2**
3. You need to know that it is important to try to make your market research as valid as possible. This could mean making the sample of sufficient size or making sure that questionnaire answers are not ambiguous, as that could lead to misleading results. **D2**
4. You need to demonstrate that you can apply the results of market research to marketing plans. The statistics are telling certain information that could result in objectives being formulated. **P4**

3. Understand how and why customer groups are targeted

3.1 Identifying customers in consumer markets

Customers and consumers

A person who purchases the goods or service is a customer, whereas the end user who uses the goods or service is the consumer. For example, if you buy a chocolate bar for your mother, you are the customer and your mother is the consumer. This means that it is possible to be the customer and the consumer. If you buy an apple from a shop and consume it, you are both a customer and a consumer.

The defining and profiling of **consumer markets** is a difficult task for marketers. Potential customers or consumers should be defined in terms of:

- what they want, or will accept, in terms of price
- what kind of distribution will be most convenient for them
- what communication channels they can best be reached through
- what they want from the product itself.

For example, a sports shoe manufacturer such as Reebok not only develops shoes for a wide range of specific sports but also realised that a significant group of customers would never go to a sports facility and that they just wanted trainers as a fashion statement. This meant they served three distinctly different groups of customers: the professional serious sports player, the casual sports player and the fashion victim.

Buyers

As long as we have the means to purchase items, we are all potential buyers. It is not just about individuals in the consumer marketplace having the potential to buy; buyers also exist in the **business-to-business** (B2B) market such as individuals who have the responsibility to purchase on behalf of the business or groups of individuals who are buying units for the business. As customers are people who are able to buy products and services, then it follows that all customers are buyers. It does not follow, however, that all consumers are buyers, owing to the differences described above.

Influencers over purchasing decisions

If a marketer can identify buyer behaviour, they will be in a better position to target products and services at them. Buyer behaviour is focused upon the needs of individuals, groups and organisations. It is important to understand the relevance of human needs to buyer behaviour. For example, for products targeted at young children, it will be the parents who will have influence over the **purchasing decision**. Similarly, for Christmas gifts for a grandmother from grandchildren, it will be the grandchildren who will be targeted as they have influence over the purchasing decision.

Similarly, in business-to-business buying, there will be an individual or a group of individuals who will have influence over the buying decision. Marketers have to try to reach this individual or group through their sales force or through other marketing communication methods.

3.2 Market segmentation

Importance of segmentation

How do we define and profile customers? Until we have managed to answer this question satisfactorily, no meaningful decisions can be made. All markets can be divided up into segments, and many marketers use the analogy of an orange being made up of a number of segments. Each segment has its own distinct profile which is defined in terms of a number of criteria, referred to as bases or variables. A market segment consists of a large identifiable group within a market, with similar wants, purchasing power, geographical location, buying attitudes or buying habits. For

Key terms

Consumer markets – individuals and households who purchase goods and services for personal use

Business-to-business – B2B refers to when one business sells to another business – for example, a stationery business selling to a firm of accountants

Purchasing decision – series of choices made by a consumer prior to making a purchase that begins once the consumer has established a willingness to buy

example, a car manufacturer may identify four broad segments in the car market of buyers who are primarily seeking:

- basic transportation
- high-performance driving
- luxury
- safety.

Segment marketing allows a firm to create a finer-tuned product or service offering and to price it appropriately for the target audience. **Segmentation**, therefore, allows organisations to develop products and plans that fit the needs of customers more effectively, thus increasing overall demand. Once the segments in a market have been discovered, the next step is to identify ones where the needs and wants of the consumer can be met by the organisation. An organisation may not have the resources to target every segment, or it may feel its expertise and resources are only relevant to one or two of the segments.

Key term

Segmentation – using marketing research to help identify groups of consumers who will respond to marketing activity in the same way, for example, first-time buyers of houses

Bases for segmentation of consumer markets – geographic, demographic, psychographic, lifestyle

Segmentation is all about identifying common needs and buying behaviour within a market. For example, a bread company (such as Hovis) might divide their market into those who like white bread, those who like wholemeal bread and those who like white bread but feel they should be eating more wholemeal.

There are no limits to how a market can be segmented. Fig. 3.3 above is typical of how a business might segment their market, dividing the whole into groups based on demographic data.

When identifying market segments and developing a marketing plan to appeal to it, the marketer needs to consider the following questions.

- Can we make a profit from the segment (is it large enough)?

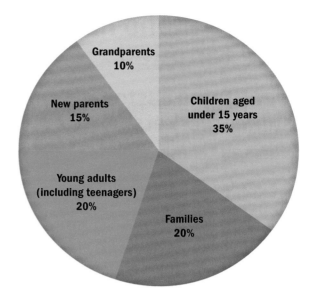

Fig. 3.3: An example of segmentation – computer game users.

- How easily can we sell to these customers (is it a sub-set of an existing customer base, or are these new customers who have not previously bought from the company)?
- How relevant is the segment? (For example, a bread company might identify that a large number of consumers are in the 50–70 age bracket, but it might not be meaningful to market a product specifically for this age group.)

The most general categories to consider when segmenting a market are:

- geographic – the location of your customers. This might split down to national or regional boundaries, or whether your customers live in an urban or rural area
- psychographic – lifestyle or beliefs. For example, if your product has environmental benefits, you might identify a customer segment that is concerned for the environment
- socio-cultural – class (this may also include income, education, and so on). A lot of magazines and newspapers categorise their readership and circulation using the National Readership Survey grades, which segment readers from A (upper middle class) to E (lowest level of subsistence), based on profession
- demographic – age, sex and so on. For example, Nivea segments its market by gender, with similar products for women and men that are packaged distinctively.

Remember

Sometimes, it is not the biggest segment that represents the biggest opportunity, so businesses will often try to profile their segment by income and so on to identify how profitable it is likely to be. In the computer game market example shown in Fig. 3.3, although the largest segment is children aged under 15 years, the most lucrative segment is probably young adults (including teenagers), as these are likely to have more disposable income.

Uses of geo-demographic systems to identify and reach target groups – ACORN, MOSAIC

A business might decide that it needs to target its customers geographically. Two neighbourhood classifications are commonly used by organisations – ACORN and MOSAIC.

ACORN is a geo-demographic tool that businesses use to identify and understand the UK population and local demand for products and services. The ACORN system categorises UK postcodes using demographic statistics and lifestyle variables to give businesses a guide to the differences between geographical regions. This information can be used to decide where to base operations (for example, opening a new store in a chain). It also helps the business to identify where marketing campaigns will be most effective.

ACORN might help a business identify that there are more high earners in Birmingham than Aberystwyth, but similarly it might help a business choose a location within a town or city that puts it closer to its target customers. For example, a Waitrose store would be better located in a residential area populated by mid- to high-range earners with concern for local produce than in an estate populated by low earners.

MOSAIC is a system that classifies households in the United Kingdom into 12 Mosaic Groups and 52 sub-groups called Mosaic Types. These Groups and Types are formed on the basis that the households comprising them share certain characteristics. A business can use this information to identify their core customer segments by cross-referencing their customer database with the profile. This helps them to make marketing decisions based on the kind of customer they attract – this could be choosing a paper in which to advertise, an area for direct mailing, or where to open a new store.

Reasons for choice of target group

Having identified the specific market segment to target, the business needs to consider the following before choosing to market to the segment.

- Will the identified segment be accessible? The business must ensure that having selected a market segment, it can reach the potential customers through effective marketing communication. If the segment is too small, then the cost of gaining access to them may make the venture too expensive.

- Will the business be able to service this segment? For example, a supermarket might identify a market for organic produce produced within 30 miles of the store, but it will not be able to service this segment if there are no organic farms within the area.

- What are the current and future prospects for this segment? The business must calculate whether the segment to be targeted will provide a good return on the investment not only now but also in the future, when changes to the product or service may have to be made.

- How profitable will this market segment be? It would be pointless targeting the segment with the product or service if the cost of production and distribution were so high that in order to make a profit, a high selling price would have to be applied, putting the product beyond the budget of the targeted segment.

- Does this segment fit in with the mission statement of the business? The values of the business are an important consideration. If it believes that certain groups of people and their beliefs are not in line with the organisation's, then it should not target these people.

By answering these questions, the business will find the choice of which specific market segment to target much easier. For example, if a business is marketing fancy wheels for sports cars, the target market will probably exclude anyone under the age of 17. Once the business has narrowed down who they think their specific market segment might be, it is time for them to test this hypothesis.

They could create a survey or send out samples of their products to the identified potential market segment.

They must define people in terms of age, gender, race, ethnicity, geographic location, religion, marital status, language, stage of life, education and profession. When the results of their research are completed, they can now analyse them and determine who the optimum specific market segment of the population is. They may find that a group they thought was within their target group is actually not, or vice versa.

For example, you would not want to spend thousands of pounds on a TV advertisement during daytime television if your target market is middle-aged men (since a high percentage of daytime television viewers are made up of women). In the process of your research, you should also determine what the best methods of advertisement are for that group. A target group of children would require brightly coloured, interactive marketing strategies, whereas a target group of older men may require something as simple as a written advertisement.

3.3 Identifying customers in business-to-business markets

Decision-making unit (DMU)

All the individuals and groups who participate in the purchasing decision process in a business are known as a decision-making unit (DMU). A DMU could include the following groups.

- Influencers are individuals whose opinion may be sought about a product or organisation. They will probably be influenced themselves by brand, company reputation and ongoing relationships.
- Users will be interested in the benefits the product offers, such as increased production rates or reduced waste.
- Buyers or purchasing officers will be concerned about easy purchasing arrangements, delivery dates and security of supply. This can mean that a business can differentiate itself from the competition by stressing its success rate and longevity (how long it will last).
- Deciders, such as managing directors, will probably be most concerned with the overall cost of the product and whether the organisation can afford it. The cost benefit of purchasing the product or

service is a key issue as it is obviously not worth the purchase if the benefits that may result do not warrant the initial investment.

- Specifiers decide on the detailed specification of the product to be purchased. They may well want technical information about such things as component performance and material characteristics.
- Gatekeepers may deny potential users information for a variety of reasons, for example, quality managers may have safety concerns or finance managers may have financial reservations. They can prevent sellers reaching the key decision makers.

As shown above, benefits for different members of the DMU include cost benefits, ongoing relationships and security of supply.

3.4 How are business markets segmented?

Bases for segmentation of business markets

The concept of segmentation applies equally to both consumer and business markets, but the bases by which they are segmented differ.

Size and value

The size of a business will make a difference to the way in which it views its suppliers and goes about its purchasing. The UK clearing banks tend to segment their business customers by size. Small businesses may need sympathetic local support from the bank, for example, when starting up. A large business may need more specialised financial advice. In a very large organisation, there may be many people involved in the buying decision and the procedure may be very complex because of the risks and levels of investment that may be involved. A small business, however, may have just one or two people involved in the decision-making process.

The value of the business is also an important criterion by which it may be segmented. If the business always makes high-value purchases, then these businesses may need a different type of approach by the selling business.

Region

Some businesses may focus their selling effort according to their geographic location. Some industries are concentrated in particular areas. For example, the financial sector in Europe is concentrated in London, Frankfurt and Zurich; therefore businesses selling to this sector will concentrate their activity in these geographic areas.

Public, private and voluntary sectors

Other selling businesses may segment their business customers on the basis of what sector they operate within. There may be different approaches by the selling business depending on whether the business operates within the private or public/voluntary sector. Selling to businesses in the public/voluntary sector involves a complex process which may involve tendering for their business. This means the selling business may have to go through a formal process of applying to provide products and services, and will be in competition with other businesses which also

hope to sell their products or services. The public sector body will then make a decision based on cost-effectiveness, quality and so on, and award the chosen business with the contract. This process does not exist within the private sector and therefore a different approach will be required.

By product and industry

Businesses may also segment by product, which means that the same product can be used in many different ways. This approach looks for customer groupings by defining a particular use for the product or service, and grouping business customers around this use.

Segmentation may also take place around a particular industry; there may be industrial sectors that are more likely to use particular products or services. For example, cash-and-carry wholesalers serve three key segments: independent grocers, caterers and pubs. Each segment will purchase different types of goods, in different quantities and for different purposes.

Assessment activity 3.3

This assignment builds upon your work for the previous assignments. You need to explain how and why groups of customers are targeted for selected products.

For this task you will need to select six different target groups for products or services of your choice – for example, Saga holidays for the over-50s. At least two of your choices must be from the business-to-business market; the remainder can be from the consumer

market. You should describe the customer profile for each of the six target groups and then explain how and why these groups are targeted. **P5**

Grading tip

Make sure that you understand the main bases for segmentation. The better a business can describe its target market, the better chance there will be of success. **P5**

4. Be able to develop a coherent marketing mix

4.1 The marketing mix

The **marketing mix** provides an excellent framework for developing marketing plans. The marketing mix for physical goods is generally accepted as being made up of four parts (the four Ps), which are:

- product
- price
- promotion
- place.

Once the marketing objectives have been agreed, marketing plans must be developed to achieve goals.

Product

A product is anything that can be offered to a market to satisfy a want or need. Products include physical goods, services, experiences, events, persons, places, properties, organisations, information and ideas. It is therefore the combination of goods and services that are offered to the target consumer. For example, you may buy a car and receive a significant amount of added after-sales service. The two aspects together make up the product being offered to the consumer.

Price

Price is the amount of money consumers have to pay to acquire the product. This can vary considerably. For example, PC World offers discounts and credit terms which all combine to alter the price different individual consumers pay for a laptop.

Place

Place describes where and how the consumer can obtain the product. Tesco has stores all over the country but place does not have to be a physical location. Nowadays consumers can buy books over the telephone, via the Internet or through their TV remote control. Producers have to choose the best method carefully to ensure consumers can find their product in an appropriate place when they decide to make a purchase.

Promotion

Promotion describes the activities undertaken to ensure the consumer knows about the product and its capabilities. It usually combines advertising, sales promotion, public relations and personal selling. These terms are explained more fully in Unit 9 Creative product promotion (see page 197).

Key term

Marketing mix – sometimes referred to as the four Ps of product, price, promotion and place, these are the ideas to consider when marketing a product

Fig. 3.4: What is a marketing mix?

Case study: Ryanair

Ryanair is a European airline that specialises in low-cost, no frills air travel. There is no free food or drink and the service on board is designed to keep costs down. They have very low fares, although they have been criticised over misleading advertising of fares compared to the actual fares charged. They do not use travel agents, and customers book online. They fly to cheaper secondary airports, which again reduces costs. They spend very little on advertising and they tend to recruit young qualified pilots and purchase aircraft at times when demand for aircraft falls. Their systems are streamlined with no check-in; seats are first come, first served.

Working in groups, how would you assess the marketing mix (the four Ps) of Ryanair?

Objectives of developing mix

A business will tailor its marketing mix to suit its objectives. The objectives may include the following.

- Support brand building.
- Satisfy needs and aspirations of targeted group of customers.

Support brand building

The marketing mix supports the building of brands through product strategies.

As we have seen, strengthening brand awareness is beneficial for a business (page 90). A strong brand allows a business to make more effective use of its marketing strategies by promoting more than one product within the brand range, and raises the profile of new products in the brand.

For example, Colgate is a brand owned by Colgate-Palmolive. The Colgate brand has a strong reputation for dental hygiene products such as toothpaste and toothbrushes. However, the strength of the brand means that the business can offer products to segments of the market – whitening, sensitive teeth, children's toothpaste and so on – while limiting the investment it puts into raising the awareness of the brand in the market. It also reassures businesses stocking Colgate products, because they can see how much value customers place on the brand and effectively judge the level of risk associated with stocking the new product.

Satisfy needs and aspirations of targeted group of customers

The four Ps of the marketing mix are the parameters that a business can control, although they are subject to the internal and external constraints of the marketing environment. The goal is to make decisions that centre the four Ps on the customers in the target market, in order to create perceived value and generate a positive response.

If a product genuinely satisfies the needs and aspirations of its target market, it stands a better chance of long-term success than a product that does not. A marketing mix should convince customers that they need the product, but the product itself (an important part of the marketing mix) needs to reinforce this message.

Importance of need for cohesion of different elements of the marketing mix

People who want cans of Coke need to find them in a variety of convenient locations, such as local shops. They are unlikely to search extensively to find a can of Coke if it is not there, and may choose an alternative. Promotion is used to make a particular product stand out from the crowd.

The secret of success lies in blending the elements of the marketing mix effectively, as each individual product requires a different blend. Coca-Cola needs to ensure that their product tastes pleasant, but the most important marketing mix elements are probably place and promotion.

4.2 Product

A product can be described as a tangible, physical entity that can be bought or sold. A product can be viewed in three different levels.

- Level 1: The Core Product (rather than the physical product) is the benefit of the product that makes it valuable to you. For example, this might be the ability to get to any destination at a time that suits you, rather than a car.

- Level 2: The Actual Product is the physical item – the car, for example. At this level, branding and added features and benefits come into play to differentiate the product from competitors' offerings. For example, the car might be a Mercedes and come with air conditioning, central locking and Bluetooth as standard.

- Level 3: The Augmented Product is additional value beyond the physical product; it usually consists of after-sales service, warranties, delivery and so on. This might be something for which a customer will pay a premium, but not always. In the example of the car, the dealer might offer an interest-free loan, a two-year warrantee and a free 10,000-mile service. In this example, these added benefits are probably free (although they will be paid for in the price of the physical item), but help to differentiate the product further from the competition.

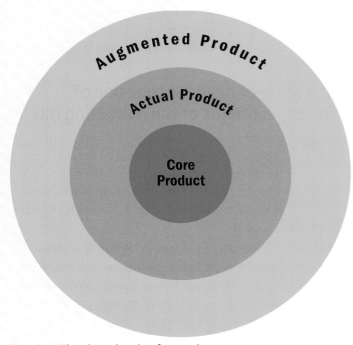

Fig. 3.5: The three levels of a product.

Product range

A business will constantly change and update its product range and mix. The extent of the mix is another significant issue. If the business has too few products, there is a chance that one will go out of date and seriously damage total sales. If there are too many products, the range could become difficult to oversee successfully and may fragment production. Whatever the decision, it is never recommended to have one product in one market. In this scenario, if the product or market fails, it could mean the complete failure of the business. The product range of a business is often limited by its area of expertise and by its size and resources. Some businesses adapt and anticipate change, while others react to the need to change. Those businesses that do not adapt will fail to survive.

PLTS

Through the activity below you will investigate the marketing of business organisations through appropriate planning in order to carry out effective research into the marketing of organisations.

Activity: Core, actual and augmented

All companies have a core, actual and augmented product or service. Fill in the missing product levels below.

Table 3.3: Examples of core, actual and augmented products.

Brand, product or service	Core Product	Actual Product	Augmented Product
Mazda car	Freedom to travel	Sports car	
Caribbean holiday	Relaxation		Holiday insurance
Manchester United Football Club	Excitement, entertainment and leisure	Sporting event	
Nike	Association with the best teams and individuals in sport		Nike Online allows personalisation of trainers
Wyevale Garden Centres		Products for gardens	Wyevale's Gardening Club

Benefits versus features of product or service for targeted customers

Once a business has identified its target customers, it should know what its products or services need to do in order to appeal to its core market. This information should inform the features of the product or service so that it produces the benefits that the target market expects or needs.

For example, a sports drink might contain a combination of glucose and caffeine (feature), which provides the consumer with more energy to continue doing their sport for longer (benefit).

However, it is important to remember that the benefits to a customer are not always practical (for example, the benefit of a car is not always that it gets from A to B). There are psychological benefits, such as status, sense of independence, happiness and so on, which can be difficult to measure and may vary from customer to customer.

Concept of product life cycle

The product life cycle concept reflects the theory that products, like people, live a life. They are born, they grow up, they mature and eventually they die. It is a useful concept for thinking about what a product has achieved and where it is heading in the future.

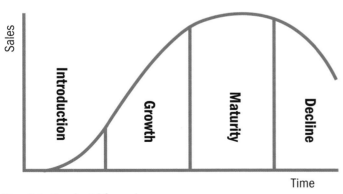

Fig. 3.6: Product life cycle.

In the introductory stage, a product takes time to find acceptance by purchasers and there is slow growth in sales. Only a few organisations are likely to be operating in the market, each experiencing high cost because output is low. They may charge high prices to cover development and the initial promotional costs, but even then, profitability may be difficult to achieve. Promotion concentrates on telling consumers what the product does.

If the product achieves market acceptance, then sales grow rapidly. In this growth stage, profits begin to materialise as higher production levels reduce unit costs. However, the growing market attracts competition and soon producers have to invest in building a brand image, product improvements and sales promotions to obtain a dominant market position.

The maturity stage follows when a product experiences stable sales. This is generally the longest period of a successful product's life. But eventually sales fall and the market finds itself with too many producers, who begin to suffer poor sales and falling profits. Some leave the market, while others employ strategies to extend the life of the product.

Most products reach the saturation stage when sales begin to fall. During this period, some brands will leave the market.

Products reach a stage of decline when sales fall significantly. Organisations progressively abandon the market, sometimes leaving a few producers who are able to trade profitably on low sales totals.

Organisations use the product life cycle to devise new product plans. An organisation will look to introduce new products to coincide with the decline of the established ones.

Case study: Kommunicate

Kommunicate, a mobile phone manufacturing company, developed a new phone that was smaller, lighter and contained many more applications than its nearest rival. The phones sold well, but are now passing from the growth stage into the maturity stage. Competitors have already entered the market.

As a member of the marketing team, suggest two promotional activities Kommunicate can use. Give your reasons.

PLTS

In this activity you will investigate the marketing of business organisations through appropriate planning in order to carry out effective research into the marketing of organisations.

4.3 Price

Price is the one element of the marketing mix that produces revenue; the others produce costs. Prices can be changed quickly. A business must set a price for a product and, in deciding the product's price, marketers must follow a six-step process.

1. **Select the price objective** – the objective could be to survive, or to maximise market share.

2. **Determine demand** – the higher the price, the lower the demand and vice versa.

3. **Estimate costs** – every business should charge a price that covers its cost of producing, distributing and selling the product, and return a profit.

4. **Analyse competitors' costs, prices and offers** – the business must take into account its competitors' costs and prices before setting its prices.

5. **Select a pricing strategy** – there are a number of pricing strategies, which are discussed below.

6. **Select the final price** – this is decided after testing on a variety of pricing points.

Premium pricing

This is where a business keeps the price of a product or service high in order to encourage customers to associate it with high quality. There can be a tendency in customers – particularly with technology, or premium foods – to assume that the high price relates to, for example, a better reputation.

Penetration pricing

This is when a product is sold into a market at a low initial price in order to generate sales before the price is increased. This helps break down any barriers to the market and generates sales volume, but not necessarily profit, so it can be used as a short-term strategy to gain market share. Next time you see a product marked with 'introductory offer', you should think of this as an example of penetration pricing.

Economy pricing

Economy pricing is the deliberate setting of a low price in order to boost sales.

Skim pricing

At the launch of a new product there will be less competition in the marketplace. Skimming involves setting a reasonably high initial price in order to get high initial returns from those consumers willing to buy the new product. As other similar products enter the marketplace, then the price is lowered to remain competitive. This strategy is often adopted by technology companies that benefit from 'early adopters'.

Psychological pricing

Psychological pricing is a customer-based pricing method, relying on consumer's emotive responses, subjective views and feelings towards specific purchases. Products such as designer perfumes need to be priced at high prestige levels, otherwise they will not sell. Customers equate higher quality with higher prices.

Captive product pricing

Captive product pricing is a strategy that can apply to products with consumable supplies – for example, printers need ink cartridges, razors need razor blades, plug-in room scents need scent refills. This is where the pricing of the supplies is high, but the initial purchase may be quite low.

For example, a new razor might cost relatively little and come with a couple of spare blades. However, once a customer has purchased this, only a specific make of razor blades will fit the razor, and these are priced comparatively highly.

Product line pricing

Product line pricing is the pricing of different products within the same product range at different price points. An example would be a DVD manufacturer offering different DVD players with different features at different prices. Product line pricing, therefore, is a pricing strategy that uses differing versions of one product. Another example would be a car model that has various model types that change with performance and quality. This pricing process relates to the customer's perception of value, the cost of production and other elements of cost and demand.

Case study: Ethically sourced chocolate

1. Working in teams, think of your favourite chocolate bar. Suggest three ways that you consider are used in marketing this particular chocolate bar. Now read and answer the questions relating to the following information.

    An ethical food company is offering an ethically sourced chocolate bar for sale. It is the same size as standard bars from other companies, and has the same kind of content as other milk chocolate bars. They want it to be a different shape to standard bars and they want it to be a way of educating people about ethically sourced food. It is to be sold around the world.

2. Discuss the pricing strategy that the company will have to consider when marketing the new ethically sourced chocolate bar. Take into consideration what the company should charge for the chocolate bar and why, and what pricing factors have to be considered when pricing a new product.

3. How would you promote the new bar? Take into consideration how you would generate interest in people buying it and continuing to buy it.

4. Discuss the reasons why not all businesses advertise on television and radio.

PLTS

In this case study, you will investigate the marketing of business organisations through appropriate planning in order to carry out effective research into the marketing of organisations.

You should attempt to generate original and creative ideas about marketing in business organisations in order to determine how organisations market their products and services.

Express carefully considered thoughts regarding the impact of marketing in business. Set your own goals when undertaking research and invite feedback on your work, considering it objectively and evaluating any outcomes to enhance your current and future learning experience.

4.4 Place

Place in the marketing mix refers to where the product is purchased from and how it is distributed. For example, most consumers of confectionery will buy products from a retail store – a supermarket or corner shop, perhaps. However, in order to sell the confectionery at these stores, the business needs to sell and distribute the products to wholesalers who will then sell to the retailers, or the business will sell direct to the retailers.

In some instances, the business may sell direct to the consumer as well as to distributors and retailers. While a consumer will typically only want one product in a range, a retailer might want a selection of products from a range, and a wholesaler might purchase a substantial quantity of products in the range. Each might expect to purchase the items on different terms – for example, the customer might want the product as soon as possible and expect to pay immediately, while the wholesaler might order a week in advance and expect to pay in 30 days' time.

Businesses need to adapt their marketing mix depending on the end customer – that is, whether they are a consumer or reseller – as each seeks different benefits from the same product.

Distribution

A business may use two different types of **distribution** method: indirect or direct. 'Indirect distribution' is the term used when a business sells its products via an intermediary, such as a wholesaler, who then

Key term

Distribution – the process of moving a product from its manufacturing source to its customers

sells to the retailer. 'Direct distribution' is where the business sells and distributes direct to the customer – for example, Apple sell products to customers via their e-commerce website and deliver direct to the consumer.

Choosing indirect distribution may mean that a business loses some of the control over the pricing of their products, as they have to offer discounts to wholesalers and retailers, who may choose to pass on savings to their customers. However, this method can be beneficial in saving the costs of distribution and making products available to customers immediately from a wide range of outlets – for example, Walkers crisps would be unlikely to benefit from direct distribution.

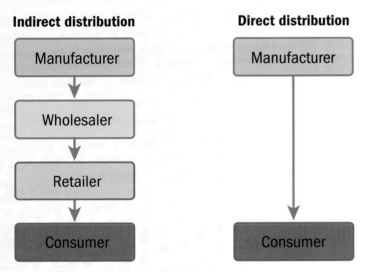

Fig. 3.7: Indirect and direct distribution.

Online and/or physical presence

The growth of online shopping has presented many businesses with a new 'place' for selling to customers. This offers a significant advantage to businesses that are interested in selling direct to consumers, because it gives them a virtual shop, from which customers can purchase items that are distributed direct from the warehouse.

This may offer the business new benefits, such as avoiding the wholesaler and therefore increasing the profit margin on their products, while still being seen to offer a discount.

4.5 Promotion

Promotion consists of the various methods of communicating with a business's target audience. This aspect of the marketing mix is designed to raise awareness of a business, its products and services, and to generate sales.

Promotion should inform, persuade and influence a customer to purchase a product or service. A common model for doing this is AIDA, which describes promotion as a four-step process, as shown in Fig. 3.8.

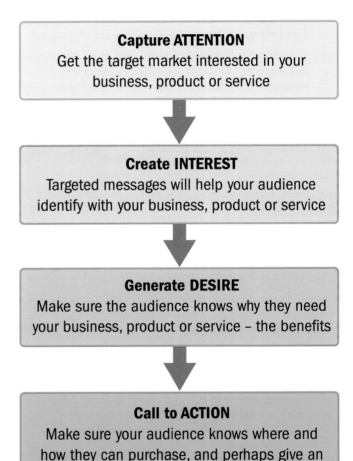

Fig. 3.8: The AIDA model.

An integrated mix of promotions is commonly used to attain AIDA and this is generally known as the promotional mix.

Promotional mix

The promotional mix involves the blending of a number of variables to satisfy the needs of a business's target market and achieve its organisational objectives. The promotional mix is a subset of the overall marketing mix. With the promotional mix, a business attempts to achieve the best blend of promotional elements to suit their promotional objectives. The components of the promotional mix are:

* advertising
* sales promotion
* personal selling
* public relations.

Advertising, sales promotion and personal selling are the most significant elements because they usually account for the majority of a business's promotional expenditure. However, all factors contribute to a successful and efficient marketing promotions campaign.

Advertising

Advertising may be defined as paid promotions through various media by businesses, non-profit organisations and individuals that are in some way identified in the advertising message and hope to inform or persuade members of a particular audience.

Advertisers have many methods to try to get the consumer to buy their products. Often, what they are seen to be selling is a lifestyle or an image rather than the product itself. Advertisers have many such tricks, for example:

* excitement: who could have imagined that food could be so exciting? One bite of a hamburger and you could find yourself surfing in California

* personality power: a famous celebrity or sports person tells you that their product is best. The audience listen without really appreciating that the personality is being paid to endorse the product

* put-downs: businesses put down the competition's product to make their own look better

* jumping on the bandwagon: advertisements encourage the audience to join the crowd. Make sure you're not left out! Everyone is buying this particular drink: why aren't you?

Do ads featuring a celebrity influence you in buying a product?

Activity: Chocolate history

Using the Internet, trace the history of advertising used by famous chocolate manufacturers. When you have gathered enough information, images, logos and so on, design a poster that would promote a chocolate product today, while considering the following.

1. What method(s) will you use?

2. Will you include a sports star or a celebrity to endorse the product?

3. Will you be more subtle?

PLTS

In this activity you will investigate the marketing of business organisations through appropriate planning in order to carry out effective research into the marketing of organisations.

You should attempt to generate original and creative ideas about marketing in business organisations in order to determine how organisations market their products and services.

Different media

Advertising primarily involves the mass media, such as television, newspapers, magazines, radio, billboards and the Internet. There are also less traditional methods, such as commercial video screens in supermarkets and cinemas, as well as messages on signs in pubs. Businesses have come to realise the incredible potential of this form of promotion and advertising is a major promotional mix element for thousands of organisations. Mass consumption and global markets make advertising particularly suitable for goods and services that rely on sending the same promotional message to a large and diverse audience.

Online techniques

Online advertisers use many techniques to try to get the consumer to purchase their products. They often blend advertising with other elements such as free downloads of music and films so that the consumer does not realise that they are being targeted. (Next time you click on a commercial site on the Internet, see if you can recognise any of these techniques.) Banner ads are an obvious form of advertising, whereas others are more subtle. For example, the creation of virtual worlds have made consumers feel they are entering a 'real' place – for example, the Optivita Village website, operated by Kellogg's. When entering these virtual worlds, consumers are surrounded by familiar terminology such as town, village and street. Advertisers want the consumer to feel that this is familiar territory and not a commercial environment. Some websites ask the consumer to enter their details before entering; they then use this information to offer personalised messages throughout the visit to the site (for example, Amazon.co.uk).

Traditional advertising does not work online and so the use of more interactive means of advertising has become the norm. Activities such as crossword puzzles and word searches are available online and can

feature brand name products or services. Interactive games featuring recognisable characters from the world of film or television seamlessly blend into what is fundamentally an advertisement. 'Free' email 'postcards' can be sent via the commercial website (this is a way of gaining email addresses for their database).

Children are a particularly vulnerable target group as they are often unaware of the persuasion of advertisements on the Internet. They are encouraged to join clubs and enter competitions to win prizes (the prizes often feature the slogan, character or logo of the company); they are often asked to submit personal information about themselves before they can join these clubs. This will allow the company to build user profiles of the children who visit the site, sell the information on to a third party and target them through their email.

Personal selling

Personal selling is a skilled task; it may require training a sales team and may be one of the more expensive aspects of the promotional mix. This is where a seller presents a product direct to a consumer, often face to face, but it can also be over the telephone and through video-conferencing and instant messaging.

Personal selling may reach a relatively small number of people (compared with TV advertising, for example), but it is generally more effective.

Public relations

Public relations covers a firm's communications and relationships with its public. This includes customers, suppliers, stockholders, employees, the government, the general public and the society in which the organisation operates. Public relations programmes can be either formal or informal. The critical point is that every organisation, whether or not it has a formally organised programme, must be concerned about its public relations. Publicity is an important part of an effective public relations effort. It can be defined as the non-personal stimulation of demand for a good, service, person, cause or organisation by placing significant news about it in a published medium or by obtaining favourable presentation of it through radio, television, Internet or that which is not paid for by an identified sponsor. Compared to personal selling, advertising and even sales promotion, expenditures for public relations are usually low in most firms. Since they do not pay for it, companies have less control over the publication by the press or electronic media of good or bad company news. For this reason, a consumer may find this type of news source more believable than if the information were disseminated directly by the company.

Sales promotion

Sales promotion relates to marketing activities that fall outside of the categories described above. These can include coupons, trade shows, displays, samples and other promotional efforts that occur on an irregular basis.

Sales promotions are often short-term and opportunistic, so may contribute to a spike (sudden, short rise) in interest in a product or service. However, they are often combined with other promotional activity to provide longer-term growth.

Assessment activity 3.4

This assignment builds upon your work for the previous assignment. You should choose one of your selected organisations. You need to complete the following tasks as part of the continuation of your research project.

1. Develop a coherent marketing mix for a new product or service. **P6**
2. Develop a coherent marketing mix that is targeted at a defined group of potential customers. **M3**

Grading tips

1. Make sure you understand what the elements are of the marketing mix, and how these can be altered to service the targeted market. **P6**
2. Look at the marketing mixes of various products. You may like to research this on the Internet and see how some successful products are managed in terms of their marketing mixes. This research should help you in developing a marketing mix for a selected product. **M3**

Just checking

1. List six techniques used in marketing.
2. Name three laws which constrain the activities of marketing departments.
3. What is the role of Trading Standards?
4. How is market research related to planning?
5. What is meant by the marketing mix and the promotional mix?
6. How is the marketing mix related to marketing planning?
7. What is the difference between primary and secondary research?
8. What is the difference between qualitative and quantitative data?
9. What is meant by the term marketing orientation?
10. Explain what a product development growth strategy is.
11. Give three examples of three socio-cultural changes that can affect the way a business operates.
12. What is the difference between a customer and a consumer?
13. Explain the usefulness of geo-demographics systems such as ACORN.
14. Describe three ways of segmenting a business-to-business market.
15. What are the four Ps of the extended marketing mix used for when dealing with services?
16. Describe the stages of the product life cycle.

edexcel

Assignment tips

1. For all the assignments, select business organisations that make available information on their use of marketing techniques, research, planning and the marketing mix. Many of the leading global companies contain on their websites information about the techniques they use. Cadbury's, for example, is an organisation which is always happy to help provide information for learner assignments.

2. Your first assignment asks you to produce a report describing, comparing and evaluating the marketing activities of two companies in relation to specified products. Include details of the constraints under which each of the selected organisations operate. Remember to produce your work in a business report format.

3. For the second assignment you may be asked to present your findings. Ensure you leave yourself plenty of time to plan and prepare your presentation. For the final two assignments, you will be asked once again to present these as business reports. Once you have completed all your assignments and they have been assessed, keep them in your portfolio in a neat and tidy order.

4 Business communication

We are always communicating – even when we are silent we are still sending a message. When we look away, we are expressing something, and when we talk, wave our hands, smile or nod, we are still communicating. Being able to write, read and speak clearly is important in communication, but having these basic skills does not mean necessarily that you can communicate well and do it effectively. When we communicate, we are giving and receiving information, which can be of many different types, with differing purposes and coming from different sources. All roles in business require effective communication, none more so than in being a manager.

Communication involves the conveying, or exchange of information. It is about all sorts of things – such as giving praise, expressing displeasure, passing opinions, maintaining or starting friendships. When you talk to someone, you often convey your feelings as well as ideas or information. When you speak, the content of the message that you send is not limited to the words spoken. The tone of your voice is a vital part of the message you send. If you can see the person that you are talking to, then gestures, use of space, body contact and facial expression will also add to your message. When you do not use words in your communication, you use what is known as body language – a way of communicating that uses the ways in which you move your body to send your messages.

Many people make the mistake of thinking that communication as a one-way process. However, if you are issuing someone with instructions, the listener is still providing the speaker with feedback. It can be the expression on the listener's face, whether they are looking at the speaker and what their body posture is. All of these tell the speaker whether the message has been heard and understood.

Learning outcomes

After completing this unit, you should:

1. understand different types of business information
2. be able to present business information effectively
3. understand the issues and constraints in relation to the use of business information in organisations
4. know how to communicate business information using appropriate methods.

Assessment and grading criteria

This table shows you what you must do in order to achieve a **pass**, **merit** or **distinction** grade, and where you can find activities in this book to help you.

To achieve a **pass** grade, the evidence must show that the learner is able to:	To achieve a **merit** grade, the evidence must show that, in addition to the pass criteria, the learner is able to:	To achieve a **distinction** grade, the evidence must show that, in addition to the pass and merit criteria, the learner is able to:
P1 explain different types of business information, their sources and purposes **See Assessment activity 4.1, page 131.**	**M1** analyse different types of business information and their sources **See Assessment activity 4.1, page 131.**	**D1** evaluate the appropriateness of business information used to make strategic decisions **See Assessment activity 4.1, page 131.**
P2 present complex internal business information using three different methods appropriate to the user's needs **See Assessment activity 4.2, page 138.**		**D2** evaluate the effectiveness of business information and its communication as key contributors to the success of an organisation, using examples to illustrate your points **See Assessment activity 4.2, page 138.**
P3 produce corporate communications **See Assessment activity 4.2, page 138.**		
P4 evaluate the external corporate communications of an existing product or service **See Assessment activity 4.2, page 138.**		
P5 explain the legal and ethical issues in relation to the use of business information **See Assessment activity 4.3, page 143.**	**M2** analyse the legal, ethical and operational issues in relation to the use of business information, using appropriate examples **See Assessment activity 4.3, page 143.**	
P6 explain the operational issues in relation to the use of business information **See Assessment activity 4.3, page 143.**		
P7 outline electronic and non-electronic methods for communicating business information, using examples for different types of audience **See Assessment activity 4.4, page 161.**		

How you will be assessed

This unit will be assessed by an internal assignment that will be designed and marked by the staff at your centre. It may be subject to sampling by your centre's External Verifier as part of Edexcel's ongoing quality assurance procedures. The assignment is designed to allow you to show your understanding of the unit outcomes. These relate to what you should be able to do after completing this unit.

Your assessment could be in the form of presentations, practical tasks and written reports.

Jason

This unit helped me realise that communication makes a business tick. I had thought that communication was just about telling somebody something or writing to someone. This unit helped me to see that listening and understanding is a key part of effective communication and very few of us are good listeners without a great deal of practice.

I enjoyed investigating business organisations in order to describe the different types of information being used – the variety of information was amazing. I particularly enjoyed the presentation exercises – although at first I was very nervous, I soon found that it wasn't half as bad as I first thought. One part of our assignment asked us to produce a leaflet to show how organisations communicate with their stakeholders. This exercise really made me think about how important the communication process between a company and its customers is, and the role played by advertising.

I found the aspects of electronic communication very stimulating and it really made me realise that we are in fact in the middle of a technological revolution as far as information and communication technology are concerned.

1. Think about how you communicate with your friends – what is your body language telling them?
2. How is this different from the way you communicate with your tutor or your manager?
3. Can you think of any times when someone has not understood your message? Why do you think this was?

Types of information

Think of time during work experience or in a part-time job. You were probably surrounded by huge amounts of information, such as sales performance data, personnel information or information for customers. Write down five different types of information that you experienced while in work. If you find this task challenging, start by retracing your steps and think of your first day. What information were you asked to provide or read? Discuss your findings in small groups and compare your types of information with those of others.

1. Understand different types of business information

1.1 What types of information are there?

Information comes from a wide variety of sources and an effective business person will research information from a range of sources before making decisions.

Verbal information

Face-to-face verbal communication is the best way to communicate. There is less scope for misunderstanding and it allows for verbal and non-verbal messages. However, with the constraints of time and budgets in business, it is not always possible or practical to meet in person. Telephone conversations are also useful ways to communicate, but it is important always to use a combination of methods.

The range of verbal communication is enormous. Speech enables complex ideas to be expressed and discussed. Although the absence of speech would not prevent us from communicating effectively by other means, for most people, talking is the most comfortable method of expression. It is immediate, it provides a huge range of choices to convey all our messages, and of course it is rapid. How often have we heard it said, in response to a particular problem, 'If only I could get to talk to him, I'm sure we could sort it out'? It is common to find that talks are arranged between two sides in a disagreement as the method of sorting out differences, such as between unions and employers, to settle wage demands and employment conditions, or nations with other nations, to discuss

economic strategies and arms control. Even our system of government, the parliamentary system, reflects the significance of discussion and debate, for the word 'Parliament' means speaking.

Key term

Information – knowledge of specific events or situations that has been gathered or received by communication; intelligence or news

1.2 Written information

Writing is the use of physical symbols to represent words. Words are the sounds that make up speech. But this definition can be broadened to include other forms of physical representation, such as diagrams, graphs and charts – in other words, all types of visual representation. All forms of numerical representation can be included under this heading as well.

We could not have reached our present state of economic, social and technological development without our ability to produce written information. Written information may come from a wide variety of sources including newspapers, books, trade journals and government publications.

On-screen information

Information may be produced on-screen. This can be seen in multimedia TV and CD-ROMs that combine text, graphics, animation, audio and video.

Did you know?

Email and telephone calls produce the highest response rate for direct marketing media channels. Even then, the rate is only just over two per cent.

Multimedia information

The term 'multimedia' simply means multiple forms of media integrated together. Media can be text, graphics, audio, animation, video, data, and so on. An example of multimedia is a web page about Mozart that has text regarding the composer along with an audio file of some of his music and a video of his music being played.

Why is verbal communication the best way to communicate?

Besides multiple types of media being integrated with one another, multimedia can also stand for interactive media, such as video games, CD-ROMs that teach a foreign language, or an information kiosk in large cities. Other terms that are sometimes used for multimedia include hypermedia and rich media.

The term multimedia is said to date back to the mid 1960s and was used to describe a show by the Exploding Plastic Inevitable, arranged by Andy Warhol. The show included a performance that integrated music, cinema, special lighting and human performance. Today, the word multimedia is used quite frequently, from DVDs to CD-ROMs to even a magazine that includes text and pictures.

Web-based information

Web-based information displays many benefits of multimedia technology. Using today's fast broadband connections, it is possible to stream sophisticated content to a computer anywhere in the world. This is an advantage for many people as the information can be received and read wherever and whenever it is convenient for them, which can be a crucial factor for a busy executive. A significant amount of interactive multimedia content is now delivered via the Internet.

1.3 What are the purposes of information?

Reliable and valid information is essential to all businesses and organisations. An organisation without information is like someone wandering around in the dark: they do not know where they are going and if they get to where they want to be, it is more by luck than by good planning. Organisations use information for a variety of purposes that include:

- updating knowledge
- informing future developments
- strategic direction and SWOT analysis
- offering competitive insight
- communicating sales promotions
- inviting support for activities.

Updating knowledge

It is imperative that businesses keep up to date with changes that are occurring within their markets. Information is required so that businesses know:

- how their markets are developing
- how labour markets are changing
- what the economy is doing
- what new laws are being passed that might affect the way they operate.

All of this information helps organisations to make accurate decisions based on full knowledge. Incorrect decisions are likely to be the result of inadequate information.

Informing future developments

A business that does not adapt, develop and grow will quickly find itself left behind by the competition. But developments need to be based on informed decisions. A business will not launch a new product, for example, unless it has ample evidence that the product is likely to sell. The BlackBerry phone would never have been launched unless a significant amount of information had been collected to show that it would sell.

Case study: Communication issues at Dalgart Ltd

Samantha works in the human resource department of a large manufacturing company called Dalgart Ltd. She has been working for some time on a project with the production manager on a new shift and bonus structure. The shift and bonus system are complex, and Samantha has decided to call a formal meeting with the union representative and shift supervisors and representatives of operatives working in the production unit. She decided that she would talk through the changes and how the bonus system would work rather than rely on cumbersome piles of paper, which would have to be distributed. The meeting took place and took twice as long as planned, as the audience kept asking for her to repeat and clarify various parts of her talk.

1. Do you think that a verbal talk or presentation was an appropriate means of communicating? Why do you think this?

2. How could have Samantha improved the communication?

Strategic direction and SWOT analysis

Strategic management is the process by which organisations determine their purpose, objectives and desired levels of attainment. It helps an organisation decide on actions for achieving these objectives in an appropriate timescale, and frequently in a changing environment. It also allows the organisation to implement the actions, then assess progress and results. Actions may be changed or modified whenever and wherever necessary.

In order to establish **strategic direction**, businesses require large amounts of information from both external and internal sources. Once this information is obtained, a very useful planning tool known as a **SWOT** analysis is used. A SWOT analysis can be used as a tool for auditing an organisation and its environment. It is the first stage of planning and helps marketers to focus on key issues. Strengths and weaknesses are internal factors.

Key terms

Strategic direction – where an organisation is going over the next year or more

SWOT – strengths, weaknesses, opportunities and threats

A strength could be:

- your specialist marketing expertise
- a new, innovative product or service
- the location of your business
- quality processes and procedures
- any other aspect of your business that adds value to your product or service.

A weakness could be:

- lack of marketing expertise
- undifferentiated products or services (for example, not presented as clearly different or better than those of your competitors)
- the location of your business
- poor-quality goods or services
- a damaged reputation.

Opportunities and threats are external factors.

An opportunity could be:

- a developing market such as the Internet
- mergers, joint ventures or strategic alliances
- moving into new market segments that offer improved profits
- a new international market
- a market vacated by an ineffective competitor.

Case study: Škoda

In 1895, in Czechoslovakia company Laurin & Klement was founded and started manufacturing cycles. The first car was produced in 1905 and the company changed its name to Škoda in 1925. Besides cars, it produced farm ploughs and aeroplanes. Škoda overcame hard times during the next 65 years. These included war, economic depression and political change. By 1991, the Czech management of Škoda was looking for a strong foreign partner. Volkswagen AG (VAG) was chosen because of its reputation for strength, quality and reliability. It is the largest car manufacturer in Europe, selling more than five million cars a year – giving Volkswagen a 12 per cent share of the world car market in the first half of 2009.

Škoda's management needed to assess its brand positioning. The image of Škoda cars in the UK was poor, with inferior quality and unreliability being major concerns. The organisation already had large manufacturing units and now Volkswagen technology was in place along with an experienced workforce. To aid its decision

making, Škoda UK obtained data from internal and external audits. This enabled it to take advantage of new opportunities and respond to threats. The audit provided a summary of the business's overall strategic position by using a SWOT analysis. The outcome of the SWOT analysis was a strategy for effective competition in the car industry.

What information do you think was required by the management team as part of the SWOT analysis?

A threat could be:

- a new competitor in your home market
- price wars with competitors
- a competitor having an innovative product or service
- competitors having superior access to channels of distribution
- taxation being introduced on your product or service.

Offering competitive insight

Businesses need to be aware of what their competitors are doing, to ensure they do not fall behind and lose sales and market share. Regular research and communication should help a business to assess its competitors' sales, marketing and development activities. Some large businesses have a section of their marketing departments dedicated to analysing competitor activity. Market research companies sometimes undertake this sort of research on behalf of an organisation. The monitoring and analysis of the behaviour of competitors is essential for many businesses in competitive markets.

Communicating sales promotions

Businesses use a variety of information and methods to communicate sales promotions to customers. They place information about products, services and special offers on their websites, and have newspaper and journal adverts, and television and radio adverts. Good market research information will offer an insight into the behaviour patterns of customers and their buying motivations. Information can therefore help businesses to promote their goods and services and so to sell more effectively.

Inviting support for activities

Information is also required and needs to be communicated in order to support business activities. This support may have to come from people inside or outside the organisation. For example, the business may wish to change the way it operates to make it more efficient; this must have the support of the workforce. Clear information will have to be given to the staff, explaining why the business needs to move in this direction.

1.4 What are the sources of information?

A business can gather information internally, from inside the organisation or externally, from sources outside the organisation.

Did you know?

It is estimated that 72.5 per cent of UK Internet users over the age of 14 will buy at least one item online in 2009. Furthermore, it is predicted that between 2009 and 2013, the number of online buyers will increase from 26.9 million to 31.8 million – this equates to over half of the UK population. (Source: www.emarketer.com)

Internal sources of information

Internal information could come from a variety of sources within the organisation. Some of the main departments are as follows.

- Finance will have a wealth of information relating to company performance, such as profit and loss figures, the balance sheet, cash flow information and the costs of running the business.
- Sales departments will often store information about customers, as well as sales records for the organisation's existing products and services.
- Human resources can provide information about the staffing and training within the organisation, such as staff turnover, number of employees, skills available, training needs and projections for future employment.
- Production will be able to give details of production costs, along with past and possible future levels of production.
- Marketing can give information about the results of research undertaken by the company, the success of previous marketing campaigns and promotional activities, as well as information about the market the organisation currently operates within.
- Customer services can tell you what customers think about the business and give you information on how customers have responded to existing products and services.

All the above functions require a considerable amount of administration, which in turn requires information.

External sources

External data exists in the form of published materials, collected by someone else outside the company. There are a number of external sources, as follows.

Government sources

These are supplied by, among others, the ONS (Office of National Statistics), the DTI (Department of Trade and Industry) and the OECD (Organisation for Economic Development). Some of the key government publications include the *Monthly Digest of Statistics*, *Regional Trends* and *Labour Market Trends*.

Trade groupings

Trade groupings are groups of businesses from the same industry or marketplaces that provide a service to representatives of their industry. They can act as pressure groups to initiate positive change for their industry. They also publish trade journals, which are a very useful resource. These are published by leaders in industries for the people working in that industry, but they also make excellent research materials. Magazines include:

- *Supermarketing* – for those in the retail food trade
- *Convenience Store* – for those owning and operating convenience stores
- *Supply Management* – for those involved in purchasing in industry.

Commercially provided databases

Many private research organisations specialise in building up databases of people who are known to have an interest in certain products and services. There are many market research agencies where lists may be purchased by businesses that wish to target these customers via direct mail. It is hoped that the response rate will be high, as these customers on the list are known to have an interest in the product. A well-known agency is Nielsen Media Research.

Research

In the broadest sense of the word, the definition of research includes any gathering of data, information and facts for the advancement of knowledge. Organisations continually conduct research to find out about their markets, customers and views of their staff. **Market research** always incorporates some form of data collection, whether it is secondary research (often referred to as desk research, and means using existing

information) or primary research, which is collected direct from a respondent.

The purpose of any market research project is to achieve an increased understanding of the subject matter. With markets throughout the world becoming increasingly more competitive, market research is now on the agenda of many organisations, whether they are large or small.

Activity: Information gathering

Information technology has changed the way businesses source their information.

1. List the different ways in which businesses are using information technology to source information:
   - internally
   - externally.

2. List traditional methods of sourcing information (not using information technology):
   - internally
   - externally.

3. Evaluate the differences between the methods using information technology and traditional methods, then make a list of the advantages and disadvantages of each.

Functional skills

English: This activity allows you to read about business information, using it to gather information, ideas, arguments and opinions.

Reliability of data sources

When gathering information, it is vital that you determine how valid the information is. Always ask yourself whether it is accurate, relevant and truthful,

Key term

Market research – systematic, objective collection and analysis of data about a particular target market, competition, and/or environment

and whether there is a bias. For example, many newspapers have a particular agenda that influences the way they interpret information for their readership. So, the *Guardian* and the *Daily Mail* might report on the same story, but may well take different slants depending on each journalist's personal opinions and the newspaper's agenda.

You should treat information that you find on the Internet with even more caution. Websites of reputable sources, such as the BBC, or the mainstream newspapers, will be reliable – although as subject to bias as printed news. However, sources such as Wikipedia or personal blogs may be biased, inaccurate or misleading. For example, anyone can alter an entry in Wikipedia – the website relies on knowledgeable readers to correct any errors.

When citing information from the Internet, it is good practice to try to find the same information from more than one source. This takes a bit more time, but helps validate your original source of information.

Assessment activity 4.1

The Assessment activity requires you to investigate the different types of business information that exist in organisations.

First, select an organisation which you are able to access in order to obtain information. The organisation could be the one that you are using for your work experience or perhaps where you work part-time. You will need permission from the owner or your line manager to obtain information about the organisation.

1. Describe the types of information used in your organisation, choosing one from each of the following categories: verbal, written, on-screen, multimedia, web based. **P1**

2. Describe where each of these pieces of information has come from. **P1**

3. Describe what the purpose is of each piece of information. **P1**

4. To achieve this criterion you will need to extend the report written for P1. You will need to analyse the different types of business information and their sources, which you have described for P1. For this task you will need to give a detailed explanation of the types of information and their sources. **M1**

5. To achieve this criterion, you have to evaluate the appropriateness of information used to make important strategic decisions. Choose two functions of the organisation, such as finance and marketing, and find out what sort of information each function requires and uses. **D1**

6. Find out what sort of strategic decisions each of these two functions make and then evaluate whether the information they used to make these decisions is appropriate. **D1**

Grading tips

1. Make sure that you choose an organisation that will be willing to give you information to complete your assignment. If you have a problem in finding a suitable organisation, see your tutor. They may be able to provide you with information to work on, perhaps in the form of a case study. **P1**

2. Most organisations should have examples of verbal, written, on-screen, multimedia and web-based information. If the organisation does not have, for example, any web-based information, then it may be possible for you to describe what information could be web based. **P1**

3. Analysis means breaking down and examining each part in detail, so you will only achieve this criterion if you extend your report significantly. Try to break down each piece information and its sources, and see if there are any connections between them. **M1**

4. Evaluation is about considering in detail the advantages and disadvantages of something, and coming to conclusions about this. Try to identify the strategic decisions made by each department and then judge whether the information they used was appropriate or not. **D1**

2. Be able to present business information effectively

2.1 Matching presentation methods to the needs of the user

When presenting business information, you should always think about how your target audience will use the information. Will they need to refer to it afterwards? What are the most important aspects of the information?

Documents

There are many different types of documents in existence within business organisations. A document is writing that provides information (especially information of an official nature). It is almost anything that is a representation of a person's thinking in the written form.

Documents are useful because they provide a lasting record of the communication that has taken place and they allow the receiver to reread the information as often as necessary to gain a good understanding of the material. This can be vital if the information is technical and/or lengthy. Documents are therefore useful when we need a record of the communication.

Different documents are required depending on the needs of the user. For example, minutes of an important meeting will have to be formal and official so that the users are clear about what has been agreed and what has to be implemented. A document produced for staff asking if they wish to attend the office Christmas party will be much less formal.

Style

The style that someone adopts is the manner in which you execute a task or action. The style that you adopt in communication will depend upon such factors as where you are communicating, with whom you are doing it, the method used and what role you are carrying out when you do it.

The style you adopt is a significant factor when it comes to both the manner and the effectiveness of your workplace communications. For example, a manager may adopt a dominant style when with their co-workers but may adopt a more submissive style during board meetings that they have been asked to attend.

Verbal presentations

Verbal presentations can be used to persuade, inform, influence and explain. All of these are important as they hold within them the potential to change things. Presentations should be:

- powerful
- passionate
- persuasive
- professional.

> ### Did you know?
>
> This method is also very useful if immediate feedback or two-way communication is needed. Perhaps your audience will need to ask questions, offer ideas or seek clarification, in which case this is likely to be a good method.

Role plays

Role-playing is when a group of people act out roles for a particular scenario. For instance, you might train salespeople by having two people act out a sales scenario as salesperson and customer. This allows trainee salespeople to practise their sales techniques. A trainer and/or other trainees may watch the role play and analyse it afterwards.

Although role plays can take a great deal of setting up and rehearsal, they can be a very effective way of delivering a message to an audience. Role plays are used extensively by organisations training staff to deal with customers, interview clients or sell products. Role plays are effective because they can also be used to give the audience or receiver the opportunity to try out new ideas and skills that have been discussed. This can be a vital method for making sure the message is fully understood.

On-screen multimedia presentations

Multimedia presentations may be viewed in person on stage, projected, transmitted or played locally with a media player. A broadcast may be a live or recorded multimedia presentation. Broadcasts and recordings can use either analogue or digital electronic media technology. Digital online multimedia may be downloaded or streamed. In a business context, a multimedia presentation is often one that is presented using a laptop and projector. It would involve a variety of media such as text slides (possibly using a program such as PowerPoint), photographs, images, video, sounds, music and links to Internet sites. Such a presentation could be delivered by a person at the front of an audience or, alternatively, if the information is compiled on a CD or DVD, the receiver could play it for themselves on their own computer at their own pace.

Did you know?

Gestures have different meanings in different cultures. For example:

- in Turkey it is disrespectful to walk around with your hands in your pockets

- it is offensive in Thailand and Saudi Arabia to show the soles of your feet

- in most North European countries it is perceived as rude to slouch.

Use of images

Images can enhance a communication to an audience, as we tend to remember more of what we see than what we hear, so showing images can be the best way to help an audience remember the message. There are some important points to remember when using images.

- Ensure the images are relevant to what is being presented.

- Co-ordinate colours.

- Do not be distracting. Flashy colours, intricate images and complicated charts are only good if they are directly relevant.

Images with impact can gain the audience's attention, illustrate the point being made, explain something more clearly and make a point very strongly.

Web-based presentations

Web presentation tools and technologies provide the means to deliver any PowerPoint-based or similar type of visual presentation to an Internet-connected audience, no matter where participants are connecting. Most web presentation technologies do away with requiring end users to have an installed copy of Microsoft PowerPoint and increasingly offer not just the ability to digitally distribute such presentations but also to create them.

Using today's fast broadband connections, it is possible to stream sophisticated content to a computer anywhere in the world. This is an advantage for many people as the message can be received wherever and whenever it is convenient for them.

Multilingual support

On occasions in business, you may have to communicate or give a presentation to an audience where some members may be non-English speakers. In such circumstances, you should consider special arrangements for them such as a translation of presentation slides or handouts, and speak clearly for those who speak English only a little.

Activity: Presentation methods

The following list includes five situations that require a presentation method. Decide which method is the most appropriate and then state why.

1. Explain to foreign visitors to your organisation what markets your organisation operates within.

2. Inform people in your department about the financial performance of the business.

3. Show information to a branch of your organisation based in Canada.

4. Send a message to your sales force about negotiation skills.

5. Present to your staff changes in the way work is organised in the company.

Working in groups, discuss the different methods of presentation. Each group should then make a five-minute PowerPoint presentation to the class on their findings.

Functional skills

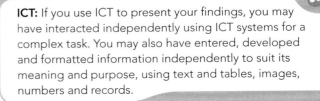

ICT: If you use ICT to present your findings, you may have interacted independently using ICT systems for a complex task. You may also have entered, developed and formatted information independently to suit its meaning and purpose, using text and tables, images, numbers and records.

2.2 What are the output requirements?

Output requirements refer to the technical information you need to know to make the best use of technology in a presentation. It is important to ensure that visual presentations are attractive to the eye and as easy to understand as possible. Important factors that you need to consider for improving presentation output include:

- resolution of images
- page layout
- text formatting
- use of tables
- combining information
- use of specialist software and hardware.

Resolution of images

Image resolution describes the detail an image holds. The term applies equally to digital images, film images and other types of images. Higher resolution means more image detail. Image resolution can be measured in various ways. Basically, resolution quantifies how close lines can be to each other and still be visibly resolved. Resolution units can be tied to physical sizes (for example, lines per inch) or to the overall size of a picture (for example, lines per picture height).

Page layout

Page layout is the part of graphic design that deals in the arrangement and style treatment of content on a page. With print media, elements usually consist of type (text), images and pictures. Since the advent of personal computing, page layout skills have expanded to electronic media as well as print media. The electronic page is better known as a graphical user interface (GUI) when interactive elements are included. Page layout for interactive media overlaps with interface design. This usually includes interactive elements and multimedia in addition to text and still images.

Some companies will have a 'house style' for particular documents (for example, trading reports or press releases). These documents will have a consistent look and feel, so the audience becomes familiar with the way in which the company presents information. This might mean that a particular font style and size should be used for body text, headings, captions and so on.

Many word-processing packages have paragraph and heading styles that are ready to use.

When producing a page layout, you should remember that your audience will find it much easier to read your document if it is well structured, uses clear headings and includes relevant images to break up the text.

Text formatting

Text formatting in Microsoft Word can add visual organisation, emphasis and structure. You can change the font, size, style, colour, spacing and vertical position of text, and add effects such as underlining. You can also control spacing and indentation, add bullets and numbers, and set alignment. You can apply formatting to either selected words or an entire paragraph. A general rule is that you can apply font properties such as font, size, colour, highlighting and effects to selected text, and paragraph properties such as alignment, bullets, numbering, shading and borders to entire paragraphs.

Key term

Text formatting – setting up the way a page of text will look by changing the fonts, bold or italic type, margins, indents, columns, tabs, headers and footers, and other attributes

Use of tables

When presenting ideas that include references to data, it can be helpful to make the point using a graph or table. These visual methods can make the point much stronger than simply describing the data. However, they also have the potential to ruin a presentation if they convey the wrong message or confuse the audience.

Graphs and tables can enhance the message you are delivering. Word processing software allows you to create tables in documents, or to import them from a spreadsheet. Tables can align information in columns and rows, so that it is all grouped neatly and is easy for your reader to interpret. This is useful for both figures and text where there should be a clear relationship between two or more columns.

Combining information

In preparing and gathering information, you will usually then have to arrange it into one document, maybe a report or PowerPoint slides ready for a presentation.

Your computer will be useful for this, as it is easy to copy and paste different information from various electronic sources into one document.

Use of specialist software and hardware

In making presentations, there are several computer programs that may help you to present your information. Microsoft Word is a versatile program that will help you to produce most printed business documents. However, if you wish to produce something more visually appealing, then a desktop publishing program such as Microsoft Publisher or Adobe InDesign can help to give a professional result.

2.3 How do you present corporate communication?

Corporate communication is the communication issued by an organisation to all its stakeholders such as employees, customers, agencies, channel partners, media, government, industry bodies and the general public. It can be described as the set of activities involved in managing all internal and external communications aimed at creating good impressions with stakeholders. Corporate communication consists of the dissemination or spreading of information by a variety of specialists and generalists in an organisation, with the common goal of enhancing people's perception of that organisation. Organisations can strategically communicate to their audiences through public relations and advertising. This may involve an employee newsletter or video, crisis management with the news media, special events planning, building product value and communicating with stakeholders and customers. An organisation can present corporate communications in ways such as:

- mission statements
- advertising
- packaging
- logos
- livery
- straplines
- endorsements
- sponsorship.

Key term

Corporate communication – activities undertaken by an organisation to communicate both internally with employees and externally with existing and prospective customers and the wider public

Mission statements

A mission statement is a statement that defines the essence or purpose of a company – what it stands for, such as what broad products or services it intends to offer customers. It should incorporate socially meaningful and measurable criteria addressing concepts such as the moral/ethical position of the enterprise, its public image, the target market, products/services, the geographic domain and expectations of growth and profitability.

The intent of the mission statement should be the first consideration for any employee evaluating a strategic decision. The statement can range from very simple to a very complex set of ideas. Below are extracts from two leading organisations' mission statements.

- 3M – 'To solve unsolved problems innovatively.'
- Walt Disney – 'To make people happy.'

Mission and values of Microsoft

As a company, and as individuals, we value integrity, honesty, openness, personal excellence, constructive self-criticism, continual self-improvement, and mutual respect. We are committed to our customers and partners and have a passion for technology. We take on big challenges, and pride ourselves on seeing them through. We hold ourselves accountable to our customers, shareholders, partners, and employees by honouring our commitments, providing results, and striving for the highest quality.

Functional skills

English: This activity allows you to read about business information using it to gather information, ideas, arguments and opinions.

Activity: Mission statement

Write a mission statement for a large chain of retail furniture shops. It may help to research existing businesses in this sector. Use the criteria above and include all elements in your mission statement.

Advertising

Advertising is a form of communication used to help sell products and services. Typically it communicates a message including the name of the product or service and how that product or service could benefit the consumer. It attempts to persuade potential customers to purchase or to consume more of a particular brand of product or service. Advertising can also be used to promote the business rather than the product or services the business sells.

Many advertisements are designed to generate increased consumption of those products and services through the creation and reinforcement of the 'brand image'. For these purposes, advertisements sometimes embed their persuasive message with factual information. There are many media used to deliver these messages, including traditional media such as television, radio, cinema, magazines, newspapers, video games, carrier bags, billboards, the post and Internet marketing.

Packaging

Packaging can be described as the enclosing or protecting of products for distribution, storage, sale and use. Packaging and package labelling have several objectives. They obviously have a role in physical protection of the product but they also present information with regard to disposal and storage of the packaging. From a corporate communication point of view, organisations can use packaging to encourage potential buyers to purchase the product. Package graphic design and physical design have been important and constantly evolving phenomena for several decades. Marketing communications and graphic design are applied to the surface of the package and (in many cases) the point of sale display.

Logos

A **logo** is the visual symbol of an organisation or brand. It might be the design of the brand name (such as the Coca-Cola or Cadbury's signature) or pure creation, such as the 'golden arches' yellow M that symbolises

Key term

Logo – symbol(s) or word(s) that carry the image of a company. Its function is to create a long-lasting, recognisable impression on the mind of a potential client or customer

What is the purpose of advertising?

McDonald's. It is a corporate communication mechanism that is fundamental to building a brand and communicating with the target audience. Logos are an integral part of a company's image and key to marketing success, so their quality is of highest importance for any business.

Livery

Livery and signage can be used effectively to reinforce and promote further a brand or the organisation – whether on vehicles, clothing, incentive items or signage. It is an extension of the brand and should not be overlooked. Company livery is an important part of an integrated corporate communication plan. Transport livery is the most common and successful form of this type of corporate communication.

Straplines

A **strapline** is a type of catchphrase for your business. Straplines are most commonly seen in adverts and on large signs; but they are useful for promoting a business message at many other times, and should really be put on the majority of business communications. Promotional material, letters, websites and business cards are four of the best places to show straplines.

The main aim of a strapline is to make existing and potential customers more aware of who the company is and what it does. A good strapline will be remembered, and will mean that people are more

likely to remember the company when they want products or services that the company provides. A good strapline can also remind customers of the qualities and aims of a business. This helps to maintain and spread the intended business image. One of the more famous straplines in the UK is Nestlé's 'Have a break, have a KitKat'.

Endorsements

Endorsement marketing is having famous or reputable people recommend your product or service to others, and can play an important part in corporate communication. Endorsers could be celebrities, star athletes, musicians and so on. A business usually chooses famous people who are related to the business and might actually use the product or service.

When proposing any endorsement deal, it is usually a win-win situation. The celebrity gets a fee and the hopefully the business's sales increase. David Beckham has endorsed numerous products over the last few years and earned sizeable fees in the process. The endorsement is usually used on all advertising and marketing material. An endorsement can increase sales fast, as it gives credibility to a company's product or service. People will usually believe a person they trust, who is not related to the business, before they will believe a representative of the company.

Sponsorship

An increasingly common form of promotional activity, which again is a form of corporate communication, is sponsorship. This is where a business supports an event, activity or another organisation by providing money or other resources that are of value to the sponsored event. This is usually in return for advertising space at the event or as part of the publicity for the event. There are television and radio programme sponsorship, sports sponsorship (such as the Barclays Premier League), educational sponsorship (such as Tesco's Computers for Schools scheme) and sponsorship of the arts.

Key terms

Livery – distinctive design and colour scheme used on a company's vehicles or products

Strapline – a term used as a secondary sentence attached to a brand name. Its purpose is to emphasise a phrase that the company wishes to be remembered by, particularly for marketing a specific corporate image or connection to a product or consumer base

Assessment activity 4.2

The Assessment activity requires you to investigate the effective presentation of business information.

For this assignment you will need either information that you have collected for outcome 4.1 or you can find new information that other organisations use. The following tasks relate to financial information but if you prefer you can use marketing, operational, manufacturing, human resource, logistics or transport information. Please check with your tutor to ensure the information you select is appropriate for the assignment.

1. Obtain financial information from your selected organisation and give a five-minute verbal presentation about what the financial information shows about the performance of the business or part of the business. Your verbal presentation should be suitable for a number of business journalists who want to report on the performance of the business. **P2**

2. Produce a brief written report on what the information shows about the performance of the business or part of the business. This report should be suitable for the directors or the senior management of the business and should include a spreadsheet or graph to help explain the financial situation. **P2**

3. Produce a leaflet, which is aimed at the staff of the business, telling them about the financial performance of the business or part of the business. The majority of the staff do not have any financial or accountancy knowledge. **P2**

4. Using the same organisation or any other of your choice, produce a corporate communication such as an advert, poster or leaflet communicating information about the business or one of its products or services. Your proposed audience will be the business's customers and potential customers. **P3**

5. Find an example of a real external corporate communication from your selected business and evaluate it as a means of corporate communication. This could be an advert they

have produced or a poster, leaflet, advertisement, packaging, logos, livery, straplines, endorsements or any sponsorship they may have undertaken. **P4**

6. Your final task is to evaluate the effectiveness of the business information and its communication as key contributors to the success of the organisation, using examples to illustrate your points. For this task you will need to research examples of effective business information and its communication in other businesses who are regarded as having effective systems of information and communication, as well as your selected organisation. You will then be able to draw some comparisons between examples of effectiveness in other businesses and your selected business. **D2**

Grading tips

1. Do not forget you can select any information from the organisation as long as it is suitable to be used to cover the criterion. **P2**

2. You have to show three presentation methods appropriate for the audiences. You cannot therefore present information to staff using technical language that they will not understand. **P2**

3. P3 is your chance to be creative in designing a corporate communication. Again, remember who it is aimed at. **P3**

4. It is important to remember that not all corporate communications are effective. Have you ever seen a billboard advert on a major road, which is very interesting and perhaps funny, but later been unable to recall what it was advertising? **P4**

5. Evaluating is about considering in detail the advantages and disadvantages of something, and coming to conclusions about this. The best companies in the world are very good at the way they communicate their information and this is a major contributor to the overall success of their organisations. **D2**

3. Understand the issues and constraints in relation to the use of business information in organisations

3.1 What are the legal issues?

There are various items of legislation (law) to protect the use of business information.

Data Protection Act 1998

Many businesses store and use information about people. The Data Protection Act protects the information held about people from being misused. The information stored by businesses on databases must be:

- obtained fairly and lawfully
- used only for the purposes stated during collection
- adequate, relevant and not excessive in relation to the intended use
- accurate and up to date
- not kept for longer than necessary
- processed in line with your rights
- subject to procedures to prevent unlawful processing, accidental loss, destruction and damage to personal data
- protected from transfer to an area outside the European Economic Area (EEA) unless adequate protection exists for that data in the area.

Freedom of Information Act 2000

The Freedom of Information Act came into effect in 2005. It provides individuals or organisations with the right to request information held by a public authority. The public authority must tell the applicant whether it holds the information, which it must supply within 20 working days, in the requested format.

There are some exemptions to this Act. For example, if the cost of a request for information exceeds an appropriate limit, the public authority may decide whether a greater public interest is being served by denying the request or supplying the information. If there is a dispute between an applicant and a public authority about a request for information, the Information Commissioner's Office may investigate and deem whether the information should be released or not.

Other relevant legislation

The Computer Misuse Act 1990 is a law in the UK that legislates against certain activities using computers, such as hacking into other people's systems, misusing software or helping a person to gain access to protected files on someone else's computer.

The Computer Misuse Act is split into three sections and makes illegal:

- unauthorised access to computer material
- unauthorised access to computer systems with intent to commit another offence
- unauthorised modification of computer material.

Activity: Start-up

A start-up company is developing a mail order giftware business and will use a computer system to hold details of customers and products ordered. The products will be advertised widely in the national press and magazines.

1. How can the business obtain income from this data?

2. What security issues would the company need to consider due to the large amount of customer information it may hold?

3.2 What are the ethical issues?

Codes of practice exist in organisations to maintain **business ethics** on:

- use of email
- Internet
- whistle-blowing
- organisational policies
- information ownership.

Key term

Business ethics – moral principles concerning acceptable and unacceptable behaviour by businesses

Use email:

- as a memo, BUT only where the text is short and to the point – the email is the electronic memo
- as a reminder/advance notice/flag of important meetings, information, and so on
- to ascertain availability for meetings, BUT only if electronic diaries are not used. Otherwise use the online meetings request facility
- to give standard information to a large group of people
- to flag where important/lengthy information is stored/being distributed, for example, public folder, Intranet, hard copy circulation when and from whom
- to gather views/initial reactions quickly (use the voting button facility)
- to disseminate urgent news rapidly
- as a telephone substitute, BUT only where a quick non-explanatory type of response, with no follow on is expected.

Do not use email:

- to send large documents/attachments, especially to large numbers of people (these are better stored in folders, on the Intranet, circulated by hard copy)
- to distribute committee papers (except for last-minute urgent late papers) as bulk reprography of papers needed in hard copy form is cheaper
- as a substitute for formal documents where construction, language and presentation are particularly important
- for long-term storage (save to networked or hard drives or delete)
- for complicated queries/ongoing dialogues/explanations (this often takes longer than oral or face-to-face contact and misconceptions can arise)
- as a substitute for face-to-face/telephone communication with colleagues (it is very important to maintain interpersonal relationships)
- to shirk responsibility, especially for difficult personal communications
- for really confidential information (hard copy delivered direct to the addressee in a sealed envelope is more secure).

Fig. 4.1: Email code of practice.

Use of email

Many organisations today have a code of practice on the correct use of email. Fig. 4.1 shows a typical example of a company's code of practice.

Internet

Many companies also have codes of practice on the use of the Internet and what their employees can and cannot use the Internet for. There are also codes of practice which govern selling on the Internet, which many businesses adhere to.

Whistle-blowing

A whistle-blower is an employee who raises a concern about a business practice – either to management within the company or to an outside organisation (for example, the press). The concern may relate to fraud, crime, danger or any other serious risk that could impact on customers, colleagues, shareholders, the public, the environment or the organisation's reputation. Whistle-blowers may receive legal protection through the Public Interest Disclosure Act, but the offence being reported must constitute a deliberate attempt to break the law.

Organisational policies

Organisations may have many **policies** to ensure that their businesses practices with regard to information can be done more ethically. This could be anything from how they manage information to ensuring marketing and other business practices are fair and just.

Key term

Policies – courses of action, guiding principles, or procedures considered expedient, prudent, or advantageous

Information ownership

The concept of information ownership is simple – if you create information in your day-to-day work, then you should be responsible for it. Suppose you write a report following a member of staff's annual review. This report is obviously confidential to some degree – it should only be viewed by a select group of people. Since you created the report, this makes you the information owner. As the information owner, you are responsible for protecting this document to an appropriate degree. If you own information, you have to protect the information's confidentiality and act with integrity when anything has to be altered with regard to the information.

3.3 What are the operational issues?

Organisations have to store and manage countless pieces of information, with some being far more important than others. Lying at the heart of any information system are two fundamental issues of ensuring that:

- the organisation receives the information it requires
- the appropriate member(s) of staff receives the information.

To make sure that information is managed appropriately, a number of policies and procedures have to be put in place, concerning:

- security of information
- backups
- health and safety
- organisational policies
- business continuance plans.

Security of information

Information security management deals with maintaining the integrity and availability of organisational information and knowledge. Much information security management focuses upon digital data; however, the subject also covers records and knowledge management.

It is important for businesses to have the right information available as and when they need it, in order to make good business decisions. For this reason, many companies keep their information on IT systems, but as the reliance on technology increases, so does the risk posed by system failure and malicious attacks (for example, viruses).

The IT security policy should take account of the common risks to the information that their business relies upon. This policy might include secure login identification for using IT systems and controls that limit access to information.

Backups

Large businesses have developed business continuity programmes to try to minimise the risk of losing vital business information stored on IT servers. This involves producing backups of information stored on the servers – some companies will create a backup every hour, while others will do so less frequently. This means that if the 'live' information is destroyed or damaged, a copy is available so the business can continue with as little disruption as possible.

Backups are stored on separate hardware from the live versions of the information. For example, a business might have a dedicated server to back up information.

Remember

Create backup copies of your work. This might seem like an inconvenience, but it could save you from having to rewrite your assignment from scratch.

This means that if the whole of the live system is affected, the backup information is not lost along with the live information.

Health and safety

Although it is unlikely that computer equipment will be dangerous in itself, it can be used in ways that can be a hazard to health of staff. Many office-based jobs require employees to spend a substantial portion of their working day sat at their desk, working on a computer. Bad posture, incorrect positioning of equipment and susceptibility to repetitive strain injury (RSI) are health and safety risks that employers are legally required to take seriously.

The Health and Safety (Display Screen Equipment) Regulations 1992, Management of Health and Safety at Work Regulations 1992, Provision and Use of Work Equipment Regulations 1992 and the Workplace (Health, Safety and Welfare) Regulations 1992 Acts all legislate the use of computer equipment.

Employers should carry out regular workstation assessments to make sure that computer screens are at the right level, and so on. If an employee suffers from RSI, they may be provided with ergonomic equipment (such as a keyboard or a mouse) which is designed to help reduce the risk of injury.

Organisational policies

Organisational policies that relate to the use of business information can help make sure that decisions affecting staff:

- are understandable and consistent
- meet legal requirements
- take full account of their impact
- contribute to productive working relationships.

Policies help make sure that staff have guidance to help them comply with legislation – for example, an organisational policy on the storage and usage of customer data should work within the requirements of the Data Protection Act. They should also help ensure that consistent decisions are made, which can be as important in internal communications as they are in handling customers.

Business continuance plans

Business continuance plans are the steps that a company puts into place to make sure it is capable of surviving a worst-case scenario. One step in the continuance programme might be to make sure

the company is producing regular backups of its information (see page 141).

The business might consider natural disasters (such as flooding or fire), accidents (such as human error) or malicious attacks (such as a deliberate breach of security, or hacking into the computer systems) in its planning. As a result of the plan, employees may need to change the way they work – for example, storing information on a central server rather than on their personal hard drive.

Costs

Most businesses would see the benefit of implementing some – if not all – of the measures listed. However, many aspects of information management can cost money – for example, while it may be desirable to store backup copies of electronic information on a remote server, a small business may not be able to justify this expense.

Ultimately, when deciding what policies to adopt and what measures to take, businesses need to consider the implementation and maintenance costs versus the benefits to the organisation. Some key considerations are:

- **additional resources needed** – would the business need to purchase new equipment or employ additional staff?
- **cost of development** – is the solution already available (for example, as an off-the-shelf product or a service), or will the company need to develop it themselves?

Increasing sophistication

One of the consequences of an increasing reliance on technology – and the increasing complexity of that technology – is that employees need to be trained to use the equipment and software required to do their job.

For example, a marketing organisation may have invested in bespoke complex customer relationship management software. The cost would be considered beneficial for the company because it would enable

Key term

Business continuance plans – the processes and procedures an organisation puts in place to ensure that essential functions can continue during and after a disaster

them to provide a better and more targeted service to their customers. However, in addition to the cost of developing and implementing the software, the business would need to make sure that all their staff were trained to use the software effectively. Without training, staff might not record customer contact correctly, or might miss out information, making the new system less effective.

Assessment activity 4.3

This Assessment activity is concerned with the issues and constraints in relation to the use of business information in organisations.

1. Use the organisation you have worked on throughout this unit or you can select another one. You have to explain the legal and ethical issues in relation to the use of information. The explanation needs to include how the business complies with current legislation and how it deals with ethical issues by means of policies and codes of practice. **P5**

2. Explain the operational issues in relation to the use of information. You can again use the same organisation or any other that is appropriate. **P6**

3. Analyse the legal, ethical and operational issues in relation to the use of business information, using appropriate examples. **M2**

Grading tips

1. Before completing this task, make sure you are familiar with various pieces of legislation as highlighted in the learning content and the ethical issues also in the learning content. You will then need to explain how the organisation administers these issues within the organisations. **P5**

2. Before completing this task, make sure you are familiar with possible operational issues as highlighted in the learning content. You will then need to explain how the organisation deals with these issues. **P6**

4. Know how to communicate business information using appropriate methods

A communicator will be able to adapt the content and manner of the communication to suit the different people receiving the information, whether this is written or verbal. We need to know the needs of the reader, or to obtain some idea of the composition of an audience before we prepare our communication. If you are preparing a presentation, for example, you need to know beforehand about the people likely to be in the audience. This will enable you to cater for the needs of everyone, including, for instance, someone who is partially sighted.

The demand for effective communication in the workplace is overwhelming and universal. Teachers, doctors, social workers, nurses, salespersons and managers are just a few of the workplace roles that demand effective communication if they are going to achieve anything. There are also some workplace roles in which skilled and effective communication is *the* primary core skill required. Being a manager is one of these.

Did you know?

Communicating is something that all managers, whatever their job titles or roles might be, are involved in, all of the time. Studies tell us that they can spend as much as 90 per cent of their time talking to others and almost a third of their time in one-to-one meetings. So being able to communicate effectively will make a considerable difference to your performance as a manager.

4.1 What are the audience's requirements?

In many encounters, the first few minutes are extremely important. First impressions have a great impact on the success of further communication. Everyone has expectations and norms as to how initial meetings should proceed and tends to behave according to these expectations. If interpersonal expectations are mismatched, communication will not run smoothly and there may be a need for negotiation if relations are to continue.

At a first meeting, formalities and appropriate greetings are usually expected, such as a possible handshake, an introduction of ourselves, eye contact and discussion around a neutral subject such as the weather or a journey. A friendly disposition and smiling face are more likely to encourage communication than a blank face, inattention or uninterested reception.

The audience's requirements will depend upon:

- age and attention span
- gender and ethnicity
- special needs and accessibility
- reading ability
- legibility
- interest
- distraction avoidance
- business-/industry-related experience and knowledge.

Age and attention span

Age and attention span have to be taken into consideration when communicating, especially with presentations and longer written documents. Consider your audience – how old are they? Younger people may have shorter attention spans than older people. Teenagers are likely to be more comfortable with using technology than pensioners.

The key to maintaining an audience's attention is variety – if a presentation or report is monotonous, the audience is likely to switch off. When thinking about how to keep your audience's attention, try to add structure to your information. Regular headings in a written document make it easier to read, and clear sections can improve a presentation's structure. Try to add some visual interest, too, such as photographs, or diagrams representing data.

Fig. 4.2: Make sure your message targets the right audience.

Gender and ethnicity

It can be easy to alienate some members of your audience accidentally by not representing them in examples. An audience is more likely to connect with your message if they see it as relating to them – even if this is a subconscious reaction.

When including examples in your communications, try to make sure they represent a balanced cross-section of your audience. Use examples that draw from the experiences of both men and women from different ethnic backgrounds positively.

Special needs and accessibility

You may need to adapt your communication depending on the needs of your audience. Large font sizes can help the partially sighted and you should remember this for PowerPoint presentations, handouts and other types of written communications. Some visually impaired learners also find certain colour combinations problematic, such as green and yellow, so you should avoid these.

You also have to consider where people are positioned in the room. People with hearing difficulties who lip read, for example, would need clear sight of your face. You should stand facing a lip reader at all times to give them maximum opportunity to receive your message. Also, those with mobility problems such as wheelchair users need wide aisles. If your presentation is to involve any sort of group activity, you might also consider grouping people so that a person with special needs works with co-operative group members.

Reading ability

You may need to adapt the language that you use for your audience. People with lesser reading ability will

Activity: Communication tools

1. Which of the following communication tools would assist people with special needs working in a business environment?
   - email
   - touch screens
   - Braille
   - sign language.
2. Using the above list as examples, identify which communication tools would assist people with the following disabilities:
   - partial sight
   - impaired hearing
   - motor disorders.

prefer you to use simpler language rather than jargon, whereas a more professional audience would expect you to use technical terms and phrases.

Legibility

Legible written material makes it easier for your audience to read. There are several factors that combine to make a document legible to the reader. Remember to consider not just your audience, but your presentation method.

Key term

Legible – able to be read or understood

If you are producing a written document, leave plenty of white space and do not produce pages that are just full of text. Use fonts that are suitable for written texts such as Arial or Times New Roman. Use font sizes of size 11 or 12. It may be appropriate to use one and a half or double line spacing, which makes the words easier to read.

Font sizes should be larger for slide presentations, and slides should be kept concise with only a few words. Use dark text on light backgrounds or the other way around.

Interest

One of the key methods to gain the interest of your audience is to get to the point quickly, and explain how the topic is relevant to them. Try to introduce variety, which helps maintain interest. Humour can also be used to good effect but be careful not to overdo it. Try to get the audience to participate by asking them questions or giving them problems to solve. You might need to know how interested your reader or audience actually is in the topic you are to communicate about. If they are already keen to hear what you have to say, then you do not need to work too hard to keep them interested, but sometimes audiences will need to be won over.

Distraction avoidance

If you are presenting information to an audience, remember to ask them to turn their mobile phones off and try to avoid – or reduce – any other distractions (such as the presentation taking place in a room overlooking a busy road).

Business-/Industry-related experience and knowledge

You must know your audience before you make a presentation. Inexperienced people will need you to explain everything. If you do not explain, they will not understand what you are saying. However, if you are presenting information to experienced business people who know the topic well, you do not need to cover the basics. In fact, if you do, your audience will probably not be paying attention by the time you get to the main part of your talk.

4.2 What are the methods of written communication?

There are different methods available to produce written communication, which has a number of differences from spoken communication. Written communication is rarely, if ever, written and read at the same time; it lasts over time, is able to be reused and duplicated, and can be revised before distribution. The various methods of written communication include:

- letter
- memorandum
- fax

- invoice
- flow charts
- publicity material
- email
- screen-based communication
- SMS (short message service)
- WWW (worldwide web).

Letter

Business letters have to reach high standards of communication as people outside the organisation judge the organisation by the letters its staff write. Letters have to be clear especially if they are issuing instructions. A letter could also give rise to legal liability if it is, for example, an acceptance of a contract. Fig. 4.3 shows an example of a business letter style. The following guidelines will help you.

- Introduction – say what the letter is about and why you are writing.
- Details – the main body of the letter should contain the information you wish to convey to your reader.
- The next step – tell your reader what they should do next in response to your letter.

Style

The style you use for your writing is important and can have a considerable influence upon how effective your writing is. You can, for example, write in ways that are:

- formal or informal
- general or particular
- specialised or lay (for those without expert knowledge)
- complex or simple

Radnor PLC
Head Office
27 Ring St
Newport
NP24 3ZT

Our ref: ST/RB

13th February 2010

Mrs D Strawbridge
Manager
Fencing Products Ltd
Wayne House
Church St
Cardiff
CF31 2RS

Dear Mrs Strawbridge,

Quotation for 6″ nails

Further to our telephone conversation on 20th January, I have pleasure in enclosing our quotation for the supply of 600,000 6″ nails.

I trust this quotation meets your requirements, but should you need any further information please do not hesitate to contact me. To place an order, please telephone our telesales order line 01892 668811 and quote the reference number on the attached quotation form.

Thank you very much for your enquiry. I look forward to hearing from you soon.

Yours sincerely,

David Lewis

David Lewis
Sales Co-ordinator

Enc.

Fig. 4.3: Example of a business letter.

- impartial or emotional
- reasoned or exhortative (urging readers).

When you choose a style in which to write a particular piece of text, you should take into account:

- the expectations and needs of the reader
- your relationship to those readers
- the nature of the document.

For example, the Managing Director of a company will adopt a certain style in writing a general letter to all of their employees but will use a different style in writing the annual report to the shareholders.

Make sure that your writing makes sense, and is no more complicated than it needs to be. People often assume that business communication needs to include complex phrases and long sentences, but this only results in impenetrable jargon. However, for a professional communication, you should use proper English and avoid slang or colloquialisms. The most important thing is to get the message through to your reader, so if something can be said clearly in ten words, say it clearly in ten words.

Memorandum

Internal memoranda are used for communication between different departments within the same organisation. These are often called memos.

Fig. 4.4 shows an example of a memo; they are normally shorter than a business letter and usually deal with one particular subject. They are not signed in the in the same way as a business letter.

Fax

Although since the widespread adoption of email they are used less frequently, faxes are still used in many businesses. A fax is a scanned document that is sent through a telephone line to a recipient. They can be used to send documents quickly if only a hard copy is available (for example, of a signed contract).

A cover sheet (including the name of the intended recipient and the sender) is usually faxed along with the message, and it is good practice to let the recipient know that you are sending a fax. Most offices only have one or a few fax machines, while they might have several hundred employees, so you need to make sure the message gets to the right person.

Invoice

An invoice is a detailed bill left by the sellers of goods and services. A typical invoice might list:

- the quantity of each item
- prices
- service description
- a contact address for payment.

MEMORANDUM

TO: Angela Preston (Department Manager)

FROM: Peter Smith (Administrative Supervisor)

DATE: 14th July 2009

SUBJECT: Health and Safety Training

The Health and Safety Department are running a number of courses for basic first aid; the first course is scheduled for the 15th and 16th August 2009. Our department needs at least three members of staff to be trained. We need to ask the staff if any would be interested in participating on this course.

I would be grateful if you could submit at least three names to me by the 20th July 2009 so that I may make the necessary cover arrangements and inform the Health and Safety Department of the staff involved.

Fig. 4.4: Example of a memorandum.

An invoice is a legal document, which can be used as evidence of an incurred debt. The recipient of the goods or services can challenge the legitimacy of individual charges, but the invoice itself is considered a bona fide debt. Sometimes a seller cannot collect on a bill immediately, so their company will send an invoice at a later date for payment. The actual daily expense of a service may be so low that a company will simply wait before sending a larger invoice to cover all of the costs at once. For example, vending machine attendants and bottled water providers may only send one invoice a month instead of billing the company a few pounds a day for supplies. An example of an invoice is shown in Fig. 4.5.

Paul's Car Parts Ltd

32 Church Road Tiltown Penshire
TZ3 2NR
Tel 0501 671285
Fax 0501 671286

INVOICE

Date/Tax Point 24th July 2009

To Purchasing Department VAT Reg. No
JL MOT Centre 324 233330
Lansborough

Order Number: 122116

Quantity	Catalogue Number	Description	Unit Price	Total Price
10	26932	Fiesta front brake pads	£21.00	£210.00
2	25781	Mondeo wing mirror	£25.00	£50.00
				£260.00
		Less trade discount @ 12%		£31.20
		Total excluding VAT		£228.80
		Add VAT @ 15%		£34.32
		Total Due		**£263.12**

Terms: 30 days
Carriage paid
E&OE

Fig. 4.5: Example of an invoice.

Flow charts

Flow charts are diagrams setting out the activities needed to complete a project. They may also include timescales. A flow chart can identify:

- how one activity may depend on the outcome of another
- the activities crucial to the successful completion of the project
- how long the project should take to complete.

Publicity material

Most organisations use publicity materials and although they vary greatly, they all carry certain essential qualities. They:

- have an eye-catching design
- inform the reader
- improve or promote the company's corporate image.

The amount of information included on publicity material will depend on the format of the material. For example, a flyer may only carry enough information to raise a customer's awareness of the company, while a brochure may include a full stock or service list, prices, a little information about the company and a range of methods for getting in touch with it.

Email

Emails are a common form of written communication in business and it is not unusual for a manager, or any staff member, to receive a hundred or more emails in a day. It is a quick way to communicate as preparing an email does not require any discussion or interaction. That does not mean that the content of the email is not produced from a lot of research or interaction, but the act itself of communicating via email is one-way. Once the email writer has sent the email they can then decide when or if they will continue the communication (for example, reading and replying to any responding email).

The biggest difficulty with emails is that they are not personal. How they are interpreted is very much down to the reader. The literary skills of the email writer will

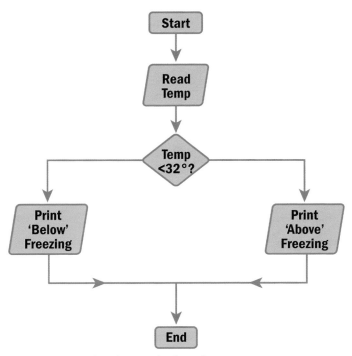

Fig. 4.6: Example of a simple flow chart.

also determine whether their message is portrayed exactly as they intended. What one person sees as factual and precise could be read by someone else as blunt and rude.

Emails can very quickly result in monologues where misunderstandings escalate and what could have been a short conversation ends up consuming far more time and energy as people carefully construct their email replies.

Screen-based communication

Screen-based communication can be read on computer monitors and on television screens. This might include publicity material (such as a website), emails (which are often read in electronic format only) or electronic copies of letters.

SMS (short message service)

Text messaging is increasingly common in business, and provides organisations with a more creative way of staying in touch with their customers. These can have a variety of uses.

- Reminders for appointments (for example, a dentist appointment) can be sent to customers 24 hours in advance.

- Some local councils encourage voters to confirm their voting registration details (if they are correct)

Functional skills

ICT: If you use ICT to present your findings in the activity below, you may have interacted independently using ICT systems for a complex task. You may also have entered, developed and formatted information independently to suit its meaning and purpose using text and tables, images, numbers and records.

Activity: Order forms

1. Collect five order forms. They can be from catalogues, the Internet or from newspapers. Write down why you think they are effective in collecting the information required. Issues to consider include:

    - the possibility of information being entered incorrectly

    - whether the forms require too much information or not enough.

2. Using your five forms as examples, list the points you consider important when designing a form.

3. Using a computer graphics package, design a form that could be used by an online clothing company. Make sure the form is clear and concise and all aspects of required information are catered for. You should keep in mind how quick and easy the form is to fill in.

by text message, rather than returning a signed form.

- Special promotional codes can be sent to a mobile phone, which may entitle a customer to special discounts on production of the message.

- Many travel companies now enable customers to have real-time travel information sent to their mobile, so they know if there are likely to be any delays on their journeys.

WWW (worldwide web)

The worldwide web has revolutionised business, and the increasing availability of broadband across the UK (and the rest of the world) has boosted the range of services offered. Many companies have now gone global from a relatively small base, and manage their relationships with their customers in much more sophisticated ways as a result of their Internet presence.

Internet technology, such as **cookies**, has enabled websites to deliver a much more customised experience to customers. For example, online stores such as Amazon.co.uk will suggest new products to a returning customer based on the items they looked at on their last visit.

> **Key term**
>
> **Cookies** – small pieces of computer code that record a user's data so they do not have to enter the same information each time they visit a site

> **Did you know?**
>
> Nearly three-quarters of businesses in Europe use email as a form of online communication tool.

4.3 What are the methods of non-written communication?

Telephone call

Communicating via the phone is more personal than email, so there is less scope for misinterpretation. With the prevalence of mobile phones, and staff often being distributed around various locations, it is a necessity in business to communicate via the phone. By using the phone, a message can quickly be communicated, making it a powerful business tool. It does not, however, replace face-to-face communication. Speaking to someone in person allows you to interpret any non-verbal communication; perhaps their body language suggests they are unhappy with the situation. Likewise, if the information to be communicated is difficult or unpleasant for the receiver, such a conversation over the telephone can seem impersonal.

Video conferencing

Some companies with more than one office use video conferencing to save travelling time and cost. Video conferencing basically allows people at two or more

different locations to see each other while talking. This can help if visual information is to be displayed (such as a slideshow). It is also easier for the participants to keep track of who is saying what than it would be if the meeting was held as a teleconference.

4.4 What technology is used for communication?

Technology has changed the ways in which businesses can communicate, and there is a wide range of tools available.

Computers

Computers are essential to modern business and enable businesses to use email, multimedia presentations, websites, instant messaging and so on, as well as newer services, such as Twitter.

Touch screens

Touch screens are often used for information points, or to create intuitive (easy to use) interfaces for customers. For example, many job centres now display all their vacancies on touch-screen hubs that allow users to refine their searches and pick areas of the country for a job search.

Some tourist information locations will also display information on touch screens. Self-service checkouts at supermarkets often use touch-screen technology, giving a large display for customers as well as a relatively easy-to-use interface.

Digital broadcasting

Digital broadcasting television services, such as Sky and Freeview, allow viewers to interact with programmes and services provided by a broadcaster. For example, viewers can find more information, or added extras, for some programmes by pressing the red button.

> **Key term**
>
> **Digital broadcasting** – a more efficient way of transmitting sound and pictures by turning them into computerised data, meaning more TV and radio services and new interactive services can be broadcast than by using the analogue system

Case study: Online bookshop

A small bookshop in a rural town has put some of their business online. They receive a lot of enquiries regarding specific books from their customers who have seen their website. The owner has informed the staff that telephone calls are to be answered within three rings. On some occasions, the owner has noticed that this policy has been ignored, resulting in some calls being missed or customers becoming irritated due to long response times.

Some of the staff have not handled the calls as well as they should and respond badly to customers.

They also neglect to record customer details correctly. The owner therefore believes the staff need some advice on how to handle telephone calls.

1. What suggestions would you give to the staff working at the bookshop?
2. Write a paragraph stating how you would deal with an irate customer who has become irritated due to their telephone call not being answered quickly.

DVD

DVDs have replaced video as the most-used visual medium. They allow businesses to provide high-quality video, supported by extra features, or can be used to store more data than a CD-ROM for computer programs. DVDs are comparatively cheap to duplicate and distribute, and the technology to play them is widespread (most new computers can play DVDs, and many TVs now include built-in DVD players).

However, DVD may soon be replaced as high-definition (HD) technology becomes more widespread.

Blu-ray eventually won the HD format war, and so is likely to be the successor for DVDs.

Mobile phones

Mobile phones enable people to keep stay in touch, even if they are out on the road. Naturally, this has proved an important development for businesses, enabling sales representatives to stay in touch and field queries from one customer while on the way to see another customer. The advent of smartphones that include email functionality has helped increase

Where can you find touch screens?

productivity, although it has created an 'always on' culture in some businesses.

Mobile phones can also be used for communicating messages to customers, as we have seen (page 149).

The Internet and WAP (wireless application protocol)

The Internet has revolutionised the way we communicate, giving people access to free web-based email accounts, allowing companies and individuals to disseminate information through websites and blogs, and increasingly allowing us to stay connected through social networks.

More and more people are beginning to use the Internet on their mobile devices. This is enabled through wireless application protocol (WAP), which allows website designers to optimise sites to work on mobiles. Websites like www.bbc.co.uk work well on full-size screens, but if reproduced on a mobile screen would be unreadable and difficult to use. If you visit this site on a mobile device, you are automatically redirected to www.bbc.co.uk/mobile, which allows you to access the same content, but uses a different presentation format.

Activity: Computer sales

You are working as a computer salesperson at a large retail outlet. A potential customer comes in, who works from home as a graphic designer and wishes to upgrade their existing computer system in order to improve their internal and external communications. At present they have a basic computer to assist with the design work and a landline telephone. The customer wants to be able to use any communication tools in and out of the office.

1. What communication tools would you advise they purchased?

2. Discuss the advantages and disadvantages of any recommended communication tools.

Activity: Choosing communication methods

Look at the following situations and suggest the best communication method for each one.

- A customer has requested a copy of an important document – they need it immediately if they are going to make a decision to purchase from the company.

- You urgently need to speak to a supplier today who is currently occupied.

- You need to order some office stationery from a new supplier for next-day delivery.

- You need to contact a customer who is expecting a delivery today and inform them the goods will be delayed.

4.5 What communication skills are required?

Formal or informal

Not all business communication is formal. Official correspondence, such as letters to customers, or business reports, use a formal structure and professional language (see page 145).

However, a lot of communication within an organisation is informal. Impromptu conversations between colleagues, most emails, text messages and instant messaging are often informal. Informal communication does not follow a prescribed structure, and may not be recorded (for example, minutes may not be produced for some informal meetings).

Verbal or non-verbal

Communication in any context can be verbal, non-verbal or a mixture of both.

Verbal

Verbal communication is communication that involves the voice. The most obvious method of this is the telephone, where only the voice is used, but this category also includes presentations, meetings, video conferencing and so on.

Activity: Telephone communication

1. Make a list of situations where you have communicated over the telephone and given either good and/or bad service to the person on the other end.

2. List examples of what points you answered well or not so well under each heading as follows.

Answered well	Answered badly

You may want to include issues such as tone of voice, polite and courteous manner, rude and hostile, or customer left hanging on the telephone for a long time.

Functional skills

English: This activity allows you to read about business information using it to gather information, ideas, arguments and opinions.

Non-verbal

Non-verbal communication relates to anything that communicates without, or in addition to, verbal communication. This might be paper-based, such as letters, memos or business reports, or screen-based, such as presentation slides or emails.

Did you know?

Research shows that the overall effectiveness of verbal and non-verbal communication between two people can be calculated as follows:

- language used: 7 per cent effective
- tone of voice: 38 per cent effective
- body language: 55 per cent effective.

Non-verbal communication also consists of a complete package of expressions, hand and eye movements, postures and so on, which should be interpreted along with speech. All forms of interpersonal communication that are not expressed verbally are called non-verbal communications. These include:

- body movements

- posture
- eye contact
- paralanguage (such as tone, hesitations, gestures)
- closeness or personal space
- facial expressions
- physiological (body) changes.

When we communicate, non-verbal cues can have greater impact on the listener than the spoken word.

Activity: Types of communication

Identify the different types of communication used every day by:

- a receptionist at a busy hospital
- a retail manager of a large furniture shop
- a salesperson travelling to customers in a defined area of the UK
- a newspaper reporter.

Guidelines for improving communication skills

- Present information in a way that its meaning can be clearly understood. Pay particular attention to differences in culture, past experiences, attitudes, abilities and so on before sending a message.
- Focus on the meaning of what you want to communicate. Aim to increase understanding

by considering how your message might be received.

- Encourage open and honest feedback from the receiver to ensure your message is understood and to avoid the receiver feeding back what they think you want to hear.
- Offer your personal viewpoint clearly and honestly to avoid confusion.
- Consider the emotional effect (for example, emotional stress) of what you are saying and communicate within the norms of behaviour acceptable to the other person (avoiding taboos).
- Avoid jargon and over-complicated language. Explain things as simply as possible. Request clarification if unclear about a message.
- Try to use language which you know will be understood. Use technical language cautiously and only when you are sure it will help communication.
- Avoid racist/sexist terms or language that may offend.
- Aim to communicate on an equal basis and avoid patronising people. You should be aware that a person in a client role may be feeling vulnerable and, therefore, if a worker communicates a superior attitude, this may do irreparable damage. Someone seeking help is unlikely to warm to such a worker.
- Try to ensure that everyone in an interaction is included, through effective body language and the use of open questions.
- If confidentiality is an issue, make sure that it is maintained and boundaries are known.
- Beware of giving unnecessary criticism as this can influence the perceived status between participants.

Did you know?

Ray Birdwhistell (1918–1994) was an American anthropologist who estimated that the face is capable of 250,000 different expressions.

The importance of communication skills in interpersonal relationships cannot be stressed too greatly. An understanding of the factors that influence communication and the possession of effective communication skills are necessary to anyone working in a business. The different types of non-verbal

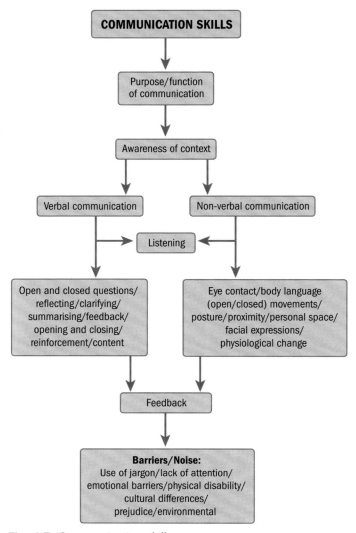

Fig. 4.7: Communication skills.

messages are equally important, and lead to a greater understanding of communication between people. To be an effective communicator, you should not only take into consideration the verbal aspects, but also the non-verbal component of the message.

Listening

Listening is a vital communication skill, but is more complex than it may seem. There is a big difference between hearing something and listening to it – listening requires an understanding of the message being communicated. In addition to this, the message may not just be in the words of the speaker; their body language may tell you more than the words, or a different story entirely.

Active listening is a very important listening skill, yet people tend to spend far more energy considering what they are going to say rather than listening to what the other person is trying to say. The following points are essential for effective listening.

- Arrange a comfortable environment conducive to the purpose of the communication, for example, warmth, light.
- Be prepared to listen.
- Keep an open mind. Concentrate on the main direction of the speaker's message.
- Avoid distractions if at all possible.
- Delay judgement until you have heard everything.
- Be objective.
- Do not think of your next question while the other person is giving information.
- Do not dwell on one or two points at the expense of others.
- Do not stereotype the speaker. Try not to let prejudices associated with, for example, gender, ethnicity, social class or dress interfere with what is being said.

As well as listening for what is being said, listen for what is not being said. Try not to leap to conclusions, and instead ask questions respectfully and patiently. Through active listening and questioning, you can often get a more complete understanding of the information.

Activity: A happy event

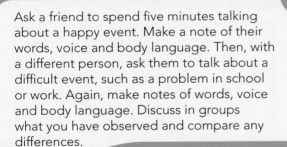

Ask a friend to spend five minutes talking about a happy event. Make a note of their words, voice and body language. Then, with a different person, ask them to talk about a difficult event, such as a problem in school or work. Again, make notes of words, voice and body language. Discuss in groups what you have observed and compare any differences.

Understanding

When you are communicating a message to an audience, it is vital that your message is understood. It is common practice to leave time at the end of a presentation for questions from the audience – although the success of this sometimes depends on the audience's ability to listen during the presentation.

An alternative approach for checking your audience has understood your message is to ask them

Activity: Observing communication

When you have the opportunity to observe communication, make a mental note of the behaviours used, both verbal and non-verbal. If this is not possible, you could examine some of the different ways interpersonal relationships are conveyed on the television.

Make notes of your observations about the following.

- Who are the communicators?
- What messages were exchanged?
- What (if any) noise distorts the message?
- How is feedback given?
- What is the context of the communication?

questions. This could be done either at the end of the presentation, throughout the key points of the presentation, or through providing a multiple-choice question paper at the end of the presentation.

As with choosing a method of communication, you need to consider your audience and message when choosing a method of checking their understanding. If you were pitching a new product to a board of directors, you probably would not set them a quiz at the end of your presentation.

Seeking clarification

As part of your listening and understanding skills, seeking clarification is essential. If you doubt that you have understood something fully, ask questions to make sure you are confident in your understanding. Asking questions is a sign of strength rather than weakness – you know yourself well enough to identify areas for improvement – and something that businesses value.

Effective questioning is an essential skill, as it can be used to:

- obtain information
- start a conversation
- test understanding
- draw someone into a conversation
- show interest in a person
- seek support or agreement.

There are two types of questions: closed questions and open questions.

Closed questions tend to seek only a one- or two-word answer and, in doing so, limit the scope for answering. For example, 'How many weeks have you been out of work?' or 'Would you like to see a counsellor?' These types of question mean the questioner maintains control of the communication, which is often not the desired outcome in a helping relationship. Nevertheless, closed questions are useful for focusing discussion and obtaining clear answers when needed.

Open questions broaden the scope for answering, as they demand further discussion. For example, 'Having indicated that losing your job has affected your home life, which areas do you feel have been most affected?' or 'What do you feel you would like to gain from this counselling session?' Open questions will take longer to answer, but they do give the other person far more scope for self-expression and encourage their involvement in the conversation.

Reflecting is the process of feeding back to another person your understanding of what they have said. Although reflecting is a specialised skill, it can also be applied to a wide range of communication contexts. It involves paraphrasing, for example, which means putting the message communicated into your own words, at the same time as capturing the essence of the facts and feelings expressed. It is a useful process because:

- you can check you have understood clearly
- the speaker gets feedback as to how their message has been received
- it shows an interest and respect for what the other person has to say, as you are demonstrating that you are considering the other person's viewpoint.

Responsiveness

As a communicator, you need to respond to the needs of your audience. Choosing an appropriate level and delivery method for your information is only part of considering your audience's needs. If it becomes clear that they need more information or if you find that their knowledge on the topic is less developed than you thought, you should respond by providing them with more information or simpler explanations.

Eye contact

Eye contact is an important aspect of non-verbal behaviour. In interpersonal interaction, it serves three main purposes.

- **To give and receive feedback** – Looking at people lets them know that the receiver is concentrating on the content of their speech. When eye contact is not maintained, this might indicate lack of interest. Communication may not be a smooth process if a listener averts their eyes too frequently.

- **To let a partner know when it is their 'turn' to speak** – This is related to the above point. Eye contact is more likely to be given continuously by a listener than a speaker. When a person has finished what they have to say, they will look directly at the other person, which gives a signal that the arena is open. If someone does not want to be interrupted, eye contact will be avoided. Good eye contact is an important practice for anyone counselling a client.

- **To communicate something about a relationship between people** – When you dislike someone, you tend to avoid eye contact and pupil size is often reduced as well. The maintenance of positive eye contact signals attraction or interest in a partner.

Activity: Nodding experiment

Experiment with nodding in the following ways during a conversation.

1. A colleague at work gives you eye contact and draws you into a conversation. Do not nod at any point in response. Note whether they end the conversation abruptly or change the subject.

2. Next time you meet, make sure you nod your head at every cue. Does your colleague react differently now? Has your different response to the conversation encouraged them to talk at greater length?

Although this is a simple exercise, it will demonstrate how positive feedback helps to make people more confident about what they are saying and encourages them to go on talking.

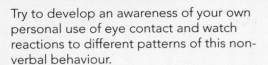

Activity: Eye contact

Try to develop an awareness of your own personal use of eye contact and watch reactions to different patterns of this non-verbal behaviour.

Observe two other learners interacting with each other and write down what you learn from your observations of their eye contact.

Facial expression

Your facial expression says a lot about how you are feeling. While you might be giving a confident pitch to investors, your facial expression might betray any nervousness or uncertainty that you are feeling.

Some speakers like to practise in front of a mirror, but you will probably find it more natural to record a short presentation. Keep an eye out for anything you do that you think your audience might find distracting. For example, do you wrinkle your brow when making serious points, or look nervous when you should be confident? What can you do to correct these behaviours before you do your presentation?

Body language

Many psychologists believe that body language can give away someone's true thoughts and feelings. Some of the traits to be aware of are below.

Body movements (kinesics)

These include gestures, posture, head and hand movements or whole body movements. Body movements can be used to reinforce or emphasise what a person is saying. They also offer information about the emotions and attitudes of a person. However, it is possible for body movement to conflict with what is said. A skilled worker may be able to detect such discrepancies in behaviour and use them as cues to a client's real feelings. A number of categories of body movements exist, as follows.

- **Emblems:** Gestures that serve the same function as a word – for example, the hand movement used when hitchhiking.
- **Illustrators:** Gestures which accompany words – for example, nodding the head in a particular direction when saying 'over there'.

- **Affect displays:** Facial expressions or gestures which show the emotions we feel. These are often unintentional and can conflict with what is said. Such expressions give strong cues as to the true emotional state of a person.
- **Regulators:** Gestures used to give feedback when conversing – for example, head nods or short sounds such as 'uh-huh' or 'mm-mm'. Regulators allow the other person to adapt their speech to reflect the level of interest or agreement. Without receiving feedback, people would find it difficult to maintain a conversation.
- **Adaptors:** Non-verbal behaviours which either satisfy some physical need such as scratching or adjusting uncomfortable glasses, or represent a psychological need, such as biting fingernails when nervous. Although normally subconscious, they are more likely to be restrained in public places. Adaptive behaviours often accompany feelings of anxiety or hostility.

Did you know?

Cultural differences in body language are many and are changing all the time. We are now exposed to these other cultural differences through the Internet, travel and movies. Mario Pei, a linguist, once estimated that there are 700,000 gestures and signals used by people all over the world, and it has been said that there are only six that are truly universal: happiness, sadness, anger, fear, surprise and disgust.

Posture

Posture can reflect people's emotions, attitudes and intentions. Research has identified a wide range of postural signals and their meanings.

Consideration will be given to two forms of posture, termed 'open' and 'closed', which may reflect an individual's degree of confidence, status or receptivity to another person. Someone seated in a closed position might have their arms folded, legs crossed or be positioned at a slight angle from the person with whom they are interacting. In an open posture, you might expect to see someone directly facing you with hands apart on the arms of the chair. An open posture can be used to communicate openness or interest to someone and a readiness to listen, whereas the closed posture might imply lack of interest.

After leaving school, Aleisha was undecided what career path to follow. Eventually, she decided to undertake the BTEC National Business Diploma. This gave her a wide understanding of the business world and, in particular, she enjoyed the advertising and communications units. Aleisha sees the decision to take this course as important as it gave her time and understanding to establish where her skills and abilities lay – such as those of working with people.

After completing the Diploma, and having initially decided against going to university, Aleisha decided to have a gap year before making a final decision. She secured a job at a call centre. One of the appealing features of the job was the ongoing training in communications skills.

After twelve months at the centre, Aleisha decided to study communications at university. The gap year and experience had paid off, as she was able to work part-time in the call centre on weekends and during holidays.

During her time at the call centre, Aleisha had learned to answer the telephone, deal with customer enquiries and had undergone training associated with verbal communication. On leaving university with a degree in communication studies, Aleisha has held several posts in call centres, but is now working at the Police Headquarters in the 999 services as a supervisor.

The job can be demanding and stressful, but counselling has helped her overcome her emotions and deal with each crisis in hand. Six months ago, the call centre was awarded recognition for excellence and this has been a great achievement for Aleisha and her colleagues. Training took four weeks and each new member of staff has a mentor – Aleisha herself is mentor to three new members of staff. She took an NVQ Level 4 in police call handling while she was working, and has found this specific course useful in dealing with distressed callers. The call centre is extremely busy with over 2,000 calls a day and Aleisha deals with an assortment of enquires covering emergency, crime recording and general information. Aleisha considers that her BTEC Diploma and university degree have been invaluable and helped her secure a supervisory position at the call centre.

Think about it!

1. Which communication skills would you suggest are important when dealing with 999 calls? (Remember you are working as a team with other people.)

2. Working in groups, compare the differences between working in the public sector and the private sector. Each group should make a five-minute presentation to the class on their findings.

3. Look up two current communications jobs advertised on the Internet. Evaluate the skills needed to be able to go for these jobs.

Mirroring is another postural signal. Notice the way a loving couple relate to each other. You might like to observe a close relationship on television. You will see that the partners' posture will match, as if one partner reflects the other. For example, if one partner drapes an arm over the back of a chair this might be replicated in the other person's position. If one partner frowns, it could be reflected in the other partner's facial expression. This mirroring indicates interest and approval between people, and serves to reassure others of interest in them and what they are saying.

Use of appropriate professional language

Formal and informal communications require different standards for language and presentation. Formal communication methods (for example, letters, business reports, presentations) should follow particular conventions, and require more formal, business-like language. As discussed on page 152, business communications do not need to be full of jargon, and messages should be conveyed simply and effectively, but you should think carefully about how you choose to do this.

For example, as an information communication method, you might text a friend to say 'U want 2 go 2 ftbl 2mrow?' However, if you were sending a message on behalf of the football club, you might send out a letter (giving more than 24 hours' notice), addressing the recipient using 'Dear', giving a brief description of the purpose of the letter and any necessary details, before closing the letter with 'Yours sincerely' (if you know the recipient's name, otherwise it would be 'Yours faithfully').

Ability to adapt communication techniques to audience requirements

Not all communication techniques will suit all audiences. When planning how you are going to present information to your audience, it is important to tailor your approach – this will give you the best chance of successfully communicating the information.

Remember, when choosing the format of your delivery, the potential technology to use, the language and level of complexity, your first concern should always be with your audience. Always ask yourself how your audience will feel about any of the decisions you are considering.

Presentation skills

Many people feel terrified when asked to make their first public talk. However, some initial fears can be allayed by good preparation, which will also help to make an effective presentation.

A presentation is a means of communication which can be adapted to various speaking situations, such as talking to a group, addressing a meeting or briefing a team. To be effective, you must consider step-by-step preparation and the method and means of presenting the information.

> ### Remember
> A presentation concerns getting a message across to the listeners and may contain a 'persuasive' element, for example, a talk about the positive work of your organisation.

The audience

Before preparing material for a presentation, consider your prospective audience. Tailoring your talk to the audience is important and you should consider:

- the size of the group or audience expected
- the age range (see page 144)
- gender (will the audience be predominantly male or female?)
- whether it is a captive audience or there from interest
- if you will be speaking in their work or leisure time
- whether they know something about your subject already or if it will be totally new to them (is the subject part of their work?)
- you are there to inform, teach, stimulate or provoke.

It is important to have as much advance information as possible about the place where you are going to speak. Ideally, try to arrange to see the venue before the speaking event, as it can be of great benefit to be familiar with the surroundings. It does much to reduce fear if you can visualise the place while you are preparing your talk. Additionally, it would also give you the opportunity to try out your voice. If at all possible, you need to know:

- the size of the room
- the seating arrangements and if they can be altered

- the availability of equipment, for example, video recorder, slide projector, overhead projector, flip chart
- the availability of PowerPoints and if an extension lead is required for any equipment you intend to use
- if the room has curtains or blinds, if you intend to use visual aids, or to ensure the correct ambience for your presentation
- the position of the light switches – check if you need someone to help if you are using audio/visual equipment and need to turn off the lights
- the likelihood of outside distractions, such as noise from another room

- the availability of parking facilities.

Irrespective of whether the occasion is formal or informal, always aim to give a clear, well-structured delivery. You should know exactly what you want to say and the order in which you want to say it. Clarity of ideas and good organisation should result in a lively, logical and compelling message. Organising the material may include:

- creative thinking – jot down all your ideas
- selecting the main points – introduction, main content, conclusion
- deciding whether to illustrate.

Case study: Presentation trouble at Paintocare Ltd

Peter had just been promoted to a position as a junior member of the marketing team at Paintocare Ltd, which manufacture paints for the automotive industry. He was asked by his line manager to give a presentation to the Marketing Director, the three Product Managers (of whom his line manager is one) and the three Sales Managers about a new type of hardwearing paint. Peter was very nervous about this as his only previous presentations have been to staff on the shop floor. With two weeks before the preparation, he decided that he would start preparing for the presentation the following week.

Before doing any planning, he decided to adopt an informal approach similar to the way he had presented to shop floor staff. Peter had been given a significant amount of information about the new paint, which was contained in a document wallet. He thought he had left it somewhere in his office, and was sure he would be able to lay his hands on it the following week.

His line manager told him that the presentation would take place in training room 3. Peter had never been in this room but assumed it was similar to training rooms 1 and 2, which he had seen and were suitable for presentations and equipped with laptops and plenty of chairs and desks. He decided to use PowerPoint for the presentation, as he felt comfortable with this.

The following week was very busy for Peter and he spent the majority of his time firefighting administrative problems. The week leading up to the presentation was equally busy and it was also his girlfriend's birthday, so he had to book a restaurant table and buy a present. The presentation was to take place on Friday morning and Peter decided that on Wednesday, he must

spend all day in his office and not get involved in other activities.

On Wednesday he began his preparation by looking for the document folder but it was nowhere to be found. Peter began to panic. He did manage to retrieve some of the information from his computer, but important information about price and target market were held elsewhere in an area that he did not have access to. On Thursday evening he had to go out with his girlfriend but he could not enjoy himself as his mind was on the presentation the following day which was only partially ready.

On Friday morning Peter put his PowerPoint slides in order and dashed off to work. He decided to go to training room 3 early to make sure everything was in place. When he entered the room he found it only had four chairs and desks. It was next to a busy road and the traffic could be heard even with the windows closed. There was no laptop in the room so he had to run around other departments trying to find another laptop.

At 10.00 a.m. Peter was to begin his presentation and the managers arrived just before 10.00 a.m. When they arrived, they saw Peter dragging extra chairs into the room, flustered and stressed. Eventually, he commenced his presentation. It was not paced well and did not cover important points that the audience were interested to hear about.

1. What mistakes did Peter make in preparing for this presentation?

2. How should he have planned this presentation?

3. What impression may the senior managers have gained of Peter?

Beware of the following behavioural bad habits that may let you down when you are nervous.

- While speaking, try to keep a tall, relaxed, open stance without hanging on to a table or lectern or trying to hide behind it. If using cue cards, do not wave them around, but keep them in one hand while gesturing with the other.

- Avoid putting your hands in your pockets, as you may start to fiddle with the contents, which will be distracting to the audience.

- Try not to hop from one foot to the other or rock backwards and forwards on the balls of your feet.

- Do not stare fixedly at one person in the room or pretend the audience is not there and talk to the ceiling or the floor.

- Do not fiddle with pens, buttons, jewellery, a tie or hair.

Ability to invite commitment to shared goals

Many presentations require the presenter to persuade others to accept a proposal or perhaps a change to working practices. In order for this to succeed, the presenter should be able to:

- clearly articulate their argument – as a general rule, people do not like change, but they are more likely to embrace it if they can see the benefits

- demonstrate honesty – if your audience feels they cannot trust you, they may not agree with your message

- answer any questions – be prepared for questions by looking at your presentation critically; if you were in the audience, what would you ask?

Assessment activity 4.4

This Assessment activity requires you to investigate communication using appropriate methods.

With reference to your chosen organisation and any other organisations, you have to outline the various electronic and non-electronic methods for communicating business information, using examples for different types of audience. **P7**

Grading tip

There are many different types of both electronic and non-electronic methods of communication. You need to consider these in relation to their suitability for different types of audience. **P7**

Just checking

1. Describe three presentation methods to meet the needs of the user.
2. Why are text formatting and page layout important aspects of written communication?
3. Why is a mission statement a very important part of corporate communications?
4. Of what benefit can sponsorship be in terms of corporate communications?
5. What are the principal requirements of the Data Protection Act 1998?
6. Why is it important that a business takes account of ethical issues?
7. Why is it important for organisations to have policies to govern their use of business information?
8. Why is it important for an organisation to have a code of practice on the use of email?
9. Why is it important to know the characteristics of the audience that you are communicating to?
10. When is it appropriate to send a memorandum as a means of communication?
11. How important is non-verbal communication? Give reasons.
12. What do you think is the most important part of the process in preparing to give a presentation?

edexcel

Assignment tips

When presenting information to your audience, take some time to think about structure. An argument is much more persuasive – and easier to absorb – if it follows a logical sequence. Some key points to consider are as follows.

- Tell your audience what you are going to tell them, tell them, and then tell them what you told them. You are not writing a thriller, so make sure that the line of your argument is clear from the start.

- Think about the logic of your sequence. What information does your audience need in order to understand each stage of your presentation fully?

- Leave time for questions, but also think about appropriate points for questions. Is your presentation complex? If so, it might be better to have regular gaps for questions so your audience does not get lost.

- Remember business continuity (page 142) – prepare for the unexpected. What happens if there is a problem with the computer, or technology fails you for some reason? How can you limit the impact?

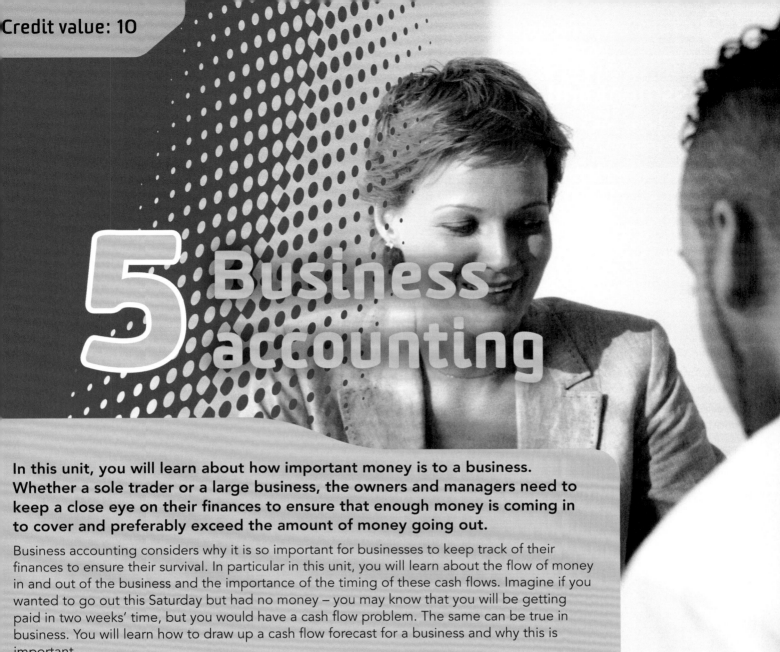

5 Business accounting

In this unit, you will learn about how important money is to a business. Whether a sole trader or a large business, the owners and managers need to keep a close eye on their finances to ensure that enough money is coming in to cover and preferably exceed the amount of money going out.

Business accounting considers why it is so important for businesses to keep track of their finances to ensure their survival. In particular in this unit, you will learn about the flow of money in and out of the business and the importance of the timing of these cash flows. Imagine if you wanted to go out this Saturday but had no money – you may know that you will be getting paid in two weeks' time, but you would have a cash flow problem. The same can be true in business. You will learn how to draw up a cash flow forecast for a business and why this is important.

You will also learn how to draw up financial records for a business so that at the end of a year, a business can work out if it has made a profit or a loss, and also what the business is worth. Most people who are in business are interested in how much money they are making and try to find ways of increasing the amount of money made by controlling the cash coming into and going out of the business.

Often learners say that they do not like finance because it is like maths. This is not true. The numbers are straightforward and really it is about money!

Learning outcomes

After completing this unit, you should:

1. understand the purpose of accounting and the categorisation of business income and expenditure
2. be able to prepare a cash flow forecast
3. be able to prepare profit and loss accounts and balance sheets
4. be able to review business performance using simple ratio analysis.

Assessment and grading criteria

This table shows you what you must do in order to achieve a **pass**, **merit** or **distinction** grade, and where you can find activities in this book to help you.

To achieve a **pass** grade, the evidence must show that the learner is able to:	To achieve a **merit** grade, the evidence must show that, in addition to the pass criteria, the learner is able to:	To achieve a **distinction** grade, the evidence must show that, in addition to the pass and merit criteria, the learner is able to:
P1 describe the purpose of accounting for an organisation **See Assessment activity 5.1, page 175.**		
P2 explain the difference between capital and revenue items of expenditure and income **See Assessment activity 5.1, page 175.**		
P3 prepare a 12-month cash flow forecast to enable an organisation to manage its cash **See Assessment activity 5.2, page 182.**	**M1** analyse the cash flow problems a business might experience **See Assessment activity 5.2, page 182.**	**D1** justify actions a business might take when experiencing cash flow problems **See Assessment activity 5.2, page 182.**
P4 prepare a profit and loss account and balance sheet for a given organisation **See Assessment activity 5.3, page 190.**		
P5 perform ratio analysis to measure the profitability, liquidity and efficiency of a given organisation **See Assessment activity 5.4, page 195.**	**M2** analyse the performance of a business using suitable ratios **See Assessment activity 5.4, page 195.**	**D2** evaluate the financial performance and position of a business using ratio analysis **See Assessment activity 5.4, page 195.**

How you will be assessed

You will be asked to help a new entrepreneur to understand the basics of business accounting and to produce and explain a 12-month cash flow forecast to them. You will then revisit the entrepreneur after they have been trading for a year and produce their first set of financial documents – a profit and loss account and balance sheet. You will then be able to help the entrepreneur understand the good and possibly not-so-good points of their first year in business by carrying out and interpreting the results of ratio analysis.

Jade

I was quite worried about this unit as I have never been very good at maths, but actually I really enjoyed it. I soon realised that all the numbers were given to me and I just had to do straightforward calculations such as add, subtract, multiply and divide. In particular I enjoyed the ability to understand how a business calculates whether it has made a profit or a loss.

The first thing I did was make sure that I understood the terms that were being used. When I prepared my presentation I ensured that I had put any terms used into language that I understood. I pretended that I was talking to a real entrepreneur and that although they had a good business idea they needed help with understanding the money aspect of setting up and running their business.

When producing the documents, I tried to be very logical and tick numbers off as I used them so I knew I hadn't missed a number out. I also used a spreadsheet with formulae in it. I found this a little tricky to start with, but managed to get it set up with a bit of help. This was really useful because it meant every time I changed a number all the sums were done for me, so I didn't need to keep recalculating them. It also meant I was less likely to make mistakes.

The East End market trader

Mitch runs a second-hand CD and DVD stall on an East End market. He opens his stall three days a week and on Saturdays, his busiest day, he is helped out by his girlfriend Vicky. Mitch is trying to earn a bit of extra cash to pay for his van's MOT, which is due soon, and so has also started to offer his services as a delivery man to other local businesses or individuals.

Draw a table with two columns for money in and money out, for Mitch's delivery man service. In pairs, try to list as many things as you can think of under these two columns. Are there any costs (the money out), that Mitch would have to pay even if he had no customers?

1. Understand the purpose of accounting and the categorisation of business income and expenditure

It is impossible to truly understand how a business operates without some knowledge of the accounting process. You may be familiar with the expression 'a picture paints a thousand words' – in business we can adapt this to 'numbers paint a thousand words'. Anyone who wants to understand how well a business is performing – such as the owner, an **employee** or a potential investor – is likely to turn straight to its accounts. However good a business idea might be, if the owner does not keep a careful eye on the business's accounts, it is almost doomed to failure.

1.1 Purpose of accounting

Accounting involves the recording of **financial transactions**, planned or actual, and the use of these figures to produce financial information. In this first section we will look at a number of reasons why accounting is important to business success.

Record transactions

Keeping business records accurate and up to date is important for the smooth running of a business. The business owner or a bookkeeper must record all of the money coming into the business (from sales) and all of the money going out, such as expenses. If a business fails to do this it may find itself not chasing payments, forgetting to pay bills or, even more seriously, in trouble with **HM Revenue and Customs** (HMRC). If the business does not record its transactions correctly, it cannot report its financial performance accurately and therefore tax payments may be wrong.

Did you know?

HMRC carries out counter evasion work to try to ensure that everyone is paying the tax they should. Incorrect tax payment may be a genuine error as a result of poor accounting or may be due to outright intention. The amount of money gleaned from reluctant taxpayers has risen from £1.13 billion in 1992 to £9.17 billion in 2007. HMRC reports that this money has come from a number of sources including individuals and companies. (Source: www.bbc.co.uk)

Key terms

Employee – a person who works for a business

Financial transactions – actions by a business that involve money either going into or out of a business – for example, making a sale or paying a bill

HM Revenue and Customs – HM is an abbreviation for Her (or His) Majesty's, and the HMRC is a British government department responsible for the collection of all types of taxes

Monitor activity

Records will be updated on a regular (ideally daily) basis and therefore provide a good indication of how the business is doing in terms of sales, receiving payments, paying expenses and so on. The owner would soon realise if money going out seemed to be on the increase while sales were dropping off. Monitoring activity should also involve keeping an eye on the bank balance to ensure there are sufficient funds to meet day-to-day expenses.

Control

The ability to control the business's accounts is a direct result of the previous two purposes. If accurate records of transactions are maintained and activity closely monitored, then actions can be taken to control the balance between money flowing in and out of the business. For example, if it appeared that expenses were creeping up but sales staying the same, then the owner could look for ways to control or cut costs.

Management of the business

A manager is someone who is responsible for the planning, monitoring and controlling of the resources for which they are responsible. A manager who clearly understands the business's accounts will be better able to make informed decisions and plan for the future. Management of a business involves careful co-ordination of resources including staff, materials, stock and money. The manager must ensure there are sufficient funds to pay wages, order new stock, pay bills and meet other demands for cash outflows by balancing this with the money coming in from sales.

Measurement of financial performance

Without financial records it would be impossible to know if the business was making a **profit** or a **loss**, or whether or not the business was owed money or in debt to others.

Throughout this unit we will consider how a business can measure its financial performance and what actions it can take to improve its performance. Key indicators of financial performance include:

- **gross profit** – this is the amount of profit left after the cost of producing the good or service is deducted from the amount of **sales revenue**
- **net profit** – this is the smaller amount of profit made after all other expenses are deducted from the gross profit
- **value owed to the business** – this is the amount of money owed to the business from sales that have not yet been paid for
- **value owed by the business** – this is the amount of money the business owes to others for goods or services purchased but not yet paid for.

So, business accounting looks at money coming into and out of a business. We will now consider these two aspects of business accounts in more detail, which are:

- the money coming in (the income)
- the money going out (the expenditure).

1.2 Capital income

Capital income is the money invested by the owners or other investors that is used to set up a business or buy additional equipment. It tends to be used to buy things that will stay in the business for a medium-to-long period of time – for example, premises, vehicles or equipment. These are called **fixed assets**. When setting up a business, capital income might also be used to buy opening stock, but as the business develops, stock should be paid for by sales income. The sources of capital income available to business owners are influenced by the type of business.

Sole trader

A sole trader is a person who owns a business on their own; they therefore have to find all of the capital income from their own sources or personal loans. Sole traders often invest their personal savings into the business or borrow from the bank using their personal

Key terms

Profit – surplus achieved when total revenue (income) from sales is higher than the total costs of a business

Loss – shortfall suffered when total revenue from sales is lower than the total costs of a business

Gross profit – sales revenue minus cost of goods sold (the cost of the actual materials used to produce the quantity of goods sold)

Sales revenue – quantity sold times selling price

Net profit – gross profit minus other expenses – for example, rent and advertising

Capital income – money invested into the business either to set it up or buy equipment

Fixed assets – items of value owned by a business that are likely to stay in the business for more than one year – for example, machinery

Assets – things that are owned by a business or individual

assets, such as their house, to secure the loan. This investment is a big risk for a sole trader, as they are ultimately responsible for the debts of the business. Being a sole trader can also limit the amount of money available and can therefore restrict the size of the business. However, if successful, the sole trader can keep all of the profits for themselves.

Partnership

A partnership is when two or more people join together to set up a business as partners. Each partner would be expected to contribute towards the capital income, hence increasing the potential amount of money available. Partners also share decision making and the profit. In most partnerships, any loans taken out are still secured by the partners' own assets, so this is still a quite high-risk option.

Shares

A company is when a business is registered with Companies House and issues shares to its shareholders (see Unit 1, page 10 for more details). The shareholders are the owners of the business and all contribute towards the capital income. Shareholders normally receive a voting right and the more shares they own, the greater their ability is to influence decision making. Shareholders are rewarded for their investment by the payment of a dividend; this is a share of the profits.

Loans

A loan is an amount of money lent to the business or business owner(s) from a bank. It is a lump sum that then has to be paid back at a set amount per month over the period of the loan, often five years, although longer-term loans can be agreed. As well as the repayment of the loan, there will be a monthly interest repayment. This is the amount of money the bank is charging for the loan as a percentage of the amount borrowed. The **interest rate** can be fixed or it may vary with changes in the economy. It is the interest payable on top of the loan that makes a loan a relatively expensive source of capital income. Monthly payments have to be made even if the business is not making a profit.

Buying a property is a big investment for a business.

Key term

Interest rate – the percentage rate a bank charges for a loan, that is, the cost of borrowing money

A bank loan can be crucial to the survival of a new business.

Banks are not guaranteed to lend money to a business, so the business would have to justify how the money borrowed would be spent and, more importantly, how they can afford to repay it. Often bank loans have to be secured against an asset (for example, the entrepreneur's home or the company's vehicles) to convince the bank that the risk being taken is not too great. This means if the business fails to meet payments, the bank can reclaim the asset.

Mortgages

A mortgage is similar to a bank loan, but it tends to be for a larger sum of money and over a longer period of time (typically 25 years). Mortgages are always secured on an asset, normally a property. Individuals will take out a mortgage to buy a house. Businesses might take out a mortgage to buy their premises – for example, a factory, retail store or warehouse.

1.3 Revenue income

As we have already seen, capital income is the money invested in the business to set it up or later buy additional assets; it is a long-term investment. Revenue income is the money that comes into the business from performing its day-to-day function – selling goods or providing a service. The nature of the revenue income depends on the activities that the business does to bring in money, and three main sources are:

- sales
- rent received
- commission received.

Fig. 5.1: What are credit sales?

Sales

Sales, or sales turnover, is money coming in from the sales of goods or services. For example, a jeans shop has money coming in each time a customer buys a pair of jeans, or a hairdresser each time a customer has a haircut. Sales turnover is therefore determined by the prices charged and the number of customers.

Sales can be either cash sales (the customer pays there and then), or credit sales (the customer buys then but pays at a later date). The significance of the difference between cash and credit sales will become clear later on when you learn about cash flow.

Rent received

A business that owns property and charges others for use of all or part of that property will receive rent as their main source of income. If a business owns a house and rents out three rooms to students, then it will receive rent from each of these students. Similarly a business may own land or offices which it rents out to other businesses.

Commission received

A business may sell products or services as an agent of another business. They sell another business's products on their behalf and for each sale they make, they get paid a percentage on that sale. This percentage is called **commission**. If, for example, you were to buy tickets for a concert from www.ticketmaster.co.uk, then Ticketmaster would receive a percentage payment for that ticket from whichever company was hosting the concert.

Key term

Commission – a percentage paid on a sale to the person or business responsible for making that sale

Christian
Sales Ledger Clerk

Christian has worked for eight months as a sales ledger clerk at Vamous Vehicles, a small independent courier business. The business operates a fleet of four delivery vans providing next-day courier services to and from anywhere in the UK.

What does your job involve on a daily basis?

I am responsible for keeping the sales ledger up to date. This is a record of all of the sales made by the business and of the payments received from customers. In effect, it lets the boss know how much is being made in sales and how much money is still owed. On a daily basis this means I have to:

- collect job sheets from drivers for the previous day's deliveries
- issue invoices to customers requesting payment for the delivery made
- check the post for incoming money received
- check the bank account online for incoming money received.

I have to input all the details accurately on to the computer. At the end of each week, I check through all the invoices that have not yet been paid. We allow our customers 30 days to pay, so if the invoice was issued more than 30 days ago and has not yet been paid, I have to chase the customer. Most of the time they apologise and say they will authorise payment there and then. If, however, I think there might be a problem, I have to tell my manager.

Do you also deal with the money going out of the business?

No, that is Tanya's job – she is the Purchase Ledger Clerk. She has to record all the purchases made by the business and authorise payment for these. For example, all our drivers have a petrol card for BP service stations. So each month Tanya will authorise the bank to pay the month's fuel costs to BP.

Why is your job important to the business?

If I don't issue an invoice and chase payment, then we would be providing a service for free! The invoice asks the customer to pay and is the first step towards getting cash into the business. If there is not enough money coming in, even if sales are being made, then the business might have cash flow problems and be unable to make payments. I for one wouldn't be very happy if my wages didn't get paid at the end of the month!

Think about it!

1. Why is it important that Christian records all sales accurately?
2. Why should Christian tell his boss if he thinks there might be a problem with a customer paying?
3. What actions might a business take if a customer does not pay the invoice on time?
4. What are the benefits to the firm of drivers having petrol cards?
5. Explain why, if Christian fails to do his job properly, the business may have cash flow problems.

1.4 Capital expenditure

Expenditure is money spent by a business and can be split into two categories: capital expenditure and revenue expenditure. We are going to start by looking at capital expenditure. This is used to buy **capital items**, which are assets that will stay in the business for a long period of time. Capital items are fixed assets and intangible assets, as explained below.

Fixed assets

Fixed assets are items owned by a business that will remain in the business for a reasonable period of time. These are shown on a business's balance sheet and include land and buildings, office equipment, machinery, furniture and fittings, and motor vehicles. These are sometimes referred to as 'tangible assets' because they can be touched.

Most fixed assets lose value over time and for this reason they are depreciated. This means that each year their value in the balance sheet is reduced in order to give a fair value of the asset.

Intangibles

An intangible asset is something owned by the business, that cannot be touched but adds value to the business. Here are three common intangibles that exist within businesses.

- **Goodwill** – when you buy an existing business, its name and reputation will already be known, and it may already have an established customer base or set of clients. This increases the value of the business and therefore increases the selling price of the business. A sum of money is added to the value of the business to reflect the value of this goodwill. However, goodwill is difficult to place a figure on – how much would you pay for a recognised brand name?

- **Patents** – a patent is the legal protection of an invention, such as a unique feature of a product or a new process. An entrepreneur or business may patent their idea to stop others from copying the idea. Having a patent allows the business to exploit this in the future by launching an innovative product at a premium (more expensive) selling price. The patent itself must therefore be worth something, but again it is difficult to know exactly how much value to place on it.

Key term

Capital items – assets bought from capital expenditure such as machinery and vehicles

- **Trademarks** – a trademark is a symbol, logo, brand name, words or even colour that sets apart one business's goods or services from those of its competitors. Trademarks can be a key influence on consumer choice and build a strong brand loyalty. A trademark therefore is of value to a business and consequently recorded as an intangible asset.

How do you decide upon the monetary value of a trademark?

1.5 Revenue expenditure

Revenue expenditure is spending on items on a day-to-day or regular basis. These are the expenses incurred by a business that are shown on the profit and loss account. The types of costs incurred vary from business to business, but some of the more common types include:

- premises costs
- administrative costs
- staff costs
- selling and distribution costs
- finance costs
- purchase of stock.

Case study: Colour wars

What do you associate with the colour orange?

When Stelios Haji-Ioannou, founder of easyJet, launched easyMobile in 2004 it was no surprise he planned to use his recognised colour – orange. However, competitors Orange, an established mobile phone company, were less than happy, claiming they were first in the mobile phone market and were recognised for the colour that goes with their name.

Orange, the company, claimed that a rival in the market using the same colour would cause confusion to customers and wanted to stop Stelios from using the colour. Orange had trademarked a specific shade of orange, but Stelios was not going to give up the fight easily, saying, 'I'm quite happy

to see them in court. I don't believe they have a case.'

Other trademarks include Heinz's distinctive turquoise cans, Cadbury's famous shade of purple and Toblerone's triangular box.

(Source: adapted from www.bbc.co.uk)

1. Should Orange be able to stop a competitor from using a specific colour? Justify your answer.
2. Why might it be important to show a value for these trademarks in a business's accounts?
3. How would you go about attaching a monetary value to these trademarks?

Premises costs

All businesses will have some sort of premises costs, from renting a market stall or using a room in the entrepreneur's home to renting factories or large retail stores. There are a number of costs associated with premises.

- **Rent** – the business may not own the premises and may therefore have to pay a regular sum of money for its use of the premises.

- **Rates** – in the same way as private residents pay council tax to the local authority, businesses pay non-domestic rates. This is a sum of money paid to the local council to go towards services such as street lights and refuse collection. This is not a set amount, but is calculated by the council based on the size and location of the premises, and the nature of the business.

- **Heating and lighting** – this covers payments for services such as gas and electricity. The business will receive regular bills, often quarterly (every three months) for the provision and use of these services.

- **Insurance** – a business is legally required to take out a number of types of insurance to protect itself from the possibility of serious losses. These include:
  - buildings insurance – to protect the physical building from damage that may be caused by events such as fire

  - contents insurance – to protect what is inside the building in terms of machinery, fixtures and fittings and stock from damage that may be caused by events such as flooding
  - public liability insurance – to protect people within the building who may be harmed or injured from an event such as an accident.

Administrative costs

Administration refers to the paperwork that goes on within a business either internally between employees or externally with suppliers and customers. Administrative costs include items such as postage, printing and stationery, which might include items such as business cards, headed paper and order books.

Telephone charges are also classed as an administrative cost and are slightly unusual from an accounting point of view. For a land line these costs are split into two; there is the line rental cost, which is paid quarterly in advance and then the call charges, which are paid quarterly after use.

Staff costs

Most businesses will employ staff. A common misunderstanding by business studies learners is that a sole trader has to do everything themselves. This is not true – they own the business by themselves, but can employ as many people as they want, need or can afford!

A larger business may try to reduce staff costs by using more machinery. A firm with a high number of staff to machines is called 'labour intensive'; one with a greater emphasis on machines is called 'capital intensive'. Staff costs can include the following.

- **Salaries** – a salary is an annual figure paid to an employee divided into equal monthly payments. For example, a trainee accountant may have a salary of £18,000 per year, meaning their gross pay is £1,500 per month. The employee will then have to pay National Insurance, tax and maybe pension contributions on this figure, so the amount they actually take home will be quite a bit less. For the business, however, the actual amount they have to pay (the real cost to the business) is higher. On a salary of £18,000 the business also has to pay **employers**' National Insurance of 12.8 per cent, an additional £2,304 plus any pension and additional benefits.

- **Wages** – a wage is an hourly rate paid to an employee, meaning there is a direct link between the number of hours worked and the amount of money paid. Paying a wage rather than a salary allows greater flexibility for both the employer and the employee, but also creates greater uncertainty.

- **Training** – a business may want to train its employees in order to help get the most out of them. Training means that employees are better able to do their job and this should ultimately lead to a better business. However, training is expensive – especially if employees are sent on courses away from the business such as external training days, have day release at college or are supported

Key term

Employer – a business that employs workers

through professional qualifications. In terms of both internal and external training, the cost is not only the financial cost in terms of paying for the training, but also the loss of time while the worker is not carrying out their job.

- **Insurance** – a business is responsible for its employees while carrying out any duties related to their work and therefore the business has to take out employers' liability insurance. This means that if the employee is injured at work, the business is protected against any claims for compensation or any legal costs incurred.

- **Pensions** – some businesses offer a pension scheme as an added bonus for employees. Both parties will contribute towards the pension fund on a regular basis. Offering a pension scheme adds to the costs of the employer. There may also be an additional cost as the business will have to pay someone to administer the fund.

Selling and distribution costs

If a business is to survive, it must make enough sales to cover all of its costs. It must be able to attract customers and get the product or service to the customer. These two crucial functions carry additional costs. Selling and distribution costs include:

- **sales staff salaries** – many businesses will employ workers with specific responsibility for sales. This

Activity: Minimum wage

Employers in the UK, by law, have to pay a minimum wage to all employees over the age of 16. When the minimum wage was first introduced in the UK in 1999, it was £3.60 per hour for employees over 22. The initial introduction of the minimum wage and each subsequent rise causes wage costs of businesses to go up.

Do you know what the minimum wage rates are today for:

- 16–17-year-olds
- 18–21-year-olds
- 22-year-olds and over?

1. Write down what you think the minimum wage is for each age group.

2. Use the Internet to check whether you are correct.

3. Carry out some research to find out how the minimum wage has changed since its original introduction.

4. Plot this information on a graph.

SALES PERSON wanted.

Car/Phone required.
Must have experience in the industry,
good communication skills,
and a positive attitude.

Basic + commission

Fig. 5.2: What are the advantages to a firm of using a commission pay scheme for sales staff?

might be a sales representative who travels around trying to generate sales, sales assistants who help the customer, or accounts managers who look after regular customers, ensuring they keep making repeat orders. Regardless of the type of salesperson, they will require paying. Often sales staff receive a commission-based salary, meaning the more they sell, the more they can earn

- **carriage of sales** – this is the cost of getting the sale to the customer and can range from something as simple as an envelope and stamp or courier delivery to something much more complex with bulky or fragile products or even products being shipped to another country. Some businesses try to pass this cost on to the customer by quoting a sales price plus postage and packaging cost

- **marketing** – this covers a whole range of costs associated with attracting the customer and convincing them to make a purchase. Possible marketing costs might include advertisements, promotional literature, promotional events, point of sale materials and so on.

Finance costs

Most businesses do not operate on a cash-only basis – they are likely to accept payments by cheque, card or direct bank transfer. They are likely to make payments in the same ways. This means that the business needs a bank account. Banks are also businesses and they too want to make a profit; they therefore charge for their services. Finance costs to a business can include:

- **bank charges** – unlike personal banking, which is generally free, banks charge businesses for each

transaction that takes place, for example, every time a cheque is paid in or written, whenever cash is deposited, and so on. Banks might offer free banking to businesses for the first year as a marketing technique, but once the first year is over, bank charges can soon start to add up to quite a large amount of money

- **loan and mortgage interest** – if the business has a bank loan or a mortgage, then interest will be charged on this. Banks may offer big businesses preferential rates if they are confident that the money will be paid back and if they want to keep that particular business as a loyal customer. Big businesses will carry out a lot of transactions and pay high bank charges, so for the bank it may be worth offering lower interest rates to keep them happy.

Purchase of stock

Most businesses providing a good or service will require some sort of stock, whether it is raw materials, finished goods to sell on or supplies to provide the service – for example, shampoo and conditioner for a hairdresser. When a business is first set up, it is likely to have to buy stock with cash as it will not have built a reputation as being trustworthy and able to pay. As a business becomes more established, it may be able to buy stock on credit (such as receiving the stock and paying 30 days later). Bigger and more established businesses may also be able to drive the cost of stock down as they will buy in larger quantities. There are other costs related to stock, such as insurance and storage costs.

How can business drive stock-related costs down?

Assessment activity 5.1

Engaging Enterprise is a local organisation that promotes enterprise in young people and offers support and help to new entrepreneurs. It has recently launched a new scheme called Acorn, a 12-week programme aimed at encouraging and helping 16–25-year-olds to set up in business.

You have been invited along as a guest speaker to give a presentation on the purpose of accounting. Your presentation should address the following questions.

- Why is it important to keep accurate financial records?
- How will these records help the entrepreneur?
- What is meant by revenue and expenditure?
- What is the difference between revenue expenditure and capital expenditure?
- What types of revenue and capital expenditure can they expect to incur?
- What is the difference between revenue income and capital income?
- What types of revenue and capital income can they expect to incur?

1. Describe the purpose of accounts. **P1**
2. Explain the difference between capital and revenue items of expenditure and income. **P2**

Grading tips

1. 'Purpose' means why something is important and how it will help. In this section of your presentation try to focus on:
   - why an entrepreneur would have to keep accurate financial records
   - how this would help them in setting up and running a business.

   You must include why it is important to have historical data to be able to check on financial performance and position, as well as the planning aspect of accounting. Remember that whenever you use technical language, it is important you explain it in your own words. **P1**

2. To effectively explain the differences between capital and revenue items of expenditure and income, you need to cover the following categorisations:
   - capital income
   - revenue income
   - capital expenditure
   - revenue expenditure.

   You should make sure you give a clear definition of each term and support with examples appropriate to new entrepreneurs. At this stage you are not expected to calculate profit or to know the impact of the income and expenditure items on profit. **P2**

2. Be able to prepare a cash flow forecast

Cash flows into and out of a business on a regular basis. A **cash flow forecast** tries to predict in advance what and when these cash flows will be. Having a healthy cash flow is crucial to the survival of a business. A healthy cash flow means that a business will have enough cash at any one point in time to be able to meet demand for short-term cash outflows. Imagine what would happen if at the end of the week a manager turned to the business's employees and said, 'Sorry, I haven't got enough cash to pay your wages this week.'

By forecasting cash flow in advance, a business can identify where there might be shortages and either try to prevent this from happening or put plans in place to deal with it.

2.1 Cash flow forecast

Structure

A cash flow forecast is a simple statement showing opening balance, cash in, cash out and closing balance. It is normally shown on a monthly basis and drawn up for a 12-month period. The **opening balance**

is how much money the business has at the start of the month and the **closing balance** how much money it has at the end of the month. For example, the closing balance at the end of January becomes the opening balance at the start of February.

Carla's Web has £1,000 available at the start of the year; Carla then predicts sales of £1,000 in January, £2,800 in February and £2,000 in March. In this case, total inflows and sales are the same, showing that Carla only makes cash sales and not credit sales.

The total cash available is opening balance plus total inflows. Carla predicts that her purchases will be £980

Key terms

Cash flow forecast – document that shows the predicted flow of cash into and out of a business over a given period of time, normally 12 months

Opening balance – amount of cash available in a business at the start of a set time period, for example, a month

Closing balance – amount of cash available in a business at the end of a set time period, for example, a month

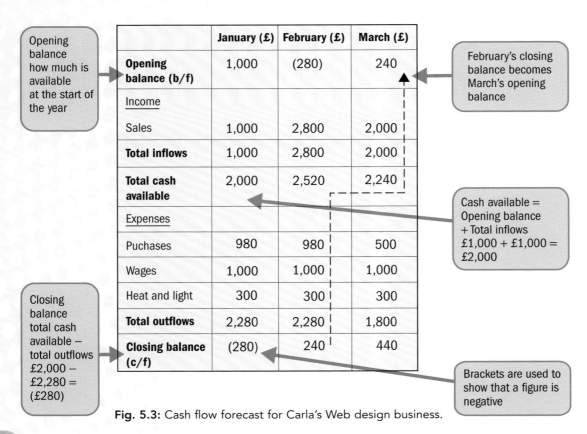

Opening balance how much is available at the start of the year

February's closing balance becomes March's opening balance

	January (£)	February (£)	March (£)
Opening balance (b/f)	1,000	(280)	240
Income			
Sales	1,000	2,800	2,000
Total inflows	1,000	2,800	2,000
Total cash available	2,000	2,520	2,240
Expenses			
Puchases	980	980	500
Wages	1,000	1,000	1,000
Heat and light	300	300	300
Total outflows	2,280	2,280	1,800
Closing balance (c/f)	(280)	240	440

Cash available = Opening balance + Total inflows £1,000 + £1,000 = £2,000

Closing balance total cash available – total outflows £2,000 – £2,280 = (£280)

Brackets are used to show that a figure is negative

Fig. 5.3: Cash flow forecast for Carla's Web design business.

in both January and February, and £500 in March, while wages will be £1,000 per month and heating and lighting £300 per month. Total outflows are all of Carla's expenses added together. The closing balance is calculated by deducting the total outflows from the cash available. Remember that one month's closing balance becomes the next month's opening balance.

Activity: Personal cash flow

Draw a cash flow table to show your personal finances for the next month. You should think about what money will be coming in from wages, EMA (Education Maintenance Allowance), presents, parents and so on as appropriate, and also what expenses you will have. These might include food and drink, presents, trips, travel and so on.

1. What is your opening balance at the start of the month?
2. What is your closing balance at the end of the month?
3. Are there any points during the month where you may have a cash flow problem?
4. What actions can you take to ensure that any cash flow problems are solved?

Timescale

The timing of the cash inflows and outflows is important. In the above example, at the end of three months Carla has a positive balance of £440, but in January she had a negative balance of £280. This means that although her cash flow was healthy at the end of three months, she had problems earlier and would have had an **overdraft** of £280 in her bank or been unable to pay one of her expenses, which could stop her from operating successfully in the following months.

Credit periods

Credit periods have two major influences on a business's cash flow.

1. The business must consider how long it gives its customers to pay. If it accepts cash sales only, then this will not be a concern, but it may have to offer credit in order to ensure a sale. The longer the credit period, the slower the money coming in. If a greengrocer gives one month's credit for a sale made in January, they will not see cash flowing into

the business until February. Yet the greengrocer may have had to pay for its stock up front.

2. Credit periods affect the ability of the business to gain credit from its suppliers. If a business can secure supplies on credit, then this will slow down the flow of cash out of a business. The longer the credit period, the later the cash flows out. Some businesses can secure credit periods of 30, 60 or even 90 days.

If a business both sells on credit to its customers and buys on credit from its suppliers, it wants the first to have a shorter credit period than the second.

Receipts

Receipts are the money coming into the business from various sources, which include:

- capital from the owner(s)
- bank loan or mortgage
- cash sales
- credit sales – these customers are classed as **debtors** as they owe the business money
- rent
- commission
- other income – this could be, for example, a one-off cash inflow from the sale of an asset, such as a machine that is no longer needed.

Payments

Payments are the money going out of the business for various purposes, which include:

- buying capital equipment (capital expenditure)
- purchases of stock
- cash purchases (revenue expenditure)
- credit purchases – these suppliers are classed as trade **creditors**, because they have supplied goods or services on credit

Key terms

Overdraft – when more money is taken out of a bank account than is in it, making the account overdrawn

Credit periods – length of time given to customers to pay for goods or services received

Debtors – customers who have purchased goods or services on credit, meaning they are in debt to the business as they owe it money

Creditors – suppliers who have provided goods or services to a business on credit, meaning the business owes them money

- staff costs, premises costs, administrative costs, selling and distribution costs (revenue expenditure)
- loan repayments, with interest
- interest on an overdraft
- value added tax (VAT) – businesses that are VAT registered must pay VAT to HM Revenue and Customs (HMRC), and this should be shown in the cash flow forecast.

A business with sales in excess of the VAT threshold, £67,000 per year in 2009, must register itself with HMRC and then record VAT received on sales and paid on purchases. A business must then work out whether it has paid or received more money in VAT, then claim a refund or make a payment as appropriate.

If a company makes a sale of £100 plus VAT, then the cost of the sale to the customer will be £117.50. In the cash flow, the company will record a sale of £100 and VAT received of £17.50.

The same company may make purchases of £50 plus VAT. The purchases therefore cost the business £58.75. In the cash flow forecast, the company will record purchases of £50 and VAT paid of £8.75.

Did you know?

The standard rate of VAT in the UK is 17.5 per cent, although from the first of December 2008, the Chancellor Alistair Darling reduced it to 15 per cent for one year.

1. Why do you think the Chancellor made this decision?
2. What would this have meant for businesses?

At the end of each quarter, the company will add up all the VAT received and deduct from this all of the VAT paid. If the amount received is higher than the amount paid, then the company must pay HMRC the difference. If the amount paid is higher than the amount received, then the company can reclaim the difference.

Opening and closing cash/bank balances

The opening balance at the start of the year will be a true reflection of the business's bank balance, whereas the closing balance will be based upon the predicted

Case study: Paddington Games

Paddington Games sells £10,000 of games per month and purchases supplies of £6,000.

Table 5.1: Cash in for Paddington Games.

Cash in	Jan	Feb	Mar
Sales	£10,000	£10,000	£10,000
VAT on sales	£1,750	£1,750	£1,750
Refund from HMRC			
Total cash in	£11,750	£11,750	£11,750

Table 5.2: Cash out for Paddington Games.

Cash out	Jan	Feb	Mar
Purchases	£6,000	£6,000	£6,000
VAT paid	£1,050	£1,050	£1,050
Payment to HMRC			£2,100
Total cash out	£7,050	£7,050	£9,150

Over the three months January to March, the total VAT received was (£1,750 × 3) £5,250 and the total VAT paid was (£1,050 × 3) £3,150. The net VAT is therefore £5,250 − £3,150 = £2,100, meaning the business has received more in VAT than it has paid and therefore must make a payment of £2,100 to HMRC.

incomes and expenditures over the period of the cash flow forecast, normally a year. One of the key purposes of the cash flow forecast is to highlight in advance any months where there is a risk of a negative cash flow, as this allows the business to make arrangements – for example, a prearranged overdraft with the bank – or to try to take actions to avoid this.

A business with a negative closing balance is often said to have **liquidity** problems and is in danger of becoming **insolvent**. In the next section on cash flow management, we will look in more detail at methods available to try to avoid these negative closing balances.

Key terms

Liquidity – measure of a firm's ability to meet short-term cash payments

Insolvent – when a firm is unable to meet short-term cash payments

Case study: Lily's cleaning services

Lily is setting up a small business providing cleaning services to offices on a trading estate in Scarborough. She has asked you to help her prepare a cash flow forecast for her first 12 months of trading.

You should produce a forecast from January to December based on the information provided below:

Sales and purchases for the 12 months are expected to be as follows.

Month	Sales	Purchases
January	£5,000	£600
February	£5,000	£600
March	£5,000	£600
April	£5,000	£600
May	£5,000	£600
June	£5,000	£600
July	£4,000	£500
August	£4,000	£500
September	£5,000	£600
October	£6,000	£650
November	£6,000	£650
December	£6,000	£650

At the beginning of January she will buy two small cars, to drive herself and staff to the offices, each costing £10,000. She will invest £15,000 of her own money and has agreed a bank loan of £7,000. Lily will receive the loan in January and start

repayments the following month at a fixed rate of £250 per month. When meeting with her bank manager, she also agreed a business overdraft that will be charged at a rate of one per cent on any negative closing balances.

In order to start trading in January, she buys £4,000 worth of cleaning equipment, including vacuum cleaners and floor buffers. In addition, she spends £150 on less durable (long-lasting) products such as dusters and mops, which she plans to replace every second month.

Lily plans to offer 30 days' credit terms to two of her bigger cleaning contracts. These two combined will account for £2,200 of her monthly sales.

Lily has rented a small lock-up to store her equipment and materials in at a cost of £600 per month. She will employ four cleaners each earning £400 per month and a cleaning supervisor earning an annual salary of £7,200. She will withdraw £1,000 a month for herself, and hopes to be able to increase this to £1,200 per month after six months.

Additional monthly costs include:

- £300 car insurance
- £20 advertising
- £100 fuel.

1. Use a spreadsheet to produce a 12-month cash flow forecast for Lily.

2. Identify and explain any potential cash flow problems she may face.

3. Do you think Lily was right to offer her two biggest customers 30 days' credit? Justify your answer.

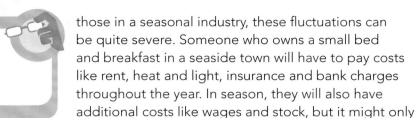

2.2 Cash flow management

A cash flow forecast can help to identify where there are potential shortfalls but might also indicate where there are large amounts of cash left at the end of a month or year. Although you may think this is a good thing, if the cash balance at the end of each month is high, it might be an indication that the business is not taking advantage of opportunities. For example, could it use this cash surplus to improve or expand the business?

Cash flow forecasts are just that, a forecast, and therefore the actual cash flow of the business should be monitored alongside the forecast to see if inflows and outflows are as expected, better or worse.

Problems within the cash flow forecast

Problems occur with cash flows when the business's outflows are greater than the opening balance plus the inflows, as this will result in a negative closing balance. This means that the business will not have enough cash to meet payments that are due.

Very few businesses have consistent cash flows throughout the year; they are likely to experience busy times and quiet times. These fluctuations are known as the cash flow cycle. For some businesses, particularly those in a seasonal industry, these fluctuations can be quite severe. Someone who owns a small bed and breakfast in a seaside town will have to pay costs like rent, heat and light, insurance and bank charges throughout the year. In season, they will also have additional costs like wages and stock, but it might only be in these summer months where there are any cash inflows.

Solutions to cash flow problems

If a business has predicted cash flow problems in advance, then there are a number of possible solutions. These include:

- **overdraft arrangements** – a business with a fluctuating cash flow cycle should be able to show the forecast to the bank and make arrangements for periods of negative cash flows. Banks sometimes offer free overdraft facilities to help businesses through these periods, but only if pre-agreed. Going overdrawn on a bank account without an agreement with the bank can be a very expensive option

- **negotiating terms with creditors** – creditors are people or businesses that a business owes money to, normally because goods or services have been bought on credit as opposed to cash purchases. A business with cash flow problems could try to negotiate a longer payment term with its suppliers – for example, an increase from 30 days to 60 days. This would slow down the flow of cash out of the business. A negative effect of this, however, may be the loss of any discounts offered for prompt or early payment

- **reviewing and rescheduling capital expenditure** – having identified cash flow problems, the owner or manager could review what cash outflows were being spent on. Such a review might identify areas of expenditure that could be cut or postponed. It is difficult to do this if the expenditure is on revenue items – for example, replacement stock – but more achievable if it is capital expenditure. A business could, for example, postpone plans to replace machinery or buy a new van.

An alternative action here could be to consider leasing an item of capital equipment rather than buying it outright. This can prove expensive in the long run, but means that rather than paying one lump sum, the business can pay to use it on a monthly basis.

Case study: Lily one year on

Business is doing well and Lily is now going to prepare a cash flow forecast for her second year of trading. She has won two new contracts, each with 60 days' credit, that will boost her sales by 20 per cent. The knock-on effect of this is that her purchases will go up by 15 per cent, she will employ one new cleaner and replace her semi-durable equipment (the dusters and mops) every month rather than every second month.

Lily's business advisor has done a quick mental calculation and has told her that this means she will now have to become VAT registered.

1. Is the business advisor correct? Use calculations to justify your answer.

2. Create a cash flow forecast for Lily for her second year of trading. You do not need to start from scratch – save your last spreadsheet as year two and then make the necessary changes, assuming all other costs stay the same.

3. Comment on any cash flow problems Lily may face in year two.

4. Recommend the actions Lily could take to solve these potential cash flow problems.

5. Test your recommended solutions by making these changes to your spreadsheet and see what happens.

	January £	February £	March £	April £	Total £
Opening balance (b/f)	0	(3,500)	(1,520)	2,500	
Income owner's capital	10,000				10,000
Bank loan	15,000				15,000
Cash sales	5,000	7,000	8,000	7,000	27,000
Credit sales	0	9,000	11,000	12,000	32,000
Commission received	0	800	950	950	2,700
Total inflows	30,000	16,800	19,950	19,950	86,700
Total cash available	30,000	13,300	18,430	22,450	
Expenses					
Cash purchases	8,000	9,500	9,500	3,500	30,500
Credit purchases	0	0	0	7,000	7,000
Heat and light	0	0	0	200	200
Fixtures and fittings	5,000	600	0	0	5,600
Equipment	5,000	0	0	0	5,000
Drawings	0	2,000	2,000	2,000	6,000
Marketing	3,000	0	1,200	0	4,200
Premises costs	10,000	0	0	0	10,000
Insurance	500	0	0	0	500
Wages	1,000	1,500	2,000	2,000	6,500
Administrative costs	1,000	750	800	1,250	3,800
Overdraft interest	0	70	30	0	100
Loan repayments	0	400	400	400	1,200
Total outflows	33,500	14,820	15,930	16,350	80,600
Closing balance (c/f)	(3,500)	(1,520)	2,500	6,100	

Fig. 5.4: Sample cash flow forecast for the first four months of a sole trader.

Assessment activity 5.2

P3 M1 D1 **BTEC**

Sharma and Ryan were both 21 when they attended the Acorn programme run by Engaging Enterprise. They were keen to learn and have since decided to act upon the advice given during the 12 weeks and to set up in business together. They have decided on a new business called SIGNature Ltd. The business will manufacture plastic road signs for builders, tourist attractions and local councils.

Sharma and Ryan have carried out substantial research into potential sales volumes, set-up costs and revenue expenses. They have approached you to help them set up and understand their first cash flow forecast. It is important that they get this right as it will form part of the business plan they are preparing to take to the bank manager in order to try to secure a loan.

1. You are to prepare a 12-month cash flow forecast for Sharma and Ryan based on the information presented below. Sales and purchases for the 12 months are predicted to be as follows.

Month	Sales	Purchases
January	£30,000	£13,500
February	£30,000	£13,500
March	£30,000	£13,500
April	£37,000	£16,650
May	£37,000	£16,650
June	£37,000	£16,650
July	£41,500	£18,675
August	£41,500	£18,675
September	£41,500	£18,675
October	£25,000	£11,250
November	£25,000	£11,250
December	£25,000	£11,250

These sales and purchases figures are before VAT has been added. VAT should be added at the current UK rate and shown in separate rows for VAT received on sales and paid on purchases. Every three months a figure should be shown to either make payments to HMRC for VAT owed or reclaim VAT if an excess has been paid.

SIGNature Ltd – a new business manufacturing plastic road signs.

Sharma and Ryan are the only two shareholders, each investing £12,500 of their own money into the business. They also secured a bank loan for £80,000 to be paid back in monthly instalments of £1,000. All of the capital invested was to be used to buy capital equipment to the value of £105,000. This was broken down into machinery worth £85,000 and fixtures and fittings worth £20,000. Sharma and Ryan had also agreed with their bank manager an overdraft of up to £20,000 at a charge of 1.5 per cent per month whenever their account was overdrawn.

They planned to rent a small factory unit at a cost of £25,000 per year to be paid in equal monthly instalments. They estimated that monthly rates on top of this would be £1,700.

Sharma and Ryan planned to employ themselves along with two other employees, but were aware of the fact that money might be tight, so decided to pay themselves the same salary as the other employees – £19,000 per year.

Other expenses were estimated to be as follows:

- telephone £300 per quarter
- post £50 per month
- courier charges £1,500 per month
- advertising £160 per month plus an additional £500 per quarter
- heat and light £500 per month
- insurance £1,000 per year, payable in January. P3

2. Write a set of notes to accompany the cash flow forecast, explaining to Sharma and Ryan:

   • why a business might experience cash flow problems

   • why this can cause difficulties

   • any potential dangers you can see specific to SIGNature's cash flow forecast. **M1**

3. Sharma and Ryan have asked for further help in preparing for their meeting with the bank manager. They have asked you to suggest actions that they could take to either avoid or help deal with cash flow problems.

   Write a letter to Sharma and Ryan explaining what actions are available and justifying why they might choose to take these actions. **D1**

Grading tips

1. Work in a logical manner, ticking off each item of information as you use it and checking that you have inputted the figures accurately. When drawing a cash flow forecast, it is easier to work from left to right rather than from top to bottom. So, for example, when working out the sales figures, do this for all 12 months before moving on to the next heading. **P3**

2. To analyse the cash flow problems, you must first of all identify where the potential problems lie. To do this, look at the monthly closing balances and then try to identify the cause of that problem and the effect of it. You should also look for trends, as a problem one month is likely to have a knock-on effect the following month. Trends might also occur across items of inflows or outflows – for example, look at whether costs are slowly rising for one particular item of expenditure, such as wages. **M1**

3. Your suggested actions should respond directly to the problems you have identified in the notes you have produced for M1. For each problem, suggest a possible action (solution) and explain to Sharma and Ryan how this action would help to solve the identified problem. In justifying your actions, you should show awareness of the dangers and costs of poor financial planning.

   One good way of supporting your actions is to actually show Sharma and Ryan how the actions would help solve the problems; you could do this by producing a reworked version of the spreadsheet with your actions in place. **D1**

Functional skills

Mathematics: Reworking your spreadsheet to show how suggested actions will solve the cash flow problems will provide evidence of your ability to draw conclusions and provide mathematical justifications.

English: Your notes to the cash flow forecast and letter will provide evidence of written documents. They should communicate information, ideas and opinions effectively and persuasively.

3. Be able to prepare profit and loss accounts and balance sheets

Up until this point we have been focusing on whether or not a business has enough cash to survive on a day-to-day basis. Beyond survival, a business is also likely to have an objective of profit. Here we will look at the financial documents that a business produces at the end (or mid-year, called interim accounts) of a financial year. There are two key documents that a firm will produce, and these are:

- **a profit and loss account**, which calculates whether the firm has made a profit or a loss by deducting all expenses from sales revenue
- **a balance sheet**, which calculates the net worth of a business by balancing what the business owns against what it owes.

3.1 Profit and loss account

Purpose and use

A profit and loss account, if produced correctly, will give an accurate calculation showing how much profit or loss the business has made. It records sales, costs and profit over a period of time (normally a year). Once produced, the profit and loss account can be used internally by management to help measure the performance of the business and inform future decision making, and used externally by potential investors and creditors. A creditor, for example, might look at the business's profit and loss account when deciding whether or not to offer trade credit.

Trading account and calculation of gross profit

To give a profit and loss account its full title, it should really be called a trading, profit and loss account, where the first part leading up to the calculation of gross profit is called the trading account. The trading account has three components.

1. **Sales turnover** is the money coming into the business from providing a trade – for example, selling goods, manufacturing goods, providing a service. The calculation for sales turnover is quantity sold × selling price.

2. **Cost of goods sold** includes the costs directly linked to providing that trade, for example, the cost of buying in the goods or the raw materials used to produce the goods. To work out the cost of goods sold, a simple calculation is done to ensure that the figure recorded for cost of goods sold can be directly linked to the goods actually sold and not just all the materials purchased. If, for example, I was to buy 12 balls of wool and knit a jumper, is the cost of wool for that jumper 12 balls? What if I had three spare balls to start with or two balls left at the end? The calculation for cost of goods sold is **opening stock** + purchases – **closing stock**.

3. Gross profit is the amount of money left or the surplus after the cost of goods sold has been deducted from the sales turnover. This is not, however, the business's final profit as there are still other expenses to deduct in the next part of the account. The calculation for gross profit is sales turnover – cost of goods sold.

Trading, profit and loss account for year ended 30 April 2010		
	£000s	**£000s**
Sales		411,529
Less cost of goods sold		
Opening stock	34,993	
Purchases	128,129	
Closing stock	21,445	
		141,677
Gross profit		269,852

Fig. 5.5: A trading, profit and loss account for Freedom Fashion Ltd.

Key terms

Cost of goods sold – the actual value of stock used to generate sales

Opening stock – the value of stock in a business at the start of a financial year

Closing stock – the value of stock at the end of a financial year

Calculation of net profit

Net profit is the money after all other expenses have been deducted from gross profit and any other revenue income has been added. Revenue income is non-capital income that is received by the business from sources other than sales, for example, discounts received and interest on positive bank balances.

Depreciation appears as an expense in the profit and loss account, as this is a way that accountants can spread the cost of a fixed asset over its lifetime. Depreciation will be explained in more detail under the fixed asset heading when we look at a balance sheet.

The calculation for net profit is:

gross profit – expenses + other revenue income

Fig. 5.6 shows a trading, profit and loss account for Freedom Fashion Ltd.

Freedom Fashion Ltd is an independent chain of fashion stores specialising in surf and outdoor wear in the south-east of England.

Why might a clothes retailer have to hold large amounts of stock?

Trading, profit and loss account for year ended 30 April 2010		
	£000s	£000s
Sales		411,529
Less cost of goods sold		
Opening stock	34,993	
Purchases	128,129	
Closing stock	21,445	
		141,672
Gross profit		269,852
Less expenses		
Rent and rates		37,554
Wages and salaries		96,221
Telephone and postage		1,359
Distribution		31,593
Advertising		15,579
Miscellaneous expenses		28,452
Depreciation		17,848
Total expenses		228,696
Revenue income		0
Net profit before tax		41,246

Fig. 5.6: Trading, profit and loss account for year ended 30 April 2010.

Commission received

A business may also receive income from commission sales in addition to its normal sales. For example, www.time2resources.com sells CDs, DVDs and games to support business and enterprise education; these are cash and credit sales. However, it also acts as an agent for SimVenture, a business simulation software company. When it sells a SimVenture licence, it receives commission on these sales.

Transfer of net profit to balance sheet

Tax is to be deducted from the net profit; this is a percentage of the profit that is to be paid to HM Revenue and Customs (HMRC). This then gives net profit after tax.

The business then has to decide how to use this profit. In the case of a company, a proportion of it may be issued to shareholders in the form of dividends. For a sole trader or partnership, it could be taken out of the business as **drawings**. Either some or all of it is likely, however, to be ploughed back into the business – this is called retained profit. Retained profits are transferred from the profit and loss account to the balance sheet.

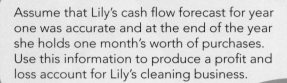

Activity: Lily's profit and loss account

Assume that Lily's cash flow forecast for year one was accurate and at the end of the year she holds one month's worth of purchases. Use this information to produce a profit and loss account for Lily's cleaning business.

PLTS

Self-managers: It is unlikely that your profit and loss account will be right on your first attempt. You will have to see this as a challenge to try to identify where all the information has not been included or where errors have been made. It is likely to take a few attempts to get your account perfect. Rise to this challenge and seek advice and support when needed.

Functional skills

ICT: If you produce your profit and loss account using a spreadsheet package, this will demonstrate your ability to select and use ICT systems independently for a complex task.

3.2 Balance sheet

Purpose and use

A balance sheet is a snapshot of a business's net worth at a particular moment in time, normally the end of a financial year. It is a summary of everything that the business owns (its assets) and owes (its liabilities). A balance sheet therefore states the value of a business.

Presentation

Balance sheets can be shown in a vertical or horizontal format, vertical being the most common and therefore the style of presentation we will use in this unit. A vertically presented balance sheet is presented as:

- intangible assets
- + fixed assets
- + current assets
- – current liabilities
- – long-term liabilities
- = net assets.

This is the first half of the balance sheet that calculates the net assets – that is, the worth of the business. Imagine if the business were to close today and you sold all of its assets, then paid off all of its liabilities. This is the amount you would be left with.

The second half of the balance sheet then asks how this has been financed. This shows the **capital employed** and is presented as:

- owners' capital
- + retained profit
- = capital employed.

For a balance sheet to balance, net assets must be equal to capital employed.

Key terms

Drawings – sum of money taken out of a business by a sole trader or partner for their own usage

Capital employed – the total amount of money tied up in the business from retained profits and capital investments

Order of permanence

If something is described as permanent, it means it is going to stay in place for a long time. When a business lists its fixed assets, it tends to list them in order of permanence, so the item that will stay in the business the longest and maintain value is listed first. This is normally land or premises as these assets maintain and sometimes even gain in value. Other assets tend to lose value, for example, machinery and vehicles. Vehicles depreciate in value at the quickest rate and are therefore listed last. Fixed assets are therefore listed in the following order of permanence:

- land or premises
- machinery
- vehicles.

Fixed assets

Fixed assets are those items of value that are owned by the business and likely to stay within the business for more than one year. These are tangible assets and include the premises, fixtures and fittings, equipment and vehicles. It is important that when these are shown in the balance sheet, they are given a realistic value. For this reason they are depreciated on an annual basis. If, for example, a business bought a delivery van for £30,000 and three years later still showed its value as £30,000, this would be unrealistic and inaccurate accounting. The balance sheet should therefore show the historic cost of an asset, the amount by which it has depreciated over its life and then a current value for the asset. This final figure is called the net book value and this represents what the asset is thought to be worth at that moment in time.

There are a number of ways to calculate depreciation but here we are going to use just one method – the straight line method. This method involves reducing the value of an asset by a fixed amount each year. To calculate the amount, the accountant must first of all make two decisions:

- how long the asset is expected to be useful to the business
- at the end of its useful life, how much it might be worth if sold on or sold for scrap.

Once these decisions have been made, the following formula can be applied.

$$\frac{\text{historic cost} - \text{residual value}}{\text{expected life}}$$

If therefore a Ford transit van cost £16,000 and it was expected to be used by the business for four years with a resale value of £4,000, the calculation of depreciation would be shown as follows.

$$\frac{£16,000 - £4,000}{4 \text{ years}} = \frac{£12,000}{4} = £3,000 \quad \text{depreciation per year}$$

Key terms

Historic cost – the cost of an asset when it was first purchased

Residual value – the value of an asset when it is disposed of by the business, for example, resale value

Expected life – how long an asset is expected to be used within a business

In the balance sheet, the net book value (the cost of an asset minus depreciation) would therefore be shown as follows.

(1) The value of the van at the end of one year: £16,000 – £3,000 = £13,000

Table 5.3: Example net book value for a Ford transit van.

Year	Cost	Accumulated depreciation	Net book value
1	£16,000	£3,000	£13,000 (1)
2	£16,000	£6,000	£10,000
3	£16,000	£9,000	£7,000
4	£16,000	£12,000	£4,000 (2)

(2) The value of the van at the end of four years matches the residual value used in the calculation above

Current assets

Current assets are those items of value owned by a business whose value is likely to fluctuate on a regular basis. Every time a business makes a transaction, the value of its current assets will fluctuate. Current assets include:

- stock
- debtors
- cash in the bank
- cash in hand.

Key term

Current assets – items owned by the business that change in value on a regular basis, such as stock

Stock is the value of stock held at that moment in time. Depending upon the nature of the business it can take three different forms: raw materials, work in progress and finished goods. A business must be careful to give stock a realistic value and not over value stock – for example, stock which they are unlikely to sell because it has gone out of fashion or is damaged.

Debtors are people who owe the business money. Although the business does not yet physically have the money, it is in effect owned by the business. Debtors are customers who have not yet paid for the good or service provided by the business and must be monitored to ensure that they do make the payment by the due date.

Current assets are listed in order of how easy it is to turn them into cash quickly. If, for example, a business has liquidity problems, it may find it difficult to turn stock into cash quickly and in trying to do so, may not receive its true value. In contrast, cash in hand is just that – cash!

Intangible assets

An intangible asset is something that adds value to the business but does not have a physical presence. One example of this that you might see on a balance sheet is 'goodwill'. This means when someone buys an already-established business, they are also buying the goodwill that that business has built up, such as brand recognition or a loyal customer base.

Long-term liabilities

A liability is something that the business owes. If it is classed as long-term, this means the business will pay it back in more than one year. Examples of long-term liabilities include bank loans and mortgages. These are likely to be used to buy fixed assets or to set up the business initially.

Current liabilities

A current liability is something owed by the business that should be paid back in under one year. Examples

Fig. 5.7: Why does the value of stock fall when a firm is forced to turn it into cash quickly?

of current liabilities are overdrafts and creditors. Creditors are people or businesses the business owes money to because it has received a good or service but not yet paid for it.

Working capital

Working capital is a very important figure for a business; it represents the business's ability to meet short-term debts. A business with insufficient working capital does not have enough current assets to meet its current liabilities. This is potentially disastrous as if the liabilities have to be paid for now and the business cannot meet these demands from its current assets, then it will have to find the cash elsewhere. This could mean being forced to sell a fixed asset without which the business cannot operate. Working capital is calculated as current assets minus current liabilities. We will look at the significance of working capital in more detail in the final part of this unit when we look at liquidity ratios.

Net assets

Net assets are the figure that represents the total value of all the assets minus the value of the liabilities. Net assets are calculated as follows.

$$\frac{\text{fixed}}{\text{assets}} + \frac{\text{current}}{\text{assets}} - \left(\frac{\text{current}}{\text{liabilities}} + \frac{\text{long-term}}{\text{liabilities}}\right)$$

Transfer of net profit from profit and loss account

The final section of the balance sheet basically asks where the business has got the money from to finance the value of its net assets. One of the answers to this question is going to be 'from profit'. The net profit from the profit and loss account is therefore transferred to the balance sheet under the heading 'Financed by'.

Capital employed

Profit will not be the only thing that has financed the business's assets. There is also likely to be some initial capital invested in the business – for example, share capital if the business is a company.

Remember

In order for a balance sheet to balance, net assets must be equal to capital employed.

	Cost	Accumulated depreciation	Net book value
	£	£	£
Fixed assets			
Premises	218,000	28,880	189,120
Fixtures and fittings	38,500	15,800	22,700
Vehicles	19,500	19,500	0
Current assets			
Stock			34,294
Debtors			21,455
Cash at bank			0
Cash in hand			381
			56,130
Less current liabilities			
Creditors			17,881
Overdraft			12,389
			30,270
Working capital			25,860
Less long-term liabilities			
Bank loans			50,998
Net assets			186,682
Financed by			
Capital			60,000
Retained profit			126,682
Capital employed			**186,682**

Fig. 5.8: Balance sheet for Freedom Fashion Ltd as at 30 April 2010.

PLTS

It is unlikely that your balance sheet will be right on your first attempt. You will have to see this as a challenge to try to identify where all the information has not been included or where errors have been made. It is likely to take a few attempts to get it perfect. Rise to this challenge and seek advice and support when needed.

Activity: Lily's balance sheet

Assume Lily's cash flow forecast for her first year was correct. Use the information from her profit and loss (P&L) account along with the additional information provided below to create a balance sheet for Lily's cleaning business.

- Fixed assets are depreciated at 20 per cent per year.

- All purchases are bought in cash.

Functional skills

ICT: If you produce your balance sheet using a spreadsheet package, this will demonstrate your ability to select and use ICT systems independently for a complex task.

Assessment activity 5.3

Sharma and Ryan have now been trading as SIGNature Ltd for a year and have again approached you to help them with producing their year end accounts.

1. You are to prepare a profit and loss account and balance sheet for SIGNature Ltd, based on the information provided. Actual sales and purchases for the 12 months were as follows.

Month	Sales	Purchases
January	£25,000	£12,400
February	£28,000	£14,000
March	£32,000	£16,000
April	£36,000	£18,000
May	£43,000	£21,000
June	£49,000	£24,000
July	£49,000	£23,800
August	£52,000	£25,000
September	£47,000	£20,000
October	£34,000	£12,000
November	£31,000	£8,600
December	£18,000	£5,000

- In their first year Sharma and Ryan received 2,080 orders.
- Closing stock was £12,000.
- Rent on their factory premises was £6,500 per quarter.
- Non-domestic rates were ten instalments of £1,800.
- Sharma and Ryan employed four machine operatives who were each paid £1,400 per month.
- The telephone bill was £60 per month and post £200 per month.

- Distribution costs via a courier were £10 per order.
- They advertised in a local magazine for the year at the cost of £35 per week, and quarterly in a specialist trade magazine at £500 per advert.

Other expenses included:

- repayment of bank loan (£1,000 per month)
- light and heating bills (£2,000 per quarter)
- insurance (£800 per annum, or year).

Sharma and Ryan had fixed assets to the value of £105,000 at the start of the year which they had decided to depreciate on a straight line method at ten per cent per year.

At the end of the year they owed £15,500 to suppliers and were owed £41,000 from customers. There was £17,160 positive balance of cash in the business.

Sharma and Ryan thought it had been a good first year and decided to reward themselves for all their hard work by paying themselves £20,000 each in dividends. **P4**

Grading tips

1. Work in a logical manner and tick each figure as you use it. When looking at each piece of information, ask yourself whether it should go in the profit and loss account, balance sheet or both. Read each piece of information carefully, taking into account the time frame. If, for example, it says a cost was £x per quarter, you must multiply this by four to get the annual figure.

2. Remember your figures can only be correct when net assets = capital employed on your balance sheet. Use a spreadsheet to present your accounts using formulae to save reworking calculations all of the time, but check your formulae are correct before you start. **P4**

4. Be able to review business performance using simple ratio analysis

You should now be familiar with the basic language of accounts and the key financial accounts produced by businesses. We will now look at what these accounts actually tell us and how an accountant can use or interpret them. Ratio analysis allows for a more meaningful interpretation of published accounts by comparing one figure to another. Ratio analysis also allows for both **inter-firm** and **intrafirm** comparisons.

Ratios will be used by internal **stakeholders** such as managers and employees, as well as external stakeholders such as investors and creditors.

4.1 Profitability

Profitability is a measure of the profit of a firm in relation to another. It allows for a more comprehensive assessment of the performance of a firm by comparing one figure to another. Imagine that there are two firms, A and B, both with a profit of £750,000 per year – how would you be able to tell which one was performing better? If, however, you were told that Firm A has sales revenue of £1.5 million and Firm B has sales revenue of £3 million, then it is clear that Firm A has greater profitability as it is generating the same amount of profit from a lower level of sales, implying it is more efficient and better at controlling its costs.

There are three profitability ratios we will look at here:

- gross profit percentage of sales
- net profit percentage of sales
- return on capital employed (ROCE).

Gross profit percentage of sales

This is calculated using the following formula.

$$\frac{\text{gross profit}}{\text{sales turnover}} \times 100$$

This ratio looks at gross profit as a percentage of sales turnover; this ratio is often referred to as the gross profit margin. It shows us for every £1 made in sales how much is left as gross profit after the cost of goods sold has been deducted. A gross profit percentage of sales of 88 per cent therefore means that for every £1 of sales made, 88p is left as gross profit.

Key terms

Inter-firm – between different firms, for example, comparing the performance of two different house builders

Intrafirm – within the firm, for example, comparing this year's results with last year's, or the performance of the York branch with the Leicester branch of a retail store

Stakeholder – anyone with an interest in the activities of a business, whether directly or indirectly involved

Table 5.4: Stakeholders and ratio analysis.

Stakeholder	Use of ratio analysis
Manager	• Assess performance of individual branches. • Monitor year-on-year performance. • Inform decision making. • Analyse relationships between revenues and expenses.
Employee	• Negotiate wages and conditions. • Assess security of firm and therefore own job. • Employees may be shareholders.
Shareholder	• Measure return on investment. • Review value of investment.
Creditor	• Assess security of firm. • Decide on credit terms offered. • Determine ability to pay debt.
Competitor	• Measure or benchmark own performance. • Make takeover bids.
Customer	• Negotiate better prices. • Assess security of long-term supplies.

If gross profit margin falls from one year to the next or is thought to be too low, a firm may try to reduce the cost of its purchases. This may involve looking for a cheaper supplier, but the firm must try to ensure that this does not affect the quality of the product. Alternatively, it may try to increase sales without increasing the cost of goods sold.

Net profit percentage of sales

This is calculated using the following formula.

$$\frac{\text{net profit}}{\text{sales turnover}} \times 100$$

This ratio looks at net profit as a percentage of sales turnover. This ratio is often referred to as the net profit margin. It shows for every £1 made in sales how much of it is left as net profit after all expenses have been deducted. A net profit percentage of sales of 31 per cent therefore means that for every £1 of sales made, 31p is left as net profit.

If net profit margin falls from one year to the next or is thought to be too low, a firm may look to reduce its expenses, for example, by moving to cheaper premises or cutting staffing costs. Before taking any action, however, the accountant must try to identify the cause of a falling figure – whether it is related to sales, cost of goods sold or expenses – as all of these factors will impact upon the net profit margin.

Worked example

Freedom Fashion Ltd

Sales turnover = £411,529

Gross profit = £269,792

Net profit = £41,246

Gross profit percentage of sales = £269,852/£411,529 × 100 = 65.5 per cent

For every £1 Freedom Fashion Ltd makes in sales, 65p is left as gross profit. A fashion retailer is likely to have reasonably high costs of sales due to the nature of their product. If it was a service industry then you might expect this percentage to be higher.

Net profit percentage of sales = £41,246/£411,529 × 100 = 10 per cent

For every £1 Freedom Fashion Ltd makes in sales, just 10p is left as net profit. A fashion retailer is likely to have reasonably high expenses due to the nature of their business. A retail business with a physical location (as opposed to e commerce) may have high overhead costs such as premises and heat and light.

Return on capital employed (ROCE)

This is calculated using the following formula.

$$\frac{\text{net profit before interest and tax}}{\text{capital employed}} \times 100$$

This ratio shows the percentage return a business is achieving from the capital (or money) being used to generate that return. It shows for every £1 invested in the business in owners' capital or retained profits what per cent is being generated in profit. A ROCE of five per cent means that for every £1 tied up in the business, 5p is being generated in net profit.

Investors will often compare ROCE to the interest rate being offered in a bank or building society to see if their investment is working effectively for them in generating a return.

Worked example

Freedom Fashion Ltd

Net profit before interest and tax = £41,246

Capital employed = £186,682

ROCE = £41,246/186,682 × 100 = 22 per cent

This means that for every £1 being used within the business, there is a return of 22p. This is certainly higher than you could expect from a bank.

4.2 Liquidity

Liquidity ratios measure how solvent a business is – that is, how able it is to meet short-term debts. There are two liquidity ratios we will look at here:

- current ratio
- acid test ratio/liquidity ratio.

Current ratio

This is calculated using the following formula.

$$\frac{\text{current assets}}{\text{current liabilities}}$$

This ratio shows the amount of current assets in relation to current liabilities and is expressed as x:1. If a firm had a current ratio of 2:1, this would mean that for every £2 it owned in current assets it owed £1 in current liabilities, and this would generally be considered acceptable. If, however, a firm had a current ratio of 0.5:1, this would mean that for every 50p it owned in current assets, it owed £1 in current liabilities. This means if the firm's bank demanded it repaid its overdraft immediately and creditors demanded payment, the firm would not be able to cover these demands from current assets. This is therefore a dangerous position to be in.

Worked example

Freedom Fashion Ltd

Current assets = £56,130

Current liabilities = £30,270

Current ratio = £56,130/£30,270 = 1.85

This means that for every £1 the business owes in short-term debt (that is, its current liabilities), it owns £1.85 in current assets. The business therefore has sufficient liquidity to meet short-term debts.

Acid test ratio/liquidity ratio

This is calculated using the following formula.

$$\frac{\text{current assets} - \text{stock}}{\text{current liabilities}}$$

The acid test is thought to be a tougher measure of a firm's liquidity. Like the current ratio, it shows the amount of current assets in relation to current liabilities, but it does not include stock. This is because stock is considered to be the hardest current asset to turn into cash quickly. The result is expressed as x:1.

Worked example

Freedom Fashion Ltd

Current assets = £56,130

Stock = £34,294

Current liabilities = £30,270

Acid test = £56,130 − £34,294/£30,270
= £21,826/£30,270 = 0.72

This means that for every £1 the business owes in short-term debts, it only has 72p in liquid assets (current assets excluding stock). This figure shows the firm to be **illiquid**, as it could not meet its short-term debts if immediate repayment was demanded. A fashion retailer is likely to have a large amount of its current assets in the form of stock, due to the nature of the firm.

Key term

Illiquid – not easily converted into cash

Activity: Comparing business liquidity

Select a business that you are interested in (or you could use the one you studied in Unit 2 Business resources). Compare the profitability and liquidity of your chosen business to that of Freedom Fashion Ltd.

Which one do you think is performing best? Justify your answer.

PLTS

Reflecting on cause and effect of financial ratios.

Functional skills

Mathematics: Use appropriate checking procedures and evaluate their effectiveness at each stage. Ensure your accounts are accurate before starting your ratio analysis and check the accuracy of each calculation before analysing the results. Draw conclusions and provide mathematical justifications. Analyse results of ratio analysis.

English: Communicate information, ideas and opinions effectively and persuasively. Evaluate ratio analysis.

4.3 Efficiency

Efficiency ratios tend to be used to assess how well management is controlling key aspects of the business, primarily stock and finances. There are three efficiency ratios we will look at here:

- debtors' payment period
- creditors' payment period
- rate of stock turnover.

Debtors' payment period

This is calculated using the following formula.

$$\frac{\text{debtors}}{\text{credit sales}} \times 365$$

If you do not know what percentage of sales were made on credit, then it is acceptable to use the sales figure as given in the profit and loss account. The ratio measures on average how long it takes for debtors to pay; it is expressed as a number of days. For example, if a business has a debtors' payment period of 60 days, this means on average it takes debtors two months to pay for goods or services purchased on credit. A business with cash flow problems will try to reduce its debtors' payment period.

Worked example

Freedom Fashion Ltd

Debtors = £21,455

Sales = £411,529

Debtors' payment period = £21,445/£411,529 × 365 = 19 days

This means that on average it takes a customer 19 days to pay for their purchases. A fashion retailer is unlikely to offer long payment terms.

Debtors' payment period will vary from firm to firm, depending upon the nature and price of items sold and whether the business deals in **business-to-business** or **business-to-consumer** sales. If it is business-to-business, longer payment terms may be given. One business may also give different payment terms to different customers depending upon the size and importance of a customer's business, reliability of payment and discounts offered.

Key terms

Business-to-business – B2B refers to when one business sells to another business – for example, a stationery business selling to a firm of accountants

Business-to-consumer – B2C refers to when one business sells to an individual – for example, a stationery business selling wedding stationery to a bride and groom

Creditors' payment period

This is calculated using the following formula.

$$\frac{\text{creditors}}{\text{credit purchases}} \times 365$$

If you do not know what percentage of purchases were made on credit, then it is acceptable to use the purchases figure as given in the profit and loss account. The ratio measures on average how long it takes a firm to pay for goods and services bought on credit; it is expressed as a number of days. For example, if a business has a creditors' payment period of 30 days, this means on average there is a one-month gap between the business buying the good or service and paying for it. A business with

cash flow problems will try to lengthen its creditors' payment period.

Worked example

Freedom Fashion Ltd

Creditors = £17,881

Purchases = £128,129

Creditors' payment period = £17,881/£128,129 × 365 = 51 days

This means that on average the firm pays its suppliers in 51 days. This may mean that some suppliers offer one month's credit and others two months.

Rate of stock turnover

This is calculated using the following formula.

$$\frac{\text{average stock}}{\text{cost of goods sold}} \times 365$$

Average stock is calculated as follows.

$$\frac{\text{opening stock} + \text{closing stock}}{2}$$

This ratio measures the average amount of time an item of stock is held by a business, and is expressed as a number of days. If a business has a stock turnover of seven, this means that on average it holds each item of stock for one week. The rate of stock turnover is very much dependent upon the nature of the firm. For example, you could expect a florist or fishmonger to have a much lower stock turnover than a fashion store or car showroom. However, if the rate of stock turnover appears high for the nature of the product, this might result in stock going out of date or out of fashion.

Worked example

Freedom Fashion Ltd

Opening stock = £34,993

Closing stock = £21,445

Cost of goods sold = £141,737

Average stock = £34,993 + £21,445/2
= £56,438/2 = £28,219

Rate of stock turnover = £28,219/£141,737 × 365 = 73 days

This means that on average the business turns its stock over, or sells its stock, every 73 days. This is just over every two months, which is what you might expect from a fashion retailer with approximately six new lines per year.

Assessment activity 5.4

Sharma and Ryan now want you to help them understand their financial accounts for SIGNature Ltd. You should prepare a set of numbered appendices to the accounts which explain their profitability, liquidity and efficiency. Only Sharma and Ryan will see these notes and therefore these should give a fair and frank explanation of their performance.

In order to produce these appendices, you should perform the following tasks.

1. Use the profit and loss account and balance sheet you created in Assessment activity 5.3 to carry out the following ratios to measure:

   - profitability
     - gross profit percentage of sales
     - net profit percentage of sales
     - ROCE
   - liquidity
     - current ratio
     - acid test ratio/liquidity ratio
   - efficiency
     - debtors' payment period
     - creditors' payment period
     - rate of stock turnover. **P5**

2. Explain what each ratio is a measurement of, and what the result means to Sharma and Ryan. Try to explain possible reasons for the ratio and the significance of it to the business's overall financial performance. **P5**

3. Make a judgement about each ratio – does it imply a good or poor performance? Explain why. **M2**

4. Write a conclusion to summarise the overall performance of Sharma and Ryan's first year of trading. **D2**

Grading tips

1. Tick off each ratio from the list as you do it, to ensure you do not miss any out. Double check each calculation for accuracy. Be careful to express each result in the correct way – for example is it a percentage, a ratio or a number of days? It is important to get this right in order to be able to progress on to M2. **P5**

2. 'Analyse' is an instruction asking you to explain what the results of the ratio analysis mean. One structure which can help with this is to consider cause and effect.

   - Cause is what factors contributed to that outcome – for example, the gross profit as a percentage of sales might be high/low because of sales or cost of materials.

   - Effect is what this now means for the business – for example, what the creditors' payment period would mean for the future cash flow of the business.

   This is not an easy skill and you should try to explain what each ratio measures, what the result means and then try to make a meaningful comment about this figure. Expressions such as 'this means that…' and 'therefore…' can help you develop lines of analysis. **M2**

3. 'Evaluate' means to make justified judgements. You should look at each ratio and consider whether this is good or bad. There are a number of things you could look at here to help make a judgement, which include:

   - how it will impact upon the future performance of the firm

   - how it compares to other businesses in a similar market

   - what the results would have been if predictions as shown in the cash flow had been true – whether performance would have been better or worse.

   When writing your overall conclusion, remember that this is a new business start-up – consider SIGNature Ltd's performance in this context. **D2**

Just checking

1. Why is it important for businesses to keep accurate accounts?
2. With the use of appropriate examples, explain the difference between capital income and revenue income.
3. How does the level of capital income available to a business vary depending upon its legal structure? (That is, whether it is a sole trader, partnership or limited company.)
4. With the use of appropriate examples, explain the difference between capital expenditure and revenue expenditure.
5. What is meant by the term intangible asset? Give at least two examples.
6. Describe the purpose and structure of a cash flow forecast.
7. Identify and explain two possible solutions to cash flow problems.
8. What is the difference between a bank loan and an overdraft?
9. What is the purpose of a profit and loss account and a balance sheet?
10. What is the difference between gross profit and net profit? Support your answer with a numerical example.
11. With the use of appropriate examples, explain the meaning of the following terms:
    a) fixed assets
    b) current assets
    c) current liabilities
    d) long-term liabilities.
12. How are net assets and capital employed calculated?
13. What is meant by the term working capital?
14. Briefly explain how a firm's profitability can be measured.
15. What is meant by the term liquidity? Why is this important to the survival of a business?
16. What is the difference between the current ratio and acid test ratio as measures of liquidity?

edexcel

Assignment tips

1. When preparing the cash flow forecast, profit and loss account, and balance sheet, try using a spreadsheet package. Check all of your formulae are correct first by putting in simple numbers and seeing if the answers generated are correct.

2. As you use each number, tick it off so you know if you have missed a figure out. Double check that you have entered the correct number into your spreadsheet – if you accidentally type a wrong number in, the spreadsheet cannot spot this.

3. When performing the ratio analysis, do each calculation twice to check it is correct. When explaining the results of the ratio analysis, try to think about the nature of the business in question.

9 Creative product promotion

Wherever you are or whatever you are doing, it is very difficult to avoid being bombarded by promotional messages. When using a computer, reading a newspaper, watching television or even sitting on the bus on the way to college, promotional messages are all around us, trying to persuade us to part with our money.

In this unit you will look at the marketing activities that help to produce successful promotional campaigns. These activities comprise a variety of tools and techniques – the promotional mix – used to influence the buying behaviour of customers or potential customers. An understanding of the parts of the promotional mix allows businesses to plan promotions to achieve their aims and objectives.

You will look at theoretical models of communication in order to understand the complexity of the factors influencing communication. The unit considers a response hierarchy model, which attempts to predict the sequence of mental stages that the consumer passes through on the way to a purchase. The AIDA (Attention, Interest, Desire, Action) model is useful for prioritising the promotional objectives at various stages of the buying process.

You will examine the role of promotion within the marketing mix as well as the other elements of the mix, such as product, price, place, people, processes, people and physical evidence. You will also explore promotional objectives and how they relate to business aims and objectives, and consider the importance to a business organisation of developing a brand.

Advertising agencies can make a significant contribution to the effectiveness of a campaign. As well as developing relevant messages, agencies can advise organisations about which media to use and how often they should be used. In the final part of the unit, you will take on the role of an advertising agency by creating a simple promotional campaign.

Learning outcomes

After completing this unit, you should:

1. know the constituents of the promotional mix
2. understand the role of promotion within the marketing mix
3. understand the role of advertising agencies and the media
4. be able to create a simple promotional campaign.

Assessment and grading criteria

This table shows you what you must do in order to achieve a **pass**, **merit** or **distinction** grade, and where you can find activities in this book to help you.

To achieve a **pass** grade, the evidence must show that the learner is able to:	To achieve a **merit** grade, the evidence must show that, in addition to the pass criteria, the learner is able to:	To achieve a **distinction** grade, the evidence must show that, in addition to the pass and merit criteria, the learner is able to:
P1 describe the promotional mix used by two selected organisations for a selected product/service **See Assessment activity 9.1, page 210.**	**M1** explain how promotion is integrated with the rest of the marketing mix of a selected organisation to achieve its marketing aims and objectives **See Assessment activity 9.1, page 210.**	**D1** evaluate and justify the use of an appropriate promotional mix with respect to marketing objectives for the selected organisation **See Assessment activity 9.1, page 210.**
P2 explain the role of promotion within the marketing mix for a selected product/service **See Assessment activity 9.2, page 219.**		
P3 explain the role of advertising agencies in the development of a successful promotional campaign **See Assessment activity 9.3, page 226.**	**M2** explain the advantages and disadvantages of using professional agencies in ensuring promotional success **See Assessment activity 9.3, page 226.**	
P4 explain the reasons behind the choice of media in a successful promotional campaign **See Assessment activity 9.3, page 226.**		
P5 design a promotional campaign for a given product/service to meet the needs of a given campaign/creative brief **See Assessment activity 9.4, page 233.**	**M3** provide a rationale for a promotional campaign **See Assessment activity 9.4, page 233.**	**D2** evaluate an existing, national marketing campaign **See Assessment activity 9.4, page 233.**

How you will be assessed

This unit will be assessed by an internal assignment that will be designed and marked by the staff at your centre. It may be subject to sampling by your centre's External Verifier as part of Edexcel's ongoing quality assurance procedures. The assignment is designed to allow you to show your understanding of the unit outcomes. These relate to what you should be able to do after completing this unit. Your assessment could be in the form of presentations, case studies, practical tasks and written assignments.

Fatima

This unit helped me to realise how much work goes on behind the scenes in order to make a customer buy a product or service. In large businesses this involves lots of people working on different aspects of marketing.

I enjoyed looking at the world of advertising and this is an area I would really like to work in, as to be successful you have to be innovative and creative, which appeals to me. I found investigating the role of advertising agencies particularly interesting – especially how they target particular customer groups. We examined some current television adverts and tried to work out who the adverts were targeted at, which was a really useful exercise.

We did lots of group and individual exercises using the Internet to look at how business organisations plan their promotions and have different promotional mixes. I really enjoyed developing my own promotional campaign, which allowed me not only to understand the important aspects of campaign planning but also use my artistic flair.

1. What type of advertising do you find effective?
2. What is your favourite advert and why?
3. What kind of information do you think an advertising agency would need to produce an effective publicity campaign for a product?

What are they trying to do?

Think of a television or newspaper advert currently being aired or printed, and answer the following questions.

1. What message is it trying to put over?
2. What theme or storyline are they using in the advert?
3. Who is the advert aimed at?
4. What is the purpose of the advert?
5. Is the advert successful in achieving its purpose?

Discuss your findings in small groups and compare your answers with other members of the class.

1. Know the constituents of the promotional mix

In a competitive marketplace, it is not enough for a business to have good products sold at attractive prices. To generate sales and profits, businesses have to communicate the benefits of products to customers. In marketing, this is commonly known as 'promotion'. Promotion is the part of the marketing process that communicates the benefits of the product or service. Promotion has an essential role in winning new customers, and keeping existing ones. A business's total marketing communications programme is called the **promotional mix** and consists of a blend of advertising, personal selling, sales promotion and public relations tools.

The challenge is to have the right mix of promotional activity to suit your business at a particular time. The combination of tools that a business uses will depend upon:

- the target audience
- the message that is sent
- the budget that is available.

1.1 The promotional mix
The marketing mix and the promotional mix

Understanding the nature of customers and their needs and wants is only the first step in successfully developing the promotional mix to sell a product. The business needs to act on the information about

Key term

Promotional mix – the elements that make up an organisation's marketing communications strategy: advertising, sales promotion, personal selling, direct marketing and public relations

What is the 'promotional mix' made up of?

the customers and create marketing activities that deliver something of value to customers. To implement marketing activities, the business uses the **marketing mix**. The marketing mix is the combination of four major tools of marketing, otherwise known as the four Ps: product, price, promotion and place.

Key term

Marketing mix – sometimes referred to as the four Ps of product, price, promotion and place, these are the ideas to consider when marketing a product

The traditional four Ps of the marketing mix are appropriate when we are dealing with tangible products such as a car or a pair of football boots, but when we look at services that are marketed (such as banking or retailing) the four Ps cannot fully describe the marketing activities that are going on. So an extended marketing mix – the seven Ps – is used. The additional three factors are people, processes and physical evidence.

The promotional mix is how a business attempts to communicate with various target audiences and is a key element in the overall marketing mix. It consists of six main elements which are:

- advertising
- personal selling
- sales promotion
- public relations
- direct marketing
- sponsorship.

Think of it like a cake mix – the basic ingredients are always the same, but if you vary the amounts of one of the ingredients, the final outcome is different. The same is true of promotions: you can integrate different aspects of the promotions mix to deliver a unique campaign.

Case study: Woodplay Ltd

Woodplay Ltd is a manufacturer of wooden toys for the very young. The product range includes wooden dolls and soldiers. The toys are quite expensive and are hand-made. The company sells largely through mail order and advertises in magazines aimed at young mothers. It has decided to increase its promotional spend and advertise through a national magazine insert in a national newspaper.

1. **Describe the target audience for Woodplay's toys.**

2. **Why do you think it has decided to advertise through a national magazine insert?**

3. **What possible national publications would you recommend that they go with?**

Functional skills

English: This case study allows you to read and understand texts and use them to gather information, ideas, arguments and opinions.

Table 9.1: The four Ps of marketing.

Product	Promotion
• Product development • Product management • Product features/benefits • Branding • Packaging • After-sales service	• Developing promotional mixes • Advertising management • Sales promotion management • Sales management • Public relations management • Direct marketing
Place	**Price**
• Access to target market • Channel structure • Channel management • Retailer image • Logistics	• Costs • Profitability • Value for money • Competitiveness • Incentives

Advertising

The American Marketing Association's definition of advertising is: 'Advertising is a paid form of non-personal presentation and promotion of ideas, goods or services by an identified sponsor'. Advertising is the method used by a wide variety of organisations to:

- communicate a message to a selected audience
- persuade people to buy a product or service
- highlight specific features or qualities inherent within the product or service.

Organisations may use advertising to develop attitudes, create awareness and transmit information in order to gain a response from the target market. There are many advertising media, including newspapers (local, national, free, trade), magazines and journals, television (local, national, terrestrial, satellite), cinema, outdoor advertising (such as posters, bus sides) and of course the Internet.

Personal selling

Many businesses employ a sales force to help in the promotional process. Personal selling is an effective way to manage personal customer relationships. The salesperson acts on behalf of the organisation. This involves interpersonal contact between the buyer and the seller with the aim of encouraging the buyer to behave and think in a certain way.

Salespeople may be well trained in the approaches and techniques of personal selling. However, salespeople are very expensive and should only be used where there is a genuine return on investment. For example, salespeople are often used to sell expensive goods such as cars or home improvements, where the profit margin is high.

Sales promotion

Businesses spend a great deal of money on sales promotions, which are often aimed at the consumer. For example, the Buy One Get One Free (BOGOF) promotion has been used by a number of businesses over that last few years. Other methods include couponing, money-off promotions, competitions, free accessories (such as free blades with a new razor) and introductory offers (such as buy digital TV and get free installation). Each sales promotion should

be carefully costed by the marketing department to ensure the investment has returned good sales and profit.

In some markets, customers have come to expect special promotional offers to accompany the brands they purchase and they will not buy or will switch if these expected offers are not available. There is also the concern with regular sales promotions for a brand that it becomes cheapened in the mind of the customer. However, generally customer perceptions of sales promotions are favourable because they are seen as offering value for money and strong incentives to purchase.

Public relations (PR)

Public relations is defined by the Institute of Public Relations as 'the deliberate, planned and sustained effort to establish and maintain mutual understanding between an organisation and its public'. There is a key difference between publicity and public relations. A business has less control over publicity, which can be either good or bad. If a food manufacturer receives publicity about a nail being found in their food product, then this publicity can be detrimental or negative to the business. If, however, it is discovered that one of their key ingredients in the product has been proven to reduce the risk of cancer, then this will have a positive effect on the business.

Public relations activities can include, for example, organising conferences, open days, hospitality events and award celebrations. A business may be expanding and planning to employ another 200 people. The public relations manager may then issue a press release announcing this and newspapers may print this, projecting a positive image of the company to the public.

Key term

Public relations – the development and maintenance of positive relationships between an organisation and its public – employees, local community, customers, suppliers, media – through activities designed to create understanding and goodwill

Direct marketing

Direct marketing is used across a wide range of consumer and business markets and has made considerable progress in recent years in overcoming its poor image as being just junk mail. Direct marketing uses databases to target any customer who has similar characteristics with the group at which the business intends to aim their products or services. The organisation can then send a **mailshot** to potential consumers and carefully monitor responses.

For example, if you are marketing medical textbooks, you would use a database of doctors' surgeries as the basis of your mailshot. More sophisticated direct marketing campaigns can target customers through the Internet.

Sponsorships

Sponsorship is where an organisation pays to be associated with a particular event, cause or image. Companies sponsor sports events such as the Premier League (currently sponsored by Barclays). The attributes of the event are then associated with the sponsoring organisation.

Major companies now sponsor many television programmes through one of their products or brands. Sports sponsorship can be one of the most prominent – and most expensive – forms of sponsorship, with

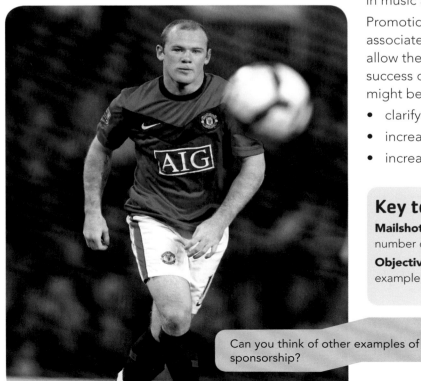

Can you think of other examples of sponsorship?

Did you know?

Bovril became synonymous with football when in 1898 they sponsored Nottingham Forest Football Club. The team advertised the drink on their shirts and went on to win the FA Cup. Sports shirt sponsorship today is worth around 70 million, with much of this revenue going to the premier or first division clubs.

teams or individuals receiving backing from businesses at local, national and international level. Businesses may also sponsor research activities (for example, a medical company may sponsor research into a drug) or competitions.

Purpose and objectives of promotional mix

Once a business has formulated a detailed profile of the customer that it wishes to target, the product and the environment, it has to set detailed **objectives** for the communications campaign.

Promotional objectives have to be precise and measureable – for example, it is not good enough to set an objective such as 'to increase awareness of the product'. With this objective we do not know who we want to become aware of the product or how much awareness we are aiming to generate. A more useful objective would be 'to generate 75 per cent awareness among under 21-year-old females who are interested in music and the arts'.

Promotional objectives can cover a multitude of issues associated with communication. Precise objectives allow the monitoring, feedback and assessment of the success of the promotional mix. Possible objectives might be to:

- clarify customer needs
- increase brand awareness
- increase product knowledge

Key terms

Mailshot – material, especially promotional, posted to a large number of people

Objectives – goals that an organisation sets for itself – for example, profitability, sales growth or return on investment

- improve brand image
- improve company image
- increase brand preference
- stimulate search behaviour
- increase trial purchase
- increase repeat purchase rate
- increase word-of-mouth reputation
- improve financial position
- increase flexibility of image
- increase co-operation from the trade.

Corporate image

Corporate image refers to the way in which a business chooses to present itself to the world. It reflects the character and philosophy of the organisation. The promotional mix that a particular business implements can support their desired corporate image. For example, BMW uses advertising in quality newspapers to promote their high-quality cars, which helps support their upmarket corporate image.

Although an organisation's logo is the most visible face of its identity, there are many other parts of the organisation that contribute to the overall corporate image. The corporate image communicates the organisation's values and character. For example, Virgin wants to establish itself as the company that provides excellence in customer service and most of its corporate communications tend to stress this aim. Similarly, non-profit organisations such as churches, colleges, charities, museums and performing arts groups market their organisations in order to raise funds and attract supporters.

1.2 Decisions to be made about the promotional mix

With so many different promotional options available, the business needs to choose carefully the methods that are best suited to the situation. We will now look at a variety of situations and the factors that should be considered when making decisions about the appropriateness of a selected promotional mix.

Costs versus benefits – short-term and long-term

A **cost/benefit analysis** is done to determine how well, or how poorly, a planned action will turn out. Although a cost/benefit analysis can be used for almost anything,

it is most commonly done on financial questions and used extensively to evaluate the usefulness of a promotional strategy.

For example, the marketing department of a manufacturing company has estimated that by spending £2 million on television advertising, they will receive an extra £15 million worth of sales, of which £5 million will be profit. In this situation, the projections indicate that this promotional spend is worth pursuing. Obviously, the proof of the pudding is in the eating and increased sales of only £5 million will significantly affect the benefit.

However, certain organisations need to take a long-term view of their investment into promotional activity. A bank might spend more on promoting its current accounts than it could hope to recoup from customers in this area. However, customers switching to the bank's current account may want to take out loans, mortgages, insurance and so on over the course of their time with the bank. Therefore, their lifetime value to the bank will be significantly more than their initial trade might imply.

Target market and exposure to the media

Businesses will choose media carefully in relation to the promotional budget that exists. However, the cheapest option will not always bring about the best return on investment.

For example, a company's target market may be relatively affluent young families in the 20–35-year-old age bracket. A TV advert on ITV1 during one of their primetime shows, such as *Coronation Street*, might expose a large portion of their target audience to their product. However, it could be one of the more expensive advertising options, so there may be a pressure to find a cheaper option. This could still be a TV advert, but broadcast at a different time of day, when the **demographics** might be different and the audience smaller, making the message less successful.

Key terms

Cost/benefit analysis – weighing up the total expected costs against the total expected benefits of one or more actions in order to choose the best or most profitable option

Demographics – selected population characteristics such as lifestyles, spending, habits, age and employment. These characteristics are used in government, marketing or opinion research to further understand the consumer or general public at large

Type of market

It is commonly agreed that there are two types of market:

- **business-to-business** (B2B), where one company will sell their products or services to other companies

- **business-to-consumer** (B2C), where a company will sell their products direct to private individuals.

Key terms

Business-to-business (B2B) – describes transactions between businesses, such as between a manufacturer and a wholesaler, or between a wholesaler and a retailer

Business-to-consumer (B2C) – describes activities of businesses serving end consumers with products and/or services

Promotional activities in these markets are often very different, reflecting the different audiences. For example, B2B customers experience more direct selling – a B2B company may identify the individual most likely to be interested in their product within another company and contact them directly. This technique is known as the push method because the business is pushing its products or services to its customers.

B2C customers are likely to have a very different experience. Companies try to raise the profile and awareness of their products, but are careful not to irritate customers in doing so. A TV or print advert for a new car is much less obtrusive than a car dealer cold-calling. This is designed to stimulate demand in the target market, and is referred to as the pull method as it pulls the customer towards the product.

Rapidly changing or relatively stable markets

Whether a market is rapidly changing or whether it is in a calm and relatively stable situation will affect the promotional strategies that an organisation uses. Rapidly changing markets require an approach that allows organisations to take advantage of the opportunities as they occur.

Volatile (unstable) markets require a promotional approach that can be devised, prepared and released quickly to make the most of opportunities in the

Activity: B2B or B2C?

Working in groups, try to identify whether the following are B2B or B2C.

1. A replacement windows representative is cold-calling around the local neighbourhood, trying to sell windows to residential householders.

2. A representative of a leading military helicopter manufacturer is visiting the Ministry of Defence to sell the helicopters.

3. A Coca-Cola representative is visiting Tesco's Head Office, hoping to persuade them to introduce a new carbonated drink into their stores.

4. A sportswear retailer is advertising premiership football kits on its website for sale to customers.

Functional skills

English: This activity allows you to practise speaking and listening, making a range of contributions to discussions.

marketplace. Promotional emails, text messages or website home pages may be suitable media for these markets, where canny marketers can make reference to recent events in their copy or design.

Stable markets are better suited to traditional methods of promotion, as the marketer can be fairly sure that nothing will have changed substantially during the production process for their promotional message. For example, an advert in a magazine will need to be conceived, designed and submitted to the magazine in time for the copy deadline; the magazine will then be printed and distributed. The magazine would then be on sale for a week, a month or even longer, depending on the frequency of the editions, and so the promotional message would need to remain accurate and current during this period.

Channel strategies and objectives

When businesses choose a route to move their products to the marketplace, the route they choose is known as the channel structure. The chosen channel will vary according to whether the business is dealing with consumer (B2C) or organisational goods (B2B). The four most common channel structures for B2C markets are:

- producer-consumer (direct supply) – manufacturer deals directly with the consumer, for example, when you go strawberry picking at a farm
- producer-retailer-consumer (short channel) – this is the most popular, and includes traditional retailing, where we enter a large supermarket and make a purchase
- producer-wholesaler-retailer-consumer (long channel) – small retail shops usually buy from a wholesaler or a cash and carry before selling to the consumer
- producer-agent-wholesale-retailer-consumer – this channel is usually found where a company wanting to enter a foreign market uses an agent to sell their products to wholesalers in that country, which in turn sell to retailers.

B2B markets also use a number of channels, which are either:

- manufacturer-user
- manufacturer-distributor-user.

The channel strategy needs to fit in with the organisation's objectives, capabilities and resources. If the objective is to generate mass appeal with rapid market penetration, then the organisation needs a channel that can distribute its product quickly over a wide area. An intensive promotional campaign would need to support this.

Positioning

A crucial decision for any business is where to position its product. Product positioning means thinking about a product in the context of the competitive space it occupies in its market. Harrod's, for example, is positioned as a high-quality, exclusive department store. In order to reinforce this positioning with its target market, Harrod's makes sure that its product ranges, its staff expertise, its displays and overall store ambience are of equally high quality.

Branding

Branding is an important element of the tangible product. It is a means of linking items within a product line or emphasising the individuality of product items. A brand consists of any name, design, style, words or symbols, singly or in any combination that distinguishes one product from another in the eyes of the customer.

Examples of brands that we see every day are Ford, Weetabix and Coca-Cola. A brand gives many benefits to the consumer, the manufacturer and the retailer.

What does 'branding' mean?

- For the consumer, it facilitates easier product identification and it communicates features and benefits by its brand name.
- For the manufacturer, it helps build customer loyalty and creates differential advantage over its competition.
- For the retailer, marketing support is given by the manufacturer and it can attract customers into the store.

Branding can therefore influence decisions about the promotional mix as messages have to be reinforced about the brand and its values.

Did you know?

Coca-Cola is one of the most recognisable brands on the market, with over one billion cans consumed every day. Strangely enough, when first invented, it was used as a medicine to cure headaches.

Case study: Tesco's Finest

Tesco's has relaunched its Finest brand with new attractive packaging and has increased its number of lines under the Finest brand to over 1,200. Tesco has already developed its Finest brand into health and beauty products. All their stores sell some non-food, with their Extra format and trial Homeplus format offering the biggest choice.

By introducing these ranges to more of their stores, Tesco can bring down prices and offer customers the convenience of shopping for value non-food along with their food and household goods. Value, Tesco standard and Finest own-brand products are available across their non-food offer.

1. What are the advantages to Tesco of developing its Finest brand?

2. What are the benefits of this brand to the customer?

Functional skills

English: This case study allows you to read about business information, using it to gather information, ideas, arguments and opinions.

Competitors

Competitors can also play a part in decisions about the promotional mix. If a competitor is having particular success with its promotional mix, then another company may want to copy these mix decisions with a similar competitive product. It may also work the other way round – for example, if a competitor is dominant as a result of its mix strategies, then another company may find it more appropriate to use a different promotional mix.

Budget requirements

All promotional activity needs to work within a set budget to ensure that it is proportional to the additional business it is intended to produce. A company may base this budget on a percentage of profits from the previous year (for example, if the business offers a service, a proportion of the profit may be reinvested to grow or maintain the revenue generated by that service), or as a portion of the anticipated profit the product or service will generate for that year.

It can be difficult to discern the financial benefit of an expensive marketing campaign, but easy to identify this on a profit and loss sheet. For this reason, promotional activities may be scaled back (particularly if the company experiences financial pressure), which may result in a less effective promotional campaign.

Timing requirements

For some products, timing can be essential for their success or failure. For example, if a toy manufacturer wants to make their product successful at Christmas, they will need to get the toy into shops from September. They will also need to raise customers' awareness of the product through increased promotional activity, probably from late summer. Realistically, the company will have started developing the product and the promotional activity at least a year in advance of its launch.

Other businesses may need to launch their products in time for an exhibition (for example, a video game developer might want to launch a new game at the annual E3 Expo), or need to negotiate a sponsorship deal in advance of the new football season.

It takes time to put all the pieces of a promotional campaign together. Salespeople need to receive training if they are to be effective, and promotional materials (for example, leaflets, flyers) need time to be designed and printed before they can be distributed.

1.3 Communications models

The primary aim of promotion is to influence the consumer's buying behaviour. Businesses therefore need to know how communication works. Models have been used to develop frameworks for the understanding of communication processes. Fig. 9.1 shows one popular model.

There are seven elements in the process plus a factor known as 'noise'. Noise covers any factors that interfere with any aspect of the communication process between the sender of the communication and the receiver. For example, noise could be not watching the television when an advertisement is broadcast that is aimed at that person. There may be many other things going on that prevent the message getting through. Noise thus either causes the message to be distorted in the receiver's mind or to fail to reach the receiver's attention at all. The other elements are as follows.

- The **sender** may be a business organisation wishing to communicate a message to a defined audience.

- The **receiver** of a marketing message may be the individuals within the targeted audience. For example, a holiday company such as Saga targets the over-50 age group.

- The **message** is what the sender wants the audience to know or understand as a result of receiving the communication. This might be, for example, 'don't drink and drive'.

- **Encoding** is where the sender's understanding of the receiver pays dividends, as the sender's message contains elements specific to a target audience. Encoding can appeal to different perceptions of a particular product.

- **Decoding** is where the receiver converts the symbols or sounds into a form that makes sense or in other words how the receiver interprets the message sent.

- The **medium** is the communication channel through which the message moves from sender to receiver, such as television, newspaper, radio or the Internet.

- **Feedback** is the part of the receiver's response that the receiver communicates back to the sender.

1.4 Consumer response hierarchy model

AIDA (Attention, Interest, Desire, Action)

The consumer response hierarchy theory is one of a number of models that stress that consumers pass through a number of stages before buying a product. The AIDA (Attention, Interest, Desire and Action) model shown in Fig. 9.2 is one of the more popular response hierarchy models.

In this model, advertising, for example, creates the initial awareness, and stimulates the interest and then the desire for the product. Only then does the trial take place. In other words, the attitude and opinion are formed before the consumer ever gets near the product.

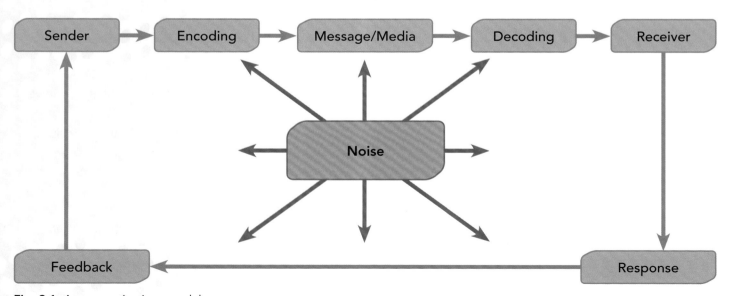

Fig. 9.1: A communications model.

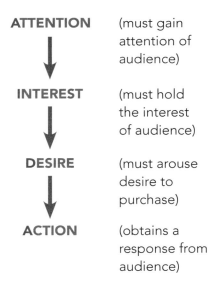

ATTENTION — (must gain attention of audience)

INTEREST — (must hold the interest of audience)

DESIRE — (must arouse desire to purchase)

ACTION — (obtains a response from audience)

Fig. 9.2: AIDA model.

Table 9.2: Promotional tools.

Stage	Most appropriate promotional tool
Attention	TV, radio advertising/sponsorship to put product in public's mind
Interest	Newspaper, magazine advertising to explain benefits, public relations to highlight product features
Desire	Advertising such as in brochures to show product being used or enjoyed, personal selling can explain benefits, sales promotion to encourage purchase
Action	Sales promotion/personal selling to convince customer to buy

Promotional methods at different stages

At each stage, differing promotional mixes may be required to maximise the benefits of the different promotional tools.

Advertising is most appropriate in the awareness stage (also known as the cognitive stage) and is designed to catch the target market's attention and generate straightforward awareness of the product.

The interest and desire stages are often referred to as the affective stage and involve creating or changing an attitude. This means giving the consumer sufficient information to pass judgement on the product and to develop positive feelings towards it.

The final stage, which is often referred to as the behaviour stage, leads to action or purchasing of the product. Some consumers may move through the stages at different rates; therefore different promotional mixes may exist within different stages targeted at sub-segments at different readiness stages. Personal selling may be appropriate at the action stage to persuade the consumer into buying.

Activity: Confectionery

A confectionery manufacturer with over £20 million to spend on its promotional campaign wants to launch its new chocolate bar targeted at 16–25-year-olds.

What promotional tools would you advise it to use to bring the new product to the attention of the target group and to create interest? Working in groups, answer this question then make a five-minute presentation to the class on your findings.

Functional skills

ICT: If you use ICT to present your findings, you may have interacted independently using ICT for a complex task. You may also have entered, developed and formatted information independently to suit its meaning and purpose using text and tables, images, numbers and records.

Assessment activity 9.1

P1 M1 D1  BTEC

For this assignment you will need to select two organisations of interest to you that are currently involved in the promotion of a product or service. You are in the role of a researcher employed by a marketing magazine and have been asked to investigate a number of promotional activities that may form the basis of future articles in editions of the magazine. By completing the following tasks, you will be able to produce the first part of the report.

1. Describe the promotional mix used by your two chosen organisations for a selected product or service. This could, for example, relate to raising sales or establishing a local profile. **P1**

2. With reference to the product or service promoted by one of the businesses chosen for Task 1, explain how their promotion is integrated with the rest of the marketing mix to achieve its marketing aims and objectives. You should explain the connection between promotional activity and the achievement of the marketing aims and objectives. **M1**

3. For the final part of the assessment, you need to evaluate and justify the use of an appropriate promotional mix in relation to marketing objectives for the selected organisation. You should have some

idea of expected gains in product sales or service uptake resulting from their campaign. You should balance this against approximate costs so that the project may be evaluated as a success or failure. **D1**

Grading tips

1. Make sure that you choose organisations where you can access information regarding their promotional mixes. If you have a problem in finding suitable organisations, see your tutor, who should be able to help. **P1**

2. Make sure you understand how the promotional mix is in effect the P for promotion within the marketing mix. Also, make sure you know the marketing aims and objectives of your chosen organisation. **M1**

3. Evaluation is about considering in detail the advantages and disadvantages of something, and coming to conclusions as a result of this analysis. Try to work out the cost of the promotional mix and set this against the possible benefits that have occurred, for example, increase in sales. **D1**

2. Understand the role of promotion within the marketing mix

2.1 Products and services

Product range

The product is at the heart of the marketing exchange process. If the product does not deliver the benefits the customer wanted, or if it does not live up to the customer's expectations, then this can be very costly for a business.

Most businesses offer a range of products. This may be a broad spectrum of different items serving different needs (for example, Tesco sells food, clothes, electronics and so on), while other companies may offer a range of different models suited to different needs (for example, Apple's iPod range includes the Shuffle, Nano, Classic and Touch). The total sum of all the products and variants offered by a business is known as the product mix or range.

New product development, product and market trials

The term 'new product' is not as clear-cut as it may sound. There are differing degrees of newness. At one extreme there could be a new pack size or colour of an existing product, while at the other extreme it could be a ground-breaking innovation that has never been seen before. There is an eight-stage framework that can guide the new product development process.

1. Ideas generation (ideas are put forward).
2. Idea screening (all ideas are reviewed and the ones least likely to succeed are removed).
3. Concept testing (sketches and mock models of the product are produced).
4. Business analysis (forecasting sales and production figures).
5. Product development (investment is made to produce the product).
6. Test marketing (product is tested in certain geographic areas and results noted).
7. Commercialisation (product is now ready for full launch).
8. Monitoring and evaluation (review of performance of the product and adjustments made).

The sixth stage is crucial for a business developing a new product, and provides a testing ground for the promotional mix chosen. An organisation may decide to run product and marketing trials in a small area, using realistic market conditions. This may involve using the promotional mix in local media and monitoring the level of demand it generates.

The business may also test the product, and try to get feedback from customers. This helps the business to identify whether any improvements need to be made to the product before the full-scale launch (which reduces the risk of wasting money on releasing a product that is not right). The business can also adapt the promotional mix if they find opportunities for getting a better response, which would help generate a better return on their investment.

Quality, style and associated services and benefits in promotion

Quality has a number of meanings – it is not always clear which meaning of quality an organisation is referring to in its promotional activity. In its simplest form, a quality product is one that meets the needs of the consumer well. Some define quality as 'fit for purpose' while others define it by the customer's perception. Some customers will equate quality with performance of the product, while for others it could be durability (how long it lasts) or reliability.

How the product looks in terms of its design and style may influence perceptions of its quality. A good example of this would be how customers perceive a BMW car as a well-designed, high-quality, stylish car. Customers are also influenced by the corporate

Activity: Customer types

Consider the four products below and try to describe the type of customer they are aimed at. Which would you describe as being quality products? Remember there are a number of definitions of quality.

1. A Ford Fiesta
2. A Cadbury's Flake
3. A Rolex watch
4. A Smart Car

image of the company that is selling the product. For example, if customers are uncertain about a product being launched by Microsoft, they may still purchase the product based on their positive perception of Microsoft – despite their reservations about the product itself.

Product features and variations

When a product does not have a strong set of features or product variations to set it truly apart from competition, the promotional activity has to create and establish a unique selling proposition or point (USP) for the product. The USP is something that the competition does not or cannot offer. A unique selling point or proposition should increase consumers' understanding of what is important about the product or service; an advertisement should concentrate on just one powerful message. The advertisement needs to stress the product's unique features, driving home its advantages over the competition with a compelling sales pitch.

The success of using a name – such as Cadbury's – across a range of products depends on the power of the brand name. The advantage is that products can be promoted cheaply and effectively. It can work where the success of previous products has been based on values such as quality and value for money. As long as these qualities remain constant across the other products, promoting a range can be effective. In contrast, multi-branding involves the introduction of a number of products and brands that are targeted at a particular market segment. For example, Mars promotes a vast number of different brands, each targeted at a particular **market segment** in the confectionery market.

Quantity and timing of promotional activity

The timing and amount of promotional activity are key to a product's success. The product design, brand and USPs may be right for the market, but the market needs to know about the product to drive demand (remember the pull method discussed on page 205).

Key term

Market segment – a group of people or organisations sharing one or more characteristics that cause them to have similar product and/or service needs

Timing may be crucial for some products. Some products rely heavily on seasonal demand – around Christmas, Easter, Valentine's Day and so on – while other products are in demand all year round. The launch date for any product will be considered carefully to assess whether timing is important, and the promotional campaign should be timed to build awareness and demand.

The quantity of promotional activity depends on the company's objectives for the product. If the company's objectives are ambitious (for example, the product is expected to bring in a large amount of revenue and/or profit), it is likely to invest substantially in promotional activity to avoid failure. However, if a product is a lower priority or not entering a competitive market, the company is likely to invest less in promotion.

2.2 Price

Importance of price

Price is one of the most important and far-reaching variables that businesses control. Pricing decisions affect profit, volume, share of market and perceptions that customers have about the product. Price is the only marketing mix element that generates income. The other parts of the marketing mix – promotion, place and product – all generate costs. So getting the price right is of fundamental importance.

Promotional activity should inform customers of the price of the product or service being promoted. Although price may be an important factor in a customer's decision about a product, it also carries implications for quality and value. If a product is too expensive for the perceived benefits, it will not sell in significant volumes. However, if the promotional activity for a product emphasises its quality, too low a price may undermine the customer's perception of the product.

Factors affecting price and pricing strategies

The first step in price setting is to consider the business's pricing objectives and whether they relate to financial targets or sales targets. Financial targets can centre on either profit or cash flow. Sales targets can relate to desired market share and the organisation's position in the market.

There tend to be three key factors that influence prices – cost, competitors and demand.

Most businesses set out to make a profit, so the cost of producing a product is often the largest influence on the price the company charges for the product. The most common strategy is to adopt a 'cost plus' approach, where a product's price is set at the cost of manufacturing plus a margin of a specific percentage. For example, if it costs £5 to produce a CD and the company's mark-up is 20 per cent, the selling price will be £6.

In competitive markets, an organisation may need to use **competitor-based pricing** – that is, basing their pricing strategy on that adopted by a competitor in order to gain market share. The business would identify the common pricing trends and set their price at the same level. If this price is low, the company will place more emphasis on controlling the cost of producing their products in order to improve their margin.

Demand pricing is one of the more complex methods of determining a pricing strategy and involves the business making an assessment of the market and their position within it. For example, by looking at the market's **disposable income** and the desirability of the product, the company may choose to set the price based on what the consumer is prepared to pay. A new CD may be priced reasonably, but higher than some of the competition, when it is first released, because it is in demand.

Another option may be **skim pricing**, where a high initial price is set to maximise the revenue potential of a product before dropping the price to attract more customers. This approach is often used in the technology market, where early adopters are more willing to pay a premium for the latest games console. A business may alternatively set their price low initially to secure early market penetration, and raise their prices later. This is known as **penetration pricing**, and can result in a company making a loss early on. Products with this pricing strategy are often on 'introductory offer' to build demand before the price is raised.

2.3 Place
Online and/or physical presence

Place or distribution is often the element of the marketing mix that causes the biggest headache to the manufacturer. Once the manufacturer has made

What methods can be used to determine a pricing strategy?

the product and it has left the factory, the product is then at the mercy of middlemen within the distribution channel. The responsibility of a business is to get the product to the customer in the right place and at the right time. In turn, the business's promotional activity should inform the customers of where they can purchase the product.

Businesses can gain some additional benefits by selling their products through wholesalers and retailers in additional promotional activity. For example, if a product is sold through Argos, it might be promoted by Argos through one of their TV adverts. However,

Key terms

Competitor-based pricing – setting the price based upon those of similar competitor products

Demand pricing – allocating a price based on what consumers are prepared to pay

Disposable income – the amount of money which an individual has available to spend on non-essential items after essential bills have been met

Skim pricing – establishing a relatively high price for a product or service to recover the costs of development and introduction more rapidly; also called high-price strategy

Penetration pricing – involves the setting of lower prices in order to achieve a large, if not dominant, market share

if a business decides to sell a product direct through their own website only, they must rely solely on their promotional activity.

Wholesale

Wholesalers offer a range of services including bulk breaking, which is the breaking down of large cases of products to enable smaller independent shops to buy smaller quantities of product. They may also offer transportation, delivery and management advice.

Cash and carries are the commonest form of wholesaler, serving the needs of small retailers which use a cash and carry just as a consumer uses a supermarket. The wholesaler can buy in bulk and pass on some of the cost savings to the small retailer, but the retailer is responsible for transporting the stock themselves. A good example of a wholesaler in the UK is Makro.

Retail

Retailers bridge the gap between the manufacturer and the end consumer. Retailers can be classified according to a number of criteria such as how they are owned, for example, as independents or as multiple chains. They can also be classified by type of store such as department store, supermarket, convenience store or speciality store. There is also the growing area of non-store retailing, which along with the Internet includes vending machines, home selling and mail order.

A small retailer may buy their goods from a wholesaler (see above), while a large retailer will buy the goods direct from the manufacturer to benefit directly from bulk-order savings.

Direct selling

Many businesses use direct selling, either instead of the traditional routes to market described above, or in addition to them. There are a number of different types of direct selling.

- **Direct mail** containing promotional information is sent to potential customers who are identified from databases as the target audience.
- **Direct response advertising** uses broadcast and print media with the aim of stimulating some kind of response from the targeted audience.
- **Telemarketing** uses the telephone to create a direct link with the customer.

- **Mail order catalogues** are sent to potential customers, allowing them to phone through orders or use the Internet.
- **Internet marketing** generates enquiries and sales through promotion and communication of information on company websites.

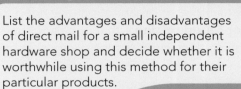

Activity: Direct mail

List the advantages and disadvantages of direct mail for a small independent hardware shop and decide whether it is worthwhile using this method for their particular products.

Role of intermediaries – push and pull

Intermediaries are independent organisations involved in the promotion, selling and distribution of a firm's goods to the end users of its products and services. There are a number of different types of intermediary.

- Resellers – these are organisations whose role is to make products more easily available to their end users. They include retailers, wholesalers, agents and other distribution companies. This means that many businesses are not selling directly to their customer, and their products can succeed or fall based on a reseller's decision to stock the product or not.
- Physical distribution intermediaries – these are usually warehouse operators and transport firms which are involved in moving goods from manufacturers to their destinations.

Businesses selling to intermediaries use different promotional techniques from those they would use when dealing directly with consumers. We saw earlier that business-to-business (B2B) organisations use the push method (see page 205) to sell, while business-to-consumer (B2C) companies use the pull method. However, in practice, some companies are a mix of B2B and B2C.

For example, Apple sell products direct to consumers via their website and Apple stores, but their products are also sold through retailers such as Argos, Tesco and Currys. Apple's B2C promotional methods include TV campaigns and print media advertisements that 'pull' customers to their products by creating desire. However, when promoting their products to intermediaries, Apple will use B2B promotional methods, with face-to-face selling, explaining the benefits of stocking their products and negotiating discounts individually.

Did you know?

In some markets, intermediaries are becoming of less importance (and in some instances, redundant) as customers deal directly with the producer. This process is known as disintermediation.

2.4 Packaging

Packaging is an important part of the product that not only serves a functional purpose in providing protection, but also communicates product information and brand character. The packaging is often the consumer's first point of contact with the actual product and so it is essential to make the product's appearance attractive and appropriate for both the product and the customer's needs.

In a crowded marketplace, the product's packaging has to be immediately recognisable and differentiated from the competition. However, the packaging also needs to reflect the brand image and convey a message about the product. This can be a tricky balance. For example, Coke Zero was launched as a sugar-free version of Coke to appeal to the male market (while Diet Coke has traditionally appealed to the female audience). The company needed to make the product reflect the brand identity of Coca-Cola (that it had the same taste), but differentiate it from Diet Coke (so that its brand values would appeal specifically to men).

The packaging therefore cannot be treated in isolation from other aspects of the product and promotional mix. Its design and the message it delivers have to be integrated with all other aspects of the marketing mix.

Producers are constantly striving to be innovative in developing packaging that can attract the potential purchaser through eye-catching design. The amount of packaging used is now being criticised on environmental grounds and supermarkets and producers are under constant pressure to reduce the amount of packaging used.

2.5 People

The quality of the buying experience and/or the service provided by a particular business is increasingly important in the customer's buying decision. For high-price items, such as cars or computers, consumers expect sales people to be knowledgeable, friendly (but not pushy) and courteous.

Businesses are increasingly recognising that they need to provide a service alongside their products to build repeat business from customers. Even for low-price repeat-purchase items, it is now standard for companies to offer a level of customer care after the initial purchase. For example, crisps or sweets will have customer care helplines to resolve any product queries or complaints quickly.

Training and development

People have an important role to play, especially in the marketing of services. Salespeople must act in a professional manner, matching a customer's needs to the products available. This can only be achieved though effective training and development programmes, which may include learning:

- how to use a product
- its benefits
- how to overcome common objections.

The capability and efficiency of salespeople can have a significant effect on services marketing. They need to be available when customers need them and be able to interact with customers in a helpful and informative manner. They must also provide a service to other departments and internal customers within their own organisation.

Consistency of image

If a company or a brand is to build a specific image or character, it needs the people involved in the promotional mix to present a consistent image. It can partially achieve this simply through uniforms and branding guidelines, but often needs to support this by training.

A business may require its staff to greet customers in a particular way, or offer a particular service (for example, a store credit card). Staff service can be monitored through mystery shoppers, who report on the success rate of staff in meeting the required criteria. Staff may then receive additional training to improve their consistency, or be rewarded for achieving the standards.

2.6 Processes

Importance of creating and maintaining a positive image

The purchasing process for a particular product or service can be a key part of the promotional mix. Many companies use technology to improve the service they offer customers, from allowing them to create accounts quickly (and avoid providing the same information each time they buy something) to order tracking so customers can see when their purchase will be delivered.

Did you know?

A positive image and easy-to-use service will encourage repeat custom, which is important for a business as it is cheaper to keep customers than attract new ones. The benefits of the process may also be used in promotional activity – free delivery, 24-hour despatch, secure ordering and so on.

2.7 Physical evidence

The engineering of an appropriate physical environment for the delivery of a service is an increasingly important part of the marketing mix. Physical evidence represents the tangible cues that support the main service product. These will include facilities, the infrastructure and the products used to deliver the service. How would you feel if you went into a restaurant and it was not very clean?

The physical environment – for example, a shop floor, display window – can combine a range of factors that help to present a specific image of the product or service to the customer. For example, lighting and colours can be used to create a particular atmosphere. Compare how a furniture store might present a show room with how a clothes store would present a window display.

The physical environment may also appeal to the customer's aural senses. Background music may be selected to encourage a specific mood or frame of mind. Staff may be trained to use specific language or a particular tone of voice when greeting customers, or answering the phone. All these factors combine to build a perception for customers that will influence their buying decisions.

2.8 Promotional objectives

Business aims and objectives and marketing and promotional objectives

Most businesses will set business or corporate objectives, many of which will be financial. For example, a manufacturing company may state that it wishes to increase sales by 20 per cent by the end of next year. This might be one of many business objectives. These objectives will then cascade down to the various departments of the organisation. The marketing department may consider that the only way of achieving this sales increase is to increase television advertising and to launch a new variety to their existing main product. This would then create two marketing objectives, which would be related to the overall business objective of increasing sales by 20 per cent. The two marketing objectives can then be translated into promotional or communication objectives. However, promotional activity must support the business's goals, as activity that complements the organisation's other activities will be more successful than activity that competes with them. Other aims and objectives may include:

- **raising awareness** – this might involve raising the profile of a specific product or an entire organisation. Improved awareness may translate into increased sales as customers seek out the brand they are most aware of. For example, when searching for something on the Internet, do you ever talk about Yahoo!ing or Binging it?

- **creating distinctive market presence** – with few genuinely unique products or services available, it is important for businesses to identify ways of differentiating their products or services. For example, Tesco supports the Computers for Schools initiative by allowing customers to receive computer vouchers in return for purchases. These can then be given to schools, which will exchange the vouchers for a computer when enough vouchers have been received. This strategy can enhance the company's image of being a caring and responsible organisation that believes in assisting education

- **increasing market share** – in competitive markets, many businesses want to improve their market share. This often means an increase in sales at the expense of a competitor's sales, and can result in increased profit (if the company sells more items at the same profit margin) or a move towards being the market leader.

2.9 Targeting the relevant audience

In order to be effective, promotional activity needs to be directed to the relevant audience who are going to respond to the messages. If an organisation does not target their identified audience effectively, the promotional campaign is likely to fail.

It is unlikely that any product or promotional activity will appeal to all customers – the range of customer needs in a given market are too diverse to boil down to one concise message. Although a product may potentially have a universal appeal, a business may decide it is better placed to serve one or more portions of the market and concentrate their efforts on this. The advantage for the business is that although this limits their target audience, it means that their promotional spend is likely to be more effective.

Attitudes, interests, opinions and demographics

Consumer buying behaviour is a very complex process, and promotional activity should reflect the attitudes, interests, opinions and demographics of potential customers. Most large organisations will undertake a significant amount of research into these factors to ensure that the promotional mix incorporates these issues into the campaign plan.

This is best seen in the magazine industry, where publications focus around the interests of their target audience. The attitudes and opinions expressed in the magazine, and in the promotional activity for the magazine, are tailored to appeal to the target audience. The target audience is categorised into demographic groups, which will give an age bracket, a gender, a professional status and so on.

Business-to-business (B2B) and business-to-consumer (B2C)

As we discussed earlier (page 205), companies may sell to other businesses (B2B) as well as direct to consumers (B2C). Although similar techniques may be applied in B2B and B2C, there are distinct differences in approach ('push' rather than 'pull').

- **Personal selling** – B2B selling can be much more direct, and is often bespoke (made to order). The business selling the product or service needs to be clear about why the other company should purchase it. As with B2C selling, the customer needs to know the benefits – although these are more likely to be based on revenue, profit, savings and/or customer demand.

- **Advertising** – trade journals and dedicated exhibitions provide opportunities for B2B advertising and promotion. If a product is to be sold through retailers, any advertising for business customers may make reference to the scale of the promotional campaign to indicate the likely levels of demand that could be generated.

The B2B purchasing process is often more complex than that for B2C. Individuals within a company may have a limited budget, and contractors may be required to fulfil a range of criteria before their services can be hired.

Promotions

A business may achieve its objectives (for example, increased unit sales) by using a promotion. There is a range of established methods including:

- buy one get one free – multi-buy offers, usually on fast-moving consumer goods

- extra free – an extra value incentive where promotional packs are larger, but sold at the same price as normal packs

- collect and claim – incentives that encourage customers to consume more of a product in return for a reward

- vouchers – a money-off coupon that entitles the bearer to a discount in any store can increase demand for a product.

Segmentation

Segmentation is about defining meaningful differences between groups of customers to form the foundations of a more focused promotional effort. Segmentation may be complex – for example, dividing your market by aspirations and interest – or relatively

Key term

Segmentation – using marketing research to help identify groups of consumers who will respond to marketing activity in the same way, for example, first-time buyers of houses

Fig. 9.3: You will see a variety of promotional methods in shops.

simple – for example, dividing your market by age bracket or gender.

Once the market segments have been identified, the promotional mix is adapted to suit the different segments better. This approach, when it works well, enables a company to get deeper market penetration than would be achievable by producing and marketing a single product. However, in order to work well, the business must conduct research into their market segments to ensure that their assumptions work.

One example of segmentation is Nivea's range of skin care products for men. Although the features of Nivea's products for men and women are similar, the promotional mix (advertising, benefits, packaging and so on) is different to appeal to the different segments of their market.

2.10 Brands

A brand is a visual identifier – usually a combination of a logo, text, symbol or design that clearly marks the product as coming from a particular company. The brand sets the product apart from competitors' products.

Some businesses spend millions of pounds developing their brand image, and protect it fiercely through rigorous usage guidelines and trademarks. So, what makes a brand so valuable?

Brand values

A business usually develops a series of brand values for their brand, and although customers may not know these (be careful not to confuse brand values

with a strapline – see page 137), they should implicitly understand them.

A brand's values may be different from the values of the company that produces the brand, but they should be complementary. Where a brand relates to a product, the values should be demonstrable – for example, if the brand value is good quality, the product should live up to this value. However, brand values can equally be applied to a service business, or to a service related to a product.

Brand personality

Brands can stimulate an emotional relationship with customers, which can be further developed by a brand 'personality'. A strong brand personality can build ties between the product and the consumer, which helps build repeat purchases and can contribute to a dominant market share.

Some brands build on their tradition and heritage – for example, Hovis or Bisto – giving a nostalgic and homely appeal, while others try to engage customers on a different level – such as WKD or Lynx.

In this way, brand personalities can appeal to a customer's:

- private personality (their self-perception and aspirations)
- public personality (how they would like to be perceived by others)
- attributed personality (how others see them).

Activity: Advertisements

1. Look at the advertisements in your local paper and make a note of the ones that attract your attention and why. Do images and illustrations draw your eye to particular advertisements? Are the larger advertisements more eye-catching?

2. Find an advertisement that you believe is successful and effective in getting the message across. Describe why you think this is a particularly successful advertisement.

3. Find an advertisement that you believe is unsuccessful and ineffective in getting the message across. Describe why you think this particular advertisement is unsuccessful.

Benefits of brand to owner

A brand can take a lot of money and time to establish, and efforts to build a brand are not always successful. However, if the brand becomes popular, it can bring a range of benefits to the owner, such as:

- **permitting premium pricing** – if a brand has a strong identity and is popular, customers will demand the products. This allows the brand owner to charge a premium price, which enables them to make a larger profit on sales
- **aiding differentiation** – a clear brand identity will differentiate a product from those of competitors. This may be through packaging (for example, in a supermarket where competing brands sit on the same shelf), or through the perceived brand values in service (for example, choosing to purchase an item from one shop rather than another)
- **allowing cross-product promotion** – an overarching brand can produce promotional efficiencies for a business. For example, a printed advert might promote several products within a range, or a display shelf in a supermarket could house a range of products from the same brand family.

Brand extension

A strong brand allows businesses to produce higher sales for new products through brand extension. This basically means using an established brand on a new product targeted into the same broad market – such as if a company decides to target a different segment of its market.

For example, Trebor is the market-leading mint sweet brand in the UK. In 2009 they extended their brand to include a chewing gum. With Wrigley's dominating the chewing gum market, Trebor is leveraging the strength of its brand to compete in this lucrative segment.

> **Did you know?**
>
> The famous online auction site eBay got its name when its founder discovered that the domain name for Echo Bay, his web consulting company, was already taken. Other little-known facts are that Google was originally called BackRub and Yahoo! was going to be called Jerry and David's Guide to the World Wide Web.

The advantages of brand extension include:

- distributors are more likely to have confidence in a new product if it comes from an established brand, so a new product is more likely to get stocked than if the company developed an entirely new brand
- customers are more likely to trust an established brand (unless they have had a bad experience in the past)
- promotional costs are likely to be lower, especially if the business is able to promote more than one product under the same brand.

Brand fingerprinting

A brand 'fingerprint' refers to all aspects of communication with customers – for example, contact with customer service staff, letters, a company's website, and so on. In each instance, the brand values should be reinforced so the customer receives a consistent experience of the brand.

For example, innocent present a very informal and friendly brand character (see page 18) in their promotional material and packaging. In addition to this, they invite customers to visit their head office if they have any suggestions or questions, or phone their switchboard. On top of this, they hold an annual AGM (which in innocent-speak stands for 'A Grown-up Meeting') where customers can come and discuss ideas with representatives from the organisation.

Assessment activity 9.2   P2   BTEC

This assignment follows on from Assessment activity 9.1, where you are in the role of a researcher employed by a marketing magazine and have been asked to investigate a number of promotional activities that may form the basis of future articles in editions of the magazine. The following task will add to the report article produced for 9.1.

For one of the organisations chosen for Assessment activity 9.1, explain the role of promotion within the marketing mix for the selected product/service. For example, the activity may be connected to

the promotion of a selected product as part of the application of the marketing mix, as the organisation selects price points, highlights product quality, secures appropriate distribution of the product or service and so on. **P2**

Grading tip

Remember that promotion can cover a number of objectives from raising awareness, to increasing sales, to increasing profit and so on. **P2**

3. Understand the role of advertising agencies and the media

3.1 Services and costs of advertising agencies

Services offered

Advertising agencies have a large role to play in creating and developing advertisements for a variety of large organisations. These organisations pay sizeable fees for the expertise which is to be found in-house at an advertising agency. Competition is fierce between agencies that have to provide a unique service to each client and to continue to develop new ideas which will promote products and services in line with their client's ethos.

The advertising function can be handled in a variety of ways. Firstly, if a potential business has sufficient expertise, it may decide to handle advertising in-house. Alternatively, a business may decide to use a 'full service' agency. This is an agency which provides a complete advertising service encompassing creative work, production, media planning and buying.

Well-known advertising agencies include Saatchi & Saatchi and Ogilvy & Mather. Agencies can be expensive, so organisations that use them tend to have high promotional budgets but limited in-house resources.

Some businesses opt to use limited-service agencies for select parts of a promotional campaign. Limited-service agencies provide services for clients in specialist areas, such as print, TV or online. Through using these services, a client may use more than one agency, or focus on some elements of a campaign in-house.

The services offered by advertising agencies include:

- **media buying** – an advertising agency will decide the best advertising options for a particular product. This involves matching the demographics of a product with the demographics of a medium, such as TV, radio, newspapers or magazines. The agency may be able to negotiate better rates than the company by bulk-buying advertising space or time for multiple clients at the same time
- **advertisement design** – the agency will combine copywriting, graphic design and typography

to design an advertisement. This will require the agency to interpret – and build on – the brand values, and use the business's branding appropriately

- **advertising production** – the development process for TV and radio adverts can be much more expensive than for print-based advertising. The agency will work with the client to identify a concept that the client is happy with, before getting the script and storyboard (which spells out the concept for an advert and gives a storyline) written and approved by the client. Only once the client has approved in principle will the recording and editing process start; this is to avoid any costly rerecording
- **engaging the target audience** – agencies can provide a range of services to engage with a business's target audience, from market research to field marketing activities (such as in-store demonstrations).

Cost options – in-house versus outsourcing

Not every business chooses to use an advertising agency for all, or even portions, of its publicity activity. The business will consider a range of factors when deciding whether to use in-house resources or to outsource, which include:

- cost
- expertise
- time
- accountability
- quality.

In-house employees are not free, so although using an agency is expensive, having the internal expertise to produce a successful promotional campaign is by no means cheap. The business would need to weigh up the pros and cons of how the money is spent, but typically a small company might use an in-house resource and a larger company might use an agency. This is often related to the volume of promotional activity.

In-house staff might know the business very well, but their experience of other companies' promotional activity might be limited. Buying in the services of an agency allows the business to access a much wider range of experience and expertise.

Briefing an outside agency, reviewing and approving early concepts, and checking draft materials all takes time. An in-house team may have been involved in developing the product from an early stage and be well versed in the features, benefits and branding.

An in-house team is directly accountable for the success of a promotional campaign – this can put a lot of pressure on them to succeed, and may inadvertently result in them sticking to tried-and-tested formulae rather than new approaches to the marketing mix. An agency may be able to develop a more creative publicity campaign, and still attract clients even if a campaign fails.

The business also needs to consider the quality of the promotional activity, which can be a difficult factor to assess objectively. Depending on the expertise in-house, a business may be able to create a high-quality campaign without using an agency. However, because an agency can provide access to a broader range of specialisms and experience, it may be able to produce more campaigns to a higher level of quality without running out of ideas.

3.2 Types of media
Local, regional, national and international

The first thing an advertising agency will consider when choosing a medium for a campaign is their target audience. The second thing they consider is how to reach this audience.

Why are television programmes a good vehicles for national launches?

At a basic level, the agency will need to establish the geographic location of the target audience. For example, if a product is being trialled in a specific location, the agency will only choose from the media that are local to that area. If a product is available in the UK, but not internationally, the agency will focus their activity on media with a large audience in the UK, but that may have limited international reach.

The agency will also need to consider how best to reach their audience. This includes reviewing the demographic and interests of the audience and comparing it with the demographic and interests of the different media identified. Some examples of how these may affect decisions are as follows.

- A national launch of a new cosmetics range for teenage girls might be advertised on TV around programmes such as *Hollyoaks* and *Coronation Street* and in national magazines such as *Sugar*.
- A local opening of a new cinema complex might be advertised on the local radio station, on prominent billboards in the area and in the local press.
- A new product in an international brand range that will be available globally might be advertised on national TV channels, in national newspapers and on websites of international interest, as well as on satellite TV and with versions of the promotional material created specifically for overseas media.
- A new distribution service for small- to medium-sized retailers might be advertised in specialist trade media, such as *Retail Week*.

Did you know?

In October 1994, Hotwired were the first company to offer a formal advertising campaign on the Internet. When they launched this campaign they had just 14 clients including Volvo and AT&T.

3.3 Criteria for media selection

Fig. 9.4 on page 223 shows seven factors that have to be considered when selecting appropriate media.

1. Budget – cost versus coverage

Advertising media have to deliver the message to the consumer and this can be very expensive. Campaigns are often developed within tight budgets and booking 20 prime-time slots on television is beyond the budgets of small businesses. A balance has to be made on what the business can afford and the coverage that is possible. This is a key consideration when considering the selection of media.

2. Promotional/Campaign objectives

The media selected must ensure consistency with the overall objectives for the campaign in terms of awareness and reach and so on. If the objective for the launch of a new product is to ensure that 50 per cent of the adult population are made aware of the product,

then it would be unlikely to succeed if advertising in a selected trade journal is the only medium chosen. Therefore, different media will be used for different types of promotional campaigns and this will depend on the objectives. If the promotional campaign needs the product to be demonstrated, it is likely that the media choice will be television. If the consumer needs a detailed explanation of the product features and benefits, then print media probably offer the best option. If the purpose of the activity is to put a brand

Table 9.3: Advantages and disadvantages of the published media.

Published media	Advantages	Disadvantages
National newspapers	• Reach large numbers of people • Short copy lead times • Colour available	• Short life – thrown away • Advertising clutter • Expensive
Regional newspapers	• Reader loyalty • Local features • High coverage within geographical area • Relatively inexpensive to advertise	• Poor readership data • Complex buying and planning
Consumer magazines	• Precise targeting of special interest groups	• Long copy deadlines • Lack of immediacy
Business magazines	• Read very closely	• Long lead times mean you have to make plans weeks or months in advance, and heightens the risk of the ad getting overtaken by events • Limited flexibility for ad placement and format • Space and ad layout costs higher
Directories	• Source of reference	• Pages can look cluttered, and the ad can easily get lost in the clutter • Ad is placed together with competitors' ads • Limited creativity in the ads, given the need to follow a set format • Ads slow to reflect market changes

Table 9.4: Advantages and disadvantages of using other media.

Medium	Advantages	Disadvantages
Television	• Mass market coverage • Flexible by region • Flexible by time of day • Audio visual/interactive • Precise targeting with digital/satellite TV	• Expensive production • Some wastage • Expensive air time • Passive audience • Possibly low • Long lead times viewing figures
Radio	• Local and time specific targeting for example, drive time • Immediacy • Relatively low cost	• Lacks creativity • Wallpaper syndrome – radio on in background, not being listened to • Some wastage • Passive audience
Cinema	• High attention span • Regional flexibility • Impactful • Easy to target	• Expensive production • Low national coverage

continued

Table 9.4: *continued*

Medium	Advantages	Disadvantages
Billboards and transport advertising	• Impactful • Flexible by region • High audience coverage in urban areas	• Long lead times • Limited amount of prime sites • Possible vandalism
Direct mailing	• Target to individual level • Personalised communication • Reinforces other advertising • Creative formats • Less visible to competitors	• No sound or movement • Associated with junk mail • Long lead times • Can be expensive
Internet	• Can reach a world wide audience • Cheap to administer • Effective targeting • Feedback available	• Open to abuse • Security issues • Not everyone has Internet access

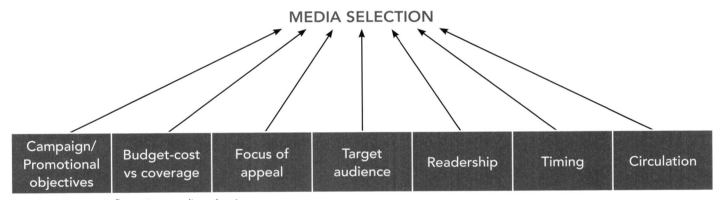

Fig. 9.4: Factors influencing media selection.

name in the consumer's mind, posters may fulfil the requirement. The choice of media revolves around three main issues:

- coverage – the percentage of people within the target audience who might see the promotional message during a certain time period
- frequency – the number of times people within the target audience will see the message in a certain time period
- media impact – conveying the product characteristics effectively; the message should be seen when the target audience is open to persuasion.

3. Target audience

The target audience is critical to guiding the detailed media selection. As close a fit as possible is required between the medium and audience. Achieving a high coverage to make sure that a large portion of the target audience is aware of the product would need a very large budget. The agency will often have to achieve a balance between:

- spreading coverage very wide, but with limited frequency, meaning that there are limited opportunities for the audience to receive the message
- narrowing the coverage and increasing the frequency (for example, just advertising on one TV station, but with the advert appearing within each advert break).

4. Focus of appeal

An advertising agency has to decide how best to appeal to their target audience. Adverts may include information-based messages, such as features and benefits, if an audience is likely to have a naturally high level of interest. For example, an advert for a new running shoe placed in a running magazine is likely to include a lot of information about technical features and how this benefits the customer.

If, however, the audience is more casual – for example, they might not necessarily be looking for a given product – the agency needs to consider how the advert will appeal to them. The impact of this appeal needs to be complemented by the medium chosen.

Table 9.5: Focus of appeal.

Focus of appeal	Promotional message
Intellectual	For example, attracting those who have savings to invest in various investment options. The message emphasises the taking of a particular course of action which will reap benefits in the future. The media choice tends to be newspapers and magazines.
Emotional	Charities target people's emotions. For example, following one particular earthquake in Italy, Save the Children deployed a team to L'Aquila to assess the needs of children in the region. It publicised this trip on Twitter and spoke to the BBC about children being emotionally affected by the earthquake. It also featured in the *Mirror* and *Guardian* newspapers, among others. The overall message fuelled people's emotions, resulting in donations for the charity.
Empathetic	This tries to get the audience to identify with the characters who are portraying a common problem, such as giving up smoking. The product, such as nicotine replacement gum, is then seen as a suitable solution to the problem.

5. Timing

The plan needs to take into account any lead-in or build-up time, particularly if the product has a strong element of seasonality. Similarly, timing is important in launching a new product, to make sure the right level of awareness, understanding and desire have been generated by the time the product is actually available.

6. Circulation

Research has to be undertaken to find out how many people read the particular publication. It may be cheaper to advertise in a publication with a low circulation, but paying more to access more potential customers may prove a better return on investment.

Activity: Post office

A small post office incorporating a convenience shop is located near the university district of Leicester. As well as the usual stamps and banking facilities on offer, the shop sells a lot of crisps, sweets and alcohol. They stock very few pet foods or higher-priced goods.

Describe the typical customer by considering some of the following.

1. What age is the typical customer?
2. Do they have a high disposable income?
3. What sort of lifestyle might they have?
4. What size might the average purchase be?

Did you know?

Most magazines and newspapers publish media packs for potential advertisers, giving profiles of their readership and circulation figures to help persuade businesses to advertise with them.

7. Readership

Readership is the number of an audience that have read one issue of the publication. The readership of any press vehicle is likely to be several times higher than its circulation. For example, I buy my daily newspaper, therefore the circulation is one. I then take it to work, read it at lunchtime and lend it to a friend. In the evening my partner reads the paper; therefore the readership is three.

3.4 The role of the Internet
Disintermediation

Earlier we saw the role of intermediaries (page 214) in the promotional mix. Disintermediation is the removal of these 'middlemen' from the process; it is a process that has been helped by the Internet.

The Internet allows businesses to deal directly with their customers through e-commerce websites. This has benefits for the business: they can make a higher profit margin by selling direct to customers at higher prices than they would have charged a wholesaler, and customer loyalty grows as the awareness of the company grows.

Disintermediation does not necessarily mean the removal of all intermediaries from a supply chain. Take publishing as an example. Traditionally, a publisher sold their books in bulk to a wholesaler. The wholesaler would then sell the books to a bookshop. The bookshop would then sell the book to the customer. At each stage, the intermediary adds their profit margin to the sale, so the customer purchases an item at a price that has generated a profit for three companies. With the advent of the Internet, Amazon.co.uk started dealing directly with publishers. Now the publisher sells direct to Amazon.co.uk. Amazon.co.uk sells direct to the customer. Although the customer is purchasing the item at a price that generates a profit for two companies in the supply chain, disintermediation allows Amazon.co.uk to offer the item at a lower price.

Direct marketing

The potential audience for direct marketing on the Internet is huge, as more and more of the world's population connect to the Internet. Disintermediation has put businesses in closer contact with their customers, which has a range of consequences for promotional activity.

- Businesses can gather data about their customers with greater ease and build effective databases of customer details. This means that they can group customers according to interests and previous purchases, and produce more targeted mailing, which often results in a higher success rate.
- Businesses can maximise their profits by removing intermediaries (as shown above).
- A business can include much more information on every product in their range than is possible in a printed brochure or than a salesperson could be expected to remember. This means a customer can choose the product they are interested in and receive all the information they need to make an informed decision.
- All businesses can appeal to international customers, and may easily produce adapted versions of their websites for specific regions.

Did you know?

Chris Anderson argued in his book *The Long Tail* that the Internet is allowing businesses to generate more profit from low sales of old products, as customers get more and more opportunities to explore their own interests.

- As a business's own website becomes increasingly important for their profit, so the business must invest more in publicising the website. At the extreme, a business may be solely responsible for informing customers about their products.

Activity: Direct marketing

Over the next few days, collect as many examples of direct marketing in newspapers, the Internet or through the post as you can. Discuss your examples in groups and consider the following.

1. Are the adverts attractive and do they tempt you to do something?
2. Did you have to do lots of reading to find out what they were trying to promote?
3. Did you believe the claims they were making?

Functional skills

English: By completing this activity, you will be practising reading, comparing, selecting and understanding texts and using them to gather information, ideas, arguments and opinions.

One-to-one communications

Increasingly there is one-to-one communication to market products and services. Usually when you have bought something online you are required to register with that company, which means giving them your email address. Although you have the right to opt out of receiving marketing information from the company, many do not cancel and receive information about products and services similar to the ones purchased. This is now increasingly happening with mobile phones.

Powerful databases are able to undertake one-to-one promotional communications; this is sometimes referred to as micro marketing. This means that companies can match new products and new offers to customers who are likely to be interested. Major retailers such as Asda and Tesco electronically contact their online customers with special offers.

Functional skills

English: By answering the questions in the case study, you will be practising reading, comparing, selecting and understanding texts and using them to gather information, ideas, arguments and opinions.

Case study: Mobile technology and ad campaigns

Society today has become more technologically savvy and typically we expect up-to-date news, weather and traffic reports, not only through traditional mediums such as newspapers, television or radios, but also through our phones and computers. In particular, content-driven websites on our computers offer access to knowledge and leisure; with a single click we are able to read articles, listen to radio or streaming music and watch video or our favourite TV programme.

Publishers have acknowledged the importance of these different medium channels but have yet to consider the significance of a mobile strategy. Mobiles can be used as a channel to promote advertising through different platforms as well as allowing applications that can be downloaded and installed on phones. With fast-changing technology and the growing popularity of this approach, publishers should determine the applications and content that assimilates their brand, as well as establish the differing services desired by their target market. By allowing the customer to read content by way of mobile applications, publishers not only strengthen their brand through ensuring access to a larger target group, but also increase their advertising inventory.

Customers expect to choose how they receive information and publishers can now position targeted mobile advertising campaigns with confidence. There are many types of advertising applications in use today, including 'click to call', which puts the customer directly in touch with the advertiser, and programmable advertising campaigns which automatically detect the settings of the device being used and adjust screen size to suit the handset.

Other mobile applications such as 'Hyper local' offer the travelling user the ability to find local information. By integrating this strategy into their marketing campaign, local publishers can offer specific, relevant information and updates to their customer base on such issues as traffic reports in their locality.

1. List a few of the advantages of using mobile technology in an advertising campaign.

2. What disadvantages can you foresee from the use of this mobile technology in any advertising campaign?

3. What products or services do you think might benefit from an advertising campaign using mobile technology?

Assessment activity 9.3

This assignment follows on from Assessment activity 9.2 where you are in the role of a researcher employed by a marketing magazine and have been asked to investigate a number of promotional activities that may form the basis of future articles in editions of the magazine. This part of the investigation asks you to assess the role of advertising agencies and the media. The following tasks will add to the report articles produced for 9.1 and 9.2.

1. Explain clearly the contribution of advertising agencies in the development of a successful promotional campaign. Again for this task you may choose one of the products or services used in Assessment activity 9.1. **P3**

2. Explain the advantages and disadvantages of using professional agencies in ensuring promotional success. **M2**

3. Explain the reasons behind the choice of media in a successful promotional campaign. You may select one of your chosen organisation's promotional campaigns to answer this task. **P4**

Grading tips

1. Make sure you know about all the activities that advertising agencies participate in, as this will help you in evaluating the contribution advertising agencies can make to a successful campaign. **P3**

2. Remember that not all advertising campaigns are successful and advertising agencies can significantly affect whether the campaign is successful or not. There are disadvantages to using an advertising agency, which need to be carefully considered. **M2**

3. Remember that the choice of media is absolutely critical. You would not, for example, use radio advertising to sell something which is purchased mainly because of its attractive colour. **P4**

4. Be able to create a simple promotional campaign

4.1 The campaign brief

For successful advertising to be developed, it is essential that the client briefs the account executive thoroughly. An oral briefing meeting should always be backed up with a written brief, to ensure the fullest understanding between agency and client.

A good brief should include, as minimum, the following elements.

a) Background to the proposed campaign: This would include comments about the internal and external environment in which the client operates and how it has shaped the need for the current advertising. For instance, the client might need to include an update on market size and shares within the market, current competitive positions and political, economic, social and technological factors as they affect the current time and near future. The client should also discuss how they intend their advertising and communications strategy to fit into the overall strategy for the brand.

b) Objectives: The objectives of the promotional campaign should be stated, following SMART (specific, measurable, achievable, realistic, time-related) guidelines – for example, 'to increase awareness of the product through advertising from 75 per cent to 85 per cent by December 2010'.

c) Target markets: The client should clearly spell out the target markets for the product – for example, females aged 16 to 25, middle income, and so on.

d) Product/service specifications: The client should provide the agency with as much detail as possible about the physical product or service to be featured in the advertising. The client should allow the agency an opportunity, not just of sampling the product or service, but of immersing themselves in the elements which go towards making it. The agency should understand as much as possible about the processes involved in product/service delivery, alongside features, benefits and how the product or service is differentiated from competitive offerings. Sometimes this last point is, in itself, the role for the advertising.

e) Budget: The agency needs to be told how much money is to be spent on advertising.

f) Timing: The advertising may need to be timed to coincide with a particular calendar date of relevance to the client (for example, Easter, Christmas, Valentine's Day).

4.2 The creative brief

The account executive must translate the client brief into a briefing document for the specific use of the creative team. The creative brief will include a summary of the seven criteria on pages 221–4. A creative brief might take the following format.

a) **Background/introduction**

b) **Target markets(s)**

This might include more than a simple listing of the target audience characteristics. It could also include an assessment of what audiences currently think about the product or service.

c) **Promotional/advertising objectives**

d) **Promotional/advertising proposition**

This links with (b) above, and answers the question 'What do we want our audiences to think?' The proposition should be summed up in a short sentence or two, stating in simple terms the response that is desired from the audience on seeing the promotional activity. Some agencies call this 'brand promise'.

What elements should be included in a good campaign brief?

e) Support

This is the backup for the advertising proposition. It would include the information or attributes that might help to produce the desired response. Support might take the form of factual benefits that a product possesses which differentiate it from the competition, or it might include findings from the research.

f) Tone of voice

This takes into account whether the advertising should be, for example, authoritative, serious, friendly and modern in approach.

g) Mandatory inclusions

Typical examples of these would be 'shot of pack must be included' or 'company logo must be easily identifiable in end freeze frame'.

4.3 Selecting the content of the campaign

Advertising is about trying to persuade people that there is something special about a company's goods and services. It is an attempt to persuade the consumer that the product or service that is being offered has features that cannot be enjoyed by purchasing an alternative product or service. Some common approaches that an agency might consider are:

- **features and benefits** – every product has a series of features, but the agency will turn these into benefits for the customer. For example: a frying pan has a non-stick surface (feature) which means you spend less time washing up (benefit). Features and benefits may sometimes be used to demonstrate superiority over the competition

- **performance** – this concerns how well a product performs, and is often used as a direct comparison to the competition. Take, for instance, the claim that a washing powder cleans better than the market leading product, even at 30°C. This clearly states that the product's performance is superior, even at lower temperatures

- **quality** – this is something that is often emphasised in advertising for food or high-price items such as cars. For food, a business may emphasise any standards or praise that set their products apart from other companies

- **reliability** – an agency may decide that consumers are concerned about the reliability of a product or

service. For example, an agency may emphasise the extent to which a car is tested before being sold to reassure customers that it is reliable. If a competitor has had some issues with reliability, this might give a business a competitive edge.

4.4 Campaign tactics

As we saw on page 200, promotional campaigns do not just consist of advertising in the media; they can include public relations, sponsorship, personal selling and a range of other methods. When an agency develops the tactics for a campaign, they consider the best ways to satisfy the client's brief using a promotional mix.

Reaching the given target group

Reaching the target audience is critical to guiding the detailed media selection. Knowing who you are talking to is the foundation of good communication. A detailed profile of the target audience increases the chances of a successful promotion. Any details, such as location, media viewing habits, geo-demographics, attitudes and values, can be used to shape the propositions contained within the campaign or to direct the creative approach and media choice.

When designing the advertisement, the agency needs to consider the AIDA framework (see page 208) and the consumer response hierarchy. This might work as follows.

- **Attention:** The smoothest shave ever!
- **Interest:** Revolutionary seven-blade design and colour-changing moisturising strip.
- **Desire:** Introductory offer – save money.
- **Action:** Hurry to your local supermarket – limited stock.

Budget

The budget (see page 207) will influence the promotional tactics chosen. A client will ask an agency

Activity: Concert tickets

Imagine you are starting up a small web-based business selling concert tickets online. Your bank has asked you to outline how you propose to advertise this business. When constructing the report you should:

- clearly state the business's aims and objectives
- identify the offline promotions you could use
- identify the online promotions you could use
- discuss the significance of the four Ps.

to work within a specific budget to make sure they are keeping control of the costs of promotion.

Even though certain tactics may be more effective at engaging a target audience or be more likely to achieve the promotional objectives, an agency may need to choose certain tactics based on the budget available.

For example, a new soft drink may stand the best chances of success if the agency organises tasting demonstrations across the country, combined with TV advertising and printed adverts. However, the budget available may not allow for all this activity, so they may prioritise the printed adverts as the most cost-effective option with the highest frequency.

Selection of appropriate media

As we saw on page 220, an advertising agency will take various factors into consideration when selecting an appropriate medium for a promotional message. These include:

- interests of the target audience
- demographic
- geographic location.

Of course, most promotional activity will include a range of media – for example, a combination of print, online, TV and radio. Each choice should reflect the target audience, increasing the likelihood of a potential customer receiving the message.

Design and presentation of promotional materials

In the early stages of a promotional campaign, an agency might produce a 'mood board' to begin to develop the look and feel of the promotional materials. A mood board consists of a range of influences on design. These might include magazine pages, competitors' adverts, samples of designers' work, website layouts and so on.

Once the influences for the campaign are identified, a designer can begin to pull together elements to produce a coherent design. The final design will include all, or a combination of, the following.

- **Images:** These could be photos or illustrations, and will be chosen to achieve a particular effect. An advert might need to make a statement and attract immediate attention, in which case an image should have impact and probably use bright colours with strong lines. Alternatively, an image might need to convey intimacy and sensitivity, so a softer focus would be more applicable, with more muted colours. If the agency wanted the audience to empathise with the advert, they might use an image with characters making eye contact with the audience.

- **Typography:** The function of the advert needs to be carefully considered. If the agency is designing a billboard poster that will be displayed on a motorway, there should be little text and it should be easily legible. Alternatively, if the advert is appealing to an already interested market, it might include a comparatively large amount of detailed text.

- **Other sensory dimensions:** Some printed adverts – particularly in consumer magazines – may include additional attention-grabbing techniques. These range from 'scratch and sniff' panels to textured paper or spot-printing effects (for example, matt finish or special pantone colours), and can help make an advert more memorable – although they tend to cost more.

Promotional materials may include functional store displays. For example, a feature display for a new Disney film might include cut-outs of the lead character with in-built shelves for holding DVDs and other merchandise. An agency would need to consider all the above factors, in addition to the practical aspects of product dimensions, when designing the display.

Text and media type

Writing for promotional activity is a specialist skill, and although adverts consist of relatively few words, agencies can spend a considerable amount of time picking and choosing the right ones. The use of words (whether printed or spoken) needs to be considered carefully with the choice of media.

For print, how big will the advert be printed, and where? How much time is your audience likely to spend reading the advert? If your advert is a poster to appear on an escalator, keep the text short and to the point – your audience will not be able to stop and read dense text, even if they wanted to.

For TV, how long is the advert? What is the most essential message to get across? How do you want your audience to remember your advert? It costs a lot of money to produce and broadcast a TV advert, so it needs to be effective. Often the most memorable part of an advert will not be what is said, but what appears on-screen.

For radio, how long is the advert? What are the essential points you are trying to get across? How are you going to call your audience to action? A radio advert relies on its script, and an agency will have to tell the audience what they are selling, why the audience should buy it and where they can buy it.

For Internet, is it a banner advert or a dedicated website? What is the function of the message – to inform or to attract? What is the intended outcome? You need to consider what you are trying to get your customers to do – purchase an item from an online store, register interest, find more information and so on.

Stages

For the printed elements of a promotional campaign, an agency may present the client with a range of concepts that have been designed to look close to the finished article. These mock-ups will demonstrate a range of ideas, and the client may pick one concept as their preferred option, or identify elements of each that they like.

The agency will then produce a proof of the chosen idea, incorporating any feedback from the client until they give their approval. This process may involve a large number of changes, but the cost of amending text or editing images is relatively low.

However, for radio and TV adverts, the cost of recording and rerecording is considerably higher. To avoid spending more money than is necessary, an agency typically follows a series of stages.

- **Storyboards:** These will spell out an initial concept for a filmed advert, giving the storyline and some

suggestions for dialogue. This can be used to test the concept with the client and to receive feedback.

- **Script:** Once the storyboard is approved, the script is written. This may include directions for visual cues or sound effects, but should also make the message of the advert clear. The client may provide the agency with feedback to incorporate.
- **First cut:** Once the script and storyboard are approved, the agency will record the video or audio and edit it together to form a package. This will be rough at this stage; it may only have limited graphics, and the sound will not have been thoroughly edited.
- **Second cut:** This will be much closer to the final advert – in fact, if no changes are made by the client, it may actually be the final advert.

Focus groups

A focus group generally consists of around six to ten members of the target audience involved in a mediated discussion. An interviewer might show them sample promotional materials (for example, a printed advert or a TV advert) and ask their opinions. The results can lead to improvements in advertising design, which may help make the message more appealing to the target market.

However, focus groups can quickly develop group dynamics and their outcomes may be skewed by strong characters.

Did you know?

Teenagers in the UK spend 60 per cent more time watching TV and playing video games than they spend in school. Hollywood has such an influence on brand inspiration that marketers building new brand strategies increasingly need to develop an integrated television, computer game and film strategy when targeting teenagers.

4.5 Developing a promotional plan

This involves a number of factors, such as choosing the promotion mix, timing and frequency, costs, mix of media and possibly use of the Internet. These are outlined in Table 9.6.

Table 9.6: Factors to consider when developing a promotional plan.

Step	Task	Comment
1	Outline your objectives from the campaign brief.	The campaign's objectives should be clear and follow SMART principles. This means they should be specific, measurable, achievable, realistic and time-related. For example, 'Raise listenership in 14–19-year-olds by 15 per cent within six months'.
2	Identify your target audience from the campaign brief.	The target audience needs to be identified, it may be a broad description (for example, homeowners in the UK) or more specific (women aged 30–40 in the ABC1 demographic).
3	Detail your promotional message in the creative brief.	The promotional message should be clearly linked to the objective of the campaign. For example, if the objective was for the target audience to perceive a soft drink as improving their sporting performance, the message would need to spell out these benefits of the drink.
4	Establish your promotional budget or cost.	The budget may define the promotional mix that can be developed by ruling out expensive options. A business will have a specific budget set aside for a campaign based on the benefits it expects to gain from it.
5	Choose your promotion and media mix.	When choosing a promotional mix, there are a number of key points to consider. • How does the promotional campaign integrate with the wider marketing mix? A business's branding guidelines (see page 218) may help build a coherent range of promotional and marketing activity. • What media should be used? The range chosen will be affected by the budget available and the target audience. How will each part of the campaign work with the other components? • Will you use the Internet, and if so, how? How will your customers know about your website?
6	Schedule the frequency and timing of your promotion.	You need to consider whether timing is important for the launch of your campaign, and what level of frequency (see page 223) is appropriate. Remember that in order for your product or service to remain in your customers' minds, promotional messages need to be repeated over a period of time.
7	Review your promotion plan.	A campaign should be regularly reviewed against its objectives to assess how successful it is and take any necessary action to improve the results or adapt the objectives. SMART campaign objectives will make this task much easier. If a campaign is not as successful as intended, it is important to identify why. Were the goals unrealistic? Has promotional activity by a competitor affected the effectiveness of your message? Has the target audience received your message? If something is not working as it should, it will be more effective for the business to adapt the tactics and promotional mix than to continue to pay to use something that is not right.

Aden Kapur
Getting into advertising at a junior level

After completing the BTEC National Business Diploma at his local college, 19-year-old Aden Kapur fully intended to pursue a career in the creative industries, which would allow him to combine his love of language and the arts. Realising the difficulties in breaking into this sector, during the BTEC Diploma, Aden purposely worked towards building an extensive and professional portfolio of his work which he could show prospective employers.

After finishing his course, Aden decided not to go on to university but instead found a job at the local leisure centre as a temporary marketing assistant. He found himself particularly inspired when asked to undertake a campaign aimed at getting mothers and toddlers to use the leisure centre – the campaign ran for six weeks and Aden was responsible for designing posters and leaflets, issuing press releases for the local paper and the leisure centre website. The campaign was a great success with a 35 per cent increase in mothers and toddlers using the leisure centre facilities.

Aden became determined to follow his career goal to work in the creative industries and in particular in the advertising sector. He was eventually interviewed by the managing director of the small advertising agency, Future Media Advertising and Designs. After a meeting with managing director, Simone Phillips, Aden was offered the position of junior copywriter at the agency.

The agency specialises in marketing and design solutions to a wide range of local and regional businesses, schools and charities. Aden's job involves assisting the senior copywriter at the agency with writing 'copy'. This entails the creation of original slogans, straplines and catchphrases as well as the research, writing of 'copy' or wording and structure for all types of advertising briefs. These can include the wording for posters, brochures and content for websites as well as verbal copy for local radio and press. Aden also works closely with the Art Director who is responsible for ideas, concepts and visual aspects of any given advertising campaign.

Think about it!

1. In what ways do you think Aden can use copy to impact on a print-based advertising campaign with a target customer aged 70 and over?

2. What do you feel are the advantages and disadvantages of a copy-only advertising campaign?

3. Evaluate the visual and copy content of your favourite website. Discuss the benefits of using a combined visual and copy advertising campaign. Can you find any evidence of a successful online advertising campaign that combines both aspects?

Functional skills

English: By completing the WorkSpace activity on page 232, you will be practising reading, comparing, selecting and understanding texts, and using them to gather information, ideas, arguments and opinions.

Assessment activity 9.4

For this Assessment activity you need to be able to produce a promotional campaign of your own. You have a friend who is setting up a sandwich and snack bar to provide lunches for workers at a local industrial estate and you have agreed to design a promotional campaign. You are also asked to evaluate an existing national marketing campaign.

1. Design a promotional campaign for the sandwich and snack bar to meet the needs of a given campaign/creative brief. For the promotional campaign, your design should follow from its associated campaign/creative brief. In designing the campaign, you should apply what you have learned about target marketing and promotional mix. **P5**

2. For this task, you need to provide a rationale or reasoning for the promotional campaign, explaining why it is expected to achieve its goals. **M3**

3. You now need to select a national marketing campaign that is of interest to you and evaluate whether you think it has been successful or not. **D2**

Grading tips

1. Look at the notes of what should be in a campaign/creative brief and follow the logical steps. Carry out some research and look at completed campaign briefs so that you get some idea of what a real one looks like. **P5**

2. For this task, you need to explain why the promotional campaign is taking place. Ask yourself why you think the organisation believes that the campaign will achieve its goals. **M3**

3. Choose a national marketing campaign that is of interest to you and one where you can access good information. Evaluation is about considering in detail the advantages and disadvantages of something, and coming to conclusions as a result of this analysis. Try to work out whether the campaign was worth the effort. **D2**

Just checking

1. What is the meaning of a brand?
2. Why are communication models useful to marketers?
3. How can the AIDA communications model help businesses design effective promotional messages?
4. Why is new product development important to businesses?
5. Why do some marketers believe that price is the most important element within the marketing mix?
6. What are the seven Ps of the extended marketing mix?
7. What is meant by media planning?
8. Why is the choice of media so important?
9. Describe what a campaign brief should contain.
10. What does a target group mean?
11. Why is it important to have promotional objectives?

Assignment tips

1. Some famous promotional campaigns have been a great success and have taken a brand which already had an excellent reputation and built upon it. In your research into successful promotional activities (Assessment activity 9.1), take a look at the following examples:

   • Sainsbury's Active Kids promotion (**www2.sainsburys.co.uk/activekids**)

   • Innocent Drinks Supergran promotion (**www.innocentdrinks.co.uk/thebigknit**).

2. There are two key categories of advertising: 'above-the-line' and 'below-the-line'. Basically, 'above-the-line' involves any work done involving media where a commission is taken by an advertising agency, and 'below-the-line' is work done for a client where a standard charge replaces commission. So television advertising is 'above-the-line' because an agency would book commercial time on behalf of a client, but placing an advert in a local newspaper is 'below-the-line,' because newspapers tend to apply their own costing approach where no commission is taken by the agency – instead the agency charges the client a fee.

3. When producing the promotional campaign for a sandwich and snack bar (Assessment activity 9.4), you will need to design a local promotional campaign rather than a regional or global one. One cheap way of advertising is through professional associations' monthly newsletters, which provide an excellent opportunity for small budget advertising. Also explore local newspapers. You can find hundreds of newspapers and weeklies with a readership only in the tens of thousands, which means their rates for ads are minimal compared to the price of a national newspaper.

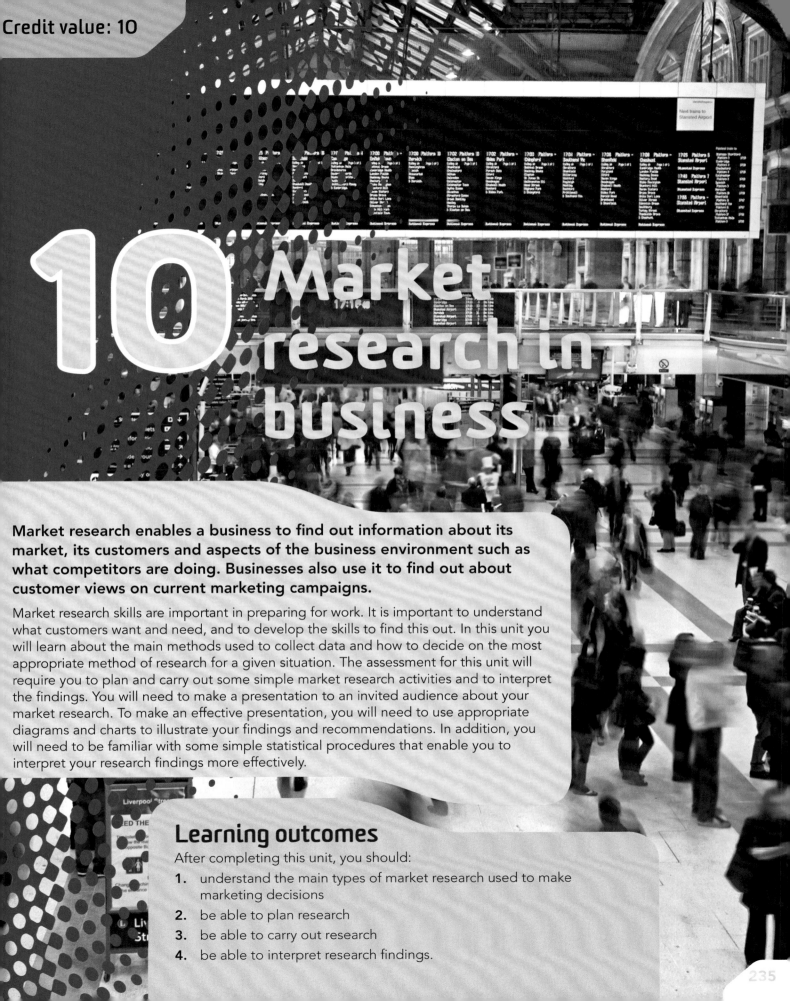

10 Market research in business

Market research enables a business to find out information about its market, its customers and aspects of the business environment such as what competitors are doing. Businesses also use it to find out about customer views on current marketing campaigns.

Market research skills are important in preparing for work. It is important to understand what customers want and need, and to develop the skills to find this out. In this unit you will learn about the main methods used to collect data and how to decide on the most appropriate method of research for a given situation. The assessment for this unit will require you to plan and carry out some simple market research activities and to interpret the findings. You will need to make a presentation to an invited audience about your market research. To make an effective presentation, you will need to use appropriate diagrams and charts to illustrate your findings and recommendations. In addition, you will need to be familiar with some simple statistical procedures that enable you to interpret your research findings more effectively.

Learning outcomes

After completing this unit, you should:

1. understand the main types of market research used to make marketing decisions
2. be able to plan research
3. be able to carry out research
4. be able to interpret research findings.

Assessment and grading criteria

This table shows you what you must do in order to achieve a **pass**, **merit** or **distinction** grade, and where you can find activities in this book to help you.

To achieve a **pass** grade, the evidence must show that the learner is able to:	To achieve a **merit** grade, the evidence must show that, in addition to the pass criteria, the learner is able to:	To achieve a **distinction** grade, the evidence must show that, in addition to the pass and merit criteria, the learner is able to:
P1 describe types of market research **See Assessment activity 10.1, page 250.**		
P2 explain how different market research methods have been used to make a marketing decision within a selected situation or business **See Assessment activity 10.1, page 250.**		
P3 plan market research for a selected product/service using appropriate methods of data collection **See Assessment activity 10.2, page 256.**	**M1** explain, with examples, how different market research methods are appropriate to assist different marketing situations **See Assessment activity 10.1, page 250.**	**D1** evaluate the market research method used by a selected organisation **See Assessment activity 10.3, page 264.**
P4 conduct primary and secondary research for a selected product/service making use of identifiable sampling techniques **See Assessment activity 10.3, page 264.**	**M2** explain the reasons for choosing the particular method of data collection for a selected product/service **See Assessment activity 10.2, page 256.**	**D2** evaluate the findings from the research undertaken **See Assessment activity 10.4, page 277.**
P5 interpret findings from the research, presenting them clearly in an appropriate format **See Assessment activity 10.4, page 277.**	**M3** analyse the research findings and make recommendations on how marketing strategies could be adapted or implemented **See Assessment activity 10.4, page 277.**	

How you will be assessed

For this unit you are expected to carry out some market research of your own. You will then need to produce a market research report setting out your findings. An oral presentation coupled with a clear written report will be an effective way of doing this. The example below should give you some ideas.

Jake

This was an interesting unit to do because it involved applying research skills that are going to be really useful in my future work. The assignment required us to plan and complete market research for a selected business. I researched a local independent cinema with three other learners. The current cinema has two screens and we were asked to carry out some research for the owner to find out whether there is sufficient demand for a third screen.

The best way to start a market research project is to clarify the research objectives. It was important to keep these in mind so that we would not get distracted in our survey work. Next we decided on the most appropriate research methods. We used questionnaires as our major tool.

Once we had collected our data we needed to analyse it – to try to identify patterns and trends. I drew a line graph illustrating changing patterns of cinema attendance in the UK and compared it with attendances at the local cinema. From this it was possible to illustrate trends (patterns). I was able to represent the views and feeling of cinema goers in a range of diagrams and back these up with supporting notes and recommendations.

Finally, my group made a presentation to the local cinema owner and to our Business Studies lecturers as well as some parents in the cinema itself. The results showed that there was a potential market for a new screen. However, it would be necessary to do further research to find out whether the cost of building and running an additional screen would pay back the investment.

Mini deodorant spray

Fig. 10.1 shows a new mini deodorant spray that has been developed by a well-known cosmetics firm. It will be sold at airports and other travel embarkation points. It is aimed to appeal to customers who have forgotten to pack a deodorant and are going on a short holiday of a week or less. It is designed to be convenient. How would you go about researching the market to find out if there is a suitable demand for the product? Who would you conduct research on?

Fig. 10.1: How would you carry out market research for this product?

1. Understand the main types of market research used to make marketing decisions

Market research can be defined as the systematic gathering, recording and analysis of data about problems relating to the marketing of goods and services. This can be broken down as follows:

- systematic – carried out in a careful and organised way
- gathering and recording of data – collection of data and setting this down in writing or (more likely) in computer records
- analysing the data – identifying patterns and trends
- problems relating to marketing – these include what price to charge, how best to advertise the goods and services, where to sell them from and so on.

A simpler definition of market research that is easy to remember is: 'keeping those who provide goods and services in touch with the requirements of those who buy them'.

There are two main methods that be used for market research. These are:

- primary research – collecting new information
- secondary research – using research that is already published.

1.1 Primary research methods

Information that an organisation collects from its own research efforts is termed 'primary'. This involves the collection of new information for a specific purpose.

Observation

Observation involves watching some type of behaviour. The main advantage of this approach is that the researcher watches behaviour first-hand rather than having to ask someone what they would do in a specific situation. As a result, observation may yield far more accurate results than alternative approaches, as observation shows what actually happens.

A good example of observation is watching customers shop. The observer can identify how long customers spend in particular aisles of a supermarket and which products they look at. This type of observation is very useful in providing information about the best possible layout for a supermarket, and the sorts of display and offer that appeal to customers.

Did you know?

Observation by market researchers who film the actions of shoppers in stores enables them to place 'special offers' in locations where customers are most likely to look for them. The research shows the best heights to place particular products in the aisles and which parts of the shop involve the highest levels of customer activity. Market research shows that 90 per cent of all purchase decisions are made at the point of sale, so observing what customers do in shops is very important.

Another example of observation is when a business sends out a 'mystery shopper'. This person will check on the products and services the business is offering. Alternatively, they can go and look at those offered by a rival. The purpose of this is to provide an impression of the quality of the customer experience and how this compares with that of rivals.

The main disadvantage of observation is that it is very time consuming and hence expensive.

Experimentation

The purpose of an experiment is to find out what happens as a result of taking a particular action. In terms of primary market research, this typically involves making a change in the marketing mix (see page 112) and then recording and analysing the results. For example, an experiment might be carried out where the price of a product is changed (usually in just one part of the total market). Other experiments might involve changing a product and seeing what happens. For example, in 2008, Oxo changed the shape of some of their gravy cubes from the traditional square shape to an X-shape. This was introduced because it was easier to crumble. This change was only brought in after careful research with consumer groups to find a suitable shape.

Surveys

Surveys are one of the most frequently used methods of market research. A survey will typically involve the use of a questionnaire (details on how to create a questionnaire are set out on page 259).

There are several ways of conducting a **survey**.

1. **Face-to-face:** this tends to be the best form of contact. It allows two-way communication between the researcher and the **respondent**, and may allow an experienced researcher to find out more detailed and sensitive information. It is also flexible, and gestures, facial and other expressions may be noted. A questionnaire put to a person in the street is likely to be less friendly and detailed than a discussion at home. A street interview is brief and impersonal whereas a home discussion can be exactly the opposite. A disadvantage of face-to-face is that it may become distorted as a result of the interpersonal relationships between interviewer and interviewee.

Fig. 10.2: What are the benefits of face-to-face interviewing?

Key terms

Survey – a careful study of a particular topic such as consumers' opinions about a specific product or issue. The survey typically involves a sequence of questions, which may be in the form of a questionnaire or interview

Respondent – someone who takes part in a survey

Did you know?

In August 2009, the *Mail on Sunday* conducted a survey to find out how readily people give their personal details to market researchers. Two market researchers stopped passers-by in central London and asked if they would fill in a questionnaire about their shopping habits in return for a £10 gift voucher. People were additionally asked to provide information about their name, address (including postcode) and date of birth. The research was really to find out how easily members of the public would provide details that could be used for identity fraud. Half of the 18 people stopped in the street provided this information. Two also gave details of their bank accounts. So be careful when giving out personal details!

2. **Postal:** the level of response to a postal questionnaire varies enormously, depending on its relevance to the reader and their interest in the topic. Response rates are typically ten per cent or lower, so answers are not particularly representative. The way to avoid this outcome is to make sure that the questionnaire is brief, and sent only to those for whom it is directly relevant. Postal surveys are cheap to administer, and can be used to survey people in a wide geographical area. The major drawback is the poor response rate.

3. **Telephone:** this is quite a useful method for business surveys as the respondents are often busy people who are otherwise unavailable for discussion. However, this method is often regarded as intrusive since it catches people unawares, especially in their home. Many telephone interviews are conducted in the early evening when the householders are home. Telephone interviews can be very annoying, meaning respondents to interviews often start with a negative view, which questioning will not necessarily help to overcome. However, it is a cost-effective way of reaching people, and the replies received are likely to be truthful. The main benefits of telephone interviewing is that it covers a broad geographical area. There tends to be a higher response rate than for postal and street surveys, and it is usually easy to analyse the data generated in this way. However, they can be costly to operate, and it is not always clear who is answering the phone and how seriously they are taking the interview.

I hope I am calling at a convenient time. Could you spare a few minutes to answer some questions?

Fig. 10.3: Do you think telephone interviews are valuable?

4. **e-mail and m-mail:** this involves delivering a survey to a computer or mobile phone e-mail address. This can work when the questionnaire is directly related to the interests of the recipient. Because the computer or mobile phone has a keypad attached it may be quite easy to fill in the survey, and may be filled in when the recipient has nothing else to do, for example, on a long train journey. However, the main problem is that many computer and mobile phone users are suffering from 'survey fatigue'. They are simply asked to fill in too many questionnaires.

E-market research

E-market research has been increasing in importance and frequency over the last ten years. Today most households in the UK have a home computer and people may spend many hours a day surfing the Internet. The share of Internet shopping has also increased at a rapid rate. It makes sense therefore to develop e-market research methods. Market research of this type is very easy to carry out. There are two main approaches.

1. Standard questionnaires. Here the computer user receives a questionnaire that they fill in related to a particular topic. The recipient can fill in the questionnaire at their leisure, saving it if they are too busy to complete it in one go. They then simply mail it back to the market research address.

Case study: Volunteered personal information

The last ten years has seen a revolution in the quantity of market research data provided directly by customers. The term volunteered personal information (VPI) refers to this type of information, much of which is collected electronically. This ranges from information such as, 'I'm interested in running so please send me information about running but not tennis or football.' They also supply information such as, 'I intend to buy a new plasma screen television in the next six months' or 'My current car insurance runs out on 20 March.' This VPI provides market research organisations with a wealth of detail about preferences, lifestyles, intended purchases, changes of address and so on. Organisations that can capture this VPI are well placed to make offers to customers that are based on their needs and requirements.

The UK VPI market is estimated to be worth £20 billion by 2020. Market research companies that

can collect this information can sell it on to others seeking market research data. This type of data falls into four categories:

- 'What I want to find out' data – £10 billion
- 'What I want' data – £6.5 billion
- 'My views and feelings' data – £2 billion
- 'Who I am' data – £1.5 billion.

1. **What type of data have you supplied voluntarily to an organisation in recent weeks?**

2. **How could this data be used for market research purposes?**

3. **How could this data then be used to inform market decisions made by businesses?**

4. **Who is most likely to benefit from the development of the VPI market?**

2. Interactive questionnaires. Here questions are presented one at a time. The sequencing of questions will depend on how the person filling in the questionnaire answers questions.

Focus groups

A focus group is a group of actual or potential customers brought together to discuss (focus on) a particular product or consumer issue. The size of the group will typically be quite small. It may contain as few as five members or extend up to 15 in larger groups.

The purpose of the focus group is to generate 'rich' information, rather than standard responses.

One approach is to use a set of cue cards containing topics or suggestions for discussion. Researchers will watch the focus group interacting and note such things as the language they use when talking about a product, or their views about the product.

Focus group structure depends on whether the market researchers have specific themes that they want exploring or whether they want a more open-ended approach that generates some new ideas.

Panels

A panel is a survey that is conducted over an extended period of time with the same group. For example, working with a consumer panel, it is possible to measure their changing buying patterns over time.

Consumer panels provide information about:

- typical items bought by consumers
- which of these items are becoming more or less popular over time
- how consumers respond to particular factors – for example, the trend to buy smaller, more fuel-efficient cars or healthier food
- how consumers respond to marketing campaigns, for example, special offers, increased advertising.

Difficulties associated with consumer panels include:

- making sure that the panel members retain their interest over time and continue to record their behaviour accurately
- problems associated with some members dropping out, and whether they can be replaced by similar people.

Field trials and piloting

A field trial involves testing a new product or service in the market before launching it. The purpose of the field trial is to find out how real consumers respond to the product. This is expensive and so will only typically take place in part of the market. By carrying out a field trial it is still possible to make changes to the product and other aspects of the marketing mix (see page 112) before the final launch takes place.

Piloting is a similar process. A pilot is a preliminary test to identify strengths and weaknesses. The term can be used to mean a field trial. The other meaning of piloting relates to the piloting of market research questions. Here questions in a survey are tried out with a sample of customers who are representative of the total market. Weaknesses can then be identified in the questions and ironed out before a full-scale market research survey is carried out.

Appropriateness of primary research methods

In choosing the most appropriate primary research methods to use, it is helpful to bear in mind a number of criteria. These are:

- **fitness for purpose** – is the method suitable for what you want to find out? For example, if you wanted to engage in a wide-scale survey, then observation may be too time consuming and a phone survey might be more appropriate
- **cost** – it is important to use a cost-effective method. The greater the cost of the research, the more opportunity there is to increase the 'richness' and quantity of information
- **accuracy** – the more representative your survey is in giving a picture of the market, the more accurate your information will be
- **time** – for example, a questionnaire takes time to construct but then it is relatively quick to administer and analyse

- **validity** – the extent to which it measures what it claims to measure. For example, a field test provides evidence of actual customer behaviours in the market. If this is what you want to measure, then this would be a valid approach to research

- **response rate** – some methods yield higher response rates than others – for example, telephone and phone research yield higher response rates than postal methods.

Table 10.1 looks at the criteria listed above in relation to the methods described.

1.2 Secondary research

Secondary research involves using existing information rather than finding out new information.

There are two main sources of secondary research:

- internal sources – information that already exists within the business

- external sources – information published by other organisations.

Internal sources

Businesses have available to them a variety of information about their market. This information is often collected for other purposes in addition to market research.

Data records

Organisations maintain a range of different types of information in their **databases**. Particularly important are their sales records, including invoices sent to customers.

Careful analysis of this data will reveal:

- who the existing customers are
- where they live
- how much they spend
- how often they make purchases.

EPOS (Electronic Point of Sale)

The bar codes on sales items generate a lot of useful information. Each bar code, or RFID (radio frequency identification), records stock coming into a business and the sales that are made. Bar codes allow businesses to record sales of products immediately – an excellent form of market research. They are now being replaced by RFIDs, which can be as small as a grain of salt.

Fig. 10.4: What are bar codes used for?

An EPOS terminal will be linked to a back office computer. The system can be used in small businesses like independent bars, clubs and hotels, as well as large supermarket chains.

When an item is sold, its bar code will be scanned and the sale recorded in the computer system. The retailer then has a record of:

- numbers of sales
- changes in the level of sales
- where sales are made (for example, by geographical store location).

In marketing terms, this information is highly useful because it immediately tells the business about customers' wants and needs. Analysing this information enables the company to respond immediately to changing demand patterns.

Website monitoring

It is essential to keep a record of browsers who have shown an interest in your website and the goods and services offered there. A **cookie** is a small file that a web server places on a computer so that it can identify who has been browsing. The next time you use the browser the web server will recognise that your computer is calling again. Most websites log visits, recording details about visitors such as:

- the pages requested
- how long the visitor browses for.

Key terms

Databases – stores of data gathered for particular purposes. Today we tend to associate databases with computer programs designed for the storage of data

Cookie – small piece of computer code that records a user's data so they do not have to enter the same information each time they visit a site

Table 10.1: Criteria for primary research methods.

Criteria	Observation	Experiment	Surveys	Focus groups	Field trials
Fitness for purpose	Useful for recording what actually happens	Useful for changing variables in the marketing mix	Can provide lots of quantitative as well as qualitative data (see page 248)	Excellent for providing 'rich' information	Provide a real representation of the marketplace in action
Cost	Expensive in requiring an observer to take detailed records – but observations can be filmed to lower cost	Time consuming as an experiment has to be set up and then studied	May be costly to create the questionnaire – but once set up, can be used for a large sample – hence low cost per unit (person) of survey	Expensive to set up – needs to take place at a specific location. Often the focus group will be observed through a one-way mirror	Expensive to administer as usually lots of participants need to be briefed
Accuracy	Yields accurate results because it involves actual observation	Depends on how well the experiment is set up and the possibility of identifying significant variables affecting behaviour	This depends on the numbers surveyed and how representative they are of the total market	Sample is likely to be small. Important therefore to try to make sure that the focus group is representative	Depends on how accurately participants keep records and the extent to which they record true behaviours
Time	Time to set up – although once organised, may be less time consuming	Experiment may have to go on for a long time before researchers have meaningful results	Takes time to create the survey; completed questionnaire may be slow in being returned, analysis may be lengthy. Computer surveys are a lot quicker	May take time to select appropriate members, explain what is required, and analyse qualitative data	Typically takes place over a longer period of time
Validity	Valid when the observed behaviour reflects what the researchers are trying to find out about	Depends on the extent to which the experiment reflects the reality which the researchers are investigating	Depends on how well the questions are structured and the extent to which those surveyed understand the questions	Good when rich data required and the focus group members are honest and clear	Excellent way of finding out how consumers behave in a setting that closely represents the real market
Response rate	As high as the observers can make it – particularly with filming of behaviours	Depends on how long the experiment is carried out for – but initially should be very high	Depends on method – some methods, for example, postal surveys have very low response rates	Because a small group is involved, most participants will contribute	Initially high but may fall over time

This information is really useful and gives an edge over traditional retailers. The e-tailer (firm selling over the Internet) not only is able to check on the buyer behaviour of those that make purchases but additionally can see the interest taken by others who simply browse the site.

E-transactions

Electronic transactions made by buyers provide a wealth of useful secondary information. The seller can see:

- who bought items
- how much they spent
- how frequently they purchased.

They can then make offers to customers. For example, when you buy a book on Amazon.co.uk, the site will suggest other purchases based on their records of what books previous purchasers of that book also bought. When you buy an air ticket from a budget airline, then the airline will send you further offers and keep reminding you about how to order through them. Often when you make a purchase there will be a box to tick that asks you if you would be liked to be sent details of future offers.

Another desirable aspect from the point of view of the website provider is for users to voluntarily submit further details, which can be stored in a database referenced against the browser's cookie.

Website providers seek to gather information about the email addresses of customers so that they can communicate directly with them. For example, a football club might seek to gain the email addresses of past season-ticket holders, in order to encourage them to buy season tickets in the future.

Did you know that when you buy a book on Amazon.co.uk the site automatically recommends the most common joint purchases made by other buyers?

Accounting and production records

Production records show how much of given products a business has made for sale in the past. What is more important are figures showing what has been sold. The accounts department will hold some of this information in computer records. It will show sales made to major customers (particularly if they have bought on credit) and the methods of payment they have used.

Sales personnel

People who work in sales for a company will be very knowledgeable about customer buying behaviour. Experienced sales members will have worked with customers for years and have knowledge about what appeals to them – for example, special offers or discounts. They will have a good knowledge of which items sell particularly well and which do not. They will know about which products and services customers tend to buy together.

Delphi technique

This is a method that is employed to predict future patterns – for example, likely consumer spending patterns. It draws on the ideas of wise people who have knowledge about the issue they are asked to examine. The Delphi technique will suggest a number of likely future possibilities.

A panel of experts are drawn up, each of whom is likely to have some knowledge and experience which they

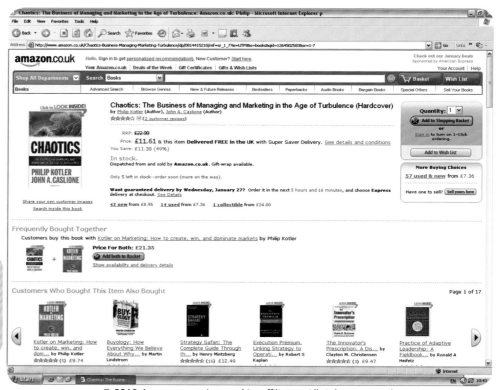

can draw on. The members of the panel provide their views. However, they do not meet together. This is so that they do not influence the views put forward by the others. One person is given the role of collecting each of the views. Extreme views are discarded first.

The person in the chairing role then sums up the main views of the panel members. The panel members then comment and fine-tune their views. Gradually a consensus view (agreement) about the likely market picture in the future emerges.

External sources

Rather than conducting their own research, many businesses use existing published research. This can save a lot of time and effort. However, purchasing an existing market research report may cost thousands of pounds. Other sources may be cheaper, such as accessing data from the Internet and government publications.

Internet

The Internet is the most accessible source of information. Researchers need to be cautious when using this source and first ask themselves what were the purposes that the information was collected for. The way that the Internet is organised makes it very easy to find out information. For example, Google ranks topics under headings according to how frequently they are searched for. This means that when you carry out a search, for example, 'market trends in confectionery', you are likely to find very recent information that is valued by other researchers.

Useful search engines that you may want to use include:

- Google – the most comprehensive of all the search engines
- Yahoo! – useful for searching for UK-based materials
- Ask Jeeves – which enables you to ask a question direct.

Government statistics

The government regularly analyses business trends and changes taking place in the economy. This information is published in reference books and journals. Many of these sources can be accessed directly through the Internet by typing in the appropriate search terms.

Examples of useful government publications include the following.

- **Social Trends** – draws together social and economic data from a wide range of government departments and other organisations. It paints a broad picture of British society and how it is changing covering key areas.
- **Monthly Digest of Statistics** – summary of information on monthly economic trends.
- **Expenditure and Food Survey** – shows what households are spending their money on and how these patterns are changing over time.
- **Regional Trends** – regional profiles, details of households, labour market information, living standards and so on.
- **Annual Abstract of Statistics** – details about population changes, social conditions, production, prices and employment.
- **Business Monitors** – statistics on output in different business sectors. The Retailing Monitor is of particular interest, covering retail sales by region.

Libraries and universities

A library is an obvious starting point to search for secondary data. The library will contain books and journals located in the business section. The library may also have market research reports, telephone directories and newspapers. Recently Google has developed a project to create an online library containing millions of books. Some of these books can be read in their entirety while others just show selected chapters.

Did you know?

A university library is likely to have a range of specialist publications, particularly if business studies and marketing are taught there. Universities also carry out independent market research on a range of specialist themes. Some of this research is sponsored directly by business.

Company reports

Public companies are required to produce an Annual General Report. These reports can be ordered by anyone and supply details of the company's current activities. The report shows the current strategy of the business and often, more importantly for market research processes, outlines current market trends in the area the company operates in. For example, if you were researching trends in the household goods market, it would be helpful to study the most recent Procter & Gamble or Unilever annual report. You can order company reports directly over the Internet from www.hemscott.net or www.ftannualreports.com

Market research reports

Market research companies produce information about markets and products. They give a good idea of trends.

Mintel is a commercial research organisation which, in return for a fee, provides a monthly journal containing reports on a variety of consumer markets – for example, bread, insurance and mobile phones. The Mintel reports are up to about 20 pages long, with information such as market size, main competitors, projected growth, market share of main firms, advertising spend of main brands and trends. Mintel also produces in-depth reports on certain markets, for example, the youth market or the sportswear market.

Datastream, produced by Thomson Reuters, provides very useful information about the current state of financial markets, including details of the exchange rate and economic forecasts.

Another organisation, Dun & Bradstreet, publishes a range of reports on industries and trading prospects within these industries. You can find all of the above at:

- www.mintel.com
- www.thomson.com
- www.dnb.com

Trade journals

A trade journal is a publication produced for businesses which work in a particular trade – for example, *The Grocer*, *Farmer's Weekly*, *Hotelier* and so on. These journals provide insider information about new developments in a particular area of business. They help a business to keep up to date with recent trends in the industry, market trends and what competitors are doing. A particularly useful trade journal for people involved in the marketing industry is *Marketing*, whose website address is www.marketingmagazine.co.uk

Criteria for selection of a secondary source

On page 243 there was a list of criteria for choosing a primary research method. Exactly the same process can be applied when choosing a secondary research method.

For example, in terms of 'fitness for purpose', it is important to use the research method that is most suitable to finding out the required information. For example, if you want to find out information about

Activity: Trade journals

A list of UK trade journals can be found if you carry out a Yahoo! search using the search term 'trade magazines'. See if you can identify trade journals that would be particularly helpful for your market research.

Functional skills

ICT: Here you have the opportunity to engage in a data retrieval activity to identify data that will be helpful in supporting your research enquiry. Use search terms related to your market research topic.

PLTS

Carry out the task using your own initiative about what to look for.

retail trends, then a Mintel report on this topic would be appropriate. If you wanted to find out about changing patterns of food consumption in the UK, then the government's Expenditure and Food Survey would be an obvious source.

In terms of cost, you will find that some published reports by market research agencies are very expensive to buy, whereas you could probably get a company report for a minimal price.

The accuracy of secondary information depends on how much effort has been put into collecting it. A newspaper or Internet report might include some inaccuracies, whereas a detailed government statistical report would be a lot more accurate.

Read specialist marketing magazines as they are a useful source of information about current marketing trends.

Case study: Secondary research about the 'staycation'

Did you know that data produced by the government's Office for National Statistics revealed the growth of the 'staycation' in 2009?

In August 2009, the Office for National Statistics published their research findings, showing that only 4.78 million people travelled abroad from Britain in June, compared to 5.98 million the previous year. In the same month, 5.7 per cent more visitors travelled to Britain from abroad compared with the previous year.

Tourism is the fifth biggest industry in Britain, employing 1.4 million people directly. It generates more than £86 billion for the economy according to the accountants Deloitte.

Company figures produced in annual reports by hotel chains Travelodge and Premier Inns showed that both companies had had the strongest summer sales on record.

The new word in the travel industry was the 'staycation' – people staying in Britain to holiday rather than going abroad. A major cause of this was the effect of the global recession in 2008–09, which led to falling incomes and rising unemployment for many Britons.

1. Identify two sources of secondary information that are mentioned above.

2. How useful would this secondary data be in helping a business owner to decide on whether to expand their hotel business in the south of England?

3. Describe and justify the use of other types of secondary data that might support the business owner in making a case to expand.

4. Would the owner be better off using primary or secondary data in making the decision to expand? Justify your answer.

In terms of time, you can access the Internet instantly, whereas going to a library to carry out research will require more effort.

The validity of different methods depends on making sure that you are clear about the purposes for which you want to gather the research information and the likelihood that the source you choose contains that information.

PLTS

This activity enables you to think creatively by pulling together what you have learned about primary and secondary information within the context of the staycation, which methods of research are likely to be most suitable and what the benefits would be of using different approaches.

Use of information technology applications

The use of information technology has made possible much more systematic and detailed collection and analysis of market research information.

Large quantities of data from questionnaires and surveys, from Electronic Point of Sale (EPOS) and other data collection methods can be stored in a vast database.

The market researcher can then use a process known as data mining to search data to identify patterns and trends and to create meaning from the data.

ICT applications can be used to:

- store information. Market research data can be placed into a database

- organise information. This information can be stored in a systematic way under key sub-headings referred to as 'fields'. Within each field the data can then be stored as 'records'

- retrieve data. It is then a simple exercise to retrieve appropriate data by carrying out a search. For example, a search could be carried out into a business database to find the names and email accounts of all customers who have browsed the company website more than five times in the last week

- report data. Reports can be set up presenting data patterns in charts and diagrams.

1.3 Qualitative and quantitative research

There are two broad types of data that can be collected by market research: qualitative and quantitative.

Qualitative research often takes longer to record as it involves collecting views and opinions which may be written or spoken. Where words are spoken, it may be necessary to record or transcribe what has been said. Most qualitative data arises from detailed interviews with a respondent or through focus group discussion.

A typical question asked in qualitative research is 'What do you think about x'? This question allows respondents to give their opinions, reasons, and motivations for thinking something or doing something. A group discussion allows different opinions to be offered. By analysing the views given

the researcher is able to identify a range of different views or sometimes a shared view.

In general, people enjoy giving their opinions, and this helps researchers. But it is vital that the audience is carefully selected to represent the target population. For example, if you wanted to find out about the views of teenagers about popular magazines like *OK!* and *Hello!* then it will be appropriate to interview teenagers who are familiar with these magazines.

Quantitative research produces numbers. These provide a measurable record or a series of values, which can then be analysed. For example, quantitative data might be produced showing what sorts of people and how many watch TV on a Friday between 7.00 p.m. and 9.00 p.m. The research will reveal two groups – those that watch TV during this period and those that do not.

The television example was based on identifying two categories – referred to as dichotomies. A lot of quantitative research involves identifying more categories or values that can be set out on a scale.

There are a number of different types of scale. Some, known as ordinal scales, are presented in order – for example an age scale involving the following groupings – 0–15, 16–35, 36–50, 51+.

Another approach to using a scale is a nominal scale. Here the scale is based on naming things to be listed. For example, the researcher may ask respondents how they cook potatoes. The list may include frying, roasting, boiling and so on. These are nominal (named) categories.

There are four components of quantitative measurement.

1. **A case** – the object, person, situation or organisation being measured and recorded.
2. **A variable** – the characteristic that is being measured and classified.
3. **A scale** – a series of values/outcomes which the research measures.
4. **A value** – what is actually recorded – the number or measure.

For example, Prakesh Patel (a case) is aged (a variable) 35 (a value) which fits into the 16–35 age category (on a scale).

Qualitative information is very good at finding out detailed views and opinions. It provides a rich depth of information. However, because it takes time to bring people together and record what they have to say, it may only be possible to research a small part of the market, which may not be truly representative of the target group.

In contrast, quantitative research has the potential to find out facts about a much larger number of people. However, the problem with quantitative research is that once questionnaires and scales have been constructed and delivered to respondents, it is not possible to change the questions. Often, gathering quantitative information leads to the wish for potential further probing questions to find out more.

Triangulation

Triangulation involves researching the same issue using several different methods (usually three methods).

The more data that market research can reveal about a particular topic or issue, the greater the chance that researchers will understand the topic being studied. If you can use more than one suitable method to research a topic, this will be helpful. For example, you could research teenagers' views about popular magazines by:

- creating a questionnaire for them
- holding focus group interviews
- observing which popular magazines teenagers pick up at your local supermarket in a given time period.

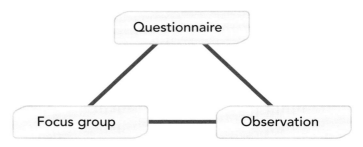

Fig. 10.5: Using triangulation to identify teenagers' views.

1.4 Marketing strategies and activities

Market research is used to make marketing decisions. These decisions are made in terms of **strategies** and **tactics**.

- **Strategic research** informs major marketing mix decisions within the organisation.

- **Technical research** identifies better ways of carrying out marketing activities. This might involve researching how well a particular advertising campaign is being received and whether adjustments can be made to it.

- **Databank research** updates and makes new entries to an organisation's databank to have to hand a ready supply of market research data. It includes details of customers and their buying patterns, records of previous promotional campaigns, details about past and current prices.

- **Continuous research** relates to finding out about customer pricing, and factors likely to affect the demand and supply of food supplies (for example, Tesco) and oil (for example, Shell) both in the short and long term, and enables businesses to regularly update their marketing strategies in line with changing conditions in their markets.

- **Ad hoc research** commissions research for ad hoc (specific) purposes, for example, to find out about customer perceptions about an organisation's brand or customer awareness of an advertising campaign.

Case study: Musical toothbrush

Julia Jones has developed a new type of toothbrush to encourage children to clean their teeth. When toothpaste and water are placed on the toothbrush, it plays a musical tune.

1. Whom would you carry out research on to find out whether this idea could be a success?

2. Identify three types of market research that could be used to find out the popularity of the idea.

3. Which of these methods would be best and why?

4. How would triangulation of your research findings help?

Key terms

Strategies – long-term plans for success

Tactics – the plans and methods used to achieve a particular short-term aim

Assessment activity 10.1

P1 P2 M1

BTEC

Two major developments in the first decade of the 21st century were the widespread use of the Internet and the growth of high street coffee shops such as Starbucks and Costa Coffee. A business opportunity that combines these two ideas is to set up a town centre coffee shop that offers wireless Internet connection, computer terminals and good-quality coffee.

An entrepreneur has asked you to carry out some market research to find out whether such a venture would work in your local town. However, she would first like to know some more details about the different types of market research that can be carried out. Produce a manual for the entrepreneur that deals with the following tasks.

1. In your manual describe the main types of market research. **P1**

2. Explain how different research methods could be used to make a marketing decision about whether there is a market for an Internet café business. **P2**

3. Explain, with examples, how the different research methods that you have identified are appropriate to enable the entrepreneur to identify whether the market is of a sufficient size for an Internet café business. **M1**

Fig. 10.6: Carrying out research for an Internet coffee shop.

Grading tips

1. Make sure that you identify in your manual the main types of market research – primary/secondary, qualitative/quantitative, internal and external. Give examples of each type and briefly outline the benefits of using this method. **P1**

2. Show how different types of market research would be helpful in identifying whether there would be a market for an Internet café business in your local town. Show how the different research methods would complement each other. **P2**

3. Make sure that you provide examples of ways in which the research methods could be used to identify the target market, what customers are looking for and whether demand would be sufficient. Justify the use of each method in terms of the sorts of results that it could provide. **M1**

2. Be able to plan research

You need to know how to plan market research. There are a number of stages which are involved, as set out in Fig. 10.7.

2.1 Stages

Research brief

The research brief is likely to be set for the market research team. It will be set out in very broad terms, for example, to investigate whether there is a market for a new type of hand cream, to see whether the market for drive-in cinemas is likely to increase over time, and so on.

The brief will set out the nature of the project for which the research is required. It will provide details of the organisation, and the project required – for example, to find out how customers are likely to respond to a new type of promotional activity.

For example, in the specification for the BTEC Business Award, one of the suggestions for the assessment is based on a market research brief:

'Stait of the Art thinks there is a market for a resalable plastic drinks container to replace cans. It wants a thorough investigation before proceeding to production, pricing and promotion.'

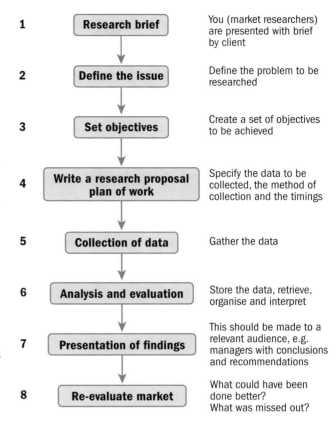

Fig. 10.7: Stages of planning market research.

Defining the issue

Given the research brief, it is now important for the market research team to clarify what needs to be researched. It is very important to be clear about the extent of the required research project and what exactly the client wants you to find out. For example, will the plastic drinks container replace all cans for drinks or just specific types of drinks?

An important aspect of defining the issue is to be clear about the target population that the research is aimed at. For example, in researching the market for plastic drinks containers, who will the target population consist of? Will this be drinkers of all types of fluids, for example, ice tea, fizzy drinks, beer and so on, or just specific groups of consumers, for example, a particular age range consuming fizzy drinks?

Setting objectives

Research projects should have clear objectives. By establishing objectives from the start, it is possible to

check whether they have been achieved by the end. It is also possible to make regular progress checks. The market research team should therefore write down three or four objectives which help to clarify the situation, for example:

- to identify whether there is a market for plastic drinks containers
- to identify the purposes for which drinks containers are used
- to identify who makes up the market for plastic drinks containers
- to identify the percentage of the market that would switch to plastic containers if these were made available.

Planning data to be collected

A plan of work is helpful in setting out the timings of the various activities that will be carried out in the market research.

Case study: Providing a research brief for organics

What's the future like for organic food?

2009 was a bad year for organic food sellers. This led some people to believe that the market had peaked. However, others attributed the fall in sales to falling incomes during the recession and a report by the Food Standards Agency (FSA) which concluded that organic food offers no additional health benefits relative to non-organics.

In response to this downturn a number of organic food brands including Green & Blacks (chocolate) and Rachel's (yoghurt) decided to appoint an advertising agency to carry out research and then carry out an advertising campaign setting out the benefits of organic foods. A group known as Sustain, which is the umbrella group for these and other organisations, set aside £1 million for the research and the ensuing campaign.

1. **Why has Sustain decided to mount a campaign to promote organic food consumptions?**

2. **Write a market research brief to inform the way in which the advertising campaign should be developed.**

Functional skills

English: It is necessary to write in clear English instructions about how the market research campaign should be developed. Set this out in no more than 200 words. You should outline clearly what the research should cover and what the purpose of the market research is.

PLTS

Demonstrate that you can create your research brief working on your own, self-managing, as you would do if given this task as a work-based activity.

The plan of work will set out:

- the methods of collecting the data
- who is responsible for collecting it
- the timing of the data collection.

It could look something like the following in Table 10.2.

Activity: Planning

When you decide on the topic for your market research, you should also create a plan like the above. Set out your plan electronically in the form of a table.

Table 10.2: Example of a plan of work.

Date	By 14 July	By 28 July	By 5 August	By 19 August	By 26 August
Project manager to plan research	*				
Create survey for street interviews (market research team)		*			
Plan focus group research (project manager)			*		
Conduct street interviews and focus group sessions (interviewers and research team)				*	
Analyse results of research (all team members)					*
Present data to client					*

Functional skills

English and ICT: In creating the table you will demonstrate the functional skills of concise presentation of key information coupled with the skills of laying out important documents using IT.

PLTS

Create the plan yourself (self-management). Once you are happy with it you can discuss it with other group members and your tutor.

Make sure that you have a clear and systematic plan for carrying out your research.

- Plan the data to be collected. Decide on the methods you will use to collect the data, for example, questionnaire, interview, survey. Decide who will collect the data, and when. Set out a time plan for each stage of the collection process.
- Decide on the data to be collected. Will the data collected be internal (already available within the organisation you are studying, for example, from customer records) or will it come from external sources, for example, using new questionnaires to use on customers? Will the data collected be primary or secondary? Usually it will be a mix of the two.
- Decide on the target population for your research. Who makes up the target market that you are investigating? Make sure you are clear about this.

2.2 Research stages

You also need to be clear about the various stages in the research.

- Be clear about the brief, when you are provided with one about what to research by an organisation that you are working for. Your tutor may generate this brief for you.
- Clarify the objectives of your research. Be clear in your own mind what objectives need to be covered, so you will know when you have completed the research and also be able to judge how effectively you have carried out the work.
- Plan the various stages of the research. Create a time plan with various headings, for example, for creating a questionnaire, carrying out pilot research, carrying out the actual research, analysing the results and so on.

Forecasting

Forecasting can be quite helpful as part of the process of planning market research. A forecast is an estimate of likely results based on the information that you already have. For example, it is possible to forecast future sales based on past sales results and the growth of sales over time. The more detailed the information that the forecast is based on, the more likely it is to yield accurate predictions of what the research will show.

Case study: Forecast sales of chewing gum 2004–2014

The following data was set out in 2009 and is based on Mintel research.

1. **What pattern can you see in the sales of chewing gum over the ten years shown?**

2. **Why is the figure for 2009 an estimate?**

3. **Why is the figure for 2014 a forecast?**

4. **How have Mintel been able to make the forecast illustrated for 2014?**

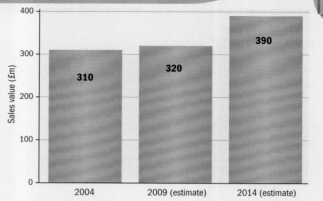

Fig. 10.8: Forecast sales of chewing gum, 2004–2014 (source: Mintel).

Functional skills

Mathematics: Interpreting these estimations and forecasts help you to demonstrate skills in interpreting simple mathematical representations of data.

Collection of data

In planning the research it is important that careful thought is given to the type of data to be collected.

- Will it be internal data/external data or both?
- Will it be primary data/secondary data or both?

When carrying out market research, the research team will need to consider how useful the data will be that already exists within the business or whether they will need to collect additional data that does not already exist within their records. Consideration will have to be given to the time and cost of collecting additional data and how useful it will be. When data does not already exist, then it will be helpful to carry out primary research. If secondary data does exist, then this can save a lot of time. However, it is important to consider the extent to which secondary data matches the specific market research objectives. For example, there may not be suitable data available about the market for plastic drink containers. If there is, it may not relate to the particular type of container that the business is considering introducing.

Analysis and evaluation of data

The data that is collected will need to be carefully stored. The next stage is that of **analysis**.

For example, you may have carried out primary research among the potential users of plastic drink containers. Analysis will reveal a pattern of results.

Key term

Analysis – making a detailed examination of the results of research, in order to find patterns and structures

- What percentage of those surveyed stated that they would purchase the new containers?
- What did they say they would use the containers for?
- How much would they be prepared to pay for them?
- Evaluation of your market research results follows on from the analysis and involves making recommendations (see below) and drawing up conclusions.

Presentation of findings

The data can be presented in charts, tables and graphs. This is covered in more detail on page 271. It is very important to choose the right sorts of tables and graphs to illustrate your points in order to provide an accurate presentation of your results.

The data should be set out in a clear way to back up any recommendations that the researchers want to make, in a clear and visual way.

Making recommendations

You will make recommendations from your evaluation of the data. For example, you may recommend that the business goes ahead with producing the plastic drinks containers because the evidence shows that there is a market for them. Your research may reveal that environmentally conscious consumers prefer reusable plastic cups rather than throwing away paper ones. Your recommendations should be clearly set out. A good way of doing this is to set out a numbered list of recommendations resulting from the research. Be concise and direct in making these.

While carrying out research, you will often find that you wish you had done something differently. For example, when carrying out quantitative research you may often find that it does not reveal enough about what consumers think and feel. It is helpful therefore to identify weaknesses in your research methods which may have led to weaknesses in your data. What would you do better if you were to start the research again?

Re-evaluation of marketing activities

You now have the opportunity to critically examine whether the marketing activities that have been carried out were the most suitable ones. What would you do differently next time?

2.3 Purpose of research objectives

It is important to be clear about what you are researching. Typical research objectives include the following.

1. **To understand customer behaviour.** Why do customers behave in the way that they do? Why do different customers behave in different ways? This covers a range of issues such as how long customers spend when they are shopping, whom they shop with, where they like to shop, what influences them to buy.

2. **To identify buying patterns.** When do customers buy goods and services? How often do they make purchases? Which goods and services do they buy together? How do buying patterns vary between different groups of customers?

3. **To identify customer preferences.** How do customers like to shop? What types of goods and services do they prefer? How do they like them to be packaged?

4. **To investigate customer satisfaction.** Are customers happy with the goods and services that they currently receive? What issues do they have? What improvements would they like to see?

Case study: Removing tattoos

In California, a tattoo removal firm has recently set up called Dr Tattoff. The company hopes to set up a chain across the United States to take advantage of the 'tattoo regret' factor that seems to grow as people get older. In 2008 a Harris Poll (market research survey) was carried out, which showed that 14 per cent of Americans have a tattoo and that a third of Americans in the 25–29 age range have one. The research showed that 16 per cent of Americans regret having a tattoo, creating a potential market of seven million laser removal customers. According to Dr Tattoff's internal data, 85 per cent of patients are women aged 18 to 44.

To remove the tattoos is expensive (£450–£900), spread over several sessions. The ink particles are blasted with a laser, which can be painful.

You have been commissioned by a tattoo removal business in the UK to find out if there is a similar market in your area.

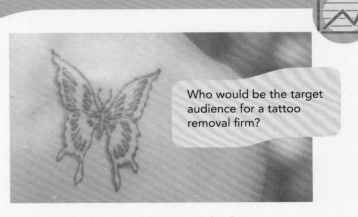

Who would be the target audience for a tattoo removal firm?

1. Define the issue to be researched.
2. Set out five market research objectives.
3. Who is the target audience for the research?
4. What data will you want to collect?
5. What methods will you use to collect the data?
6. Who will collect it and when?
7. How will you present the data?

5. **To identify sales trends.** Are sales improving, staying the same or falling?

6. **To reveal brand awareness.** Are customers aware of a particular brand? Customers are most likely to make purchases of brand names and brand images that they are familiar with.

7. **To reveal advertising awareness.** What percentage of customers can remember a particular advert? Do they associate the advert with the product? This reveals how successful advertising has been. Have consumers been encouraged to buy as a result of seeing an advert?

8. **To measure the success of a product development.** Product development involves introducing new lines and varieties of products. Market research can be conducted to see how successfully the new developments have been received.

9. **To identify new product opportunities.** Is there a market for new products that can be developed?

10. **To identify changes in the market.** Modern markets change rapidly. Customers are continually on the lookout for better offers.

11. **To identify the emergence of new markets.** Are there new markets for existing products?

12. **To carry out a PESTLE analysis.** Unit 3 Introduction to marketing introduced the concept of a PESTLE analysis (page 102). Researchers can carry out an analysis of changes in political, economic, social, technological, legal and environmental changes that are likely to affect the business and its products.

13. **To understand customer activity.** What are your rivals doing? How are they changing their marketing mix elements such as the nature of their products and prices charged?

Activity: Planning

In planning your market research, make sure that you are clear about the objectives of your research. Which of the 13 types of objectives listed above are you most concerned with? You should clarify in your research plan which market research objectives that you are focusing on.

Assessment activity 10.2

  BTEC

Following on from Assessment activity 10.1, where the local entrepreneur has asked you to find out whether there is a market for an Internet café business in your local town, she wants you to carry out a thorough investigation before recommending whether she should set up or not.

You need to create a research plan that sets out:

- the research objectives that you want to focus on
- the methods you will use to carry out the research
- a justification of the chosen research methods explaining why you have rejected alternatives.

The plan should identify the target audience, and the timing of the use of the research methods and who will be responsible for carrying out the research.

1. Plan research for a selected product/service using appropriate methods of data collection. **P3**

2. Explain the reasons for selecting the particular method of data collection for a selected product/ service. **M2**

Grading tips

1. Set out a clear plan using clear headings. Carefully discuss the alternative methods of market research with your tutor and other learners. Decide on the methods that are most valid for this particular piece of research and make sure that you justify their use. **P3**

2. Make sure that you explain clearly why the methods you have chosen are likely to produce valid data. You will most likely use more than one method, so explain how the methods complement each other and are likely to provide additional insight into the research topic. **M2**

3. Be able to carry out research

3.1 Census versus sample

The next stage of market research is to carry out the research. You will need first of all to consider the size and choice of sample that you want to research.

A possible approach is to take a **census**. This involves researching everybody in a particular population. For example, if you were going to research the demand for sandwiches at a proposed new local sandwich shop, then you would need to interview all potential sandwich purchasers in your area. Immediately you can see the difficulty in terms of time and cost. A census tends to be used for market research purposes when the population size is very small.

The alternative then is to take a **sample**. This involves questioning a selection of respondents from the target market. In order to ensure that the results of a sample survey are accurate, the market research process must identify a **representative cross-section** of customers.

Choosing a sample

A respondent is someone that takes part in a market research survey. There are two main ways of sampling (see Fig. 10.9).

The choice of sampling method depends on how much importance the researchers attach to getting an accurate picture of typical customer behaviour and the time available to collect the data. The more systematic the sample, the greater the time required to plan and carry out the research.

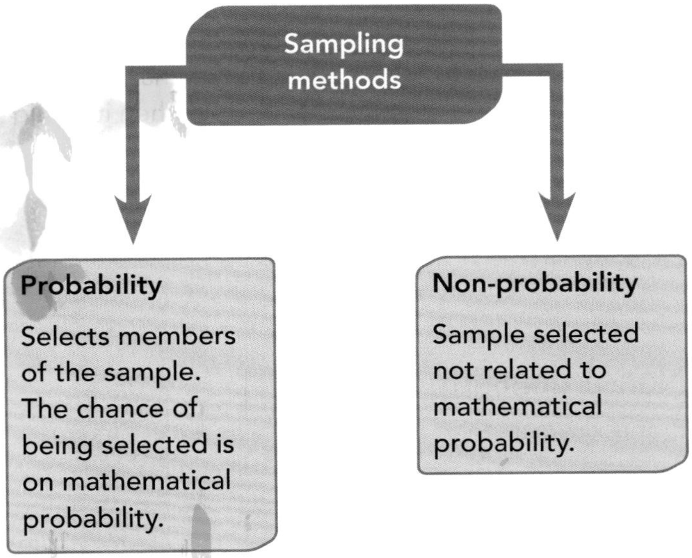

The sampling units must be defined clearly. In market research, these are the people who are going to be sampled, for example:

- people who buy butter
- members of a particular sports club.

A **sampling frame** is then compiled. This is a list of the population by **sampling units**. The sampling frame should be the same as the target population. For example, if the population is 'learners in a particular year in a school or college', the sampling frame would be the registers (or other lists) showing the names of these learners. This would be easy to obtain. A sampling frame should be as accurate and up to date as possible.

It is not possible to create an accurate sampling frame for many market research purposes. For example, while it is possible to get a list of people who live in a particular street, some of these people may have moved or provided inaccurate details.

Probability sampling

This approach involves using a systematic method of selecting respondents for market research. The chances of somebody being part of the sample could be expressed as a mathematical **probability**.

In statistical terms, probability means the relative frequency of occurrence in a long series of trials of the event of interest. For example, if a new bread roll has been extensively test-marketed across the UK, and it

Sampling methods

Probability

Selects members of the sample. The chance of being selected is on mathematical probability.

Non-probability

Sample selected not related to mathematical probability.

Fig. 10.9: Sampling methods.

Key terms

Census – study of all members of a population

Sample – study of carefully selected group that is regarded to be representative of total population

Representative – containing typical specimens of all of the members of a sample, for example, typical tattoo wearers in your area

Cross-section – a sample designed to be typical of the wider population

Sampling frame – list of population by sampling units

Sampling units – people who are going to be sampled

Probability – how likely an event is likely to occur, measured by the ratio of the extent to which an event is likely to occur compared to the total number of cases possible

is found that seven out of ten people like it, then it is likely that if an additional person is interviewed, the probability is seven out of ten that this person will like the roll and seven out of ten people in the total UK population will like the new roll (provided the sampling has been done correctly).

Random sampling

This is a simple method that is used when the whole population can be included in the sampling frame – for example, everyone with a tattoo. Everyone with a tattoo has an equal chance of being picked out, in the same way that lottery balls are drawn in the National Lottery.

Systematic random sampling

This method is similar to that described above and requires a list of all of the members in a particular population, for example, householders living in your town whose names are listed on the electoral register (those who have registered to vote). You would then select everyone at a set number on this list, for example, every tenth person listed.

Excuse me, sir, would you like to try this bread roll? Our marketing research shows that there is a seven in ten chance that you will like it!

Fig.10.10: What are the benefits of probability sampling?

Stratified sampling

One criticism of random sampling is that it may not accurately reflect the weighting of different groups within the population. Stratified sampling ensures that different groups are properly represented and allows the random selection of items within each group. For example, about 50 per cent of the population is female. If you wanted to make sure that women were given this weighting in your survey, it would be better to use stratified sampling, which enables this weighting to be given. Your sample would need to contain 50 per cent females and 50 per cent males. There may be other factors that you would need to take into account, such as age. You would then build these factors into the sample you select.

Multi-stage sampling

This involves a number of stages in selecting a sample and is used to reduce the time and cost of research while at the same time keeping a random approach.

For example, if you wanted to research advertising awareness of a particular advert in your school or college, you could first choose a random sample of five subject classes or groups. From each of these groups you could then take a sample from the learners within the class. The same type of process could be used for sampling across the UK, for example, taking a sample of geographical locations within the UK and then households within these geographical locations.

Cluster sampling

Sometimes it is possible to divide the total population into clusters (groups) of individuals whose behaviour patterns/buying patterns and so on are similar to those of the whole population. For example, if clusters of households across the country have similar purchasing patterns for washing powder, then it would be reasonable to research a small number of clusters in chosen geographical areas. This would save the time and expense of sampling across the whole of the country. The problem of cluster sampling is that it depends on clusters having similar characteristics to the total population.

Non-probability sampling

Probability sampling produces very good results but can take time and be costly both in planning and carrying out the research. Other methods can therefore be used which do not involve mathematical probability, such as the following.

Quota sampling

A quota sample is widely used in market research. The population is first divided into groups by age, sex, income level and so on. The interviewer is then told how many people to interview in each group but is not given instructions on how to locate the respondents to meet the quota. This approach is widely used in street interviews in shopping centres. It is quick, uncomplicated, and any member of the sample can by replaced by another with similar characteristics.

The disadvantage of quota sampling is that it is non-random. As a result there is a possibility of bias in choosing the sample. The interviewer may choose, for example, people who appear most co-operative. Because the surveys are carried out in shopping areas, people are excluded who do not shop there.

Judgement sampling

Here it is left to the judgement of the researcher to choose those who they think are most likely to represent the views of the target population. This depends on the skill and experience of the researcher and may be less appropriate for inexperienced researchers.

Convenience sampling

This involves interviewing those who are most convenient to sample, for example, people walking down the high street, regardless of their characteristics. This is a simple method, but the results are not likely to be particularly reliable. For example, it may involve interviewing people who are not part of the target population.

Observation

Earlier (see page 238) we looked at observation as a market research technique. Observation involves watching and recording data such as buyer behaviour. The advantage of this technique is that it enables the observer to record actual behaviour rather than what the customer states that they do. It is possible to record how long customers spend looking at particular types of displays in shops and the behaviour that they engage in, for example, trying on clothing, reading the labels of food produce and so on.

Focus groups

A focus group is brought together because it is felt that it is representative of a particular population. The group is asked to discuss issues related to products, services or other activity such as advertising. The focus group is usually costly to set up. Its meeting may be filmed or some other recording method may be used. A difficulty is that group members are more likely to represent those with time available to engage in such activity rather than the wider population.

Implications of different samples

In carrying out your research, it is important to think out the implications of the different sampling approaches.

Table 10.3: Cost and accuracy of using different sampling techniques.

Sample	Cost	Accuracy
Random	Expensive	Excellent
Systematic random	Expensive	Excellent
Multi-stage	Cheaper than the above	Good
Stratified	Expensive	Good
Cluster	Cheaper	Good
Quota	Cheaper	Good
Judgement	Cheaper	Depends of skills and experience of researcher
Convenience	Cheaper	Can provide inaccurate results
Observation	May be cheaper but not very cost-effective	Reveals actual behaviour
Focus group	Expensive to set up	Gets to the heart of detailed views

3.2 Questionnaires

Questionnaires are structured lists of questions used in market research. The questionnaire can be used in a variety of different ways, including postal questionnaires, face-to-face interviews, phone interviews and other means.

Activity: Research brief

You have been given a research brief by the marketing department for your centre to find out what new courses learners would like to see being offered as part of the post-16 curriculum.

1. How would you select an appropriate sample to carry out this research?
2. Identify two possible methods, setting out the strengths and weaknesses of each method.

Design

The design of a questionnaire is very important in influencing the **response rate** and the quality of responses.

You should start a questionnaire by making it clear what the purpose is of the questionnaire and show your appreciation of the time taken by the respondent. For example: 'The purpose of this questionnaire is to find out about your preferred choice of breakfast cereal.'

This could be followed up with: 'The questionnaire will take no more than ten minutes to complete. Thank you for sparing the time to answer these questions. Your views will help us to improve the products/services that we provide for you.'

Key term

Response rate – the percentage of responses to the number of questionnaires sent out or interviews requested

Questions to be asked

Questions asked will typically consist of both:

- factual questions, for example, name, age, sex, location
- questions asking for views and opinions, for example, 'What do you think about the quality of the service provided by…?'

The language used within a questionnaire is important. It must be neutral, easy to understand and not designed to influence the opinions of the respondent. Questions should be phrased as unambiguously (clearly) as possible to avoid misunderstanding.

A good questionnaire will:

- ask questions that relate directly to information needs
- not ask too many questions
- not ask leading or intimate questions
- fit questions into a logical sequence
- use the language of the target group
- not use ambiguous questions
- not rely upon the memory of the respondents, particularly if it is an event that happened many years ago
- include 'check' questions, where you expect people to provide unreliable answers. For example, people often round off their ages to the lowest decade. A date of birth question could be inserted later in the form to double-check their first answer.

Types of question

Sequencing of questions

Sequencing the questions logically is very important. It may be useful to start with a few factual questions that are easy to respond to. These may be followed by some form of multiple-choice questions before introducing questions that require the respondent to think about the issues being researched.

Key term

Sequencing – placing questions in a logical order that makes sense to the respondent and enables easier analysis of the data

Dichotomous questions

A dichotomy refers to two entirely different things, meaning that here there are two alternatives to choose from. These questions are simple to understand. They can be used as a filter to determine which question the respondent should move on to next. They are a particularly good way of saving time when filling in online questionnaires because the respondent will only see the questions that are relevant to them. For example:

6. Do you shop at Waitrose?
   Yes ☐
   No ☐
   If your answer is *No*, please proceed to question 15.

Multiple choice questions

Here the respondent is usually provided with four or five alternatives to choose from. They are required to tick the answer that most closely matches their opinion or behaviour in relation to a particular issue. An example would be:

> Which of the following supermarkets do you use for regular shopping (that is, once or more a week)?
>
> Tesco ☐
> Waitrose ☐
> Morrisons ☐
> Sainsbury's ☐
> Asda ☐

Scaled questions

Sometimes you will want to find out the strength of feeling that a respondent has about a particular issue, product or brand.

A Likert scale is frequently used to show how strongly the respondent feels about a particular statement. The illustration below shows a five-point Likert scale.

Open-ended questions

Open questions allow the respondent to give an opinion and may encourage them to open out at greater length. For example, in the questionnaire in the case study, respondents were encouraged through an open-ended question to identify improvements to the blood donor service. Open-ended questions encourage qualitative responses where the respondent expresses views and opinions. Closed questions require answers picked from a range of options. Most questionnaires use mainly closed question so that they can be answered quickly and efficiently, and the answers are easier to analyse.

Length of questionnaire

Questionnaires need to be long enough to provide suitable data to work with. However, if they are too long, it will take a lot of time to analyse the data. The respondent may also get tired and frustrated, and may not complete the questionnaire. It is suggested that a questionnaire should contain no more than 20 questions if the researcher is going to be able to interpret the data provided successfully.

You can use skip questions where the respondent can miss out questions that do not directly relate to them.

Bias

You need to be careful in creating questions not to present them in such a way that they suggest a right answer. For example, if you posed a question in the following way: 'Many people think that Brand A is best – do you agree with this view?', you are suggesting a particular answer.

It is actually quite difficult to avoid some form of **bias** in structuring questions, particularly those that ask respondents to state their views.

Bias also results from poor sampling, for example:

- the lack of a good sampling frame – for example, using the telephone misses all those who do not have a telephone
- the wrong choice of sampling unit
- non-response by some of the chosen units.

Key term

Bias – a distortion of results caused by the way in which they are collected

17. Do you agree that our supermarket:	Strongly agree	Agree	Neither agree nor disagree	Disagree	Strongly disagree
provides a high level of customer service	☐	☐	☐	☐	☐
is open at convenient times	☐	☐	☐	☐	☐
provides an appropriate selection of well-known brands	☐	☐	☐	☐	☐

Customer satisfaction survey

The following survey was produced by a blood donor service. Key objectives of the research were to find out customers' views of the service and ways in which the service could be improved.

We need your help to assess and improve the service that we provide for you. Please place an X in the relevant box to indicate how you feel about your most recent visit (or the N/A box if appropriate). Please mark only one box for each question. Thank you.

	Totally dissatisfied									Totally satisfied	
	N/A	1	2	3	4	5	6	7	8	9	10
1. The overall experience	☐	☐	☐	☐	☐	☐	☐	☐	☐	☐	☐
2. Welcome on arrival	☐	☐	☐	☐	☐	☐	☐	☐	☐	☐	☐
3. Waiting time	☐	☐	☐	☐	☐	☐	☐	☐	☐	☐	☐
4. Finger-prick test	☐	☐	☐	☐	☐	☐	☐	☐	☐	☐	☐
5. Insertion of needle	☐	☐	☐	☐	☐	☐	☐	☐	☐	☐	☐
6. Friendliness of staff	☐	☐	☐	☐	☐	☐	☐	☐	☐	☐	☐

What would have made you score us higher in the above areas?

How well have we met your expectations in the following areas?

	Expectations totally unmet							Expectations fully met			
	N/A	1	2	3	4	5	6	7	8	9	10
7. Did we make you feel valued and appreciated?	☐	☐	☐	☐	☐	☐	☐	☐	☐	☐	☐
8. Did we treat you with consideration?	☐	☐	☐	☐	☐	☐	☐	☐	☐	☐	☐

9. Thinking about your experiences as a donor, are you likely to recommend blood donation to a friend or colleague?

Yes ☐   No ☐

Think about it!

1. Identify the probable purposes of one of the questions in the survey. Do you think that the questionnaire would have been successful in finding this out?
2. Do you think that the questions are appropriately sequenced?
3. Identify the strengths and weaknesses of each of the questions asked.
4. Write an additional question that could be added to the list and explain why you chose to add it.

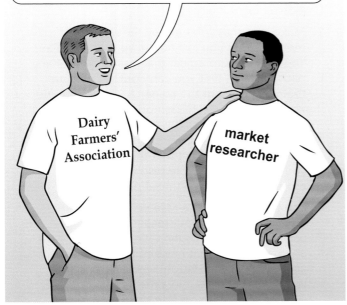

Fig.10.11: What is biased market research?

Relevance

Some questionnaires are designed so that respondents can concentrate on the questions that are relevant, and then skip over the questions that do not relate to them. A respondent will quickly become frustrated if they are asked to answer a series of questions that do not appear to be relevant to them.

Response

The response rate to a questionnaire is determined by the extent to which the respondent feels that the questionnaire is going to help them. The most important factors in increasing the response rate are:

- creating an incentive to complete the questionnaire, for example, a prize or reward
- explaining the purpose of the survey and showing how and why it is relevant to the respondent
- using an appropriate means of delivering the questionnaire – face-to-face use of questionnaires will yield a much higher rate of response than an anonymous online approach
- making sure that the respondent is clear about how to fill in the questionnaire and what to do when it is completed.

Pilot stage

Every market research survey should first be piloted with a small number of members of the target population. They should be asked to fill in a trial (pilot) questionnaire. They should also be asked to state whether they found the questionnaire easy to understand and whether there were any questions they found confusing. The pilot research should then analyse the results of the questionnaire to see that they make sense.

3.3 Survey

It is important to distinguish between a survey and a questionnaire – although there is considerable overlap.

- A questionnaire is simply a structured set of questions that can be given to one or a number of people.
- A survey is a research tool that is used to find out the general view of a large number of people on a particular topic.

Questionnaires can be used to gather data as part of the process of the survey. To be part of one, the questionnaires would be used with a relatively large number of respondents. In addition, interviews can be used as part of the survey.

The objectives of carrying out a market research survey are to find out answers to questions about:

- what
- where
- when
- how.

For example, if you were going to do a survey into the mobile telephone use of 16–21-year-olds, you would ask questions such as the following.

- What types of mobile do you use? What do you use the mobile for?
- Where do you buy your phone? Where do you use it?
- When do you pay for your phone services?
- How do you use your phone? How do you pay for it?

Carrying out this survey work might involve the use of questionnaires and interviews.

Assessment activity 10.3

P4 D1 BTEC

This Assessment activity is based on carrying out your research and provides lots of opportunities to demonstrate personal, learning and thinking skills and functional skills.

When you carried out Assessment activity 10.2, you planned to carry out research for a particular research brief. This Assessment activity involves carrying out the research that you planned earlier. You will need to use appropriate methods and select and justify appropriate samples.

1. Conduct primary and secondary research for a selected product/service, making use of identifiable sampling techniques. **P4**

2. Evaluate the research method used by a selected organisation. **D1**

Grading tips

1. Make sure that you employ the research methods that you justified in your earlier plan. You may want to adjust these as a result of any pilot research that you carry out. Make sure that you carry out the research in a systematic way. You will need to demonstrate use of a sampling method(s). It is very important that you understand why you chose the particular sample and the effect that this has on enabling you to produce reliable results that are representative of the target population. **P4**

2. You can compare the research methods that you have used for your research with those used by a specific organisation. This could be an organisation that has been covered as a case study in your taught sessions, one that you have read about in a marketing journal such as Marketing, or one that you have researched on the Internet. **D1**

4.   Be able to interpret research findings

Having designed your research, carried out the research and generated a wealth of data from your market research survey, you will next be in a position to interpret and present your results.

It is important to know how to make sense of the research statistics and to present the data in an appropriate manner to whoever commissioned the research.

4.1 Statistical procedures

You need to be familiar with some simple statistical procedures for analysing research findings.

Because surveys seek to find out the views and behaviour of typical buyers, it is important to be able to present a picture of the average person, group or groups that you have surveyed. There are a number of ways of calculating averages, as shown in Fig. 10.12.

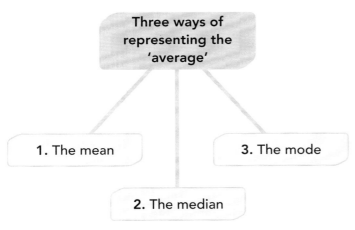

Fig. 10.12: Representing the average.

Arithmetic mean

The arithmetic mean is the most commonly used way of calculating an average. It represents the average of a set of numbers. For example, Table 10.4 shows the number of motorcycles registered for the road by the top ten motorcycle businesses in the UK in July 2009 (source: Motor Cycle Industry Association, July 2009).

To calculate the mean (average) number of bikes sold per company, we need to divide the total number of bikes sold by the number of companies.

$$\text{mean number of bikes} = \frac{7,692}{10} = 769.2$$

We can see therefore that the mean number of bikes sold by the ten companies was about 769 bikes.

Table 10.4: The number of motorcycles registered for the road by the top ten motorcycle businesses in the UK in July 2009 (source: Motor Cycle Industry Association, July 2009).

Business	Sold	
Yamaha	1,835	
Honda	1,291	
Suzuki	1,044	
Triumph	793	
Piaggio	693	
Kawasaki	590	
BMW	556	
Harley-Davison	427	
Aprilia	272	
Ducati	191	
Total	**7,692**	

The median

The median is a second way of calculating an average figure. It is simply the middle value in a set of numbers. For example, if we look again at sales by the top ten motorcycle companies, we can see that the middle values (the fifth and sixth numbers in the list) are 590 for Kawasaki and 693 for Piaggio. The median lies halfway between these two figures – about 641 (641.5 to be exact).

This shows that the average (median) Top Ten motorcycle company was selling about 641 bikes in the UK in July.

In the example above there is an even number of companies – ten. There are therefore two middle figures (the fifth and sixth companies). The median lies midway between the sales of these two companies. Where there is an odd number, the median is simply the middle value. For example, if there were only nine companies the median would be the number of sales made by the fifth company in the set.

The advantage of using the median rather than the mean is that this prevents distortion of the average by extreme values. For example, it could be argued that the relatively high sales by Yamaha (1,835) distorted the average figure upwards (in the mean calculation), whereas 640 is more a typical figure for the top ten sellers.

The mode

The third way of calculating an average is to identify the most popular (frequent) figure in a set of numbers. This would not be of any use for motorcycle sales because we are only looking at ten figures, which are all different.

We can illustrate the mode by looking at the number of items bought by shoppers at a supermarket on a Sunday morning in Table 10.5.

The mode is 12 items because eight customers bought this quantity of goods. The next highest number was 11, with four customers buying this number of goods.

The mode is most useful as an averaging technique when there are lots of numbers in a data set and many of these numbers cluster around a central point. The mode is not very helpful when the data you generate only includes relatively few numbers, most of which are different.

Activity: Mean and median

Use the data shown in the table below for supermarket purchases to calculate the mean and the median.

Range

In working with statistics, it is often important to examine the dispersion of sets of figures – are figures clustered around the average, or are they widely dispersed? For example, in market research we may find that for some of the questions where we ask customers to rate a particular product on a ranking scale, then their responses are all close to the mean figure. For other questions, there may be considerable differences in opinion – that is, wide dispersion.

We use the range to identify the difference between the highest and lowest figures. For example, in a customer satisfaction survey involving 12 customers, ratings for satisfaction revealed the results as shown in Table 10.6.

The range is therefore 40: from the highest rating of 90 to the lowest rating of 50.

Inter-quartile range

The inter-quartile range is another important measure that is used in statistical research because it indicates the extent to which the central 50 per cent of values within a data set are dispersed.

In the same way that we can use the median to divide a data set into two halves, it can be further divided into quarters by identifying the upper and lower quartiles. The lower quartile is found a quarter of the way along a data set when the values have been arranged in order of size; the upper quartile is found three-quarters of the way along. Therefore, the upper quartile lies halfway between the median and the highest value in the data set while the lower quartile lies halfway between the median and the lowest value. The inter-quartile range is found by subtracting the lower quartile from the upper quartile.

For example, a panel of customers is asked to rate an advertisement which they see from 0 to 100, as listed in Table 10.7.

The median lies at the mid-point between the two central values (tenth and eleventh) = halfway between 60 and 62 = 61.

The lower quartile lies at the mid-point between the fifth and sixth values = halfway between 52 and 53 = 52.5.

The upper quartile lies at the mid-point between the fifteenth and sixteenth values = halfway between 70 and 71 = 70.5.

The inter-quartile range for this data set is therefore 52.5 to 70.5, which is 18, whereas the range is 43 to 80, or 37.

Table 10.5: Number of purchases made by 25 different customers.

12	10	8	24	12	6	24	8	12	10	11	12	9	12	11	18	2	6	11	9	12	11	12	6	12

Table 10.6: Ratings for satisfaction with the service provided by the business (out of 100).

50	55	57	60	65	68	72	75	80	82	85	90

Table 10.7: Customer ratings of an advertisement from 0 to 100, arranged in order of magnitude.

43	48	50	50	52	53	56	58	59	60	62	65	66	68	70	71	74	76	78	80

Case study: Confectionery makers' UK market share

The following table is extracted from Mintel data. It shows the share of the UK confectionery market held by the top five firms in 2008. A figure is also shown for the share of all the others.

Table 10.8: Confectionery makers' market share (2008).

Company	Percentage of market share
1. Cadbury Trebor Basset	23
2. Nestlé	22
3. Wrigley	16
4. Mars confectionery	9
5. Haribo	8
Others	22
Total	**100**

1. Calculate the figures for the mean and median market shares.
2. Which of these values would be most useful and why?
3. Explain whether using the mode would be a suitable way of calculating an average.
4. In 2008, Mars acquired Wrigley. What would be the impact on the mean and median figures for the other confectionery makers in the top five? Show your calculations.

Functional skills

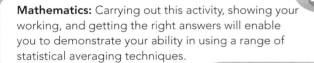

Mathematics: Carrying out this activity, showing your working, and getting the right answers will enable you to demonstrate your ability in using a range of statistical averaging techniques.

Scatter diagrams

A scatter diagram can be used to plot the relationship between two variables. One variable is regarded to be the dependent variable. The other is the independent variable. Changes in the dependent variable result from changes in the independent variable.

For example, customer awareness of an advert (the dependent variable) may increase with the number of times the advertisement is shown on the television (the independent variable).

In a scatter diagram the dependent variable (customer awareness) is plotted on the horizontal (y-axis) and the independent variable (showings of the television advert) are shown on the vertical axis (see Fig. 10.13).

The term *correlation* is used to describe the relationship between the dependent and the independent variable. In the illustration above there is a positive correlation. As the independent variable increases the dependent variable increases.

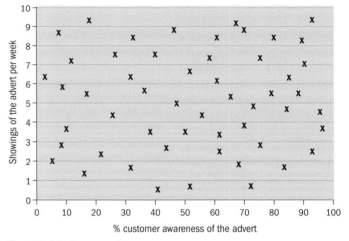

Fig. 10.13: Scatter diagram.

Time series

Time series are very useful in demonstrating patterns that emerge over time. Earlier in this unit (see page 252) we saw that a group called Sustain is commissioning research to promote the sale of organic groceries. The question was whether organic groceries have reached a stage of maturity in their life cycle.

The following illustration demonstrates a time series chart showing the growth in sales of organic groceries over a ten year period. It provides a very clear picture of rising sales up until 2008.

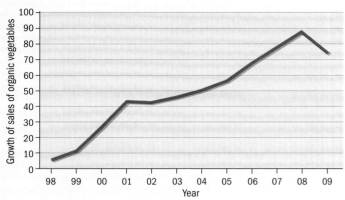

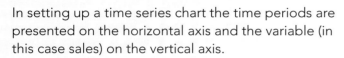

Fig. 10.14: Growth in sales of organic groceries (£m).

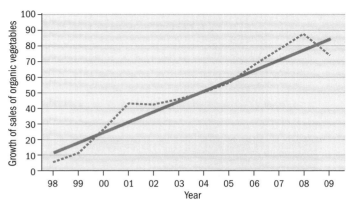

Fig. 10.15: Trend line for organic groceries.

In setting up a time series chart the time periods are presented on the horizontal axis and the variable (in this case sales) on the vertical axis.

Trends

A trend is a pattern that appears in a set of figures. Sometimes there is no clear trend that can be seen in a set of figures. However, often it is possible to identify a rising or falling trend.

A trend can be illustrated on a line graph. First of all join up the points on your line graph. A line of 'best fit' can then be drawn through the line graph. The illustration above shows how this could be done for organic groceries, although it is difficult to predict what will happen after 2009, given the downturn illustrated from 2008.

Use of spreadsheets for analysis

A spreadsheet program is a very large grid of 'cells', which contain text, numbers or formulae, and are used for numerical problems where a large number of figures can be calculated. Microsoft Excel (a spreadsheet program) is the most widely used of these programs and it will enable you to illustrate business trends by converting a spreadsheet of numbers into graphs and diagrams. On page 272 we go on to discuss the benefits of bar charts, pie charts and other ways of presenting data in graphic form.

The number in any one cell in a spreadsheet can be calculated from the number in other cells (or combinations of cells) using the spreadsheet to perform the calculations. When any one number is

Activity: Plotting market share of motorcycles

We have already outlined the sales of motorcycles in the UK in July 2009. You can now use Microsoft Excel to illustrate this data.

1. Find Microsoft Excel in the Microsoft Office suite of programs on your computer. Click on the program.

2. An outline spreadsheet made up of rows and columns appears on your desktop.

3. You can put a title into the spreadsheet in cell 1A. Put in the title: 'Units Sold in the UK, July 2009.'

4. In the first column, enter the names of the different companies: Yamaha, Honda, Suzuki, Triumph, Piaggio, Kawasaki, BMW, Harley-Davidson, Aprilia, Ducati.

5. Now, in the second column enter these figures: 1,835, 1,291, 1,044, 793, 693, 590, 556, 427, 272, 191.

6. Using the mouse, highlight the area of the table that you have completed the data for. Now look for an icon that resembles a bar chart at the top of your window. This will enable you to select a number of different ways of presenting your data.

7. Present your data as a bar chart. Then present your data as a pie chart.

8. What do these charts tell you about the market for motorcycles?

changed, the result on other cells is seen immediately, saving long calculations. The spreadsheet is an excellent tool for presenting market research data and enables immediate analysis of results. For example, plotting consumer ratings of customer service provided by a particular firm into a spreadsheet enables you immediately to calculate mean figures and the range (including interquartile range) for these ratings. Plotting the sales figures of competing companies over time into a spreadsheet enables you immediately to convert this data into a line graph revealing trends over time.

4.2 Presentation of findings

An important part of your work for this unit is to make a presentation to an invited audience about your market research findings. This section therefore outlines ways in which you can make a first-class oral and written presentation (report) of your market research project.

Oral report

The first thing to bear in mind is that your oral report should cover the ground that you first set out when you planned your research. The key things to cover are:

- the nature of the research brief
- the research objectives
- how you decided to collect the data and why
- an analysis and evaluation of the data
- the key findings and recommendations
- any improvements that you would make if you were to conduct the research again.

Make sure that you cover each of the points outlined above.

You can now build these essential elements into a typical outline for a presentation. This could take the following shape.

1. Introduction. Introduce the team making the presentation. Give an outline of the market research brief that you were working to. Briefly outline the structure of the presentation. Outline the key research objectives.

2. Explain the methods that you used to collect your data – for example, primary/secondary, quantitative/qualitative. Nature of the samples chosen. Why specific methods were chosen.

3. Analysis of the data. Present the data in a suitable form – for example, pie charts, bar charts, trend lines, range of figures and so on. Explain why you have chosen to present your data in the way that you have. Make sure that this section of the presentation is well organised with a clear structure.

4. Findings and recommendations. Here you should be responding to the original research brief. What have you found out? What does it mean in market research terms?

5. Any improvements that you would like to make if you were to carry out the research a second time.

6. Questions from the audience and list of references that you have used in your research.

Because the assessment for this unit requires you to make a presentation, it is helpful to make some further remarks about how you should conduct your presentation.

1. If you are making the presentation in a team, make sure that each of the team members contributes equally to the preparation of the presentation and to the delivery of the presentation. This will ensure that everyone has a fair opportunity to score a high mark and feels that they are a member of the group.

2. Make sure that you prepare the PowerPoint slides well before the presentation takes place and have more than one trial run through the presentation.

3. The overhead slides should not contain too much text. A few bullet points are best. You have plenty of opportunity to use visual charts to represent your market research findings. If you put too much text on slides, you will end up reading from them and this will make your presentation sound dull.

4. Do not stand in front of the screen as this will obscure the view of the slides.

5. Make sure you know what you want to say about each slide. Because the presentation is about your own research, you will be familiar with the material, so there is no need to read it out. If you use prompt cards, only put the minimum amount of detail on them.

6. Organise the presentation in a clear sequence and make sure that each presenter knows when they are expected to contribute.

7. Use eye contact with your audience. There is no substitute for good eye contact and confident delivery. The two go together.

8. Do not speak too slowly or too quickly. Alter the speed of your delivery to add interest. If you feel embarrassed, then slow down rather than speed up. This will help your confidence to return and your audience will be more likely to be switched on to what you have to say.

9. Make sure that the presentation starts with an introduction, has a main body and ends with a clear conclusion.

10. Never turn your back on your audience.

Fig. 10.16: Do not stand in front of the screen in a presentation, retain good eye contact and try to look confident.

Written reports

A written report is produced with a target audience in mind. A formal report would be produced for a client who has commissioned market research work and would provide a lot of formal detail. In market research work, a lot of tables and charts will be produced. Only put the most important tables in the main body of your work. You can put the remainder in the appendices.

You will probably want to use a numbering system for each of the sections of your report, for example, 1.1, 1.2, 2.1, 2.2 and so on.

A formal report will take the shape of something like Fig. 10.17.

An alternative to the formal report outlined above would be an informal report, which would be a lot

1. Title page
Title of research project, the name of the client, the name of the market research organisation, date presented.

2. Contents
A numbered guide to the sections of the report.

3. Research brief
An outline of the research brief.

4. Objectives
A summary of the market research objectives.

5. Summary of conclusions and recommendations
This should be written last i.e. when you have put together all of the other sections of your report. It provides a brief summary and is always helpful to the reader when they first pick up the report.

6. Methods employed
Outline the methods that were used, briefly giving the justification for the choice of each method.

7. Findings
Set out key findings including the most significant charts and tables. This should be clear and easy for the reader to navigate.

8. Conclusions/recommendations
A more detailed set of conclusions and recommendations than point 5 above.

9. Appendices

10. Supporting materials that are cross-referenced in the research findings section of the report

Fig. 10.17: Example of a formal report.

less detailed. This could be used to show provisional findings before the research has been completed.

Visual aids

In making a presentation or producing a written report, it is helpful to use visual aids where appropriate. The next section (below right) outlines a variety of charting techniques that you can use to make a presentation more exciting. Computer graphics are particularly helpful in illustrating the key points that you want to make. Pictures can be scanned into a presentation. It is particularly important to make sure that the visual aids relate directly to the presentation or written report rather than distracting attention from it.

Sometimes it is helpful to use a consistent theme throughout the presentation or written report such as a consistent colour scheme (perhaps representing the corporate colours of the client), the same type of font size, background and overall look to the slides. When you are making a presentation to a client, it is helpful to use their logo or brand image so that they immediately feel ownership of the presentation – you have just done the work for them.

Conclusions and recommendations

It is very important that these are set out in a clear and unambiguous way. Throughout the presentation there should be a consistent message about what the recommendations are. This is why it is important to set them out at the outset of the presentation, and then to return to them later on. The conclusions and recommendations should be presented in the same way in both the written and the oral report.

Audience

A presentation or written report is produced for a target audience. For this work, your tutor will invite a business representative (or more than one) to your presentation. This representative will either be from an organisation that has commissioned research directly from you or will be someone with experience of market research processes. It is essential therefore to target your work at this person/people as well as at your tutor.

An oral report should be less formal and detailed than a written report. This is because it is easier to take in what is produced in a written report because the reader has more time to do so and can reread sections that are less clear.

Sense of audience is very important in producing any report. The writer or presenter needs to focus constantly on what the reader or listener wants and is able to take in.

- It is essential that there is a clear structure and that this is made clear to the audience.
- It is very important that points that you make are backed up by examples and factual detail.
- It is essential that good, clear communication skills are used.
- It is essential that the audience is clear about how the presenter/writer arrived at the conclusions which they set out.

Effectiveness and quality of information

It is very important to make sure that the information provided in a report supports the key messages that the presenters are making. So make sure that:

- you provide sufficient information to support particular points or conclusions
- tables and charts are clearly explained – a chart or table rarely speaks for itself, and needs some form of explanation
- the essential points do not get lost in a mass of other detail
- the research brief, the research objectives, the methods employed and the recommendations all line up. Have you met the research brief?

Facilities

Check out the facilities for the presentation beforehand. You need to familiarise yourself with how the projector works and how you want the seating to be arranged for your audience.

4.3 Diagrammatic analysis and presentation

Market research reporting typically involves a lot of visual material. One reason for this is that in order to explain key points to other members of an organisation and to their clients, market researchers can save a lot of time and have a direct impact by presenting materials in a visual way.

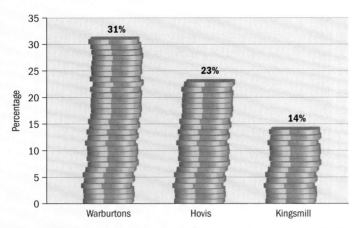

Fig. 10.18: Bread brands, UK market share (percentage) 2009.

Pictograms

Pictograms are frequently used to display data. A pictogram is a diagrammatic form of display that uses pictures or symbols as well as numbers. The symbols used are explained in a key.

For example, the pictogram in Fig. 10.18 illustrates the market share of the top three bread brands in the UK in 2009.

Pie charts

One form of statistical representation used widely in newspapers, marketing articles and marketing research reports is that of the pie chart. In a pie chart, each 'slice' represents a component's contribution

to the total amount. The pie adds up to 360°. Each component of the pie therefore needs to be converted into degrees.

The following method can be used to convert each relative proportion to degrees.

$$\frac{\text{proportion}}{\text{total}} \times 360°$$

For example, we know that Warburtons had 31 per cent of the bread branded market in 2009, Hovis had 23 per cent, Kingsmill 14 per cent, and other brands 32 per cent.

This can be converted to the following (Fig. 10.19).

Bar charts

Although pie charts provide a simple form of display, they show only limited information and it can be difficult to make accurate comparisons of segment sizes unless the numbers are also written into the segments.

In bar charts, the areas of comparison are represented by bars, which can be drawn either vertically or horizontally. The length of the bar indicates the relative importance of the data.

Functional skills

Mathematics and ICT: This case study allows you to demonstrate these skills by creating bar charts. Remember to put headings to the charts and use scale carefully on your axes.

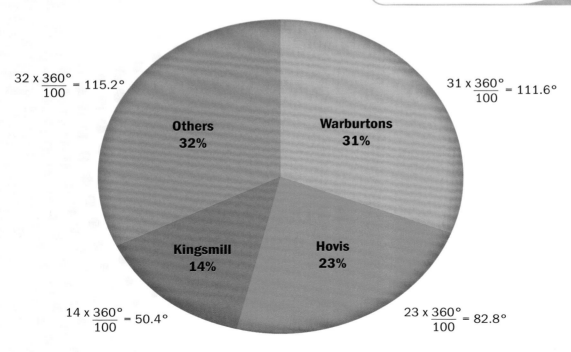

$$\frac{32 \times 360°}{100} = 115.2°$$

$$\frac{31 \times 360°}{100} = 111.6°$$

$$\frac{14 \times 360°}{100} = 50.4°$$

$$\frac{23 \times 360°}{100} = 82.8°$$

Fig. 10.19: Pie chart illustrating UK market share of the key bread brands in 2009.

Case study: Sales of ice cream in the UK

The horizontal bar chart in Fig. 10.18 shows sales of ice cream in the UK comparing different categories of ice cream (source: Euromonitor International).

The top bars show the total value of sales of ice cream. The other bars relate to categories of ice cream, such as impulse ice cream (for example, ice cream that you might buy at the cinema or a service station), take-home ice cream (that you buy in a supermarket freezer cabinet to store at home), frozen yoghurt and artisanal ice cream (specialist ice cream such as handmade ice cream sold from an ice cream van).

1. What is a horizontal bar chart?
2. What does the horizontal bar chart illustrated above show?
3. How useful is the chart for showing the growth of ice cream sales over time?
4. Set out the bar chart in vertical form. What are the advantages and disadvantages of converting the bar chart from a horizontal to a vertical format?

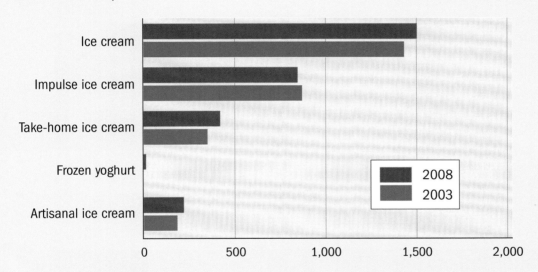

Fig. 10.20: Ice cream value sales by category (£m) (source: Euromonitor International).

Histograms

A histogram is a form of bar chart that has a number of unique features. It is used to illustrate grouped **frequency** distributions using bar chart techniques. The key difference between a standard bar chart and a histogram is that the width of each bar on a histogram relates to a numerical scale, and the width of each block reflects this. The number of observations relating to each variable is represented by the area covered by the bar on the chart, and not necessarily the height of the bar.

When you draw a histogram you must not leave gaps between the bars on the horizontal axis.

To illustrate a histogram, it is best to start by setting out a frequency distribution table. Table 10.9 shows the sum of money spent by customers in a shop in a given week, set out as a frequency distribution table.

Table 10.9: Frequency distribution.

Amount spent	Frequency
Less than £10	5
Between £10 and less than £20	15
Between £20 and less than £30	20
Between £30 and less than £40	15
Between £40 and less than £50	10

Key term

Frequency – the number of times an event happens in a given period of time. Frequencies are often measured in market research, for example, the frequency with which a particular individual or group of customers will buy specific items

This can now be set out in a histogram as Fig. 10.21 illustrates.

Frequency curves

The same data can be illustrated in the form of a frequency curve. This simply involves constructing a histogram, marking off the mid-point of the top of each rectangle and then joining the mid-points together (see Fig. 10.22).

Line graphs and scatter graphs

We have already illustrated line graphs and scatter graphs on pages 267–8. The line graph is particularly good at showing changes over time for example, in consumer awareness of a brand or advert. Time will be shown on the horizontal axis.

Scatter graphs are particularly useful for charting the relationship between two variables. Market researchers are often asked to find out the relationship between marketing activities and the sales of a product. For example, they may want to plot the relationship between money spent on advertising and promotion and the sales of a product over time.

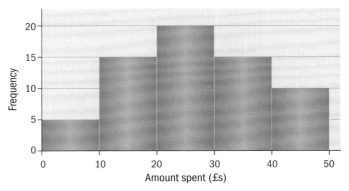

Fig. 10.21: Histogram showing expenditure by customers in a shop.

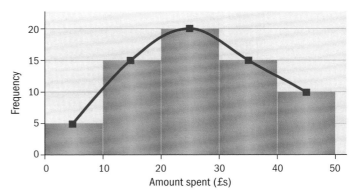

Fig. 10.22: Frequency curve illustrating levels of expenditure in a shop.

Activity: Consumption of confectionery and snacks by children

A group of learners carried out research to find out the consumption of confectionery and snacks among children by age, as percentages. Table 10.10 shows their results.

1. Illustrate the data from the table, using an appropriate method of representing the data.

2. Identify one other method that you might have used.

3. Justify your choice of method for presenting the data, explaining why it is more suitable than an alternative method.

Table 10.10: Consumption of confectionery and snacks.

Product type	Consumption by percentage of children aged 7–10	Consumption by percentage of children aged 11–14
Crisps	99	61
Chocolate/sweets	90	63
Biscuits	85	62
Ice cream	83	42
Fruit	82	50
Cakes	81	45
Yoghurt/fromage frais	78	30
Cereal bars	60	30
Chocolate spread	50	15

Appropriate use of techniques

In preparing your market research presentation, it is very important to use appropriate techniques to represent your data. You may want to use the techniques already described.

- Pie charts – percentage market share of a particular product, possible market share of a new product, percentage of those researched who answered yes or no to a dichotomous question, other illustrations where you want to show that your research indicated that opinions fell into clear segments.

- Bar charts – sales values of several different items (for comparison), consumption of different types of product, awareness of an advertisement, growth in something over time.

- Histograms – number or value of purchases by customers, number of customers in a store in different times of the day, number of purchases of goods in different price ranges.

- Frequency curves – frequency with which customers spend different amounts of money in a shop, frequency with which different respondents to a questionnaire give responses in particular ranges of answers.

- Line graphs – changing patterns/trends over time, rise or fall in consumer awareness of an advert or brand, sales of products over time.

- Scatter diagram – changing trends over time, the relationship between two variables, for example, advertising spending and sales.

Interpretation of results

How you interpret the results of your research is very important. Before writing up your main findings, you should first set them out in rough on a piece of paper. At the top of the paper, write down your research objectives and then list the various research methods that you used. Under each research method, write down a list of what you consider to be the most significant results that the method revealed. Then list the main types of evidence that supported these results.

Some of the evidence will clearly back up the results, whereas other evidence will be less clear. It is important that you make it clear in your final write-up how clear the evidence appears to be. For example, you may find out using questionnaires that seven out of ten young people in your town would use an Internet café at least once a month if it was available. This seems to provide substantial support for the idea. However, if in follow-up focus groups you find that the majority of these would only use it for checking their emails when in town, and would be unlikely to buy coffee and other items on sale, then you may need to be more cautious about the claims you make about the demand for the café.

When you find that the correlation between an independent variable and a dependent one is weak, make this clear in your findings rather than exaggerating the relationship.

One of the problems when young people set up in business is that they often tend to be overoptimistic about market research results. Because they are eager to start out, they tend to look just at those results which indicate a market for their business, rather than other results that suggest the importance of caution. For example, nine out of ten people might say that they would visit your shop – but how many of them would actually make purchases or pay the prices that you are charging?

This is why triangulation of research methods is so important (that is, using more than one method to collect and check data). You also need to triangulate your results to check that the results stemming from one aspect of your research back up results from another area.

4.4 Limitations of research

An important aspect of the presentation of your research findings is to identify the limitations of your research. Set out the weaknesses and areas for improvement.

It is likely that in carrying out your research project that you have only been able to use a limited sample, so make this clear. You have only had limited time to carry out your research, so make it clear what else you would have done, given more time.

A number of possible limitations to your research are outlined below. These are similar to the problems that market researchers face in the workplace and include:

- excess of information and e-business feedback overload
- reliability of sample
- bias
- subjectivity.

Excess of information and e-business feedback overload

We saw earlier in this unit that modern consumers provide huge quantities of information about themselves to organisations (volunteered personal information, or VPI). Organisations are therefore moving from a situation where they had too little information about customers to one where they almost have too much. This is termed e-business feedback overload.

The important thing is to collect data that is specifically related to developing a relationship with individual customers. Tesco, for example, collects huge quantities of information from customers through its Club Card scheme about what they buy, when they buy and what items they buy together. As a result of this research, the company is able to make offers to individual customers based on the understanding they have built up about the buying behaviour of that customer.

When used well, this information can give an organisation a clear advantage over rivals. The important thing is to be able to decide which information is useful and which is not. You will find exactly the same problem in your research. Try to concentrate on your research objectives. Collect and analyse data that fits in with these objectives, and present information that relates to these objectives.

A problem for many learners in carrying out market research is that they sometimes put questions into questionnaires and interviews without carefully thinking through the usefulness of the data that it will generate. Careful planning of research, and piloting of interview techniques, is essential. Also important is your ability to discard data that is clearly leading you nowhere.

Reliability of sample

Surveys that you carry out are likely to cover less than 100 per cent of the target population. These are therefore sample surveys. The important thing is to

make sure that your sample is representative of the population.

Make sure that you clearly define the target population from the outset, for example:

- potential users of an Internet café
- 16–25-year-olds with tattoos.

Bias

To make your sample more reliable and to reduce bias, give careful attention to:

- providing an appropriate sampling frame – try to create an accurate list of all those that constitute your sample (where this is possible)
- choosing the most suitable sampling unit
- encouraging as many people as possible to respond to your interviews and questionnaires, for example, by being polite and encouraging. Also make sure that your questions are easy to understand for all members of your sample.

Bias can also result from the approach of the person conducting the survey. For example, the interviewer may not interview someone who appears to be unco-operative. The style of questioning (tone of voice, for example) may also create an element of bias.

Awareness of these potential sources of bias can help an interviewer to conduct a survey more accurately.

Subjectivity

The final issue of concern in market research is that of **subjectivity**.

Market researchers have their own views about a particular topic or product. They may unwittingly influence those being researched to take on some of their own views and perceptions. In a similar way, researchers may see and hear things that they want to see and hear rather than what actually happens. Quantitative research is felt to be more objective (based on facts) and qualitative research to be more subjective. However, it is important to recognise that in writing questions for quantitative research, there is plenty of scope for the way the questions are written to influence the responses provided.

Key term

Subjectivity – looking at things from a personal viewpoint rather than being impartial

Assessment activity 10.4

The final assignment activity is to present the research findings.

1. Interpret your research findings and make a presentation of them to an invited audience. Your tutor may want to invite a business person with experience of market research to attend this presentation. Alternatively, you may make a presentation to a business owner on whose behalf you have been conducting market research. **P5**

2. Produce a written report analysing your research findings, recommendations and conclusions, and make recommendations on how marketing strategies could be adapted or implemented. The outline for a formal research report was provided on page 270. **M3**

3. Evaluate the findings from the research undertaken. **D2**

Grading tips

1. Make sure that you have clear visual aids that clearly demonstrate appropriate use of graphical techniques and sampling methods.

You need to focus on the key aspects of the data that you generated from your research. Structure it in an appropriate way and explain what it means. Use charts and diagrams to illustrate the key points. Make sure that you explain key terms such as median, and mean as well as time series and other trends. **P5**

2. Your presentation and supporting written report should demonstrate ways in which your analysis of your data backs up the recommendations that you are making for the organisation researched to improve its marketing strategies, including elements of the marketing mix. **M3**

3. Make it clear how your findings provide supporting evidence for the recommendations and conclusions that you have drawn from your research. Make it clear what the strengths and weaknesses of your research methods, data collection and analysis have been, and what improvements you would make if you were to conduct the research again. **D2**

Just checking

1. What is the difference between primary and secondary research? When would primary research be more useful than secondary research?
2. Explain the difference between internal and external research. What sorts of market research data does a business have internally?
3. Explain one technique that could be used to conduct quantitative research and another for qualitative research. Which of these approaches is more subjective?
4. What is the purpose of triangulation in carrying out research?
5. Identify the key components of a market research plan.
6. How do you calculate the mean from a set of figures? How does this differ from the median and the mode?
7. Explain what is meant by range and inter-quartile range.
8. When would you use a line graph to display data?
9. Is there a difference between a bar chart and a histogram? If so, what?
10. What advice would you give to someone making a market research presentation?

edexcel

Assignment tips

1. The most enjoyable and effective market research involves working for a real organisation. The research should be carried out on a local basis.

2. The most productive research methods for your research will be questionnaires and small focus group discussion. Clarify your target market from the outset. Always pilot the research methods you use, and give yourself plenty of time to analyse your results.

3. Do not make up the results. A common failing of market research is that the researchers seek to adapt the results to what they want to find out, for example, that a new product will be a success. However, it is better to find out exactly what consumers want and are looking for. This might mean modifying or rejecting an original idea.

4. Justify your choice of sample size. Present your findings using appropriate tables and charts. Pictograms should be easy to understand.

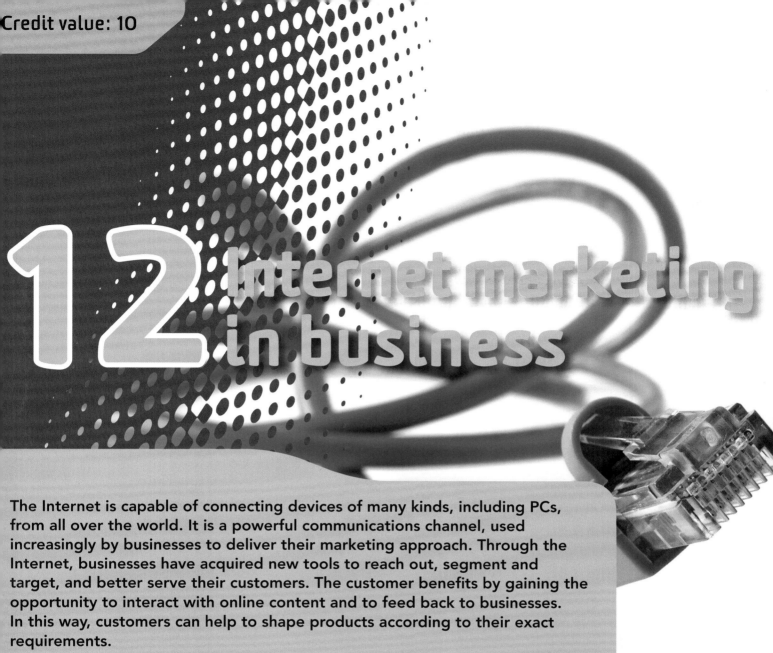

12 Internet marketing in business

The Internet is capable of connecting devices of many kinds, including PCs, from all over the world. It is a powerful communications channel, used increasingly by businesses to deliver their marketing approach. Through the Internet, businesses have acquired new tools to reach out, segment and target, and better serve their customers. The customer benefits by gaining the opportunity to interact with online content and to feed back to businesses. In this way, customers can help to shape products according to their exact requirements.

In this unit, you will explore the use of the Internet in achieving marketing success. You will learn how the medium creates tremendous opportunities for businesses, helping them to find out exactly who and where their online customers are. You will see that Internet marketing offers innovative ways of giving service and consulting customers.

Finally, you will learn that there are challenges too. Mistakes in the digital world can be costly. It is worth careful planning.

Learning outcomes

After completing this unit, you should:

1. know what role Internet marketing has within a modern marketing context
2. understand the benefits of Internet marketing to customers
3. understand the opportunities offered to businesses by Internet marketing
4. understand the challenges faced by businesses using Internet marketing.

Assessment and grading criteria

This table shows you what you must do in order to achieve a **pass**, **merit** or **distinction** grade, and where you can find activities in this book to help you.

To achieve a **pass** grade, the evidence must show that the learner is able to:	To achieve a **merit** grade, the evidence must show that, in addition to the pass criteria, the learner is able to:	To achieve a **distinction** grade, the evidence must show that, in addition to the pass and merit criteria, the learner is able to:
P1 describe the role Internet marketing has within a modern marketing context **See Assessment activity 12.1, page 293.**	**M1** analyse the benefits of Internet marketing to customers **See Assessment activity 12.2, page 297.**	**D1** evaluate the effectiveness of Internet marketing in meeting customer needs for a selected business **See Assessment activity 12.2, page 297.**
P2 describe how selected organisations use Internet marketing **See Assessment activity 12.1, page 293.**		
P3 explain the benefits to customers of a business using Internet marketing **See Assessment activity 12.2, page 297.**	**M2** analyse the marketing opportunities and challenges faced by a selected business when using Internet marketing **See Assessment activity 12.3, page 309.**	
P4 describe the benefits and opportunities to the business of using Internet marketing within the marketing mix of a selected business **See Assessment activity 12.3, page 309.**		
P5 explain how Internet marketing has made a selected business more efficient, effective and successful **See Assessment activity 12.4, page 317.**		
P6 explain the challenges of globalisation facing a selected business when using the Internet as a marketing tool **See Assessment activity 12.4, page 317.**		

How you will be assessed

This unit will be assessed by an internal assignment that will be designed and marked by the staff at your centre. It may be subject to sampling by your centre's External Verifier as part of Edexcel's ongoing quality assurance procedures. The assignment is designed to allow you to show your understanding of the unit outcomes. These relate to what you should be able to do after completing this unit.

Your assessment could be in the form of presentations, case studies, practical tasks and written assignments.

Tom

I liked investigating Internet marketing. Being able to build on my understanding of marketing really helped when I looked at the web presence of businesses. I love gaming and sport, but I soon learned to investigate a wide variety of websites. I chose sports outlets, a local council, a car dealer… quite a few, actually. Then I looked at the sites and found the features where I could see they were making a particular marketing effort. One thing I did was to see where businesses asked people to register online. This helps them to keep track of who their online users are and to build relationships.

I felt I was in charge of the way I learned. I was free to search around and really be creative. Understanding different kinds of Internet offers was interesting! Seeing who does it well, who could maybe do better and how the businesses and customers can benefit was quite fun. At the university interview, they were interested in hearing about my work on Internet marketing, even though I was hoping to specialise in business finance. The university's admissions tutor must have been impressed at my knowledge – after all, I did get in!

Time spent online

According to Ofcom August 2007, women aged 25 to 34 now spend more time online than men in the same age group.

In your view, does this fact have any relevance to an online marketer? Justify and explain your answer.

1. Know what role Internet marketing has within a modern marketing context

1.1 Modern marketing

The function of marketing in a private sector business, operating to generate profit, is to attract and keep customers. Customers might be private individuals, in so-called B2C (business-to-consumer) markets, or they may be other businesses in B2B (business-to-business) markets.

Markets exist wherever goods and services are bought and sold. There is a market for clothes and a market for cars; there are industrial markets and markets for food produce. Wherever people and organisations want or need goods or services, there is a market.

In the modern world, it is crucial for businesses to know about the markets they serve, so that they can work to serve these better. Marketing is the whole process of finding out what customers need or want, continually striving to meet their requirements in full and to relate products to these requirements.

Marketing is a function within business that has become increasingly important over the years. Long before the growth of the web, it was essential for businesses – if they were to compete successfully – to think about how their products would meet the needs of the people who might buy them. If they failed to do this, people would stop buying the products.

The Internet is a medium that can help the marketing process. Not only does it help, it alters and reshapes what businesses can do. However, before looking at the distinctive features of Internet marketing, it is necessary to have some grasp of traditional marketing principles and processes in the physical world. Unit 3 introduces the marketing function and it may be worth revisiting that unit before exploring the special features of Internet marketing here.

The marketing mix

Traditional marketing is based on a combination of the four Ps: product, price, place and promotion. Marketers work with these to create a tactical mix, designed to achieve business aims and objectives.

Product

The marketing function considers the features of a product offered to a market or part of a market (called a segment). What is it? Who is it aimed at? What does it do? What should it do? **Product development** decisions are based on the answers to these questions. Some new cars feature improved benefits for drivers, such as heated seats or adjustable mirrors. Some shampoos may be combined with new conditioners. These features rely on considerations of what customers require from products.

Key term

Product development – taking an existing product and adding new features so that it sells more or appeals to different groups

Price

The marketing function also considers the price a product should be set at. What sort of customers will buy at a particular price? What will be the best price to attract a particular kind of customer? What price might get more people to buy? What price might create the best image? What might be the effect of a change in price?

Different 'pricing strategies' are available according to what the business is aiming to achieve.

- **Penetration pricing** sets a price at a level that will gain a foothold in a market.
- **Destruction pricing** sets a price that will drive others out of the market.
- **Competitor pricing** bases the price on those of competitors.
- **Skimming** (or **creaming**) the market sets a high price because you have a unique product.
- **Discrimination pricing** sets different prices for different customers.

Place

Marketing specialists have always considered how a product will find its way to a place where consumers can make a purchase. This includes physical distribution and merchandising. Goods must be transported from the manufacturer into storage, through other distribution centres then to wholesalers, then to the high street retailer. Businesses working in between a manufacturer and a retailer are known as 'intermediaries'.

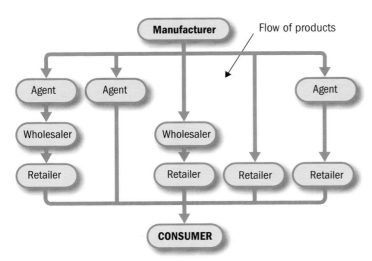

Fig. 12.1: Traditional channels of physical distribution.

Promotion

Marketing professionals have to consider ways of bringing products to the attention of potential customers. This includes advertising in the various mass media, as well as other ways of promoting products in the eyes of consumers, such as special offers. These activities, in the physical world, are designed to 'push' products and services out towards the eyes and ears of potential consumers.

> **Remember**
>
> The four Ps are the basic set of marketing tactics that can be manipulated in order to attract customers.

The extended marketing mix

In our modern economy, many organisations do not sell physical products; they provide services that we cannot touch or feel. In the UK we now live and work in a 'service economy'. This means that there are more organisations and people working to offer services than there are working in manufacturing.

The marketing of services is different to the marketing of physical products. This has led some people to

argue that the four Ps are not adequate by themselves to describe the marketing of services. They have added three further Ps to create an extended **marketing mix**. These are people, processes and physical evidence.

> ### Key term
>
> **Marketing mix** – sometimes referred to as the four Ps of product, price, promotion and place, these are the ideas to consider when marketing a product

People

People are at the centre of service delivery. When customers go to a restaurant, shop, café, bank or school/college, their satisfaction hinges on how the people there deal with them. For example, on the bus to school or college, if the driver is unfriendly or aggressive, that is what one remembers.

Processes

When customers use a service, they may have to take part in various activities or processes. For example, a café may require customers to use a self-service counter, or they may interact with a waiter. In a bank, is it an attractive waiting environment? Do customers have to wait long to get service? Do they have forms to fill in?

Physical evidence

This refers to the environment in which the service is delivered. For example, customers often check how restaurants look or how retail stores are laid out. They often look for tangible evidence to judge whether a service is what they want.

> **Remember**
>
> The marketing mix extends to seven Ps when discussing the marketing of services.

The marketing mix has to be put into practice by everyone in an organisation, guided and led (perhaps) by marketing professionals. Marketing consists of more than mere tactics; it is an entire style of doing business. The following sections show how marketing influences this style, and how Internet technologies are changing this day by day.

Relationship marketing

It is far more expensive to acquire new customers than it is to keep existing ones. For this reason, many businesses work hard to establish long-term relationships with their customers. This means that products and services offered to a market have to be highly appropriate. It is impossible to build a relationship with a customer who will never again return to your business.

Web technology is able to make use of detailed images and customer interaction. This allows customers to manipulate web pages and customise products to suit their preferences. One use of this is by allowing the customer to assist in the product design process.

Web technology enables customers to interact with products and change them on screen to suit their own preferences. This is an added web benefit that outperforms a physical environment. For instance, on its DIY website (www.diy.com), B&Q offers customers the opportunity to design their own kitchens, bathrooms and bedrooms.

Another technique in relationship marketing is to monitor and analyse customer feedback constantly, and then respond flexibly to their wishes. Business websites usually offer 'feedback' mechanisms or

'contact us' links. These help the business to relate closely to customers.

Internet technology can help a business to target specific groups. This enables the business to develop goods and services that accurately meet customer needs. By discovering the preferences and wishes of a group, a business is more likely to be able to offer the best product. (See 'Internet-enabled segmentation and targeting' on page 286.)

Remember

Marketing is often about long-term relationships. The web helps businesses to build these both in B2C and B2B markets.

Identifying new product and market developments

Because of the rapid explosion of the Internet and its increasing (if uneven) penetration worldwide, business leaders today make important strategic decisions about the purpose and potential of an online presence. Managers have to take account of industry-wide factors to decide how effective or relevant the company's Internet presence can be.

Web technology expands businesses into new products and markets and achieves significant aims and objectives. This can happen through:

- **market penetration** – businesses can increase their market share by offering better customer services or promotional information within the markets they already serve
- **market development** – businesses can enter new markets and potentially increase their market reach overseas because of the relatively low cost of advertising
- **product development** – a business can develop new information products and these can be digitally delivered over the web.

Activity: easyJet

Visit www.easyjet.com. How is the website helping easyJet achieve its goals?

Remember

Business strategy and objectives are attainable by using the Internet to enter new markets or develop products in existing markets.

Using the Internet to achieve objectives

When a business makes a strategic decision to create an Internet presence, possibly to sell online, management will set objectives for the new channel. These objectives should be specific targets, designed to lead the company towards its overall aims.

Online business objectives could be to:

- increase revenue from the Internet by ten per cent
- achieve a top five ranking in market penetration in a particular country
- make cost savings of ten per cent
- increase customer retention by 20 per cent
- increase sales by 25 per cent to 25–40-year-olds
- improve customer response times to a two-hour limit.

Objectives should therefore be specific, measurable, achievable, realistic and time-related (SMART). To assist in this, the Internet offers a number of methods for businesses to gain accurate measurements about how a website is performing.

Case study: B&Q and easyJet: online business objectives

When B&Q decided it was going to open an online sales channel called B&Q Direct through its website, www.diy.com, the subsidiary business managing the project was given a four-year Internet contribution target at the outset. The website had to reach specific levels of revenue.

easyJet (www.easyjet.com) originally launched its online booking facility with a two-year plan. The online revenue contribution needed to be 30 per cent in two years.

1. Why is it helpful for businesses such as these to set specific targets?
2. What other specific objectives might a business establish for its website? Justify these suggestions.

PLTS

When investigating the B&Q Direct site, analyse the ways in which the business is trying to meet customer needs, as well as its own objectives, in order to practise independent enquiry.

Segmentation and targeting

We saw at the start of the unit that there are markets for all goods and services produced, otherwise businesses would have no reason to produce them. However, markets do not contain individuals or businesses that are all the same. For example, although we say that there is a market for cars, they come in all sorts of sizes, shapes, colours and styles. This reflects the fact that we as consumers have different:

- preferences
- budgets
- reasons for buying.

One person might buy a car because they want something reliable to get them to and from work; someone else might buy a car because they want people to know they are a success in their business.

One of the functions of marketing is to make sense of the different groupings within markets. This process is called segmentation. By segmenting markets, businesses are able to see particular characteristics within them and target products and marketing tactics to suit that segment. Fig. 12.3 shows the process.

Segment the market by using market research.

Identify customer needs within each segment.

Target chosen **market segments**, using the tactics available from the seven Ps of the marketing mix.

Fig. 12.3: The segmentation process.

Internet-enabled segmentation and targeting

Segmentation and targeting online is undertaken using a number of different variables:

- demographic
- psychographic
- economic
- usage-based.

There are some comprehensive sources of web trends and analyses. Three of these are:

- www.clickz.com
- www.nua.ie/surveys
- www.webtrends.com

These online services provide business planners with detailed statistics and analysis of Internet trends.

PLTS

Try creatively extending your analysis of using WebTrends by suggesting ways in which other businesses might use the service.

Case study: WebTrends Marketing Warehouse

WebTrends Marketing Warehouse™ is designed to meet Internet marketing needs. The enterprise-class Microsoft SQL Server database provides a platform for collecting, enriching and analysing visitor-level behavioural data, so a business can gain insight and drive actions to improve the **bottom line**.

WebTrends Marketing Warehouse helps to:

- drive sales, marketing – visitor-level tracking helps to segment and target individuals who visit a website more effectively
- uncover customer and business trends – dedicated analysis tools help to track and correlate the actions of unique visitors, and even target the most valuable customer segments.

Key term

Bottom line – the last line in an audit; the line that shows profit or loss

This is illustrated by an article in *Marketing Week* from October 2007.

'Low-cost airline easyJet has appointed digital agency and services provider WebTrends to oversee strategy for its online web and marketing initiatives.

WebTrends will measure the success of the low-cost carrier's online marketing communications and web content to assess its effectiveness in the increasingly competitive online travel market.'

1. In what ways do you think a business will be able to target customers more effectively using this WebTrends product?

2. Why is it important for an online business to track visitors to their website?

3. Take two businesses and analyse the benefits from this kind of marketing intelligence.

Demographic

Demographics are about the make-up of your population. We can study population trends all over the world. Another form of demographics is Internet demographics, and this directly relates to Internet marketing. In Internet terms, it is useful for businesses planning an online strategy to know how many Internet customers there may be.

Potentially, a website gives a business global reach. However, levels of 'Internet penetration' vary widely, depending on the proportion of the population within different countries and continents having access to the web. To make a well-informed decision about targeting requires an understanding of Internet access and availability in different countries.

A number of services give comprehensive data about Internet facts and figures. Nielsen NetRatings, for example, provides statistics on home Internet use by country.

Psychographic

This kind of segmentation uses lifestyle and personal characteristics as a way of segmenting a market. It addresses the question: 'What are our possible customers like?' Using this basis, an online business can blend its marketing tactics to suit the segment. Psychographic profiles of different Internet users are based on detailed research, carried out by marketing services companies. The following case study gives an example of this kind of segmentation.

Table 12.1: Number of active home Internet users by country, May 2009 (source: The Nielsen Company).

Country	April 2009	May 2009	Growth (%)	Difference
Australia	10,929,536	11,237,351	2.82	307,815
Brazil	25,460,307	25,566,439	0.42	106,132
France	29,457,939	31,099,132	5.57	1,641,193
Germany	36,158,816	36,706,500	1.51	544,684
Italy	17,662,655	17,769,768	0.61	107,113
Japan	48,567,721	49,711,242	2.35	1,143,520
Spain	19,375,214	19,826,831	2.33	451,617
Switzerland	3,721,585	3,765,629	1.18	44,044
UK	29,063,326	29,048,332	-0.05	-14,994
US	154,525,974	156,557,641	1.31	2,031,667

How can demographics be used in marketing?

WorkSpace — Five personalities of broadband users

Broadband users are often characterised as 'one homogenous group of people', says Josh Crandall, Managing Director of Media-Screen, a strategic market research firm that published 'Netpop Portraits' as part of its Netpop Research series of data.

Nearly 650 million households will have broadband Internet service by 2013 and although growth is slowing in the USA, it is increasing in less developed countries. Its adoption is said to have created a population of five segments with unique characteristics:

- content king – looks to the web for entertainment, games and so on, and spends an average 2.5 hours online each weekday

- social clicker – young or old, uses the Internet as a means of communication – more than half of social clickers' time (57 per cent) is spent on communications; the remainder is spent on news and information (10 per cent) and shopping (8 per cent)

- online insider – consumes content, contributing to Internet content or information each month, including posting to blogs, community sites and chat rooms. The group spends upwards of US$130 each month on e-commerce

- fast tracker – typically uses the Internet to seek out news and information; they use the Internet to research products but typically buy in stores

- everyday pro – looks to the Internet to fulfil needs for personal productivity and efficiency, such as online banking or retailing.

Source: Adapted from an article by Enid Burns on www.clickz.com, 16 November 2006.

Think about it!

1. In what ways do you think that a potential online business might make use of this kind of psychographic profiling?

2. Which profile, if any, would you place yourself in?

3. Give examples of two online businesses that in your view could make valuable use of this psychographic profiling.

Economic

On a global basis the economic prosperity and conditions within different countries determine the extent to which e-commerce (buying and selling on the Internet) is likely to succeed in them. A business considering an online strategy that depends on an increasing volume of sales in, say, Eastern Europe, would do well to acquaint itself with economic data about the area. The Economic Intelligence Unit, available at www.eiu.com, provides detailed data.

Activity: New markets

Produce a report for a business considering expanding into new markets in China and the Far East. In the report, summarise the main economic and demographic factors that you would suggest the business takes into account.

Usage-based

This kind of data informs business leaders about how the Internet is being used in different parts of the world. The service provided by ClickZ (www.clickz.com) offers detailed insights into traffic patterns on the web, as the case study below illustrates.

Activity: Survey

Design and conduct a survey in which you find out from teenage people in and around your own school/college, whether the categories listed in the case study apply. Make sure you analyse the results carefully and highlight any differences.

Remember

Marketing techniques involve breaking a market up into smaller groups with shared characteristics. From this, marketers 'target' these segments by blending the elements of the marketing mix.

Case study: Reaching the teenage market

The following is based on an article by Heidi Cohen of ClickZ.com (www.clickz.com), July 2009. It deals with the ways in which teenagers (particularly in the USA) use various kinds of media.

Teens communicate via phone with their friends. Today's teens use mobile phones for voice and text communications to privately share the details of their lives. Experian finds that older teens (18–20) use text and email equally. Teens are three times more receptive to mobile advertising, according to 2008 Nielsen research. Following this logic, it is understandable that Twitter, which many users access via mobile devices, does not reach teens because it is a more public communication vehicle that does not meet teens' needs.

Marketing implication? Add targeted text campaigns to reach teens, and use other mobile marketing formats to attract them.

Teens listen to music. They are the biggest buying segment of recorded music. Today's teens are their own DJs, using personal, portable music devices, mobile phones, and computers. Nielsen reports that globally 39 per cent of teens listen to music on an MP3 player and 33 per cent listen to music on a home computer. Additionally, 75 per cent of global teens still listen to some CDs each week.

Marketing implications? Assess potential to provide or sponsor music and/or ringtone download. Incorporate music-related marketing, such as tour and live event sponsorships and tie-ins…

Teens tend to have limited access to money. As a result, they seek free and cheap alternatives. They tend to spend their money on clothes, good looks and entertainment. Teens are known for finding loopholes to get free products and to share content, music and software. Therefore, it is no surprise that they do not want to pay for content such as newspapers and music.

Marketing implications? Consider the pricing impact of teen-related offerings.

(Source: ClickZ.com)

1. In what ways does this insight into teenage behaviour offer marketers a chance to improve targeted marketing?

2. Analyse the teenage characteristics described by Heidi Cohen. For each one, write out a statement in which you give an honest appraisal of yourself in relation to using media.

Business interactions

Buying and selling involves interactions between different kinds of customers and suppliers. Business-to-business transactions are known as B2B. These are less frequent but of much higher value. Businesses purchase raw materials and buy services such as ICT from other businesses.

Private consumers are individuals like us. We need bread, carpets, pens, clothes and so on. We buy these things from businesses; hence they are referred to as business-to-consumer (B2C) transactions. On the Internet, consumers can buy from consumers, for example, on eBay. These consumer-to-consumer (C2C) transactions use bidding on an auction basis.

Disintermediation

In the physical business world, a product originates with the raw materials from which it is made. Timber, for example, can be used to make garden furniture. The timber is transported from its original source to manufacturers who produce the garden items. From the manufacturers, the items may go to a distribution centre and from there to a garden centre, close to where customers live – the third 'P' marketing tactic of 'place' (see page 282). This is a supply chain, which is the way that goods get to where you buy them.

The businesses that work between the original manufacturer of the furniture and the customer are known as intermediaries. Their job is to move, store or package the items to be sold.

With the Internet, there is often no need for intermediaries, as many products can be shipped directly to your home. This is **disintermediation**. One of the most well-known examples of an online business doing this is Dell Computers (see next page).

Remember

The Internet allows businesses to sell directly to consumers without using an intermediary. This saves both time and cash.

Direct market communication

Direct marketing communications are now very common. Producers can directly mail potential buyers either online or through the post. Leaflets, booklets, catalogues and flyers are sent out daily, directly offering goods from manufacturers to end users.

Key terms

Disintermediation – the removal of intermediaries ('middle men') from the process of getting products to where consumers can buy them

Direct marketing – sending messages directly to potential customers, for example, by email, without using indirect promotions such as advertising

1.2 Internet marketing

Internet marketing can help businesses to deliver their strategy. Unlike traditional marketing communications media – TV, radio and printed material – which all *push* mass marketing messages out from a business, in one direction, the web is a *pull* medium. This means individual customers choose to visit a website when they feel like doing so. On the web, a marketing message is always delivered on a one-to-one basis.

Internet marketers use a number of techniques to take advantage of this. They remix the seven Ps described on pages 282–3 to offer different tactics.

Online promotion

Promotion on the Internet spreads widely. It relies on a combination of methods.

- **Search engine optimisation** – register with the big search engines such as Google or Yahoo! and make sure that the website contains the correct keywords so the site appears high up in the relevant searches that people carry out.

- **Banner advertisements** – advertisements for products or services that appear at the head of a web page, often animated.

- **Affiliate programmes** – placing linked advertisements for products or services on another business's site.

- **Email promotion** – an easy but potentially damaging method of promoting a business. 'Permission-based' mailing works best (where an organisation obtains the permission of the potential customer first).

Activity: Online display advertising

Investigate what is meant by 'online display advertising'. Present a poster display showing examples.

Did you know?

Despite the poor economic climate, online display advertising activity in the UK during the first four months of 2009 was up 21 per cent on the same period during 2008 (source: The Nielsen Company).

Remember

The Internet differs from traditional marketing communications because it is not a push medium, one to many; it depends on individual customers selecting a website and interacting one to one. Therefore, communication techniques are different and have to stimulate interest.

Individualising market attention

In B2C markets in particular, because a web visit is always an individual choice, a one-to-one relationship is possible. Web technology means online businesses can personalise their response to suit an individual.

Amazon.co.uk is perhaps the best-known online business for **personalisation**. The screen shot in Fig. 12.4 shows a personalised Amazon.co.uk page. Based on information about previous visits to the website, the next page makes individual recommendations, promoting other products that the individual customer may be interested in.

Mass customisation

The Internet offers the opportunity for businesses to let customers tailor or customise products to suit their individual tastes. An example is Dell Inc., an online computer retailing service that allows customers to select the various components to build their own PC configuration. As this service is available from some businesses to *all* of their online customers, it is known as 'mass **customisation**'.

Key terms

Personalisation – adjusting the web page that is returned to a visitor so that it offers information that is personal, based on their previous visits to the website

Customisation – opportunity for the customer to manipulate and change the online presentation of a product

Activity: Customisation of Internet products

Visit the following websites and write a report about 'customisation of Internet products'.

- www.ic3d.com
- www.nike.com

In what ways, if any, do you feel that customers benefit from this customisation?

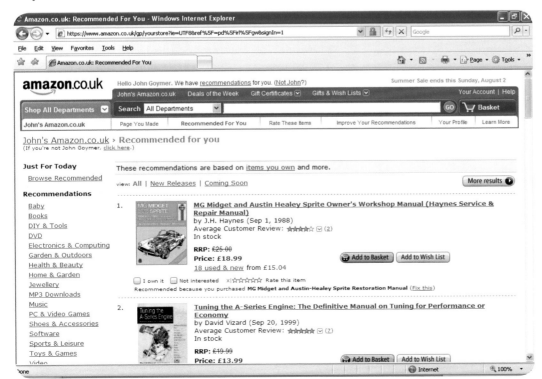

Fig. 12.4: What is online personalisation?

Fig. 12.5: What benefits does customisation offer to the customers of Dell Inc.?

© 2007 Dell Corporation Limited. Dell and the Dell logo are either registered or unregistered trademarks of Dell Inc. Dell disclaims any proprietary interest in the marks and names of others. Dell Corporation, c/o Box 69 Milbanke House, Western Road, Bracknell, Berkshire, RG12 1RD.

Increased information and product impact

There are obvious limitations in offering physical products for sale online. Depending on the product, customers may prefer to examine the look and feel of products. The web allows businesses to compensate for this by extending products with added information and impact.

Extending online products is done by:

- extensive product endorsements from previous customers
- lists of customers
- warranties
- money-back offers
- additional customer back-up services
- 'cross-selling' of related or complementary products
- offering expert advice.

These facilities help to give customers confidence in an online purchase.

Websites usually offer detailed product information – including images and customer interaction – allowing customers to compare features, prices and costs (see, for example, www.diy.com).

Activity: Extending online products

Explore the web and try to find examples of at least three sites where products are being sold using some of the above techniques.

1. How effective do you feel these are?
2. Would you recommend this to a business considering an online channel?

Reaching wider markets

A glance at the table showing European Internet usage (Table 12.1, page 287) is enough to show that by using the Internet, a business can instantly achieve a far wider and more distant geographic reach than by using other means of marketing.

Did you know?

EMarketer forecasts that mothers will account for 39.6 million of the international online audience by 2012 (source: ClickZ.com).

Case study: Buy It Direct

Buy It Direct (www.buyitdirect.co.uk), is an online discount retailer that sells air conditioning systems as part of a range of electrical goods.

Monthly sales at Aircon Direct, one of seven websites the company operates, soared by over 400 per cent to £485,000 between April and June in 2009. On one hot Monday in June, the company took over 550 orders, generating 65 per cent of its total daily profit.

Nick Glynne, Buy It Direct's managing director, says:

'People have air-conditioning in their cars so they expect a comfortable working environment too. We deliver [the systems] directly the next day. They are a seasonal purchase, but they are an important source of business in what is usually a quiet time.'

Since its launch nine years ago, Glynne has built a strong firm that is snatching business from recession-hit rivals. Over the past 12 months, the Huddersfield-based firm has invested over £1 million on an IT system that captures and analyses data on sales, stock and logistics. Customer service has been improved and a

more experienced management team has been appointed.

Like other websites, Buy It Direct is benefiting from the drift away from traditional retailers as value-conscious shoppers search online for bargains. The company is also winning customers from competitors that have gone into administration.

Overall turnover has grown 15 per cent in the past six months and revenues are forecast to reach £100 million in 2009, up from £67 million last year.

(Source: Catherine Wheatley, www.telegraphbusinessclub.co.uk, 2009)

1. Describe the elements of the marketing mix that are being improved by Buy It Direct's use of the Internet.

2. Analyse the ways in which customers are gaining benefit from Buy It Direct's online approach.

3. Evaluate the effectiveness of this Internet marketing effort in terms of both customer benefits and business success.

Mix between online and offline activities

Much of the continued evolution of e-commerce has built on existing businesses that have established their reputations and customer bases in the physical world. Long-established names like Next, B&Q, Topshop and Tesco now combine offline and online sales channels. These are known as **clicks and mortar businesses**, as they have both physical buildings ('bricks and mortar')

and an Internet presence ('clicks' of the mouse). Many of these businesses also combine their offline and online promotional activities.

Key term

Clicks and mortar businesses – businesses that have physical buildings and an Internet presence

Assessment activity 12.1

  BTEC

You are employed as an assistant to the Economic Development Officer in your local Planning Authority. You have been asked to put together some helpful information for presentations they are giving. You have two important tasks.

1. Describe the role Internet marketing has in a modern marketing context. **P1**

2. Describe how selected organisations use Internet marketing. **P2**

Grading tips

1. You need to consider the broad role of marketing in meeting customer needs. How does an Internet presence help certain businesses to give better service? You might consider giving customers better information about products or services; you might consider personal service; speed of service; finding out about the market and customers. **P1**

2. You should choose at least three business organisations doing different things (for example, one selling, another giving information and another voluntary body). Have a look closely and study their websites. In which ways are these organisations developing their marketing effort online? **P2**

2. Understand the benefits of Internet marketing to customers

2.1 Customer benefits

The increasing availability of so many products and services on the Internet has introduced many opportunities and benefits for customers.

Comparing and selecting providers

The Internet allows a great deal of **price transparency** for consumers. This means they can compare prices easily between many potential suppliers. Prices are stored digitally in databases, and software (robot shoppers, shopping bots or price search engines) is used to search for the best prices available on the web (for example, www.kelkoo.com). Some sites, such as the BBC's Internet shopping service at www.beeb.com, provide instant price comparisons, and at www.letsbuyit.com, customers can join together in order to lower prices. This has the effect of giving online customers much greater bargaining power.

> ### Key term
>
> **Price transparency** – when everyone who visits your website can see all of your prices

Instead of prices being set by businesses and passively received by the market, the Internet is capable of turning this situation upside down. Priceline.co.uk (www.priceline.co.uk), for instance, allows consumers to set their own prices, and at several online auction sites such as eBay (www.ebay.co.uk), consumers are able to place bids for consumer products after viewing the minimum (reserve) price acceptable to the seller. The website www.confused.com offers an easy service comparison and is heavily backed by TV advertising.

Comprehensive and up-to-date product information

In both B2C and B2B markets, the Internet offers businesses the opportunity to provide total product information. Private customers shopping online do not have the chance to touch, smell, taste or sample products; businesses looking for industrial components or business services might not have the chance to make contacts with a range of representatives. These drawbacks are bypassed because of the web's power to store and communicate information. RS Components' e-commerce site, for example, offers detailed information for business buyers of electrical parts.

Fig. 12.6: What other websites make effective use of interactivity on the Internet?

For prospective buyers on any site, the essential product details are:

- price
- descriptions of features and specifications
- colour options, if relevant
- images
- drawings
- promotional deals.

From a well-designed website, customers can fully check specifications and quickly make email contact with staff. The whole transaction process is quickly completed. In the case of RS Components, the site even offers a procurement software tool for use by a B2B purchasing organisation.

Ibstock Brick Ltd uses a website that makes very effective use of the interactivity of the web. Customers can access a wide range of features including a brick selector, calculator and design assistance.

2.2 Dynamic pricing

Customers can gain excellent cost savings by making use of the Internet's ability to alter pricing in real time to reflect market conditions. The airline industry and hotels are two examples where customers can save due to **dynamic pricing** (or fluid pricing). When few seats are sold, availability is good and prices are set very low. As the flight time draws nearer, and fewer seats are available, prices increase, depending on seat availability. The website and supporting technology can respond instantly to market changes. The price is constantly on the move.

Online auctions can make use of the same principle. Prices are open and available for all potential bidders to see. As bidding progresses, asking prices move according to the interest that is shown.

> ### Key term
>
> **Dynamic pricing** – the facility of the web that enables online businesses to adjust prices quickly, according to market conditions

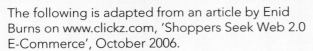

Case study: The importance of online product information

The following is adapted from an article by Enid Burns on www.clickz.com, 'Shoppers Seek Web 2.0 E-Commerce', October 2006.

E-commerce sites lose as many as 67 per cent of consumers; many abandon their shopping carts due to a lack of product information. The 'Online Merchandising Survey' research brief, released by Allurent, details consumers' perceptions of online shopping.

Increased interactive elements and innovative ways to display and purchase products would encourage Internet purchasing for 83 per cent of survey respondents.

Enhanced features that would also help could include mix-and-match outfits, where shoppers can put together an entire outfit on screen (44 per cent); 360-degree product views (78 per cent); side-by-side comparisons (63 per cent) and personalisation or customisable products (53 per cent).

In Reuters.com, May 2009, it was reported:

'Allurent, the market leader in powering superior online shopping experiences, today announced that Charlotte Russe Holding, Inc., a specialty apparel and accessories retailer, will bring interactive merchandising to its e-commerce site using Allurent software that increases customer satisfaction and site conversion by quickly and cost-effectively deploying merchant-controlled widgets to retailers' existing websites.

Charlotte Russe shoppers are on the cutting edge in terms of fashion and trends, and they want interactivity and freshness as they shop online. The retailer's merchandising team works to create differentiated, engaging displays that strengthen customer satisfaction and loyalty. Charlotte Russe chose "Allurent on Demand" to improve this process with greater flexibility, control over costs and best-in-class interactive experiences.'

1. Find at least three other websites where customer interactivity is used, and assess whether in your view it really adds to customer satisfaction.

2. Take one of these interactive websites and evaluate its main features.

Case study: Dynamic pricing by PC vendors

PC vendors planned to introduce dynamic pricing to sell more stock online. IBM, Compaq, Dell Inc. and Hewlett-Packard were among those 'actively investigating' dynamic pricing models, according to a report by InfoWorld.

Prices change as customers order multiple items on certain offers. Dell Inc. is considering extending the method to its whole product line by the end of the year.

All this means that system prices could change constantly, and catching a bargain would be down to Internet surfers' lucky timing. However, surfers can be easily annoyed if they discover that a company has been using a dynamic pricing system that it had failed to publicise – for example, to make regular customers pay more than first-time users of the site.

1. In what ways might 'dynamic pricing' make buying online more appealing?

2. Why would customers have been annoyed by dynamic pricing?

2.3 Responsive transactions

The Internet offers customers the chance to conduct transactions straight away and immediately have the satisfaction of knowing that they have made a booking. Booking an airline ticket through an online facility such as www.easyjet.com offers an easy process and great convenience.

2.4 Customer service

Marketers must constantly look at customer needs and wants. Customer service is of paramount importance if a business is to remain competitive in today's business world. Products and services may be very similar; it is customer service that can clinch the business, whether in B2C or B2B markets.

The Internet offers businesses a number of ways of delivering improved customer services. Websites are available 24 hours a day. They almost all include links to FAQ (frequently asked questions) pages, and 'About us' and 'Contact us' sections. These all help to give online customers a better level of service.

Digital complaints

Online complaints services exist that can help customers to lodge a complaint about an online product or service. Consumers benefit because they can add their voice to those of others who have complained. This gives a collective view. A fee is paid to the complaints service company, which then contacts the business concerned and explains customer concerns.

Fig. 12.7: Why is customer service on a business's website so important?

Chat

The Internet offers people the chance to participate in real-time online chat groups. This is especially useful to consumers who can add their opinions and read those of other consumers (C2C).

How can internet chat groups be useful to consumers?

Assessment activity 12.2

  BTEC

Building on your research and investigations so far in your work as an assistant to the Economic Development Officer, complete the following tasks.

1. Explain the benefits to consumers of a business using Internet marketing. **P3**
2. Analyse the benefits of Internet marketing to consumers. **M1**
3. Evaluate the effectiveness of Internet marketing in meeting customer needs for a selected business. **D1**

Grading tips

1. Select at least three websites such as www.diy.com, www.topshop.co.uk and www.tesco.com or your own local council. Describe the marketing features of these websites that offer benefits to their customers. **P3**

2. To analyse the benefits, you must give full details about each marketing feature and explain the ways in which customers gain. For instance, product comparisons are available

in the physical stores too; why is this felt to be 'beneficial' just because it is online? (Is it ease of use?) You might say that the features are available at the click of a button without any searching around, asking staff, and so on. How have Internet marketing activities built on conventional offline marketing activities? How is the mix exploited differently? **M1**

3. To evaluate means, in this case, that you must review the information you have presented about one online business. This is a challenge because you must outline your own views based on your judgements about something. For example, you may decide to consider whether customers really benefit from having the chance to chat about products online. Your view may be that this is a gimmick. However, you must be able to justify that view fully. On the other hand, you may discover a 'chat' or 'discussion' service about a product that you think is very useful (for example, the Apple iPod discussion forum at www.apple.com). You must back up your views with evidence from the websites. **D1**

3. Understand the opportunities offered to businesses by Internet marketing

The Internet presents businesses with great opportunities to improve their marketing effort and perhaps gain competitive advantage. However, the extent to which a business takes up these opportunities depends on some important considerations.

- Does the firm deal in appropriate products for online sales?
- Does the firm have the internal IT resources and skills to monitor and maintain a transactional website?
- Does the business leadership have a strategic plan for e-commerce?
- Are there competitive forces within the industry that are driving firms to e-commerce?
- What are the financial and technological capabilities of the business?

Assuming a business has considered these things and has a clear strategy for its online channel, then the marketing benefits available from the Internet can be built into practice. Internet marketing can benefit a business in the three main areas of:

- communications
- product development
- business efficiency.

3.1 Opportunities to access customers and markets

Trading online gives businesses in both B2C and B2B markets the chance to access new customers, in new markets, on a global scale. Web technology allows a business to present products and services in detail, together with substantial supporting information. Once this is done, the business can use a well-planned website to capture data about customers, such as their names, addresses, postcodes, telephone numbers and email addresses. The business is able to build up a database of customers. From this point – as we saw earlier – the web page offered to returning customers can be customised to give them a web page personalised according to their previous purchase history (for example, www.amazon.co.uk).

Once a business is able to make contact with a customer, it can use email to send further product details or news about the business. For example, through its registration process and 'Clubcard' points system, Tesco tries to build a relationship with its online customers and is able to give them product offers and recommendations based on their buying history.

In B2B markets there is also a need for firms to use effective communications in order to build relationships. In industrial markets, for example, B2B exchanges can be vital to the prosperity of a firm. Think of almost any business and there will be suppliers that are crucial to its operation. A printing business must have paper, ink, machine components and so on; a fish and chip shop must have fish! It follows that communications between these partner businesses need to be good.

B2B relationships in general improve by establishing good online relationships. Businesses can co-operate better over the long term. Transactions can be quicker and the records of them more reliable and accurate. The whole question of dealing with customers efficiently can be handled online with the use of Customer Relationship Management (CRM) software. This is software that can automate sales responses, respond to customer queries, record visits, and manage emails, direct mails and campaigns.

Customer service is now a central element of a business's competitive drive. Prime considerations when choosing firms to work with are product suitability, reliability and quality; after these are established, it is the quality of service that makes the difference.

Did you know?

Research summarised by Reichheld and Schefter (2000) showed that acquiring online customers is so expensive (20 to 30 per cent higher than for traditional businesses) that start-up companies may remain unprofitable for at least two to three years. The research also showed that by retaining just five per cent more customers, online companies can boost their profits by 25 to 95 per cent (source: DaveChaffey.com).

Communicating for promotion

A website in itself is a promotional tool. Online businesses seek to create a look and feel that appeals to the self-image of their **target market**. Often, this is a hidden message to do with lifestyle.

New product launches are possible online. Software downloads can be made available on a trial basis and promoted widely online. The capacity of the web to carry lots of detailed product information makes it an ideal place to attract interest in new product developments. Businesses can use multimedia presentations, interactivity and movies as well as written information.

Case study: Subaru's interactive product launch

Subaru needed to build awareness of its new luxury vehicle, the Impreza. The company hired an agency to develop an online campaign. Site visitors were encouraged to 'opt in' to receive information by email as soon as it became available.

Subaru then implemented a three-phase launch of the product online. There was a slow release of images of the new car. This occurred in the autumn. Then there was a staged reveal phase, when the official site was launched in the January.

Subaru's dedicated site, www.subaru-impreza.co.uk (no longer active), featured video that was specifically shot for the site to capture the essence of the range of cars, including Subaru's rally heritage. Subaru intended to create a 'rich' experience for potential customers. Pictures and features were added to the site over time to stimulate interest and make people want to visit their local dealerships.

1. What is meant by 'opt-in' e-mailing?

2. Why do you think Subaru chose to use an opt-in tactic for customers to receive emails about the new car?

3. Can you think of another product type that could suitably use the Internet for a launch? How might this help its launch?

4. Why might a consumer wish to get 'interactive' with a product launch? Does it matter? Justify your response.

Key term

Target market – the segment that marketers aim for when they create their marketing message

Did you know?

Online services can help e-businesses to understand specific website audiences by:

- demographics
- lifestyle (leisure, life events, electronics ownership)
- traditional media behaviour (TV, radio, print)
- online media behaviour (email newsletters, online subscriptions)
- shopping and purchase behaviour (online and offline).

(Source: The Nielsen Company.)

3.2 Opportunities to improve availability

Businesses can use the Internet to create 24-hour availability of their services and products, and make them more easily available.

On the Internet, customers initiate contact. This means the business immediately has – for a limited time at least – 100 per cent of the customer's attention. To be successful, the website must present information that is both interesting and relevant to a visitor. Traditional marketing communications go out to everyone; Internet marketing on the other hand can suit individual visitors, whether they are consumers buying leisure items or trades people on the lookout for tools or equipment.

Two online businesses that have made a special e-commerce effort and been recognised for doing so are RS Components (http://uk.rs-online.com) and Screwfix (www.screwfix.com). In both these cases, the buyer can register with the site and, thereafter, the site will record purchases and offer a customised set of menus to suit the next visit.

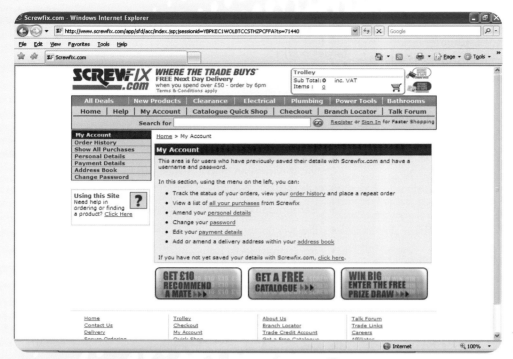

Fig. 12.8: How can online businesses take full advantage of the Internet's marketing opportunities?

Activity: Screwfix

Investigate the services offered to trade customers from www.screwfix.com

In what ways does this site represent evidence of an online business taking full advantage of the Internet's marketing opportunity? Justify your response with reference to the features of the website.

Identifying product development opportunities

The Internet may be used by online businesses to gather detailed information about customer perceptions of an online product or service. Alternatively, it can be used to gather marketing research information. As an example of the former, Egg (www.egg.com) takes care to ask customers about their feelings about the online service. The business attitude is: 'How can we improve things?'

Other online businesses have found that the Internet has generated new business opportunities. RS Components was a traditional B2B wholesaler of electrical parts. The business discovered that ten per cent of its online sales were to private consumers. The Internet allows businesses to target new subsets of larger markets that it may not have considered before.

The Internet enables companies to offer digital delivery of new, information-based products. They can

offer newsletters or services to meet new demands for web-based applications. Sunderland-based Leighton Group, for example, has developed an online collaborative service called 4Retail.

Immediate sales of products

Another advantage of the Internet is that online services – particularly those that are information-based – are immediately accessible. People can use online insurance or banking services and gain peace of mind within minutes.

Substituting online products

The Internet is a multimedia channel that is capable of delivering digital content in the form of downloads to a home device. It is now commonplace to download music, films, radio and TV programmes. These services are an easy alternative to visiting offline providers and, in the case of radio services or TV broadcasts, offer great flexibility in that users can choose when to listen to or watch them.

Podcasts

A podcast is a small multimedia file that can be downloaded using the Internet. Podcasts are most commonly used by broadcasters such as the BBC, which makes podcasts of news summaries or snippets of shows. In theory, any business can make use of podcasting to deliver marketing information.

Fig. 12.9: Find out what 4Retail offers to customers.

Market development

The Internet gives online businesses the chance to expand into new markets without the huge expense of mass advertising using traditional media. A website creates instant reach into wide geographic areas and is capable of generating new export sales. This opportunity must be balanced against the costs and the red tape involved in exporting to different parts of the world.

It is easy to assume that as the Internet is a global phenomenon, a business can launch its website and immediately generate immense sales all over the world. However, there are risks involved in an online strategy. A business may not achieve profitability for a long time,

Fig. 12.10: What sort of information can businesses gather thanks to the Internet?

despite the fact that it achieved multi-billion dollars' worth of sales. Online goods and services have to be delivered to consumers. Depending on the nature of the product, delivery involves shipping, packaging and acknowledgement, and the company needs back-up staff to support the online transaction.

In some cases, however, the opportunities offered by the Internet have transformed businesses. The following case study illustrates this.

Case study: Card Corporation

Card Corporation (www.cardcorp.co.uk) was founded in 1988 by Ivor Jacobs. The business set out to plug a market gap by producing short-run print items such as business stationery. These days the business is making extensive use of Internet technology.

Card Corporation has very few direct competitors and, with sales snowballing, turnover is increasing at an annual rate of 80–90 per cent. Its pioneering role in the industry has also allowed Card Corporation to grow through word of mouth, rather than through extensive marketing campaigns. 'People tell other people about our site because they've had such a good experience from it,' says Ivor. 'Other people's take-up of faster bandwidths and general misunderstanding of what technology is all about is a barrier.'

As an early adopter of an e-business strategy, Card Corporation's response is to help move its trading partners forward as well. It does this by building into its system simple but powerful features that will provide demonstrable benefits to clients. For example, the company has built in sufficient flexibility that it can develop new offerings in response to client requests, and has also set up an automated online approval tool. This adaptability helps clients to see the benefits of technology and encourages them to electronically enable their own businesses.

1. Investigate Card Corporation through its website at www.cardcorp.co.uk
2. Produce a report outlining and evaluating the business's use of the Internet.
3. How does the business benefit from the Internet?

Lower entry costs for small businesses

The Internet gives smaller businesses a relatively low-cost strategy for competing on the same online terms as much larger corporations. This is known as 'equality of Internet presence' and refers to the fact that to Internet surfers, all businesses can appear to be operating on the same scale.

Virtual services

Digital media are able to break down the barriers that naturally occur in the physical world. This is why it is common to speak of a 'virtual' world and a physical world.

We spend most of our lives in the physical world, in which we are bound by physical realities such as distance. In the virtual world, digital media can create a realistic impression of these physical realities, enabling the user to experience them without moving from their seat. This allows estate agents, for example, the opportunity to offer buyers 'virtual tours' of properties. Computer-generated images of rooms are uploaded on to the site. A prospective buyer can then select areas of the property and 'walk through' the rooms at a click of the mouse button.

24-hour service online

Not only do digital media break down physical constraints, but they also eliminate time constraints. A website is available 24 hours a day, seven days a week. For service businesses this offers tremendous advantages, as clients with Internet access can use the service any time, anywhere. Online services where this applies include:

- banking
- insurance
- education
- retail.

Bricks and clicks

Internet marketing is a strategic tactic that depends on the willingness and capacity of a firm to take advantage of the facilities that are potentially available from the web. Not all firms are ready for full participation on the Internet. They can participate at one of various levels.

In their book *Internet Marketing* (Prentice Hall, 2003), Chaffey, Mayer, Johnston and Ellis-Chadwick suggest a hierarchy of participation levels, as shown in Fig. 12.11.

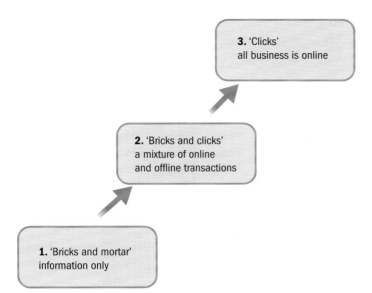

3. 'Clicks'
all business is online

2. 'Bricks and clicks'
a mixture of online
and offline transactions

1. 'Bricks and mortar'
information only

Fig. 12.11: Hierarchy of Internet participation levels.

- The first level of Internet activity consists of businesses that offer information only from their website. They do not offer sales of any kind and the site serves as a promotional tool only – for example, Bells Fish and Chips (www.bellsfishshop.co.uk).

- The 'bricks and clicks' level consists of businesses that use both an online and an offline sales channel. This has been a growing category in recent years; well-established names like Next, Topshop, Tesco and B&Q fall into the 'bricks and clicks' grouping.

- Finally, there are the so-called 'clicks'. These businesses, such as the insurance business elephant.co.uk, only trade online and have no physical sales operations at all. (It is worth noting that even Amazon.co.uk uses some physical warehousing and distribution outlets.)

Market diversification

The Internet's capacity to help offer services such as those mentioned earlier have allowed big retailers like Tesco's to operate in new markets. In other words, they have been able to diversify by offering new online services. This is called **market diversification**.

Key term

Market diversification – expanding a business by offering new products and services

3.3 Opportunities for business efficiency

The increasing availability of the web gives businesses of all kinds the opportunity to speed up their interactions with both suppliers and customers. This can lead to a number of efficiencies.

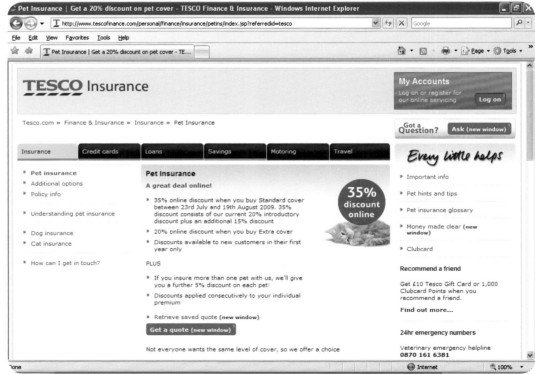

Fig. 12.12: How does the Internet help Tesco to diversify its services?

Supply chain efficiencies

In B2B markets a business is often a link in a 'supply chain'. Such a business will be both a buyer and a seller, buying products from other businesses and selling to others, or private consumers.

A company that manufactures replica strips of football teams, for example, has to buy (or 'procure') the materials it uses before it can sell finished garments to the retail outlets. The Ford Motor Company uses in excess of 10,000 components for each car it produces. Outside firms manufacture individual car components, and they too use other components from other companies. Each company is a link in the supply chain.

For businesses working within supply chains, creating smoother, faster ways of dealing with the firms they regularly buy from – or sell to – can substantially save on costs and get their products to market more quickly.

Many people across an organisation are engaged in supply-chain activities. This involves delivering sales or services to customers, shipping products, negotiating with suppliers and trading partners, managing inventories, tracking orders or other critical tasks. The Internet offers businesses a chance to manage the supply chain, speed up supplies and integrate businesses along the chain.

The case study on the next page about the Irish firm Kingspan is particularly related to how people can work together in supply by using the Internet. It shows how the Internet can be used to enable all firms within a supply chain to share and communicate relevant information. Kingspan encourages its customers to use the web to specify their requirements clearly. This improves their ability to give customers exactly what they need.

If Kingspan becomes aware of technical changes required in cladding or insulation, this information is made available where it is needed. In this way, an integrated response by the different participating firms is made possible. Important external factors such as local regulatory or economic changes that might affect demand (such as unemployment) can be identified, then shared and acted on.

The Internet offers an ideal electronic link between organisations and it has the potential to eliminate distortions in information about market conditions that is crucial to proper business operation.

Participating as a connected business within the supply chain therefore offers businesses a real opportunity to be more informed, efficient and competitive.

One important way in which shared information can be useful is in product planning. Businesses need to make forecasts for buying (procurement) and replacing stocks, or for deciding whether stocks need replacing at all. They may need to make plans for increased (or reduced) production. Should new products be introduced to the market, or existing ones developed?

Remember

A supply chain moves goods along from business to business, eventually to the end consumer. The Internet helps to manage and co-ordinate this, and brings businesses closer together.

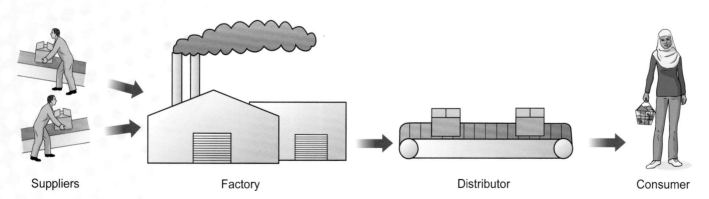

Suppliers   Factory   Distributor   Consumer

Fig. 12.13: A typical supply chain.

Case study: Kingspan

Kingspan Insulated Roof and Wall Systems are part of the Kingspan Group PLC. They are market leaders in the manufacture of superior-quality insulated roof and wall cladding systems for the building industry, and they are based in County Cavan, Ireland.

In 1998 Kingspan appointed a company called Cadapters to develop and launch the www.kingspanpanels.com website – a static site, simply designed to offer company and product information to the industry.

Market information

The market for roof and wall insulation systems works like this.

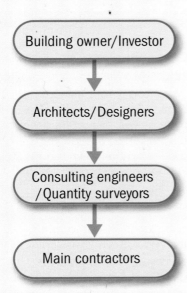

Fig. 12.14: Market information.

Kingspan wanted to create an online ordering system that allowed for fast, accurate order processing. Roofing and cladding contractors, architects or anybody else considering Kingspan products needed to be made to feel that products could easily be researched and specified, and prices clarified, via the website. Added to this would be helpful detailed graphical images of panels and a range of complementary products.

The Kingspan online ordering system has dramatically reduced errors in order processing. The system highlights mistaken combinations in an order and automatically suggests corrections – this would be impossible in a paper-based system. This helps to save time and make the supply of Kingspan products much more efficient.

While 45 out of 47 structural steel contractors in Ireland use the Kingspan ordering system, in the roofing and cladding sector, things have developed more slowly. This sector seems to be less IT literate or confident. Kingspan therefore needed to be able to identify a customer's member of staff who could deal with the information about its products and use its system. IT literacy, combined with Kingspan product understanding, was important if the online system was to work properly.

Kingspan has been at the forefront in innovation using Internet technologies and is influencing the roofing/cladding market. It plans to develop further an entirely online cladding solutions package to meet the different needs of each customer in the market.

(Source: developed with the permission of Tom Prendergast, Kingspan.)

1. Describe the ways in which the supply of Kingspan products has been made more efficient by use of the Internet.

2. In what ways do you think that Kingspan has used the Internet as a marketing opportunity?

3. Evaluate the Kingspan online experience from the point of view of customers. Do you feel they can gain real benefits? If so, how?

Activity: Supply chains

Think of a manufactured product such as a piece of pine furniture. Try to consider the supply chain for this product.

1. Where did the raw materials come from?

2. Where were they assembled?

3. How did the furniture find its way to where it was purchased?

Draft a summary explaining how the Internet can help with such a supply chain.

Remember

Selling directly to consumers cuts out intermediary businesses. This direct channel might cause conflict if you use intermediary businesses for other products you sell.

Opportunities to increase sales from existing customers

Businesses that adopt an Internet **marketing strategy** do so because they can see opportunities either to improve sales within the markets they already serve or to enter completely new markets. As Internet penetration increases and more businesses use an online strategy, the web will become the accepted method for marketing. The car accessories retailer Save and Drive at www.saveanddrive.co.uk secured its business and expanded into new product lines directly by using an Internet strategy.

Key term

Marketing strategy – the general direction in which marketing decisions take a business – for example, a business may be looking to increase its sales overseas or to target a smaller market segment

Did you know?

Services are available to allow a business to measure a website's total audience from PC and mobile Internet users (source: The Nielsen Company).

Case study: UK SMEs missing out?

Managing costs and optimising how a business operates could be the key to finding a successful way out of the economic downturn. The 2009 'Business Pulse' report shows that many UK SMEs find that technologies, such as 'Business social networking', can have interesting ways of generating new customers.

Larger SMEs are more likely to have changed the way they operate during the recession. These firms (101 to 250 staff) were shown to have adopted a more proactive attitude towards technology for business advancement. Technology that is able to merge communications (voicemail, email, etc.) into a single system has shown benefits. Faster broadband speeds have really helped the larger businesses.

The age of people running businesses makes a difference too. The Pulse report showed that 46 per cent of business people under 30 thought it was essential to 'be at the forefront of technological adoption'. Mobile devices, social networking are regarded as vital to the success of younger managers. Younger people also consider 'location independence' as vital.

The 'killer technologies' today for business people are seen as faster broadband, better websites and eCommerce capability, as well as mobile devices. Many firms have now started to use Twitter and Facebook, and develop their own forums for a range of marketing and customer service activities.'

(Source: 'Small Business Week 2009' – Business Pulse Report)

The 2009 report surveyed 7,200 respondents.

1. What advice would you give to an SME manager who simply said, 'Let them get on with ICT; it's business as usual for us'?

2. Write a summary explaining why a business might increase sales from 'Business Social Networking'.

3. In what ways would it be possible for an SME to use networking sites such as Twitter or Facebook to improve their marketing effort?

Opportunities to monitor competitor activity

Businesses must constantly monitor the external forces around them so that they can follow strategies and objectives that will enable them to stay competitive. In an increasingly global business world, competition can come from anywhere. It is best to stay informed.

In 1980, Michael Porter set out a 'five forces' model for business managers to use to watch out for external threats. These were:

- the bargaining power of buyers
- the bargaining power of suppliers
- the threat of substitute products
- barriers to entry
- rivalry between existing competitors.

The Internet offers business leaders a quick and cost-effective way of monitoring what competitor businesses are doing. The case study on Euromonitor (below) illustrates how it is possible to check trends and developments in the market for a single product line.

Opportunities to buy online promotion

There are various forms of online promotion that businesses can buy.

3.4 Search engines

An Internet visitor might type 'flight tickets India' into www.google.co.uk, for example. On the right-hand side of the screen will be a panel showing a list of businesses that have sponsored certain links. Many businesses pay for **search engine advertising** so that their business shows up on the first page of a relevant search.

Activity: Internet marketing

A local entrepreneur has approached the consultancy firm you work for and requested a report on Internet marketing.

Describe the benefits and opportunities to the business of using Internet marketing within the marketing mix of a selected business.

3.5 Promotion on websites

Online advertising is now an important component of some of the most successful campaigns. In just ten years it has overtaken cinema and surpassed radio.

Online display advertising spend rose to over £235 million in 2008, contrasting with a decline in TV and radio advertising spend. Online display advertising is generally used to make a bigger audience aware of a brand but it can also generate direct customer response.

The most obvious form of display advertising is banner ads. If you have spent any time surfing the web, you will have seen plenty of these small rectangular advertisements. Although they vary considerably in subject matter, they all share a basic function: if you click on them, your web browser will take you to the advertiser's website.

Sometimes a business can misjudge the power of the Internet in its promotional effort. The off-licence chain Threshers thought it had a winning idea. However, as the case study on page 309 shows, the Internet can be a monster if marketing ideas go wrong!

Key term

Search engine advertising – paid-for links that are presented by a search engine when a user requests a particular search

Case study: Deodorants in France

Euromonitor International's 'Deodorants in France' report offered a comprehensive guide to the size and shape of the market at a national level. It offered the latest retail sales data, allowing people to identify the sector's driving growth. It identified the leading companies and brands, and offered strategic analysis of key factors influencing the market, whether new product developments,

packaging innovations, economic/lifestyle influences, distribution or pricing issues. Forecasts illustrated how the market was set to change.

(Source: adapted from www.euromonitor.com)

1. What sort of useful data do you think a service such as Euromonitor can offer a business?
2. How do you think this could be used?

Fig. 12.15: Have you ever noticed and clicked on banner ads on the Internet?

Here are some online advertising facts to consider.

- There are now 32 million people online, 65 per cent of the total GB adult population (BMRB Internet Monitor August 2008 and TGI.net wave 15).
- The UK online advertising industry is valued at £1,682.5 million for the first half of 2008, taking a 18.7 per cent share of the UK advertising industry (IAB/PwC, October 2008).
- Search accounts for 58.3 per cent of all online advertising, display 19.8 per cent and classifieds 21.5 per cent. The IAB has continued to track spend on solus email campaigns which accounted for 0.4 per cent of the market (IAB/PwC, October 2008).
- Search revenues grew by 28.7 per cent year-on-year, display by 16.3 per cent and classifieds by 30.2 per cent (IAB/PwC, October 2008).

Did you know?

As consumers spend more time online, brand marketers know that traditional media placement alone does not cut it when targeting their core audiences. Shifting spending to include online advertising is therefore a critical component of any successful media plan (source: The Nielsen Company).

3.6 Links

Businesses can use other low-cost methods of generating traffic to their websites by making sure they have links on other sites.

- **Reciprocal links** are two-way links between two businesses and, as such, they are free.
- **Affiliate links** are agreements whereby a link to your site is placed on another site. In return, the site receives payments for 'click-through' sales.

Case study: Threshers discount vouchers

The First Quench Group went into administration in November 2009 meaning that 391 stores were to close with the loss of over 2,000 jobs. One of the group's brands was the famous Threshers wine stores. Threshers had tried hard to embrace new technology in its marketing and promotional offer, not always with the outcomes that were intended. Three years ago threshers anticipated an onrush of customers after millions of bargain hunters downloaded an online discount offer.

The 40 per cent discount offer was for champagne and wine purchases at 2,500 stores nationwide and applied between 30 November and 10 December 2006. Spokesman for the business, Dirk Kind, said, 'The initial email was sent to our suppliers and we did say it could be sent to friends and family. We knew it was a bit of a grey area but it has just absolutely snowballed way beyond anything we anticipated.'

The chain initially mailed the coupon to a limited number of suppliers at the end of November. It then appeared on the website of Stormhoek, a South African wine company which estimated the coupon

was downloaded more than 800,000 times. The voucher quickly spread among the public by email.

All recipients had to do was print off the coupon, fill it in and present it at a store. Threshers said it would honour all vouchers presented. Kind said the business had not made it clear on the coupons that the offer was intended for limited use.

Robert Dirkovski, head of interactive media at the Direct Marketing Association, said the case demonstrated the power of the Internet.

'The Internet lends itself perfectly to passing things on from your friends and relatives. This "viral marketing" is a very good way for a business to collect data. Once you have taken up the offer, a business can send you emails.'

1. What do you think the Thresher Group had to gain from offering the downloadable 40 per cent vouchers on the web?

2. What lessons (if any) do you think Threshers will have learned? What would you advise?

3. What advice would you have given Threshers in the situation it faced in early December 2006?

Activity: Online promotion

Write a report on at least five different forms of online promotion activity. You should include banner ads, pop-ups, affiliates, reciprocal links and

search engine advertising. Try to illustrate the latter using examples from three different searches.

Assessment activity 12.3

  BTEC

You have been asked to prepare a presentation for a local business about using Internet marketing.

1. Prepare to give a talk, supported by written slides and notes, in which you describe the benefits and opportunities to a specific business in using Internet marketing within its broader marketing mix. **P4**

2. Using your selected business, analyse the marketing opportunities and challenges it faces in using Internet marketing. **M2**

Grading tips

1. You should include a description of both benefits and opportunities for a business. A clue to the structure might be given in the reference to the marketing mix. You might describe the various tactics under the seven Ps and outline benefits and opportunities for each one (for example, product features or availability, promotional material, pricing, personalised menus). **P4**

2. Here you need to look at several of the opportunities that the business is taking up online and carefully analyse what the business is hoping to achieve. Additionally at this level, you should show an awareness of the various challenges facing an online business (for example, meeting orders, increased competition). **M2**

4. Understand the challenges faced by businesses using Internet marketing

While the Internet offers marketing benefits and opportunities, it also throws up many challenges generated by an increasingly global marketplace. These challenges have to be prepared for, faced and overcome if a business is to compete successfully in the online world.

Traditional thinking about business activity looks at the chain of value-adding processes the organisation undertakes – for example:

- acquiring materials
- storing materials
- working with materials to produce something
- packaging the product
- warehousing (storing) it
- marketing it
- selling it
- moving it.

Many modern businesses have grown to encompass several of these spheres of activity within the one organisation. By networking these systems and being able to draw on accurate digital data, a business can connect with the outside world with increased confidence. However, just as the Internet represents a new area of opportunities, so it may cause potential conflict and challenges. Internet activity is measured by the value it adds to the business. If it fails to add value, then the strategy either has been poorly thought through or is inappropriate for the business.

4.1 Competition through global website visibility

The following 'challenges' are threats that online businesses must face.

Disintermediation and channel conflict

The Internet offers the chance to use a direct channel of supply to clients or customers, wherever they are. This process, called disintermediation, is the tendency to cut out the middle man, as illustrated in Fig. 12.16.

This creates obvious efficiencies and savings, but at the danger of destabilising many older traditional channels that might still be valuable sources of revenue to the business. These two scenarios show how this can occur.

- Example 1: A manufacturer sells PCs directly to customers. Several long-established and valued retail outlets for the product object to this and refuse to sell it any more.

- Example 2: A distributor is employed to deal with physical placement of products and is made redundant for some products but not others.

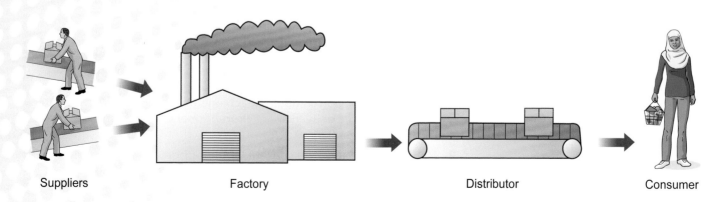

Suppliers   Factory   Distributor   Consumer

Fig. 12.16: A typical supply chain.

Established businesses considering adding an online distribution channel (either to their **buy-side** or **sell-side** channels) therefore have to consider the impact such a move may have on existing methods of distribution. If a new online channel causes problems with an established set of business relationships, this is known as **channel conflict**.

Dave Chaffey argues in *Internet Marketing* (Prentice Hall, 2003) that today's firms have to identify what their core competency is. What do they do best? Once their core business is identified, they can then build key channel partnerships, collaborating with other firms who do other things better. Consider these examples.

- Example 1: A manufacturer works with a retailer to offer better online customer support. Both share customer data. Both work to create the brand identity.

- Example 2: B&Q Direct (at www.diy.com) works in partnership with Spark Response, the latter providing customer service, a call centre, warehousing and product fulfilment.

- Example 3: Ford Motor Corporation in the USA works in collaboration with its dealer network on an 'Internet Approved' programme, giving training and expertise to promote Internet-based customer relationships. In this way, Ford has developed direct customer relationships over the Internet without conflicting with its highly valued dealership network.

Payment security

Consumers are often concerned about **payment security** with transactions via the Internet. There are frequent stories about attacks by hackers, 'identity theft' and so on – all of which leave us feeling vulnerable. Therefore, many people are reluctant to give their credit or debit card numbers online, which deprives them of access to products and services that cannot be found elsewhere.

Whether a business sells to private consumers or other businesses, payment transactions are necessary. It is a matter of management policy how payments are to be taken, and how to reassure potential customers. Cost considerations, security considerations, customer service and image considerations have to be taken into account. If a business refuses credit cards, there will always be other businesses that will accept them. It is a question of keeping up with the competition.

Did you know?

The major issue for many consumers and corporate organisations is security. For online customers to verify that they are in a secure connection, it is necessary to take two elements into account. Firstly, if the page is in secure connection mode, the URL begins with 'https' ('s' for secure). Secondly, a padlock icon, which indicates security in the closed position, is present on the browser and shows the level of 'encryption' (for Internet Explorer). This means the data has been scrambled so it cannot be read by a third party.

Key terms

Buy-side – the part of the business in which orders originate

Sell-side – refers to firms that take orders from buy-side firms

Channel conflict – where the introduction of an Internet sales channel threatens relationships with businesses working in existing channels

Payment security – setting up online payments systems so that customers' personal details remain hidden

Fig. 12.17: Direct selling.

Meeting customer expectations

The Internet continues to raise customer expectations and this is a challenge to all online business. The 24/7 availability and convenience of the Internet has been reinforced with increased personalisation and price transparency. Even more importantly, customers are starting to expect higher levels of reliability, responsiveness, convenience and speed – speed in terms of both the time taken visiting the website and in delivery of items once the order is placed. Taken together, these are heavy demands on the online business.

We have seen that through the Internet, merchandise is becoming available in mass customised form, enabling customers to enter personal measurements online (for, say, a pair of jeans) before ordering or to configure their machines (such as a computer) when they order it. Customers will increasingly demand or expect this one-to-one online attention.

The process of engaging the customer is fundamental to good online marketing. Yet it generates a fierce level of expectation that what is asked for *is* delivered and that every scrap of supporting information is available and correct. A beautifully constructed website, with tremendously informative content, competitive prices,

and smooth and easy transaction arrangements all count for zero (or less than zero) if a customer's product or service expectations are not fulfilled.

A Forrester Technographics survey of 9,000 users who had made online purchases found that 80 per cent of them had visited a manufacturer's site first before visiting the retailer selling the item. These people then revisited throughout the buying cycle and knew exactly what they wanted. Buyers on the Internet are increasingly showing this willingness to bypass the retailer to get product information. They are usually well informed.

Remember

Online customer expectations are very high – higher than in an offline environment.

The challenge for online marketers is to anticipate and understand what customer expectations will be, whatever the market context. One of the best-known failures of the dot.com boom was a US online delivery service called Kozmo. This was a retailer promising free delivery of any online order. The idea was born in

How can websites meet customer expectations?

New York City, where many people living in high-level apartments might decide they suddenly want a DVD or a pizza at any time. The business proved to be neither realistic nor cost-effective.

Marketing should lead to customer expectations being satisfied profitably – so the moral is: do not make outrageous promises.

A business strategy for managing customer expectations has been suggested by Chaffey in *Internet Marketing* as follows.

- Find out what customers expect by doing some research. Include in the site a feedback form if necessary. Always work to rectify any shortcomings.

- Make realistic promises and communicate them clearly. Do not make impossible promises.

- Deliver commitments with the help of staff as well as physical fulfilment.

> ### Did you know?
> Online marketing services are available that can provide businesses with a visual map to give a comprehensive understanding of key brand information (source: The Nielsen Company).

Overload of market feedback

Internet marketing opens up a business to the entire global market it hopes to serve, as well as its customers and its competitors. As a result, the business will accumulate a massive amount of data, and its employees and systems can quickly be overloaded. There is therefore a need, at the outset, to consider the kind of data that is crucial to the business and from that, to think of the processes and information systems necessary for handling that data.

In B2B markets especially, customer profiles are usefully built up. Customer profiles characterise each customer in terms of the products they have bought. This sort of information helps to place customers in their **market segment** and the business can form an appropriate marketing relationship with them. It is vital to capture the relevant information and act appropriately on it.

Businesses need to be aware that information is not knowledge – data has to be interpreted and made sense of. What does it mean? Managers and individual staff within the organisation should have good access to relevant data, assistance with its interpretation and the ability to act on it. This of course generates more information and so the cycle goes on. Eventually, however, the sheer volume of profiles and the complexity of the data can create overload. This is known as **information fatigue**.

There are many specialist marketing advisory services available to help businesses make good use of marketing information.

> ### Did you know?
> Factsheets, reports and guides from Scavenger (www.scavenger.net) could provide vital reading for anyone starting up a business in the UK. The Business Opportunity Profiles are downloadable reports on specific UK industries. With over 800 reports in total, the range includes everything from 'Children's Day Nursery' profiles to 'Coffee Shop' profiles to a profile on 'Wedding Planners' (source: Bytestart.co.uk).

Many organisations incorporate a FAQ panel on their website. Most serious online businesses also include an email address and telephone number within a 'Contact us' link. This facility is likely to generate a considerable degree of customer feedback. The online business must be prepared to allocate resources designed to deal with this effectively, otherwise it risks damaging its reputation. If necessary, large portions of an Internet marketing strategy may need to be revised in response to aspects of feedback. The business must process feedback and be prepared to act on it if required.

> ### Remember
> Online businesses can successfully acquire a lot of market data. However, the business has to sort and prioritise this before it can act on it.

> ### Key terms
> **Market segment** – a group of people or organisations sharing one or more characteristics that cause them to have similar product and/or service needs
>
> **Information fatigue** – having so much data that it becomes meaningless and impossible to use

Keeping pace with technological change

As Internet business gathers pace, most businesses in competitive markets are facing up to the challenges of whether to go online, what to do, when to do it and how. Technological change has always been with us. Without it, there would have been no progress at all. Our own economy has evolved from agriculture to manufacturing, and in recent times to services. These days we are evolving into a digital economy in which change is accelerating at a quicker pace than ever before. Businesses are under pressure to innovate (find new ways of doing things) in virtually all markets.

Businesses must respond to new ways of working. The digital economy is a **knowledge-based economy**, based on providing better products, faster and more efficiently than others. In this economy, speed wins – and for management this adds pressure.

Remember

Businesses today must constantly keep pace with change. Look back at the case study on page 306 about UK SMEs.

Key term

Knowledge-based economy – an economy based on the creation of advanced information services that inform both businesses and citizens

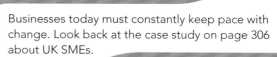

Case study: Wolters Kluwer

Three years ago publisher Wolters Kluwer has invested nearly £1 million in business intelligence tools that are increasing the effectiveness of its marketing campaigns.

The company, which publishes both print and electronic materials on health, safety, legal and finance issues, has grown by acquisition and in the process acquired several sets of customers that it did not necessarily know a lot about. Data existed about which publications and services customers subscribed to, but it was locked up in separate systems, which made it difficult to get a quick view of each account. Because of this, Wolters Kluwer's marketing team had a difficult time working out which of its products to pitch to which customers.

The company asked for quotations from software suppliers and chose SAS marketing automation software. Turner said, 'It could do all we needed it to do.' He also liked the 'joined-up approach' of the SAS products. The other short-listed option entailed buying software components from a lot of different vendors and 'gluing them together', he said.

The result has been more targeted and lucrative marketing campaigns. During a seven-week pilot of the SAS software earlier in 2006, response rates went up and one campaign returned three times the expected revenue.

The availability of up-to-date customer profiles means marketing staff are able to plan more

strategically, said Wolters Kluwer's Turner. They can now figure out which products customers might be interested in and which formats – email, direct mail, telemarketing – are most effective.

The new system has proved fairly easy for workers to learn – after just a few months, the vast majority of users are comfortable with it and 'can't imagine life without it', said Turner.

Another benefit is that staff will no longer be needed to maintain older databases which contained customer info, as all the data has been migrated to the new system – and these staff can now be redeployed elsewhere.

Turner said if the company continues to see the benefits and savings it has experienced so far, it is on track to meet the board's goal of a return on investment over the next three years, which is worth 'just short of £1 million', according to Turner. 'So far the project has stuck to our schedule, goals and objectives,' he said.

(Source: adapted from 'Publisher gets smart about marketing', by Sylvia Carr, 28 November 2006, www.silicon.com)

1. In your opinion, why does Wolters Kluwer feel it needs better 'business intelligence'?

2. Explain how Wolters Kluwer has been able to use the better business intelligence to their marketing advantage. How, in your view, has their marketing work improved?

Ensuring maximum exposure through ISPs and search engines

Internet Service Providers

Internet Service Providers (ISPs) are firms that offer an Internet connection service to both private householders and businesses. Their primary function is to provide a link to the Internet, and many ISPs also host websites on their own servers.

The crucial point for business management is to ensure that the ISP is offering a satisfactory level of service for a reasonable price. ISPs have to be able to deal with fluctuating and perhaps growing traffic. Speed of access is crucial. We have seen earlier that customers online demand speed. One way of helping in this respect is to have a dedicated server – that is, one which is serving only content from your business. Additionally, bandwidth is an important factor in the speed of content delivery. The bigger the bandwidth, the quicker data can pass (like a pipe). Bandwidth is measured in kilobits (1,000 bits) per second and is written as Kbps. A typical modem operates at 56.6 Kbps. This is the bandwidth that small businesses often use.

A further issue with ISPs is the amount of time that a website is made available to customers. Ideally a business needs to ensure that the site is available 24/7.

Not all sites are made available 100 per cent of the time and this means lost revenue.

Search engines

Search engines are extremely important for the promotion of a website, as we saw earlier. More than 80 per cent of web users are known to use them and if a business has not registered with the search engines, it is unlikely to be found unless it has an extremely well-known brand name. Registration and website design are basic and fundamental to the site profile – registration for making the search engines aware of the site and website design for elevating the site in the search engine listings. There has been a growing trend, too, for businesses to use paid-for listings ('sponsored links').

Security and payment systems

As the following chart in Fig. 12.18 shows, the Internet has become a global phenomenon within an increasingly global marketplace.

Millions of Internet-based business transactions are taking place every minute. Confidential, sensitive and potentially damaging company data is increasingly accessible over the Internet. Viruses, hackers and other undesirables are a constant danger. Malicious individuals or firms can attack a business's data, make fraudulent claims or simply attempt to steal the data.

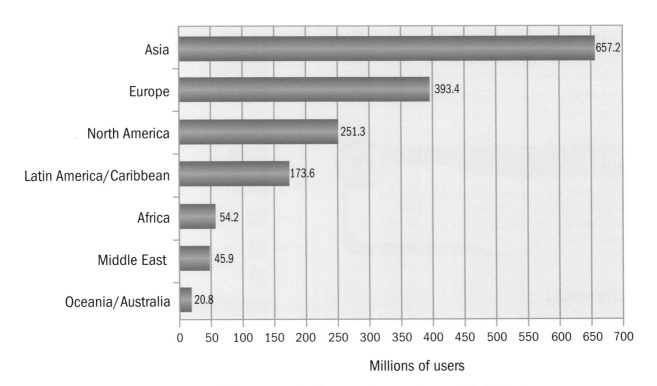

Fig. 12.18: Internet users in the world by geographical regions (source: Internet World Stats).

At least half of all credit card fraud is known to be Internet-related; for the e-tailer (retailer selling on the Internet) there is a significant risk of fraudulent purchases. Repudiation of orders (ordering goods online, and then denying it) is a common problem. Private consumers are just as open to attack. Consumer reassurance is a primary marketing task for an online business.

The challenge for business leaders is therefore to plan for security. This means, right at the outset, devising an e-business strategy that takes security issues seriously. There are several ways of doing this.

- **Authorisation** – the business determines who has access to certain applications and information. It establishes a consistent policy and ensures this is centrally controlled and monitored.

- **Encryption** – this is a method of changing data into a hidden format. The actual meaning of text, numbers or symbols becomes almost impossible to recognise by anyone other than those who have access to the 'key' that translates it back again. Businesses in the digital world have to embrace encryption. Confidential documents such as contracts, personal data, pricing details and product research data are vulnerable to theft or attack. Encryption of emails is the equivalent of slotting a document into a sealed envelope to keep it private. Both SSL (Secure Sockets Layer) and SET (Secure Electronic Transactions) are standards that ensure the encryption of Internet traffic. SET encompasses a whole payments system, while SSL encrypts only traffic between a web browser and server.

- **Authentication** – customers must identify themselves through a login and password procedure.

Remember

Online consumers are naturally worried about security of personal information when they make purchases. An online business must reassure customers that the order process is secure and safe.

Legal complexity

If you buy a product from an online retailer based in the USA and it is shipped to you, only for you to find that you are not satisfied with the product, whose legal system applies – the UK's or the USA's? What rate of taxation, if any, applies to the purchase?

A business setting up a website to sell across Europe, possibly worldwide, must satisfy the legal requirements that might exist in the different European or other nation states.

In 2002 the European Union enforced an Electronic Commerce Directive which was designed to set a framework for electronic commerce in the EU. There is little doubt that a business needs to consider legal regulations if it is intending to sell online. The UK government's BERR website offers information services for small businesses (www.berr.gov.uk).

Linguistic and cultural sensitivity

As use of the Internet continues to grow, more and more users are expected to be non-English speakers. English-speaking audiences are not likely to dominate the Internet for long.

It is important for any business that is seriously attempting to expand to consider translations on their site. However, creating literal translations from one language to another is not as straightforward as it might appear. Here are a few examples of translations that went disastrously wrong!

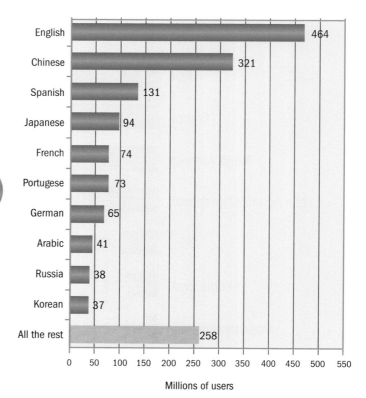

Fig. 12.19: Top ten languages in the Internet millions of users (source: Internet World Stats).

- The Pepsi slogan 'Come alive with the Pepsi generation' was translated into Taiwanese as 'Pepsi will bring your ancestors back from the dead'.
- The Kentucky Fried Chicken slogan 'Finger-lickin' good' came out as 'Eat your fingers off' in Chinese.
- US car manufacturers General Motors realised why it was not selling any of its Chevrolet Novas in South America when it found out that 'no va' meant 'it will not go'. The company renamed the car the 'Caribe' for Spanish markets.

It is also important to be aware that adding translations is only the first step. A website must also take account of users' cultural expectations, which vary around the world.

> **Did you know?**
>
> Alibaba (www.alibaba.com) is a leading B2B e-commerce company based in China. It provides a marketplace connecting small- and medium-sized buyers and suppliers in China to the rest of the world (source: DaveChaffey.com).

> **Remember**
>
> Cultural differences need to be taken into account when a business sets up a website that is intended for overseas markets.

Cultural attitudes to payments

A report by NetSmartAmerica ('America.com: What makes America click') showed that 70 per cent of online shoppers in the USA paid by credit card. In Japan, the most common payment method was cash on delivery. A spin-off from this was that in Japan many more websites were obliged to be membership-based, as this enables members to pay by direct bank deposit.

Cultural issues for designers and marketers

Web designers of the future will increasingly need to consider cultural differences at great length. Differences in perception are significant. Oriental scripts (Japanese, Korean, Chinese) are justified and read vertically, and Arabic is read from right to left, whereas English is read from left to right. These differences are significant. Will a Chinese user find a left-justified web page appealing?

Some societies can be said to be very family- or group-oriented (China, for example), while others are much more individualistic (USA, UK, Western Europe). This difference needs to be reflected in marketing communications. Get the message wrong and real long-term online damage can be caused. In marketing, as you know by now, it is vital to know your market.

Assessment activity 12.4

You have been asked to prepare some background information in readiness for a meeting with the management of a local business by responding to the following tasks.

1. Select a particular business to use as an example and explain how Internet marketing has made it more efficient, effective and successful. **P5**
2. Explain the challenges of globalisation facing a selected business when using the Internet as a marketing tool. **P6**

Grading tips

1. You need to consider each of the factors mentioned in the criteria. How can Internet marketing create efficiency or effectiveness, and how do these lead to success? One way could relate to direct selling by missing out the middle man; another way could be because customers get lots of product information, cutting out chances of making mistakes; another factor could be global visibility. There is much content to be found throughout this unit relating to these things. **P5**

2. There are many challenges caused by globalisation. The most obvious is the challenge of responding to increasing competition from all over the world, particularly from economies in Asia, where labour costs are low. How can a UK-based business offer something better? In what ways can the Internet help? **P6**

Just checking

1. What do you understand to be the main purpose of marketing?
2. List at least four ways in which the Internet helps a business to find out about its customers.
3. Describe what is meant by targeting customers.
4. Describe what is meant by segmenting a market.
5. Describe and give three examples of personalisation of web pages.
6. What do you understand by the term mass customisation?
7. How could the Internet offer customers improved purchasing value?
8. What is dynamic pricing?
9. List and describe three ways in which businesses can use Internet marketing opportunities.
10. Describe three challenges that a business going online might have to face. Why are they challenges?

edexcel

Assignment tips

1. When you are investigating the ways in which organisations use the Internet to help their marketing function, start with the first four Ps in the marketing mix. How could the Internet help with pricing, placement, product and promotion? Then develop your work to extend your analysis by including the other elements such as people, personalisation and process.

2. To make sure you use contrasting organisations, see if you can include a public sector and a voluntary organisation as well as a private business. If you would prefer to stick to the private sector, choose businesses in different economic sectors – for example, insurance, retail and manufacturing.

3. When you give a presentation, always remember to give it a clear structure. What are you going to say? Say it. What have you said? Do not feel embarrassed. It is the content that matters.

4. When you are asked to think about the challenges of using the Internet, consider things from the point of view of inside the organisation. Can staff cope if there is increased demand? Will orders be fulfilled? Does the business have the capacity to deal with things? Is the organisational structure OK?

13 Recruitment and selection in business

Recruitment and selection describes the process that organisations follow to attract potential employees and then choose the best person for the job. It is important that a business gets this right so that they can get employees who will be happy and work hard.

This unit will take you through the stages of recruitment and selection. You will learn about the processes involved before a vacancy is advertised and the reasons why a business might need to recruit additional staff. You will learn the difference between vacancies that are advertised inside the business and those outside the business. As part of this process, you will become familiar with the different paperwork that is involved and how the selection of candidates is made at each stage from the application form through to a selection interview, where the successful person is offered the job.

Recruitment and selection must comply with legislation from the UK and European Union, so you need to be aware of different laws that have been brought into force and the effect they have on recruitment – for example, equal opportunities and minimum wage. You will be given an insight into some of the ethical issues that relate to recruitment and selection, such as making sure every candidate is asked the same questions to ensure that everyone is treated equally.

Learning outcomes

After completing this unit, you should:

1. know the processes involved in recruitment planning
2. understand the implications of the regulatory framework for the process of recruitment and selection
3. be able to prepare documentation involved in the selection and recruitment process
4. be able to participate in a selection interview.

Assessment and grading criteria

This table shows you what you must do in order to achieve a **pass**, **merit** or **distinction** grade, and where you can find activities in this book to help you.

To achieve a **pass** grade, the evidence must show that the learner is able to:	To achieve a **merit** grade, the evidence must show that, in addition to the pass criteria, the learner is able to:	To achieve a **distinction** grade, the evidence must show that, in addition to the pass and merit criteria, the learner is able to:
P1 identify how two organisations plan recruitment using internal and external sources **See Assessment activity 13.1, page 329.**		
P2 explain the impact of the legal and regulatory framework on recruitment and selection activities **See Assessment activity 13.2, page 333.**		
P3 prepare the documents used in selection and recruitment activities **See Assessment activity 13.3, page 342.**	**M1** compare the purposes of the different documents used in the selection and recruitment process of a given organisation **See Assessment activity 13.3, page 342.**	**D1** evaluate the usefulness of the documents in the interview pack for a given organisation, in facilitating the interview process **See Assessment activity 13.3, page 342.**
P4 plan to take part in a selection interview **See Assessment activity 13.4, page 353.**	**M2** analyse your contribution to the selection process in a given situation **See Assessment activity 13.4, page 353.**	**D2** evaluate your experience of planning and participating in the recruitment and selection process **See Assessment activity 13.4, page 353.**
P5 take part in a selection interview **See Assessment activity 13.4, page 353.**		

How you will be assessed

To achieve Unit 13, you will investigate and prepare for recruitment and selection. This means you will produce documents, make judgements about their use and actually take part in an interview situation.

Iokasti

I have always been interested in working in human resources, so I found this unit really interesting. I really enjoyed the part that related to body language. I did not realise how important this was before. I now know that most of what I do rather than what I say will influence what others think about me.

Knowing the differences between documents in the recruitment process and looking at the best templates for those has also helped me to produce higher-quality documents myself.

Taking part in the interview process was so enlightening. We had a local employer who came in to do the interview, so I was really nervous. However, she gave us lots of hints and tips on how we could continue to improve in the future and it was very useful when I went for my university interview.

Overall, I have really enjoyed this unit and believe that it has not only developed my understanding but has also given me real practical skills that I can use at work.

Your experience of work

In pairs, think about how you have applied for part-time jobs or work experience placements that you have completed.

1. How did you actually communicate with the employer?

2. What information did you outline or send?

3. What happened in the interview situation?

4. How did you receive feedback on the process?

Now draw a diagram of the process that can be displayed on the classroom wall.

1. Know the processes involved in recruitment planning

The first stage of recruitment that you may be aware of is as an **applicant**. This is after the organisation has placed the advertisement and you have applied for it, but a lot of work happens before this stage. Part of recruitment planning involves the organisation working out if they need to recruit anyone at all. There may be lots of reasons why an organisation may think about recruiting. The organisation will then need to consider whether to undertake **internal recruitment** or **external recruitment**, and how that process is going to take place. You will need to be aware of the different possible methods and influences on which choices an organisation makes.

1.1 Recruitment planning

Reasons for a vacancy

There are many different reasons that an organisation may decide to recruit someone to a position. The most common reason is that someone is leaving to go and work for another organisation, and their position needs to be filled. There are lots of other reasons that may also be possible, as shown in Fig. 13.1.

The person being recruited for the vacancy may be needed to work on a **temporary** or **permanent** basis. A person may be recruited to cover another employee when they go on to maternity leave or if they are ill for a long time and their work needs to be done

by someone else. This work would be as part of a temporary contract.

Sometimes vacancies happen because the business is getting busier or needing to expand, perhaps to another country or area. The organisation would need to find additional employees to work for them and provide resources and training for them.

Key terms

Applicant – the name given to the person applying for a job

Internal recruitment – recruiting someone who already works for the business to do a different job

External recruitment – recruiting from outside the business

Temporary – for a limited amount of time specified – for example, a month or a year

Permanent – until that person decides to leave or the job ceases to exist

Fig. 13.1: Different reasons for recruitment.

Case study: Dr Oetker

In March 2009, Dr Oetker, who are responsible for the production of Pizza Ristorante, were reported as considering moving some of their production from Germany to Lancashire. Increasing production often means it is necessary to recruit additional staff to cope with the extra tasks that need to be performed. In small groups, work through the following questions.

1. Which types of vacancy might Dr Oetker require when moving production from Germany to the UK?

2. What might happen if they did not recruit the right staff?

3. What effect would their recruitment have on the local area?

4. Which other factors should be taken into account when moving production from one country to another?

Functional skills

English: Practise your speaking and listening skills by listening to other people and contributing relevant and useful suggestions to the discussion.

Did you know?

According to Energise (2009, www.liberateyourtalent.com) there will be huge changes needed to the way that employers recruit and treat employees. Energise predict that:

- due to increasing road congestion, employers will need to recruit more home workers
- more young people will be setting up their own businesses and will need support to do so
- people will retire later and therefore will need to work longer
- employers who develop flexible working practices will recruit and retain the best employees.

Organisations are changing as well as expanding, so although the amount or volume of work may not go up in an organisation, the type of work that is needed may change and this may need new staff to be recruited.

Some organisations will need to recruit to cover their female staff if they decide to take maternity leave to have a baby. In 2009, mothers were entitled to up to 52 weeks' maternity leave and maternity pay for some of that period. Employers need to be able to cover this leave and so will employ temporary staff as cover. New regulations were also proposed in September 2009 to make maternity leave more flexible and allow it to be shared with new fathers as paternity leave, instead of just providing the statutory two weeks' leave. This might mean that a mother and father could share the leave between them.

Activity: Maternity and paternity regulations

1. Look up the changes in the regulations for paternity leave flexibility and find out whether the regulations were agreed and in force for April 2011.

2. At the same time, it was also proposed that maternity leave should be extended from being paid for nine months to a full year. Find out if these changes were also agreed. What would be the advantages and disadvantages of this change?

Sometimes employees are ill and employers also need to cover for illness. The length of time for cover will depend on how long the person is going to be off. Other employees may be able to cope with extra work for a week or so, but if someone is going to be off for weeks or months, someone may need to be employed to cover.

Decision to recruit

Before an organisation actually recruits a new person to do the job, it will make sure that it really needs to recruit that person permanently and that the work cannot be done by somebody else. You may have heard of organisations being 'restructured'. This is when an organisation has looked at the employees working for it and has decided that rather than recruiting someone into the same job, they will redivide the work in the organisation.

The organisation may also look at how productive its employees are being. This means how much work they are producing per person. The organisation may decide that some people have capacity to do extra work so they do not need to recruit a new person to cover the difference. To be competitive, businesses need to be very careful about how they spend their money; therefore, if they are able to save money on staff costs, they may do so.

A further decision that an organisation may consider is whether or not the vacancy is going to exist in the future or if technology might replace the need for the person's job. Many organisations work online so staff in shops or branches may not be needed, but staff in call centres or staff operating online services may need to increase. Organisations will take this into account.

Once the decision has been made about whether to recruit or not, the next stage of the process is to consider how to recruit and whether or not the person chosen should come from inside or outside the organisation.

Internal recruitment

Internal recruitment means that the person recruited to do the job will be taken from inside the organisation. This means that the person will already have an idea of the type of organisation that they are working for and the skills needed to work there. Sometimes this type of recruitment will also give current employees the chance for promotion or additional responsibility, so it can be motivating for them.

Organisations will sometimes decide to advertise a vacancy internally first; if no suitable employees apply for this job, they will advertise outside as well. Of course, if a vacancy is advertised internally and someone changes jobs to fill the role, somebody new may be needed to replace them in turn. This may extend the recruitment process and may be a problem for the organisation if they need to recruit quickly.

Table 13.1 lists some of the key advantages and disadvantages of recruiting internally.

Table 13.1: Advantages and disadvantages of recruiting internally.

Advantages	Disadvantages
Cheap to advertise	Limited choice of candidates
All candidates known to the organisation	May cause problems among employees due to the change
Candidates also already know the organisation	Employees may be stuck in their ways
More likely to have smaller number of applicants	May not generate new ideas
Can encourage career progression	The successful candidate will need to be replaced, needing another recruitment plan

External recruitment

External recruitment is the opposite of internal and is the process of recruiting from outside the organisation. There are a number of ways this can be done and these include the organisation recruiting themselves or making use of job centres, consultants and recruitment agencies.

Table 13.2: Advantages and disadvantages of external recruitment.

Advantages	Disadvantages
Higher number of candidates	Takes longer
Candidates may have new ideas	Person appointed may not be as good as they appear
Potential for new skills to be brought into the organisation	More expensive to advertise

Organisations recruiting new employees externally will need to manage every part of the recruitment process themselves from deciding the type of skills and salary needed for that employee to where to advertise the vacancy to get the right type of applicants. You will learn more about advertising on page 326.

An organisation may not able to manage the process of recruiting themselves because they are too busy or do not feel able to do it. They may therefore decide to use other agencies. Job Centres are popular places for employers to advertise vacancies as this is where people go to get advice on different jobs and benefits that they may be entitled to. Job Centres work with employers to provide additional training and support to local areas so that employees can be found to fill vacancies that are needed. Many job vacancies are available online for people looking for work (www.jobcentreplus.co.uk) so it is a popular method of recruitment. Job Centres are also able to offer employers extra training and support so that they can recruit employees, for example, by giving advice on recruitment from other countries within the EU or how to manage vacancies.

Some employers prefer to work with consultants to manage their vacancies. Specialist consultants can give advice and work with employers to give suggestions about where and how to recruit.

Consultants may also work with prospective applicants to find out whether or not they would be suited to a particular organisation or job vacancy. They will then match the applicant to the right organisation for a fee. This means that the organisation will not have to spend time working with people who are unsuitable.

Recruitment agencies work in a similar way to consultants in that they provide employers with details about potential applicants. Often recruitment agencies will provide staff on a temporary or permanent basis. This means that an employer may have a chance to see how an employee is likely to work out by putting them on to a three-, six- or twelve-month contract first. This is a cost-effective option often for employers, particularly if their business changes rapidly and they may not need to keep staff permanently.

Table 13.3: Advantages and disadvantages of using an agency.

Benefits of using an agency or consultant	Disadvantages of using an agency or consultant
The organisation can concentrate on running the business and not looking for new employees.	The organisation must pay the agent and the new employee, adding to costs.
The organisation does not have to employ a recruitment team.	The agency/consultant may not find the right person for the job as the agent does not work within the organisation.
The agency/consultant will have access to lots of different people and will screen out those unsuitable.	They may not care as much about employing the right person for the job as someone working for the organisation.
They will not tell competitor organisations that you are recruiting, but your own advertisements will.	
They can offer specialist support or people for the area needing recruitment.	
They can offer advice about what is happening in the employment area.	

Activity: Jefferson Maguire

Jefferson Maguire is a headhunting agency based in Hampshire. They recruit employees for leading companies including M&S, Harrods, Littlewoods and Thorntons. Their activities include:

- targeting high achievers
- presenting candidates to clients
- interviewing candidates
- helping candidates to resign from their current employer.

They also conduct assessment days so that employers can receive details about applicants' previous knowledge, experience and ability before the recruitment process starts.

In pairs, answer the following questions.

1. What is a recruitment agency?
2. What are the advantages and disadvantages to businesses of using headhunters to recruit new members of staff?
3. 'Headhunters are only useful to recruit the most senior employees.' Discuss the extent to which you agree with this view.

Functional skills

English: Practise your speaking and listening skills by listening to the other person and contributing relevant and useful suggestions to the answers for the questions.

Cost and time considerations of external sourcing

External sourcing of applicants means the process of sourcing employees from outside the organisation. Recruiting new employees, whether it is being done directly or through an agency, takes a long time and can require a lot of money. This is because time is needed to outline the vacancy and the type of person required, for the advertising and then the selection process itself. In addition, if an applicant is already working for another organisation, they will have to work their notice. The amount of notice required will depend on the type of job but it could be anything from one week to six months. If it is not possible to fill an empty vacancy when the current employee leaves, this may cause a problem for an organisation and therefore damage its customer service or even its reputation or results. If an employee is recruited from within the organisation, this is less likely to happen and they may be able to move more quickly to their new post.

Cost is another factor when considering external sourcing. The cost of recruitment should be measured in two ways: the cost to actually advertise or the fee that needs to be paid to an agency for recommending an employee, and **opportunity cost**. Money that is spent on external recruitment cannot be spent elsewhere in the business, so this is an opportunity cost for that organisation.

Key terms

Work their notice – the time an employee must work for their current employer before they are allowed to move to their new job

Opportunity cost – the cost to an organisation of making one decision over another – the cost of the lost opportunity

Did you know that internal advertising is often completed by email?

1.2 Recruitment advertising

Once the decision to recruit has been made and the choice as to whether or not that vacancy should be advertised internally or externally has been made, the process of actually getting the advertisement into circulation needs to take place.

Internal advertising

Internal advertising is the simpler of the two types of advertising for a vacancy. This is because it only needs to be shown to employees who currently work for the organisation. There are a number of ways this can take place and these include the staff notice board, email, web page, company magazine or staff meeting. The details of the job need to be given, together with any increase in pay or responsibilities. These must be made available to all members of staff so they can decide whether or not they want to apply. Organisations sometimes ask employees to provide a 'declaration of interest' for a vacancy. This means that they write a letter to their employer or speak to their employer about why they are interested in a particular job and why. The employer can then see how many potential people would apply for an advertised job and make a decision as to whether this is the best way to recruit.

External advertising

External advertising is more complicated than internal advertising, as it can be achieved in a number of different ways. Some organisations use newspapers or radio, others a poster in a window, some keep an up-to-date list of interested people to email and others rely on industry-related magazines. Online advertising through websites is becoming increasingly popular. The most suitable place to advertise a post is where potential applicants will read it. Advertising, as you have already learned, may also be done by using an agency or job centre.

One of the cheapest methods of advertising a position is a poster in the window of a business or on a notice board. You may have seen this type of notice when you were looking for a part-time job. Employers will put it in the window and anyone in the local area will see it and then may decide to apply. Any applicants will already know a bit of information about the company. This type of advertising does limit the number of possible people applying, because only those who have been past or in to the organisation will see it.

Online advertising is also becoming a popular method of recruiting new employees. Many employers have a section of their website devoted to giving details about possible vacancies with the organisation. This means that access to vacancies is possible from outside the country and 24 hours per day, which makes it very time-effective. If the advertisement is hosted on the organisation's own website, it may also be free. The problem with this method of advertising is that applicants need to keep going back to the site to see if there are any vacancies, and applicants who may not really be interested might apply just to see how they would get on. To avoid this problem, some organisations use an external agency to host the advertisement for them. One such online recruitment agency is www.fish4.co.uk. They advertise vacancies on behalf of employers and agencies in one place so that potential applicants can source them. Potential employees are also able to advertise their skills and CV on the site so they can be seen by employers.

Activity: Employer guide

Produce a guide for employers detailing the critical information that is needed within any recruitment advertisement. Remember to give justification for those choices.

PLTS

Practise your creative thinking skills to think of all the critical information that employers need.

As well as advertising online with a recruitment agency, many organisations still make use of recruitment agencies to advertise their vacancies both online and offline. Some agencies have posters in the window for people to go in and look at potential new jobs. Using the local and national newspaper is also still a popular way for both agencies and individual organisations to recruit. Many newspapers offer employers the opportunity to have their advertisement seen in print and online, so they have access to two audiences.

Radio is also used if employers are looking to recruit a number of people at the same time and want to interview them as a large group at an event like a recruitment fair.

Advertising can be very expensive and take a lot of time. The cost will depend on where the vacancy is advertised. Many organisations have a 'house style' for their advertisements. This means that they will use the same layout for each vacancy they advertise. This is very important for external advertising, as it makes it easy for potential applicants to recognise a job opportunity with the organisation. Sometimes the advertisement might have the company logo on it or be printed in a particular text or a particular colour. The size of the advertisement will also be important as employers or agencies usually pay per square centimetre in a printed newspaper. Many organisations choose to advertise all their vacancies in one place so it makes it easier for people to see how many vacancies they have at one time. Other organisations, for cost reasons, use smaller advertisements without their logo or further information.

The type of advertisement will depend on the job. The advertisement will be based on the job description and person specification (see page 335) already produced. Vacancies for some jobs may include a lot of information including pay and conditions written into the advertisement itself, whereas senior managerial jobs may have pay and conditions negotiable.

A further consideration of advertising externally is that employers must make sure that they take into account the legal implications of recruitment advertising. You will learn more legislation relating to recruitment on page 330. External advertising to comply with the law must be fair and not discriminate. This means that advertising that stops equal access for everyone must be avoided, whether this is on the grounds of age, sex, race, sexual orientation or anything else. Making sure that an advertisement complies with legislation is very important. Mistakes can be costly if employers are fined as result of it being proven that their advertisements were discriminatory. As a result of the Employment Equality (Age) Regulations 2006 that came into force on 1 October 2006, employers now also need to be careful when wording advertisements to ensure that they do not contain words that may be linked to age such as 'mature' or 'lively'. This is because applicants must not be treated any differently because of their age.

these on page 337.
Letters make use of traditional post so the time taken to send the application in needs to be taken in to account when drafting the advertisement. It should also take into account the amount of time needed to send out an information pack, if necessary, to applicants. This can make the process quite lengthy.

PLTS

Practise your self-management skills to carry out this research.

Activity: Recruitment advertisement

Read the recruitment advertisement below that was advertised in your local paper and answer the following questions in small groups.

1. Which information is missing from the advertisement and what do you notice about its quality?

2. What are the advantages and disadvantages of using the local paper to advertise for vacancies externally?

3. To what extent does the quality of the advertisement affect the number of people applying for the job?

WANTED

Part-Time Administration Asssistant

£200 per week

39 hours per week

Please write or fone for more infomation to

C Wythe

Enterprising Solutions Ltd

Tickleton Road

Lorrencester

LR4 8PQ

Fig. 13.2: Example of a job advertisement.

Methods of application

When an advertisement is put out so that people can apply, the employer must clearly outline how they actually want people to apply. There are three main methods that are used, which are letter, online and telephone.

Letter

This is the traditional method of application. A letter is requested to be sent in with either an application form or curriculum vitae. You will learn more about

Online

Online applications are becoming increasingly popular. They take two main forms; the email application and the online application form. Email applications are very similar to the letter application but instead of sending the information through the post, it is emailed, which makes it much quicker. Some employers will ask applicants to send their CV by email or to download and fill in an application form that can be sent as an attachment by email. This saves time and postage costs for both the employer and prospective employee. Many employers have also moved to complete online applications. This means that rather than filling in an application to send in, the application is online so the information is sent to the employer and can be immediately stored within an online database. This method of application is very cost-effective for employers as data can be sorted before the employer needs to sift through an application, reducing processing costs. An example of this might be an employer asking that potential applications have a double Merit for BTEC National Business. When the online application reaches the online database, those details will be checked for. If the candidate has a double Merit, their application will go through, but if they do not, it will be immediately discounted.

Telephone

Employers are also increasingly using the telephone to help with applications. This means that applicants telephone a recruitment number and are often screened by answering a series of questions. If their responses are good, they will be put through to the next stage of the process; if they are not good, they will be unable to go forward. Large employers including Barclays Bank and M&S use this form of application. Smaller employers can also use the telephone as part of the application process as prospective employees may be asked to telephone for an information pack or application form. This way the employer can get an idea of how successful their advertisement has been and, as a result of it, how many people have applied.

Table 13.4: Purposes, advantages and disadvantages of interviewing methods.

Method	Description	Advantages	Disadvantages
Letter	Applicants write a letter about their suitability for a job and post or fax it to the organisation	• Gives the organisation the ability to compare • Allows applicants to demonstrate their suitability for the job	• Applicants are likely only to show their strengths and not weaknesses • No standard format • Post may take a long time or get lost • Fax can be read by others or may not be kept confidential
Online	Applicants send letters and CVs direct to organisations or fill out online application forms	• Organisations can advertise on their website for free • Can increase the number of candidates which is very useful for specialist employers • Data can be sent in to the organisation very quickly and needs little processing • Can happen 24 hours a day, seven days a week • People looking at company information may see the job by accident and apply for it • Can be accessed by people with disabilities on an equal basis	• Technical problems, for example, the website or email not working • Jobs advertised on the web may receive too many applicants so employers may take a long time to choose candidates • Not everyone has access to the web so it may reduce the number of possible applicants and may not be accessible to some people • May be difficult to prove where the information has come from; electronic signatures can be used but are not used widely yet
Telephone	Applicants call a number and notes are made about them. Sometimes tests are also done on the applicants to try to work out their personality type	• Can be used for large numbers of applicants as the information can be put into a database and sorted • Allows the applicant to speak to someone from the organisation and ask questions	• The telephone may be busy or engaged and good applicants may not get through • May involve using an automated service so applicants may be put off or service may not operate outside office hours

Assessment activity 13.1

For the first part of the assessed work for this unit, you must demonstrate that you have gained an understanding of the way that two organisations plan their recruitment. Before you start the task, think carefully about the organisations that you would like to study and for which you will complete assessed work.

Identify how two organisations plan recruitment using internal and external sources. **P1**

Grading tip

Remember you will need to show you understand the reasons why vacancies occur, and the factors which influence organisations to recruit. You will need to consider internal and external recruitment and the time and cost implications of each method. You must include two organisations in your work, so make sure you choose them carefully. **P1**

2. Understand the implications of the regulatory framework for the process of recruitment and selection

As recruitment and selection is a very important part of any organisation, there is a lot of legislation that companies need to comply with. This is to ensure that the process is fair and that everyone can have equal access to job vacancies.

2.1 Current UK and EU legislation

The UK is governed by two key areas of legislation:

- laws passed within the UK
- laws passed within the European Union.

The European Union consists of the 25 European states of Europe who have joined together to become integrated and have free movement of people, goods and services across them. The European Parliament is responsible for passing EU legislation that affects all the states of the EU. The EU also brings into force directives such as the Equal Pay Directive (75/117) that stops discrimination on the grounds of sex in relation to pay. Each of the main pieces of legislation that are currently affecting the UK as part of the EU are briefly outlined here. You will need to check government websites and publications for the latest information when working on your assignment. The law is changing all the time and you need to be aware of the latest changes and the effect on recruitment and selection.

Sex Discrimination Act 1975/97

These Acts make it law that men and women are treated equally. People must not be discriminated against because of their marital status, sex or if they have had their gender reassigned. Indirect and direction discrimination are both unlawful in the Sex Discrimination Acts.

Direct discrimination means a less qualified man could not be given a job over a more qualified woman.

Indirect discrimination is when a job has requirements that one sex is unable to perform, for example, 'must be six feet tall' – very few women are this tall.

Sometimes jobs do not have to comply with the Sex Discrimination Act if they must be performed by a particular sex; for example, a youth worker specialising in helping young women may have to be female. If a group is underrepresented, positive steps can be made to encourage that particular group such as offering free management courses to women in a particular organisation because there were not enough.

Race Relations Act 1992

This Act makes it unlawful for anyone to be discriminated against on the grounds of race, colour, nationality, ethnic origin or national origin. Employees must be protected from discrimination, victimisation and harassment, and can use an industrial tribunal to force employers to change the way they operate or to seek compensation. Indirect and direct discrimination can also be applied to the Race Relations Act.

Direct discrimination would be a job being advertised as only suitable for someone of black skin, so it would discriminate against anyone with white skin.

Indirect discrimination would be when a job requires someone to only be fair haired so it would be discriminating against people who do not have fair hair.

Activity: Sparkplugs Motors Ltd

Read the recruitment advertisement below that is to go in a local paper and answer the following questions in small groups.

'Blonde-haired person wanted for car technician post in local garage. Must be physically fit and at least 6'2" tall. No previous experience necessary but should be willing to learn and be prepared to get dirty. Pay subject to negotiation. Closing date 26 June.'

1. How does this job discriminate directly and indirectly?
2. Rewrite it in a more appropriate format.
3. To what extent can a job advertisement affect the level of discrimination in the workplace?

PLTS

Practise your creative thinking skills to create an eye-catching advertisement.

Equal Pay Act 1970

This Act forces employers to pay men and women equally. This includes all aspects of pay including benefits, childcare allowances, sickness benefits and car allowances. When the Act was brought into force the gap between the pay of men and women was 37 per cent (source: Women and Equality Unit). This Act makes sure that men and women are paid the same amount of money when they are doing:

- the same jobs
- equivalent jobs
- jobs of an equal value.

In April 2009, the Equality Bill was published with a view to making it law in 2010. The purpose behind the Bill was to support equality between men and women, as women in 2009 were still being paid less than men.

Activity: Equality Bill 2009

Carry out research into the latest status of the Equality Bill 2009.

1. What is published within it?
2. Has it become law yet?
3. What are the advantages of having equal pay for men and women?

What is the purpose of the Equal Pay Act 1970?

Did you know?

Even in 2009, men and women were still not being paid the same amount for the same work, with women earning on average less. Some people say this is because of a 'glass ceiling' which does not allow women to progress into more senior positions at work.

Disability Discrimination Acts 1995 and 2005

These Acts make it unlawful for a disabled person to be treated less favourably because they are disabled, unless there are very good reasons. Reasonable adjustments must be made to premises so that disabled applicants or workers are not put at a substantial disadvantage. Making reasonable adjustments might be adding ramps for wheelchair access or a hearing loop for a person who is hard of hearing. In April 2005 the Disability Discrimination Act 2005 was brought in and came fully into force from December 2006. It amended or extended the provision of the DDA 1995. This makes it:

- unlawful for operators of transport vehicles to discriminate against disabled people
- easier for disabled people to rent property and for tenants to make disability-related adaptations
- unlawful for private clubs with 25 or more members to keep disabled people out, just because they have a disability
- possible for people who have HIV, cancer and multiple sclerosis to be protected by the legislation from the moment they are diagnosed
- possible for discrimination law to cover all the activities of the public sector
- a requirement for public bodies to promote equality of opportunity for disabled people.

Activity: Disability equality

Find out the latest information on the Single Equality Duty that employers must work within. How does this Duty support people with disabilities at work?

PLTS

Practise your self-management skills to carry out this research.

European Working Time Directive

This directive introduced the idea of a maximum working week of 48 hours to be maintained over a period of 17, 26 or 52 weeks by workforce agreement. It also provides:

- restrictions on the maximum length of nightshifts
- rest periods
- annual leave of four weeks.

Employers have to keep records of how many hours an employee has worked to avoid any disputes.

Employment Acts 2002 and 2008, and the Work and Families Act 2006

The Employment Act 2002 covered a number of areas within employment law and these included the rights to maternity and paternity pay, for parents to be able to ask for flexible working arrangements and the monitoring of equal opportunities.

The Work and Families Act 2006 extended some aspects of the Employment Act 2002 by offering enhanced legislation for employees and families, including:

- extended maternity pay from six months to nine months for mothers of babies born after 1 April 2007
- extended rights for carers of adults to have flexible working hours
- extended paternity pay for fathers (with or without pay, depending on the mother's situation)
- the introduction of better planning and other measures for employers to deal with planned leave
- improved communication between employers and employees during maternity leave.

The Employment Act 2008 enhanced the areas of employment law that already existed, including changes to:

- the enforcement of minimum wage by introducing a new penalty for employers who underpay their workers
- Trade Union membership to allow a member of a union to be asked to leave because they are members of a political party
- the age of children for which parents can ask for flexible working – now up to 16 years of age
- the way that disputes are resolved
- holiday pay entitlement.

National Minimum Wage

The National Minimum Wage is the amount of money set by the government as recommended by the Low Pay Commission. Each year the amount goes up but it is the minimum amount that workers aged 16 or over must be paid for doing a job. There are very few exceptions to this amount of money and specific rates are given for workers aged 16 and 17 as well as 18 to 21 and 22 or over. These amounts are the minimum rates that must be paid, but of course employers can choose to pay more if they wish.

In October 2009, the rates were:

- the full rate of £5.80 an hour for adults (people aged 22 and over)
- a 'development rate' of £4.83 an hour for workers aged 18 to 21 inclusive
- £3.57 an hour for young people (those older than school leaving age – the end of summer term of the school year in which a person turns 16 – and younger than 18).

(Source: www.direct.gov.uk)

If employees are not being paid the minimum wage, they can ring the Pay and Work Rights Helpline to report their employer and either give their name or call anonymously.

Data Protection Act 1998

The Data Protection Act 1998 came into force in 2000 and aims to protect an individual's right to privacy in relation to their personal data. Personal data does not just mean personal information, for example, medical information; it means any data relating to a living person. This means it includes information about current employees and anyone who applies for a job such as their address, pay, bank details, date of birth, training record or references.

This information can only be stored if a person has consented to it being stored or if it is necessary for the performance of the person's job. The Data Protection Act seeks to provide a balance between the interests of an organisation that holds data and the individual. The individual has rights under the Act to:

- access the information
- stop information being held about them
- prevent the information being passed on for marketing purposes
- have compensation made and to ask the data controller to rectify errors.

Activity: Data Protection Act

Find out the latest information on the Data Protection Act and the amendments and regulations that have been made to the Act since 2000. Present your findings as a written paper or poster.

PLTS

Practise your creative thinking skills to think of all the ways that the Data Protection Act affects employees at work.

2.2 Ethical issues

The final aspect of recruitment and selection that you need to consider is the ethical issues that relate to the process. These are issues that are not governed by law but are the right things that should be done.

Asking candidates the same questions

The first ethical issue that has already been outlined is asking the candidates the same questions. This makes it fairer for everyone as their answers can be compared more easily. It is only discriminatory to ask different questions to candidates if they are unfair to those candidates, so this is not a legal obligation but an ethical one.

Interviewers not related to candidates

It is not ethical for a member of staff to interview candidates if they are related to them by marriage or if they are directly related. This is because this personal link may cause a conflict of interest. **Interviewers** may also let their employer know they cannot interview if they are friends or former colleagues of a person and therefore may be biased, whether positively or negatively. This can avoid the suggestion that a candidate only got the job because of who they were related to or who they were friends with. This makes the process much more open and fair. Many application forms now ask applicants to make it clear if they have personal links with any member of the senior management team or other significant individuals within the institution.

Gender and ethnic balance on panels

The final part of the process that needs examining from an ethical perspective is making sure that the interview process, including the interview panel, reflects a balance of employees or managers of both genders and different ethnic groups, for example, white, black or Asian. This is important because different ethnic group members might provide a more balanced judgement of a candidate and choose different qualities that they think are important in an employee. This rounded judgement should ensure that the right candidate is chosen to fit in with everyone.

Key term

Interviewers – the employer or organisation interviewing potential people for a job

Why is gender and ethnic balance on panels important?

Assessment activity 13.2

For the second part of the assessed work for this unit, you must explain the different laws and regulations that you have been made aware of and how they influence the recruitment and selection process. Before you start the task, think carefully about any examples from the workplace that you can include in your work.

Explain the impact of the legal and regulatory framework on recruitment and selection activities. **P2**

Grading tip

Remember to include as many work-based examples in your work as you can. These will help your thinking to become clearer and will show that your knowledge is good. **P2**

3. Be able to prepare documentation involved in the selection and recruitment process

You have learned about the process of planning to recruit, how different organisations choose to recruit and also the regulatory framework that impacts on them. However, you also need to understand and be familiar with the paperwork that is used to support the process. The key documents that you need to be able to prepare are the job description and the person specification. You also need to prepare other documents to make an application, including the application letter and curriculum vitae.

3.1 Job description

The purpose of the job description is to give information to prospective employees about what the job actually involves by giving the purpose of the job and the types of responsibilities and duties that will be expected as part of that job. Different organisations will have their own particular extra information that they will include within a job description, but there are a set of key elements that are always included and they are shown in Table 13.5.

Fig. 13.3 is an example of a job description that shows how they actually look on paper.

Money Management Ltd

Job Description

Job Title	Finance Assistant
Department	Accounts
Responsible to	Sarah Pearson
Scope of the post	The Finance Assistant's main role is to assist the Finance Manager.
Responsibilities	The post holder is expected to help with company accounts using Sage Accounting Software. This requires preparation of accounts for budgets within the organisation and assistance in the production of annual accounts for external agencies.

Duties performed by the post holder include:
- reconciliation of accounts and problem solving of any variances
- preparation of invoices
- raising orders
- general office duties such as travel claim processing
- ad hoc reports as and when required
- any other duties as commensurate with the post.

Compiled by	C Taylor
Date	8 March 2010

Fig. 13.3: Example of a job description.

Table 13.5: Elements of a job description.

Element	Description
Title of the job	This is really important as it is used to give a person an idea of what the job involves and an indication of the level of responsibility, for example, Finance Manager.
Department and location	A job description will be written for a particular department in an organisation, especially if the organisation is very large.
Broad terms	This gives a very rough idea of what is involved in the post. Many job vacancies have **open-ended terms**, meaning that they can change slightly to take into account the needs of the business or employee.
Responsible to whom	This tells the employee whom they must report to with any problems or queries.
Responsibilities	This tells the employee about any people or resources they are responsible for.
Scope of post	This gives them guidance on how far reaching their post is, for example, whether or not they have the possibility to supervise others or can make management changes.
Education and qualifications	Some organisations will also include details about the level of qualifications and experience that the job requires, for example, 'graduate required'. Such information may also be included in the person specification.
Name of compiler and approver	This is the person who designed and agreed the job.
Date of issue	This is when the description was issued. In a fast-changing business world, it is important to know when the last changes were made to the job.

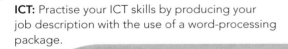

Activity: Job description

In pairs, write a job description for the post of Office Administrator. Carry out research online, in books, journals or newspapers to help you. You may need to interview a member of staff to complete this activity.

1. Compare your job description with others in your class. What are the similarities and differences?
2. What are the advantages and disadvantages of having a job description?
3. To what extent is an accurate job description necessary in the recruitment process?

Functional skills

ICT: Practise your ICT skills by producing your job description with the use of a word-processing package.

3.2 Person specification

The job description essentially concentrates on providing information about the job. The **person specification** is a direct contrast; it provides information about the type of person that the organisation is looking for to do the job.

The person specification gives a list of requirements, but these relate to the person doing the job. It will have an introduction at the start of the person specification giving details about the job like job title, post reference number and management responsibilities (including whom the employee needs to report to and is responsible for). It will then detail **attributes** that the organisation wants that person to have, for example, their type of personality or intelligence level.

Key terms

Open-ended terms – terms that are written very vaguely, allowing the employer and employee some flexibility about what they actually require – for example, an employer might write into the job description a statement that covers 'any other reasonable duties as required by the post'

Person specification – list of attributes needed by the person to perform a job, such as personality type or experience

Attributes – the personal characteristics that someone has, for example, outgoing or conscientious. The attributes needed will change depending on the type and level of the job

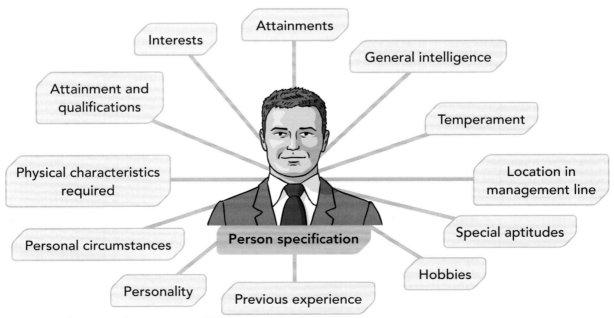

Fig. 13.4: Elements of a person specification.

Table 13.6: Person specification.

Element	Description
Title of the job and reference number	This is really important as it gives a person an idea of what the job involves. The reference number makes it easier for the organisation to send out details and keep information on file.
Location in management line	A person specification will give clear details about how senior the post holder will be. This helps a potential applicant to work out whether they are suitable for the job.
Essential and desirable characteristics	The person specification will list characteristics that a person needs to be able to perform the role, for example, excellent communication skills or the ability to speak an additional language.
Physical characteristics	If it is essential for someone to have certain physical characteristics for the job, these may be listed, for example, physically fit, or if someone needs to be a certain gender (while still complying with discrimination legislation, see page 330), this may be listed.
Attainments, qualifications and general intelligence	This information details the education level and qualifications that the person should have. Employers will sometimes write 'must have degree-level education' or 'Level 3 education'.
Previous experience	The level of experience needed for the job should be outlined. This must be done in a way that does not discriminate against older or younger employees, so should not state a number or years but could say 'extensive experience'.
Special aptitudes	These are special skills that a person doing this job needs to have, for example, ability to use IT or minimum typing speed.
Temperament and personality	Someone applying for this job needs to be able to demonstrate a certain type of personality so indicators will be provided to help applicants understand what is required, for example, 'able to work under pressure' or 'good sense of humour needed'.
Hobbies and interests	Hobbies and interests may be included if these are relevant to the job. This may be included as something desirable in the person specification, for example, ability to play music.
Personal circumstances	Without discriminating against any applicants it may be possible to include personal circumstances on the person specification, for example, 'must be willing to undertake extensive overnight travel'. This is indicating that such work will be needed and therefore should be prepared for.

Fig. 13.5 shows an example of a mini person specification.

Some organisations will also use ratings in their specification. This means that they will rate how important a part of the person specification is to a job, with 1 meaning that this attribute is very important and 4 not important.

Person Specification
Post Title: Finance and Administrative Officer
Grade: Clerical 3/4

Criteria	Essential	Desirable
Qualifications/Knowledge:	• BTEC National Diploma in Business • GCSEs in Maths and English plus 3 others at Grade C or above or equivalent • ICT functional skills, particularly spreadsheets and databases	
Work-related Experience:	• 1 or 2 years general office and/or financial experience • Good level of numeracy	• Experience in higher education
Skills/Abilities and Special Attributes	• Good organisational skills • Able to prioritise workloads • Good communication skills • Team-working ability	• Previous experience or willingness to work in an open-plan environment

Fig. 13.5: Mini person specification.

Activity: Person specification

Write a person specification for the job of Office Assistant. Using each of the categories contained in your person specification (see Table 13.6), describe what is needed and then rate how important that attribute is. An example is started below to help you.

Previous experience: 3

Able to work to deadlines: 1

Previous experience might be rated 3 because it is not essential for some jobs, but working to deadlines is given a 1 because it might be essential to get work in on time for this job.

1. When you have finished your person specification, compare it with person specifications from others in your class.

2. How can a person specification help an employer to choose the right person for the job?

3. 'A person specification may limit an organisation's ability to get a range of applicants for a job.' Discuss this view.

Functional skills

ICT: Practise your ICT skills by using a word-processing package to produce your person specification.

3.3 Application documentation

The main documents used as part of the application are the:

- letter
- application form
- curriculum vitae.

Letter

A letter of application should highlight all the positive aspects of the applicant and the special skills that they have.

Table 13.7: The main documents used as part of the application.

Document	Description
Letter	Letters are used by applicants to outline why they are suitable for a job. Applicants can use a letter to highlight any special skills and attributes they feel they have that make them suitable for the job. Applicants should use the job description and person specification when highlighting their particular strengths so that an employer can match them to the job.
Application form	Application forms ask for a standard set of questions and boxes to be completed. This makes it easy for the organisation to compare candidates. Application forms ask set questions and information and therefore will avoid the employer having to read information that they do not need. Paper-based forms may take time and money to be sent out and then will need to be processed and put into a system to compare them. This may take a long time. Online forms have the advantage of doing this automatically. Care should be taken with online application forms to ensure that they are completed using appropriate English and not 'text language', as this might not give the right impression to an employer.
Curriculum vitae (CV)	Applicants write all their details including education and history on a two-page sheet, including referees. The organisation can see immediately everything about an applicant. CVs only focus on positive aspects of an applicant, so it may be difficult to compare candidates. CVs may also have been used to apply for lots of jobs so may not be specific to a particular role. It is important to review a CV regularly or to adapt it for each individual job if an applicant really wants that job.

38 Thornton Lane
Teeton
TR8 7 PU

18 December 2009

Money Management Ltd
8 Marks Square
Teeton
TR7 8NK

Dear Mr Halford

Application for the post of Finance Assistant

I am writing to apply for the position of Finance Assistant as advertised in 'The Local Paper' on 16 December.

I have spent the past two years working for Smart Money Finances in Teeton. As part of my role I am required to process invoices and enter them on to the computer. I also type letters as required for clients and answer the telephone. Within my role I work with two other Finance Assistants so I am used to working as part of a team. I really like working in this way and would like to do so in the future.

I am a well-organised person with good communication skills and believe that I would make an excellent employee for your organisation. I developed my skills while I was studying BTEC National Business at Teeton College. This course gave me excellent knowledge of business and in particular finance, so I have been able to use these skills at work.

In my personal life I am a keen football player and have represented the county on more than one occasion. I am also interested in travelling and have visited lots of different European countries including Spain, France and Italy.

I believe I would be a very useful addition to your team. I am a hardworking and very conscientious employee and would be pleased to bring my skills and experience to your company. I am enclosing my Curriculum Vitae for your information and would be available for interview at your convenience.

Yours sincerely

Andy Brown

A Brown

Enc.

Fig. 13.6: Letter of application.

Application form

Application forms are another way of gaining information in a standard format that makes it easier for employers to compare applicants (see Fig. 13.7). They can be completed online or in paper form. The information in the questions can be directly related to the individual business needs.

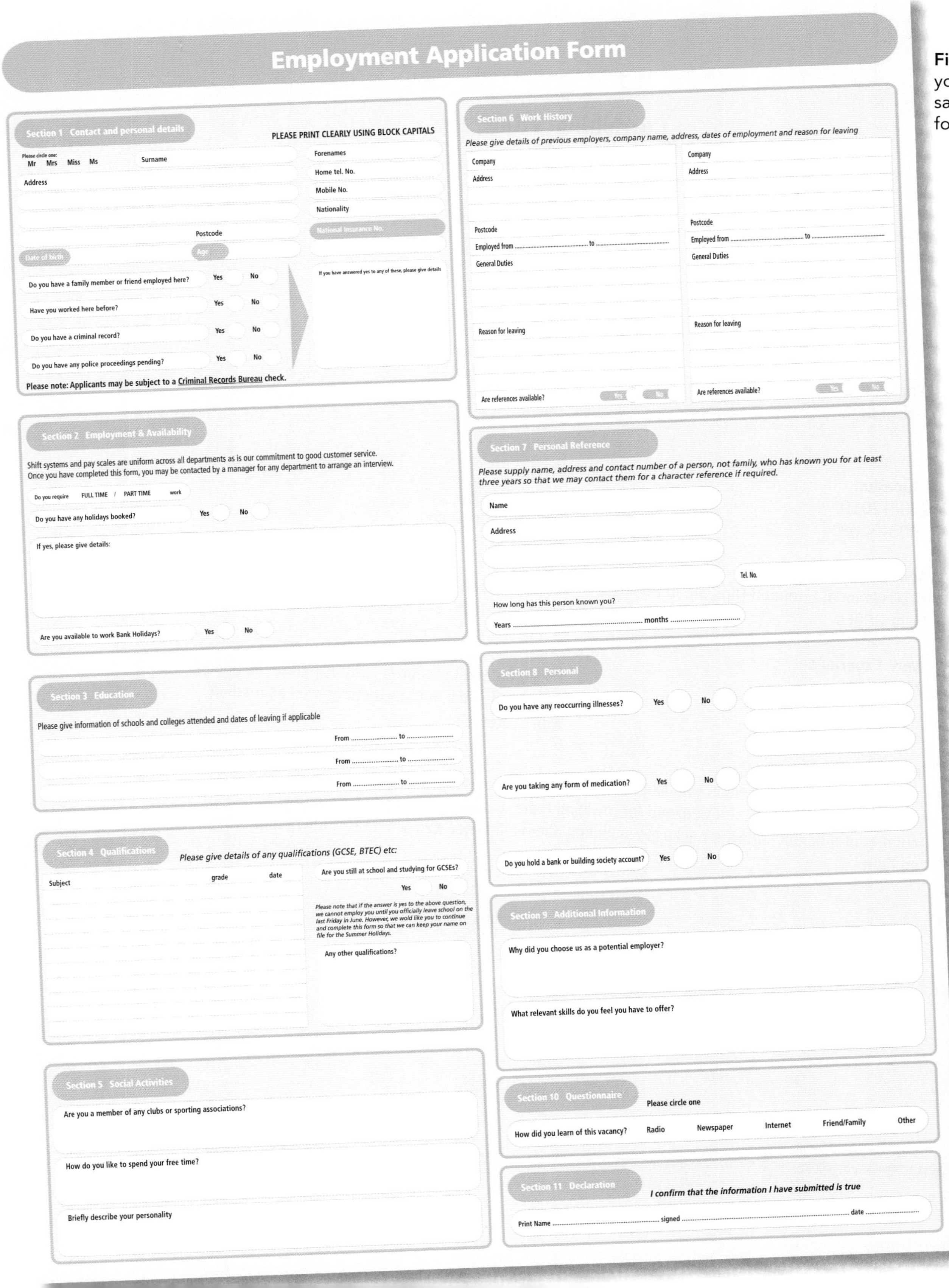

Employment Application Form

Section 1 Contact and personal details

PLEASE PRINT CLEARLY USING BLOCK CAPITALS

Please circle one: Mr Mrs Miss Ms

Surname

Address

Postcode

Date of birth

Age

Forenames

Home tel. No.

Mobile No.

Nationality

National Insurance No.

Do you have a family member or friend employed here? Yes No

Have you worked here before? Yes No

Do you have a criminal record? Yes No

Do you have any police proceedings pending? Yes No

If you have answered yes to any of these, please give details

Please note: Applicants may be subject to a Criminal Records Bureau check.

Section 2 Employment & Availability

Shift systems and pay scales are uniform across all departments as is our commitment to good customer service. Once you have completed this form, you may be contacted by a manager for any department to arrange an interview.

Do you require FULL TIME / PART TIME work

Do you have any holidays booked? Yes No

If yes, please give details:

Are you available to work Bank Holidays? Yes No

Section 3 Education

Please give information of schools and colleges attended and dates of leaving if applicable

From .... to ....

From .... to ....

From .... to ....

Section 4 Qualifications

Please give details of any qualifications (GCSE, BTEC) etc:

Subject grade date

Are you still at school and studying for GCSEs? Yes No

Please note that if the answer is yes to the above question, we cannot employ you until you officially leave school on the last Friday in June. However, we wold like you to continue and complete this form so that we can keep your name on file for the Summer Holidays.

Any other qualifications?

Section 5 Social Activities

Are you a member of any clubs or sporting associations?

How do you like to spend your free time?

Briefly describe your personality

Section 6 Work History

Please give details of previous employers, company name, address, dates of employment and reason for leaving

Company

Address

Postcode

Employed from .... to ....

General Duties

Reason for leaving

Are references available? Yes No

Company

Address

Postcode

Employed from .... to ....

General Duties

Reason for leaving

Are references available? Yes No

Section 7 Personal Reference

Please supply name, address and contact number of a person, not family, who has known you for at least three years so that we may contact them for a character reference if required.

Name

Address

Tel. No.

How long has this person known you?

Years .... months ....

Section 8 Personal

Do you have any reoccurring illnesses? Yes No

Are you taking any form of medication? Yes No

Do you hold a bank or building society account? Yes No

Section 9 Additional Information

Why did you choose us as a potential employer?

What relevant skills do you feel you have to offer?

Section 10 Questionnaire

Please circle one

How did you learn of this vacancy? Radio Newspaper Internet Friend/Family Other

Section 11 Declaration

I confirm that the information I have submitted is true

Print Name .... signed .... date ....

Fig. 13.7: Have you ever used sample application forms?

Curriculum vitae

Fig. 13.8 shows an example of a CV.

Did you know?

Some organisations ask you to remove some of the personal details from your CV or application, such as your date of birth, to help to ensure that you are not discriminated against on the grounds of age.

Curriculum Vitae

Personal Details
Name

Gita Powell

Address

18 Hill Lane
Southampton
SO15 5RL

Telephone
Date of Birth

023 80511822
02/02/1992

Education
2008–2010
2003–2008

Topton College
Besthampton School

Academic Qualifications
BTEC National Extended Diploma in Business
Eight GCSEs

MMP Awarded
including Maths and English

Work Experience
2007–2010

Part-time employment at Next using the till, pricing stock and stock management as well as dealing with customers

Personal Statement
I am a really outgoing person who likes to play sport. I am a member of the Badminton Team at College and also play at the weekend for my local team. I enjoy computing and am able to use a number of different software packages including Microsoft Office XP. I am hard-working and always on time.

Referee
Kate Sharp
76 Laxford Avenue
Southampton
SO26 8PU
Tel: 02380 876233

Fig. 13.8: Example of a curriculum vitae.

Debenhams use their website to provide information for applicants. The site uses drop-down boxes to help potential applicants search for job vacancies that might be relevant to them. They then give their email address to Debenhams and start the online application. This means that Debenhams have contact information from the earliest stage and can monitor who is interested in their vacancies.

The online application form screens applications by asking questions about aspects such as:

- their age
- previous criminal convictions
- relationships with others at Debenhams
- previous employment with them
- hours available to work
- equal opportunities information, for example, marital status, religion, ethnic group
- customer service experience
- skills and qualities
- interests and hobbies
- occupational skills
- absence record
- gaps in employment history.

Think about it!

1. How do Debenhams use online applications as part of recruitment?

2. What are the advantages of using such a system?

3. Are there any disadvantages?

4. Compare and contrast the online application process for three different organisations that you are aware of. To what extent are common features contained within these processes? How important is conformity in recruitment?

Assessment activity 13.3

P3 M1 D1 · BTEC

For the third part of the assessed work for this unit, you must show that you produce documents and that you understand their appropriate use.

1. Prepare the documents used in selection and recruitment activities. **P3**
2. Compare the purposes of the different documents used in the selection and recruitment process of a given organisation. **M1**
3. Evaluate the usefulness of the documents in the interview pack for a given organisation in facilitating the interview process. **D1**

Grading tips

1. Remember when you prepare the documents, you will need to be doing them for a specific vacancy and therefore link them together. **P3**
2. When comparing, you will need to compare the different documents with each other in the context of the vacancy and note the different types of information and how it will be used in the process. **M1**
3. To evaluate means to make judgements that are being used by an organisation. Write about what makes them useful and not so useful. Overall, how useful are they and how could they be improved? **D1**

4. Be able to participate in a selection interview

Now that you are aware of the early stages of the recruitment process, it is important that you are able to participate in a selection interview. There are various stages to the process that you will learn about and each is very important. These stages include:

- pre-interview
- interview
- post-interview.

4.1 Pre-interview

For an employer to make decisions about who to ask for interview, they need to look through the application information that has already been sent to them to make decisions. The type of information provided will depend on whether or not the organisation has used an application form or curriculum vitae to collect the information. The organisation will want to decide who to interview and will be looking at:

- experience
- qualifications
- skills
- references
- the quality of the documents themselves, including typing or handwriting.

Selection criteria for short-listing

Applicants will be aware that employers will be using the person specification as the primary method for short-listing, by matching the skills and attributes listed with those of the applicants. Depending on the number of applicants applying for a vacancy, this may be easier or more difficult. Applicants should try to match their experience as closely and clearly as they possibly can.

Employers may use a form to make comparison easier by making notes on each individual applicant and then looking at them altogether. Table 13.8 shows an example of a simplified form.

An alternative short-listing grid may also be used by writing the selection criteria next to each application so that each area can be ticked or crossed. Again, this makes comparison much easier.

It is important at every stage of selection that reasons are clearly outlined for why an applicant has been chosen to go forward and why another has been rejected. This is to avoid discrimination. If an applicant wishes to find out why their application was rejected, they are entitled to do so and an employer will need to have clear reasons

Table 13.8: Selection criteria.

Candidate	Communication skills	Qualifications	Ability to work as part of a team	Shortlist
1	No evidence provided	5 GCSEs at C grade	No evidence provided	No
2	Evidence of telephone skills and good standard of report writing	BTEC National Extended Diploma (D*D*D*)	Working in a bank for the past two years in a team	Yes
3	Typing skills (30 words per minute or wpm) Reception skills	A-levels in Spanish, French and English	No evidence	No
4	No evidence provided	3 GCSEs including Art	No evidence	No
5	Reception skills, typing skills (60 wpm)	BTEC National Diploma (MM)	Part-time restaurant supervisor of a small team	Yes

to feed back to them. Employers must also only use the information that they have been given in front of them and not make any assumptions about candidates; this should avoid stereotyping and discrimination.

Application packs and information for candidates

In order to help candidates understand the process after the application has gone through, they are sent application packs with more information including the process that is going to happen.

The application pack often includes additional information about the organisation they are applying to and the structure of the day(s) that they need to take part in, including any tests or additional tasks that they might need to undertake. This information is important for candidates, as it may help them to decide whether or not they actually want to go through the recruitment process.

References

References are written statements that an employer, college or personal friend supplies in support of an application. It is usual to have an educational and employment reference as part of the process. The reference usually contains information about the applicant's employment history, timekeeping, sickness and experience to help the new employer to make judgements about whether to take that person on.

References are a very important element of the recruitment process. They may be taken up before or after the recruitment process. It is common for

references to be taken before the process starts if the job involves working with young or vulnerable groups. References can indicate whether or not someone is likely to be suitable for a job. They must be written very carefully as they should be factually correct and give opinions that present the candidate in a reasonable way. Employers need to be very careful about how they write a reference, as if a reference is written in a way that is too negative and leads to the withdrawal of a job offer, employees may be able to sue if it is inaccurate.

Employers should make sure:

- opinions are reasonable and that facts are correct
- the reference does not give an unfair impression
- it is clear if they are only able to offer a limited opinion of an applicant.

Employers should not:

- give misleading information
- provide a reference if they do not wish to; there are few legal obligations for an employer to provide a reference
- write a reference that they do not wish the subject of it to see (as the person has a right to see the reference as part of the Data Protection Act).

Types of interviews

As part of the pre-interview stage, the employer will need to decide which method of interview is to be used as part of the selection process. There are six main methods of interview that can be used:

- group
- individual
- team
- panel
- telephone
- multi-stage.

343

Group

Group interviews are when a number of candidates are invited to visit an employer to receive a presentation from the recruiting organisation, talk to other candidates and ask questions about the job. They take place if large numbers of staff are needed by an organisation. Group interviews may be used as the first stage of the process to select candidates who seem more interested in the job or who ask suitable questions. It can be a good opportunity for a candidate to decide whether or not they wish to go forward with their application and for an employer to get a first impression of the candidates. In a group interview it is important for candidates to stand out from the rest of the people and this may be difficult to do. Employers may give candidates a task to complete as part of a smaller group to monitor how well they work with each other.

Individual

This type of interview is very intense as the candidates are expected to meet in a one-to-one situation to talk about why they want the job. This type of interviewing is expensive as it requires each candidate to be spoken to individually. It is likely that only very promising candidates will be picked to go through to this stage.

Team

Team interviews are those conducted by a team of personnel who will be asking different questions of candidates. These are normally taken from a number of different areas within the organisation such as finance, personnel or marketing. Each person brings a different set of skills to the interview so will be looking for different features in the candidates. Usually each member of the interview team will have equal weighting of their opinion. This means that each person's view will be taken into account as important.

Panel

Panel interviews are similar to team interviews in that a group of people are brought together to interview the candidates. A chairperson is appointed and each member of the panel is given the opportunity to ask questions as directed by that chairperson. Each member of the panel will have their questions ready to ask. This type of interview is often used in public sector organisations such as hospitals or colleges. Panel interviews often ask the same questions of all candidates to make effective comparisons.

Telephone

Telephone interviews are often conducted with candidates who are applying to work in a customer service environment such as in a retail store or in a call centre. The telephone interview can take place at any time and the interviewer chats to the candidate to judge whether or not they have the right skills to work for their organisation. The interviewer may ask all sorts of questions about organisational skills or other information to make decisions about the suitability of the candidate. Telephone interviews can be a useful way of screening out unsuitable candidates at an early stage as they do not require the candidates to travel to a location. This cuts out time and costs for both parties. As telephone interviewers often have a set of standardised questions, the process may be completed by less-experienced interviewers and is therefore more cost-effective for the organisation. As part of the interview, candidates may be asked a number of questions including calculations, so they should be prepared for this.

Multi-stage

Multi-stage interviews mean that more than one interview takes place in order for a candidate to be chosen. This may mean different types of interview are used and candidates must go through each stage

Fig. 13.9: When do group interviews take place?

What is a panel interview?

to eventually get the job. The first interviews might be less formal, for example, an informal chat with some members of staff from a relevant department. The next stage might be a more formal interview with a manager or human resources employee. The final stage could be a panel interview with the senior management team. Candidates must pass through each interview stage to finally get the job, so it can be a good way of seeing how candidates perform at different levels and in a variety of situations.

Tasks and tests used to complement the interview process

There are a number of different tasks and tests that may be used as part of the interview process and these are categorised into four main areas:

- occupational preference tests
- attainment tests
- aptitude tests
- psychometric tests.

Occupational preference tests

These are tests that measure skills that are important for the job – for example, if a person needs to be very customer-focused, the test will measure this. A roleplay may be used to do this where a candidate is asked to deal with an 'angry customer'.

Attainment tests

This may be measured by observing candidates performing in a group to see which level they are working at. It shows the level at which candidates work within a group, such as high or low achiever.

Aptitude tests

These assessments try to measure suitability for a job and may be more practical, for example, putting tasks into order of priority or demonstrating the management of small groups.

Psychometric tests

Psychometric tests are those that try to measure intelligence or personality type to assess how good a person will be at a job. These may be multiple-choice tests that are paper-based or completed online.

PLTS

Practise self-management skills to answer the questions on your own or in small groups.

Activity: Research into psychometric testing

Conduct research into the use of psychometric testing in your area. You may wish to conduct online research or interviews/questionnaires to gather this information.

1. Which companies are using it?
2. How are they using it?
3. How do you think they benefit from it?

Fig. 13.10: What are psychometric tests used for?

Use of specialists in the interview

It is important that within an interview, specialists are being used. This means that accurate judgements can be made and the appropriate processes are followed. Often a member of the **Human Resources Department** will be present as they process all the paperwork and check the process has happened fairly and keeps to UK and EU legislation.

Specialists may also be used to give advice and guidance to the interviewer or interview team. These may advise on the results of any tests that have been set or are used to give an opinion on the expertise that an individual holds. Advisors may be brought in for short-term projects to help businesses recruit the right individuals.

Assessment and interview questions

Assessment and interview questions are critical to the success of any interview. If candidates are not asked the right questions, it is difficult to assess whether or not they are suitable for the job. It is also important to ask all candidates the same questions to make sure the process is fair. There are some questions that a business may never ask about and these include:

- race
- colour
- sex
- religion
- nationality
- sexual orientation.
- birthplace
- age
- disability
- marital status
- children

Asking questions about any of these topics means that a business is breaking the law.

Questions that are good to ask an employee relate to things they feel they have done well in the past, any relevant experience they have highlighted in their application and how they would approach a particular role.

Assessment questions are direct questions which ask employees about a specific aspect of the role that they are applying for. They will include specific information that relates to the knowledge needed to perform that role; for example, if a legal secretary would need knowledge of legal terminology they are therefore likely to be asked assessment questions relating to legal terms. An accounting technician could be asked a specific question about an auditing process. Through

assessment questions, the interviewer is trying to establish the ability of the **interviewee** to do the job.

Key terms

Human Resources Department – this deals with the management of policies and procedures relating to the people who work for an organisation, covering areas such as payroll, sickness monitoring, and grievance and disciplinary procedures

Interviewee – person who has applied for the job and is being interviewed for it

Procedure for informing candidates on interview decisions

Candidates will also be told what is going to happen during and after the interview, such as when they will be informed about the outcome of the interview – for example, by the end of the day, next day or week. This is important as it helps the candidates to know how long it might be before they are informed about their performance.

4.2 Interview

The process of interviewing itself is complex as there are agreed rules about what happens within the interview situation and what happens to the information created as part of the process during and after it has taken place. Body language as well as the spoken word is important, so you need to understand the impact of these areas on the interview itself.

Interview protocol

Interviews need to follow interview protocols. These are expected rules and guidelines that are not written down but the candidate(s) and the interviewer(s) are expected to follow. These may be things like:

- candidates arriving at the interview early
- the need to dress smartly with a clean and tidy appearance
- the interviewers shaking hands with candidates when they enter the room
- the candidate speaking highly of their last or current employer and not saying bad things about them
- candidates not chewing gum
- at the end of the interview, the candidate thanking the employer for the interview.

Wearing formal clothing is part of interview protocol.

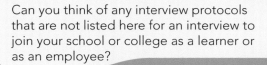

Activity: Interview protocols

Can you think of any interview protocols that are not listed here for an interview to join your school or college as a learner or as an employee?

Confidentiality

Candidates will also be told what will happen to their personal information if they are not successful. It may either be destroyed or some organisations ask candidates if they are able to keep the information for another six months so that if a job should be advertised again, they will be considered. Keeping this information secure is part of the organisation's responsibility to maintain **confidentiality**.

Key term

Confidentiality – keeping information secure and only allowing it to be given to people who have received permission to see it

Fairness

You will learn more about fairness when you consider the ethics and legal aspects of the interview process. It is important that all candidates are treated fairly in terms of their seating arrangements, the questions used, the information about the process and so on. This means that all interviewees can be compared equally. This also includes making sure that every candidate is allocated the same amount of interview time and receives the same information.

Interview environment

The interview environment should be made as comfortable as possible, taking into account any potential health and safety issues. Candidates should have equal access to any relevant equipment. Distractions or interruptions should be avoided so that each candidate is given the time and space to perform to the best of their ability.

Agreed questions

As you have already learned, agreeing appropriate questions is a key part of the process to make sure that the interview is conducted fairly. The same questions should be asked of each of the candidates and these should be agreed before the interview starts. Often during interviews where there is more than one interviewer, the interviewers will agree which questions they will each ask, focusing on their own area of expertise.

Checking of personal information

Checking personal information is also an important part of the process. This may take place in the information stage of the process, for example, where a member of the human resources team photocopies the candidate's certificates or other personal information, such as birth certificate or driving licence. During the interview a verbal check of that information takes place using the application form or CV to help the interviewer.

Interview checklist

Many interviewers will use an interview checklist. This is particularly helpful if there is more than one stage to the process. Some organisations will include both formal and informal interviews to help them make decisions. A checklist helps the organisation to ensure that all questions have been asked and responses noted. Candidates may also make use of a checklist to help them work out if they have fully prepared for the interview. During the interview they may use their own checklist to ask any questions that they wish to ask. It is important that the checklist is not used too much by candidates in the interview, as it may not give the employer a good impression of the candidate if they keep needing to refer back to their information rather than answering questions directly.

Control of interview

To control the whole interview process, a member of that team will need to co-ordinate the questions to make the interview flow well. Candidates also need preparation and control. Candidates often feel under pressure in interview situations and will therefore need to control themselves mentally (by giving focused and well-thought-out answers) and physically (by giving good eye contact and body posture). They are usually given an outline of the format of the interview, for example, how long it will last and the type of questions that they will be asked. This allows them to try to do their best. It is important that appropriate and fair questions are asked of candidates so that each person has an equal chance of getting the job.

Decision criteria and documentation

It is important through every stage of the process that the correct decision criteria are used to make decisions about which employee to offer the job to. Documentation should also be kept with notes about the candidates to help decide which candidate is eventually going to be offered the job. A comparison chart like the one used in the selection of candidates stage of the process (page 343) may be used to help employers make effective comparisons between candidates. This may also make it possible to give a rank number to candidates to indicate who is best for the job.

Communicating the decision to candidates

During the interview, candidates will usually be told when and how they will be informed about who has got the job. It is usual for candidates to all complete their interviews and then for the employer to telephone them later that day or the next day. This may be done by the person interviewing them or by someone from the Human Resources Department. Sometimes interviews may need to take place over more than one day so it is important to communicate this to candidates so they are aware of how and when they will be told about the decision.

Communication and listening skills

Communication skills are necessary for both the interviewer and the candidate during an interview situation. Being able to communicate clearly what you mean and being able to listen to answers is really important. Questioning techniques and the types of

questions are important, but so are listening skills in order to really hear what people are saying and whether or not they would be suited to a particular employer or job. Whether the interview is by phone, face-to-face or by videoconference, listening and analytical skills are required. Sometimes interviewers will use summarising skills to help them. Summarising is a form of recapping, or going over, what has been said before. If a statement is made, the interviewer may start by saying, 'I think you are saying… is that correct?' Summarising allows the interviewer to confirm their understanding and show the candidate that they are listening.

Body language

Eye contact and smiling are extremely important and help to communicate that you are open and trustworthy. A firm handshake is also a way of showing that you are confident and a suitable person for the job, but being overconfident is as bad as being shy and nervous, because that may make the interviewer perceive you as big-headed. The way you sit in the interview chair can also give signals to the interviewer. If you slouch backwards during the interview or tap your foot, you may appear not to be interested in the position.

There are other non-verbal barriers that may affect how you communicate. Dress is an extremely important issue within recruitment and selection. How you dress will communicate to your interviewer something about whether or not you will fit into the organisation. It is usual within the business world to wear smart clothes in an interview such as a suit, and for men, a tie. Your choice of dress may be a barrier to communication if you dress in a way that the interviewer does not expect. Wearing clean clothing, being washed with combed hair and appropriate general body hygiene also influences the interviewer subconsciously. Someone who smells too much of aftershave or

Did you know?

According to research by Dr Paul Ekman, you make 'microexpressions' that are involuntary. These give indications about how you are feeling that you are not aware of, such as feeling happy or sad. Other people can see them and this may influence how they feel about you in an interview situation.

perfume can often be as off-putting as someone who has body odour, so this needs to be managed carefully!

Fig. 13.11: What does body language in an interview reveal about an applicant?

Questioning techniques

The use of effective questioning techniques is also very important. Asking the right questions will help the candidate to give the right answers.

Open questions

These are questions that give the candidate the opportunity to give an open answer, for example:

- What is your biggest strength?
- How would you deal with this problem?

They may also be used to check information given.

Closed questions

These are questions that only allow a candidate to give a limited answer, for example:

- How long did you work at ABC Ltd?
- How many GCSEs do you have?

Using a variety of types of question will allow the interviewer to get a good idea about the candidate, so

Activity: Type of questions

Look at the questions below and decide which are closed questions and which are open. Check your answers with someone in your class.

1. Which skills do you think are needed for this job?
2. Do you have a BTEC National Business qualification?
3. Can you type?
4. How long did you work for your last company?
5. What do you think is your biggest weakness?
6. What do you know about our organisation?
7. Is your name Frances Mills?

Imagine you are one of the people asked to interview candidates for the post of Sales Assistant in a shop. They are responsible for customer service, taking money, dealing with the till and filling shelves. Produce a list of closed and open questions that you could ask and practise using them by doing a roleplay in pairs.

it is essential that the questions are prepared before the interview, especially if the interview is going to be done by a team or panel. Questions need to be fair and appropriate.

Barriers to communication

Overcoming barriers to communication is about ensuring the recruitment process is made available in the right places to attract the widest range of candidates possible. Examples of this include jobs being advertised in Welsh and English for vacancies in Welsh-speaking parts of Wales to make them more accessible for English speakers, or advertising vacancies for jobs where women or ethnic groups are underrepresented in cultural or single-sex magazines. New methods of encouraging variety in terms of numbers and types of candidates also include online applications and text messaging information services.

In addition, most organisations have an equal opportunities policy that states how they work to maintain equality of opportunity within their organisation. Equal opportunity policies are designed to encourage candidates to apply for jobs that they may not have considered before. They also give the organisation good publicity, as they are seen as fair.

Analysing and summarising

Analysing answers and making sense of them may lead to further questions. It is therefore important that the interviewer has good listening and analytical skills in order to be able to probe the candidate on their suitability for the post in a fair and controlled manner. After all, this may be the only chance the interviewer has to ask questions and compare candidates before deciding who will be chosen for the job. It is crucial that the interviewer can analyse and judge the answers in order to make a decision. One way to do this is by summarising what a candidate has said to them and checking it back to ensure that what the interviewer thinks is being said is really being said.

4.3 Post-interview

When all the candidates have been interviewed, the job of choosing the best candidate must be carried out. This can be done in many different ways, but a popular method is rating the candidates against criteria with a score. The individual scores are then added up and the totals compared. The candidate with the highest score is the one that gets the job. By doing this, the organisation is trying to make the process fairer and more objective. It is important to recognise that the candidate with the highest score will not necessarily be the one with the most qualifications or experience to do the job. It is the person that is 'best' for the job. Someone with too many qualifications can be just as unsuitable as someone with not enough.

Informing candidates

Once the candidates have been rated and the person chosen for the job, the next stage is to write any other relevant information on the other applicants and why they have not been chosen for the job. This is needed for lots of reasons but the four main ones are to:

- feed back the information to candidates so they can improve in their next job application
- keep notes on why the person was not suitable for the job for the organisation's own records
- monitor equal opportunities, looking at all the different types of people who applied for the job and did not get it – this demonstrates the organisation carried out the process fairly and legally
- keep candidates' notes on record, with the candidates' permission, for consideration of other possible vacancies.

Case study: Southampton City Council

Southampton City Council are an equal opportunities employer. They have an equality statement that is given to every applicant for employment with them. They also carry out equal opportunity monitoring as shown below.

Equality Statement

Southampton City Council has a positive approach to Equal Opportunities and encourages applications from all sections of the community. Southampton City Council will ensure that your application will be judged solely on its merits, irrespective of race or ethnic origin, marital status, sex, sexual orientation, gender reassignment, religion, disability or age.

Equal Opportunities Monitoring

Southampton City Council aims to effectively monitor the success of its Equal Opportunities Policy and Practice. Monitoring Equal Opportunities Data within the recruitment process is a vital element in ensuring achievement in this area. Please ensure that you fully complete and return the Equal Opportunities Monitoring form with your application. This information will be used for monitoring purposes only and will not be considered part of the selection process.

(Source: Southampton City Council)

1. What is the purpose of an equality statement?
2. Why do you think Southampton City Council (SCC) monitors the success of its equal opportunities policy?
3. What benefits do you think SCC gain by having an equal opportunity policy?
4. To what extent can an organisation remove both indirect and direct discrimination from the organisation through its equal opportunities policy?

Activity: Office Junior

To allow you to think about how a simplified rating system works, rate two candidates based on the histories below. Discuss in small groups which of the two would get the job and why.

The job is for an office junior with the possibility of accounting training in the future. The pay is minimum wage and the hours are 35 per week. The two candidates are as follows.

- Emma Champion has three years' full-time work experience in an office but gave up to go and work in a hairdressing salon after a disagreement with the office manager. She has a BTEC National Award in Business completed at Pass level.

- Atif Iftikhar has been working on Saturdays in hotel reception while at full-time college doing BTEC First Business. He is willing to learn new skills.

Rate the candidates on each of the following criteria and give them an overall total.

Table 13.9: Emma and Atif's ratings against the job specification for Office Junior.

Criterion	Emma's rating	Atif's rating
Qualifications required BTEC National Diploma in Business or equivalent at double Merit grade or above		
Demonstrates good customer service skills		
Able to respond to, and follow instructions		
Well organised and adaptable to change		
Able to work under pressure		
Total		

Making a job offer

The successful candidate receives a job offer at this stage. It is usual for the successful candidate to receive communication first so that in the event they decide not to take the job, the other candidates could be contacted afterwards.

Verbal/non-verbal offers

A verbal offer is usually the first way of offering the job and commonly this is done by telephone or face to face. In jobs where the candidates have been through one or two days of recruitment interviews, this is usually done in the evening after consideration by the interviewer(s). The candidate accepts or declines the job verbally. If they accept, a written offer letter is sent to confirm the offer with them.

Contents of job offer

The written offer letter gives details of all the relevant information that the employee may wish to know, including the:

- start date
- salary or wages
- hours of work
- holiday entitlements.

This makes the offer very clear to the candidate. Fig. 13.12 shows an example of an offer letter.

Other conditions

Sometimes employers will want to make the offer subject to additional conditions such as the taking up of references from previous employers, medical or health checks or even the passing of examinations. This is known as a conditional offer. Fig. 13.13 shows an example of such an offer letter.

Expense claims

Often candidates are able to claim expenses for travel, hotels or meals – this is very important if they have travelled a long way. They need to give their receipts to the organisation either on the day of the interview or afterwards by post. It is important that they are given information about how to submit expenses claims at the start of the recruitment process so they are aware of what they need to do. Offering expenses is a good way to attract applicants who are out of the immediate area and therefore can give a wider range of candidates to choose from.

Barnacles Ltd
17 East Street
Brompton
BR9 8KU

Dear Kalpesh

Job Offer for the Post of Finance Assistant

Further to your interview of 18 October, I am pleased to offer you the position of Finance Assistant. The post will commence on 1 January. The starting salary, scale point 8 with a salary of £16,000 per annum. Your working hours will be from 8.30 until 4.30 pm Monday to Friday and you will be entitled to six weeks holiday per year.

Please could you send written confirmation that you wish to accept this job offer as soon as possible.

Yours sincerely,

Mr Crabb
Managing Director

Fig. 13.12: Example of a job offer letter.

Barnacles Ltd
17 East Street
Brompton
BR9 8KU

Dear Kalpesh

Job Offer for the Post of Finance Assistant

Further to your interview of 18 July, I am pleased to offer you the position of Finance Assistant. The post will commence on 1 September. The starting salary, scale point 8 with a salary of £16,000 per annum. Your working hours will be from 8.30 am and until 4.30 pm Monday to Friday and you will be entitled to six weeks' holiday per year.

This offer is subject to a health check with our medical team and you passing your BTEC National Diploma with Double Merit

We will also be taking up references at this stage.

Please could you send written confirmation that you wish to accept this job offer as soon as possible subject to these conditions.

Yours sincerely,

Mr Crabb
Managing Director

Fig. 13.13: Example of a job offer letter, showing additional conditions.

Candidate feedback

Candidate feedback is also important at the end or after the interview has finished. This may be to gain extra information about candidates or ways that the interview process could be improved next time. Gaining information from candidates can also be a good way of finding out what they thought of the organisation and if they would apply again. If candidates go away with a negative impression of an organisation, they may not apply for other jobs there in the future.

Taking up and checking references

Taking up and checking references is a critical stage of the process. It is important because it can confirm where a candidate has worked before and any relevant experience or details from that employer. Some employers will ask for references to be taken up before interview so that a quick decision can be made; other employers will take up references after the interview.

Police and/or medical checks

Police checks are conducted by the CRB (Criminal Records Bureau) in conjunction with the Independent Safeguarding Authority (ISA). These are particularly important if the job involves working with young or vulnerable people. The candidate will complete an application form that the organisation will then send to the CRB to be checked to see if the person has a criminal record. They are also required to work with the ISA to check that the person is appropriate for such employment. The organisation needs to pay for these services but they help to ensure that young and vulnerable people are not put in the care of unsuitable employees.

Medical checks can be completed in two ways:

- by the employee going into the workplace and having a medical completed
- by the organisation writing to the candidate's doctor.

If the organisation chooses to use a medical, the candidate must go into the organisation and have a

Table 13.10: Advantages of taking up references before or after the interview.

Taking up references	Advantages	Disadvantages
Before the interview	• Employers will have all the relevant information before they interview the candidates.	• References will be taken for candidates who will not be offered the job and this takes a long time. • Employees may not wish their current employer to know that they have gone for a job unless they are successful.
After the interview	• References will only be taken up from the successful candidate, so this takes less time. • References will not be taken for somebody who is going to turn down the job offer if they have been asked whether they would like the job in interview.	• The candidate has already been chosen by the organisation and a negative reference at the final stage may mean that the employer needs to rethink the whole job offer.

medical examination completed. The candidate must be given the reason why the examination is needed and what is being looked for. If a health issue is then highlighted, reasonable steps should be made to help that employee be able to do the job as part of the Disability Discrimination Act.

If the organisation uses the doctor to complete a medical check, they must make sure that the information they ask for does not discriminate against the candidate due to disability. The information must also comply with the Access to Medical Records Act and the Data Protection Act. This means that the candidate must be aware that this information is being collected and their written permission given.

Rejection of unsuccessful candidates

Often employers will decide not to reject unsuccessful candidates until they are certain that their preferred candidate has accepted the job. It is important that decisions and information about why applicants were unsuccessful is noted so that they can receive feedback to help them with future applications. This should make the reasons for the appointment and non-appointment very clear. It is important that the reasons for someone not being employed are kept in case they ask for further verbal or written feedback. This should avoid any suggestion that the reason they were not appointed was discriminatory, for example, due to gender, race or age.

Assessment activity 13.4

For the last part of the assessed work for this unit, you must show that you can produce documents and that you understand their appropriate use.

1. Plan to take part in a selection interview. **P4**
2. Take part in a selection interview. **P5**
3. Analyse your contribution to the selection process in a given situation. **M2**
4. Evaluate your experience of planning and participating in the recruitment and selection process. **D2**

Grading tips

1. Remember when you are planning to take part in the selection interview to think of and answer as many questions as you possibly can to practise. **P4** **P5**

2. Think about ways to make yourself relax or cope with nerves. You will need to think about all the skills you have read about and developed during the interview. **M2** **D2**

Just checking

1. Give three reasons for a vacancy.
2. What are two disadvantages of external recruitment?
3. Why do some organisations choose to advertise only internally?
4. To what extent have online applications taken over from more traditional paper-based methods and why?
5. When might the Data Protection Act 1998 be used at work?
6. Name two elements of the Employment Acts 2002 or 2008 and how they influence people at work.
7. What are the advantages and disadvantages of the National Minimum Wage?
8. Name two different documents that are used as part of recruitment.
9. What is the difference between a job description and a person specification?
10. Name three different elements that you would expect to find in a person specification.
11. Explain why an interview checklist is important.
12. Name two different questioning techniques that can be used in the interview situation.
13. What is the difference between a verbal and non-verbal job offer?
14. To what extent might barriers to communication influence the ability of an employer to pick the right candidate for a job?

Assignment tips

1. You may find it helpful to include charts or grids in your work to illustrate your thinking rather than producing written work only.

2. You may find it helpful to include mini case studies and examples of legal cases that you have researched to improve your explanations.

3. Make sure you include the paperwork that you have considered in your appendices and include reference information that you have researched in your work, using a bibliography.

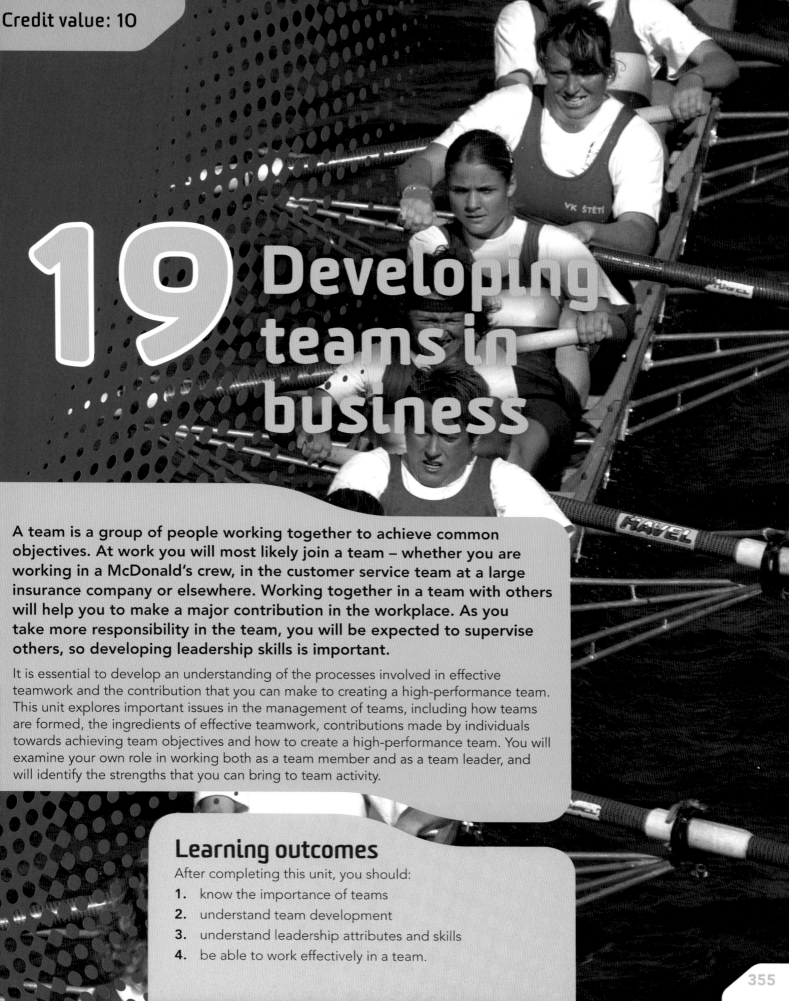

Credit value: 10

19 Developing teams in business

A team is a group of people working together to achieve common objectives. At work you will most likely join a team – whether you are working in a McDonald's crew, in the customer service team at a large insurance company or elsewhere. Working together in a team with others will help you to make a major contribution in the workplace. As you take more responsibility in the team, you will be expected to supervise others, so developing leadership skills is important.

It is essential to develop an understanding of the processes involved in effective teamwork and the contribution that you can make to creating a high-performance team. This unit explores important issues in the management of teams, including how teams are formed, the ingredients of effective teamwork, contributions made by individuals towards achieving team objectives and how to create a high-performance team. You will examine your own role in working both as a team member and as a team leader, and will identify the strengths that you can bring to team activity.

Learning outcomes

After completing this unit, you should:

1. know the importance of teams
2. understand team development
3. understand leadership attributes and skills
4. be able to work effectively in a team.

Assessment and grading criteria

This table shows you what you must do in order to achieve a **pass**, **merit** or **distinction** grade, and where you can find activities in this book to help you.

To achieve a **pass** grade, the evidence must show that the learner is able to:	To achieve a **merit** grade, the evidence must show that, in addition to the pass criteria, the learner is able to:	To achieve a **distinction** grade, the evidence must show that, in addition to the pass and merit criteria, the learner is able to:
P1 describe different types of team and the benefits of teams for an organisation **See Assessment activity 19.1, page 362.**	**M1** compare the roles of the different members of a team **See Assessment activity 19.2, page 374.**	**D1** evaluate the team's overall effectiveness in meeting its objectives, making recommendations for improvements **See Assessment activity 19.4, page 392.**
P2 explain how to build cohesive teams that perform well **See Assessment activity 19.2, page 374.**	**M2** compare the effectiveness of different teams **See Assessment activity 19.2, page 374.**	
P3 define the attributes and skills needed by a team leader **See Assessment activity 19.3, page 381.**		
P4 demonstrate working as part of a team towards achieving specific goals **See Assessment activity 19.4, page 392.**		
P5 demonstrate working as part of a team towards achieving specific goals, dealing with any conflict or difficult situation as a team leader **See Assessment activity 19.4, page 392.**		
P6 review the team's overall effectiveness, together with your contribution to achieving the goals, receiving and providing feedback to other team members **See Assessment activity 19.4, page 392.**		

How you will be assessed

The assessment requires you to demonstrate understanding of what makes an effective team and to demonstrate team working and team leadership skills. Working in a small team, you are required to produce a presentation for a business about teams. This presentation is part of a management training exercise for trainee managers seeking to develop into the business leaders of the future.

Imran

At the start of the unit we were asked to form into teams of five learners. We filled in a questionnaire to identify our preferred teamwork styles. Using this information we then chose to work in teams with others with different preferred styles to our own. We chose a team leader, and decided to rotate the team leadership every two weeks. We planned to produce a poster setting out the purpose of working together in a team.

While we were preparing for the presentation, we kept a log of our activities as team members and team leaders. We made out an audit list identifying situations in which we had demonstrated different teamwork and leadership skills. Later we provided this evidence to our tutor.

Different members of our team were allocated roles. For example, the resource investigator collected all the presentation resources, the team leader acted as the chair, the monitor-evaluator checked on whether we were meeting our objectives and so on. When the second team leader took over, he allocated various parts of the presentation to different individuals. There was a little bit of conflict here but I thought the team leader handled this well, making it seem as if both the individuals in dispute got what they wanted – a win-win situation!

Capitals

First, work on your own for two minutes to answer the following. Next, work with two or three other learners to answer the questions, again during two minutes.

What countries are the following the capitals of?

- Nairobi
- Brussels
- Tel Aviv
- Madrid
- New Delhi
- Warsaw
- Manila
- Wellington.

(Answers can be found on page 393.)

How did your scores compare between the first and second times?

1. Know the importance of teams

When you start work, it immediately becomes clear why teamwork is important. For example, more experienced team members can provide you with excellent advice and workmates can help you when you have difficulties.

1.1 Types of team

A team can be defined as 'a collection of people with a shared purpose and a commitment to working together'. The definition shows why teams are so powerful – everyone in the team knows the purpose of the team, and they are committed to achieving this together. Can you think of examples of where you have already worked in a team?

Formal and informal teams

A **formal team** is one that is created for a specific purpose – for example, to interview applicants for a job. In carrying out this task, members of the team will have specific tasks to do. Other examples of formal teams that you may become part of at work include a 'customer service team' or a 'welcome team' to meet new starters.

A formal team is recognised as being official and will normally be set up to perform a set task or group of tasks. Managers in your workplace will typically be organised in a formal management team.

Another type of formal team that has become popular in business is the 'Quality Circle'. This will be made up of eight to twelve employees who meet at regular intervals to discuss ways of improving the way in which they carry out their work. The Circle will be led by a team leader. Everyone in the Quality Circle will be encouraged to suggest ideas, which may then be taken up to improve the way that work tasks are completed.

An **informal team** develops in a less structured way. For example, a group of new employees might start a

discussion in the canteen about a way of improving a work practice. They might then suggest the idea to a supervisor or manager.

Formal teams have more rules and clearer expectations about the parts that team members should play. For example, a committee will have roles such as chair, secretary, treasurer and so on. The formal team may have written rules.

Key terms

Formal team – team that has been set up by the organisation itself with the purpose of achieving specific objectives. There will often be rules and guidelines about how and when the team should meet, and some form of leadership structure

Informal team – a group of individuals, not officially set up by an organisation, that sees the benefit of working together to achieve given purposes. Informal teams are usually less highly structured and rule-bound than formal teams

Activity: Formal and informal teams

Discuss the following in a small group of learners.

1. What formal or informal teams have you been part of recently?
2. Were they small or large teams?

Compare your answer with those of others in your group.

PLTS

Group members should first list the teams to which they believe that they belong. Then the members of the group should share their lists and see if they can jointly identify which of the teams listed are formal and which are informal teams. Sharing ideas is a useful communication skill. Practise your listening skills by listening carefully to what others have to say.

Did you know?

Quality Circles were first developed widely in Japan. The idea is that ground-level employees can make invaluable contributions to improving work practices, rather than leaving everything to managers.

Size of teams

The size of a team needs to be appropriate to the mix of individuals needed in the team, the task in hand and the speed with which decisions have to be made. If an important decision needs to be made by tomorrow, there is little point in having a very large team to discuss the problem – this will only slow things down.

It has been suggested that the **optimum team size** is five people, because:

- the odd number will prevent a deadlock in decision making
- the team is sufficiently large to avoid the mistakes that result from insufficient information, or the power of one individual with a fixed view
- the group is small enough to involve everyone.

Others argue that a modern team should include between five and fifteen members. The team will be large enough to provide sufficient resources, but small enough to function efficiently. If the size of the team grows too big, it will be as difficult for the members to manage themselves successfully as it would be for a supervisor to manage them.

Activity: Optimum team size

1. Think of your own experience of working in teams on project-based work for this course. What was the best size of team and why?

2. Contrast this with another activity you have been involved with, where a different team size was more effective. Why was the size of team more appropriate in this situation?

Temporary and permanent teams

Temporary project or task teams are set up for a relatively short period of time to complete a task. They come together to agree on a team plan, and they split up when the project is completed.

Key term

Optimum team size – the best size for the team in terms of open communication, all members being able to voice an opinion, and achieving good results

For example, creating advertisements often involves bringing together teams of marketing specialists with different skills working for a particular client. For example, they may work on a television advertisement for a large car manufacturer like Honda. Once the brief is completed, team members may then split up to work on different advertising campaigns for different clients. In creating a temporary team it is very important to:

- clarify the nature of the task or project so that everyone is clear about the purpose of the team
- allocate clear roles within the team so that everyone is clear about what is expected of them.

In contrast, a permanent team is one that works together continuously. Their work is frequently ongoing. For example, if you have had retail experience, you may have worked in a particular sales team. The same sales team will interact with customers in similar ways over an ongoing period of time. Roles and patterns of behaving become established in the team.

Activity: Temporary and permanent teams

Identify one temporary and one permanent team that you have been a member of.

1. Was the nature of relationships in the team different because of the length of time that the team was together?

2. Were there any other noticeable differences?

PLTS

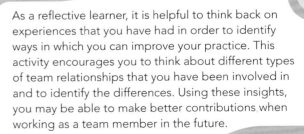

As a reflective learner, it is helpful to think back on experiences that you have had in order to identify ways in which you can improve your practice. This activity encourages you to think about different types of team relationships that you have been involved in and to identify the differences. Using these insights, you may be able to make better contributions when working as a team member in the future.

1.2 Benefits of teams

Teamwork can make a major contribution to departmental and organisational **productivity** and **effectiveness**. Teams are smaller components in larger departments and organisations. It is essential that each team is clear about the targets it has been set and how these can contribute to helping the department and the organisation to achieve its objectives. Teams are all about collective effort rather than individuals working separately. They are thus a very powerful driving force at the heart of any department or larger organisation.

Project teams can be formed to help organisations on specific projects. The nature of a project is that it is a one-off process with a given start time and finish (although these might need to be adjusted). A good example of a project is when an organisation introduces a new way of working. This could involve introducing employees to new information technology applications or health and safety procedures. Alternatively, it could relate to the launch of a new product. Once the product is launched or once staff have sufficient knowledge of the health and safety procedures, then the team is no longer required.

Often a project team will have a project manager who is responsible for making sure that the project is implemented well and the team meets deadlines. It can be very exciting to work in a project team because it often involves working with new people. It is important that the objectives of the project team are made clear from the start and that there is an agreed way of working. The project manager and team should also agree to deadlines and timescales.

Target setting and monitoring

Targets can be set for teams and for the individual team members. For example, in a sales team of ten there may be a target to sell 50,000 units of a product per month. This target might be distributed evenly within the team (that is, 5,000 units each) or different targets may be set according to the type of customer that team members are dealing with.

The team leader will play an important role in setting team targets and agreeing individual targets. Ongoing monitoring can then take place to check whether the team is meeting targets.

Key terms

Productivity – the relationship between output and resources. In terms of teamwork this means the amount and quality of work achieved with a given number of team members. When this increases or improves, productivity will have increased

Effectiveness – the value of the work carried out. An effective team will achieve high-quality results

Innovation – the generation of new ideas

Monitoring performance

There are various ways of monitoring performance of individuals within a team. The most widely used is performance review. Typically this will involve individuals agreeing targets with their team leader. The team leader will periodically review whether individuals are meeting these targets and these will form the basis for discussion at a formal review meeting.

Reduction of alienation

Being alienated means feeling that you do not belong or are not part of something. Alienation can result from being part of too large an organisation. Teams help to break the organisation down into more friendly components.

Everyone has a part to play in a team and this helps motivation. Individuals feel that they have a stake in the decisions that are made. They also feel proud of their contribution to the team.

Fostering innovation

Teamwork approaches also encourage **innovation** because people feel empowered to be creative. They know that if their ideas are exciting, other team members will be enthusiastic; but if their ideas are not appropriate, someone else in the team will modify them constructively.

Sharing expertise

It is possible to share the knowledge base of team members – everyone can contribute ideas. In this way it is possible to share expertise. For example, in a sports team, one member may be able to advise others on how to make the defence work better together. Another may be able to give some useful tips about attacking moves. Another may have played for a rival team and so can tell the others about what playing patterns to expect from their rivals.

In a similar way, in a management team, one person may have expertise of marketing or sales, another of finance and accounts, another may have worked for a competitor, and so on.

Case study: Virgin Airlines air crew

Working for a busy airline like Virgin requires teamwork and co-operation. For example, on the busy route between London Heathrow and Delhi, the cabin crew work an eight-hour shift, serving two in-flight meals, serving drinks, selling duty-free items and attending to the needs of hundreds of passengers.

Cabin crew work in dedicated customer service teams led by a more experienced team leader. All crew will have had extensive training before they make their first flight. Once they are part of the team, they will be looked after by a team leader who is there to coach them and to provide them with support and guidance. In training, the emphasis is on making sure that the team learns to work together and to focus on providing customers with the best possible service. New crew members are encouraged to ask questions and seek advice. Team leaders are trained to be patient and to focus on giving encouragement and help.

Virgin has a dedicated set of staff working the London to Delhi route, although the make-up of the teams will vary from flight to flight.

1. Are Virgin cabin crew members part of a permanent or temporary team?

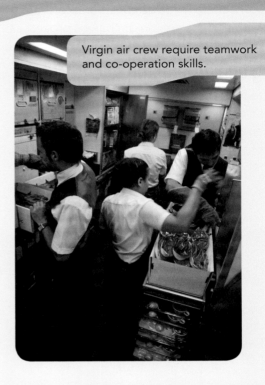

Virgin air crew require teamwork and co-operation skills.

2. Are they part of a formal or informal team?
3. What actions are taken to make Virgin crew members feel part of a team?

Case study: The other tool in the box

Joe Brown has been working as a customer service manager in his local garage for 20 years. He has a number of young apprentices working for him. Joe shows them the ropes when they first start and keeps an eye on the quality of their work. However, he also likes to encourage them to think for themselves.

One of the things that he is forever telling them is that as well as the traditional tools in their toolbox, there is an additional compartment labelled 'initiative'. Rather than waiting to be told what to do all the time, at least once a day they should go to this compartment and try out a new solution, provided there are no major risks involved.

The apprentices often tell Joe that they have used the compartment labelled 'initiative'. It gives them a real pride in what they have achieved. Joe knows that if they are struggling they will ask another apprentice for advice. If the worst comes to the worst, Joe will take responsibility and seek to put things right himself.

1. How does being part of a team encourage initiative?
2. Can you give an example of your own where being part of a team has encouraged you to be innovative?

Implementing changes

Teamwork provides an ideal vehicle for managing change in an organisation. Managing change refers to introducing change in a planned and structured way. Employees can be resistant to change if it is forced on them from above with little explanation. Introducing change through a team involves considerable shared involvement with and discussion of change processes, leading to a greater sense of ownership of the change.

Identifying and developing talent

An effective team needs to be made up of people with different skills and abilities to contribute to the team. For example, Meredith Belbin (see page 366) carried out research in which he identified a number of team roles that help a team to work well. Some of his

roles included people who make sure that a task gets completed; other team roles related to making sure that the views of everyone in the team are listened to.

One of the important roles of a team leader is to make sure that the team recruits people with the full range of skills required so that a team works well. Just as a sports manager will need players who perform different roles – for example, defending the goal or attacking the goal – the team leader of any team needs specialists that are appropriate to the team.

Teamwork also provides an opportunity for managers and supervisors to identify talent within their team, and to provide the development and training opportunities to build on that talent. This is sometimes referred to as talent management.

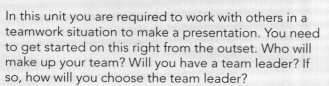

Assessment activity 19.1   **BTEC**

In this unit you are required to work with others in a teamwork situation to make a presentation. You need to get started on this right from the outset. Who will make up your team? Will you have a team leader? If so, how will you choose the team leader?

Next, you need to clarify the purpose of the team. The purpose is to make a presentation using multimedia. Different members of the team need to be allocated roles. Working together reduces alienation and increases motivation.

Part of your presentation asks you to identify different types of team. Who is going to do this? Who is going to check that the work has been carried out successfully? You also need to identify the benefits of working in a team. Who will do this?

You can now start work on this activity. Identify different types of teams and try to provide actual examples of situations where you have come across these teams, for example, project teams, temporary/permanent, formal/informal and so on. You can also

produce a display poster outlining the benefits of teams. It would be useful if you could show how teams can be helpful to a particular organisation.

Describe different types of team and the benefits of teams for an organisation. **P1**

Grading tip

You should develop a set of your own notes which identify different types of teams. It is particularly helpful if you can provide examples – for example, in carrying out this part of the assignment you are working as part of a project team. At work you may be part of a permanent or temporary team. You also need to identify the benefits of teams. Focus on a particular organisation, for example, your local sports centre or place of work, to show how this organisation benefits from effective teamwork. **P1**

2. Understand team development

2.1 Team building

Since good teamwork is a key feature of a successful organisation, it is important to study team building. Teamwork is most likely to be successful when it operates in a supportive environment. Senior managers and team leaders play an important role in creating high-performance teams. However, it is also important to have team members with complementary skills – as outlined by Belbin (see page 366) and others.

Team building starts with recruiting the right mix of team members and then coaching and mentoring members to create a high-performance team. This can be represented in an input, processes and output diagram, as Fig. 19.1 shows.

Recruitment

One of the key responsibilities in managing and supervising people at work is managing the flow of new people into the organisation and retaining those who are already there. Team managers and supervisors therefore have considerable responsibility for overseeing the successful running of a series of integrated activities involved in team building, as Fig. 19.2 shows.

The recruitment process involves identifying the skills and competences that will be required in new team members. This is referred to as job analysis, and from this a person specification can be drawn up setting out all the qualifications and qualities that a new team member would be expected to have.

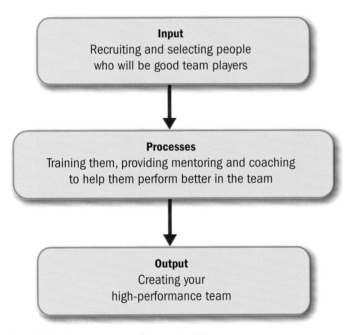

Fig. 19.1: The process of team building.

Activity: Person specification

Set out a person specification for the recruitment of a new team member who would be expected to act as a finisher/completer in a project team brought together to create a new advertising campaign for a cereal bar.

Functional skills

English: A person specification sets out the attributes that an individual needs to have to do a particular job well. In setting out a clear specification, you will demonstrate your ability to present complex ideas in a simple and structured way.

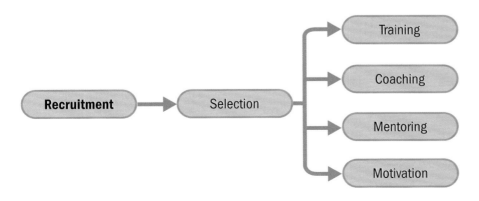

Fig. 19.2: Integrated activities involved in team building.

Induction and training

An induction programme is a series of activities designed to introduce new employees to an organisation, its members and its working practices. Research has shown that tailor-made induction programmes improve staff retention. The induction period is the time when individuals are introduced to their team. It should be seen as an opportunity for team building.

A good induction programme should include:

- describing where the facilities are, for example, toilets, canteen
- showing how the new employee fits into the team
- health and safety information – this is a legal requirement
- an explanation of working terms and conditions
- details of the organisation's history, its products and services, and its values (especially team work)
- a clear outline of the job role/requirements. The requirements of the job and the job role should be explained in terms of how it fits into the team structure.

There are two broad approaches to training people in team working: experiential learning and counselling.

Experiential learning is learning by carrying out real or simulated tasks. This may involve analysing case studies. More often it involves carrying out a number of brief tasks which can be completed successfully with the necessary team skills. After each task, the team, with the guidance of the trainer, analyses the lessons learned from the exercise. In a teamwork situation, experiential learning would involve some form of team simulation or real teamwork exercise. For example, this might include some form of problem-solving activity that has to be carried out in a team structure.

A counselling approach is usually more appropriate with management teams. The trainer is a consultant and advisor and works both with the team and with its individual members.

Coaching and mentoring

Both coaching and mentoring involve an experienced person helping a learner to become more effective. However, there are four key differences between mentoring and coaching, as Table 19.1 shows.

Did you know?

The term coach is used in sport as well as business. A coach is someone who gives advice and support to a coachee. The coach sets targets for the coachee and regularly provides feedback on how they are doing and how they can make improvements. A mentor at work is usually a more experienced employee who gives advice and help to the mentee in a relationship outside of the line of command (that is, rather than in the superior/subordinate role). Some mentors act as supporters and advisors, whereas others take on a more stretching role to help the mentee to extend themselves.

PLTS

Most if not all of you will have benefited from informal coaching from a tutor or friend. Others will have had formal coaching, for example, from a sports coach. Use these experiences to reflect on the questions outlined above.

Table 19.1: Key differences between mentoring and coaching.

	Coaching	Mentoring
Duration	Can cover a long time span, but it can also be limited to a single session	A long, if intermittent, relationship
Benefit for those giving it	A valuable skill for line managers and supervisors	Separate from that of line manager, and the same person should not carry out both
What it covers	Concerned more with day-to-day work	More concerned with longer-term issues such as working relationships and career paths
Group or individual	Can be public – groups of people can be coached	Conducted in confidence on a one-to-one basis

Case study: Coaching to secure change

An international pharmaceutical company has used coaching in recent times as part of a programme of change designed to get the organisation closer to its customers. Managers have had to change the way they operate, from the old-fashioned way of telling employees what to do to encouraging them to make decisions for themselves when working in teams.

Each manager has been assigned a coach. Each pair has between six and eight one-to-one sessions, each two or three hours long, over a six-month period. The manager sets the goals, but it is up to the coach to guide the process. After each session the manager works on the subject covered, and reports on progress next time. One subject covered was coaching skills. Success was measured by feedback from those who worked in teams responsible to the managers.

1. What sort of person would make a good coach?

2. In what ways is the coaching described above different from mentoring?

3. Why did the managers need to change from their previous approach of telling employees what to do?

4. How do you think the employees might have felt about this new approach?

Motivation

Motivation is an important part of supervising and managing team members. It involves making sure that everyone feels part of a team, and that they are given the right training and development opportunities to contribute to the team. Mentoring and coaching can be used to encourage team members, and to provide targets for them to achieve that are manageable, rewarding and motivating.

Team knowledge

Team selection involves identifying potential team members with a specific contribution to make to the team. Team selection will be concerned with identifying a range of personality traits, such as the ability to:

- listen to others
- encourage others to share their ideas
- help the team to move forward
- contribute to a shared decision-making process.

Managers will also need to have an awareness of team members' strengths. An understanding of Belbin's roles helps in the selection of team members. These can be selected to fill the appropriate **team roles**. While working as a team member during this unit, you should reflect on the types of skills demonstrated by other members of your team and also about your own skills.

This is where it will be helpful to keep a **log**. This is a written document that you start when you begin to work together as a team and which you regularly maintain. Failure to keep this log will make it very difficult for you to score higher grades. Try to update your log at regular intervals. Identify who did what in the team. You can then examine Belbin's list of team roles and relate the actions of your team members to these roles. Of particular importance is your own contribution to team roles. Try to extend the range of roles you play as you work through the team activities. Keep regular log entries about your experience of trying out these roles.

You will find that as you work through the unit, your ideas will become more focused as you learn more and more about how teams operate together.

It is worth putting the following major sections into your log from the start.

1. How I worked as a team member helping the team to achieve specific goals (in this case, to produce an effective presentation).

2. How I dealt with conflict and difficulty when acting as a team leader.

3. How well the team worked together to achieve goals.

4. The parts played by others in team activities.

Key terms

Team roles – parts played by individuals within the team. Each part involves behaving in defined ways and bringing specific skills to the team. An individual can play several different roles

Log – a record kept in writing, usually set out in date order

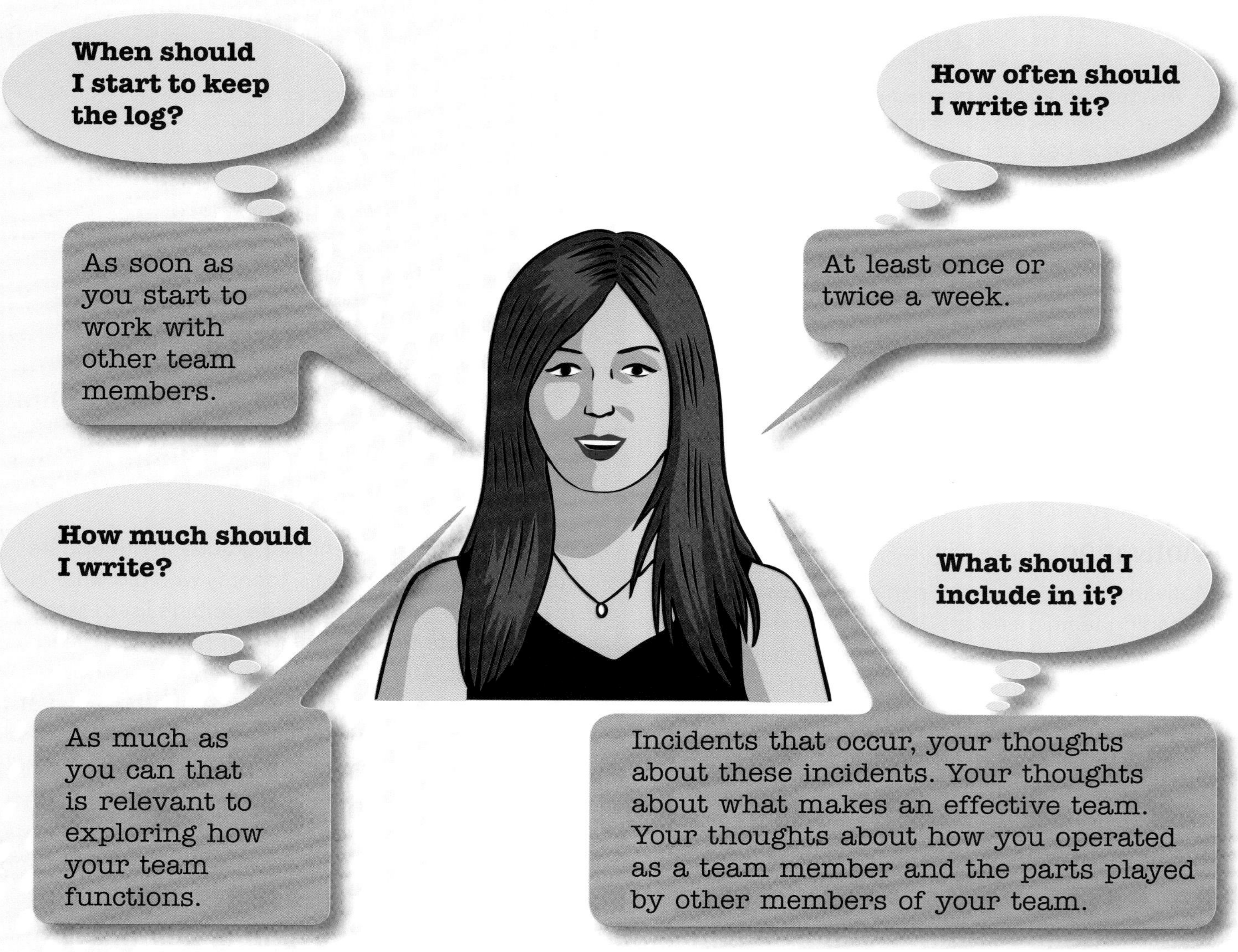

When should I start to keep the log?

As soon as you start to work with other team members.

How often should I write in it?

At least once or twice a week.

How much should I write?

As much as you can that is relevant to exploring how your team functions.

What should I include in it?

Incidents that occur, your thoughts about these incidents. Your thoughts about what makes an effective team. Your thoughts about how you operated as a team member and the parts played by other members of your team.

Fig. 19.3: Do you know how to keep a log?

Your tutor will provide you with helpful additional guidance about how to keep a log.

Team roles

Dr R. Meredith Belbin identified ways in which people behave when put into syndicates or teams. He identified eight major roles, and argued that teams work particularly effectively when they consist of members who are able to play all of these eight roles. An individual may play more than one role. The important thing is to have all of the eight roles covered. The different roles include the following.

1. The **chair** co-ordinates the team efforts and ensures all resources are used effectively in achieving goals.

2. The **shaper** sets the objectives and priorities, and guides the team towards completion of the task.

3. The **plant** is the creative 'ideas' person.

4. The **monitor-evaluator** is shrewd and analytical, and can analyse problems and evaluate progress.

5. The **resource-investigator** is extrovert and good at making outside contacts and reporting developments outside the organisation.

6. The **company worker** is practical, loyal and task orientated.

7. The **teamworker** is caring and very person orientated, keeps the team together and improves communications within the team.

8. The **finisher** maintains momentum and ensures the completion of the task.

Case study: Teamwork assignment

A group of learners was working as a team to complete an assignment looking at the value of working in teams.

Sanjay paid particular attention to making sure that the team was focused on getting the task completed on time. When others were slacking, he set out to remind them of goals and priorities.

Sumita felt that if the team was going to work well, then it would be essential to involve everyone. She spent a lot of time talking to and encouraging others in order to make everyone feel part of the team.

Lloyd felt the team would only work well if it had clear direction. He saw himself as a leader, pulling together the various components of the teamwork and making sure that each of the components of the team had the necessary resources.

Mohammad realised that if the group was going to get high marks, then it would be necessary to tackle the project in unconventional ways. He therefore sought out exciting new methods of working and new ideas to give his team an edge over rivals.

Sandrine was good at looking at what had been achieved and weighing up progress in order to inform other members of the team about what remained to be done. She was good at analysing information and building it into reports.

Sylvester saw himself as a 'mover and shaker', with lots of contacts that he could draw on for advice and information. He was able to use these contacts to benefit the team project.

1. Can you identify the nature of each of the roles described in terms of Belbin's teamwork roles?

2. Which of these roles are more concerned with building the processes of team working and which are more concerned with completing the task?

3. What roles appear to be missing in terms of creating an effective team?

4. Describe two or three individuals who could complete the team by filling the missing roles.

Team development

Staff development is an important role for team leaders and supervisory managers. Planned staff development is the process of identifying development opportunities that meet the needs of individuals in your team – what new skills they can learn that will help them with their work. For example, there may be learning opportunities for new IT packages such as presentation software and spreadsheet packages.

Tuckman and the creation of the high performance team

Tuckman's study of the development of teams is helpful in showing how groups can be developed into real teams given the right sort of support. This is illustrated in a diagram (see Fig. 19.4) with two dimensions – group effectiveness and time.

Tuckman identifies four stages.

1. **Forming** – a number of individuals come together. They are a loose collection with no clear sense of purpose.

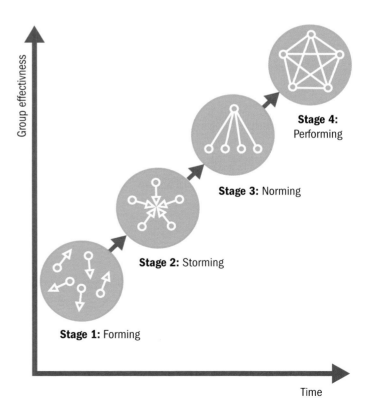

Fig. 19.4: Stages of small group development.

Activity: What is your preferred teamwork style?

Belbin's work showed that successful teams are made up of groups of individuals with complementary skills. Try out this questionnaire to find out where you would broadly fit into Belbin's team. Answer this honestly. We can then identify the broad teamwork role that you like to play. Answers are given on page 393 so you can score your answers to the questions.

In working in a team which of the following best describes the approach you typically adopt?

1. In team decision making…
   a) I like clear action steps that can be implemented in a practical way
   b) I like decisions that are agreed upon, so that the whole team is happy
   c) I like decisions based on the best solution – discovered through clear reasoning.

2. In seeing a task through…
   a) I like solutions that have involved all team members
   b) I like solutions based on detailed knowledge and understanding
   c) I like solutions that are efficient and practical.

3. When working with others…
   a) I like to listen to everyone's view
   b) I like people who can turn ideas into practical solutions
   c) I like to share my knowledge with the team.

4. A good description of my team role is that I am…
   a) disciplined, reliable and efficient
   b) enthusiastic and communicative
   c) creative, imaginative and unorthodox.

5. In my view, the most useful member of a team is someone who is…
   a) able to solve difficult problems
   b) able to listen, build on the ideas of others, and avert friction
   c) able to deliver on time.

6. Which of these descriptions best fits the contribution you make to a team?
   a) Implementer (putting things into practice)
   b) Team worker
   c) A solver of difficult problems.

7. One of my weaknesses in working in a team is that…
   a) I am reluctant to delegate responsibility to others
   b) I worry too much about other people's feelings
   c) I am too preoccupied to communicate my ideas clearly.

8. Another of my weaknesses is that…
   a) I tend to dwell on technical points
   b) I lose enthusiasm once the initial enthusiasm is passed
   c) I can be easily provoked when people do not focus on the task.

9. I would describe my team role as being primarily…
   a) cerebral (thinking/ideas)
   b) people-oriented
   c) action-focused.

10. In working in a team…
    a) I like to get the project completed
    b) I like to build strong team bonds
    c) I like to use brain power to come up with good ideas.

2. **Storming** – the group begins to exchange ideas, but there is as yet little structure to the group, and there are no clear plans to take the group forward.

3. **Norming** – the group beings to share ideas – a team begins to form. A leadership pattern may begin to emerge, and the group starts to conform to a given set of ideas. Decisions begin to be formulated.

4. **Performing** – the group transforms into a high-performance team. A clear organisational pattern is formed, based on mutual respect, the sharing of ideas and the drawing out of plans and proposals from all members of the team. Every member of the team is therefore able to make the best possible contribution to the group process.

Did you know?

Research into the way that learners form teams for assignment work shows a slightly different picture from that set out by Tuckman. When learners are allowed to choose team mates, they will usually pick their friends. So there may be quite a lot of norming that takes place at the outset. However, learner teams often fail to engage in getting on with the task when they are in a friendship group. This changes when deadline dates loom and this can lead to quite a lot of disagreement and blaming. Hopefully these issues are then resolved. However, in some teams the blaming continues, resulting in poor work. What are the implications for how you choose a team?

Supporting team members

Team leaders have an important responsibility for helping to build team morale by supporting and encouraging their team members. Good team leaders make it their business to try to support all team members. The team leader who motivates the team and makes them feel valued is able to retain valued employees (enabling the organisation to be more effective and to reduce costs). Good team leaders also know when to delegate. You do not have to do everything yourself; you need to know when to trust other team members. Trusted team members are typically the most committed ones.

Understanding weaknesses and sensitivities

Good team leaders and team developers understand the strengths and weaknesses of their team members. For example, some team members are good at coming up with ideas, while others are good at the process side of things – that is, making people feel comfortable within the team.

Good team leadership and team membership involves being sensitive to the skills and abilities of others. For example, if someone has good ideas, it helps if others are encouraged to listen to these ideas. If someone is good at finishing and completing a project, then they can be given more responsibility in the later stages of the project.

Activity: Teamworkers

The following have been identified as the qualities of a successful teamworker. The teamworker:

- has good listening skills
- has good persuasive communication skills
- is able to express technical ideas lucidly (clearly) to persuade other people
- is receptive to new ideas
- is not afraid to look foolish by airing new or unconventional ideas
- understands and is committed to the team's objectives
- can give and take constructive criticism
- trusts and is trusted by fellow team members
- expresses feelings honestly and openly
- does not claim personal credit for a team success.

Which of the above characteristics do you honestly believe you have recently shown in team situations?

PLTS

Here is another opportunity to build up the entries in your log, which is an excellent tool to support reflective learning. Write about the characteristics outlined above that you most frequently display. Then try to develop some of the other characteristics that you feel are important. By reading back through your log, you will be able to keep a record of how your skills of working in a team are improving over time.

2.2 Team performance

Business organisations place a strong emphasis on performance. There are four main ways of measuring team performance.

1. Individual's contribution to the team. This can be measured by how the individual works with other team members. For example, this could be shown by the extent to which they contribute to team meetings, whether they volunteer for team projects, how they communicate with others (for example, in a supportive or threatening way).

2. Individual results from teamwork. The work carried out by a team member that contributes to the final team product could be assessed.

3. Team performance. This could involve looking at team dynamics; for example, how well the team works together, the effectiveness of team meetings, the ability of the team to achieve agreement and so on.

4. Team results. The team performance could be measured in terms of its work results, for example number of cases or products completed, the use and acceptance of the team's report, and so on.

In judging how well a team is working, you need to decide on which measures to use – probably a combination of several of the above.

Performance indicators

In business it is good practice to create **performance indicators** (PIs). A performance indicator helps to measure the extent to which an individual or team meets targets.

Key term

Performance indicators – measures of specific aspects of performance, which might involve things which you can attach a number to, or indicators that something did or did not happen in the required way

Team performance indicators (TPIs) can be set out in terms of processes or in terms of products or outputs. For example, a team effectiveness process indicator might be that 90 per cent of team members attend team meetings, and that teams agree to arrive at a consensus view by voting on issues where there is disagreement.

Output/product indicators are measured in terms of the results of team activities. For example, you could measure the effectiveness of a sales team in terms of the number of sales that the team makes.

Target setting

Team performance indicators act as targets for teamwork activity. Examples might include:

* the team will meet at regular weekly intervals
* everyone in the team will have the chance at some stage to chair a team meeting
* the team will set out to make sure that the views of all participants are listened to.

In addition, the team might set work-based targets, for example:

* the team will increase output by five per cent per month
* individuals in the team will each increase their output by five per cent per month.

It is then a fairly straightforward task to monitor the success of the team in meeting its targets. Regular checks need to take place to make sure that performance is on track. For example, in a learner project, targets are set that in two weeks' time Davinder will have researched the topic, Mohammad will have prepared a PowerPoint presentation, Claire will have interviewed the managing director of a company, and so on. A review can then be carried out to check that these individual targets have been met so that the team is on track to complete the project.

Monitoring and review of performance against targets

It is then possible to measure each individual's performance and the team's performance against these targets. It is possible that certain team members have fallen behind. This indicates that they may need extra support and encouragement. For example, Mohammad may not have completed the PowerPoint presentation because he lacks the right sort of skills, or because Claire has not given him the information he needs to put into some of the slides.

Support and development of team members

Sometimes team members will require additional support to make up for current weaknesses. For example, Mohammad's team leader might put his name forward to go on a training course to develop his information technology skills further. The training and development manager in an organisation will liaise closely with team leaders to try to identify training and development needs of individual employees. A TDNA (Training and Development Needs Analysis) can be used to identify areas of weakness in an employee. Using this analysis, it is possible to identify the types of training programmes that enable individuals and teams to perform better.

Fig. 19.5 shows an improvement cycle for team performance.

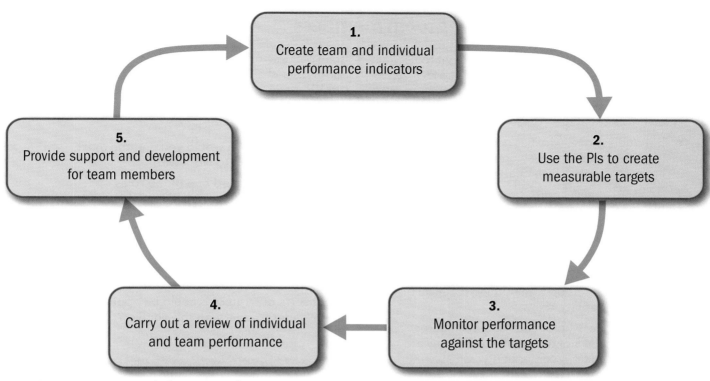

Fig. 19.5: Improvement cycle for team performance.

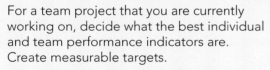

Activity: Performance indicators

For a team project that you are currently working on, decide what the best individual and team performance indicators are. Create measurable targets.

Then, once the team project is underway, set a date/dates at which performance will be monitored. Carry out a review at this point. Decide how support will be provided for individuals and the team if the project falls behind plan.

PLTS

Keep a record in your log of the type of function that you perform within the team and whether you think that this is a good thing or not. If you feel that you the team would benefit from you performing a different role or function, then try to make a change. Reflect in your log about what happens when you make a change in your practice.

2.3 Team cohesion

In **cohesive** teams, some members tend to concentrate on task functions while others focus on process maintenance roles.

Task functions help the team to get the task done. They include:

- proposing objectives
- clarifying goals
- seeking information and opinions
- keeping the group on track
- summarising ideas
- suggesting ways forward
- evaluating contributions.

Process maintenance roles include:

- supporting other group members
- ensuring all members of the group are included
- reconciling disagreements and reducing tension
- making suggestions for compromise
- monitoring the group.

Key term

Cohesive – sticking together, united

371

Case study: Belbin's other team members

We saw earlier that Belbin identified eight roles that are required for effective teamwork. However, Belbin did not mention some of the other more negative players that you are likely to come across in teamwork situations. These include:

- the clueless one, who has no idea about team goals and confuses everyone by identifying irrelevant issues which bear no relation to team goals

- the idler, who promises to do all sorts of things by given deadlines, but the work never materialises, so the rest of the team becomes demotivated

- the critic, who knocks down everyone else's ideas but comes up with nothing practical or realistic to replace them

- the rude one, who offends and intimidates other members of the team, so that they are discouraged from contributing

- the apathetic one, who does not join in and looks disenchanted

- the 'doesn't-turn-upper', who is not there, does not want to get involved and has not done the required work in any case.

1. Which of the above would you find the most frustrating to have to work with?

2. Have you ever played one of the roles described above? If so, what sort of impact do you think you had on team motivation and performance?

3. Which of the above is most likely to spoil group cohesion? What sort of conflict is likely to arise?

4. What sorts of strategies could be applied by a team leader to deal with this conflict?

Problems with cohesion

Lack of cohesion in teams can occur for the following reasons.

- Team goals are poorly defined. If you do not know what the goal is, how do you expect to achieve it? How can people pull in the same direction, if they do not know what that direction is?

- High turnover of team members. There is no continuity or stability. What the team had previously agreed on may be disputed by new members. High turnover is typically a sign of poor motivation.

- Little opportunity for career progression. Commitment to the team will be limited because most people want opportunities for personal development and career progression.

- Contributions are not recognised or rewarded. People will be less inclined to contribute next time. They do not like being taken for granted or having the credit for their work taken by someone else. They feel cheated.

- Weak or authoritarian team leadership. Under weak leadership a team quickly loses direction. Under an authoritarian leader, team members may be frightened to voice their ideas and innovation is stifled.

- Internal challenges to team leadership. This can lead to disputes, disagreements and lack of focus on team goals. Both the process and the task performance begin to lack clarity. This is also the case when actual or potential conflict between members exists. In these situations, team members concentrate on individual differences rather than team goals.

- The team is unable to be a **self-managing team**. In the absence of the team leader or supervisor, the ongoing effectiveness of the team suffers.

- Particular members are not suited to the nature of the work. For example, a team leader in a situation requiring democratic discussion may be too used to operating in an autocratic way (where just one person is in charge).

- Personal problems. Members' personal problems may prevent them from concentrating on their work.

- Frequent resort to crisis management (also known as firefighting). Rather than planning ahead, and deciding on priorities and ways of tackling problems when they arise, teams may be faced

Key term

Self-managing team – a team that has had the training and developed the skills to work on its own to solve work-related issues

with problem after problem, all of which need to be resolved immediately, and have no clear framework for dealing with them.

In the event of team under-achievement, corrective measures will need to be applied. Many of these will relate to the process, and some will relate to both the task and process. For example, in situations where the team leader may be away on important business, the team needs **empowerment** to operate as a self-managing team, making decisions for itself, with appropriate structures for working independently without supervision.

In order to create team cohesion, it is essential to develop a number of team management strategies to avoid the problems noted above.

Definition of team goals

From the outset it is essential to set out clear team goals. What is it that the team is seeking to achieve? For example, if the goal is to play entertaining football, then this is quite different from the goal of trying not to lose a match. In the former, the team might concentrate on attack; in the latter, the emphasis might be more on defence. If team members are clear about their goals, they are more likely to concentrate effectively on them.

Management of group conflict

It is very important to develop strategies for managing conflict. Actual conflict occurs when there are obvious disagreements. Different team members want things to be done in different ways. Team managers can also anticipate potential conflict. For example, in a team with an ideas person who is a poor finisher, others may be frustrated by the inability of the ideas person to complete tasks. It is therefore essential to be aware of this potential difficulty, perhaps by allowing the ideas person to generate ideas but not have responsibility for task completion.

Management of group turnover

Group turnover is another major issue in business. This means new people come into the team while others leave to work elsewhere. This can be harmful if a key member of a team leaves at a crucial time.

Ways of dealing with this include preparing succession management – that is, training someone to take over the role of the person who is leaving, before they go. In preparation for the Rugby World Cup in 2007, the

Key terms

Empowerment – the process of spreading power and decision-making responsibility across the organisation and within teams, rather than a few key individuals retaining it

Group turnover – the rate at which the members of a team change

New Zealand rugby management made sure that they had two people to fill every position on the field – just in case of injury.

Other ways of reducing turnover include providing incentives for people to stay in the team. A good way of doing this is to offer opportunities for career progression at work. A team member could be promoted within the team, so they have no cause to go elsewhere. Other strategies involve recognising the contributions of team members; this makes them feel good about what they are doing – so they feel that they are valued members of the team.

Team leadership

Weak leadership can be another reason why teams lack cohesion, as teams need to have some sort of direction. It is important to have the right leadership for the team, as there are different leadership styles.

- An authoritarian leadership style is one where a particular individual is controlling and likes to make most of the decisions. This works in teams where the rest of the team is happy to be told what to do. However, many people resent authoritarian styles.

- A consultative style is where a leader consults with other team members, asking them for advice before coming to a decision for the team. Members feel more involved, although ultimate direction is with the team leader.

- A democratic style is the opposite of an authoritarian one. Here there are lots of leaders. Everyone is listened to and plays a part in team decision making.

Activity: Leadership styles

1. Which of the styles outlined above would you prefer to work with in teamwork situations?

2. Which of the leadership styles do you tend to adopt?

3. Can you think of situations in which each of the styles described would be most appropriate?

Activity: Corrective measures

What corrective measures can you suggest for the following situations? An example is given to get you started.

Table 19.2: Situations requiring corrective measures.

Situation	Solution
Lack of recognition of members' contributions	Articles in company newsletter naming individuals and their good ideas; bonuses for particularly good ideas
Persistent reliance on crisis management	
Poor definition of team goals	
Weak team leadership	

Assessment activity 19.2

To carry out this activity you will need to be working as part of a team of learners with the responsibility for creating a PowerPoint presentation which sets out:

- the characteristics of a high-performance team
- obstacles in the way of creating a high-performance team
- ways in which these obstacles can be overcome through effective team management
- a description of the way in which your learner team has set out to overcome any obstacles to your team development, and how you have created a high-performance team.

1. Explain how to build cohesive teams that perform well. **P2**

2. Compare the roles of different members of a team. An effective way to do this is to keep a log setting out the roles that you and different members of your team play within the team in which you are working. **M1**

3. Compare the effectiveness of different teams. To do this you should identify a number of team situations in which you have been involved, good and bad. In the light of this unit and further reading, create a critical commentary on why some of the teams that you have worked in have been more effective than others. **M2**

Grading tips

1. You could examine the characteristics of high-performance teams and then use examples of successful teams and show how these examples fit with the theory that you have outlined. You could also give illustrations of obstacles to high team performance by quoting examples, such as a well-known team that suffered because one of the members made life difficult for others. Use the example of your own learner team to outline ways in which high-performance processes may or may not be achieved. **P2**

2. As soon as your team has been decided on, you should start to keep a log of incidents that took place within the team and who did what. Once you have started to read about Belbin's theories and tried some of the associated activities, you will be able to reflect on the roles that you and others play within the team you are working in. **M1**

3. Make a list of all the team situations you have been involved in and then identify which of these involved effective and which ineffective team work. For the critical commentary, compare situations in which there was effective or ineffective teamwork and the reasons behind this. **M2**

3. Understand leadership attributes and skills

3.1 Leadership

Leadership skills are important. Leaders get things done and they make change happen. The leader gives direction to others and enables them to follow a chosen path.

An important distinction is often made between management and leadership. Management involves making sure that various tasks are carried out well and that resources are used efficiently. Leadership goes further than this because it involves getting things done in new and different ways, and persuading others to follow your direction.

Table 19.3: Good management versus good leadership.

Good management	Good leadership
Getting tasks done well	Getting tasks done differently
Working within the existing patterns and rules and doing this well	Changing the existing patterns and rules for the better
Getting other people to do their jobs in the expected ways	Getting others to do their jobs in new ways
Inspiring and motivating other people to do what is expected of them	Inspiring and motivating other people to do new things in new ways

Most modern organisations operate in a competitive setting in which frequent changes are required. Leadership skills are therefore required to drive change.

3.2 Leadership styles

A **leadership style** is the way in which a person tries to lead others over a period of time. Their style is their chosen approach and will determine the way others see them and react to them. There are four types of leadership style:

- autocratic
- democratic
- participative
- laissez-faire.

Autocratic leaders give instructions that they expect other people to carry out. This may work in situations where employees need to have very clear instructions and where the leader has a lot of knowledge. However, key weaknesses with this approach are that most employees do not like being ordered around, and that the ground level employees may have lots of good ideas that they could share with their leader if given the chance.

Democratic leaders like to listen to the points of view of those that they work with. They tend not to make a decision until they have heard others' ideas. They will consult rather than tell.

Participative leaders encourage those that they work with to participate in decision making. They will delegate responsibility for certain tasks and encourage subordinates to come up with suggestions for making changes and give them an input into decision making.

Laissez-faire leaders leave the decision making and the responsibility for decisions made to others. The advantage of this approach is that the leader is encouraging others to think for themselves. However, this can lead to frustration with employees complaining 'he doesn't give any leadership' or 'she heaps all the responsibility on to our shoulders'. It can also lead to a lack of structure.

Key term

Leadership style – the predominant type of behaviour that a leader uses when leading a team, for example, to be domineering, or to be cautious. The leader does not necessarily use this style all of the time

The impact of different leadership styles

The type of leadership style employed will have an effect on team performance. There are three factors to consider, which are:

- the preferred management style of the leader
- the style of leadership that team members are used to or prefer
- the situation in which the team is operating.

An autocratic style will work best when team members hope to be directed in this way and when the situation

Activity: Leadership styles

1. Have you worked with any of the four types of leaders described? How did they make you feel? Were you motivated to do your work?

2. Look at the following photographs showing well-known leaders. If you do not know much about these leaders, carry out some research on the Internet. Members of your team could choose to research a different leader each. When you have carried out your research, discuss where you would place these leaders on a grid with autocratic at one end and democratic/participative at the other end.

or task requires a clear command structure. For example, in some situations where urgent action needs to be taken, and only the team leader has knowledge and experience of what to do, then autocratic leadership may be suitable.

In contrast, where team members have considerable skills, knowledge and experience about decisions that need to be taken, then it would be better to use a democratic or participative style.

PLTS

Here is a good opportunity for you to demonstrate team working skills when working with others. Carrying out the task will encourage you to listen to each other, and to build on each others' ideas. Try to make sure that everyone gets involved in the discussion.

Activity: Good and bad leadership

1. Can you provide examples of team situations that you have experienced in which you have preferred a particular style of leadership?

2. Can you give examples where the style of leadership has been unsuitable both for the team members and in the situation?

PLTS

In our everyday life in family situations, at school/college, at work and when socialising with friends, we regularly operate as part of a team in which there is some form of leadership structure. Reflect about a number of situations in which you have felt that the leadership style was inappropriate for the team and for you. What can you learn from this?

Adapting leadership style according to situation

It is likely that the appropriateness of using an autocratic or democratic style depends on whether the situation facing management is 'favourable' or 'unfavourable'. A favourable situation would exist when:

- the leader is popular and trusted by members of the team
- the task is well defined
- the power of the leader is high.

The 'best-fit' approach suggests that different styles are most suitable in different circumstances. The degree of fit can be measured on a scale running from 'tight' to 'flexible' as illustrated in Tables 19.4 and 19.5.

The good fit in Table 19.4 is represented by a situation in which a democratic leader is working with employees seeking to be empowered in a situation requiring flexibility. The poor fit in Table 19.5 is illustrated by a similar situation but with an autocratic leader.

Activity: Your leadership style

Consider your leadership style in working as part of a team in a given situation.

1. Do you want to control your team?
2. Are you happy to discuss things with your team?
3. Do you believe that you know more than them, so should be making the decisions for others to follow?
4. Do you think that some opinions of team members are not worth listening to?
5. Do you mind having to wait to get a consensus view from the team before moving ahead to a decision?
6. Do you want to create an agenda and to take charge of important decisions?
7. Do you want all of the team members to get involved in decision making?

If your answers are yes to questions 1, 3, 4 and 6, then you are probably an autocratic leader.

If your answers are yes to questions 2, 5 and 7, then you are more likely to be a democratic or participative leader.

Table 19.4: An example of good fit.

Tight							Flexible
Task							x
Leader							x
Subordinates							x

Table 19.5: An example of poor fit.

Tight							Flexible
Task							x
Leader	x						
Subordinates							x

3.3 Leadership skills

Much has been written about the qualities of leaders. Some of this writing contradicts other work. Some writers suggest that leaders may have certain traits or personality and physical characteristics. For example, Charles Handy suggests that research shows that leaders:

- tend to have a dynamic and assertive personality
- are of above average intelligence without being brilliant
- tend to be either of above average height or relatively small.

He also suggests that leaders are able to take a 'helicopter view' of what is going on around them. In other words, they can see the situation from above rather than getting tangled up in small details.

Did you know?

Napoleon Bonaparte is often cited as an example of a leader who was of below average height. Can you think of people with strong leadership qualities who are below or well above average height?

Power and authority

A distinction is sometimes drawn between power and **authority**.

- Power involves the ability to force through decisions.
- Authority involves having the legitimate right to make decisions (for example, because you are the managing director of a business, or the team leader).

A good team leader will have both power and authority. Their authority rests in their title of team leader, and their power rests in their ability to use that authority and their personality to get other members of the team to do things.

There are a number of different types of power that a leader has.

- **Charismatic power** – this is power that an individual has because of their personality. For example, it could be argued that Barack Obama has a lot of **charisma**. People listen to him because they are swayed by his personality.

- **Legitimate power** – this is based on a leader's official title and the legal power that goes with it. Barack Obama has legitimate power as the President of the United States to make many important political decisions. Alan Sugar of *The Apprentice* fame has legitimate power to fire people on the show (as well as in his own company because he is the Managing Director).

- **Expert power** – this is based on having a high level of knowledge and skills. For example, when decisions are made in a college of education about spending money to hire new lecturers, the views of the college accountant will be listened to. They have expert power based on their knowledge of the financial situation about the college.

- **Reward power** – leaders have considerable powers when they are able to reward members of their team. They have the 'carrot' of being able to reward those doing well and the 'stick' of being able to take rewards away from those that step out of line.

- **Coercive power** – this power stems from the ability to be able to force somebody to do something. Bullying is one example of coercive power.

Key terms

Authority – legitimate power to do something, usually based on the position or experience of the person in authority

Charisma – having a strong personality, usually one which captivates and motivates others

Activity: Power

Which of the five types of power described above are going to be most suitable for leading a learner team? Think about this within the context of the presentation that you have been asked to put together for this unit.

Authority and responsibility

Leadership brings with it the authority to make decisions, providing it is backed up with appropriate sources of power. As a team leader your team will expect you to perform a leadership role. Your ability to carry out this role depends on what sorts of power you exercise and how willing team members are to accept this power.

The other side of being given authority is that you will also be in a position of responsibility. You will be responsible for the decisions that the team makes and you will be responsible for the members of your team.

Team, task and individual needs

John Adair developed a very helpful model of leadership, which is useful for anyone taking up a team leadership position. The model shows how a good leader can lead any type of team.

Adair carried out research into the leadership of teams and larger organisations and found that 'good leaders' command three main areas. He illustrated these as three overlapping circles.

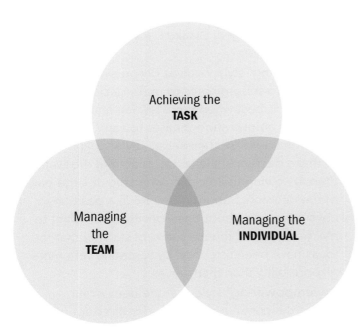

Fig. 19.6: John Adair's model of leadership.

When a team leader is able to balance these three factors well, this will enhance team morale and increase the productivity of the organisation.

How to successfully achieve the task

- Clearly define the task to be carried out.
- Clarify what resources and people are needed to complete the task.
- Create a plan to achieve the task.
- Establish who is responsible for what and when.
- Set the standards that need to be met.
- Control the task activities to check that they are being carried out properly.
- Monitor how the task is being carried out compared with your plan.
- Report on progress to the team.
- Adjust the plan if necessary.

Managing the team

- Agree and communicate expected performance standards to the team.
- Set out the approach that the team will use.
- Anticipate and resolve conflicts that may occur.
- Develop a teamwork approach.
- Agree team roles (who will do what).
- Identify training needs of team members.
- Give the team feedback on their performance.

Managing the individual team members

- Treat each person as an individual.
- Understand the personality, skills, needs and fears.
- Assist and support.
- Set individual objectives for team members.
- Help individuals to create a personal plan to fit into the team plan.
- Recognise and praise the achievements of team members.
- Give some freedom to individuals to make personal contributions.
- Reward team members for their efforts.
- Use the strengths of the individual team members.
- Provide training opportunities for individual team members.

A continuum of leadership styles

Many researchers have explored different styles of leadership. Managers are interested in this work, particularly in deciding on leadership roles that they and others should play in organisations. Management training typically involves study of management styles. In your own research you are likely to come across a number of articles about different approaches to leadership styles. One of the best known of these is the continuum approach outlined below.

Tannenbaum and Schmidt described the factors which influence a manager or team leader's choice of leadership style. Their research led them to argue that there are three main forces influencing the style adopted.

- **Personal forces**, including the leader's own background, personality, confidence and preference for a leadership style.
- **Characteristics of others involved in the decision-making process** (for example, subordinates), including the subordinate's background, personality, confidence and preferred leadership style, and the willingness of subordinates to take responsibility.
- **The situation**, including the typical patterns of behaviour within the organisation, the nature of the decision that needs to be made, the time available to make the decisions, and the existing ways of working.

They set out a continuum of leadership styles as Fig. 19.7 shows.

In Fig. 19.7, as we move upwards to the right the manager is using less authority and is instead allowing a greater amount of democratic decision making.

The 'best' style of management depends on the situation and the people involved.

- A **'telling'** style is best when subordinates are not prepared to take responsibility for themselves. They want the leader to tell them what to do. They may be unable and/or unwilling to take responsibility and therefore need to be directed.
- A **'selling'** style is best when subordinates are only moderately ready to take responsibility themselves. This approach offers both direction about what to do and support to those who are unwilling or unable to take responsibility. The leader will direct subordinates but also explain to them what they need to do and give them feedback on their performance in order to maintain motivation. Leaders therefore go out to 'sell' new ideas and decisions to employees, for example, by saying, 'Look this is a great idea – if you buy it, you will reap the benefits.'
- A **'testing'** style involves allowing subordinates to try out decision-making processes for themselves. The leader may test out new ideas on subordinates, encouraging them to start to take some of the responsibility and ownership for carrying out the decision and seeing it through themselves. However, if things do not work out, there is still scope for managers to take back full responsibility for the decision.
- A **'consulting'** style involves giving even more freedom to subordinates to make decisions. This style is best when there is a fair amount of readiness among subordinates to carry out and make decisions for themselves. By enabling others to make decisions, the leader is able to motivate them by giving them clear ownership of large parts of the decision. Subordinates are in a position to consult leaders about decisions that they want to make. This gives them a sense of security that their ideas have been screened by someone with more responsibility than themselves.
- An **'empowering'** style is at the democratic end of the continuum. The leader does not use authority over others. This would be the case in a self-managing team in which each individual has a key contribution to make to the decision-making process. Everyone is broadly at the same level and therefore takes an equal share of responsibility.

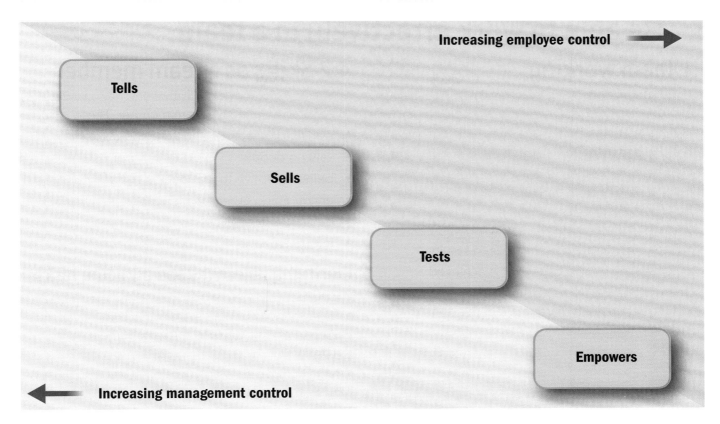

1. Tells – Management decides, then tells staff.

2. Sells – Management gets input from staff before making decisions.

3. Tests – Employees test out the decision making process for themselves.

4. Empowers – Employees empowered to take responsible decisions themselves.

Fig. 19.7: Continuum of leadership styles.

Assessment activity 19.3 P3 BTEC

This outcome activity will help to provide evidence of P3 – define the attributes and skills needed by a team leader.

1. Decide in your team how you would like your team to function. If you are going to appoint a team leader, which approach would you like the team leader to adopt? Each member of the team should justify in 250 words the approach that they would be most in favour of. This should be neatly set out and kept as evidence. It should provide the basis for a group discussion.

2. Next, in your team you should discuss Adair's three circles approach. How can you make sure that your team covers each of the three areas well? Come up with a collective plan that sets out how each of the areas outlined by Adair can be successfully achieved.

3. Individually create a poster setting out the attributes and skills of a team leader. P3

Grading tip

Make sure that you are clear about Adair's model first. Working in your team, discuss the different styles of leadership and which of these you would like your group to adopt. Revise your own ideas in the light of group discussion. Put a picture of your ideal team leader at the centre of your poster. Your poster should be put into your evidence for this unit. P3

4. Be able to work effectively in a team

4.1 Team working

An important aspect of your work on this unit is being able to demonstrate your ability to work as a member of a team.

Working in a team enables individual members and the team as a whole to achieve far more than from independent work. We have seen that high-performance teams:

- share a clear picture of what is to be achieved
- pull together to achieve the desired results
- jointly feel responsible for what is achieved.

It is this notion of joint responsibility that is particularly important. When team members feel this, then they seek to help each other rather than to compete with each other.

Activity: Team purpose

Make sure that all of the members of your team are clear about the purpose of working together as a team. The purpose is to achieve a particular goal – that is, to make a presentation to an invited business person to outline key aspects of team working. This is to be seen as a management training exercise, so you need to carry it out professionally. Make sure that all team members understand how structured collaboration will increase individual and team efficiency, and individual and team productivity.

PLTS

Working in your small team of learners, you need to demonstrate team working and effective participation skills in deciding on how you will work together to create a presentation about effective teamwork. Make sure that you can come to an agreement about what you collectively understand to be good teamwork, and agree that this will be the approach you will use in preparing your presentation.

4.2 Skills as a team member

There are a number of skills that you need to develop to become an effective team member. These include:

- clarifying objectives and agreeing tasks
- valuing people
- being receptive to feedback
- encouraging other team members
- dealing with conflict
- interpersonal skills.

Clarifying objectives and agreeing tasks

If a team is to be successful, then team members need to be aware of what the team is trying to achieve. Failure to do this will lead to disagreement and frustration.

When you have clarified your objectives, you must then identify the tasks that have to be completed to ensure that the objectives are achieved.

PLTS

You will be able to demonstrate effective participation through involvement with the activity (opposite), and team working through preparing the plan together.

Valuing people

For a team to work, the people that make up the team need to want to be a part of it. They also need to show respect for and value the other members of their team. Belbin demonstrated that teams require different types of role. Not everyone wants to play some of these roles. By valuing other members of your team, you will find that this encourages them to make contributions that you are not able to make yourself.

People frequently have an ability to surprise us with their knowledge and skills. By encouraging them and respecting their contribution you are most likely to make others feel valued and encourage them to make important contributions. You can show that you value people by:

- listening to their ideas
- encouraging them to voice their views
- praising their efforts.

Activity: Assessment brief

At the start of this unit your tutor will provide you with an assessment brief. The assessment brief requires you to work together as a team to carry out a particular task. Here it is suggested that the task should be to make a presentation about teamwork to a business person.

In order to clarify your objectives, it will be helpful if each member of the team writes down a few sentences about what they see as being the objective of working together as a team, and what they understand the task to involve. Discuss this as a group. Then create a poster setting out your shared understanding of the task, and the objectives of working together as a team. Display this poster in a prominent position.

As a team, you also need to create a chart displaying the sequence of tasks required to be completed. The chart could look something like the following. This only has some of the details filled in. You will need to decide on the actual sequence of activities and procedures for the final delivery of the presentation.

Table 19.6: Sequence of tasks to be completed.

Task	Description	Carried out by
Set objectives	Discuss and decide on the objectives of working together as a team	All team members
Identify the task	Make sure what the overall task is	Team members working with tutor
Choose team leader	Choose a team leader – it is likely that you will want to either share out the team leader role or change the team leader from time to time	Team members
Break down the task	Identify the various sub-components of the task into a flow chart	Team leader and team members
Choose a business leader	Choose a business leader to whom the end presentation will be made	Team leader working with tutor
Research benefits of teamwork	Research the literature and class notes to identify the benefits of teamwork	All team members. Team leader may delegate one member of the team to present this information
Research theories of teams	Research theories of the roles of team members, Belbin and so on	As above
Research theories of team leadership	Research theories of leadership – for example, Adair's ideas	As above
Prepare structure of presentation	Decide on how the presentation will be conducted – who takes responsibility for what?	Team leader and team members
Prepare presentation	Prepare the resources, plan how the parts of the presentation will fit together	Individual members of the team under the leadership of the team leader
Evaluation of teamwork	Discuss how well the team worked together	Team members
Evaluation of leadership roles	Discuss and comment on the effectiveness of individuals in carrying out leadership roles	Self-evaluation and feedback from at least one other team member
Evaluation of team member roles	As above	Self-evaluation and feedback from team members

Being receptive to feedback

Other people are able to see things about you that you may not be able to see yourself. Sometimes they will detect weaknesses in the approach you use or the way you make suggestions. Hopefully they will give you feedback about what you do (right or wrong) rather than about your personality. If you want to move forward, it makes sense to listen to feedback rather than taking it as criticism. It is helpful to thank someone for useful feedback and to take on board what they say when it is appropriate to do so.

Encouraging other team members

Other team members are always capable of suggesting improvements to the way that a task is carried out and the way in which the team is working together. In many instances, these improvements will help to improve teamwork. An important team skill is therefore to encourage your team mates to suggest improvements. There are various ways of doing this through asking questions.

- 'Has anyone got any good ideas for…?'
- 'How can we make improvements?'
- 'What else can we do?'

Dealing with conflict

In any good relationship there will always be some disagreement. However, this disagreement needs to be managed in a constructive way. It is important to distinguish between criticism of the individual and criticism of the idea. In the former case, it is important to deal with this immediately and to try to conciliate (end the conflict and reach an agreement) between the various parties. Failure to do so can lead to 'toxic teams' – which are not really teams at all.

People do not have to like each other, but they need to show respect. It can be helpful therefore to set out an agreed set of rules that create the boundaries for interpersonal team relations.

Criticism of ideas is far more constructive and should be encouraged – provided it does not conflict with team objectives such as completing a task on time. Within the team it is healthy to discuss disagreements, provided it is made clear what the purpose of the discussion is (for example, to come up with the best solution to a problem from alternatives).

Interpersonal skills

High-performance teams communicate frequently along well-defined channels of communication. A good communicator in the workplace will possess the following qualities:

- active listening skills
- questioning
- body language
- assertiveness.

Active listening skills

When someone else is talking, try to listen in such a way that you get a clear picture of the point that they are seeking to get across. Often they will be making a point that you agree with. If you do not listen, you may find the discussion going at cross purposes. Be prepared to sit back and listen rather than just concentrating on the points you want to get across.

Active listening involves three steps.

1. Hearing – listening hard enough to catch what the speaker has to say. For example, the speaker might be talking about team roles and says that it is important to have a leader. You can demonstrate that you have listened carefully by rephrasing what the speaker has said and verbalising it in a friendly and appreciative way.

2. Understanding – you take in what has been said and understand it in your own way. When you heard the speaker say that it is important to have a leader, then you understand that the speaker could be suggesting that the team should have a leader.

3. Judging – if you understand what the speaker has said, you will want to judge whether it makes sense. Has the speaker put forward a good case for having a leader? What were the arguments put forward? Were they sound arguments? To get to stage three you really need to listen carefully.

Questioning

Learn to ask questions that help the team and others. These include seeking information: 'Does anyone know?', 'Has anyone had any experience of…?', 'Does anyone know how to…?'

Questions can also be used to clarify: 'When you said… did you mean that?', 'Can you explain that again?', 'Can you give another example?', 'Do you mean that…?'

Questions can be used to find out the prevailing opinion of the team: 'How many of you think that…?', 'Do most of us believe that…?'

Questions may move the team forward: 'Can we move on to the next point now?', 'Do you feel that we have discussed this for long enough now?'

Body language

Body language is of central importance in any form of effective communication. It works well when members of a team mirror each others' body positions, and when they sit forward and look interested. In contrast, body language is not helpful when individuals look too defensive, or when they point and jab fingers in an aggressive way.

> ## Key term
>
> **Body language** – use of the body, for example, facial expressions or gestures, as a means of communication to support other forms of communication such as speech

Assertiveness

An assertive approach allows you to work well within your team and help the team to work well together. Common weaknesses when working in a team are either being too aggressive or too passive. But being assertive helps your team to work much better.

Assertive behaviour involves standing up for your own rights in such a way that you do not violate another person's rights, and expressing thoughts, feelings and beliefs in direct, honest and appropriate ways.

In practice, this means that an assertive person:

- talks calmly at a dignified pace
- sticks to the point or repeats a point
- uses a questioning style
- does not raise their voice.

Non-verbally, an assertive person may use their hands to explain a point, or nod to show that they support another person's point of view or that they are listening.

The consequences for the assertive person for behaving like this are that it allows them to:

- receive the attention and respect that they deserve
- be emotionally honest
- remain in control
- value themselves and others.

The consequences for others are that they:

- feel valued and respected
- feel that they have something to contribute.

However, being effective at being assertive takes time, and there are particular techniques that you may need to practise in order to feel confident at being assertive. These include:

- be smart with your non-verbals: maintain eye contact, try to control your facial expressions even if you are feeling really angry or upset, and remember

Fig. 19.8: What is wrong with each of these body positions in a team meeting?

that nodding helps to show you understand even if you do not agree

- reduce conflict: try not to interrupt the other person, and when you feel they have finished, show that you have registered their point of view. For example: 'I can understand why you might think that…' You can then have your say, state your point of view by continuing with the word, 'however…'

- persevere positively but politely: you need to ensure that your message has got across and has been understood. Depending on the situation and the composure of the person you are talking to, this may take some time. Remember to control the volume and tone of your voice and to remain composed at all times

- handle criticism being specific: the skill here is to decide when it is valid and then how to handle it. Ask for an example of when you behaved in a particular manner. Then try to find out what aspect of your behaviour they are unhappy with and try to reason out the situation calmly. If you are criticising someone's behaviour, be specific and try to explain how their behaviour upsets you.

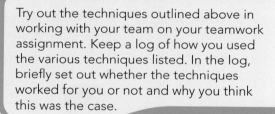

Activity: Assertiveness techniques

Try out the techniques outlined above in working with your team on your teamwork assignment. Keep a log of how you used the various techniques listed. In the log, briefly set out whether the techniques worked for you or not and why you think this was the case.

4.3 Responsibilities as a team leader

We have already outlined important aspects of the role of the team leader on pages 375–81. The responsibilities you take on as a team leader are very important in preparing you for work practice once you complete this qualification.

The team leader needs to act as a role model for other team members. This involves being prepared to put in the extra hours and to show extra commitment to the team.

Common purpose

A key responsibility of the team leader will be to make sure that the team has a common purpose. When you are acting as team leader, what actions can you take to make sure that this common purpose is clear and that everyone is working towards it?

It will be helpful to publish team goals – perhaps in a written statement. The leader then needs to refer to these goals continually and stress ways in which tasks are goal oriented. Successes of the team should be related to team goals.

Integrity

Another quality of the team leader is that of integrity. If the team leader lacks this quality, then it is unlikely that the team will be taken seriously. Integrity relates to keeping confidences. If one member of the team tells you something in private, then you should not repeat this to other members.

The team leader also needs to make sure that the team is operating in an honest way and is not taking short cuts. The team leader must model this quality and demonstrate it through the actions they take. If you are chosen as team leader, how will you go about modelling integrity?

Fairness

Being fair involves:

- allocating responsibilities so that some individuals do not feel that they are bearing an unequal share of the burden

- making sure that team members have sufficient time to carry out tasks

- not having favourites who are given some of the more attractive tasks to do.

Consistency in decision making

Being consistent is a very important work practice. As a team leader you will be required to make a number of decisions. At work these decisions will be implemented on a daily basis. Team members know where they stand with a consistent team leader. A team leader who makes contradictory decisions will confuse the team.

4.4 Skills as a team leader

There is a range of skills required by a team leader that are listed in the **audit** document for the following activity.

Key term

Audit – a formal examination of something to see that it is true and fair

Activity: Leadership skills

Copy out the following document. You should then provide evidence of how you have demonstrated each of these skills when performing a team leadership role. Make it clear what the context was/is in which you are or were acting as a team leader.

Table 19.7: Evidence of leadership skills.

Leadership skill	Evidence of having demonstrated this skill (what you did)
1. Verbal communication	
2. Non-verbal communication	
3. Planning	
4. Team building	
5. Leading by example	
6. Providing and receiving feedback	
7. Setting objectives	
8. Motivating	
9. Consulting	
10. Problem solving	
11. Valuing and supporting others	
12. Stretching people's talents	
13. Monitoring	
14. Preventing and resolving conflict	
15. Fostering creativity	
16. Adapting leadership style to situation	

High quality local cheese – everything must go today!

Surbhi was appointed team leader for an *Apprentice*-style challenge in which her team of BTEC Business learners had to compete against a rival team. The brief was to sell locally produced cheese at the Saturday market in the local town. A local cheese manufacturer had provided the two teams with a large quantity of cheeses. They had to choose which of the cheeses to trade on a market stall and how to price and promote the cheese.

Before the exercise started, Surbhi decided that her team would only stock high-quality, high-price cheese. At the team meeting, she presented this idea to the team and was surprised that there was quite a lot of opposition to the idea. Some of the other learners felt that it would be more sensible to sell cheaper cheeses and to try to sell everything on the market stall.

Eventually Surbhi compromised and decided that the team would sell under the banner 'High-quality local cheese – everything must go today!' There was some grumbling about this but Surbhi insisted that this is what they would do. She decided that there should be sufficient time for discussion. Unfortunately this did not leave much time for planning the pricing campaign and a strategy to promote the cheese. There was a bit of a rush to collect the cheese from the suppliers and the team found that some of the cheeses they wanted to stock had already been taken by the other team.

Think about it!

1. What do you think Surbhi did well in leading the team?
2. What should she have done better? What changes would you suggest?
3. Make a list of the leadership skills that Surbhi employed. Which skills do you think were missing?

Communicating

You are likely to be familiar with *The Apprentice* television series. Each week, teams compete against each other on a task set by Sir Alan Sugar. One member of the team is chosen as the team leader. Some of them do it well and others perform badly.

In *The Apprentice*'s challenges, the team leader only has a limited amount of time to decide on a course of action. Having good communication skills is therefore very important. The sort of communication skills that are required are to:

- clarify the nature of the task facing the group
- listen to the views of the team as to how to carry out the task
- make a list of what needs to be done
- inform the team about who will be doing what
- often organise some sort of sales pitch
- make a presentation of what has been achieved
- report back to Sir Alan.

In communicating verbally you will need to speak clearly and with confidence. Make sure that you know what you are talking about. Focus on the key message that you want to get across, and avoid getting sidetracked into irrelevant issues. Avoid long pauses and 'ers' and 'ums' that break up the flow of the message.

You will also need to apply the active listening skills that were outlined on page 384.

Your body language needs to be open and positive. Eye contact is important as well as a confident – but not over-confident – stance.

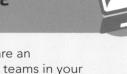

Activity: *Apprentice* challenge

Encourage your tutor to prepare an *Apprentice*-style challenge for teams in your class to compete against each other. This could involve competing to sell a product for a local company, or to prepare an advertising campaign for them.

An *Apprentice*-style challenge provides a good opportunity to assess team leadership and teamwork skills.

Planning

Creating an effective plan is an important management skill. Plans are usually set out on paper (or electronically). For the purpose of your team exercise, a simple plan using the following format as shown in Table 19.8 would be helpful. Set out the purpose of the plan briefly in one sentence.

Team building

Teams need to be built. The leader needs to take an active role in building the team. In business, team building may involve organised team-building exercises such as 'away days' where the team tackles a series of challenges together. The challenges are designed to encourage co-operation.

Table 19.8: A sample plan.

Action to be carried out	By whom	By when	The evidence required to show that the action has been completed successfully

In a similar way, it can be helpful to carry out activities in your team that encourage co-operation.

Leading by example

Good team leadership typically involves 'leading from the front'. This involves demonstrating to other members of the team that you are prepared to get your hands dirty where necessary and that you are prepared to do those things that you ask others to do for the team.

Providing and receiving feedback

When you give feedback to another member of your team, it is always helpful to ask them to give their point of view first. For example, after carrying out an activity, the team leader could ask 'How do you think that went?' rather than immediately giving their own opinion. This approach helps the team leader to see things through the eyes of their team and also gives the message that the team leader values the views of others.

The team leader should also ask for feedback. This might involve creating a feedback form to evaluate an activity or simply leading a discussion to monitor progress.

Setting objectives

Ultimately it is up to the team leader to make sure that objectives are set for the team. This is an important starting point for any series of activities. In the bustle of everyday working activity, some members of the team can lose sight of the objectives – for example, the football player who gets involved in a fight with

a member of the opposing team and is sent off has forgotten that the objective is to win the game! The role of the team leader is to keep the team focused on the objectives and to remind the team of how well they are performing.

Motivating

Motivation is the desire to achieve given objectives or to carry out tasks. Motivation comes from within an individual. However, the team leader can influence motivation by creating the desire to achieve within individuals and the wider team.

Earlier we looked at Adair's three circles (see page 379). One of these focused on leading the team and another on leading individuals. They showed the importance of motivating. The team leader can use a range of motivational strategies, including:

- continually encouraging the team and getting to know them as individuals
- helping to establish ambitious yet achievable targets
- encouraging participation in agreeing and setting objectives
- making sure that the reward system reflects effort and achievement
- rotating work within the team to maintain interest and involvement
- identifying factors that hold back achievement and making sure that something is done about them.

Consulting

Consultation involves asking people for their views and opinions. When team members are consulted, they feel a sense of ownership of the decisions that are made. Rather than feeling that a decision has been made for them, they will feel that in some ways they have played a part in making that decision.

In consulting others you will need to use questions such as:

- 'I would like your opinion on…'
- 'What do you think of this idea?'
- 'Which alternative do you think is the best and why?'

Problem solving

Team leadership can be seen as ongoing activity to solve problems so as to help a team meet its objectives. There are different types of problem.

Open-ended problems are problems where there are no set answers. New ideas may be helpful in solving these problems. Team leaders can use a number of problem-solving techniques to encourage the team to come up with ideas. One possibility is a brainstorming activity. The team leader poses a problem and then asks the team to come up with suggestions. The team leader writes all of the ideas on a flipchart or whiteboard. At this stage there is no discussion of the ideas – they are simply listed. After a suitable period of time, the team leader will ask the team to look at the various suggestions to see which are the most suitable. Criteria may be set out to evaluate the options.

With closed problems, there is likely to be a 'best answer'. The leader poses the problem and the team then works to find the best solution. The problem may be a 'deviation' problem. This is where the team is deviating (moving away) from a pre-established plan. The purpose of the problem-solving activity will be to find the best way to get the team back on plan.

Valuing and supporting others

Good team leaders support all the members of their team. They look on the positive side and are typically encouraging. When reviewing progress, you should focus more on what went well, although you need to identify the weaknesses in a fair way. You can value others by pointing to their successes, identifying who did what well.

Stretching people's talents and managing aspirations

Team leaders in the workplace play an important role in developing their team members. Everyone has talent; it just needs bringing out. When you play the team leader role, try to identify the particular qualities of your team members. How can these be built on both for the sake of the individual and for the good of the team? In addition, you need to find out about people's aspirations. Everyone has ambitions and hopes. All too frequently they are ignored at work, leading to frustration. Within the context of your teamwork assignment, see if you can spot opportunities for individuals within the team to do those things that they feel they are good at.

Monitoring

Monitoring involves checking how well things are going and spotting problems. The principal tool for doing this is the initial plan that you will have set out, as discussed earlier. Team meetings provide the opportunity to check on progress against the plan. By spotting areas where the team is falling behind the plan, it is possible to allocate additional resources and time to getting back on track.

Activity: Monitoring

Interview someone who has had team leadership experience, and ask them what is involved in monitoring progress at work. Create a poster entitled 'The role of the team leader in monitoring the work of a team'. Add a photograph of the team leader at the centre if possible, and create a spider diagram illustrating the activities they have to carry out in monitoring team progress.

Preventing and resolving conflict

Preventing and resolving conflict is important in reducing tension in a team and raising team morale. You can resolve conflict by stepping in when there is a disagreement. One way is to try to identify and maintain the positives in both positions; this will make it a 'win-win' situation.

It is even better if you try to anticipate conflict. Conflict will occur when people:

- have different ways of working
- have different characters
- give different values to their contribution to the team.

Try to anticipate where conflict is likely to occur and take actions to prevent this. For example, if you think that one person is likely to try to force their view on others without listening to alternatives, then encourage others to put forward their views first.

Fostering creativity

Creativity is important in any team. Coming up with creative solutions differentiates stronger from weaker teams. For example, a well-led team in *The Apprentice* with a creative solution to a problem often wins the day. The important thing is not to stifle creativity. You can foster creativity through the following.

1. Identify creative individuals in your team.

2. Encourage activities such as brainstorming that encourage your team to think more imaginatively.

3. Establish creativity and originality as important objectives of your team.

4. Praise and reward individuals who come up with creative ideas.

Adapting leadership style according to the situation

Earlier in this unit we examined a 'best-fit' approach. This involved matching the leadership style with the style in which team members want to be led and the situation in hand. In taking up a leadership role you should apply this understanding.

- What is your preferred leadership style?
- How do your team members like to be led?
- What is the most appropriate leadership style for the tasks that you are required to do?

Activity: Leadership style

Decide on a leadership style that you think is suitable for making sure that the assignment for this unit is carried out well.

- If you are the team leader, choose the most appropriate 'best-fit' leadership style.

- If you are being led, then make it clear to the team leader how you like to be led and what you consider to be the best leadership style for the tasks you are being asked to complete.

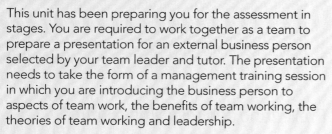

Assessment activity 19.4

P4 P5 P6 D1 **BTEC**

This unit has been preparing you for the assessment in stages. You are required to work together as a team to prepare a presentation for an external business person selected by your team leader and tutor. The presentation needs to take the form of a management training session in which you are introducing the business person to aspects of team work, the benefits of team working, the theories of team working and leadership.

You must also report on how well your team functioned as a team, and the leadership qualities demonstrated by the team leader/leaders. Additionally, you are required to provide evidence for your tutor of the various team working skills and team leading skills that you possess.

1. Demonstrate working in a team as a member towards specific goals. **P4**

2. Demonstrate working in a team towards specific goals, dealing with any conflict or difficult situation as a leader. **P5**

3. Review the team's overall effectiveness together with your contribution to achieving the goals, receiving feedback and providing feedback to other team members. **P6**

4. Evaluate the team's overall effectiveness in meeting objectives, making recommendations for improvements. **D1**

Grading tips

1. It is essential that you keep a log or record of how the team functioned and the part that you played in helping the team to function. Make sure that you keep the log in the way identified at the start of the unit or in ways suggested by your tutor. The log should provide you with useful evidence to demonstrate how you have worked in a team during the study of this unit. **P4 P5**

2. With feedback, other people are able to see things about you that you may not be able to see yourself. If you want to move forward, it makes sense to listen to feedback rather than taking it as criticism. Try to take on board what they say when it is appropriate to do so. **P6**

3. 'Evaluate' means to make justified judgements. Make it clear how your findings provide supporting evidence for your team's overall effectiveness in meeting objectives, and for your recommendations for improvements. **D1**

Answers

Answers to 'Capitals' activity on page 357

- Nairobi: Kenya
- Brussels: Belgium
- Tel Aviv: Israel
- Madrid: Spain
- New Delhi: India
- Warsaw: Poland
- Manila: the Philippines
- Wellington: New Zealand.

Answers to 'What is your preferred teamwork style?' activity on page 368

Question	Answer (a)	Answer (b)	Answer (c)
1.	action orientation	team orientation	cerebral orientation
2.	team orientation	cerebral orientation	action orientation
3.	people orientation	action orientation	cerebral orientation
4.	action orientation	people orientation	cerebral orientation
5.	cerebral orientation	team orientation	action orientation
6.	action orientation	team orientation	cerebral orientation
7.	action orientation	people orientation	team orientation
8.	cerebral orientation	people orientation	action orientation
9.	cerebral orientation	people orientation	action orientation
10.	action orientation	people orientation	cerebral orientation

When you have identified which of the three categories your answers match most, refer back to page 366 to identify how you fit with the teamwork roles Belbin suggested.

- **Action orientation:** wanting to get things done and therefore focusing on the task more than the relationships between people involved in the team.
- **People orientation:** focusing on relationships, seeing these as more important in achieving team goals than the focus on the task itself.
- **Cerebral orientation:** quiet thinkers, focusing on the ideas primarily – these types may come up with creative and insightful ideas, and may see some of the problems in the suggestions of others.

Belbin felt that all three types were important in teamwork.

Just checking

1. How would you define a high-performance team?
2. What is the appropriate size for a team?
3. List four benefits of organising employees in a hairdressing salon into teams.
4. Why is it important to set clear team objectives?
5. Which two of Belbin's team members do you see as being most influential in helping to create a successful team?
6. What is the difference between 'storming' and 'norming'? What needs to be done to take 'norming' through to 'performing'?
7. What do you consider to be the most important communication skills required in teamwork?
8. What do Adair's three circles represent? Describe one of these in detail.
9. What do you think are the most important team leadership skills? Why?
10. In terms of the continuum of leadership styles, which approach are you most likely to employ and why?

edexcel

Assignment tips

1. The assessment requires you to focus on two main themes of:

   - having the underpinning knowledge and understanding about how teams work and the roles of team members and leaders

   - actually working as part of a team and being aware of your skills as a team member and team leader.

2. Make sure that you work on these two areas right from the start and that, at the outset, the team you work in sets clear objectives and tasks to complete by given dates. If you do this, completing the assessment task will be relatively easy.

3. The assessment requires you to create a presentation as part of a management-training exercise to inform an invited business person about teamwork and teamwork skills. Make sure that you prepare and target your presentation with this in mind.

4. Take it in turns to perform team leadership roles. Keep a record of how and when conflict arose in your team, and the strategies that were used by team members and the team leader to deal with this.

33 The impact of communications technology on business

Communications technology is a force changing business, life and the world. This unit is important in understanding business today. It takes you through some history of the Internet and the web, covers a range of ways in which the Internet can be brought to use by businesses and outlines some of the latest digital communications technologies.

It then deals with some possible pitfalls and problems, before outlining some of the benefits – for both businesses and customers – that can be the result of good online business. Finally, the unit covers some of the ways in which businesses and individuals can plan and prepare for a world in which we can all benefit by doing 'digital business'.

Learning outcomes

After completing this unit, you should:

1. know how the Internet operates and the facilities available
2. be able to use the Internet and related technology for a range of business activities
3. understand how organisations adapt to trends in the use of e-business
4. understand the key features of planning for the increased use of e-business at different levels.

Assessment and grading criteria

This table shows you what you must do in order to achieve a **pass**, **merit** or **distinction** grade, and where you can find activities in this book to help you.

To achieve a **pass** grade the evidence must show that the learner is able to:	To achieve a **merit** grade the evidence must show that, in addition to the pass criteria, the learner is able to:	To achieve a **distinction** grade the evidence must show that, in addition to the pass and merit criteria, the learner is able to:
P1 describe how the Internet operates **See Assessment activity 33.1, page 407.**		
P2 describe examples of how the Internet is used by selected, contrasting businesses **See Assessment activity 33.2, page 419.**		
P3 use the Internet for different types of business activities **See Assessment activity 33.3, page 434.**	**M1** demonstrate how to solve problems in Internet use for four different types of business activity **See Assessment activity 33.2, page 419.**	
P4 describe the actions taken to reduce risks to security while using the Internet for different types of business activities **See Assessment activity 33.3, page 434.**		
P5 explain the competitive pressures on selected, contrasting business organisations to develop their use of e-business **See Assessment activity 33.3, page 434.**	**M2** explain how two selected, contrasting business organisations have responded to competitive pressures to develop their use of e-business **See Assessment activity 33.3, page 434.**	**D1** evaluate how successful a selected business organisation has been in preparing for the growing use of e-business **See Assessment activity 33.3, page 434.**
P6 explain how the government supports the development of e-business **See Assessment activity 33.4, page 437.**		
P7 produce a personal development plan to help an individual prepare for increased use of e-business **See Assessment activity 33.3, page 434.**		

How you will be assessed

The assessment requires you to prepare presentation materials and web-blogs on e-business developments. You also need to produce a portfolio of evidence of your own business-related skills, a SWOT analysis of your own skills and an action plan for your own updating and development.

Kulbinder

In my group some of us were lucky enough to have an iPhone so we were able to use that as a starting point to think about what communications technology used to be like. After discussion we arranged to survey some local businesses to see how they were using mobile technology possibilities and then did a presentation that included case studies.

When we started investigating the way that things were changing it was interesting to see how many businesses and organisations were relying more and more on the Internet. Even our own college used the Internet for buying and managers were issued with BlackBerries so they could always be in touch. Most members of staff used laptops now and could access their emails and the intranet from anywhere with a wireless connection.

1. Do you think some businesses rely more (or less) on the Internet than others? Give examples.
2. What benefits do you think the Internet has for Kulbinder's college?

Facebook

The social networking site Facebook had 120 million members in 2009 and was one of the most-visited sites on the Internet. There are many other social networking sites, some of them specialising in particular interests such as Geni.com for people interested in family history, Goodreads for book lovers and Ravelry for knitting and crochet.

Write out a list of the main ways you feel a business could make good use of specialist and general social networking sites.

1. Know how the Internet operates and the facilities available

1.1 How the Internet works

The Internet and the worldwide web

It is a common mistake to confuse the worldwide web (www) and the Internet. Technically, they are not the same thing; the Internet has existed for over fifty years, long before the web. While it is the 'web' that has made the Internet such a vital part of our lives today, without the basic techniques that enable computers to talk to each other, the web would be useless.

The 'Internet' refers to the massive network of connected computers stretching all over the world. In fact, the word Internet comes from the two words, **inter**connected and **net**works. The Internet is a linked network of computer networks.

This in itself does not quite explain how so many PCs are able to connect together and exchange information. Computers on the Internet do not all link to the same central 'mega-computer' that holds all of the information or services we need. Within each sub-network on the Internet, some PCs hold the information we need and others just access the information. This arrangement is known as 'client–server' architecture.

Remember

The worldwide web and the Internet refer to two different things that evolved at different times. The Internet has existed since the 1960s. However, without the worldwide web, there would be limited use for the Internet.

Servers and clients

The Internet works on the basis that some computers act as **servers**. These computers offer services for other computers that are accessing or requesting information; these are known as 'clients'.

Key term

Servers – higher-capacity computers that offer services to client computers that can connect to them

So, sitting in your room at home, or your school or college computer workshop, you are able to access the Internet because the PC you are using has a connection to a server. Your PC will have a piece of software loaded on it called a browser. This software (often Internet Explorer, but possibly Netscape or Mozilla Firefox) takes your request for Internet access and services, and then displays the results on your PC. To do this, your browser mainly reads Hypertext Mark-up Language (HTML); this is the simple code created by Tim Berners-Lee.

You might require different types of information or services from the Internet. You might want a written document from a website, or a catalogue, multimedia presentation, photograph, video, piece of music or email. Different kinds of servers can deliver different services. Server types include:

- web servers
- email servers
- application servers.

Types of connections to the Internet

There are different ways of connecting to the Internet. This includes the speed with which you can connect and get access to services – a very important consideration for most users. A 56K modem (modem being an abbreviation of **mo**dulator **dem**odulator) uses an analogue connection using the phone lines. Every time you need access to the Internet, analogue or ISDN (Integrated Services Digital Network) modems must dial a number to secure a connection. The modem's job is to convert analogue signals (which are continuous rather than pulsed or discrete) received into digital format so your PC can understand them.

A growing trend is for more and more Internet users to switch to a broadband connection. Broadband gives permanent, 'always on' connectivity, so there is no need to dial a number. DSL and cable are types of broadband connection; these are much faster than analogue or ISDN links. Broadband connection (as the 'broad' part of the name suggests), carries more data, at a faster rate than dial-up. Because of this, it is becoming more popular both for home and business use.

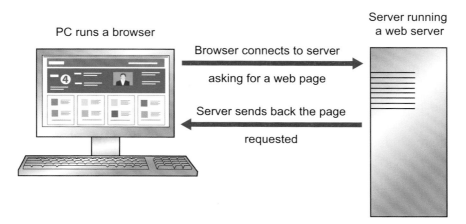

Fig. 33.1: Client–server architecture.

Internet service providers (ISPs)

An Internet service provider is a business that offers Internet access services for both businesses and individuals. The main function of an ISP is to provide a link to the worldwide web. Many ISPs these days also host websites and offer email services. Examples of ISPs are Wanadoo, BT Internet, Tiscali and Pipex.

Protocols

A protocol is a particular way of doing something. When computer scientists in America were first developing the Internet, there had to be common agreement about how computers would 'speak' to each other. What has emerged is a set of protocols that everyone using the Internet must follow. Important ones are:

- Internet Protocol (IP)
- Transmission Control Protocol (TCP)
- Hypertext Transfer Protocol (HTTP).

Internet Protocol (IP)

Internet protocols establish a unique name for every computer on the Internet. This is a ten-digit number, for example, 216.24.62.133; each number separated by the point is called an 'octet'. This identifies every network, host and organisation on the Internet.

Key term

Internet protocols – agreed ways of doing things so that everyone on the Internet connects in the same way

Transmission Control Protocol (TCP)

IP addresses let the Internet find the right route for messages, so that they get to where you want them

Remember

Computers are able to speak to each other because of a series of protocols that everyone agrees to follow.

to go ('get me in touch with Yahoo! please'). But it is Transmission Control Protocol (TCP) that takes the overall piece of data (whatever it is), breaks it down into 'packets' (units of data routed between an origin and a destination on the Internet or any other packet-switched network) and checks for errors, reassembles the packets at the other end and resends anything that gets lost.

Imagine yourself in New York, wanting to send a message home. All you have is four postcards, each with space for only one word. You write 'Hello' on one, 'Having' on the next, 'Nice' on the next and 'Time' on the last. You stick these in the post and hope for the best. At home your folks receive, Time, Hello, Having and Nice – eventually. It does not make much sense. TCP is the transport system of the Internet which sorts this out. It does its best to ensure delivery of sensible data across the inter-network. TCP takes each of your packets of messages, puts them in proper order at the other end and checks that each packet has been received. Together, the TCP/IP protocols make the Internet work.

Hypertext Transfer Protocol (HTTP)

The Hypertext Transfer Protocol (HTTP) was created by Tim Berners-Lee while working for CERN (a research centre based in Geneva, Switzerland) in 1991. Berners-Lee is therefore correctly regarded as the creator of the worldwide web. The function of HTTP is to specify the way in which browsers and web servers transmit data to each other.

The essence of this protocol is to establish which computer speaks first, how they then speak in turn and the format of the data they exchange, which is HTML. Without HTTP, the Internet would be a vast network of variable networks, all struggling to speak with each other – very limited indeed. It would not be a worldwide web.

Domain names

The IP addresses containing ten-digit numbers could never be remembered by people. So web servers hold lists of names made up of letters (sometimes called 'symbolic names') called domain names.

Unlike IP addresses, you will probably know many domain names by heart, for example, www.yahoo.com, www.google.co.uk, www.msn.com

Worldwide Web Consortium (W3C)

Although no one actually owns the worldwide web, there are leading bodies which try to ensure it develops in an open and accessible way, so that it will benefit as many people as possible. A major contributor is the Worldwide Web Consortium (known as W3C) and they, among others, attempt to define web standards.

A web standard is made up of elements and structures. The purpose of developing a core of web standards is to ensure as far as possible that web-based content is designed and structured in such a way that the greatest benefit will be gained by the greatest number of web users (see www.webstandards.org).

Did you know?

Every website can be checked for HTML standards by running it through the W3C validation software (see http://validator.w3.org).

Internet Society

The Internet Society is a global voluntary group that works to co-ordinate and develop an accessible Internet and its underlying technology. It was founded in 1992 and is based in Virginia, USA.

1.2 Networking of computers

Computer networks have spread fast. They have revolutionised the way we live and do business. As we shall see, networking technology (how we create networks) is improving quickly. The Internet is one huge network of computers.

Networks and wireless networks

But what is a network? Imagine a fishing net and you may picture a series of connected fine ropes forming see-through squares. Each of the corners of the squares is knotted and has ropes shooting off in four different directions.

Now think of these corners of the 'net' as being formed of PCs. Each PC is linked using cables/lines to form a virtual 'net'. Some points in the net have bigger computers feeding the others. This is the basic structure of a computer 'network'. These days, however, some networks are 'wireless' and therefore do not have cables.

Networks can be confined to an organisation; this is known as an **intranet**. Your school or college probably has its own intranet. Some organisations open up their intranet to some outside partners. Entry is protected by passwords; this creates an **extranet**. On the biggest scale is the global network, the Internet, connecting all computer networks together.

Key terms

Intranet – restricted computer network confined to a specific organisation

Extranet – restricted network that extends outside an organisation to include other computers

Activity: Benefits and dangers of a computer network

Discuss the benefits and dangers (see 'threats' later) of a computer network with other learners and plan to either interview or talk with the manager of your school or college network about these.

Current related technology

There are different technologies forming computer networks. These are developing all the time. A few of the emerging network technologies include:

- wi-fi
- bluetooth
- 3G mobile phones
- Personal Digital Assistants (PDAs)
- smartphones.

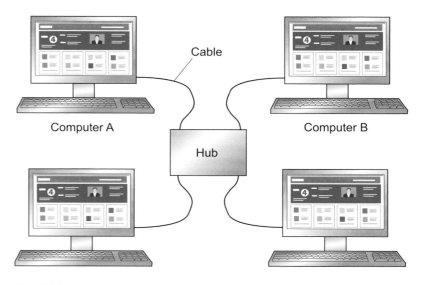

Fig. 33.2: A computer network.

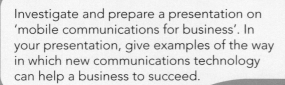
Activity: Mobile communications for business

Investigate and prepare a presentation on 'mobile communications for business'. In your presentation, give examples of the way in which new communications technology can help a business to succeed.

PLTS

When you are planning your work, make sure you break down tasks into sub-tasks.

Wi-fi

It is now possible to connect computers without the use of physical wires – a wireless connection. **Wi-fi** (**wi**reless **fi**delity) uses specified radio frequencies to send and receive data. More and more wireless laptops are being used. These devices have to be connected and enabled to work with wi-fi. A wireless-enabled laptop contains a wireless access card that is able to connect to other cards on other laptops directly, creating a 'point to point' connection. More likely, the laptop and any other client device will connect to a router to join a much larger network.

Wi-fi has become the most popular way of connecting to the Internet both in home computing (who wants to network devices at home using cables dragged under carpets?) and when working on the move. More and more staff carry their own laptops while away from the office.

Bluetooth

This is a low-speed, short-range wireless protocol designed to allow a variety of enabled gadgets to connect. (Do you exchange ringtones using bluetooth?) Once a device fitted with a bluetooth chip is within a ten-metre range of other bluetooth devices, it can connect by using a small 'personal area network' (known as a piconet).

Key term

Wi-fi – way of connecting to the Internet without physical wires

Once connected, each device announces its presence on the piconet and it can then pair off with others. Devices can be phones, laptops, printers, fridges, freezers – anything fitted with the chip.

Remember

The Internet consists of a global network of connected computer networks. People and businesses can connect to these using either cables or wireless connections.

3G mobile phones

This is the 'third generation' of mobile phones. These devices use WAP (wireless application protocol) technology to offer 'always on' connection to data services as well as a range of other features. These phones can send and receive data by connecting to the Internet, albeit at a significantly slower rate than modern broadband connections.

Personal Digital Assistants (PDAs)

A PDA (see the Locators Ltd case study on page 417) is a handheld computer that runs a reduced version of standard software. A PDA comes with personal information management software and can be used as an organiser or a diary planner that is portable and capable of connecting, using bluetooth or wi-fi, to a PC. It is capable of connecting to the Internet; it can act as a global positioning system (GPS) and run multimedia software.

Smartphones

A smartphone is either a PDA that has mobile phone capabilities, or a mobile phone with PDA features. A smartphone therefore combines the features of both.

Activity: Salespeople

A typical small- to medium-sized business might use a number of travelling salespeople. Think about ways in which specific devices and technologies may be able to help in these roles.

Netbooks

Netbooks give wi-fi access to the Internet and are smaller, cheaper and lighter than notebooks. They have a smaller screen (less than 9") and no DVD or CD drive. Although they are less powerful, they are very

What are the functions of a PDA?

useful for people who are regularly travelling away from their business base. Because they are cheaper, they are attractive to both businesses and consumers.

1.3 Use of the Internet and worldwide web by business organisations

The web is now a key aspect of business life for a growing number of businesses. Nevertheless, there are still some large businesses today that do not have a website; they could be called 'siteless' or 'sightless' if you prefer. Eventually, all businesses will probably be on the Internet. They will all have a 'web presence'. In just about every case, their websites will be interactive, meaning that visitors can make use of the information, change it and get something back.

We saw earlier that the Internet is a lot older than the worldwide web. However, it is the web that has made the Internet such a valuable tool for business. This is because businesses can do many things using the Internet and the worldwide web.

Did you know?

Brazil, Russia, India and China are the leading countries in terms of growth in mobile phone subscriptions (source: ClickZ.com).

Procurement

Procurement means buying. Businesses that are seeking to make profits have to procure the things they need to pursue their activities. Some need raw materials for a production process; others have to buy finished products to resell in their stores.

Every public sector organisation, such as your local authority, has to buy things: stationery, desks, furniture, road materials and so on. Primary Care Trusts have to buy drugs, equipment, scanners and cleaning materials on behalf of NHS hospitals.

Research

Businesses need to be aware of things that are happening around them. Modern business managers are under increasing pressure to provide everything that customers need or want. They have to be competitive in their market; otherwise they risk being overtaken by events.

The Internet offers all sorts of opportunities to research market developments and keep in touch with the wider world. Businesses can investigate their own markets, investigate industrial trends through participating in industrial portals, and keep in touch with sales trends in places far away from their headquarters. The web is a rich source of business intelligence.

Developing an online presence for sales

After the 'dot.com bubble' of the late 1990s, many people were far too quick to dismiss the Internet as a passing fad that would blow away. How wrong they were. In fact, what has happened is that many long-established businesses have added an online sales channel to their existing business. Big organisations like Tesco (www.tesco.com), Next (www.next.co.uk), Sainsbury's (www.sainsbury.co.uk) and B&Q (www.diy.com) all offer home shopping. There are so many that some people are now complaining that online shopping is killing the high street!

Promotion

In the USA, online advertising in 2009 represented about ten per cent of total media spending and the proportion is growing. Businesses have increased spending on Internet advertising, particularly using banner ads and pop-ups. The newer mobile channels are a big advertising opportunity too, with some new techniques employed to persuade people to look at the ads.

Customer service

Customer service is about meeting the needs and requirements of every single customer. Businesses may have exactly the same products that do exactly the same thing, so how do we choose one rather than another? The answer lies in customer service. By offering excellence in service, businesses compete better.

Today there is software that can offer businesses templates and techniques for offering excellent customer service on the Internet. People who shop online expect the very highest standards in care. Delivery, product descriptions, FAQs (frequency asked questions), catalogues, images and added design services are all features of the web. 'Contact us' pages can also help. In a last resort, telephone contact can be made with the online business.

Case study: E-procurement

Large companies have achieved some excellent savings using e-procurement software available on the Internet.

- **Compaq** achieved a 50 per cent reduction in process costs and a direct saving on purchased goods and services of over £30 million.

- **Boeing** achieved similar cost savings but also reduced their supplier base by over 80 per cent in some commodity areas.

- **Xerox** predicted that it would save in excess of $10 million per annum through the introduction of e-procurement.

(Source: Business Gateway.)

1. These savings appear impressive. However, are there any extra costs involved in adopting an e-procurement system?

2. How does e-procurement lead to cost savings?

3. In your view, is an e-procurement system a good thing to adopt? Why?

Case study: Virgin Mobile US

'Virgin Mobile USA is giving hard-up youngsters the chance to make free phone calls in return for watching ads. The "yoof-oriented" cellco has hooked up with ad outfit Ultramercial to launch the ad-for-airtime service called "SugarMama".

'Punters interested in SugarMama must first fill out a "demographic profile" before confirming that that they are at least 13 years old. Once the administration has been done, they can watch a streaming video ad. Customers get free airtime depending on the number of correct questions they can answer about the ad. Alternatively, they can respond to text-based ads to earn free minutes.

'Either way, the suits behind the scheme are looking to generate revenue from mobile advertising. For advertisers, it is yet another way to get their brand or product across to this hard-to-reach youth audience. "Everyone is racing to shove ads into the mobile channel," said Howard

Handler, top marketing bod at Virgin Mobile USA. "But the last thing young people want is spam on their phones."

'Earlier this year mobile marketing firm I-movo began recruiting punters to test a new service that offers mobile phone users in the UK the chance to send text messages for free, in return for viewing ads on their phones.'

(Source: from an article by Tim Richardson in *The Register*.)

1. This is an innovative way of getting young people to take notice of the advertisements on their mobiles. How would you justify it as a possible promotional strategy for a business?

2. How would you 'sell' this form of promotion to a business entrepreneur? What do you feel are its major selling points?

3. What drawbacks, if any, can you see in this form of promotion? Justify your points.

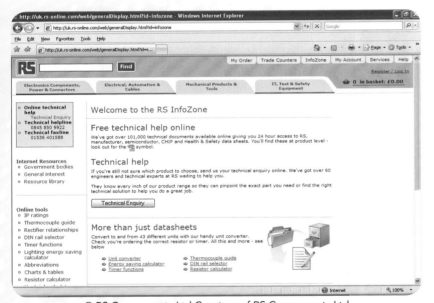

© RS Components Ltd Courtesy of RS Components Ltd

Fig. 33.3: RS Components offers procurement on the web.

Fig. 33.4: Next sells a variety of products and services online.

Activity: Organisations using the Internet

In groups of three or four, prepare a presentation showing the rest of your group how three different kinds of organisation use the Internet to help their business.

Functional skills

English: When searching for information, remember to use your functional English skills to critically appraise the source of information. Is it reliable? Is there any bias?

© The Co-operative Bank p.l.c.

Fig. 33.5: The Co-operative Bank uses its website to demonstrate its ethical approach to business.

Public relations

Public relations (PR) is about giving out a good message about a business and its activities. A website allows businesses to state loudly and clearly what they do and what they do well. The Co-operative Bank is an ethically aware business that takes great care to say clearly what it does.

Providing information

Every web page gives us information. Local councils and government departments increasingly use the power of the Internet to give information that will be useful to citizens. Private businesses, large and small, can give out information to potential customers and stakeholders. As the case study on the following page shows, online shoppers want good product information before they buy.

Influencing others

Because the web is full of information, and can be used as a powerful tool for research, it can also be used to try to influence others. This can happen in a number of ways.

Many websites allow discussion forums where site users can leave comments. There was a problem with an initial batch of the Apple iPod Nano when the screens cracked after only a short period of use. Apple's initial refusal to deal with the problem was overcome when an aggrieved customer set up a website. The fear of bad publicity across the Internet forced Apple into action.

Pressure groups such as Friends of the Earth, Greenpeace, Corporate Watch and others can use the global spread of the Internet to try to change people's views.

Activity: Influencing others

Investigate three websites that in your view set out to 'influence others'. Prepare a short presentation saying how they attempt to influence and whether, in your opinion, they might succeed.

Communications – emails, intranets and extranets

We know that computer networks make up the Internet. The crucial thing for business organisations is that this enables rapid communications beyond and within a business. People can work remotely, either at home or on the move, by connecting to an intranet or extranet using a password and username. It is possible today to email from a range of portable devices such as your phone or a handheld PDA.

The Internet phone revolution is well underway, and many companies are now taking advantage of free telephone services through online providers. Now that ADSL (Asymmetric Digital Subscriber Line) has become widely available across Europe, Internet phone services have become a compelling new way to communicate and to reduce costs.

Skype (www.skype.com) is free technology. Anyone with an Internet connection can use the system to speak with anyone else who is also registered. The most useful function is being able to speak, for free, from computer to computer; but Skype is also built to allow calls to landlines, although to use this feature there is a small charge.

In order to use Skype, a user must either have a microphone and speakers activated on a computer, or an Internet telephone handset. These are widely available and have the advantage of being more private than using the speakers in a PC. Skype also works as an instant messaging system in a very similar way to MSN Messenger.

Remember

Businesses can connect to the Internet for a number of reasons. They can buy and sell, advertise and promote, tell the world about themselves and communicate.

1.4 Uses of related mobile technology by business organisations

Mobile technology allows people to use information technology without being tied to the office. Many organisations have staff who work away from their office. The availability of wi-fi, 3G mobiles and PDAs (see page 402) has enabled fast communication of data, images and audio in a much more flexible way.

> ### Key term
>
> **Mobile technology** – portable devices that can connect to the worldwide web

Mobile technology can improve the speed of service for clients. For instance, a carpet fitter can come to your house, measure the areas to be carpeted, store these digitally using a laptop and send the estimate to the store. This way, the carpets can be cut more quickly because information transfer is speeded up. In another business, travelling sales staff can give presentations or store appointments on a handheld computer.

Voice-over Internet Protocol (VoIP)

Mobile technology such as VoIP allows you to call anyone in the world and talk for as long as you wish. This, together with all the other portable devices with connection ability, gives much greater flexibility to business practices. More and more people today

have the flexibility to work from home thanks to these developments.

1.5 Trends in Internet developments

Increasing penetration and speed

The Internet is a global phenomenon with six billion users, and the numbers of people using it grows day by day. The increase in availability and access to the Internet is a major trend that encourages businesses to get online. However, there are still parts of the world where Internet penetration – that is, the percentage of the population who have regular Internet access – is relatively low.

Connection speeds are increasing as technology improves, which makes it even more desirable for businesses and individuals.

Falling costs

Other factors can encourage greater access and use of the Internet. The cost of broadband connection is

Table 33.1: Top 20 countries with highest number of Internet users (source: Miniwatts Marketing Group, Internet World Stats).

#	Country or region	Population 2008 est	Users latest data	% Population (penetration)	Growth 2000–2008	% of world users
1	China	1,330,044,605	298,000,000	22.4%	1,244.4%	18.7%
2	United States	304,228,257	227,190,989	74.7%	138.3%	14.2%
3	Japan	127,288,419	94,000,000	73.8%	99.7%	5.9%
4	India	1,147,995,898	81,000,000	7.1%	1,520.0%	5.1%
5	Brazil	196,342,587	67,510,400	34.4%	1,250.2%	4.2%
6	Germany	82,369,548	55,221,183	67.0%	130.1%	3.5%
7	United Kingdom	60,943,912	43,753,600	71.8%	184.1%	2.7%
8	France	62,150,775	40,858,353	65.7%	380.7%	2.6%
9	Russia	140,702,094	38,000,000	27.0%	1,125.8%	2.4%
10	Korea South	48,379.392	36,794,000	76.1%	93.3%	2.3%
11	Spain	40,491,051	28,552,604	70.5%	429.9%	1.8%
12	Italy	58,145,321	28,388,926	48.8%	115.0%	1.8%
13	Mexico	109,955,400	27,400,000	24.9%	910.2%	1.7%
14	Turkey	75,793,836	26,500,000	35.0%	1,225.0%	1.7%
15	Indonesia	237,572,355	25,000,000	10.5%	1,150.0%	1.6%
16	Canada	33,212,696	23,999,500	72.3%	89.0%	1.5%
17	Iran	65,875,223	23,000,000	34.9%	9,100.0%	1.4%
18	Vietnam	86,116,559	20,993,374	24.4%	10,396.7%	1.3%
19	Poland	38,500,696	20,020,362	52.0%	615.0%	1.3%
20	Argentina	40,481,998	20,000,000	49.4%	700.0%	1.3%
Top 20 countries		**4,286,530,622**	**1,226,184,091**	**28.6%**	**342.7%**	**76.8%**

falling, which encourages more people and businesses to use the web and get more from it.

As businesses see opportunities and realise that greater numbers of people are accessing the web, and as costs, speed and reliability continue to improve, the Internet evolution is likely to accelerate.

Activity: Global Internet penetration

The figures for global Internet penetration are growing. Do you think that this presents business opportunities? How?

Assessment activity 33.1

For the first part of the assessed work for this unit, imagine that you are a consultant advising a local entrepreneur.

Create a set of presentation slides with notes to describe how the Internet works. **P1**

Grading tip

A structured set of slides, with notes, should describe the basic architecture of the Internet as a network of networks based upon servers and clients. The role of ISPs should be covered, along with domain names, different types of connection, the www and the different protocols (for example, HTTP) that are used. You should also explain the role of the W3C and the Internet Society. **P1**

2. Be able to use the Internet and related technology for a range of business activities

Business activity is increasingly taking place on the Internet. Businesses can buy and sell from each other (B2B transactions) as well as selling to private consumers (B2C transactions).

The number of B2C transactions on the Internet far outweighs B2B, yet in money terms it is the B2B business that has the greater value. Consumers will frequently purchase fairly low-value items, such as a book or a CD. However, less frequently, a big business might purchase a high-value piece of equipment.

When a businesses wishes to alter its strategy and open up an online presence, it has a number of things to consider. One of the most basic of these is the question of capacity to meet increased demand. Can the business cope with a potential global interest in its products? This is all part of the business planning process. If management decides that an online sales channel is potentially of benefit, then it must consider a number of issues as outlined below.

the shape of PCs that connect to the web, using either cabling or wireless technology. The costs of these are falling and if a business buys in bulk, then the costs can be reduced further. In addition to the PCs there are the costs of cabling, modems or routers, and printers as well as the software.

To connect effectively to the Internet for business purposes, there must be a 'host' for your website. This means that the site will be placed on a server with its domain name, and there will be costs associated with this. The price of a domain name is quite low; hosting services will depend on the kind of website it is. The average cost of a website in 2003 was quoted as £3,000 (Chaffey, Mayer, Johnston and Ellis-Chadwick, *Internet Marketing*).

Protecting a computer system

When setting up a PC for Internet use, it is essential to protect it against a number of **security threats**. There are several ways of doing this.

- A firewall helps protect a computer from hackers who might try to delete information, crash your computer, or even steal passwords or credit card numbers.

- High priority operating system updates are critical to the security and reliability of a computer. They offer the latest protection against malicious online activities.

- Antivirus and anti-spyware software protect a computer against these two kinds of usually malicious software. Antivirus technology helps prevent viruses (see page 428 for various kinds of virus), and needs to be regularly updated.

A business facing these various threats must take measures to back up data and to ensure policies are adopted for staff usage of the computer system.

Activity: Digital Britain

In pairs, investigate the report called 'Digital Britain' and summarise the main points. What do you feel the implications of the report are for business?

2.1 Setting up an Internet-linked computer

Equipment requirements and cost

To make use of the Internet, a business must invest. First of all, obviously, there will need to be hardware in

Key term

Security threats – openings in the software or networking arrangements of an e-business that allow intrusion, data theft or virus infections

Activity: Security measures

1. Demonstrate how to download two important security measures for a business to give:
   - firewall protection
   - antivirus protection.
2. Access www.personalfirewall.comodo.com and demonstrate, using a download, how to create a firewall protection for a network.
3. Look up a freely downloadable antivirus software package, such as AVG. Demonstrate how to download the package and show evidence that you can do so. Produce a short explanation for the business of why such measures are important.

2.2 Use of Internet for business research

All businesses have to take account of their external environment. They need to be aware of things that are going on and be aware of the forces that could affect their own performance. The web offers many opportunities for research. The ability and the willingness of an organisation to use these opportunities is governed by the degree to which a business has embraced digital media.

There are different levels of Internet business. As we have already seen, some businesses have no website of their own and simply place an entry on a business listing (for example, www.yell.com); others have a basic site that provides information about the company and products. The next stage is a more interactive site, allowing users to query the information and search the site. Finally, a growing number of businesses have fully interactive sites where people can make purchases and where the site contains the full range of marketing functions.

Types of data

E-business has generated a new type of research. When a business goes fully online and uses the Internet extensively, there is often a great deal of investment involved. **Web analytics** refers to a series of methods by which the contribution and performance of a website can be measured. How many

people visit the site? How long do they stay? Where do they 'click through' to? What do they purchase? WebTrends (www.webtrends.com) offers this service.

The web also offers a series of specialist services that can be of use to a business, including on:

- demographics
- competitor analysis
- environmental analysis
- legislation and specialist sites.

Demographics

Population statistics and trends have an obvious influence on the online business. How many people are online, where are they and what are the trends? There are some useful online services provided by specialist sites such as ClickZStats (www.clickz.com) or www.demographicsnowuk.com, where business managers can analyse what is happening and take more informed decisions.

Competitor analysis

A well-formulated business strategy takes account of all external forces. Among these, it is very important to be aware of what competitors are doing.

Yahoo! (http://finance.yahoo.com) offers information on its financial pages about many firms around the world; Dun & Bradstreet (www.dnb.co.uk) has data on millions of worldwide companies.

Environmental analysis

All businesses function within their industrial environment. Increasingly, we live and work in a global economy. This means that many different environmental factors will have an impact upon the performance of a UK-based business. To take an obvious one, the price of fuel affects business; so does the price of commodities.

The Internet makes the world a much smaller place. The availability of instant communications helps to keep a business in touch with what is happening.

Key terms

E-business – a business that has digitised many of its internal functions by using computer systems. These are often connected to the web

Web analytics – software services that can track users of websites, measure click-through patterns and provide data to assist in web strategic planning

Fig. 33.6: How does the Internet help businesses keep in touch with their industrial environment?

Activity: Coffee café

Imagine you own a café selling high-quality coffee and related products. In what ways will the web offer you a chance to stay in touch with your business environment?

Legislation and specialist sites

In general, weather conditions, climate change, global population trends, political change in a region and the threat of global terrorism are all of importance to some very significant industries. Businesses will also use specialist sites to find out technical information as well as data on legislation that will affect them, transport information and so on.

Activity: Global terrorism

Global terrorism is a big threat not only to individuals, but to big business interests too. In your view, which industrial sectors are most vulnerable to the threat of terrorist attack?

Efficient use of search engines

Search engines are directories that list everything on the web. There are hundreds of them. The most popular for personal users may not be the most suitable for professional or business users. For general use, here is a selection:

- www.google.com
- www.ask.co.uk
- www.excite.co.uk
- www.yahoo.com

For a business user, Copernic (www.copernic.com) is an automatic search of other search engines. A query raised on Copernic can be sent to multiple search engines simultaneously.

Different types of search

For a business (and a learner), using better search techniques can improve the chances of finding useful information.

Example – refining a search

A manager wishes to search for printers. A Google search might return 55 million entries. If this is refined by entering inkjet printers, the return falls to 4.5 million entries. By enclosing inkjet printers within quote marks, the search result drops still further to 2.2 million.

Some search engines allow a user to include some special commands to be more precise. Using the '+' in search engines before the word means that it must be included in the matched page. Placing a '-' before the word means that it must not be included in the matched pages.

For business users of the web, there are many directories and newsgroups that are also of use. You can find a list of all UK newsgroups at www.usenet.org.uk

Case study: Industrial suppliers

Buyers of industrial equipment and services look to the web to source goods, but the distributors they want to locate are slow to build an online presence. That's according to a survey conducted by GlobalSpec, a vertical search engine for the engineering, industrial and technical communities.

'Today, you find far fewer companies that don't have a website, it's really more about how they've embraced the Internet and online,' said Chris Chariton, VP of marketing at GlobalSpec. 'It takes them out of their comfort space a little bit.' Traditional means of sourcing new suppliers, trade shows, sales calls and catalogues are being replaced by web searches. Seventy-three per cent of buyers of industrial equipment look for new sources on search engines and online directories. Search engines are the first place to query for new vendors; online industrial directories account for 21 per cent of first searches. Online sources exceed initial searches through traditional channels like recommendations from colleagues, manufacturer sales calls, trade magazines and direct mail.

'The audience has moved online, and the first place they're going to look for new sources is the Internet,' said Chariton. 'From a time saving standpoint, the engineering and tech audience really embraces the Internet as a place to find information and news sources.'

When finding a source on the web, up-to-date content and technical specifications are the most important functions of a site.

(Source: from an article by Enid Burns, 19 May 2006: www.clickz.com)

If you were an 'industrial buyer', you would be responsible for the purchase of many thousands, perhaps millions of pounds' worth of materials and equipment.

1. What does the article by Enid Burns tell you about the uses of the Internet for buying?

2. Is this information of use to business planners?

3. What points would you make to the management of a small- or medium-sized business to encourage them to take up Internet opportunities?

Fig. 33.7: How can the Internet help businesses do specific searches?

Bookmarking sites

When a website resource is discovered that offers useful information or resources, it is possible to 'bookmark' the site in the Netscape browser, or 'Add to Favourites' in Internet Explorer. This means the site's web address is stored ready for quick access the next time it is required.

Social bookmarking

Social bookmarking has become more popular as the Internet has increasingly become a social phenomenon. This allows users to store, organise, search and share the bookmarks of web pages. Users can choose to share with one or many people within a network. Social bookmarking services are available providing 'web feeds' to lists of bookmarks as they are saved or tagged by others.

Filtering sites

Business organisations as well as home users will seek at times to block certain websites. By using filtering software, websites containing distasteful or inappropriate content can be filtered out and blocked.

Validity of data sources

The Internet offers the capability to conduct extensive secondary research and extract detailed primary data through web analytics. A business using the web can analyse how a site is being used.

A recent report, Marketing Sherpa's 'Buyer's Guide to Web Analytics' described more than 50 different tools for measuring website traffic – and said there were at least 50 others. The report did not include companies that provide traffic measurement services using panels of web users (such as comScore Media Metrix and Nielsen/NetRatings) or those that collect behavioural information from users via telephone or online surveys.

While site administrators are awash in data, many have found that the numbers generate as much confusion as understanding.

2.3 Use of Internet for procurement

Every business organisation has to buy (procure) things. Business could, in fact, be summed up as just that – buying and selling. The trick for a private sector business is to buy things at a low cost, add value and sell them for more. For a public sector organisation, efficiency is vital because it is spending tax payers' money. Procurement is, therefore, crucial to the success of any organisation.

Selection of suitable sites

The Internet can offer a range of procurement services and there are web services specially tailored for both private businesses and public bodies. There are several advantages in using the web for procurement purposes, as follows.

- Comprehensive purchasing intelligence – some web-based services offer analytical applications ranging from simple Internet reports to data warehouse-based workbooks. This helps a business to measure performance and identify the most significant opportunities to save money.
- Self-service purchasing – this provides purchasing activities which reduces irresponsible spending by staff and speeds up the buying process.
- Self-guiding catalogue – this enables users to find catalogue items quickly using a powerful text-based search engine.
- Supplier collaboration – web-based applications can link suppliers and partners together and integrate the supply chain.
- Global solution – web-based services can support dealings in multiple languages and currencies for

Case study: Making sense of data

Greg Swanson, director of Internet sales for Lee Enterprises, just wanted to know two things.

- How many people were visiting the websites of his company's 44 newspapers?
- How often did they visit?

The problem was, the answers Swanson got did not make sense to him. In Montana, for instance, the *Billings Gazette* had a Sunday readership of about 52,000 people, but the website had almost ten times that many visitors in a month and the average site user was visiting the site just one or two times per month.

'We had unbelievably large reach – which in some months exceeded the entire population of the state of Montana. Huge reach, but incredibly low frequency,' Swanson said. 'For advertisers, it was

as if we were putting a message on the side of a bus and driving though a crowded downtown area once a month.'

Swanson ultimately concluded that the problem stemmed from the inaccuracy of the tools his company was using to measure website usage. At newspaper websites, he is one of many people who have been frustrated by the difficulty in getting answers to seemingly simple questions about their online audiences.

(Source: from Rich Gordon: The DigitalEdge.com © 2005 Newspaper Association of America.)

1. How would you describe web analytics to a new e-business?

2. Do you think this case study shows that web analytics do not work? Why?

businesses of all sizes, with services and support offered around the clock and around the globe.

Intermediary sites

Efficient buying in B2B markets relies on good information. The Internet offers these services via 'intermediary sites'. These are websites that exist between buyers and sellers, bringing them together. The web offers access to a number of business directories. These allow managers to check things out in their own markets and specialist areas.

Activity: Business directory websites

Look at business directory websites, such as www.yell.com, www.scoot.co.uk and www.uktradeinvest.gov.uk. As a small-business advisor, draft a report specifying how these online directories could help a small- to medium-sized enterprise to develop its e-business.

Remember

The Internet helps to bring partner businesses together so that they can share information and act more quickly in buying and selling.

Security symbol

Anyone using the web to conduct business must consider the level of security. It is wise to look at the security setting shown by the browser and to set the level appropriately. This is displayed by a security symbol that appears on the browser.

Remember

Always check the level of your browser security by looking for the security symbol.

Secure payment methods

A business that opens up an online channel will hope to take credit card payments. In doing this there are natural fears about **secure payments** from all parties. Two web standards have been designed to try to make credit card payments secure on the Internet.

The first of these, SSL or Secure Sockets Layer, acts by encrypting (making something unreadable to anyone who doesn't have a 'key' for it) traffic between a web

Key term

Secure payments – payments system on a website that offers security to customers as they know that their credit or debit card details cannot be stolen

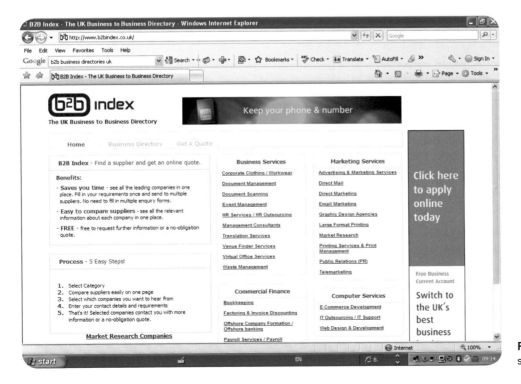

Fig. 33.8: What are 'intermediary sites'?

Fig. 33.9: What does this symbol mean?

server and a web browser – in the payments context this means the consumer's computer (the client) and the online seller's computer (the server).

The SET standard (Secure Electronic Transactions), unlike SSL, was designed exclusively for Internet financial transactions. The SET standard goes further than SSL and offers more protection for e-businesses. Using digital certificates, each participant within a transaction can be verified and authenticated, and each message can be checked for alteration. This means that no one can legitimately deny later that they placed an order, because all orders have to be digitally signed and a digital signature cannot be forged. SET defines:

- the way a transaction flows
- the formats of messages
- the forms of encryption used.

The confidentiality and integrity of SET-based financial transactions is said to be high.

Remember

Customers thinking of buying online want to be reassured that their card details are secure.

Many software vendors are entering the payments security market and offering packages that build upon security standards. One example is FraudShield, created by ClearCommerce, which sets up rules so that any transaction is automatically validated and checked at the point of sale.

Financial transactions between banks have for several years been digitised. The level of security has necessarily been high. The Society for World-Wide Interbank Financial Telecommunications (SWIFT) is a private intranet that is used by financial organisations to exchange funds between them (see www.swift.com).

Further means of securing the payments network are available from VeriSign (www.verisign.org), which adopts a policy based upon checks across the whole process of an electronic transaction. The VeriSign approach is that a transaction is capable of being monitored along its entire life cycle – in other words, from first customer payment effort, through initial processing, to settlement.

Activity: Security

Investigate at least four contrasting businesses that operate online. Search their websites and for each business, summarise their main messages to customers/clients about security.

Online services and ways to reduce risks

Many online users now like to use the Internet for purchasing music or software. In fact, the web offers free downloads of software (freeware) and music sharing packages are now well established (for example, Amazon.co.uk). Online banking has also become more popular as a convenient way of managing personal finances. However, all of these services should only be used in the context of antivirus software and with Internet security browser settings set to at least 'medium'. In this way, the risks of infection to a PC are reduced.

Legal protection and limitations

A business advertising goods or services via a website, interactive TV or mobile phone must comply with the E-Commerce Regulations 2002. Anyone selling anything online is certainly affected. The UK's E-Commerce Regulations 2002 came into force on 21 August 2002. At the heart of the Regulations there are new information requirements.

- Adverts online must provide the full name of the business and contact details including geographic address.
- Prices must also give details of any associated taxes or delivery charges.
- If online activities are subject to VAT, the VAT number must be shown.
- Details of association with a trade or professional body must be shown.

If email campaigns are used to promote goods or services, the Regulations mean that the following must be observed.

- Make it unambiguous who the email is being sent by, or on behalf of.
- Any description of discounts or promotional offers must set out all the qualifying conditions.
- If email is unsolicited, it needs to be clear to the recipient that it is unsolicited without the recipient having to open the email.

If customers can place orders online, there are some further things to do.

- It must be clear at what point in the ordering process a customer has committed themselves.
- Users must be able to view, store and print business terms and conditions.
- The business must acknowledge receipt of orders electronically and without undue delay.

Remember

Using the Internet to set up an extra online sales channel can provide tremendous opportunities for a business; however, the E-Commerce Regulations set out important rules that protect the consumer. These must be followed.

2.4 Use of Internet for promotion

To promote a business can involve all sorts of techniques; some paid for, others free. Paid advertisements traditionally used the printed media, the radio or TV. The Internet has offered new forms of advertising and has become a multi-million-dollar industry.

Websites

Some businesses simply wish to promote their activities on the Internet. They have no interest, or no scope, to actually 'transact' on the web. There are many businesses where having at least this basic level of web presence can contribute to their aims.

Banner advertising

A space across the top of a web page, often with animated content, advertising products or services from another business, is known as a banner. A click on the banner by a visitor to a site leads to a referral through to the site of the advertising business. This is known as a 'click-through'.

Fig. 33.10: Where does a banner ad lead?

The banner size 468 by 60 pixels is a common ad size, often used at the top or bottom or even mixed in with content of a website.

Case study: Mobile marketing

Mobile marketing – sending adverts directly to people's mobile phones – has long been both a promise and a challenge. The massive growth of mobile devices over the last few years means the audience has grown fantastically. The phone is unlike any other consumer electronic device. Just about any other media channel marketers use to advertise must be actively encountered by consumers: they turn on their televisions, computers and radios. They decide to go to the cinema.

The phone is clearly different. It is, for most of us, always with us and always turned on. The increase in smartphone ownership just makes this all the more true. The more features we are able to access with our phones and the more of our messages we are able to get through the phone, the more crucial it becomes. Mobiles should be an absolute marketer's paradise.

The Mobile Marketing Association is anticipating a 26 per cent jump in mobile marketing spending this year.

We are on the cusp of seeing a new sort of device that will defy categorisation in the near term. Already we have Amazon.co.uk's Kindle, which is certainly not a computer and definitely not a phone. However, it has a large screen and a wireless data connection. Apple is expected to release news soon about a different kind of iPod that has a much larger screen, is able to download applications and contains (at least) a wi-fi antenna.

(Source: based on an article by Gary Stein, ClickZ, June 2009, www.clickz.com)

1. What do you understand by the term 'mobile marketing'?

2. What do you feel are the advantages and disadvantages of sending adverts directly to mobile devices?

3. Make a list of products or services that you feel could suitably be advertised on mobile devices. Present a case to an appropriate business evaluating this opportunity.

The choice of which sites to place the banner on will be considered by marketing specialists. There are several specialist sites offering services to help in placing, or targeting, banners. Banner ads can be exchanged between sites offering complementary products or services, or they can be specifically targeted on to sites where it is felt that the audience will be appropriate.

Activity: Camping equipment

Imagine you run a business selling used camping equipment. On which websites might you consider placing a banner advert?

Link registration

Once a business has a website up and running, then it is important to register the site with the search engines. Search engines are extremely important for the promotion of a website. The majority of web visitors use them and if a business has not bothered to register with search engines, then they are unlikely to be found unless they have an extremely well-known brand name.

Remember

A business setting up a new website should register with one of the well-known search engines. This is free and easy to do.

We saw earlier that a vague search by a user can throw up literally millions of websites. Even a carefully refined search possibly offers thousands of websites containing at least some reference to what is being looked for. For a business to make sure that its website has a good chance of coming up in a search engine, it must register with the search engine and ensure that the keywords in the site header are relevant.

Direct emails

It is simple to send out hundreds, even thousands of emails, to unsuspecting people. The trouble is that sending out 10,000 emails might get 50 people interested in whatever product a business has to offer and 9,950 people thoroughly annoyed. The practice of sending out unrequested email is known

as 'spamming'; the term spam is said to mean Sending Persistent Annoying (e)Mail, sometimes known as 'junk'. If PR is the effort to promote an effective and positive image on the Internet, spamming tends to have the opposite effect. Internet users are simply learning to delete spam.

If Internet marketers are going to tap into the potential benefits of email, they need to consider ways of bypassing any accusations of spamming. To do this they might use **opt-in emailing**. This means that, before sending anyone any mail they seek permission first, hence the sometimes-used term, 'permission marketing'. Users must actively check a box giving the organisation permission to mail them in future.

The benefits of permission-based emailing are considerable, according to a survey quoted in eMarketer. The survey, by Quris, found that 67 per cent of consumers believed that the quality of opt-in emails positively influenced their opinions about the companies sending them and 53 per cent said that such emails had an influence on what they purchased.

Marketers must be extremely careful when considering both emailing and PR on the Internet. Because the Internet is a network, the effect is that news travels very fast. Internet marketers can and do use this effect to the benefit of their businesses, but they must be aware of the negative effects of bad mailing practice or bad PR. **Viral marketing** is the term used to describe the way in which marketing messages can be rapidly spread around the Internet through word being passed on, either through emailing (virtual word of mouth) or actual word of mouth.

Key terms

Opt-in emailing – collecting permissions from customers to send them emails detailing future services or promotions

Viral marketing – marketing through word of mouth on the web, very rapidly indeed, whether the news is good or bad

Remember

Direct emailing can access millions of potential consumers; however, spamming carries the danger of getting a business a bad name. It is better to seek permission before mailing people.

2.5 Use of Internet for business communication

Businesses can profit from the increased speed and efficiency of Internet communications. However, they have to be careful about how they use the technology.

Email

The speed with which computer networks can now connect means that documents and messages can move rapidly around them. Within most modern organisations there are intranets; email has become the norm in business internal communications.

Emails can be addressed to single individuals using an organisational email account, or they can be globally addressed to all staff. By using the 'CC' facility (CC stands for 'carbon copy'), a copy of a mail is sent to further email addresses.

It is possible to use another facility in email services such as Outlook, which allows an email sender to send multiple copies to many recipients, but not show this to the individuals. These are 'hidden (or blind) CCs – BCCs – and avoid the irritating situation for some people who do not appreciate being one of many recipients.

Using email in an organisation is today the norm for just about everyone. All businesses have company policies on emails. Staff are expected to use email professionally and sensitively. Any abusive content or inappropriate content can be traced and action taken.

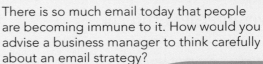

Activity: Email strategy

There is so much email today that people are becoming immune to it. How would you advise a business manager to think carefully about an email strategy?

A corporate business strategy for email must include security practices. This will ensure that attachments – always a dangerous source of possible viruses – can be scanned and appropriate warnings given before they are opened.

Other important aspects of email include tone and style within emails. It can be easy to offend via email. Users should always:

- ensure correct grammar
- adopt a suitably professional tone
- be careful about emailed data.

Remember that emails can be a permanent record. They may be quick to write but they need to be produced with care.

Case study: Locators Ltd

Locators Ltd (see www.locators.co.uk) is a provider of forklift trucks and storage equipment for industry. In 2008 the business implemented a mobile communications system and as a result has seen a number of benefits.

The company employs a small mobile workforce of 15 engineers. Previously, a paper-based system was used to organise service calls. The decision was made to implement a mobile communications solution in April 2008.

As a result, Locator now receives real-time updates from the field as engineers complete electronic sheets. Engineers use TyTN II PDA devices, which incorporate signature capture for clients to sign at the completion of a call.

Staff training was initially provided by an external consultant, but this is now provided internally when required.

In addition to the benefits mentioned, Locators has experienced improved speed of invoicing and improved customer service resulting from use of the mobile solution.

1. In what ways do management, engineers and customers benefit from Locators Ltd decision to introduce their mobile communications system?

2. What do you feel are the possible disadvantages for each group of stakeholders above?

3. In what other business contexts can you see a role for mobile communications technology? For each context you mention, explain and justify your position.

Digital cameras and video images

The web is a quick and convenient way of sending digital photographs and video images. While these are very useful facilities, especially for businesses such as estate agencies, users need to treat digital cameras and the use of digital images with care.

Voice-over Internet Protocol

As already mentioned, VoIP allows users to make phone calls over a computer network. Once they have the specialist handsets needed to convert voice data into computer data, businesses with a broadband connection can make free calls (including international calls) to other broadband users with VoIP equipment. All the users pay for is their Internet connection.

According to a survey by Inclarity of 500 small-business managers, while only 12 per cent of firms made phone calls over the Internet, those that did saw their telephone bill drop by 23 per cent and IT costs fall by 13 per cent.

Video conferencing

Video conferencing involves a range of technologies used in many situations. Sometimes it is not just video and audio being transmitted, but also data, allowing a business with multi-site operations the chance for collaborative working though shared applications.

Video conferencing may be used in:

- one-to-one meetings, also known as point-to-point communications, with full two-way audio and video

- one-to-many meetings, involving full audio and video broadcast from the main site, where other sites may be able to send audio

- many-to-many meetings, known as multi-point communication, providing audio and video between more than two sites. With most multi-point systems only one site in a conference can be seen at a time, with switching between sites either controlled manually or voice activated (that is, the loudest site is on screen).

What sort of technologies does video conferencing involve?

For a business to set up video conferencing, the basic hardware components are:

- camera, usually attached to the top of the monitor
- microphone
- speakers – even where speakers are built into a workstation, external ones will provide better quality audio. Alternatively, headphones may be useful, particularly in a shared office
- video board – to capture the signal from the camera and convert it to digital form
- network card – usually an Ethernet card for connection to the LAN (local area network), or an ISDN card.

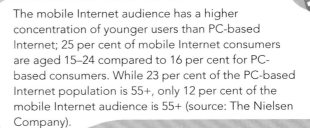

Did you know?

The mobile Internet audience has a higher concentration of younger users than PC-based Internet; 25 per cent of mobile Internet consumers are aged 15–24 compared to 16 per cent for PC-based consumers. While 23 per cent of the PC-based Internet population is 55+, only 12 per cent of the mobile Internet audience is 55+ (source: The Nielsen Company).

Remember

Video conferencing can allow a business with separate operations located geographically far apart to engage in video, audio discussion and instant data transfer.

Assessment activity 33.2  BTEC

You are advising a group of local small- to medium-sized businesses which are considering creating fully transactional websites. Now your clients want to know more about how the web can help their businesses.

1. Investigate and describe in a presentation examples of how the Internet can be used for different types of business activity (for example, selling, persuading, promoting, Informing, offering a service) using contrasting types of business. **P2**

2. Demonstrate how to solve problems in Internet use for four different types of business activity. **M1**

Grading tips

1. There are so many websites online for business purposes these days you have a vast range of sites to choose from. Consider B2B use as well as B2C. Additionally, consider including a public sector organisation in your description. Remember to use contrasting sites. To do this you could show a business selling via the web and contrast it with an information service such as Confused.com. Your work should pick out the main business purposes you can identify from the website. For instance, how does the website try to persuade visitors to buy or stay? **P2**

2. Doing business online inevitably brings problems as well as potentially improving performance. Here you must demonstrate your awareness and knowledge by creating clear instructions (possibly using screen shots) on how to overcome certain important problems in Internet use. **M1**

3. Understand how organisations adapt to trends in the use of e-business

3.1 Marketing benefits

Responding to competitive forces

The world economy is increasingly global. This means that today our industry faces growing and far more sophisticated competition from all over the world, particularly from fast-emerging economies like China and India. Wherever they are, businesses can compete on price, on quality of the products offered, on quality of customer service, on product features or on availability. The use of e-commerce via the Internet has now become almost a necessity. Having an effective, well-managed web presence can help a business to compete.

A survey in 2006 on e-business trends in manufacturing by SVM (www.svmsolutions.com) showed that:

* 78 per cent of manufacturers intended to increase spending on their website
* 60 per cent intended to increase investment in email marketing
* 48 per cent were boosting spending on search engine marketing
* 25 per cent were reducing spending on magazine advertising
* 17 per cent were reducing spending on trade shows.

The evidence is strong that businesses are taking up Internet opportunities in many sectors. As the SVM survey clearly shows, one of the key areas of take-up is in marketing.

Marketing benefits

The Internet helps businesses to acquire a good knowledge of customers because it is a way of connecting everyone who is online. Millions of pounds, dollars, euros and many other currencies pass through wires linking computers all over the world. According to ClickZStats (www.clickz.com), the worldwide Internet population in 2010 is 1.8 billion.

Of course, eventually growth will slow down, but it will not stop completely, as more and more of the newly developing world (China, India, Russia, Eastern bloc countries and perhaps even the Third

World) increasingly come online. The number of users will continue to grow and, more importantly, so will the frequency of use and the time spent online. Technological improvements and increasing availability of broadband will guarantee this.

> **Remember**
>
> China has a population of 1.3 billion and only 5.5 per cent of these people are online. Imagine the growth of the Internet population when China begins to approach the levels of Internet use such as those of nations like Canada (60 per cent).

Not only will more people be online, but the comfort and ease with which they use the Internet will improve and fears about security issues will diminish.

Reformulating the marketing mix

Traditional marketing uses tactics based on the marketing mix: product, price, place and promotion. Internet marketing specialists refer to a 'remix' of these, so that traditional marketing is re-applied in different ways in the online world. This **e-marketing remix** changes the traditional marketing tools and adds one or two new ingredients designed specifically for the online community.

To make visitors want to stay, a website has to offer something that is of value to a visitor. This is an **online value proposition** (OVP) and it is a similar concept to the unique selling proposition (USP) commonly referred to in traditional marketing. In the case of the USP, marketers are trying to communicate something unique about a physical product that will make people want to buy it more than other products. Similarly, the OVP is the special set of characteristics about a website that will make people want to stick around on the site and make a purchase.

> **Key terms**
>
> **E-marketing remix** – new marketing tactics designed to market a web-based business
>
> **Online value proposition** – characteristics about a website that make people want to use it

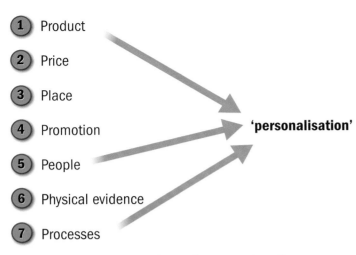

1. Product
2. Price
3. Place
4. Promotion → 'personalisation'
5. People
6. Physical evidence
7. Processes

Fig. 33.11: Implementing the marketing remix online.

Did you know?

The fact that almost seven and a half million Britons now access the web through their phone shows that mobile Internet is fast becoming a viable way for advertisers and publishers to reach important demographic groups (source: The Nielsen Company).

24-hour global presence and flexible location

The use of the Internet in marketing means that products may be displayed and offered online 24 hours a day, all over the world. Catalogues can be made available showing images and giving full details. Promotion can happen 24 hours a day using search engine marketing (SEM) and banners. Prices are competitive because of lower overheads. Prices can also be dynamic; they change according to market conditions and feedback from customers. Products (non-digital) can be made available anywhere, because there is the possibility of flexible location; digital products download immediately. People can contact call centres or use email. Finally, processes, for example, easyJet flight bookings, are simple.

Personalisation and feedback

One of the longest participating online businesses is Amazon.co.uk (www.amazon.co.uk). Anyone who registers with Amazon.co.uk and makes a purchase will find that the next time they visit the site they have **personalised** recommendations. Amazon.co.uk's web software remembers what customers have ordered and promotes similar products – from books to cameras

to PC games. There is also the opportunity to gain valuable feedback from customers through the use of interactive websites.

Opportunities for competitor analysis

The Internet offers the opportunity to do careful and accurate analysis of what competitors are doing online. Each company that goes online immediately becomes open and transparent as it does so. Marketing activities have to include keeping a close eye on the tactics, ideas and offerings of competitor businesses. The websites themselves can be looked at and are a primary source of information.

Marketing specialists look for new ideas, offers and tactical manoeuvres, particularly from organisations competing for the same segment of the market. The idea is not to copy a website but to gain an insight into competitor strategy. As we saw earlier, there are organisations offering this kind of intelligence as a service on the web (for example, http://finance.yahoo.com and www.dnb.co.uk).

Opportunities to communicate with customers

The web allows a business to capture contact details of customers through registration. Again, this also can mean better customer feedback. Communication is made through opt-in emails or regular email news bulletins. Some software, known as customer relationship management (CRM), can automate communications and keep detailed records of important staff in B2B contexts.

3.2 Cost benefits
Premises and location

The Internet gives immediate geographic spread, without the need for relocation. A business considering growth through expansion could consider the web option as a way of saving on capital costs. Customers target the business online, rather than a business having to seek out customers.

Key term

Personalisation – adjusting the web page that is returned to a visitor so that it offers information that is personal, based on their previous visits to the website

Because an online business is virtual, dealing in digital information, there is no immediate need for investment in physical premises. These could, if necessary, be confined to third party distributors, depending on the nature of the product sold. In addition, the positioning of premises can be an important factor when an organisation does business online. For example, some retailers can sell their products, using the Internet, from a base in the Channel Islands to gain tax advantages for themselves and so offer lower prices to their customers – gaining an edge over their competitors.

Reduced staffing costs

The potential for cutting staff costs is strong for businesses that begin to use the web for e-transactions. In a traditional business, there is an enormous amount of paperwork and records that need to be kept, such as invoices, orders, delivery notes, credit notes and so on. An organisation has to employ administrative staff to deal with paperwork. However, when a business uses electronic means of conducting transactions, it reduces the need for administrative records and also therefore administrative staff.

Cash flow advantages

A business depends on good cash flow. Cash flow refers to the stream of revenue that comes into a business from sales activities so that working capital can be maintained. This allows it to pay for wages and salaries as well as operating costs. Many businesses fail because of poor cash flow. By opening up a new web-based sales channel, there is an opportunity to improve income.

Remember

The Internet can generate impressive increases in sales revenue. For example, the following was reported by SHL Group (an HR consultancy firm) in 2005: '40 per cent increase in web revenue to £14.6 million (2004: £10.4 million).'

Disintermediation of the supply chain

Everything has to come from somewhere. A business that makes railway carriages depends on other businesses that produce the parts that go into railway carriages. The parts that go into railway carriages are themselves made from raw materials or other component parts. The supply chain refers to the way in which raw materials and parts find their way eventually to the customer.

The supply chain can consist of many links. Once raw material (for example, timber) is sourced, it is then transported to a merchant. The merchant may alter the raw material in some way before selling to a customer for use. The transport, the merchant, or distributors are all 'intermediaries'. This means they work in between. The web is capable of cutting out these intermediaries – a process known as **disintermediation**. This helps to cut costs.

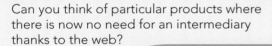

Activity: Disintermediation

Can you think of particular products where there is now no need for an intermediary thanks to the web?

3.3 Benefits to customers

The Internet offers a vast range of products and services to customers. These products and services are accessible 24 hours a day, from anywhere. Customers are now able to choose products from a wider range of businesses, irrespective of their location.

A new type of intermediary has grown up on the web. Traditionally, wholesalers and distributors were the intermediaries between manufacturers and retailers – and then consumers. Today, 'infomediaries' provide consumers with the ability to compare prices and quality of service. One of these is Kelkoo (www.kelkoo.com).

Personalised offers

We saw earlier how a website can offer a personalised page that suits the personal preferences of a visitor. Amazon.co.uk does this very effectively and so do the supermarkets – for example, remembering your shopping list favourites week after week when you do your grocery shopping online.

3.4 Operational implications of trends on organisations

A number of factors deserve consideration before a business sets up a transactional (buy and sell) website. These factors all affect the way an organisation works. The day-to-day running of a business is known as operational management. There can be a number of

operational implications for a business that starts to trade online.

Expectations and product fulfilment

Having a good-quality website can give an organisation a real advantage over rivals. However, it is crucial that the business considers operational implications. For instance, does it have the background systems and processes that can meet an increase in demand, possibly from a worldwide customer base? This means there must be stock available at all times and online orders have to be fulfilled.

Customer expectations

Consumers who shop online are quite demanding. They have expectations that a website will be quick to load in a browser. They will want all site links to work and for the site to have a minimum of annoying pop-ups. References to products in catalogues should be up to date and accurate. Prices should be easily available along with terms and conditions. The web shopper also requires a chance to give feedback or view an FAQ page. Finally, the online shopper expects privacy and complete security.

Increased competition

A business that opens up online immediately makes itself vulnerable to increased competition. Competitors can see the entire product range, promotional offers and prices changes. The online business will be subject to online price comparisons. Offline businesses will be attempting to meet and improve upon prices and services.

New providers of old services

In some business organisations there has been a change caused by the fact that the business is now operating in new markets on the web. Tesco.com, for example, now offers music downloads from its website.

Further examples of this include new telecommunications services offered through VoIP (see page 418) and the huge growth of online shopping for everything from lingerie to household groceries.

3.5 Strategic implications of trends on organisations

The general direction a business takes involves the bigger issues. These things are not about whether, for example, to buy paper from one source rather than another; they are about whether to:

- enter new markets
- produce new things
- open or close premises
- relocate or trade online.

However, before opening up a new web presence, a business has to consider certain strategic implications. What will be the effect of a big change in direction on that business?

Competitive pressures

The huge growth in online trading and the increasing tendency for global businesses to use digital communications technology is increasing competitive pressure. Competition online can increase in a number of areas, including prices and recruitment.

Prices

The web-based business is faced with very competitive pricing. A survey by Sage showed that most businesses expected a squeeze on profits caused by increased

Case study: Pricing on the Internet

The following is adapted from an article by Lester Haines in *The Channel Register*, November 2005 (www.channelregister.co.uk).

'"Sony and other manufacturers have been accused of asking online retailers for 10 to 15 per cent more for wholesale electronic goods than they charge their traditional counterparts," *The Times* reports.

'This "dual pricing" strategy – designed to narrow the price differential between net and high street – was allegedly initiated by Sony and quickly adopted by other suppliers. Big-name retail chains have exerted pressure on the electrical giants at a time of falling high street sales in the face of cut-price Internet offers.

' "The cost of distribution through the Internet is about 20 per cent of sales, compared with 45 per cent of sales for a bricks-and-mortar store, and consumers have greatly benefited as a result of online operations," argues retail management consultant Edward Whitfield.'

(© The Register)

1. What is meant by dual pricing?

2. What is a bricks and mortar store? (See page 293 if you need a reminder.)

3. If you were advising a high street store selling mainly electrical goods, how would you suggest that it improved its preparation to meet growing Internet competition?

price competition. Businesses deciding to trade online are often obliged to publish lists of their prices. These lists are then quoted by price comparison services such as Kelkoo or Dealtime. This is known as price transparency.

Recruitment

When it comes to competitive pressures on business, access to quality staff is still top of the list, according to the Sage report. The web creates a fiercely competitive recruitment environment.

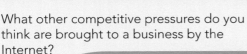

Activity: Competitive pressures

What other competitive pressures do you think are brought to a business by the Internet?

Relocations, takeovers, closures and mergers

We saw at the beginning of this unit how Internet shopping is growing in popularity and looks set to continue growing at a rapid rate. This has caused particular pressure on the retail sector. When firms face declining market share, and are unable to compete, there is a tendency to look for ways of strengthening the position. This can include relocations and sometimes takeovers by or of another business. The extreme response is to close an outlet altogether. Alternatively, mergers with other firms can sometimes create a stronger business that is better able to compete.

The implications of a decision to close down a business operation can be immense for a region or a community. Jobs are lost that will affect families. This loss of jobs can have a knock-on effect on other businesses in the area. The whole effect can snowball.

Refocusing business

Some business activities have been completely changed in order to take up Internet opportunities, as can be seen in the following case study.

Case study: Save and Drive

Save and Drive (www.saveanddrive.co.uk) is a 'clicks and mortar' motor accessories supplier – this means it has a physical store and a web-based transactional website. It is based in Sunderland, in north-east England. The business began as a motorist discount centre, selling car accessories in 1977. In those days there was a strong market for car parts and accessories.

By the 1990s, the market for car parts was in decline. Cars had become much more reliable. Design improvements meant that many replaceable components were obsolete; engines had evolved into 'black boxes' that were computer managed. Modules could be unplugged and replaced. It was now the era of the 'throw-away car'. People had stopped coming into the centres for do-it-yourself car maintenance and repair.

Save and Drive had to refocus its business or close down. The owners decided to set up a website that promoted their full range of accessories. They found, for instance, that there was a market for roof boxes and that these could be marketed online. Indeed, the whole range of accessories could be offered online.

Today, Save and Drive uses a promotional and e-commerce website. People can purchase online in a secure payments system. All of the information a customer needs is available from the site. If not, staff are available to give advice and personal assistance.

One of the dangers of adopting an online strategy such as this is that local customers will stop visiting the physical store. In fact, Save and Drive has succeeded in keeping local people interested in the physical range of products while at the same time extending its market reach online.

1. Describe how Save and Drive has changed its business. Do you think that their staff would have needed new skills?

2. Explain how far you think that the owners of Save and Drive have refocused their business.

3. Could it be argued that Save and Drive has not refocused at all, but just opened up a new sales channel? Explain and justify your answer.

4. What would a business have to do to completely refocus its activities?

3.6 Organisational adaptations to trends

Strategic-level decisions

Strategic decisions at organisational level have a big impact on which direction a business takes and, of course, on whether it succeeds or fails in its marketplace. The Leeds business Card Corporation took a strategy decision based on e-commerce that intended to make full use of Internet technology.

Location of manufacture and service provision

The Card Corporation website illustrates another aspect of the Internet. People can access data and interact with designs from a distance. This means that the potential for online collaboration is significant, as location does not matter.

In manufacturing, global businesses are increasingly giving consideration as to where is the best location to carry out production activities. It is often felt that these businesses will relocate only in areas where labour is cheap.

One of the major business functions capable of relocation is customer services. A big incentive to do this is the availability of a large local supply of personnel. The mobile telecoms company, Three Network, offers its customer service provision from India.

Some businesses adopted an e-commerce website and outsourced their customer service function. The Kingfisher Group's DIY.com outsourced product enquiries and customer service to another company called Spark Response, at Follingsby Park, Gateshead. Customers surfing to www.diy.com placed an order, made an enquiry or a request and all of these were dealt with by Spark Response personnel, although there were also B&Q managers on site.

Re-engineering of business processes

The re-engineering of business processes is a systematic method of examining everything a business does, from top to bottom. Why are particular processes done? What is the reason for them? Are they still needed?

A business that adopts an e-business strategy will need to look again at all of its functional areas to see how they integrate with the whole business. There is no place for separate 'silos' of data (see page 16) that are used only by one specialist function. All data within the organisation is related to the whole purpose – everyone must base their day-to-day activities, planning and objectives upon the same sets of data.

This reinforces the need for a high-quality, secure network that is accessible to all decision makers.

> **Remember**
>
> An e-business must have processes that make use of digital data. Process re-engineering checks all processes (ordering, stock taking, selling and manufacturing, quality controls) to make sure they are contributing to the organisation's objectives.

Redefining the supply chain

Supply chains differ for different products. A supply chain for the factory in Fig. 33.13 consists on one side of a network of suppliers that the business deals with and on the other side a network of customers.

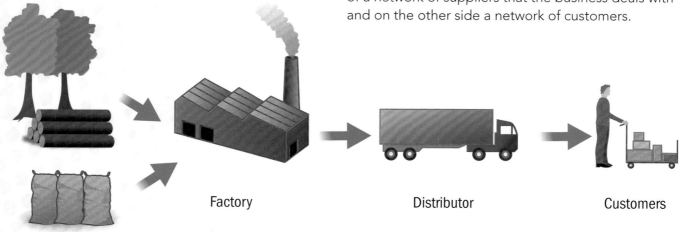

Suppliers   Factory   Distributor   Customers

Fig. 33.13: An example of a supply chain.

The Internet allows firms working together in a supply chain the chance to become much closer in the ways they work. As has been described, there can be a process of disintermediation where distributors or wholesalers are no longer needed. The supply chain becomes integrated and shorter. Ideally, customers benefit.

Investment in information technology

Obviously, businesses must invest in IT if they are to succeed in making productive use of the opportunities from e-business. This investment can include:

- hardware and software requirements
- security issues to consider
- website design and maintenance
- network technologies to weigh up.

From a strategic view, the question is whether a business should outsource the IT function. This means that the installation and maintenance of IT become subject to an external contract with another business. The internal operation of IT systems remains with the organisation's own staff.

Acquisition and development of appropriate skills

Basic IT skills are becoming essential for staff in all organisations. If a business is to go ahead with an e-business strategy, it is even more important that its employees are IT literate. Many employees can learn on the job by training at their desk. Often, IT contractors can train staff as part of the initial contract and this has the advantage that they are most familiar

with the software and the systems that they have been responsible for implementing. Ideally, in such a situation, the IT contractor will have consulted with staff users before a computer system is implemented.

Alternatively, staff can be trained by external IT trainers in-house or off the premises.

One of the methods by which a business could become more prepared for e-business is by setting up individual Personal Development Plans (PDPs) for staff. The following sections and questions need to be answered in designing a person's PDP.

- Objectives – what do I want the staff member to be able to do, or do better?
- Success criteria – how will I measure how successful they have been?
- Actions – what actions will I take to get them to achieve the learning objectives in the plan?
- Implementation – how will I get the staff member to implement the things they have learned?

Remember

Staff training is essential if a business is to make effective use of IT. Staff should be aware of the implications of IT and know how it will affect their jobs.

Risks of an Internet connection

A business with only physical premises to look after still needs to consider security; a business that presents itself on the Internet immediately has many other forms of threat.

When a business begins the process of transferring much of its operations online, it tends also to computerise most of its internal functions. This means that sales figures, staff details, financial performance and much other confidential information is at risk. In this situation, a fully fledged e-business (that is, one that uses digital data extensively) must take steps to protect the business.

There are some annoying issues that can affect an online business at any time and these must be considered and monitored at the outset. These include:

- **spam** – unrequested rubbish or junk mail, which can be blocked through easily installed filters on email accounts

Case study: Business Link

The government's own Business Link service offers practical business advice about selecting IT suppliers from its website (www.businesslink.gov.uk).

1. What sort of advice is given to businesses on the site about choosing an IT supplier?
2. Write a summary of the advice for people considering an e-business strategy.
3. Do you think that businesses need the kind of advice service offered by Business Link? Why?

What are the risks of an Internet connection?

- **spyware** – 'aggressive commercial' software that uses various methods to get installed on your PC and attempt to sell you things or, in some cases, steal money from you by stealing your passwords or card numbers (avoid spyware by setting 'Internet options' > 'Tools' > 'Security options' to medium or high)
- **adware** – irksome advertising and snooping software
- **scams** – for example, phishing, where users are taken to spoof websites pretending to be legitimate businesses, where they are asked to 're-register' – do not ever do this! Newer browsers have an anti-phishing scanning feature to counteract this.

Viruses, Trojans and worms

The term 'computer virus' has come to be a catch-all means of referring to any sort of malicious code introduced unwittingly, or deliberately, into a computer. There are three main variants:

- viruses
- Trojans
- worms.

Software programs consist of hundreds of thousands of lines of code that act as individual instructions for the computer. A virus is a small piece of program code that is designed to enter computer systems and which then spreads to infect more and more files and systems. The virus spreads from computer to computer, carried by any sort of file that is transferred by portable disc or email attachment. Increasingly, in these days of global interconnectedness, viruses spread very rapidly across the Internet.

Some viruses enter systems and are set to wait until something triggers their infection. This could be a date (for example, the Michelangelo virus was set to infect on 6 March, the date of his birth) or a particular time. The deletion of someone's payroll number from a database has been used to trigger a virus. Other viruses just attack immediately on introduction.

Sub-types of virus

There are several sub-types of virus. One of the more serious is a boot sector virus. The boot sector is a small area on the computer hard drive or disc where information about the drive or disc structure is stored. Whenever the computer is started (booted up), the virus is loaded into the memory. This could mean that every time you start up the machine, all files and removable media, such as floppy disks, are infected as well. In some of the worst cases, these viruses can recognise antivirus software programs and delete them before they run. A boot sector virus often sends error messages on start-up or refuses to boot at all.

Program infector viruses attach themselves to the .exe files of programs so that each time you run a particular application, such as Word, the virus loads itself into the system. Every other program that is started after that is also infected. Programs infected with this sort of virus tend not to run as they should. Warnings are therefore given quite early on that infection has occurred.

Macro viruses work by infecting files from other programs that run macros. A macro is a prescribed sequence of actions. A common example would be where a spreadsheet is designed to carry out a calculation at a certain point, or a Word program checks for spelling errors. Macro viruses can spread quite easily because they infect files rather than programs. They are platform independent, meaning they can easily spread from one operating system to another.

A Trojan is a piece of programming language that works by appearing to be something else. It is disguised as either something useful or entertaining, or perhaps something mysterious. These are often attachments to emails, or they may be downloaded from the Internet. A Trojan will enter a system and then wait until it is ready to strike. Trojans can sometimes simply be destructive and ruin files; more commonly they are used to create back-door entrances into

Fig. 33.14: Computer viruses can spread rapidly.

systems so that intruders can access data or gain control of computers.

A worm is a rapidly self-replicating (recreating) program that does not necessarily infect other programs. Instead it spreads across networks and the web. Sometimes this can happen extremely quickly – the 'Slammer Worm' propagated (multiplied) at a rate in which during the first minute of its release it doubled in size every eight seconds – infecting millions of users. Worms work in hidden parts of a system and, like other virus forms, can simply be a nuisance, slowly undermining and destroying a system. However, they can also be dangerously sinister by creating weaknesses and entry points for later access to data within systems.

'Blended' threats

So called 'blended' threats combine the characteristics of worms, viruses and Trojans to cause widespread damage. They propagate rapidly by a range of methods: embedding themselves into HTML code within files on a server; sending unauthorised emails with a worm attachment, infecting visitors to a website (seriously damaging to an e-commerce site). Blended threats often exploit known vulnerabilities in operating systems to gain access points by scanning the Internet for servers to attack.

Loss of data

E-businesses are seriously vulnerable to security breaches. This vulnerability can come as much from perception (how things are seen) as from reality. Whatever kind of business is under discussion, security breaches such as wrongful access to information, falsely transferring funds, destruction of data or other malicious attacks can happen in a number of ways. Some of these are external threats and some can come from inside.

Activity: Computer viruses

In pairs, investigate reports of at least three computer viruses. Describe their:

- scope
- effect
- impact.

Case study: Melissa

In 1999, a macro virus known as 'Melissa' was discovered. An email was headed 'Important Message From…' Within the text body were the words, 'Here is the document you asked for, don't show anyone else ;-)'. A Word document was attached called List.doc that contained a list of the URLs for 50 pornographic websites.

The Word document attached to the email contained a macro which was executed once the document was opened. Written in Visual Basic, a powerful and simple way to create macros, this one accessed as many email directories as it could within Microsoft Outlook's mailing lists, pulling

50 addresses from each one and sending the document with your name on it to these people. Microsoft was forced to close down its mailing services for a while in order to get rid of the virus.

1. In view of the situation that occurred with Melissa, what general advice would you give to staff in a new e-business?

2. Offer a summary of the main antivirus software that a business might consider.

3. As a manager in an online business, what precautions would you require staff to take relating to various computer threats?

Software problems

Hundreds of new software vulnerabilities are reportedly discovered every week.

Businesses usually do not have the staff resources to develop their own applications software and therefore tend to purchase well-established packages or acquire 'open source' programs (computer software for which the source code is freely available) from outside. These programs sometimes introduce bugs that can create serious security loopholes. A bug in software terms is an unintended problem caused by the program. These can have the effect of creating an undesirable 'doorway' into a computer system and its data. This can be used by malicious hackers to extract private information or introduce further unwanted programming code that corrupts data in a system.

As an illustration, in February 2004, Microsoft was forced to issue a critical security alert because of the discovery that some of their programs were vulnerable to a problem called 'buffer overflow'. A buffer is a piece of memory in a computer that can store a set amount of data. Sometimes, usually because of a software bug, more data is sent to the buffer than it can hold, causing it to overflow into the next piece of buffer memory. This makes a computer vulnerable to hackers because, by deliberately causing buffer overflow, they can force the machine to execute their own illegal code. Hackers insert malicious program instructions into areas of memory that should contain only authentic data; the computer is then made to execute the hacker code. In this way, anyone's private data – stored in a Microsoft operating system – could be either corrupted or stolen.

It is obviously in the interests of Microsoft, as well as anyone using its software, to eliminate these bugs as and when they are discovered. Microsoft has a policy of investigating and fixing bugs as soon as it is alerted about them. This is done by issuing downloadable software 'patches' that have the effect of closing security loopholes.

Software design is crucial in helping to create computer system security. An e-business, by its nature, is Internet-facing. The business has to be part of the open web to be part of the online community. This means that any weaknesses in software design

can allow unauthorised access to all sorts of data. Software design should, for example, ensure correct user validation (confirming the user is who they say they are) and a program should flow in ways that are in line with business intentions. The latter problem in programming tends to be referred to as a 'logic error'. This occurs where the program flow can be manipulated or changed by a hacker so as to gain access into the system. In extreme cases, a hacker can gain total control of an operating system.

In some instances, it is neither software bugs nor software design that causes a security threat. Incorrect configuration of some software (such as a firewall setup) may inadvertently allow hackers to read corporate data. The application's software might be fine, but the security setup is wrong.

Activity: Software bugs

Investigate the issue of software bugs. Write a simple explanation – in plain English – of how these might introduce vulnerabilities into a computer system.

Theft of identity

This is sometimes called 'spoofing'. It occurs when a hacker pretends to be someone else and thereby gains access to data. One method of spoofing is by pretending to be a certain IP address. Many web-facing computer systems are restricted to a limited set of IP addresses. Hackers can gain access to the system and gain an entry point that will disclose other, more sensitive data.

Physical insecurities

Business managers need to be aware of simple poor practices that can have dramatic effects on data security. By carelessly discarding old media, such as floppy disks or CDs, data that can allow access to a system can be picked up by outsiders. Just by picking through a rubbish bin, people can gain all sorts of sensitive information, including passwords, code numbers or access information. No amount of technical security can overcome this sort of oversight. Similarly, technical steps are no match for physical intrusion into a building or office.

Internal security threats

Many security problems do not come from outside, but within the organisation – mainly from untrustworthy employees. Usually, the aim of unauthorised intrusion is to:

- gain information from databases
- access research data
- view sales reports
- view marketing statistics or human resources records.

Information can be valuable to others and is sold; occasionally data can be tampered with and corrupted.

A 'root password' is the main means of authorised entrance to a full system. The trusted individuals with access to this password will have full rights to do virtually anything with the system and therefore its data. If this password is carelessly issued, or communicated using unprotected methods, damage can deliberately or mistakenly be done to a system.

'Cracking', 'hacking' and 'bombing'

Computing terminology is evolving and different computer interest groups worldwide have different preferences. Not so long ago, 'hacking' would have been taken to refer to unauthorised access and tinkering with computer systems for fun, in order to satisfy pure intellectual curiosity. But now a whole underground of hacker groups exists, some of them intending to do malicious damage, some merely in it to show off and for the technical buzz. Many hacker groups claim to operate for legal purposes; some even claim to be a force for good. These groups prefer the term 'hacker' to be seen as respectable, whereas a 'cracker' is the criminal.

'Bombing' is an activity in which large amounts of email are sent to an individual or organisation with the aim of completely filling the recipient's hard disk with immense, useless files. This causes at best irritation and at worst complete system failure.

Measures to reduce risks

To help reduce the risk to computer security, organisations can implement sensible procedural precautions, such as:

- IT technicians switching off features that automatically open attachments to emails
- ensuring that operating system updates are always installed
- instructing staff about the dangers of opening email attachments from unknown senders.

In addition to this, antivirus software is also required.

Antivirus software

Antivirus software is essential protection for any business organisation that is connected to the Internet. This software needs to be applied not only to single PCs but to the network as a whole. This should ensure that viruses carried by floppy or zip disks or any other removable media are stopped. Additionally, antivirus software should be able to scan incoming mail.

Many software vendors offer antivirus products. Most of them are similar in terms of what they do. The most effective are those that offer an updating of virus definitions as part of their service. Updates are usually available on demand or are sent out automatically via email. Typical of this sort is Norton AntiVirus (see www.norton.com); also see www.drsolomons.com, or www.mcafee.com

Good antivirus packages tend to offer three components as part of their service.

- They scan all files on local or hard disks, floppies or network drives.
- They shield automatically in the background, looking out for viruses while downloading takes place or a floppy disk is put into a PC.
- They clean a file system or disk of viruses once they have been found. This is done by scanning a database for established remedies. Most antivirus solutions erase a virus immediately and it is expected that the recipient of a virus informs the sender straight away so that the source can be eliminated.

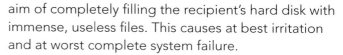

Activity: Hackers

1. Research and find out the various categories of 'hacker'.
2. Produce a clearly sectioned poster, warning about the different kinds of threat.

Firewalls

A firewall is a security system implemented in software or hardware that is used to prevent unauthorised access to or from an intranet (private network). Firewalls are frequently used.

A good illustration of how this works is the medieval castle. In Fig. 33.15, we can see that the 'treasures' of the internal networks are all hidden behind a high external firewall, which itself hides another security firewall. Each level of security – from the inside out – gets progressively more robust and strong. Internally, less security (but still good security) is required because the outer layers are strong.

Firewalls can work by filtering packets of data as they enter or leave a network – on the basis of preconfigured rules. Alternatively, they apply security to particular applications. Firewalls are the first line of defence for networks.

Remember

Any computer connected to the Internet can be subject to attack from elsewhere on the web. Everyone should take steps to protect their PC.

Information technology policies

When an organisation uses a computer network, it tends to have computerised systems across all its internal functions. This means that finance, human resources, sales, production and other functions all depend on digital data. The security methods outlined will offer good protection from external threats, but internal threats also exist. Poor staff practices, and inappropriate Internet use, can cause damage to a business.

A business therefore needs to have a set of IT policies (see Fig. 33.16). These will establish the ground rules for all staff to follow. Such measures as passwords, authentication, firewalls and restrictions will all have to be implemented.

Backing up data

A simple security measure that is advisable for individuals as well as businesses is to back up the data that is stored on computer. A business that uses an intranet will have a lot of crucial data on file. Malicious hacking or loss of data can be very harmful to the organisation. Computer systems are often configured to back up all data automatically. This means creating an additional copy of all files and storing this separately.

For individuals, backing up important data on CDs, or other portable media such as a data stick, is good practice.

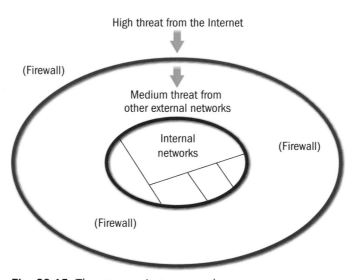

High threat from the Internet

(Firewall)

Medium threat from other external networks

Internal networks

(Firewall)

(Firewall)

Fig. 33.15: Threats to private networks.

AN INTERNET POLICY FOR YOUR EMPLOYEES

ACCESS RULES

Give employees proper training before they use the Internet. This should cover:

- how to use your Internet software

- your Internet policy, and how it works

- efficient use of the Internet.

Make sure employees follow your access procedures: Configure software to maximise security.

Do not allow employees to change settings or use other software.

Depending on the nature of your connection, employees may need to disconnect once they have finished using the Internet.

You can set your Internet connection to close down after a specified time if it is not being used.

Only give employees remote access (for example, using a laptop) to your network or Internet connection when it is absolutely necessary.

Fig. 33.16: Sample Internet policy information from the HSBC Knowledge Network.

3.7 Implications of trends on customers

The Internet offers great opportunities for those who have the skills and understanding, or the cash, to be able to take advantage. For those who do not have such opportunities, there is disadvantage. Many people, mostly those already poor or socially disadvantaged in some other way, cannot or do not have access to the new technologies and the opportunities they bring. These people – the 'socially excluded' – are said to be on the wrong side of the 'digital divide' because they lack the technical literacy skills to access the range of full digital services available to others.

Income, education and age are the biggest factors in creating the digital divide, according to a European Union report ('e-Inclusion revisited: the local dimension of the Information Society'). It reveals that women are taking to technology in greater numbers than ever, and the over-55s are also gaining computer skills. But poor, badly educated people are still lagging behind.

Those who do not have Internet access are the ones with the most to lose if high street businesses are forced out of operation. We saw earlier that the retail sector is under pressure. The loss of physical outlets or services will hit these people harder, increasing social disadvantage.

Activity: E-Inclusion revisited

1. Research the report 'e-Inclusion revisited: the local dimension of the Information Society' (you can find a link to this on www.einclusion-eu.org). Summarise its findings and write a report offering your own conclusions.

2. 'Poorly educated people have no chance of accessing the Internet properly.' Do you agree with this statement? Explain your response.

Assessment activity 33.3

Grading tips

You have been asked to help a local business that is experiencing a downturn in its business. To do this you decide to help them to use the Internet.

1. Visit www.nielsen-netratings.com and look for the 'solutions by country' panel on the left of the home page. Survey the site and draft a short report for the business on the kind of data that this service can bring. **P3**

2. Carry out research using a search engine such as www.google.co.uk. Discover a full range of prices and product comparisons for laser printers suitable for business use. Create a written summary for the business explaining how you searched for the information. **P3**

3. Prepare a presentation that describes (using examples) the kinds of actions that various organisations can take to reduce security risks arising from operating online. **P4**

You are also required to prepare materials explaining the various competitive forces causing them to consider developing a more web-based e-business.

4. Explain the competitive pressures on selected, contrasting business organisations to develop their use of e-business. **P5**

5. Take two contrasting businesses and explain, using examples, how they have responded to competitive forces to develop their use of e-business. **M2**

6. Evaluate how successful a particular business organisation has been in preparing for growing use of e-business. **D1**

You are then asked to advise a local medium-sized business which is considering launching an e-commerce website designed to open up new customer bases in both the EU and Asia. The MD has particularly asked for your advice on producing a PDP for sales staff.

7. Prepare an outline personal development plan for sales staff that are unfamiliar with Internet business. **P7**

1. You need to actually use the Internet for a business purpose. In this context you are required to show a business manager how the Internet can be used to gain useful marketing information and to demonstrate how a simple (but careful) search can be used to gain product information. **P3**

2. The presentation should cover a variety of steps including the use of software such as firewall protection; anti spyware and antivirus measures. There should be full coverage of the kinds of IT usage policies and procedures that are common today. **P4**

3. You must show understanding of what these forces are. For example, the price of Chinese goods may be much lower than those made in Britain because they have much lower wage costs. On the other hand, British technological expertise may be superior in many areas, allowing a business to compete on non-price factors. **P5**

4. You need to show a good analysis of two practical cases of real businesses adopting e-business practices to compete more effectively. The emphasis may be on marketing, product development, pricing or customer relations. Many websites have excellent summaries of this kind of information. **M2**

5. This grade is reserved for high-level evaluative thinking that focuses on one of the businesses. **D1**

6. Your plan should show a good understanding of the main issues the staff member will meet when working in a selling context using Internet technology. These may include email practices, online diaries, databases, searches, product information, online customer relations and so on. **P7**

4. Understand the key features of planning for the increased use of e-business at different levels

4.1 Government support

The Internet does not belong to any one country; it is a 'stateless' phenomenon that crosses national and international boundaries. Both the UK and the European Union – of which the UK is a part – have adopted policies designed to encourage both private and business Internet use. The UK government has had a policy to make the UK 'the best place in which to do e-business'. The European Union has a stated aim of creating an 'information society' among all member states.

Digital Britain

In January 2009, the government published the Interim Digital Britain Report. This set out an agenda for action involving both the private sector and government. Five objectives were identified and these were:

- modernising and upgrading the UK's wired, wireless and broadcasting framework to sustain Britain's leading position as a digital economy
- providing a favourable climate for investment and innovation in digital content, applications and services
- securing a range of high-quality public service content, particularly in the news
- developing the nation's digital skills, at all levels
- securing universal access to broadband, increasing its take-up and using broadband to deliver more public services more effectively and more efficiently.

Legislative framework

E-Commerce Regulations 2002

In 2002, the EU issued instructions to all member states to implement the E-Commerce Regulations. Any business intending to trade online must take these into account. The key features of the Electronic Commerce (EC Directive) Regulations 2002 are as follows.

- Online selling and advertising is subject to the laws of the UK if the trader is established in the UK. Online services provided from other member states may not be restricted. There are exceptions, particularly for contracts with consumers and the freedom of parties to choose the applicable law.

- Recipients of online services must be given clearly defined information about the trader, the nature of commercial communications (that is, emails) and how to complete an online transaction.
- Online service providers are exempt from liability for the content that they convey or store in specified circumstances.
- Changes were made to the powers of enforcement authorities, such as Trading Standards Departments and the Office of Fair Trading.

The purpose of the Directive (and the Regulations) is to ensure the free movement of 'information society services' across the European Community and to encourage greater use of e-commerce by breaking down barriers across Europe.

Consumer Protection Distance Selling Regulations

Distance selling means selling and buying by phone, mail order, the Internet or digital TV. Such transactions are covered generally by normal buying and selling legislation, but they are also covered by special Distance Selling Regulations.

Distance Selling Regulations give protection to consumers who shop by phone, mail order, via the Internet or digital TV. This protection includes:

- the right to receive clear information about goods and services before deciding to buy
- confirmation of this information in writing
- a cooling-off period of seven working days in which the consumer can withdraw from the contract
- protection from credit card fraud.

Data Protection Act 1998

The Data Protection Act 1998 (see also pages 94, 139 and 332) is the law that governs the processing of personal information held on living, identifiable individuals. Businesses must comply with the Act if they process personal information about people.

The Act requires that a business is open about the use of information and follows certain principles for processing that information. These principles are known as the eight data protection principles. The Act also provides individuals with certain rights, including the right of subject access.

Business support and education

The UK government offers free training and advice for businesses that are considering adopting a strategy of e-commerce. Business Link (www.businesslink.gov.uk) gives advice on training, grants and support schemes. The national government Department for Business, Innovation and Skills has the following purpose: 'We want to make sure that Britain is the best place in the world to run an innovative business or service – this is critical to the UK's future prosperity, our quality of life and future job prospects' (www.berr.gov.uk).

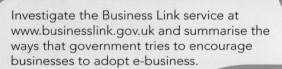

4.2 Individual level

Growth of home computing

In 1981 IBM launched the first home computer, the IBM 5051. At today's prices the machine would cost you £2,500. In 1982, a British entrepreneur, Sir Clive Sinclair, launched a mass-market ZX Spectrum machine which cost just £125 (about £307 at today's prices). The ZX held only 16K of memory (PCs today are said to give 11,000 per cent extra capacity!).

However, it was the start of home computing. Before then computers were confined to large obscure rooms usually located in basements within workplaces. Since 2001, the market for home computing has grown by 52 per cent. More than 6.5 million home computers will be sold in the UK in 2006 and according to Jupiter, a research company, 70 per cent of UK homes have a PC.

This means that home computing is continuing to grow. Computers are becoming the central entertainment area in households. More and more families are connecting their computers to flat-screen TVs; the TV screen becomes the computer screen. The computer has evolved into the home entertainment centre rather than being something that just produces, for example, spreadsheets.

Employability and ICT skills

Individuals increasingly have to consider their personal level of ICT skill. Employers can offer IT training, as we saw earlier. However, for those who are out of work or considering a career change, it is essential that they possess at least the basics in computer literacy. The British Computer Society's European Computer Driving Licence (ECDL) has been used by 1.5 million people in the UK to acquire the basics.

If the UK is to compete successfully in the wider European knowledge economy, the ICT skills of the entire workforce need to be improved, according to IT trade body Intellect.

Increase in flexible working models

Some organisations today employ only a reduced full-time permanent core of multi-skilled staff. There is an increase in secondments – temporary transfers to another job within the same organisation – part-time or flexible working patterns, and work being contracted out to freelancers (self-employed individuals). Because information technology allows novel forms of communication between individuals and organisations, people can adopt more flexible work patterns.

From an individual staff viewpoint, there is the likelihood that at some point in their working life they will need to change job roles and get new skills. Lifelong careers have been replaced by lifelong learning.

Case study: Woolley & Co. Solicitors

'We run as a virtual firm; all our lawyers and typists/support staff work from home on total flexi-time and flexi-holidays. We have no offices.

'We get incredibly high-quality lawyers from top firms joining us because of the lifestyle they can achieve. We would never attract those lawyers to a small firm like ours without this flexibility. We have never had any issue with trust or how long people have worked, and so on. Good professional people know what hours to work and don't need it enforced.'

(Source: Andrew Woolley, Woolley & Co. Solicitors, www.family-lawfirm.co.uk)

1. Describe what is meant by flexible working.

2. Do you think that flexible working depends on IT skills?

Assessment activity 33.4   BTEC

You have been asked to prepare a presentation in which you explain how the government supports the development of e-business. To construct your presentation you decide initially to look at the following:

* www.businesslink.gov.uk
* www.berr.gov.uk

Explain how the government supports the development of e-business.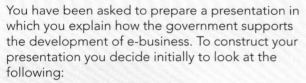

Grading tip

You should look at the kinds of advice the government gives to business. This will cover initial considerations about setting up a website, e-commerce regulations, staff skills required, security and data protection. Keep your explanation simple, well structured and clearly presented. **P6**

Just checking

1. How would you distinguish between the Internet and the worldwide web?
2. What is a wireless network?
3. Describe how a business might make use of a range of mobile devices for Internet access.
4. What is e-procurement and what are its advantages?
5. How could a business make use of the Internet for promotional purposes?
6. How could a business conduct research on the Internet?
7. What are the main security issues for a business considering doing online business?
8. What is meant by 'competitive forces'? How can the following potential advantages of e-business assist a business to meet them?
   - increased sales
   - cost savings
   - wider market reach
   - better marketing opportunities.
9. What is the supply chain and how does the Internet help this?
10. What are the main legal considerations for a possible e-business?
11. What sources of advice would you recommend for a possible e-business and why?
12. What is meant by process re-engineering and why might it be needed for a newly developing e-business?

Assignment tips

1. When you are describing how the Internet works, see if you can be creative but clear. Use easy-to-understand diagrams and include simple notes. You do not have to be highly technical.

2. The Internet can be used in many ways for many purposes. Try to show a broad understanding by showing different kinds of use. This means not just selling; what about things like health and police services?

3. When you are looking at competitive forces you can work in a group, each taking one sort of force (for example, technological, price) and share what you have found out.

4. Just about every website that exists to promote online sales has a section designed to reassure customers about security. This is an obvious source of information on the topic.

Credit value: 10

34 Website design strategy

In June 2009, James Hall in the *Daily Telegraph* quoted a major new survey by PayPal, the online payment system, saying that sales in physical stores will plummet by up to £8.3 billion by the end of 2011. However, in the same period, online sales will rise to £21.3 billion. The report shows that nearly nine million adults shop online at least once a week.

Carl Scheible (MD of PayPal) said, 'In our experience the retail winners from this recession will be those that work hard to meet expectations. If customers have come to expect fantastic service on the high street, retailers must make sure they aren't disappointed if they head online. Customers want good value, simplicity and security when they decide where to spend their money online.'

According to the report, 24 per cent of UK adults now believe that online shopping will become the norm and that the high street will eventually die out. Over half of consumers polled believe that high-street retailers could significantly improve their websites and sales processes to 'enhance the customer experience'.

A strategy for excellence in web design is vital for any business hoping to tap into the growing world of online sales.

In this unit you will examine the huge range of organisations now using their own websites for a variety of business purposes. You will examine the various features that have an impact on usability and appeal for users of websites. Finally, you will look at the practical matters to be addressed in designing a modest website of your own.

Learning outcomes

After completing this unit, you should:

1. know the purposes of a range of websites
2. understand the main elements in web design for usability and visual appeal
3. be able to plan the development of a website for an organisation.

439

Assessment and grading criteria

This table shows you what you must do in order to achieve a **pass**, **merit** or **distinction** grade, and where you can find activities in this book to help you.

To achieve a **pass** grade the evidence must show that the learner is able to:	To achieve a **merit** grade the evidence must show that, in addition to the pass criteria, the learner is able to:	To achieve a **distinction** grade the evidence must show that, in addition to the pass and merit criteria, the learner is able to:
P1 describe how three contrasting organisations use their websites for business purposes **See Assessment activity 34.1, page 453.**	**M1** analyse how a selected website has been designed to meet the requirements of its target audience **See Assessment activity 34.2, page 464.**	**D1** evaluate the extent to which the design of a selected website helps the originating organisation to meet its objectives **See Assessment activity 34.2, page 464.**
P2 explain the usability features of the websites of three contrasting organisations **See Assessment activity 34.2, page 464.**		
P3 describe how the websites of three organisations have been designed to appeal visually to their users **See Assessment activity 34.2, page 464.**		
P4 design a website for a specified organisation to meet stated purposes for a defined target group **See Assessment activity 34.3, page 475.**	**M2** assess how own website design contributes to fulfilling the organisation's purpose through meeting the requirements of the target audience **See Assessment activity 34.3, page 475.**	**D2** make justified recommendations for how a website design and launch plan could be improved **See Assessment activity 34.3, page 475.**
P5 draw up plans to assess the design of a website aimed at meeting a specified purpose **See Assessment activity 34.3, page 475.**	**M3** explain the appropriateness of the plan for the launch of a website for a specified organisation **See Assessment activity 34.3, page 475.**	
P6 draw up a plan for the launch of a website for a specified organisation **See Assessment activity 34.3, page 475.**		

How you will be assessed

For this unit you are required to investigate websites from different categories and produce a report on an example of each one. You will need to produce a website for an organisation for a specified purpose and targeted to a defined audience, and a plan for the launch and maintenance of the website.

Sophie

I'd never thought about design in web terms – clothes, yes please. When I thought about it, I realised that the way a web page looks and is laid out is very important. We had a web designer talk to our class. He told us that in his opinion, 'less is more' and we shouldn't be thinking about animations and jazzy colours all over the site. This is OK for experimenting and playing, but we must think about what the user of a website will feel. I enjoyed the unit; it was great fun and really made me think about the web in a different way.

Website design

'While retailers close tens of thousands of bricks-and-mortar stores, few are making severe cuts in their e-commerce teams. In fact, many e-retailers see a big opportunity for retail websites to appeal to increasingly price-conscious consumers at a time when physical stores are cutting back on staff and stock, or disappearing altogether.' (Source: Don Davis; Internetretailer.com, 2009.)

List the things about website design you feel are the most important for a selling website. Are they the same for all websites?

1. Know the purposes of a range of websites

It is sometimes said that there are now more web pages available online than there are stars in the sky. Certainly, in the UK alone, several thousand organisations have websites that act as global shop windows. Today, there are so many different kinds of organisation using the web that it is helpful to try to make sense of this by placing them into categories.

In broad terms, it is possible to distinguish two kinds of commercial (that is, buying and selling) relationships online. The two most common interactions occur on business-to-consumer sites (B2C) and business-to-business (B2B) sites.

1.1 Commercial relationships
Business-to-consumer (B2C)

A B2C website offers to sell or provide a service to private consumers rather than other businesses; B2C businesses respond to consumer demand.

Walk around any shopping area and you will see a range of retail outlets offering goods for sale to us, private consumers. Before the development of the Internet, shopping was restricted to particular times and places. Shops were only open at certain times and you had to travel to them. By contrast, an online shop is unlimited in time or space and there are no limits to what an Internet retailer (known as an 'e-tailer') can offer to consumers. There are only limits as to what they can actually do, as some early dotcoms found out.

These e-tailers are usually part of an established retail firm. There is a big difference between adding an online sales channel to an existing firm and trying to set up a completely new online retail outlet. Most of the growth in e-business is due to physical businesses adopting an e-strategy.

Amazon.co.uk is one of the most successful online businesses and a model for every online firm. Amazon.co.uk started off as a bookseller and today offers nearly five million books, together with information about them all, as well as personalised recommendations based on past choices from the site (see more on this on page 421). Amazon.co.uk has diversified its product range to become a multi-product online business: as well as books it now sells CDs, DVDs, toys, electronic items and sports equipment, to name just a few. The Internet not only gives e-tailers the chance to offer a wider range of choices, but also allows them to offer more back-up services to consumers.

The problem of the abandoned online shopping cart is a major issue for the e-tailer. Slow Internet connections and download times, fears about intrusion and fears about security will often drive even the most enthusiastic consumers away from Internet shopping. Online shoppers often drop out at the cart stage because of lack of speed. Despite this, online shopping continues to increase. Faster broadband Internet connections may be the solution, but online suppliers still have to make a real Internet offer to gain sales.

Business-to-business (B2B)

In the online world, B2B is reported to be bigger than B2C. Transactions between businesses may be less frequent over the Internet, but they account for more in terms of money value.

The B2B business is buying from and selling to other businesses. It is buying either for its own internal maintenance, repair and operations (MRO) purposes, or for items used as part of what is sold to another business in a supply chain.

A report by eMarketer (www.emarketer.com) predicted that these kinds of transactions would soon amount to almost 90 per cent of total e-commerce. In 2006, it was reported that:

- 93 per cent of business decision makers used the Internet every day
- 70 per cent thought their use of B2B websites would increase.

Why has B2B Internet trade become so significant? The reason is that there are many more opportunities for big-deal transactions between businesses than there are for transactions with private customers. Fig. 34.1 illustrates this.

Business organisations are likely to have several suppliers and the suppliers themselves will have suppliers.

Online marketplaces for components are becoming more common. For example, Ford and General Motors have joined forces and moved their US $300 billion and US $500 billion supply chains online.

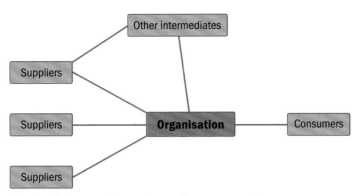

Fig. 34.1: B2B and B2C interaction compared.

Remember

For commercial websites offered by profit-seeking organisations, a basic distinction can be made between B2C websites targeted towards private consumers and B2B websites aimed at business buyers.

1.2 Purposes of commercial websites

The basic purpose of a commercial website is, of course, to generate revenue from sales. There are a number of business models achieving this online. We saw on page 298 that many long-established retailers have added an online sales channel to their existing offline (physical) stores. There are some notable businesses (Amazon.co.uk being the most well known) that have established a purely online presence – you will not (yet) find an Amazon.co.uk shop down your road.

Direct online sales

The Internet offers the ability to sell directly to consumers from a website, thus bypassing other intermediaries (for example, wholesalers).

Computers and software

One company that built its business solely on this model is computer manufacturer Dell (www.dell.co.uk). The strategy adopted by Dell Inc. was that it would not have any physical retail outlets. Consumers would simply visit Dell online, specify their computing requirements, and Dell would build and deliver on this basis.

In recent years, Dell seems to be changing its strategy by considering a move into high street retail sales. It has recognised that private consumers need to

experience through 'touch and feel' the products they are considering buying.

Music and software products lend themselves to purely digital formats. These can therefore be sold and delivered solely via the web. In the case of expensive software, individuals and business customers appear less willing to pay large sums upfront for a CD packed with coding. The preferred model is to buy a contracted deal whereby the software is offered on an ongoing maintenance arrangement. This way, purchasers would pay as they use, with support offered via a contractual agreement. The software industry is changing.

This is an important development. For businesses, software products are a means of making far better use of the Internet. Software applications such as customer relationship management, database management and project management can help firms to automate their processes and gain a competitive advantage.

The Leighton Group's 4Projects application is an example of the kind of software that businesses can purchase with ongoing maintenance and support.

Music

Music downloads are now a must for many, if not all, teenagers. The Apple iTunes application and others such as Amazon.co.uk allow for both peer-to-peer file sharing and music purchases directly online.

Online sales with physical delivery

Retail stores such as Tesco, Asda, Sainsbury's, Next, M&S, B&Q and many more have opened up online sales channels, adding to their physical stores. Clearly the goods they sell are incapable of direct delivery over the web, so they have to be physically delivered, sometimes using a third party service.

In the case of PC World, the sales strategy has included online promotion with offline collection. This is a helpful sales strategy combining the convenience of the web with the practicality of physical collection.

Pre-sales models

All pre-sales business models can make excellent use of the web because of its suitability to carry detailed information about products. Internet shoppers can get as much information as they require before making a decision to buy. This means that brochures and online catalogues are very suitable vehicles for product promotion. Businesses seeking to generate sales from a website can embark on email campaigns too.

Case study: 4Retail

4Retail is a North-East based company, offering a comprehensive on-demand software solution designed to enable retailers to collaborate effectively and communicate more efficiently. This particularly applies to the design to delivery cycle, where designers, buyers, technicians and suppliers must work closely together to deliver a product on time and to specification.

Delivered via SaaS (Software as a Service), 4Retail is an extranet-based platform. This means that firms buying into the application enter into a secure wide area network (WAN) along with other partner companies. Immediately the problems inherent in the Internet or public email accounts are overcome. Extranets are robust, secure and flexible.

The on-demand software is designed to be totally flexible and capable of being configured to meet many requirements. The application consists of a number of component modules including:

- document management
- task management
- versioned forms
- calendar management.

1. Can you describe another example of software available directly on the web?

2. What are the advantages of this kind of software for a business in construction?

3. In what other contexts do you think that software like 4Retail could be used? Do you think it adds value to a business? How?

4. How are demand and supply interrelated in the marketplace?

How can physical delivery or collection help a business?

It is important for any business looking for sales via an email campaign to recognise that unrequested emails are a source of great irritation to many people. **Spam** is a nuisance. Research has shown that where permission has been sought and agreed, email campaigns can be very fruitful. The message for online businesses is: always request permission to email before sending out a campaign.

Key term

Spam – unsolicited emails, often referred to as junk mail

Post-sales models

The web is useful for helping communications between customers and the selling business. The customer is in a stronger position to give feedback once a sale has been made. As businesses adopt an online business approach, some feel that automated responses in customer services can be a help.

Software applications are now available to manage the entire relationship with customers. This means that two businesses that work closely together in partnership within an industry (for example, a fence manufacturer that always purchases the wood from a particular producer) can be digitally bound together. There are databases of, for example:

- staff
- product codes
- technical support staff
- technical information
- sales staff.

If someone wishes to make contact, the software can allow this to happen easily.

Remember

The relationship between businesses in a B2B context can be helped by the use of customer relationship management software. These are applications that manage the interactions between two businesses, making sure that each one is satisfied.

Websites not related to sales

Although the web is a proven vehicle for generating sales, there is also a use for the medium in supporting other activities of the core business.

Most websites include pages that are intended purely for corporate communications. Some websites (for example, Bells – see page 462) have no intention of generating sales because of the nature of the business.

The B&Q-owned e-business Screwfix uses its website for some PR work, as do many others. It is worth remembering that the web is a vehicle for carrying information. Clearly it is in the corporate interest of all businesses to sell themselves as well as their core products.

Other websites exist to inform the consumer about the available choices. The CNET website at www.computers.com only contains reviews and price comparisons.

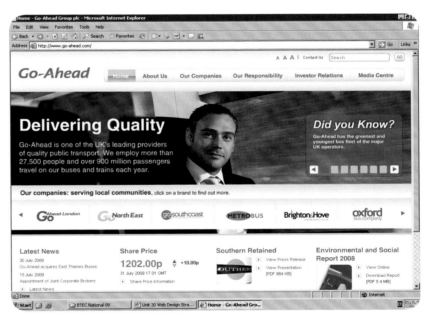

Fig. 34.2: How many links from this home page are intended purely for communications purposes?

1.3 Non-commercial business relationships

Whereas commercial websites set out to generate consumer interest and (hopefully) sales, non-commercial websites set out to do something else. This depends on whether they are:

- government
- national government

- voluntary sector bodies
- campaigning groups.

Local goverment

Local government is delivered through local councils. Local councils are democratically elected bodies that have the responsibility to offer local services according to the wishes of Parliament. All local councils get their powers from Parliament. Services such as education, social services, planning, trading standards and rubbish clearance are all carried out by your local council because they are required to do so by Parliament.

Local government is important. We tend to ignore our local council. But think about the following.

- If your neighbours decided to build a big extension to their house, it would be the council that would give or refuse permission.
- If a road was to be built near you, it would be the council making that decision.
- If a parent wanted their child to attend one school rather than another, it would be the council that finally decided.

It follows that if your local council has a website, it is likely to carry information that is important to you.

These days, most local councils have a website. The purpose is to provide information about services they provide and, in some cases, to make services available online. Of course, apart from information about services, councils know that the local electorate have the power to vote them out of office. It is therefore in their own interest to promote the work they do. Local voters are aware that councils cost them money. Tax payers like to know what the council is doing and a website is an ideal way of communicating.

> **Remember**
>
> Local councils use websites to promote their services and inform people about what is going on in their area.

National government

National government offers services and deals with concerns that affect us all. The Internet is a great way to offer certain services across the country in an efficient and cost-effective way. Because national government covers so many issues and concerns, many government departments have their own website. Some typical government websites are:

- www.berr.gov.uk (Department for Business, Enterprise and Regulatory Reform)
- www.dcsf.gov.uk (Department for Children, Schools and Families)
- www.defra.gov.uk (Department for Environment, Food and Rural Affairs).

Fig. 34.3: Local council website for south Tyneside.

One way to give the public access to a broad range of online services is to use a national government **portal**. You can find the national government portal at www.directgov.gov.uk, for example.

The national government sites that have been mentioned so far address the needs of both private individuals and businesses. As its name would suggest, the Department of Trade and Industry specialises in offering advice and service to industry.

Key term

Portal – a gateway site that offers many links into other sites related to the same theme

Remember

The web is capable of being used by private businesses and national and local government to carry information that can either inform or persuade.

Voluntary sector groups

The voluntary sector also uses the web to great effect. Voluntary bodies rely on the public for support for their particular cause. These bodies do not have the pursuit of profit as their main aim. They exist to further a particular cause and hopefully gain public sympathy for it, for example, to help artistic talent within inner cities or to inform people about the work of the Youth Hostels Association (www.yha.org.uk).

Campaigning groups

Some groups come together to raise a specific issue, by bringing it to the attention of the government and the public. There are many issues that are of national and indeed global importance. Perhaps the most obvious of these are to do with our natural environment. The Greenphase portal shown in Fig. 34.4 illustrates how well environmental organisations are represented on the web.

Apart from the environment, there are many other specific causes that are represented by organised groups.

- Some of these exist to exert pressure on the government to change policy (for example, the campaign for divorced fathers at www.wifesgone.com)

- Others exist to represent the interests of a particular group (for example, www.rcn.org.uk, the body representing nurses).

Remember

The Internet carries websites that intend to persuade people to support voluntary causes (such as Fairtrade); it also carries websites from pressure groups such as Greenpeace and interest groups such as trade unions.

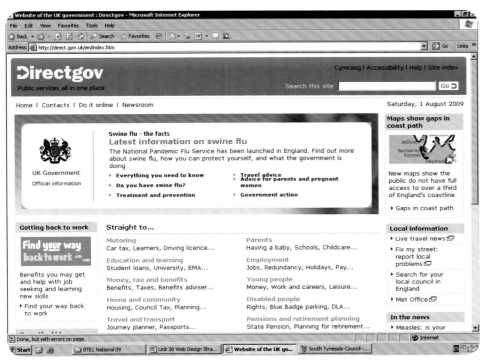

Fig. 34.4: The national government portal offers links to many government services.

Case study: ActionAid

International development charity ActionAid is launching a new website inspired by the success of community site MySpace to offer support to fundraisers. Users can join an online community to publicise upcoming events, collect donations, then blog [write about experiences, like an online diary] about their experiences.

While collecting money online is well established, the new site allows users to swap tips on successes and disasters. Fundraisers can upload blogs and pictures, swap ideas and discuss their sponsored sing-along, marathon run or coffee morning with like-minded people. One area of the site offers users the chance to share tips on getting fit for sponsored runs.

www.myactionaid.org.uk aims to be easy to understand and allows users to create their own colourful fundraising page 'in a matter of minutes'.

Simon Molloy, head of community fundraising at ActionAid, says, 'ActionAid's fundraisers ride bikes across Malawi, kayak through the Brazilian jungle and throw themselves out of planes to help fight poverty. We wanted to create an online community that would give everyone who raises money for ActionAid the chance to show the world what they're planning and make it easy for them to raise as much money as possible.'

(Source: adapted from *The Guardian*, 13 February 2007.)

1. Why do you think that voluntary sector bodies find using the web useful?

2. What features of the web are being employed by this website? Do you think they will work?

3. Study the website mentioned in the article. Evaluate the extent to which you think it will meet the voluntary sector objectives outlined.

Fig. 34.5: This site offers links to other environmental websites.

1.4 Purposes of non-commercial websites

Non-commercial websites are intended to carry information. Is the information meant to persuade, influence or inform, or all of these? Is the website designed to collect data from people and organisations?

Website designers, as we will see on pages 458–64, need to spend a great deal of time with the people seeking to go online to discover the purpose(s) of the website. It is vital that these intentions are known. The whole look and feel of a website, its design, layout, imagery and content are governed by its basic intention.

Activity: Organisational purpose

1. Investigate two websites – one from a profit-seeking business and another from a non-profit seeking organisation.

2. Create a simple presentation to explain the way each website helps the organisation to achieve its purpose(s).

PLTS

You can independently investigate and analyse the ways in which a web presence helps both profit-seeking and non-profit-seeking businesses to achieve their objectives.

1.5 Key marketing concepts

Marketing is the set of professional activities designed to satisfy an organisation's customers, whoever and wherever they are. This applies increasingly to the public sector as well as to the private sector. For example, in creating a website, your local council is trying to improve citizens' views about it and provide a better service.

For the private sector (the sector that first took up marketing in response to global pressures to do so), marketing has evolved into a sophisticated and important function. Private sector businesses want to attract and retain customers.

There are three key marketing concepts:

- targeting
- segmentation
- the marketing mix.

Each of these is assisted by the availability of the Internet.

Think about the word 'marketing' for a moment – we all know that a market is a place where people buy and sell things. In a market, sellers display their goods and buyers come looking for the best deals.

Marketing is, as we have seen, about making sure that goods and services meet customer expectations. To do this properly means that marketers try to make sense of the whole 'market'. Two basic techniques help in this:

- targeting
- segmentation.

Targeting and segmentation

Some products (for example, Mars Bars) could be said to be aimed at everyone who enjoys chocolate – in other words, a mass market. However, others are targeted at specific groups. An example of targeting a market might be a magazine that is clearly aimed at teenagers. Others would be particular razors, cosmetics, jewellery and clothing.

Marketers use various criteria for **targeting a market**. They can use age, social class, lifestyle, psychographics (the use of demographics to study and measure attitudes, values, lifestyles and opinions) and geographic location. Each of these can then be used to isolate particular characteristics and meet their specific needs.

Key term

Targeting a market – tailoring communications in order to attract sales from a specific group of people

Associated with targeting is another tool known as segmentation. Here, an entire market is divided into subgroups sharing similar characteristics. A market segment is then available for targeting particular products. Just as an orange has separate segments making up the whole, so a market has many segments. Marketing professionals find out what the segments are, then aim the marketing approach to satisfy that segment.

The marketing mix

Once marketing professionals have discovered their market segments and determined the groups they wish to target, the next set of decisions revolve around the tactics used to meet the needs of the target group. These tactics come from the marketing mix. The marketing mix is often described as the 'four Ps', and has been extended to the 'seven Ps':

- product
- price
- place
- promotion
- people
- physical evidence
- process.

Each P describes the methods that marketers can use to address the needs of a target market. The last three Ps were added because of criticism that the original four Ps did not take into account that many businesses today are in **service industries**, and therefore factors other than product, price, place and promotion are important.

The marketing mix can be summarised as follows.

Product

The marketing function considers the features of a product offered to a market.

- What is it?
- Who would it be aimed at?
- What does it do?
- What should it do?

The product could be a **tangible** thing (for example, a toothbrush with a manoeuvrable head). Alternatively, it could be an intangible service (for example, a delivery service).

Price

The marketing function also considers the price a product should be pitched at.

- What sort of customers will buy at a particular price?
- What is the best price to attract a particular kind of customer?
- What price might get more people to buy?

Key terms

Service industries – industries not dealing in physical products but offering services such as finance or insurance

Tangible – something you can touch

- What price might create the best image?
- What might be the effect of a change in price?

Place

Marketing specialists consider how a product would find its way to consumers to a place where they could make a purchase. This would include physical distribution and merchandising. Physical goods must be transported from the manufacturer into storage, through distribution centres to wholesalers, then to the high street retailer. Businesses working in between a manufacturer and a retailer are known as intermediaries.

Promotion

Marketing professionals have to consider ways of bringing products to the attention of potential customers. This includes advertising via the various media, as well as other ways of promoting products in the eyes of consumers, such as special offers. These activities, in the physical world, are designed to 'push' products and services into the eyes and ears of potential consumers.

These four Ps are a set of tactical ingredients, to be mixed according to what a firm's marketing strategy is designed to achieve – hence the term marketing mix. The 'extended mix' (that is, the last three Ps) has been added to deal with services.

People

Service products are delivered by people. If a bus driver on your way to school or college this morning was horrible to you, you would be upset. If people are nice to you, you might return for more business. People make businesses!

Physical evidence

If you go somewhere to receive a service (for example, a meal in a restaurant), you expect it to be in pleasant surroundings. Businesses try to make sure that there is a good physical environment for customers.

Process

If you want to use a service, what is the process of getting it? Is it easy, or so complicated that you give up and go elsewhere? Marketers need to consider people's views about this and respond.

The website in the marketing mix

The Internet has added to the range of marketing tactics and tricks available to marketing professionals.

A business website, depending on what the business does, can be its product. In the case of businesses selling other physical products, the website becomes the shop window. In either case, the technology offered by the web lets businesses modify the marketing mix in a number of ways. This is sometimes referred to as the 'marketing remix', as Fig. 34.6 shows.

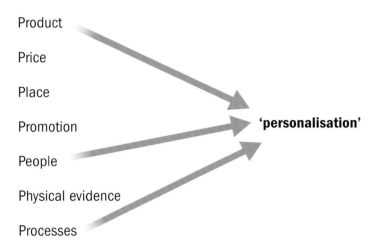

Product

Price

Place

Promotion

People

Physical evidence

Processes

'personalisation'

Fig. 34.6: The Internet e-marketing remix – the seven Ps.

Each element of the Internet marketing remix can be affected by a website.

- **Products** are displayed and described in detail. Indeed, online, the web makes an individual offer because it is a one-to-one relationship when a customer accesses a website. This allows for personalisation. As an example, try registering with Amazon.co.uk, browsing some particular products and then returning to the site. The website will offer you recommendations and show you what products you have recently viewed. Products can also be extended by giving additional offers of guarantees or other enhancements. In Internet terms, this is known as bundling products together.
- **Prices** are visible; they are often lower because costs are lower.
- **Place** is affected because people can often download from a website if the products offered are in digital format (for example, software, music or film). Often there is direct selling. This means that 'middle men' are cut out of the chain.
- **Promotion** can be placed on all websites. Businesses can carry banner adverts and affiliate links to other business sites. They can have strong PR stories on their sites and they can make special

offers. Promotion is very effective online, if used well.

- **People** are behind every website. However, online customers do not meet people face to face. If a problem occurs in a transaction there need to be back-up support staff. Very often this is done through contact centres. A website should inform customers how to make contact. There could be features like FAQs (frequently asked questions), virtual assistants and auto-responders built into the site. In the case of a website offering a personalised service, there is a one-to-one relationship.
- **Physical evidence** is only represented by the look and feel of a website, which in effect becomes the replacement for the environment a service is delivered in. Customers have to feel comfortable in the site and know their way around.
- **Process** refers to how easy it is to receive a service or product. If a site visitor decides to take advantage of an available product, how easy is it to get what they want? EasyJet has a famous three-click process for ordering a flight ticket. This can be a major selling point and again can be done on a personalised basis.

Remember

When a business goes online it can design features into the website that add to the marketing impact. The marketing mix is remixed with some added ingredients to give customers a positive experience.

Websites in the promotion mix

Modern businesses use their websites to offer lots of promotional material, both for themselves and, through affiliate programmes, for other businesses. Promotional activities in the marketing mix can take several forms; this is referred to as the promotion mix. Websites can:

- carry advertisements
- have sales promotions
- assist in personal selling
- carry PR materials
- help in direct marketing.

Not only does a website help a business to deliver these promotional strategies very quickly and cost-effectively, but the website also assists in targeting the correct audience by using email. A business can customise a message to suit a particular market segment. All of this can help to build better relationships with customers.

1.6 Current and future developments

In the Internet world, technological developments happen very quickly. One of these – broadband connection to the web – is extremely fast-growing.

Broadband in homes

Broadband Internet connections are much faster and smoother than the now old-fashioned dial-up connection. Films, music and software downloads are now speedy and relatively easy to achieve on broadband, and more and more households are switching over.

Telephone developments

One of the most important parts of customer service provision is to ensure that telephone calls are handled efficiently and quickly. More than 80 per cent of customer communication is still by voice. The latest software products can automate responses and reroute calls quickly to a member of staff.

VoIP (Voice-over Internet Protocol) allows a person to make telephone calls using a computer network over a data network such as the Internet. VoIP converts the voice signal from a telephone into a digital signal that travels over the Internet, then converts it back at the other end so you can speak to anyone with a normal phone number.

Scalability in planning a website

Typical website development occurs gradually. The key aspect at the initiation of many web design projects is **website scalability**. This means that while the website may have certain features and facilities now, in all likelihood there will be additional requirements in the future that are not applicable now.

This is a typical scenario, where companies like the website's usability and structure, but want to provide for expansion without having to go back from the beginning again, with all the associated implications.

Key term

Website scalability – the capability of a website to grow alongside the growth of the business

Case study: Broadband in the UK

There were 17.4 million broadband subscriptions in the UK by the end of 2008, according to the latest statistics from broadband statistic experts Point-Topic. The overall growth in broadband was 10.6 per cent, which is much less than in 2007 where there was a 19.9 per cent growth in broadband subscriptions.

There were around one million new broadband subscriptions in the first half of 2008 and only 675,000 during the second half of 2008. The slower growth could be from a couple of factors, first being the saturation of broadband in the UK – with many already having broadband, there are not that many new people trying to get it – and also with the recession and the 'credit crunch' in the UK, many are starting to tighten their belts to save money and possibly see broadband as a service they can afford to live without at the moment. With the roll-out of fibre broadband from BT we could soon see broadband speeds increasing and larger bandwidth available.

(Source: Mark Ward/BroadbandWatchdog.co.uk)

1. What is meant by the term 'saturation of broadband in the UK'?
2. What are the current statistics for broadband connections in home users?
3. What would you say is the business case for having a broadband connection?

Activity: Marketing mix

Carry out a search for two contrasting profit-making businesses working online. Make notes about how these businesses are using the web to deliver their marketing mix. Be ready to give a three-minute verbal explanation to your tutor.

Remember

A website is designed to help a business achieve its aims and objectives. If it succeeds, the business may grow and the features of the website will have to grow with it. This means scalability.

Assessment activity 34.1

P1   BTEC

You work for the local council's Economic Development Unit, which is keen to encourage new 'e-business' into the area. You have been asked to do a preliminary investigation and prepare a short presentation about how different businesses can use the Internet.

Describe how three contrasting organisations use their websites for business purposes. **P1**

Grading tip

To meet the pass criteria, you need first to consider why an organisation has a website. Is it to sell, offer a service or inform? Then look at the features of the websites of the contrasting organisations and describe what they offer users. Say how you think this online presence helps the organisations achieve their goals. **P1**

2. Understand the main elements in web design for usability and visual appeal

The Internet has emerged as a key aspect of many modern businesses. When planning and designing a website, the intention is not only to attract visitors, but also to retain their interest. We saw in the previous section that organisations have many diverse functions and purposes. However, there is little point in having a web presence at all if users simply visit your site, then quickly pass through. For this reason, design features relating to usability and **visual appeal** are very important.

A website should encourage a visitor to look at the site content, easily find something of value and draw them step by step into the site. Fig. 34.7 shows the ideal sequence. To achieve this, there are several important considerations, including:

- usability
- navigation
- language
- efficiency
- speed of response
- respect for privacy
- design of web pages
- accessibility.

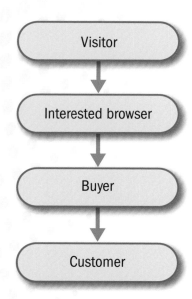

Fig. 34.7: Turning a website visitor into a customer.

2.1 Usability

How easy is a website to navigate? Have you ever visited a site that was difficult or frustrating to use? There can be many reasons for this, for example:

- links on the site do not work
- the page takes a long time to load into your browser
- images do not show properly
- the site does not show in the browser you are using.

For a website to be successful, it must do what the user wants. In other words, it must do what it is designed to do and demonstrate **usability**. This means it should offer clear and useful information. Links that are intended to take users elsewhere should work, and images within the site should serve a clear purpose and not take too long to load.

Web customers are slow to please and easy to deter. One slip, one faulty link or one confusing page and a user will quickly leave. It is important to recall that 'the door' is merely a click away.

Retaining customers

Customer retention is a key purpose of usability. It is far cheaper to retain a customer than it is to acquire new ones. Once visitors have entered the site, there should be a strong enough reason for them to stay. The site should have a value to users. They should find it easy to:

- see what they want
- buy what they want.

An initial visit should, ideally, lead the customer painlessly through to a purchase.

Key terms

Visual appeal – a pleasant and appropriate look and feel that is appropriate to the organisation

Usability – the ease with which staff and visitors can use a website

Customer retention – keeping customers so that they come back to your site to make repeat purchases

Case study: www.diy.com

'You can be totally confident when you shop with www.diy.com! We are so confident about the payment security we offer on our site that we will back every purchase with our security guarantee.

- Our site uses Secure Server software that encrypts your credit or debit card information to ensure your transaction with us is private and protected as it travels over the Internet.

- Every payment transaction we process is checked by our fraud control systems to validate the authenticity and validity of the payment cards used, as well as indicators of possible fraudulent use.

- In the unlikely event of fraudulent or unauthorised use of your payment card in online transactions, most banks and card issuers that subscribe to the Banking Code either cover all the charges or may limit your liability to just £50.00.'

(Source: www.diy.com, the online sales channel for B&Q.)

1. Why do you think that online customers sometimes feel insecure about paying online?
2. What would you recommend a possible new online business do about security fears of a website?
3. How effective do you feel that website security reassurance is when it is done like the above? Will this approach work? Justify your response.

Trust in the website

Web visitors need to be given reassurance when they visit a site that it is trustworthy and secure.

Factors affecting usability

There are a number of factors that affect the usability of a website.

- **Navigation** – Creating good website navigation is the most important task a web designer has to accomplish in the web design process. Website navigation is the pathway people take to navigate through sites. It must be well constructed, easy to use and intuitive.

- **Language** – Language problems on the web can arise if a website is intended for international use and the only language available for users is English. Software is available to translate languages online. They can also arise if language used on a site is too technical. It is important to remember that web information should be accessible to as many people as possible.

- **Efficiency** – The website should be efficient. This means it should be quick to load and should offer speedy navigation, with all links being up to date and working. People online expect things to work.

- **Accuracy** – The information contained on a website should be up to date and accurate. People could leave the site never to return if they have no confidence that the content is correct.

- **Speed of response** – If customers place orders or make enquiries, it is crucial that they receive a prompt response. There should therefore be systems within the business that ensure online queries or orders are dealt with.

- **Respect for privacy** – Online customers value their **privacy**. If customers entrust an organisation with personal information, they have a right to expect that the information will be kept private unless they have given explicit permission for the data to be given to someone else.

Key term

Privacy – the level of security of personal information – a crucial factor in a website's status in the eyes of users

Remember

Usability is one of the most important factors affecting the success of a website.

Each of the key factors influencing a website's usability can be worked on by developers as shown in the following sections.

2.2 Navigation

As we saw earlier, website navigation should help users to find their way quickly and easily around a website. There are several design techniques to build navigation into a site. A good website should always provide a set of text-only navigation links to enable non-graphical browser users to navigate your site. Other navigation techniques include the following.

- **Mouseover image navigation** – Mouseover images add entertainment value and impact to the user's experience of visiting a site. A mouseover is an image that reacts when users place their mouse over the image, by swapping to another image in exactly the same place and the same size.
- **Rollover image navigation** – This is similar to mouseover, but the image can appear in a different part of the web page and can also be a different size.
- **Drop-down menu navigation** – Navigation can be created in layers that allow links to appear and disappear in sections when activated by the user.
- **Navigation images/graphics** – Navigation opportunities can be highlighted to users with images.

These techniques should take account of user types and their needs – for example, whether the target audience is other businesses or teenagers.

> **Remember**
> When developing a website, make it easy for users to find their way around the different pages.

Ability to complete transaction

For most website visitors on sites where buying and selling takes place, the ability to complete the transaction is vital. There is no point at all in all the links, images and navigation options working well if at the end of the process there is no chance of placing an order and making or taking payment. (We noted earlier on that many people abandon their online shopping.) This is **completing the transaction** – something is exchanged or promised at the time of the visit.

> **Key term**
> **Completing the transaction** – actually making the sale from the website; funds are transferred with the promise of the product

2.3 Language

The web is an information-based medium. Content is therefore everything. Web designers must think carefully about the style and tone associated with website content. The words used on a website must have meaning for typical users. Language problems can be caused by a lack of understanding of English or excessive technical jargon, or they can be caused by inappropriate tone. So just as in face-to-face interactions, the user of website information can be distracted and lose interest if the words used are not well thought out.

> **Remember**
> The words used on a website should be very clear and easy for users to understand.

Legible text

If something is legible, it can be read. If something is illegible, you are not able to read it. (Ever heard a tutor say that your handwriting is illegible?) It is important for web designers to make sure that the text used on a site is legible. Careful selection of font style and font size is essential.

Another factor that we will examine later is accessibility for those who have sight problems. Web designers should take note of the law in relation to this.

2.4 Efficiency

A business website must be efficient for the user. There should be something online that is of value to the customer, and this should be available quite quickly and easily. For example, easyJet has, as a selling point, its three-click online booking process to get an airline ticket.

The information and presentation of the navigation options through the site should be economical and time efficient. Users are always impressed if a process is easy.

2.5 Speed of response

The Internet carries data using a set of protocols (see page 399). The most significant of these in relation to speed is TCP (Transmission Control Protocol). Data is broken down into packets for transfer, then reassembled at the receiver's end. The rate of transfer is slow if data packets are lost. These days, when more and more consumers and businesses are using the Internet, the transfer speed has become a real selling point.

Web developers use several technical tricks to ensure that a user's experience on a website appears to be smooth and easy. One of these is called AJAX. This is JavaScript code that requests only a small portion of data is transferred. An example would be where a user is registering with a website and is asked to choose a username. The user moves on to the next action while in the background, AJAX coding has already sent a request to check whether the selected username is available. If it is not, the user quickly receives a polite message suggesting they try another name. The effect of this coding is, of course, to speed up the process experienced by the user.

When a customer types a URL (Uniform Resource Locator or web address) into the address bar of the browser, there may be a subconscious sense of frustration caused by the fact that it takes even a few seconds for a web page to load. This is made worse if the web page takes longer than those few seconds to load. Anything a web designer can do to speed up the process of response will make customers happier.

Web designers in the past have been guilty of incorporating all sorts of images and multimedia features into websites at the expense of speed. Users of websites need to be able to see what the content is for. There should be a logical flow of content, and the text and visual content needs to be attractive and interesting.

2.6 Respect for privacy

The privacy of personal information is a big concern of many Internet users and web designers need to consider this issue.

Businesses trading from a website receive and store certain types of information whenever you interact with them. Many websites use cookies (see pages 458 and 469) and obtain certain types of information when a customer's web browser accesses the website.

Information can be collected and analysed using technology that is not obvious to you, for example:

- the Internet Protocol (IP) address used to connect your computer to the Internet
- your login, email address and password
- computer and connection information such as the browser type and version, operating system and platform
- the full URL, click streams to, through and from the website, including date and time
- cookie number
- pages viewed or searched for
- your site history and phone number used to make contact.

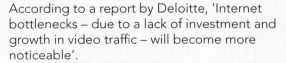

Case study: Internet reaching capacity?

According to a report by Deloitte, 'Internet bottlenecks – due to a lack of investment and growth in video traffic – will become more noticeable'.

The report said that one of the key possibilities is that the Internet could be approaching its capacity.

'The twin trends causing this are an explosion in demand, largely fuelled by the growth in video traffic and the lack of investment in new, functioning capacity,' said Igal Brightman, global managing partner at Deloitte. 'Bottlenecks are likely to become apparent in some of the Internet's backbones, the terabit-capable pipes exchanging traffic between continents.'

(Source: www.pcpro.co.uk, 19 January 2007.)

1. Why do you think that some business websites use video images in their site? Give examples.

2. Analyse why video and images are useful in some business contexts.

3. For one of your examples, evaluate the extent to which video and other visual media contribute to the organisation's objectives.

Cookies

Cookies are pieces of information that can be transferred to your computer's hard drive through your web browser when you are viewing a website. These pieces of information allow the website to act on information that will make a customer's use of the website more rewarding. Cookies enable a business system to recognise your browser and provide features such as easier login and greater security, and store information about you between visits.

Activity: Privacy

Investigate the websites of at least three trading organisations.

1. Can you identify any statements on these sites about privacy?
2. How do you feel about the privacy issue?
3. Do you think that businesses should make it clear to web customers that personal information is being collected?

PLTS

When you are investigating the statements made by businesses about privacy for customers, you can reflect on the importance of personal privacy to people and recommending the measures that could be taken to reassure them.

For a business to be successful on the web, it is essential that its website makes no intrusive or irrelevant requests for information. Users frequently want to know why information is needed and to what purposes such information will be used. People have fears about third parties being given their personal details.

For the web designer, it is wise to be open and honest about:

- what, if any, information about customers is being collected
- how the data is being collected
- the uses to which data will be put.

Remember

Respect for customer privacy can be a selling point for an online business. People have a right for their privacy to be respected. They also have a right to be made aware of what information is being collected about them and the ways such information may be used.

2.7 Design of web pages

Remember that the point of web design is to give the user (not the designer) a satisfying and useful experience while on the site. There are many things to consider in relation to this, including:

- user paths through the site
- ranking information
- search engine operation
- design for usability and visual appeal
- conflicts between different aspects of usability.

User paths through the site

The most basic difference between reading a web page and reading a page like this in a textbook is that in the case of the web we are looking at **hypertext** and in the book we are reading linear text.

- Linear text is read from left to right in order for us to make sense of what it is saying.
- Hypertext contains hyperlinks that allow us to jump all over, from page to page and document to document (even from site to site).

Key term

Hypertext – text available on the web that contains hyperlinks to other web pages

This has immediate repercussions for web designers. People can skip from one page to another in an instant – and frequently do. Rarely do visitors read text on a web page in a linear fashion. What web visitors do is skim across text, often looking for relevant links. The web designer must try to ensure that links offer clear pathways to relevant pages within a site.

Ranking information

Depending on the site, its purpose and the target audience, a web page should not usually contain large blocks of text (a 'wall of words'). Information on the page should be ranked using headings in a clear hierarchy. Text should be broken up with headings and bulleted lists. The reader of the web page should be given convenient visual resting points such as a list or an emboldened piece of text.

Visitors to a website could arrive on the site at any page, not just the home page. Designers should make it easy to get back to the home page with simple navigation.

Activity: Age profile

Investigate the age profile of the UK population.

1. How has this changed over the last 30 years?
2. Considering the changing age profile of our population, what would you recommend the web design community does to help older users make use of a website?

Remember

Always try to break up text on a web page by ranking headings in order of importance and by using bulleted points.

Search engine operation

One of the most vital jobs of good web designers is to bear in mind that search engines automatically search for pages using sophisticated software that is looking at content. A website should be 'search engine friendly'. Google, for instance, reads whole web pages. How is the page 'marked up'? Has the designer used good HTML (HyperText Mark-up Language)?

The days are long gone when designers could simply pack the headers with keywords to draw the search engines on to a site. Today, designers work with copywriters to make sure that web pages hang together in content and HTML tags. If they are done well, search engines will rank them highly. As more users visit the site, because the content is good, the ranking becomes even more secure.

Case study: Gareth Rushgrove, web designer

Gareth Rushgrove, a Durham University Physics graduate, is a professional web designer dedicated to making the Internet work for both businesses and their customers. Working for a rapidly growing new media company called THINK (www.think.eu) that is based in Newcastle-upon-Tyne, Gareth takes a very user-centred view of the design process.

'Web design must be done with users in mind. Often I will consult with senior management in an organisation, and they will carefully outline what they expect from a website. Of course, I listen carefully and note their requirements. I go back to the office and produce a "low fidelity" version of the site, precisely as they believe they want it. Then I go and speak to people in the corridor (staff) and show them the outline site on a laptop. I call this the "Hallway Test". This inevitably leads to changes. Next, I will do what I call the "Tesco Test", often involving people having coffee in Tesco! This leads to even more changes. Gradually, the website evolves to become user friendly.'

The point is that Gareth sees his role as giving the users of a website a satisfying online experience – knowing that by doing this, organisational leaders will discover that their website achieves their objectives. While management may think they know what they want, this is not always what is needed by their own staff or their customers and clients.

1. What do you understand by the term 'user-centred design'?
2. What do you feel are the advantages and disadvantages of the so-called 'Hallway' and 'Tesco' tests?
3. Evaluate the idea that senior managers may not always appreciate the real needs of staff or client users of a website. Can you find any evidence of this in a website you have experienced?

Other ways to do this are by building links into your site with a view to attracting more visitors.

Design for usability and visual appeal

The look and feel of a website are key to attracting visitors and getting them to stay on the site long enough to make a purchase. Ideally, design should not only cause visitors to want to stay on the site, but also it should encourage them to return. To achieve this, both usability and visual appeal must be good.

Remember

Search engine optimisation is a central part of modern web design. A business must ensure that important search engines find its site. People may judge a website within a 20th of a second on their first visit.

Conflicts between different aspects of usability

Some of the features that make a website appealing to visitors may conflict. There are a number of ways in which this can happen and often a designer may have to compromise.

Personalisation versus speed

The web offers businesses a superb opportunity to personalise content. Web pages are capable, if they are designed this way, of remembering a previously registered visitor to a site, then personalising content the next time the user visits (for example, Amazon.co.uk). However, if this causes the site to slow down, the user may be deterred. Design factors must therefore consider how important personalisation is to the business objectives.

Visual appeal versus speed

The temptation to include all sorts of images, font colours and animations is always present for a novice website creator. However, we have already noted that such features can dramatically slow down the load time of a web page. Bearing in mind the case study below, perhaps the old saying 'less is more' would be appropriate in many instances. Efficient load-up may be more fruitful, rather than flashy images in an attempt to create visual appeal.

Visual appeal versus legibility

Visual appeal should not affect the ability of the visitor to actually read the page content. Some websites include colourful backgrounds, but these can make it very difficult to read the text.

Case study: Good web design

Canadian research suggests that web users make up their minds about the quality of a site or e-commerce store within a 20th of a second.

Dr Lindgaard, who conducted the research, said, 'As websites increasingly jostle for business, companies should take note. Unless the first impression is favourable, visitors will be out of your site before they even know that you might be offering more than your competitors.'

The research does seem to confirm the disappointment that we all get looking at cheap sites or where the design has been homogenised (made the same) by a committee.

Companies need to spend longer on the design of their websites and to refresh the look of them regularly. Design must be very individual for each site and adapt the offline personality of the brand to the special characteristics of the web.

The use of animation is a controversial aspect of the home pages of many brands and was not covered in the reported research. Some web designers prefer to take the client straight to the front page, meaning it must be beautifully designed. If the researchers are right, a slow animated introduction to a site may not convince visitors, who will already be on their way to another site.

(Source: adapted from an article by Jonathon Briggs on www.othermedia.com, 16 January 2006.)

1. What do you think is meant by the phrase 'adapt the offline personality of the brand to the special characteristics of the web'?

2. What do you think are the important messages from the article for a business commissioning web design?

3. What are your views about the claim that people make their mind up within a 20th of a second about a website's worth? Explain your views and justify them with reference to a real business website.

Remember

Websites always have a purpose beyond visual appeal. It is no use having a great look to a site if users find the site difficult to use.

2.8 Accessibility

The Website Accessibility Initiative (WAI) outlines the international guidelines on **accessibility** in web design. The WAI is affiliated with the Worldwide Web Consortium (W3C) and works with organisations around the world to increase the accessibility of the web. As part of this work, the WAI published the first version of the Web Content Accessibility Guidelines (WCAG) in 1999. These are accepted as the definitive set of international guidelines used for building accessible websites. All other guidelines and standards are derived from these.

The UK government recommends that web pages comply with the WCAG guidelines. Web designers and those commissioning web pages therefore have a responsibility to ensure that their website design does not discriminate against visitors with disabilities.

Disability Discrimination Act (DDA)

The part of the Disability Discrimination Act (DDA) that states websites must be made accessible came into force on 1 October 1995. The Code of Practice for this section of the Act was published on 27 May 2002. There is now a legal obligation – following the implementation of section 21 of the Disability Discrimination Act (1995) – to make reasonable adjustments to ensure blind and partially sighted people can access a web-based service.

The DDA 1995 expects web designers to make 'reasonable adjustments' to their sites to accommodate and assist those who may have a sight problem.

Remember

The Disability Discrimination Act 1995 expects web designers to make 'reasonable adjustments' to a website to help the visually impaired. This may include things like larger fonts.

2.9 Visual appeal

If a website can clearly and efficiently show a potential customer that the company is knowledgeable and up to date in its field of expertise, the customer becomes confident and trusting of the services offered. A website is a multi-functional medium that serves as a communication tool. Thus it plays a central role in improving the impact and image of a brand.

A website is a personal interaction with both current and potential consumers. Yet however gripping a website's content may be, it is the design elements that have a dramatic, if not crucial, impact and contribution to make. There are a few prominent aspects of a website that are greatly influenced by web design.

Whatever the place of a website in the life of a business, the visual appeal, commonly referred to as the look and feel of the website, is an important factor when planning the site.

Use of fonts and graphics

The basics of any website include the fonts used for the various levels of text and the graphics used to convey the right impression, or give the right information, to the visitor. The case of Bells, a fish and chip shop (see page 462), illustrates how some of these factors are considered in even the most basic websites.

Advantages and disadvantages of using multimedia

Multimedia elements within web pages allow for a user to play video streaming or audio files through their browser. There are alternative techniques to design these features into a page. For example, it is possible to have a link to an external media player and only allow for very short clips to be played on the page. Alternatively, the media could be designed to use a fully downloaded media player such as Apple's QuickTime player.

Key terms

Accessibility – the ease and comfort with which websites can be used by those with disabilities

Multimedia elements – the facility on a web page to show streaming video or sounds to back up the textual information

Activity: Multimedia

Consider the following organisations with an online service or product. In your view, which of these would benefit from a multimedia feature available from a website? Copy and complete the table and fully justify your responses with suggestions.

Table 34.1: Businesses suitable for multimedia on websites?

Business	Yes	No
A fish and chip shop		
An estate agent		
A law firm		
A photographer		
A bus company		
A school or college		
A building firm		

There are advantages for many organisations in building multimedia into a website.

Obviously many websites depend on sound as a key element of their purpose (for example, YouTube). However, for designers looking to incorporate sound effects into their design, there are online services offering options.

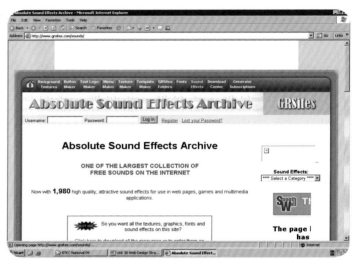

Fig. 34.8: A website requiring sound effects.

Case study: Bells Fish & Chips

Fish and chip shops probably do not spring readily to mind when you think of an Internet presence. Firstly, it is impossible (so far!) to buy a portion of fish and chips over the web. Secondly, the typical fish shop would appear to have little to gain from being online.

Bells Fish & Chips shop owner Graham Kennedy decided otherwise.

'I'm not a computer geek by any means and I hardly know how to type,' says Graham. 'I just felt that as a nation we were turning out to be an online economy. If my fish shop didn't have an online existence, it wouldn't be long before others did. In any case, at Bells we do have something to shout about, so why not let people know online?'

Graham consulted a local web designer, Scott Oliver, and discussed a number of important things. 'I wanted to know how much it would cost. Scott gave me a figure and I thought it was fair enough. So I then gave him an outline of what I wanted. Within three days Scott had sent me about six alternative "looks" for the website. From these I chose two that I felt were the right image and after discussions with Scott I selected one that we both liked.'

After this agreement there was a process of communications between Graham and Scott as the site developed. For instance, Graham insisted that the font for the Bells wording at the top was changed and he checked out the photographic images.

The Bells website offers a crisp, clean image that gives all the essential information and includes good-quality images that tell visitors something about the shop.

1. Given the type of business that Bells is, which aspects of 'visual appeal' do you feel the owner has tried to achieve?

2. Take a look at www.bellsfishshop.co.uk and, together with the information you have been given above, analyse the visual aspects of the site and comment on the functions, usability and the visual and media design of the site.

3. Evaluate the Bells website and one other business site of your own choice. To what extent do you feel the features mentioned above on these websites contribute towards the achievement of the businesses objectives?

Use of white space

White space is the space between the elements on a web page. If there is no or too little white space, a web page will appear disorganised. Web designers should try to make the page look clean, simple, and easy to read and navigate.

Appealing to a target group

It is, of course, possible to design a successful website without a specific target group. However, this suggests that the business does not have an online strategy. Some people have a very clear target audience in mind when designing their websites, even without any formal documentation – usually one-person start-up businesses that are designing their site according to their own enthusiasms or knowledge of a special interest group.

If someone transfers a 'bricks and mortar' business (one that operates offline) to the Internet, they usually have a pretty good idea who the target audience is – basically the same people as in their established business.

The more an online business knows its target audience, the more it can target a design. This is about the choice between design and practicality. Targeting both form and functionality to a target audience is more likely to ensure web success.

Consistency with brand image

Branding is a centrally important creative activity in a businesses marketing strategy. Could you identify, for example, the Tesco brand, the M&S brand or the Ford Motor company brand?

Successful branding means that a business and its products have an instantly recognisable identity or **brand image**. The brand communicates a corporate image.

Key term

Brand image – the creation of an easy-to-spot identity that consumers get to know well

It is a known marketing fact that strong brands, with their associated values, sell. There are many retailers in the market – for example, Virgin, M&S, Sainsbury's and Tesco – which have proven that with a strong brand, it is possible to diversify from core product offers, such as clothing, food and travel, to include new services such as banking and insurance.

Consumer confidence in a strong brand enables retailers to sell new ranges that traditionally would not have been considered. Consumers are comfortable with the brand and what it represents, and are confident enough to purchase additional services.

How do you know if a brand image is successful?

Consistency in a brand is therefore vital in order to achieve this. For many retailers operating in a market where customers are fickle (for example, the fashion industry), it is important not only to identify the factors in the core brand, but also to employ them consistently at every point the customer comes into contact with the company. In a competitive market, creating brand loyalty is essential in order to stay ahead.

Customer contact may be in-store, from catalogues or online. In some instances, this may also include customer call centres or service departments where the employee may be dealing with customers over the phone. Online, this presents a challenge – conveying the same image that a customer may experience from good service in-store.

Assessment activity 34.2

You are employed in the Economic Development Unit of a city council. One of the key areas of policy of the council is to encourage new businesses into the area, and to help existing businesses to develop and expand. Both of these things will help to encourage economic development in the area.

Your line manager has been given some investigative work to do as part of the background research required to prepare for a series of 'road shows' in which the council will present materials to local business managers. The general topic of the road shows is 'the e-economy'. Your manager has delegated the following research tasks to you.

You decide to create a set of well-organised portfolios in the form of notes and handouts.

1. Explain the usability features of the websites of three contrasting organisations. **P2**

2. Describe how the websites of three organisations have been designed to appeal visually to their users. **P3**

3. Analyse how a selected website has been designed to meet the requirements of its target audience. **M1**

4. Evaluate the extent to which design of a selected website helps the organisation to meet its objectives. **D1**

Grading tips

1. This involves looking at aspects of websites that are designed to help users. Does the site offer help features? If so, explain why they are there. What functions does the site offer? **P2**

2. Why do you feel that these organisations have designed certain features such as attractive images or multimedia into their sites? **P3**

3. You need to identify the attributes of the target group and relate these requirements to the design of the website, outlining its advantages and disadvantages. (For example, what is Topshop hoping to achieve from its website's entire 'look and feel'?) **M1**

4. You must arrive at well-explained and justified conclusions about the design of a selected website and relate this conclusion to the organisation's objectives. **D1**

3. Be able to plan the development of a website for an organisation

Before a company creates an e-business website, there are a number of important factors to consider. We saw from the case study on page 462 that even for a small business with little or no potential for sales transactions to be carried on the Internet, it is necessary to give some thought to what a website is designed to achieve. This implies an online strategy that places a website within context.

3.1 Strategy
Business objectives

All businesses work on the basis of an overarching set of aims and **objectives**. Aims revolve around strategic direction. A small- to medium-sized engineering firm, for example, may set as an aim, the desire 'to increase our share of the aerospace components market'. To achieve this, there has to be a degree of planning that will specify a series of actions to be taken. Once these practical actions have been decided, management will set business objectives based on SMART criteria (specific, measurable, achievable, realistic and time-related). One such SMART objective in the above case may be to increase sales of a particular product by ten per cent within six months.

There are obvious implications for a website involved in this objective.

- It should include excellent technical information.
- It should include communications and relationship management features.
- It should be well designed with clear information. Potential customers should be made to feel (from the website) that this is a company that sets high standards and will meet all their needs.

Marketing objectives

Part of the strategy involves establishing marketing objectives.

- What do customers in particular markets want?
- Is there to be a targeted market, or an undifferentiated marketing message?

- How can a website be used to target the market a business wishes to break into?
- How can the business satisfy and exceed customer needs?

The business that is planning a website has to think about the ways in which it is going to promote its activities and products. At the design stage, managers and web designers have to work together, considering the ways in which the website can deliver better service to customers.

A website can be promoted both online and offline. The site can be linked through affiliate promotion on industrial portals or industrial networks. Given that small- to medium-sized businesses enjoy a certain level of 'equality in online presence' on the Internet, a business can use a good website to raise the company profile in the eyes of possible buyers.

The website should offer a value proposition to potential customers that encourage them to enter the site, stay there for a while and see enough of interest that will cause them to come back. These things are known as **website stickiness**.

Consumer/customer profile and expectations

In the process of planning to target a particular segment of a market, a business may develop a **customer profile** by collecting information about them. For example, what will be the expectations of young people 18 to 25 years of age? What are their expectations? The characteristics of a young person's lifestyle should be taken into account.

> ## Key terms
>
> **Objectives** – goals that an organisation sets for itself – for example, profitability, sales growth or return on investment
>
> **Website stickiness** – the capacity of a website to make people stay on the site and eventually make a purchase
>
> **Customer profile** – the characteristics of a typical person or business that buys from your website

The information a business needs to collect depends on the type of business. For example, to sell to individual consumers (B2C), information is needed about their:

- age
- gender
- location
- spending habits
- income.

If selling is to other businesses (B2B), information is needed about:

- what sector they are in
- how big they are
- how much they spend
- what other suppliers they use.

The CIM (Chartered Institute of Marketers) recommends finding out as much as possible about existing customers. This can be done by analysing sales records, talking to customers and, if more information is required, carrying out a survey. A business can build up a database of information about customers. In doing this, it includes as much feedback as possible about how highly customers rate products or services. A business's own records are used to add details of purchasing behaviour, such as:

- the products each customer tends to buy
- when and how the customer buys.

These information-gathering activities are all helped by being online. The website can be used to capture customer data. By using web analytics (see page 409), the business can discover how the site works and how customers are responding to it.

Consumers' technical environment and user experience

Another factor to bear in mind when designing a website is the level of customers' technical expertise as well as their experience in using the web. Many more people today are competent in finding their way around websites. However, as we saw earlier in the unit, people are easily deterred if they lack confidence either in themselves or the business they are trying to deal with.

Web designers must think 'ease of use' and 'simplicity' if there is any doubt about customer web experience or confidence.

Analysis of competitor websites

A competitive analysis provides information on a website's usability, strengths and weaknesses, compared to existing or potential competitors. It can also provide a measure of how a website compares to the overall market.

By examining competitors' offerings (for example, in terms of information, architecture, navigation, interaction styles), businesses can identify the features, functionality and design elements of their competitors' sites that work well for customers. Once identified, they can apply these elements to the planned website and often present opportunities for further innovation to stay ahead of the competition. More importantly, a competitive analysis can find out which aspects of your competitor's sites are not usable and help a business involved in website planning to avoid the same pitfalls.

Remember

An online strategy can place a business in a much stronger marketing position if a website is designed with customer needs in mind.

3.2 Functions of a website

The following things determine the functions that can be offered to customers from the website.

- The nature of the business.
- The resources available.
- The corporate strategy surrounding a company's decision to go online.

We have seen a number of examples of **website functionality**. Take a look at the example in Fig. 34.9 from Kitchens2yourdoor.com.

Website functionality – what the customer can do on the site and the functions the site offers

Transaction arrangements

Most retail websites offer a shopping basket function allowing customers to select items and place them in the basket. The site calculates the total value of the items in the basket and gives an option of a checkout. At the end of the online shopping process, customers are given payment options involving giving credit/debit card details.

Fig. 34.9: www.kitchens2yourdoor.com

Activity: www.kitchens2yourdoor.com

Visit www.kitchens2yourdoor.com and create a summary of the functionality designed into the site.

To what extent are these functions essential in the website, given the nature of the business?

PLTS

If you work with another learner in doing this activity, you could be an effective team worker. If you work alone, you can be a creative thinker by finding an interesting and clear way of presenting your findings.

PayPal

PayPal allows any business or consumer with an e-mail address to send and receive payments online. This is vital if a business is to conduct transactions.

Remember

For a transactional website, there must be payment facilities offered to the customers that are secure and easy to use.

Other background functions

When a business decides to operate an online sales channel, it is often assumed that there are adequate background functions and systems that will support the website. A website has to be kept up to date with current information on products. This may mean that there need to be staff who are able to monitor this and make adjustments when and if they are needed. Many transactional websites depend on background databases to supply the information that is essential to them. These databases might contain:

- product details
- staff details
- prices
- images
- details of registered customers.

A full e-business today might have an integrated set of digital systems that should be capable of avoiding data duplication.

3.3 Personalisation of web experience

When online customers visit a website, it is always a one-to-one (personal) experience. Web developers have therefore tried in the last few years to develop sites that can remember customers and tailor a message precisely for them.

The underpinning thinking behind this is that it benefits both a business and a consumer by establishing a relationship between them. Because we are known to the online business, we are automatically given information we really need. Because we feel

Joe's Brew
a business experience

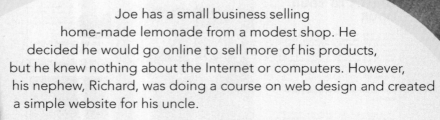

Joe has a small business selling home-made lemonade from a modest shop. He decided he would go online to sell more of his products, but he knew nothing about the Internet or computers. However, his nephew, Richard, was doing a course on web design and created a simple website for his uncle.

In the first two weeks, Joe received just two email enquiries. He decided to get in touch with the local press. They carried a story about him titled 'Local lemonade business is booming'. The following day, Joe was interviewed by every newspaper and radio station in the region. A few more enquiries came in, but still not as much as Joe had hoped for.

Two weeks later a national Sunday newspaper printed a feature on Joe headed 'The online brewer makes it'.

The next day, Joe received about 3,500 emails, most of them trying to place orders for lemonade. However, there was no online facility for customers to pay. Joe asked some people to send cheques or credit card details with their orders.

From having no business online, Joe was now getting between £4,000 and £5,000 worth of orders a day, but because he could not keep up with his business, he did not know about most of them. To make matters worse, other sites had started to put links to Joe's site and his traffic increased even more. Finally, complaints started to come in from people unable to buy his products. Joe eventually closed down his site.

Think about it!

1. For a business attempting to sell lemonade, what functions do you feel the website should offer?
2. For a business like Joe's, who would be the target audience? Justify your response to this.
3. Make justified recommendations about the range of functions that a new website of Joe's would need.

valued by the business and we always receive the things we want, we are more inclined to go back to that site. In this way, a relationship is built.

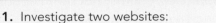

Activity: Personalisation

1. Investigate two websites:
   • one operating within a B2B sector
   • one operating in a B2C sector.
2. Write a report summarising the benefits for both the businesses and the customers within these contexts. Do you feel that the B2B situation merits personalisation?

PLTS

You can reflect when you are analysing the benefits for both the businesses and the customers from the design features of different websites.

However, although web technology allows for personalisation, this does not necessarily mean that it is a useful thing to have in all contexts. There are several reasons why some Internet advisors may argue that personalisation is not suitable.

• Customers do not want relationships with businesses. As customers smile at the sound of a store assistant's greeting, they are actually responding to a person, not to a corporate message. They do not all want warm personal 'relationships' with the retail businesses they use the most.

• Personalisation requires data. Amazon.co.uk, the master of personalisation, makes the technique successful because book purchases send it a constant stream of detailed data about individual customers. Most transactions, though, do not provide such easy preference data.

• Personalisation technology understands consumers poorly. A recommendation for a needlework book as soon as you order that 'ideal gift' for your favourite aunt makes even the most inexperienced consumers realise that they and an online bookstore are not that close.

Personalisation does work effectively in some cases; it simply does not work in every case.

There are several tools available to web designers that can assist in customer information-gathering activities.

Cookies

A cookie stores information about you for the next time you visit that site – information such as where you went on the site and what you did. Cookie files enable a website to remember you when you next visit.

3.4 Resources required

When a business seeks to have a website, not only does the site have to be designed and planned, but it also needs **hosting** on a web server in order to make it available on the Internet. Hosting can involve housing, serving and maintaining files so that visitors are able to view the content of the website.

Key term

Hosting – a website being held on a server – this is a service offered by ISPs or specialist providers

Hosting a website involves a number of different factors, each of which can have a significant impact on its overall success. These key factors are as follows.

• **Site functions** (discussed on pages 466–7) – The range of features offered, the ways in which it presents content to the user, and how the content is kept fresh and updated.

• **Performance** – The speed at which it loads pages and responds to user requests.

- **Reliability** – How high the availability of the site is and how frequently it suffers from downtime.

Hosting can be done in-house (within the business) or it can be bought in as a service. There are pros and cons to each approach.

In-house hosting

In-house website hosting is always an option. However, it does require significant resources. Not only will the business need a web server, but also it will need a high-speed connection to the Internet. The firm will be directly responsible for its day-to-day operation and 24-hour support. There will also be the cost of software licences to consider. In-house hosting has various advantages and disadvantages, as Table 34.2 shows.

Table 34.2: Advantages and disadvantages of the in-house approach.

Advantages	Disadvantages
There is full control over access to the website.	The cost of purchasing web server hardware, associated software and high-speed Internet connectivity.
The choice of hardware, including the ease and expandability of upgrades, is internal.	Technical skills that staff will require in order to develop, maintain and upgrade the website, and to keep up to date with the latest technical developments.
There is full control over the operating environment – the software and systems that run on the web server.	The need for resources capable of providing round-the-clock support for the website in order to ensure its availability for users.
Web storage space and performance can be managed effectively.	The need for specialist security expertise in employing tools and techniques to maintain the security of the website.
There are no contractual or legal issues associated with using an Internet service provider (ISP).	

The in-house option is probably best suited to larger companies, and/or those with a specialist IT department, as considerable resources are required to handle the ongoing development and support

activities. For smaller businesses, external hosting with a content editing system is an option. (See also the case study about Bells Fish & Chips, page 462.)

Using an ISP for hosting

Paying an Internet service provider (ISP) for web hosting is an external hosting solution where the ISP is responsible for providing the business with connection to the Internet. ISPs can provide different types of hosting services, as follows.

- **Shared server** – The server is owned by the ISP and is located in its offices. The server is used to host several other websites. This represents a cost-effective approach, but may not be an option if complex technologies are required such as personalising web pages for different users.
- **Dedicated hosting** – A website is the only one that is hosted on a dedicated server. This option is better suited to large websites with high user traffic, or those requiring special software or particularly high levels of security. These approaches offer the most powerful and secure solution, but they are more expensive.

As with in-house hosting, there are various advantages and disadvantages to using an ISP, as Table 34.3 shows.

Table 34.3: Advantages and disadvantages of using an ISP.

Advantages	Disadvantages
There is no need to invest in your own web server.	You need to trust the ISP to maintain the availability and security of the website.
Most ISPs have very fast connections to the Internet.	The website's performance may be compromised if the ISP is hosting too many other sites on a shared server basis.
The ISP's server should offer a very high degree of availability (uptime) and reliability.	
The ISP should have a secure operating environment, high-quality virus protection and the latest software patches to ensure the security of your site.	

Software options

To help with web development at a level that will offer real e-business solutions, there are a number of software applications.

Online shop software

Online shop software allows the web development process to incorporate into a website the many benefits of online shopping. This can include:

- secure 24/7 online ordering and payment collection
- collecting customer information for direct marketing data
- analysis and web analytics.

Online shopping software can build in features that emulate (try to recreate) a real-life shopping experience. Customers visit a virtual department, choose their merchandise, go to the checkout, choose a shipping option and pay by credit/debit card. The software confirms their purchase and emails them a transaction confirmation, along with the business's customised message.

Use of web authoring tools

Web pages are typically created using HyperText Mark-up Language (HTML). While HTML is a relatively simple code to learn, several companies specialise in developing highly sophisticated authoring software for website creation. These make it possible for even an amateur developer to work within a WYSIWYG (what you see is what you get) environment, to create useful and usable web pages. Authoring tools do the HTML automatically.

There are several advantages to using web **authoring tools**, for example:

- speed of creation

- ease of use by non-HTML experts
- ability to create large numbers of consistent pages.

Macromedia Dreamweaver is an industrial standard authoring package. It has been available for several years in different versions. It is both an HTML editor and a site management tool. Each version has encompassed new features and improvements.

The typical Dreamweaver working environment shows the main menu bar running along the top of the screen, allowing a website developer to:

- create new files
- modify a page's properties (set a background colour or image)
- insert several choices (tables, images)
- select font styles or colours.

The 'site' option on the bar allows the developer to view and manage a whole site structure. Most websites contain several pages functioning as an interlinked group. Dreamweaver maintains and checks the links site-wide and offers a visual reference guide during development.

Dreamweaver, among other visual web development tools, offers a powerful means to create web pages within an environment that could be said to be 'developer friendly'. The effects being sought can be seen immediately. However, these industrial standard authoring packages are relatively expensive to buy and license.

Security measures

Websites are gaining in importance as the public face of many businesses. The additional revenues generated by e-commerce systems mean that organisations are becoming ever more reliant on them as significant elements of their business strategy.

With this high level of dependency on the services provided by e-commerce systems, it is essential that they are protected from the threats posed by hackers, viruses, fraud and denial-of-service attacks.

E-commerce systems are based on the web, and this provides open and easy communications on a global basis. However, because the Internet is unregulated, unmanaged and uncontrolled, it introduces a wide range of risks and threats.

Fig. 34.10: What does the security symbol mean?

Remember

Trading on the Internet involves an element of security risk and this must be considered in the design process.

A serious e-business should introduce sufficient security controls to reduce risk to its e-commerce systems. The following are typical measures used to protect against attack.

Authentication

There are several techniques used for **authentication**, to identify and verify someone seeking to access an e-commerce system. These include:

- a username and password requirement, where the password can vary in length and include numbers and characters

- 'two-factor' authentication requiring something the user has (for example, an authentication token) and something the user knows (for example, a personal identification number)

- a digital certificate that enables authentication through the use of an individual's unique signing key

- a person's unique physical attribute (referred to as a biometric). This can range from a fingerprint or iris scan through to retina or facial-feature recognition.

Key term

Authentication – proving that someone is who they say they are

Access control

This restricts different types of users to subsets of information and ensures that they can only access data and services for which they have authorisation. These include using:

- network restrictions

- application controls.

Changes to access privileges must be controlled to prevent users retaining them if they transfer between departments or leave the business.

Firewall

This is a hardware or software security device that filters information passing between internal and external networks. It controls access to the Internet by internal users, and prevents outside parties from gaining access to systems and information on the internal network.

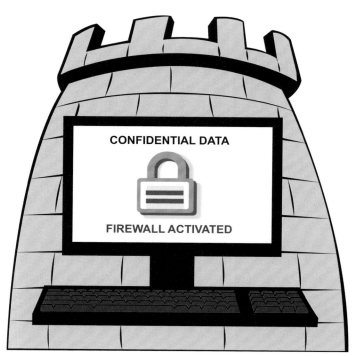

Fig. 34.11: What does firewall software help to protect?

Encryption

This technique scrambles data and is used to protect information that is being either held on a computer or transmitted over a network. It uses technologies such as virtual private networks (VPNs) and secure socket layers (SSLs).

Intrusion detection

Intrusion detection software monitors system and network activity to spot any attempt being made to gain illegal access. If a detection system suspects an attack, it can generate an alarm such as an email alert.

Costs of developing a small website

The costs associated with developing a website depend on the level of sophistication that is built into it. This governs the amount of time and the level of skills that are needed. A number of components go together to determine cost.

- **Graphics** – This includes the page layout and images to create the look and feel of a site. If a business needs graphic designers to create logos and colour schemes, this can add to the costs.
- **Photography** – The business may require photographs placed on the site. If photos are already held in stock then this brings the cost down.
- **Coding** – This is the creation of an interactive site. Web browsers understand the code known as HTML (see page 471). The complexity of the code required governs the time taken and hence the cost.
- **Content** – Website 'copy' refers to the words that are placed within web pages. Copywriting services can be bought and are charged according to the amount of work involved. Often clients requiring a website provide the copy themselves.
- **Web hosting and domain name** – Web hosting has already been covered on pages 469–70. The business adopting a website will pay for the hosting of the site on a web server and will also need to purchase a domain name. Domain names can be bought quite cheaply from as little as about £8. Ongoing site maintenance and hosting can cost between £90 and £200 for two years.

The answer to the question 'How much?' is therefore not a straightforward one. The easy response is to say that it depends on the kind of site required. For a cheap site that simply acts as an online billboard, the cost can be as little as £300. For a small- to medium-sized enterprise looking for a modest, functioning and transactional site, the cost is likely to be about £1,500–£2,000. For the top-class sites with all of the functionality available, the costs will go above £5,000. Add to these design costs the cost of hosting and domain name.

3.5 Evaluation

One of the most fundamental things overlooked when developing a new e-commerce website is user acceptance **testing**. Many web developers underestimate what is involved in testing an e-commerce site from the user's perspective. System testing and load balancing are important. If a new site is not user friendly or does not meet the expectation of the target audience, it can cost a new Internet business dearly. The following steps need be taken to ensure thorough testing of a new website.

Key term

Testing – trying out the website to make sure it allows ease of use by both staff and customers

1. Complete all system testing and quality assurance (QA) before commencing user acceptance testing. This allows the testers to focus on usability issues and not technical defects.
2. Use ordinary online users to test the site. Do not use the development or production team. This ensures people testing the site are new to this online shopping experience. First impressions are important.
3. Write a testing plan explaining in plain English what needs to be tested and how. Construct testing routines for every page in the site, detailing expected results of all the functionality. From these, the tester can easily identify the appropriate outcome from every action response.
4. Test on all target platforms and browsers. These should be outlined in the site's technical specification. But make sure they are listed again in the test plan document.
5. A senior project leader rather than the testers should conduct prioritisation of defect fixing. This ensures that change control tasks are allocated to the right people. The project leader should also

make sure the development teams change the status of a defect once it is fixed.

6. Conduct at least three rounds of testing. This ensures after change control has been completed, any 'fixes' do not have an impact on any other functions on the site.

7. After the site is deployed, conduct a final full loop test on the 'live' server (password protected only) with technical and production staff to make sure all defects are corrected and signed off.

Accessibility testing

Given the new regulations outlined earlier in the unit (see page 461), it is important that new websites are tested to ensure they are available to those with impaired vision. This process should be planned into the testing procedure.

3.6 Launch of website considerations

After all of the pre-launch planning has been carried out, the day will come when the new website goes live on the web. But even at this stage the site should not be forgotten, because there are several considerations that will affect the performance.

Maintenance and updates

Remember that a website is only as good as its content. The statement 'content is king' is true as far as the web is concerned. With poor or outdated content, a website is discredited and useless to potential customers. Credibility is essential. Because of this, it is well worth making every attempt to ensure that the site is checked, updated and maintained on a regular basis. From a strategic viewpoint, the question is: 'Should content be maintained internally or should an external agency carry this out for us?'

Customer feedback

One of the advantages of the web is the ease with which clients and customers are able to give feedback to the website. This entails building into the site a feedback facility which could be in a form on the site, or a 'contact us' page.

Promotion of a website

A website is a huge potential source of business and goodwill if the online personality and impact is right. Therefore it is well worth extra expenditure to promote the site both offline and online. Offline promotions can appear on vehicle livery (such as B&Q, Sainsbury's and many others); online promotion can be through affiliate links strategically placed on other sites. Both of these tactics can help to drive traffic through to the new site.

Security of ICT systems

Once the site is launched, it is also worth checking on the security measures that have been put in place in response to any concerns about this. Security issues change every day and it is unwise for any management simply to assume that security is always tight.

Business continuity plans

A business making big strides online can find itself in difficulty if it becomes dependent on Internet technology only to discover that when there is a technical disaster, the business is put immediately under threat. This means that the managers would be sensible to have contingency plans based on 'What if…?' scenarios.

- What would they do if something went wrong?
- What would customers do?
- How would orders be dealt with?

Typical costs of a small website

The costs of hosting and maintaining a small website can be anything between £90 and £200 per year.

Assessment activity 34.3

You are working for a web development firm and have been given the following brief, with some comments attached from your boss: 'This is a fairly flexible project, but the clients are particularly fussy. Use your imagination and try to come up with something that is appropriate.'

The Copt Hill Preservation Society: background

Copt Hill is a well-known local landmark thought to be a prehistoric burial site. It is topped by seven large trees known in the region as the 'Seven Sisters', which can be seen for miles around. Archaeological digs completed in the 19th century found evidence of several burials and quite a number of historic artefacts.

The Copt Hill Preservation Society (the client) aims to maintain and improve the Copt Hill site. The society wishes to encourage visitors by informing people about its importance as a site of historic interest. Educational materials are felt to be a good idea and a new membership scheme, the 'Friends of Copt Hill', is envisaged.

It has been decided that a website would be a good way of promoting the activities of the society and reaching a broader audience. Perhaps such a website would encourage many more visitors from abroad.

Your design brief: You have an idea of what the site should do. It is to be largely promotional and raise the status of the Copt Hill landmark. It has to be informational, educational and encourage membership. The client needs a site that is easy to use and navigate. People must know whom to contact to get more information; people should enjoy looking at the site; the site should be accessible through a range of browsers; and it should meet the requirements of the Disability Discrimination regulations on website accessibility.

Your test plan: All pages and all links must be tested as the site is developed. If a site is to include advanced features such as JavaScript or other scripts, these will be tested as the site is uploaded on to the web.

1. Design the website for the Copt Hill Preservation Society (CHPS) to meet its specific purposes for the defined target group. **P4**
2. Draw up plans to assess the design of the website. Does it meet the specified needs? **P5**
3. Draw up a plan for the launch of the site. **P6**
4. Assess how your own website design contributes to fulfilling the CHPS purposes, through meeting the requirements of the target audience. **M2**
5. Explain how your launch plan is appropriate for the CHPS. **M3**
6. Make justified recommendations for how the website designs and launch plans for the Copt Hill website could be improved. **D2**

Grading tips

1. The design could be initially produced on paper explaining the design features you envisage for each page in terms of the needs of the client and the target audience. Using either your own valid HTML code, or a suitable authoring package, create a functioning site that will serve as a basis for your client to view. **P4**
2. This should be a list of the steps you would take in the evaluation process. How would you involve the client? Who would you consult? Is the information it contains accurate and appropriate for the target audience? Who will maintain and update? How will you test the site? **P5**
3. This should be a well-thought-out consideration of issues such as pre-launch promotion of the site, checking content, client feedback, security and antivirus measures. **P6**
4. Explain why certain features you have planned have been included. What is their purpose as far as target users are concerned? You need to show an understanding of the organisation's objectives. You may also think about potential unforeseen users of the website. **M2**
5. Explain why your launch plans will help the client. You could consider timing, promotional media and message. What will you do with feedback? **M3**
6. Consider honestly your design in terms of the target group(s). What features do you think could be improved? Why? Possibly your design skills need to be further developed. Make recommendations for both the design and the launch plans. **D2**

Just checking

1. What is the distinction between B2C and B2B transactions?
2. Which of these types of transaction has grown the most?
3. List four different kinds of organisation using the web and describe their basic online activities.
4. Why do you think that government bodies use the web? Give examples from your own local council.
5. Select a website that you are familiar with and assess its usability. What features help the user?
6. What do you understand by 'multimedia' in a website? Select an example and say why you feel it is used in that context.
7. What do you understand by the term 'target group' of a website?
8. Select two different websites to illustrate two contrasting sorts of 'visual appeal'. Explain the different techniques that have been used.
9. Give an example of a website designed to meet specific objectives for a private business. Do you feel that it succeeds?
10. Why is it considered necessary to 'test' a new website?

Assignment tips

1. Remember that the websites you look at can contrast in terms of size, sector and purpose of their website. They should include organisations from both the profit and not-for-profit sectors.

2. Try to consider website design from the viewpoints of different types of users, including those with particular access requirements. Think about how a range of people from different backgrounds and ages respond to different websites.

3. It would be very useful to gain experience of using web authoring tools such as Dreamweaver, FrontPage or the functions in MS Office, for example, converting a Word document into a web document, and to experiment with multimedia tools such as Flash.

4. When designing a website, consider what the attributes of the target group are. Think about physical abilities, interests, technical abilities, environment and an understanding of the organisational objectives.

Glossary

Accessibility – the ease and comfort with which websites can be used by those with disabilities

Analysis – making a detailed examination of the results of research, in order to find patterns and structures

Applicant – the name given to the person applying for a job

Asset – something that is owned by a business or individual

Attributes – the personal characteristics that someone has, for example, outgoing or conscientious. The attributes needed will change depending on the type and level of the job

Audit – a formal examination of something to see that it is true and fair

Authentication – proving that someone is who they say they are

Authoring tools – software packages that offer a WYSIWYG user-friendly environment allowing for website design without knowledge of HTML

Authority – legitimate power to do something, usually based on the position or experience of the person in authority

Average stock – the opening stock plus the closing stock, divided by two

Bank loan – an individual or organisation borrows a sum of money for a period of time, and then pays back so much a month which includes repayment of the sum borrowed plus interest

Bias – a distortion of results caused by the way in which they are collected

Body language – use of the body, for example, facial expressions or gestures, as a means of communication to support other forms of communication such as talk

Bottom line – the last line in an audit; the line that shows profit or loss

Brand awareness – extent to which a brand is recognised by potential customers, and is correctly associated with a particular product

Brand building – enhancing a brand's equity directly through advertising campaigns and indirectly through promotions such as supporting causes or event sponsorship

Brand extension – a marketing strategy in which a firm marketing a product with a well-developed image uses the same brand name in a different product category

Brand image – the creation of an easy-to-spot identity that consumers get to know well

Branding – entire process involved in creating a unique name and image for a product in the consumers' mind, through advertising campaigns with a consistent theme

Business continuance plans – the processes and procedures an organisation puts in place to ensure that essential functions can continue during and after a disaster

Business environment – all of the outside influences on a business. These include government actions, actions by competitors and changes in the law

Business ethics – moral principles concerning acceptable and unacceptable behaviour by businesses

Business objectives – the goals a business sets to increase productivity and sales

Business-to-business – B2B refers to when one business sells to another business – for example, a stationery business selling to a firm of accountants

Business-to-consumer – B2C refers to when one business sells to an individual – for example, a stationery business selling wedding stationery to a bride and groom

Buyer behaviour – how people behave in certain ways before and when making a purchase

Buy-side – the part of the business in which orders originate

Capital – funds that are invested in business

Capital employed – the total amount of money tied up in the business from retained profits and capital investments

Capital income – money invested into the business either to set it up or buy equipment

Capital items – assets bought from capital expenditure such as machinery and vehicles

Carbon footprint – this measures the impact of an activity on the environment by doing things like burning fossil fuels to heat factory buildings. A carbon footprint is measured in tonnes or kilograms of carbon dioxide equivalent

Cascade – to pass information on to a succession of others

Cash flow forecast – document that shows the predicted flow of cash into and out of a business over a given period of time, normally 12 months

Census – study of all members of a population

Channel conflict – where the introduction of an Internet sales channel threatens relationships with businesses working in existing channels

Charisma – having a strong personality, usually one which captivates and motivates others

Clicks and mortar business – a business that has physical buildings and an Internet presence

Closing balance – amount of cash available in a business at the end of a set time period, for example, a month

Closing stock – the value of stock at the end of a financial year

Cohesive – sticking together, united

Commission – a percentage paid on a sale to the person or business responsible for making that sale

Competitor-based pricing – setting the price based upon those of similar competitor products

Completing the transaction – actually making the sale from the website; funds are transferred with the promise of the product

Confidentiality – keeping information secure and only allowing it to be given to people who have been given permission to see it

Consumables – goods that customers have to buy regularly because they wear out or are used up, for example, food and clothing

Consumer market – individuals and households who purchase goods and services for personal use

Contract – legally binding agreement between two or more parties, who promise to give and receive something from each other

Contribution – how much money each unit of an item sold brings in towards paying off the fixed costs of a business (revenue, or income, minus variable cost)

Control – the process of making sure that things are done in expected ways

Cookies – small pieces of computer code that record a user's data so they do not have to enter the same information each time they visit a site

Corporate communication – activities undertaken by an organisation to communicate both internally with employees and externally with existing and prospective customers and the wider public

Cost/benefit analysis – weighing up the total expected costs against the total expected benefits of one or more actions in order to choose the best or most profitable option

Cost of goods sold – the actual value of stock used to generate sales

Credit period – length of time given to a customer to pay for goods or services received

Creditors – suppliers who have provided goods or services to a business on credit, meaning the business owes them money

Cross-section – a sample designed to be typical of the wider population

Current assets – items owned by the business that change in value on a regular basis, such as stock

Customer profile – the characteristics of a typical person or business that buys from your website

Customer retention – keeping customers so that they come back to your site to make repeat purchases

Customisation – opportunity for the customer to manipulate and change the online presentation of a product

Database – a store of data gathered for a particular purpose. Today we tend to associate databases with computer programs designed for the storage of data

Debtors – customers who have purchased goods or services on credit, meaning they are in debt to the business as they owe it money

Demand and supply schedules – tables showing quantities that will be supplied and demanded at different prices

Demand pricing – allocating a price based on what consumers are prepared to pay

Demographics – selected population characteristics such as lifestyles, spending, habits, age and employment. These characteristics are used in government, marketing or opinion research to further understand the consumer or general public at large

Digital broadcasting – a more efficient way of transmitting sound and pictures by turning them into computerised data, meaning more TV and radio services and new interactive services can be broadcast than by using the analogue system

Direct marketing – sending messages directly to potential customers, for example, by email, without using indirect promotions such as advertising

Directives – these bind member states to objectives to be achieved within a certain time limit. However, it is left to national authorities to decide how to implement them. Directives have to be implemented through national law

Disintermediation – the removal of intermediaries ('middle men') from the process of getting products to where consumers can buy them

Disposable income – the amount of money which an individual has available to spend on non-essential items after essential bills have been met

Distribution – the process of moving a product from its manufacturing source to its customers

Drawings – sum of money taken out of a business by a sole trader or partner for their own usage

Dynamic pricing – the facility of the web that enables online businesses to adjust prices quickly, according to market conditions

E-business – a business that has digitised many of its internal functions by using computer systems. These are often connected to the web

Economic growth – a period of month-by-month increase in goods produced and consumed in an economy, coupled with rises in average incomes

Effectiveness – the value of the work carried out. An effective team will achieve high-quality results

E-marketing remix – new marketing tactics designed to market a web-based business

Employee – a person who works for a business

Employer – a business that employs workers

Empowerment – the process of spreading power and decision-making responsibility across the organisation and within teams, rather than a few key individuals retaining it

Equilibrium – position at which demand equals supply, so that producers and consumers are happy; disequilibrium is the opposite

Expected life – how long an asset is expected to be used within a business

External recruitment – recruiting from outside the business

Extranet – restricted network that extends outside an organisation to include other computers

Financial transaction – action by a business that involves money either going into or out of a business – for example, making a sale or paying a bill

Fiscal policy – policies involving changes in government spending and government taxation

Fixed assets – items of value owned by a business that are likely to stay in the business for more than one year – for example, machinery

Fixed cost – the costs of running a business, such as rent and wages

Formal monitoring – when managers are officially checking, watching or recording the employee in some way

Formal team – team that has been set up by the organisation itself with the purpose of achieving specific objectives. There will often be rules and guidelines about how and when the team should meet and some form of leadership structure

Frequency – the number of times an event happens in a given period of time. Frequencies are often measured in market research, for example, the frequency with which a particular individual or group of customers will buy specific items

Gross profit – sales revenue minus cost of goods sold (the cost of the actual materials used to produce the quantity of goods sold)

Group turnover – the rate at which the members of a team change

Historic cost – the cost of an asset when it was first purchased

HM Revenue and Customs – HM is an abbreviation for Her (or His) Majesty's, and the HMRC is a British government department responsible for the collection of all types of taxes

Hosting – a website being held on a server – this is a service offered by ISPs or specialist providers

Human Resources Department – this deals with the management of policies and procedures relating to the people who work for an organisation, covering areas such as payroll, sickness monitoring, and grievance and disciplinary procedures

Hybrid vehicles – cars that run on a combination of petrol and alternative fuels such as battery-powered electricity; they can switch between the two

Hypertext – text available on the web that contains hyperlinks to other web pages

Illiquid – not easily converted into cash

Incentives – additional rewards or payments that employers give to employees as a reward for working even harder or better

Inflation – the general increase in prices in an economy

Informal monitoring – when managers are making more subtle judgements about how an employee is fitting in or if they have a problem

Informal team – a group of individuals, not officially set up by an organisation, that sees the benefit of working together to achieve given purposes. Informal teams are usually less highly structured and rule-bound than formal teams

Information – knowledge of specific events or situations that has been gathered or received by communication; intelligence or news

Information fatigue – having so much data that it becomes meaningless and impossible to use

Infrastructure – the skeleton of the economic system which supports the rest of the economy. It includes communication links such as transport networks, and Internet and telephone systems

Innovation – the generation of new ideas

Insolvent – when a firm is unable to meet short-term cash payments

Interdependence – the linking together and mutual dependence of parts of a system on each other

Interest rate – the percentage rate a bank charges for a loan, that is, the cost of borrowing money

Inter-firm – between different firms, for example, one house builder may compare its performance against anther house builder

Internal recruitment – recruiting someone who already works for the business to do a different job

Internet protocols – agreed ways of doing things so that everyone on the Internet connects in the same way

Interpersonal skills – skills that enable us to get on with other people and promote positive relationships in the workplace

Interviewee – person who has applied for the job and is being interviewed for it

Interviewers – the employer or organisation interviewing potential people for a job

Intrafirm – within the firm, for example, comparing this year's results with last year's, or the performance of the York branch with the Leicester branch of a retail store

Intranet – restricted computer network confined to a specific organisation

Job description – a list of working conditions that come with a job – for example, pay, hours or duties

Knowledge-based economy – an economy based on the creation of advanced information services that inform both businesses and citizens

Labour market – this consists of employers requiring (demand) employees and people seeking work (supply)

Leadership style – the predominant type of behaviour that a leader uses when leading a team, for example, to be domineering, or to be cautious. The leader does not necessarily use this style all of the time

Legible – able to be read or understood

Legislation – UK and EU laws

Line of control – where individuals are responsible to a line manager or supervisor. The senior colleague will be responsible for making more important decisions

Liquidity – measure of a firm's ability to meet short-term cash payments

Livery – distinctive design and colour scheme used on a company's vehicles or products

Log – a record kept in writing, usually set out in date order

Logistics – processes involved in moving and supplying goods to where they are required. Logistics involves organising transport and storage of goods

Logo – symbol(s) or word(s) that carry the image of a company. Its function is to create a long-lasting, recognisable impression on the mind of a potential client or customer

Loss – shortfall suffered when total revenue from sales is lower than the total costs of a business

Mailshot – material, especially promotional, posted to a large number of people

Manufacturing – making things (in the secondary sector)

Market diversification – expanding a business by offering new products and services

Market leadership – position of a company with the largest market share or highest profitability margin in a given market for goods and services

Market research – systematic, objective collection and analysis of data about a particular target market, competition, and/or environment

Market segment – a group of people or organisations sharing one or more characteristics that cause them to have similar product and/or service needs

Marketing concept – philosophy practised by producers of goods and services that focus on satisfying the needs of consumers

Marketing mix – sometimes referred to as the four Ps of product, price, promotion and place, these are the ideas to consider when marketing a product

Marketing planning – developing marketing strategies that will help a business attain its overall objectives

Marketing research – systematic gathering, recording, and analysis of data about issues relating to marketing products and services

Marketing strategy – the general direction in which marketing decisions take a business – for example, a business may be looking to increase its sales overseas or to target a smaller market segment

Marketplace – any situation in which customers demanding products interact with suppliers supplying products

Mobile technology – portable devices that can connect to the worldwide web

Monetary policy – policies related to money available in the economy. The government can change the quantity of available money or the cost of borrowing money (interest rate) as a result of advice from the Monetary Policy Committee

Multimedia elements – the facility on a web page to show streaming video or sounds to back up the textual information

Net profit – gross profit minus other expenses – for example, rent and advertising

Objectives – goals that an organisation sets for itself – for example, profitability, sales growth or return on investment

Online value proposition – characteristics about a website that make people want to use it

Open-ended terms – terms that are written very vaguely, allowing the employer and employee some flexibility about what they actually require – for example, an employer might write into the job description a statement that covers 'any other reasonable duties as required by the post'

Opening balance – amount of cash available in a business at the start of a set time period, for example, a month

Opening stock – the value of stock in a business at the start of a financial year

Opportunity cost – the cost to an organisation of making one decision over another – the cost of the lost opportunity

Optimum team size – the best size for the team in terms of open communication, all members being able to voice and opinion, and achieving good results

Opt-in emailing – collecting permissions from customers to send them emails detailing future services or promotions

Overdraft – when more money is taken out of a bank account than is in it, making the account overdrawn

Payment security – setting up online payments systems so that customers' personal details remain hidden

Penetration pricing – involves the setting of lower prices in order to achieve a large, if not dominant market share

Performance indicator – a measure of a specific aspect of performance, which might involve things which you can attach a number to, or an indicator that something did or did not happen in the required way

Permanent – until that person decides to leave or the job ceases to exist

Person specification – list of attributes needed by the person to perform a job such as personality type or experience

Personalisation – adjusting the web page that is returned to a visitor so that it offers information that is personal, based on their previous visits to the website

Plant – place where an industrial or manufacturing process takes place

Policies – courses of action, guiding principles, or procedures considered expedient, prudent, or advantageous

Portal – a gateway site that offers many links into other sites related to the same theme

Price transparency – when everyone who visits your website can see all of your prices

Primary sector – extracting raw products from nature

Privacy – the level of security of personal information – a crucial factor in a website's status in the eyes of users

Privatisation – transferring the ownership of a business from the government to private owners

Probability – how likely an event is likely to occur, measured by the ratio of the extent to which an event is likely to occur compared to the total number of cases possible

Product development – taking an existing product and adding new features so that it sells more or appeals to different groups

Productivity – the relationship between output and resources. In terms of teamwork this means the amount and quality of work achieved with a given number of team members. When this increases or improves, productivity will have increased

Profit – surplus achieved when total revenue (income) from sales is higher than the total costs of a business

Promotional mix – the elements that make up an organisation's marketing communications strategy: advertising, sales promotion, personal selling, direct marketing and public relations

Public relations – the development and maintenance of positive relationships between an organisation and its public – employees, local community, customers, suppliers, media – through activities designed to create understanding and goodwill

Public service – emphasis on providing high-quality service to the public rather than focusing on narrow self-interest

Purchasing decision – series of choices made by a consumer prior to making a purchase that begins once the consumer has established a willingness to buy

Quantitative easing – increasing the quantity of money in the economy

Range of businesses – the variety of different types of business. Three useful ways of classifying business are: according to where they operate; what the businesses are trying to achieve, and the sector of business activity they are involved in

Recession – when for two quarters (a quarter is three months) in a row, the value of all the goods sold in the economy falls

Recruitment – taking on employees

Refurbishment – when a business gives a new look to its offices or stores. It can help keep staff and customers happy

Regulations – laws that are directly binding on member states created at European Union level

Representative – containing typical specimens of all of the members of a sample, for example, typical tattoo wearers in your area

Residual value – the value of an asset when it is disposed of by the business, for example, resale value

Respondent – someone who takes part in a survey

Response rate – the percentage of responses to the number of questionnaires sent out or interviews requested

Retailing – selling things in small quantities (shops in the tertiary sector)

Retention – keeping employees at the workplace for as long as possible, to benefit from their experience

Running costs – day-to-day costs incurred in operating a firm or facility

Sales revenue – quantity sold times selling price

Sample – study of a carefully selected group that is regarded to be representative of total population

Sampling frame – list of population by sampling units

Sampling units – people who are going to be sampled

Search engine advertising – paid-for links that are presented by a search engine when a user requests a particular search

Secondary sector – transforming those raw products into finished or part-finished goods

Secure payments – payments system on a website that offers security to customers as they know that their credit or debit card details cannot be stolen

Security threats – openings in the software or networking arrangements of an e-business that allow intrusion, data theft or virus infections

Segmentation – using marketing research to help identify groups of consumers who will respond to marketing activity in the same way, for example, first-time buyers of houses

Self-managing team – a team that has had the training and developed the skills to work on its own to solve work-related issues

Sell-side – refers to firms that take orders from buy-side firms

Sequencing – placing questions in a logical order that makes sense to the respondent and enables easier analysis of the data

Server – higher-capacity computer that offers services to client computers that can connect to it

Service industries – industries not dealing in physical products but offering services such as finance or insurance

Skim pricing – establishing a relatively high price for a product or service to recover the costs of development and introduction more rapidly; also called high-price strategy

Solvency – when a business is able to pay its expenses as it has money available within the business

Spam – unsolicited emails, often referred to as junk mail

Stakeholder – anyone with an interest in the activities of a business, whether directly or indirectly involved

Strapline – a term used as a secondary sentence attached to a brand name. Its purpose is to emphasise a phrase that the company wishes to be remembered by, particularly for marketing a specific corporate image or connection to a product or consumer base

Strategic direction – where an organisation is going over the next year or more

Strategic plan – a plan for the whole organisation setting out its aims and the major resources that will be used to achieve these

Strategy – a long-term plan for success

Subjectivity – looking at things from a personal viewpoint rather than being impartial

Subsidy – sum of money provided by government to provide additional finance for a business to support selected activities

Succession planning – when employees are recruited and developed to fill each key role within the company

Supply chain – made up of a series of links starting with raw materials, and converting them into finished products

Survey – a careful study of a particular topic such as consumers' opinions about a specific product or issue. The survey typically involves a sequence of questions, which may be in the form of a questionnaire or interview

SWOT – strengths, weaknesses, opportunities and threats

Tactics – the plans and methods used to achieve a particular short-term aim

Tangible – something you can touch

Target market – the segment that marketers aim for when they create their marketing message

Targeting a market – tailoring communications in order to attract sales from a specific group of people

Team role – the part played by an individual within the team. The part involves behaving in defined ways and bringing specific skills to the team. An individual can play several different roles

Temporary – for a limited amount of time specified – for example, a month or a year

Tertiary sector – providing services to individuals and businesses

Testing – trying out the website to make sure it allows ease of use by both staff and customers

Text formatting – setting up the way a page of text will look by changing the fonts, bold or italic type, margins, indents, columns, tabs, headers and footers, and other attributes

Usability – the ease with which staff and visitors can use a website

Variable cost – cost that varies with the level of output or sales

Viral marketing – marketing through word of mouth on the web, very rapidly indeed, whether the news is good or bad

Visual appeal – a pleasant and appropriate look and feel that is appropriate to the organisation

Web analytics – software services that can track users of websites, measure click-through patterns and provide data to assist in web strategic planning

Website functionality – what the customer can do on the site and the functions the site offers

Website scalability – the capability of a website to grow alongside the growth of the business

Website stickiness – the capacity of a website to make people stay on the site and eventually make a purchase

Wi-fi – way of connecting to the Internet without physical wires

Work their notice – the time an employee must work for their current employer before they are allowed to move to their new job

Bibliography

Unit 1

If you want to find out about the origin of some of the UK's most exciting enterprises try starting with an Internet search with the name of one of the UK's most enterprising people of recent years, such as:

- Levi Roots
- Lakshmi Mittal
- Anita Roddick
- Richard Branson
- Martha Lane Fox
- Reuben Singh
- Toni Mascolo.

To find out more about a specific organisation, try one of the following.

- www.asos.co.uk – ASOS, an online clothes retailer
- www.costacoffee.com – the Costa Coffee chain of coffee shops
- www.easyjet.com – easyJet, a low-cost airline
- www.innocentdrinks.co.uk – innocent smoothies
- www.lastminute.com – last-minute travel and entertainment
- www.marksandspencer.com – Marks & Spencer
- www.tesco.com – Tesco online.

For online company reports access:

- www.carol.co.uk

Two useful government sites are:

- www.businesslink.gov.uk – a support service for businesses providing a wealth of information about businesses and government support for business
- www.statistics.gov.uk – official UK statistics.

For online business information about the European Union access:

- www.eubusiness.com

Another useful resource is:

- www.thetimes100.co.uk – a specialist site providing business case studies about well-known UK and overseas businesses. Search the website index to find cases about stakeholders, business ownership, business organisation and environmental influences.

Books, magazines and newspapers

Useful business magazines are:

- *Business Review* (Phillip Allan Publishers – see www.phillipallan.co.uk
- *The Economist* (*The Economist* Newspaper Group Inc).

Good newspaper reports about business and economic issues can be found in *The Guardian* newspaper.

A useful text is:

Worthington and Britton (2006) *The Business Environment*, (Financial Times/Prentice Hall).

Unit 2

Books

Alred, A., Garvey, B. and Smith, R. (2006) *The Mentoring Pocket Book*, Alresford: Management Pocket Books

Bartol, K. and Martin, D. (1997) *Management*, 2nd rev. ed., McGraw-Hill

Chaffey, D. (2002) *E-Commerce and E-Business Management*, Harlow: Pearson Education

Gillespie, A. (2002) *Business in Action*, London: Hodder & Stoughton

Kirton, M. (ed.) (1989) *Adaptors and Innovators: Styles of Creativity and Problem-Solving*, London: Routledge

Harvey-Jones, J. (2003) *Making It Happen: Reflections on Leadership*, London: Profile Business

Parsloe, E. and Wray, M. (2000) *Coaching and Mentoring*, London: Kogan Page

Martin, M. and Jackson, T. (2002) *Personnel Practice (People and Organizations)*, London: Chartered Institute of Personnel and Development (CIPD)

Journals

Business Review

Personnel Management

Websites

- www.acas.org.uk – the Advisory, Conciliation and Arbitration Service
- www.adviceguide.org.uk – Citizens Advice Bureau with guides to the workplace
- www.businesslink.gov.uk – Business Link advice for businesses
- www.cbi.org.uk – Confederation of Business and Industry
- www.cipd.co.uk – Chartered Institute of Personnel and Development
- www.coachingnetwork.org.uk – useful tips on coaching and mentoring
- www.compactlaw.co.uk/free_legal_articles/health_and_safety.html – including information about health and safety and intellectual property
- www.dti.gov.uk – Department of Trade and Industry
- www.envirowise.gov.uk – government-funded campaign giving practical environmental support to businesses
- www.fact-uk.org.uk – Federation Against Copyright Theft
- www.investorsinpeople.co.uk – Investors in People
- www.managementqualifications.co.uk – advice on management qualifications
- www.mindtools.com – tools that can be used to help managers
- www.mybusiness.co.uk – information on management issues for small businesses including resources
- www.patent.gov.uk/patent.htm – the Patent Office
- www.personneltoday.co.uk – human resource information provider (UK)
- www.statistics.gov.uk – National Statistics published by the government

Unit 3

Books

Brassington, F. and Pettitt, S. (2007) *Essentials of Marketing*, Harlow: Financial Times/Prentice Hall

Cave, S. (2002) *Consumer Behaviour in a Week*, London: Hodder Arnold

Chaffey, D. and Smith, P.R. (2008) *eMarketing eXcellence: Planning and Optimising Your Digital Marketing (Emarketing Essentials)*, Oxford: Butterworth-Heinemann

Dibb, S., Simkin, L., Pride, W.M. and Ferrell, O.C. (2005) *Marketing Concepts and Strategies*, Boston, MA.: Houghton Mifflin (Academic)

Hall, D., Jones, R. and Raffo, C. (2004) *Business Studies*, 3rd Edition, Causeway Press Ltd

Kotler, P., Armstrong, G., Wong, V. and Saunders, J. (2008) *Principles of Marketing*, Financial Times/ Prentice Hall

Kotler, P. and Keller, K. (2008) *Marketing Management: International Version*, Pearson Education

Palmer, A. (2009) *Introduction to Marketing: Theory and Practice*, OUP Oxford

Proctor, T. (2005) *Essentials of Marketing Research*, FT Prentice Hall

Stokes, D. and Lomax, W. (2007) *Marketing: A Brief Introduction*, Thomson Learning

Journals

Business Review Magazine (Phillip Allan Publishers)

Campaign (Haymarket Business Subscriptions)

Journal of Marketing Education (Sage Journals Online)

Journal of Marketing Theory and Practice (M.E. Sharpe, Inc.)

Marketing (Haymarket Business Subscriptions)

Marketing Week (Centaur Communications Ltd)

The Economist (The Economist Newspaper Group, Inc)

Websites

- www.adassoc.org.uk – the Advertising Association
- www.amazon.com – Amazon
- www.asa.org.uk – the Advertising Standards Authority
- www.bized.ac.uk – business education website including learning materials and quizzes
- www.businessballs.com – free business resources; free career help, business training, organisational development
- www.businesslink.gov.uk – free government-run organisation offering advice and information for businesses
- www.cadburys.co.uk – Cadbury Trebor Bassett confectionery manufacturer

- www.cim.co.uk – the Chartered Institute of Marketing
- www.easyjet.com – easyJet low cost airline
- www.marketingminefield.co.uk – advertising and marketing guide
- www.marketingteacher.com – free marketing resources for learners, teachers and professionals
- www.statistics.gov.uk – official UK statistics
- www.swatch.com – Swatch watches
- www.tesco.com – Tesco

Unit 4
Books

Argenti, P. (1998) *Corporate Communication*, Irwin McGraw-Hill

Blundel, R. and Ippolito, K. (2008) *Effective Organisational Communication: Perspectives, Principles and Practices*, Financial Times/Prentice Hall

Bovee, C. and Thill, J.V. (2009) *Business Communication Essentials: International Version*, Pearson Education

Brounstein, M. et al. (2006) *Business Communication: Communicate Effectively in Any Business Environment (Wiley Pathways)*, J. Wiley & Sons

Bruckmann, C. and Hartley, P. (2001) *Business Communication: An Introduction*, Routledge

Davies, C. (2004) *Finding and Knowing: Psychology, Information and Computers*, Routledge

Lowe, M. (2009) *Business Information at Work*, Europa Publications

McClave, H.J. (2008) *Communication for Business*, Gill & Macmillan Ltd.

Niederst, J. (2001) *Web Design in a Nutshell: A Desktop Quick Reference*, O'Reilly

Stuart, B.E., Sarow, M.S. and Stuart, L. (2007) *Integrated Business Communication: In a Global Marketplace*, John Wiley & Sons

Woolcott, L.A. and Unwin, W.R. (1983) *Mastering Business Communication (Macmillan Master Series (Business)*, Macmillan

Websites
- www.bbc.co.uk – the British Broadcasting Corporation
- www.bized.co.uk – business education resources
- www.brc.org.uk – trade association for the British Retail Industry
- www.businesscommunication.org – business communication resources
- www.businesslink.gov.uk – free government-run organisation offering advice and information for businesses
- www.cnx.org – an education resource site
- www.howstuffworks.com – online resource offering information and advice
- www.lessonplanet.com – education website offering learning materials
- http://news.bbc.co.uk/1/hi/business – the business pages of the BBC website
- www.thetimes100.co.uk – *The Times* 100 case studies

Unit 9
Books

Belsch, G. and Belch, M.A. (2008) *Advertising and Promotion: An Integrated Marketing Communications Perspective*, McGraw-Hill

Cave, S. (2002) *Consumer Behaviour in a Week*, Hodder Arnold

Chaffey, D. (2003) *E-Business and E-Commerce Management*, FT Prentice Hall

Chaffey, D., Mayer R., Johnston K. and Ellis-Chadwick, F. (2008) *Internet Marketing: Strategy, Implementation and Practice*, Prentice Hall

Clow, K.E. and Baack, D.E. (2009) *Integrated Advertising, Promotion and Marketing Communications: Global Edition*, Pearson

Dibb, S., Simkin, L., Pride, W.M. and Ferrell, O.C. (2005) *Marketing: Concepts and Strategies*, Houghton Mifflin

Harte, L.J. (2008) *Introduction to Internet Marketing; Search Engine Optimisation, Adword Marketing, eMail Promotion, and Affiliate Programs*, Althos

Needham, D. and Dransfield, R. (1994) *Marketing: Everybody's Business – Covering European and International Marketing*, Heinemann

Shimp, T.A. and Delozier, M.W. (1996) *Advertising, Promotion and Supplemental Aspects of Integrated Marketing Communications*, Dryden Press

Smith, P.R. (1993) *Marketing Communications. An Integrated Approach* (Kogan Page)

Journals

Advertising Age (Crain Communications Subscriptions)

Campaign (Haymarket Business Subscriptions)

Journal of Marketing Communications (Vol.15, 2008)

Marketing (Haymarket Business Subscriptions)

Marketing Week (Centaur Communications Ltd)

Websites

- www.amazon.com – online shopping
- www.bbc.co.uk – British Broadcasting Corporation
- www.bized.ac.uk – business education website including learning materials and quizzes
- www.businessballs.com – free business resources: career help, business training, organisational development
- www.cim.com – the Chartered Institute of Marketing
- www.easyjet.com – low-cost airline
- www.ebay.co.uk – online auction site
- www.freemarketingzone.com – free advice on all aspects of marketing
- www.marketingminefield.co.uk – advertising and marketing guide
- www.marketingteacher.com – free marketing resources for learners, teachers and professionals
- www.tesco.com – Tesco
- www.the-dma.org – the Direct Marketing Association
- www.tutor2u.net – free marketing resources for learners, teachers and professionals

Unit 10

Books

Dibb, S. et al (2005) *Marketing Concepts and Strategies*, Houghton Mifflin

Proctor, T. (2005) *Essentials of Marketing Research*, FT/ Prentice Hall

Websites

- www.carol.co.uk – company annual reports
- www.cim.co.uk – the Chartered Institute of Marketing

- www.keynote.co.uk – market research reports
- www.mintel.com – Mintel is a global supplier of consumer, media and market research
- www.marketingmagazine.co.uk – marketing magazine provides excellent case studies based on market research findings
- www.statistics.gov.uk – National Statistics provided by the government
- www.thetimes100.co.uk – contains some useful market research case studies
- www.thomsonreuters.com – company financial information

Unit 12

Books

Chaffey, D., Mayer, R., Johnston, K. and Ellis-Chadwick, F. (2003) *Internet Marketing, Strategy, Implementation and Practice*, Prentice Hall

Goymer, J. (2004) *BTEC National e-Business Book 1*, Heinemann

Websites

- www.4retail.com – an online collaborative service
- www.acmewhistles.co.uk – investigate whistle performance 'virtually'
- www.amazon.co.uk – online store
- www.beeb.com – BBC's Internet shopping service, providing instant price comparisons
- www.bellsfishshop.co.uk – 'bricks and mortar' company, with an information-only website
- www.berr.gov.uk – Department for Business, Enterprise and Regulatory Reform, offering information services for small businesses
- www.cardcorp.co.uk – company producing business cards
- www.clickz.com – Internet trends and statistics
- www.davechaffey.com – guide to digital business
- www.diy.com – B&Q's online service, which has a variety of interactive features
- www.easyjet.com – low-cost airline with a dynamic pricing facility
- www.ebay.co.uk – online auction site connecting private customers

- www.egg.com – Egg's website collects detailed information about customer perceptions of its financial services
- www.eiu.com – the Economic Intelligence Unit
- www.fightback.com – a consumer response service
- www.ibstock.com – interactive brick manufacturer
- www.ic3d.com/index.html – an interactive shopping site that lets the customer modify clothing before ordering
- www.kelkoo.com – an online service listing the best prices available on the web
- www.nike.com/index.jhtml – Nike sports footwear group
- www.norton.com – antivirus software online
- www.priceline.co.uk – site allowing consumers to set their own prices
- www.rswww.com – RS – supplier of electrical components and accessories, with a successful B2B and B2C website
- www.saveanddrive.co.uk – successful 'clicks and mortar' motor accessories supplier
- www.screwfix.com – DIY business, with a successful customised buyer menu
- www.searchenginewatch.com – search engine marketing
- www.statistics.gov.uk – a rich source of government statistics
- www.tesco.com – Tesco, a very successful 'bricks and clicks' supermarket
- www.webtrends.com – WebTrends, an analytics service

Unit 13
Books

Bartol, K.M. and Martin, D.C. (2001) *Management*, Irwin

Bratton, J. and Gold, J. (2003) *Human Resource Management: Theory and Practice*, Palgrave Macmillan

Cuming, Maurice W. (1993) *The Theory and Practice of Personnel Management*, Butterworth-Heinemann

Edenborough, R. (2002) *Effective Interviewing: A Handbook of Skills and Techniques*, Kogan Page

Fowler, A. (2000) *Writing Job Descriptions (Management Shapers)*, Chartered Institute of Personnel and Development (CIPD)

Gillespie, A. (2002) *Business in Action*, Hodder & Stoughton

Grout, J. and Perrin, S. (2002) *Recruiting Excellence: An Insider's Guide to Sourcing Top Talent*, McGraw Hill

Martin, Malcolm and Jackson, Tricia (2002) *Personnel Practice (People and Organizations)*, Chartered Institute of Personnel and Development (CIPD)

Journals

Personnel Management

Personnel Review

Personnel Today

Websites
- www.cipd.co.uk – Chartered Institute of Personnel and Development website with lots of information on all types of recruitment and advertising activity
- www.direct.gov.uk – government website with information on public services and including information on legislation such as the Disability Discrimination Acts
- www.dti.gov.uk – Department of Trade and Industry with information on recruitment and training processes
- www.ico.gov.uk – Information Commissioner's Website providing information about the Data Protection Act and other information issues
- www.jobcentreplus.gov.uk – Job Centre website with links and information about current vacancies
- www.lawontheweb.co.uk – information on law relating to all aspects of recruitment including discrimination

Unit 19
Books

Adair, J. (1987) *Effective Teambuilding: How to Make a Winning Team*, Pan Books

Belbin, M. (1996) *Team Roles at Work*, Butterworth-Heinemann

Honey, P. (2001) *Teams and Teamwork*, Peter Honey

Leigh, A. and Maynard, M. (2004) *Leading Your Team*, Nicholas Brealey

Websites
- www.belbin.com/belbin-team-roles.htm – what are team roles?
- www.belbin.com/onlinetest.htm – online Belbin questionnaire
- www.chmaeraconsulting.com/tuckman.htm – information related to Bruce Tuckman
- www.reviewing.co.uk/toolkit/teams-and-teamwork.htm – links about teamwork

Unit 33

Books

Amor, D. (2002) *The e-business (r)evolution*, Prentice Hall

Chaffey, D., Mayer, R., Johnston, K. and Ellis-Chadwick, F. (2003) *Internet Marketing*, second edition, Prentice Hall

Goymer, J. (2004) *BTEC National e-Business Book 1*, Heinemann

Websites
- www.berr.gov.uk – a government department for business, innovation and skills
- www.businesslink.gov.uk – free government-run organisation offering advice and information for businesses
- www.clickz.com – specialist online service
- www.nielsen-online.com – source of Internet research facts
- www.norton.com – Norton Antivirus
- www.saveanddrive.co.uk – motor accessories supplier
- www.searchenginewatch.com – search engine marketing

- www.statistics.gov.uk – National Statistics (ONS)
- www.theregister.co.uk
- www.usenet.org.uk – news groups site
- www.webstandards.org – web standards project

Unit 34

Books

Chaffey, D., Mayer, R., Johnston, K. and Ellis-Chadwick, F. (2003) *Internet Marketing*, 2nd edition, Prentice Hall

Goymer, J. (2004) *BTEC National e-Business Book 1*, Heinemann

Websites
- www.4projects.com – Project Management processes website
- www.acmewhistles.co.uk – website that uses the web's ability to carry multimedia effects
- www.amazon.co.uk – online retailer
- www.bellsfishshop.co.uk – good example of a website with visual appeal
- www.berr.gov.uk – government department for Business, Enterprise and Regulatory Reform
- www.computers.com – unbiased reviews of the latest computer technology
- www.covisint.net – website of a company that specialises in connecting people and systems across industries
- www.diy.com – B&Q's online business: a good idea of website functionality
- www.emarketer.com – market research on e-business and online marketing
- www.wifesgone.com – pressure group

Index

accounting 163–96
acid test ratio 78, 79, 193
ACORN classification 109
actual product 113, 114
Adair, John 379
administration of organisation 56
advertising 119–20, 136, 202, 209, 217
  codes of practice 94–95
  online 120, 290, 307–08, 415–16
advertising agencies 197, 220–21
Advertising Standards Authority 94–95
affiliate programmes 290
AGM (Annual General Meeting) 10
AIDA model 118, 197, 208–09
aims of business 19–20
  private sector 21–23
  public sector 23–24
AJAX coding 457
alienation 360
allocated budgeting 72
Amazon.co.uk 65, 244, 291, 421
Annual Report 10, 245–46
Ansoff, Igor 90
Apple 92, 214–15
  iPhone 34
apprenticeships 44
Asda 50, 59
aspirational demand 30
assertiveness 385–86
asset turnover ratio 81
assets 77, 78, 167
  see also current; fixed; intangible
attitudes to work 44
Audit Commission 23
augmented product 113–14

backing up data 141–42, 432
balance sheet 184, 186–89
Bank of England base rate 26, 28
banks 26, 65
banner advertising 290, 415–16
bar charts 272–73
Belbin, M. 363, 366, 372
Bluetooth 401–02
body language 123, 150, 153–54, 157, 159, 385
  and interviews 348–49
bookmarking 411–12
brand awareness 89–90
brand building 92, 113
brand extension 92, 219
brand image 136, 463–64

brand/branding 90–92, 206–07, 215, 218–29
  benefits to owner 219
  brand personality 218
  fingerprinting 219
  global brands 34
  and price sensitivity 34
break-even 21, 73–75
bricks and clicks 302–03
broadband 39, 398, 452
budgets 72–76
buildings and facilities 65, 66
business continuity plans 141–42, 474
business environment 1–46, 102
  and strategic planning 20–21
Business Link 40, 427, 436
business names 41
business purposes 6–9
  making profits 7–8
  not-for-profit 8–9
business-to-business (B2B) market 107, 205–06, 217, 290
  online 298, 413, 442–43
  segmentation 110–11
business-to-consumer (B2C) market 205–06, 217, 290, 291
  websites 442
buyer behaviour 91, 107

call centres 16, 36
capital
  employed 188
  expenditure 171
  income 167–68
  movement of 35–36
  working 55, 75–76, 188
captive product pricing 116
car industry 20, 35, 37, 38
carbon footprint of businesses 45
cash flow forecast 176–80, 181
  opening/closing balances 176, 178–79
  problems 180
  receipts and payments 177–78
cash flow management 180–82
cash flows 163
changes, implementing 362
channel conflict 310–11
channel structure 205-06
charities 3, 5, 8–9, 10–11, 37
Child Protection Agency 10
China 30, 31, 34, 35

cinema advertising 222
coaching 364–65
Coca-Cola 34, 113, 136
coffee shop chains 6–7, 250
communication 123–62
  audience requirements 144–45
  corporate 135–38
  formal and informal 152
  global 34
  Internet 405
  methods 143–61
  and noise 208
  non-verbal 153–54
  professional language 159
  skills 152, 348–49
  in teams 384–86, 389
  technology 150–52, 395–438
  verbal 126, 152–53
  written 126–27, 144–50
  see also information
communication models 208
communities as stakeholders 11
company law 40–41
Competition Commission 37, 43
competitor analysis 409, 421, 466
competitor-based pricing 213, 282
competitors 191, 207, 424–25
Computer Misuse Act (1990) 139
computer networks 400–02, 405
computer security 408-09
computers, home 436
confidentiality and recruitment 347
consumer 25, 107
  confidence 26
  protection 41–42, 93, 94, 435
  see also customer; segmentation
Consumer Credit Act (1974/2006) 41–42, 93
Consumer Price Index (CPI) 27
Consumer Protection (Distance Selling) Regulations 94, 435
Consumer Protection from Unfair Trading Regulations (2008) 93
consumerism 95
contract of employment 42, 60
contract law 41
contribution 21
control, lines of 13
cookies 242, 458
copyright 69
core competency of business 311
core product 113, 114

corporate image 204
corporate social responsibility 45
corporation tax 38
costs and budgets 72–76
creativity and initiative 53
credit: cost and availability 28
credit agreements 41
credit periods 177
creditors 177, 180, 191
creditors' payment period ratio 194
cross-functional teams 52
culture, professional 52
current assets 78, 187–88
current ratio 78, 192–93
curriculum vitae 337, 340
customer service 15–16, 129
    Internet 296–97, 298, 403
customers 11, 14, 83, 107, 191
    expectations 312–13
    retention of online 454
customs duty 38

Data Protection Act (1998) 56, 94, 139,
    332–33, 435–36
Debenhams recruitment 341
debtors' payment period 80–81, 193–94
decision-making unit (DMU) 110
Delphi technique 244–45
demand 29–30, 32–34
    aspirational 30
    elasticity of 33, 34
demand curve 29, 32
demand pricing 213
demographics 43–44, 102, 108, 204,
    217, 287, 409
destruction pricing 282
digital broadcasting 150, 435
direct marketing 203, 223, 225, 290
direct selling 214, 311
Disability Discrimination Acts 331, 461
discrimination pricing 282
discrimination in recruitment 327,
    330–32
disintermediation 224–25, 290, 310–11,
    422–23
distribution 117–18, 213–15, 283, 450
diversification 90
dividends 9
DVD and Blu-ray 151
dynamic pricing 295–96

e-business 420–23
    government support 435–36
    see also Internet
E-Commerce Regulations (2002) 414–
    15, 435
economic environment 25–29, 102

and credit availability 28
    growth and recession 21, 26–27
    impact of changes 26–27
education and training 40, 44
efficiency ratios 193–94
email 148–49, 240, 290, 417
    code of practice 139–40
    monitoring 56
emergency provisions 66–67
employability skills 60–64
employees as stakeholders 11, 191
employer associations 11
employers as stakeholders 11
Employment Act (2002)(2008) 332
Employment Equality (Age)
    Regulations (2006) 327
employment law 42, 60, 327, 332
Employment Rights Act (1996) 60
encryption 472
endorsement marketing 137
environmental analysis 409–10
environmental issues 45, 102
EPOS information 242
equal opportunity policies 349–50
Equal Pay Act (1970) 331
Equal Pay Directive 42
Equal Treatment Directive 42
Equality Bill (2009) 331
equipment 54–55, 66
equity 77
ethics 45, 139–41
European Union 31, 37, 40, 42
    Working Time Directive 332
experimentation 238, 243
eye contact 153, 158–59

facilities for staff 55–56
fair trade 45
fax 147
field trials 241, 243
film industry subsidies 38–39
finance department 15, 129
financial accounting 15
Financial Ombudsman Service 93
financial resources 47, 70–71
financial statements 72–81
    balance sheet 77–78
    costs and budgets 72–76
    profit and loss 76–77
    ratio analysis 78–81
firefighting 57
firewalls 432, 472
fiscal policy 29
fixed assets 78, 167, 171, 186–87
fixed costs 21, 72
flexible working 437
flowcharts 148, 149

focus groups 230, 241, 243
foreign direct investment (FDI) 36
4Projects case study 444
Freedom of Information Act (2000) 139
functional areas 15–17

GDP (Gross Domestic Product) 30
gender roles, changing 44–45
geographic market segmentation 108
geographical location of organisation
    14
global economic crisis (2008/9) 25–29
    see also recession
global products 34
globalisation 4, 34–36
    movement of capital 35–36
    supply chains 34, 35
goodwill 171
government 10, 11, 23, 26, 29, 39
    information 130, 245
    regulation of global business 36
    statistics 245
    subsidies 31
    support for businesses 37, 38–40
government agencies 10
grants and loans 38, 71
graphs and charts 271–75
greenfield investment 35
gross profit 167, 184
gross profit percentage ratio 79, 191
groups see team
growth, economic 26, 27
growth strategy 22–23, 87, 90

Handy, Charles 378
health and safety 55, 66–67, 142
Health and Safety at Work Act (1974)
    55, 66–67
histograms 273–74
hours worked by country 44
households, changes in 44
human resources 16, 47, 50–64, 129,
    346
    encouraging creativity 53
    incentives 51, 52–53
    Information System (HRIS) 50
    liaison with other departments 52
    meeting targets 50–51
    monitoring 50–51, 56–57
    outsourcing decisions 53–54
    recruitment and retention 57–64
Human Rights Act (2000) 56
hybrid vehicles 37

identity theft 430
Ikea 65
immigration 43

in-house versus outsourcing 53–54
incentives for employees 51, 52–53
incentives for new enterprises 37
income tax 38
India 5, 30, 31, 34, 35, 36
inflation 27
information 126–31
  commercial databases 130
  communication methods 143–61
  documents 132, 134
  effective presentation of 132–38
  issues and constraints 139–43
  operational issues 141–43
  ownership 141
  policies 141, 142
  reliability of 130–31
  security of 141
  sources of 129–31
  style of presentation 132
  see also communication
Information Commissioner 139
information fatigue 313
infrastructure, provision of 39
innocent 5, 13, 18, 20, 219
innovation and teams 360
insolvency 179
insurance 67
intangible assets 171, 188
intellectual property 68
inter-quartile range 266
interdependence: levels and types
    34–36
interest rate 28, 168
intermediaries 214–15
international businesses 1, 4
Internet 402–05, 406–07, 408–19
  for business communication 417–19
  and business efficiency 303–07
  for business research 409–12
  codes of practice 140
  communications 149–50, 405
  company policies 432–33
  cost benefits 421–23
  customers 312–13, 423, 433
  data loss 429
  hierarchy of participation 302–03
  as information source 131, 245
  networks 400–02
  operational implications 423
  organisational adaptations 426–33
  payment security 312, 315–16, 413–
    14
  for procurement 403, 412–15
  protocols 399–400
  refocusing business 425
  risks 427–33
  security threats 431–32

strategic implications 423–25
time spent online 281
users by country 315, 407
working of 398–400
and worldwide web 398, 402
see also websites
Internet marketing 214, 279–318,
    449–52
  24-hour presence 299–300, 421
  advertising 223, 308
  benefits 294–95, 420–21
  challenges 310–17
  cultural issues 316–17
  customer service 296–97, 298
  customisation 291–92
  global customers/markets 298
  marketing strategy 306
  markets 284–85, 292, 301–02
  monitoring competitors 307
  online/offline activities 293
  personalisation 291, 421, 423
  products 284–85, 294–95, 300–01
  promotion methods 290, 403, 415–16
  responsive transactions 296
  usage-based 289
  website links 308
Internet Service Providers 315, 399
interpersonal skills 62, 384–86
interviewing skills 63–6
invoice 147–48
IT equipment 66

Japan: GDP 30
job description 60, 334–35
joint ventures 35

Kingspan case study 305
knowledge-based economy 314

labour market 28–29, 31, 43
lastminute.com 5
leadership 373, 386, 391
  Adair's model 379–80
  continuum of styles 380–81
  power and authority 378–79
  skills 378–81, 387–92
  styles 375–77, 380–81, 392
legal factors 40–43
legislation 40–41, 42, 43, 102
  consumer 41–42, 93–95
  health and safety 142
  Internet 414–15
  recruitment 330–32
letters, business 146–47
liabilities 77, 188
limited liability 9, 10, 40–41
line management 14

line and scatter graphs 274–75
liquidity 75–76, 179
liquidity ratios 192–93
listening skills 154–57, 159, 384
livery and signage 137
local businesses 1, 4
local councils 10
log, keeping 365–66
logistics 31
logos 136–37
loss 167
Low Pay Commission 42

mailshot 203
management accounting 15
managers 191
  troubleshooting 57
manufacturing companies 6
market development 90, 285
market diversification 303
market leadership 89
market penetration 90, 285
market research 83, 97–101, 130,
    235–78
  bias 276
  diagrammatic presentation 271–75
  e-market research 240–41, 244
  forecasting 253–54
  interpreting findings 265–76
  limitations 100–01, 275–76
  objectives 237, 255–56
  pilot stage 241, 263
  planning 251–56
  presentation of findings 269–71
  primary research 97, 238–42, 243
  qualitative and quantitative 98–99,
    248–49
  questionnaires 259–63
  research brief 251
  research methods 97–98
  sampling methods 257–59
  secondary research 97, 238, 242,
    244–48
  stages of 253–55
  statistical procedures 265–69
  validity and reliability 100–01,
    241–42, 243, 247
market research analyst 103
market-orientated business 86
marketing 15, 83–122, 129
  constraints on 93–95
  definitions 86–87
  objectives 89, 90
  role of 86, 282
  strategies 106, 249
  techniques 90–93
  see also Internet marketing

marketing mix 15, 106, 112–13, 197, 201, 282–83, 449–50
  e-marketing remix 420–21, 451
  extended 283, 450
marketing planning 102–06
marketplace 32
  global 31, 34–36
materials and waste 65
maternity/paternity regulations 323, 332
mean, median and mode 265–66
media 120
  selection 221–24
  teenage use of 289
  types of 221, 222–23
memorandum 147
mentoring and coaching 364
minimum wage 42, 332
mission statements 17–19, 135
mobile marketing 415
mobile phones/technology 149, 151–52, 226, 402, 406
  advertising 404
monetary policy 29
Monetary Policy Committee 26, 28
monitoring employees 50–51, 56–57
monopoly and merger legislation 43
mortgages 168
MOSAIC classification 109
motivation of teams 365, 390
multimedia 126–27
  presentations 132–33
  websites 461–62
multinational companies 35–36
music downloads 443

National Health Service 23, 54
National Insurance 38
National Lottery Commission 37
negotiation skills 63
Nestlé 11, 34–35
net assets 188
net profit 76, 77, 167, 185
net profit percentage of sales 79, 192
non-verbal communication 153–54
not-for-profit organisations 5, 7

objectives 87–89, 90
  cascading 19, 90
  hierarchy of 90
  marketing 89
  SMART 19–20, 87–88, 89, 104
  team 390
observation 238, 243
Office of Fair Trading 93, 95
Office for National Statistics 27, 247
older people, increase in 43–44

online presence 118, 213–14, 403
online shopping 403, 425
  statistics 129, 439
  see also Internet
online value proposition (OVP) 420
organisational charts 14
organisational structures 13–15
outsourcing decisions 53–54
ownership of businesses 9–11, 35
  and objectives 9
Oxfam 8–9, 18, 20

packaging and labelling 136, 215
partnerships 9, 167
  limited liability 10
patents 69, 171
PayPal 439, 467
penetration pricing 116, 213, 282
people in marketing mix 215–16, 283, 450
  e-marketing mix 451
performance indicators 370
performance monitoring 360
performance ratios 80–81
person specification 335–3
personal selling 121, 202, 209, 217
personal skills 61–64
PESTLE 102
physical evidence 216, 283, 450
  e-marketing mix 451
physical resources 47, 64–67
pictograms 271–72
pie charts 272
place 15, 112, 117, 213–15, 282–83, 450
  e-marketing mix 451
plant and machinery 65–66
podcasts 301
political factors 37–40
positioning 206
postal surveys 239
Poundland 8, 22, 23
power and authority 378–79
premium pricing 116
presentations 132–38
  corporate communications 135–38
  of research findings 269–71
  skills 159–61
  use of images 133, 134
  using technology 134–35
  web-based 133
pressure groups 95, 447
price/pricing 15, 112, 424
  e-marketing mix 451
  equilibrium 32
  and promotion 212–13
  sensitivity 33–34
  strategies 116–17, 282, 450

Primary Health Care Trusts 24
primary research methods 238–42, 243
primary sector 6
Prince's Trust 71, 75
private businesses 4–5, 9
private limited companies 10
private sector
  aims and objectives 21–23, 87–88
  break-even strategy 21
  growth strategy 22–23
  profit maximisation 22
  survival strategy 21–22
privatised public businesses 5
processes in marketing mix 216, 283, 450
  e-marketing mix 451
product 15, 112, 282, 450
  benefits versus features 115
  e-marketing mix 451
  life cycle 115
  range 114
  three levels 113–14
product development 90, 282, 285
  Internet 300–01
production concept 86
production function 129
production managers 15
professional culture 52
profit 167
  calculating 22
profit and loss account 76–77, 184–86
profit maximisation 7–8, 22, 87
profitability ratios 79–80, 191–92
promotion/promotional campaign 15, 112, 118–21, 197–234, 283, 450
  budget 227, 228–29, 231
  campaign brief 227
  creative brief 227–28
  design of materials 229–30
  e-marketing mix 451
  focus of appeal 223–24
  media selection 229
  objectives 216–17, 222–23
  one-to-one communication 225
  online 415–16
  plan 230–31
  and pricing strategies 212–13
  role of 211–19
  tactics 228–30
  targeting 217–18, 227, 228, 231
  timing 207, 212, 224, 227
promotional mix 118–21, 197, 212
  cost/benefit analysis 204
  decisions and issues 204–07
  elements of 201
  and marketing mix 200–01
  objectives 203–04

promotional mix – *continued*
   target market and media 204
   type of market 205
   websites in 451–52
psychographic segmentation 108
   and Internet marketing 287–88
psychometric testing 345
Public Interest Disclosure Act 141
public limited companies 10
public relations (PR) 121, 202, 405
public sector businesses 4–5, 9, 24
   aims and objectives 23–24, 88
   cost limitation 23
   privatised 5
   subsidies 37
   value for money 24
public service 23
publicity 121
   material 148
published media 222

quantitative easing 28–29
questioning 349, 384–85
questionnaires 97, 99, 100, 259–63

Race Directive, EU 42
Race Relations Act (1992) 330
radio advertising 89, 222
range of businesses 4–6
rate of stock turnover ratio 194
ratio analysis 78–81, 191–94
raw material availability 31
recession 27, 29, 102
   2009 global 1, 5, 7, 25–29, 87
   ripple effect 27
recruitment agencies 324–25
recruitment and selection 57–64,
   319–54
   advertising 326–28
   application form 337, 339
   application letter 337–38
   application methods 328–29
   candidate feedback 352
   communication skills 348–49
   ethical issues 333
   EU and UK legislation 330–32
   fairness 347
   internal and external 324–26
   interview protocol 346–47
   job description 334–35
   job offers 351
   person specification 335–3
   post-interview 350–53
   recruitment planning 322–26
   selection criteria 342–43
   selection interview 342–350
   tasks and tests 345

references for job application 343,
   352–53
Register of Companies 41
relationship marketing 92, 93, 284
religious requirements 44
reports and organisational charts 14
Resale Price Maintenance 43
resources 47–82
   and business operations 54–57
   types of 47
restrictive practices 43
Restrictive Practices Court 37
retailers 6, 214, 283
retaining staff 58–59
return on capital employed (ROCE) 80,
   192
revenue expenditure 171–74
revenue income 168–69
role plays 132
running costs 7
Ryanair 19, 112

Sale of Goods Act (1979) 41, 93
sales concept 86
sales function 16, 129
sales ledger clerk 170
sales promotion 121, 202
sales revenue 167
sales turnover 169, 184
sampling methods 257–59
scatter diagrams 267
Schmidt, W. 380–81
search engine optimisation 290, 307,
   459–60
search engines 315, 410–11
secondary research 97, 98, 242, 244–48
secondary sector 6
security of buildings 67
segmentation 83, 107–10, 217–18, 449
   bases for 108–10
   business-to-business 110–11
   Internet 285–88, 313
servers and clients 398, 399
services 6, 7
   virtual 302
Sex Discrimination Act (1975/97) 330
shareholders 9, 10, 41, 191
shares 167
silos, working in 16–17
skilled staff 60
skills, employability 60–64
skim pricing 116, 213, 282
Skype 405
SMART objectives 19–20, 87–88, 89, 104
SMEs case study 306
social class segmentation 108
social factors 43–45, 102

social networking sites 397
software licences 68
software problems 430
sole traders 9, 167
solvency ratio analysis 78–79
span of control 14–15
sponsorship 121, 137, 203
staff costs 172–73
staff turnover 58, 59
staffing, adequate 54
stakeholders 3, 11, 12, 20, 191
statistical procedures 265–69
stock exchange 10
stock turnover ratio 80
straplines 137
strategic management, SWOT 128–29
strategic planning 17–20
   aims and objectives 19–20
   and business environment 20–21
   business type and ownership 21
subsidiaries, foreign 35
subsidies 31, 37, 38
substitutes 30
succession planning 50
suppliers 11, 25
supply 30–31
   changes in 32–33
   and profitability 31
   supply curve 31, 32–33
supply chains 34, 35, 310, 422–23
   global 35
   and Internet 304, 426–27
surveys 238–40, 243, 263
survival strategies 21–22, 90
SWOT analysis 104, 128–29

takeover bid 10
Tannenbaum, R. 380–81
target audience 223
target market 109–10, 449
   promotions 217–18, 227, 228, 231
target setting: teams 360, 370
taxation 5, 37–38
teams 62, 355–94
   benefits of 360–62
   building 363–69, 389–90
   cohesion 371–73
   conflict 373, 384, 386, 391
   formal and informal 358
   high-performance 367–68
   induction and training 364
   interpersonal skills 384–86
   measuring performance 369–71
   monitoring 51, 391
   motivation 365, 390
   roles 363, 366, 372
   selection 365

self-managing 372
size 358–59
skills of members 382–86
stages of forming 367–68
teamwork qualities 369
temporary and permanent 359
see also leadership
technological developments 102
technological resources 47, 64, 67–69
telemarketing 214
telephone calls 150
telephone developments 452
telephone surveys 239–40
television advertising 222
tertiary sector 6
Tesco 5, 23, 34, 35, 50, 91, 303
online 403
profits 7
text messaging 149
Thresher Group case study 309
time series 267–68
tone of voice 123
touch screens 150, 151
trade journals 130, 246
trade unions as stakeholders 11
trademarks 171
training, cascading 68
transactional marketing 92–93
Tuckman, B. 367–68

uncertainty, economic 27
Unilever 35
United States: GDP 30

validity of research 100–01, 241–42,
243, 247
values 17–19

variable costs 21, 72
variance analysis 72
VAT (value added tax) 38
verbal communication 126, 152–53
verbal presentations 132
video conferencing 150, 418–19
viral marketing 416
Virgin 5, 92
Virgin Airlines case study 361
Virgin Mobile US case study 404
viruses, computer 428–29, 431
Voice-over Internet Protocol (VoIP) 406,
418, 452
Volkswagen 34, 89–90, 128
voluntary sector 5, 9, 37, 88, 447
Voluntary Service Overseas 5
volunteered personal information 240

waste reduction 65, 66
web analytics 409, 412
web conferencing 52
Website Accessibility Initiative 461
website planning 465–75
access control 472
authentication 472
costs 473, 474
customer feedback 474
customer profiles 465–66
evaluation 473–74
functions 466–67
hosting 470
launch of 474
personalisation 467, 469
promotion of website 474
resources required 469–73
security measures 471–72, 473
software options 471

strategy 465–66
transaction arrangements 466–67
web authoring tools 471
websites 439–76
accessibility 461, 474
campaigning groups 447–48
commercial relationships 442–43
direct sales 443
efficiency 456
government 445–47
language 456
monitoring 242, 244
navigation 455, 456
non-commercial business 445–48
physical delivery 443, 444
post-sales models 445
pre-sales models 443, 445
privacy of information 457–58
purposes of commercial 443–45
scalability 452
speed of response 456–57
target group 463
usability 454–55, 458, 460–61
visual appeal 454, 461–64
see also Internet
WebTrends 286
whistle-blowing 140–1
wholesalers 214, 283
Wi-Fi 401
Wolters Kluwer 314
Work and Families Act (2006) 332
worker co-operatives 10
working capital 55, 75–76, 188
worldwide web *see* Internet
written communication 126–27, 144–50

zero budgeting 72